Design and Technology

Second edition

JAMES GARRATT

CAMBRIDGE UNIVERSITY PRESS
Cambridge, New York, Melbourne, Madrid, Cape Town, Singapore,
São Paulo, Delhi

Cambridge University Press
The Edinburgh Building, Cambridge CB2 8RU, UK

www.cambridge.org
Information on this title: www.cambridge.org/9780521556071

© Cambridge University Press 1991, 1996

First published 1991
Second edition 1996
10th printing 2008

Printed in Dubai by Oriental Press

A catalogue record for this publication is available from the British Library

Library of Congress Cataloguing in Publication data applied for
Garratt, James.
Design and technology/James Garratt. – 2nd ed.
    p.   cm.
Includes index.
ISBN 978-0-521-55607-1 paperback
1. Engineering – Juvenile literature.   2. Engineering design – Juvenile literature.
3. Engineering design – Experiments – Juvenile Literature. [1. Design, Industrial.
2. Engineering.]
TA 149.G37   1996
620–dc20

ISBN 978-0-521-55607-1 paperback

Second edition prepared by Stenton Associates

Acknowledgements

The author wishes to thank the former Principal, Christopher Evans, and the former Deputy Head, Peter Green, of Countesthorpe Community College, for their support and cooperation during the writing and production of this book, and all the pupils whose work is photographed or illustrated in the book. The help of colleagues within the Design and Technology department is also gratefully acknowledged. Finally, he wishes to thank his wife Jenny for her invaluable help and support.

To the student

Design and Technology has been written for you to use for GCSE and at Key Stages 3 and 4 in the National Curriculum. You should use this book to look up information when you require it rather than trying to read it from cover to cover. For this reason it has a very simple layout designed to make the information contained easy to understand and locate. Sometimes you may need to read a whole chapter, in which case you should refer to the contents list on page 3. Alternatively use the index at the end of the book to locate more specific information. For project briefs and ideas use the project index. Chapter 1 describes the **stages in the design process** which embody the National Curriculum attainment targets. It is suggested, therefore, that you read the introduction and chapter 1 first.

Contents

Introduction

We live in a **high technology society**. In simple terms this means that our way of life, our standard of living and the wealth of our country is dependent, to a large extent, upon the manufacture of sophisticated products and, of course, all of these have to be **designed**. Indeed, everything which has ever been made was designed by someone. I wonder how many different things *you* have designed without actually realising it? The layout of a room perhaps, a flower bed in the garden, the cover for a school book and so on. But what 'makes' someone design something? It happens because human beings like to be creative and when a person recognises a need, the reaction is to try to do something about it. Look at the photographs here and see if you can work out the needs which inspired the designs.

In your design and technology course, you will be expected to **recognise** the different **needs and preferences** of potential product users, and to investigate the design and manufacture of familiar products to help you to develop appropriate designs to meet user needs.

To our early ancestors, with only limited materials and skills, design was probably a very 'hit and miss' affair. Today we have numerous different materials and access to an enormous range of information, knowledge and skills. Further, we have the facilities for using these resources to their best advantage to ensure that our designs **work well**, **look good**, are **safe to use** and so on. Even so, it is important to realise that the manufacture, use and disposal of any product will have both beneficial and detrimental effects upon people, wildlife and the environment. Look at the photographs again and think for a moment about how the various technologies identified are beneficial and in what ways they can cause harm. For example, chemical technology has provided farmers with insecticides and artificial fertilizers. The benefits include increased crop yields and cheaper food in the shops. Among the negative effects, however, is the pollution of rivers and lakes.

Chemical technology: crop spraying

Materials technology: product packaging

Vehicle technology: heavy transport

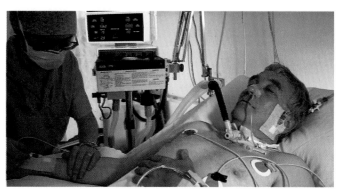
Medical technology: intensive care unit

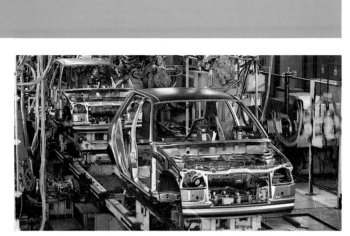

Control technology: automated production

Power technology: electricity generation

Aircraft technology: intercontinental flight

Information technology: police records department

Clearly, designers and technologists have an enormous responsibility for the well-being of people in our society, of all the peoples of the world, and of the very future of planet Earth. When studying design and technology at school, *you* will be expected to act as a responsible designer whilst **generating designs** to solve problems or satisfy needs.

Whenever anything is made, of course, from the simplest to the most complex product, **materials, components** and **tools** will be used, and **skills** and **knowledge** will be required. A thorough understanding and application of these resources, therefore, is necessary to ensure a high quality product. When studying design and technology at school, *you* will be expected to identify how **materials** and **manufacturing processes** have been used in existing products and to learn to use these resources to their best advantage when **planning** and **making** products yourself.

For **economic** reasons, designers try to make sure that their products appeal to a large number of people. Imagine for a moment going into a shop yourself to buy a new pair of 'trainers' – you wouldn't buy 'just any pair'. You would try them on to see if they were comfortable, examine them to see if you liked the style and appearance, think about the quality of the materials and whether they were good value for money, and so on. In other words, you would **evaluate** them. Whilst studying design and technology at school you will be expected to evaluate existing products and the products *you* make. This is an important process for designers and technologists, not only because they need to assess the product's sales potential, but also because their **products** (as we have seen) **have the potential to affect all our lives.**

Studying design and technology, therefore, will help you to: identify needs, generate designs, plan and make products and to evaluate your own work and that of others. In the next few pages, two pupils, Pauline and Nick, help to illustrate the **stages in the design process** through which these skills can be developed.

CHAPTER ONE

Stages in the design process

Situation

Designers and technologists are men and women who set out to solve **practical** problems which arise out of life's **situations.** Here is an example of a situation in which Pauline and Nick became involved.

On reaching old age, some people find it very difficult, and often frightening, to climb up and down stairs. The solution might be to live downstairs, to move house, or maybe to go into an old people's home. Mrs Brown didn't want to do any of these things. She wanted to continue to live as she had always lived.

Analyse the situation

Before attempting to solve a problem, it is important to **analyse** the situation to sort out exactly what the problem is. (For further details see p.10.)

Write a brief

Once the problem is fully understood, the next step is to write a design **brief.** A brief is a short statement giving the general outline of the problem to be solved. (For further details see p.10.)

Carry out research

Sometimes a problem can be solved 'straight out of your head' using your own knowledge and imagination. However, to obtain the best possible solution you will almost certainly need to gain some new knowledge and information, and this will require **research.** (For further details see p.11.)

Write a specification

Having researched the problem you should have a good understanding of what is required and a clearer understanding of the design limits which will affect what can ultimately be achieved. A **specification** can now be prepared. This must outline specific details of the design which must be satisfied, and identify the design limits. (For further details see p.12.)

Work out possible solutions

Possible solutions to the design brief should now be considered. Draw some ideas on paper. Your first idea will not necessarily be the best, so try several different designs (at least three). By combining your own ideas and information obtained from research. you should begin to move towards a good solution. (For further details see p.13.)

Select preferred solution

A decision must now be made. You must decide which solution to develop. Ideally, the chosen solution will be the one which best satisfies the specification – but this is not always possible. (For further details see p.13.)

Prepare working drawings and plan ahead

At this stage, working drawings of the chosen design should be prepared. They should contain all the **details** of the design which are important to its construction.

Planning for the work ahead is also important at this stage to ensure that you complete the work on time. (For further details see p.14.)

Construct a prototype

You are now ready to **make** the product – this is sometimes called realisation. In industry a prototype is usually built first, and the final product is a development of this. In school, the prototype is often all you have time to make (or sometimes just a model), but this is probably the most interesting part of the work. It involves building, testing and modifying the design to try to satisfy the specification. (For further details see p.15.)

Test and evaluate the design

The prototype, or final product must now be **tested** to see if it solves the problem outlined in the specification. Very few designs are perfect. To discover how successful your project has been, you must ask questions like: How well does it function? Does it work reliably? Can it be used safely? And so on. (For further details see p.17.)

Write a report

Finally, a report must be written on the project. In school your report provides **evidence** of your ability to analyse, plan, design, carry out practical work, evaluate and communicate. In industry the report has other uses. (For further details see p.18.)

Note you can see photographs of this project on page 163.

The design process flow chart

The design process can be illustrated using a 'flow chart'.

The large arrows show how you normally progress from one stage to the next. However, you will soon discover that problem solving is not always this straightforward. Often you will have an idea, or discover something which will make you re-think an earlier stage. This process is sometimes called **feedback**. The side arrows show how feedback may occur.

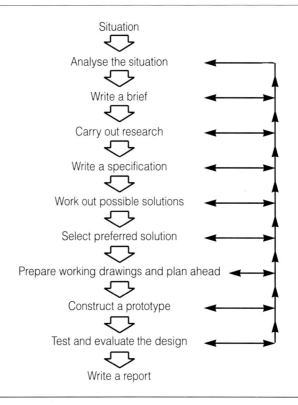

Situation
⇩
Analyse the situation
⇩
Write a brief
⇩
Carry out research
⇩
Write a specification
⇩
Work out possible solutions
⇩
Select preferred solution
⇩
Prepare working drawings and plan ahead
⇩
Construct a prototype
⇩
Test and evaluate the design
⇩
Write a report

Further details of the design process

Analysis of the situation

The process of analysing a situation will help you to sort out in your mind exactly what the problem is. Asking questions about the situation is one way of sorting out the problem.

Pauline and Nick talked to Mrs Brown in her home to learn more about the problems which old people face in getting up and down stairs.

Sometimes it can help you to sort out a problem if you actually 'put yourself in the situation'.

Putting someone else in the situation and observing their actions and reactions is another useful approach.

Because different people respond in different ways to a situation, a questionnaire can be another useful means of analysing a problem.

All your observations and thoughts should be recorded. Use a notepad, sketchbook, camera, tape recorder or even a video camera, for this purpose.

I feel so unsteady and I don't have the strength I used to have.

The brief

Once a problem has been analysed, it should be possible to write a short statement describing the problem to be solved. This is called a **brief**.

It may be a very short statement, such as 'Design a burglar alarm for use in the home', or be more precise 'Design a burglar alarm for use in the home which warns of false entry through windows and doors by sounding an alarm'. It is important that the brief is not so vague that the designer is unclear about what is needed, e.g. 'Design a burglar alarm'. Alternatively, it must not be so detailed that the designer doesn't have the freedom to be creative.

An example of a project brief is shown here. It is the brief which Pauline and Nick wrote after analysing the problem illustrated on page 6.

BRIEF

Climbing up and down stairs can be difficult and often frightening for some elderly people. The problem is made worse when they try to carry things as well. We think there is a need for some kind of lift device or other aid to help them to go up and down stairs safely.

Research

Having written a brief, you are now ready to seek out information which will help you to produce a successful design. This is called **research**. Use the chart below to help you to get started. First ask yourself the questions 1 to 6. Then read the column headed **Areas of research**. This will suggest areas of research which are relevant to the questions.

Areas of research

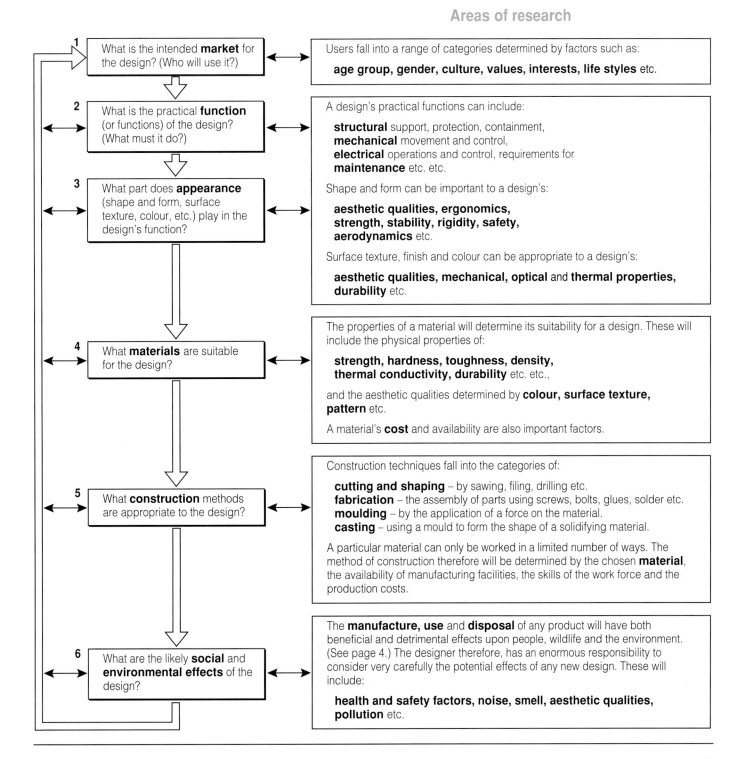

1. What is the intended **market** for the design? (Who will use it?)

Users fall into a range of categories determined by factors such as:

age group, gender, culture, values, interests, life styles etc.

2. What is the practical **function** (or functions) of the design? (What must it do?)

A design's practical functions can include:

structural support, protection, containment,
mechanical movement and control,
electrical operations and control, requirements for
maintenance etc. etc.

3. What part does **appearance** (shape and form, surface texture, colour, etc.) play in the design's function?

Shape and form can be important to a design's:

**aesthetic qualities, ergonomics,
strength, stability, rigidity, safety,
aerodynamics** etc.

Surface texture, finish and colour can be appropriate to a design's:

aesthetic qualities, mechanical, optical and **thermal properties,
durability** etc.

4. What **materials** are suitable for the design?

The properties of a material will determine its suitability for a design. These will include the physical properties of:

**strength, hardness, toughness, density,
thermal conductivity, durability** etc. etc.,

and the aesthetic qualities determined by **colour, surface texture,
pattern** etc.

A material's **cost** and availability are also important factors.

5. What **construction** methods are appropriate to the design?

Construction techniques fall into the categories of:

cutting and shaping – by sawing, filing, drilling etc.
fabrication – the assembly of parts using screws, bolts, glues, solder etc.
moulding – by the application of a force on the material.
casting – using a mould to form the shape of a solidifying material.

A particular material can only be worked in a limited number of ways. The method of construction therefore will be determined by the chosen **material**, the availability of manufacturing facilities, the skills of the work force and the production costs.

6. What are the likely **social** and **environmental effects** of the design?

The **manufacture, use** and **disposal** of any product will have both beneficial and detrimental effects upon people, wildlife and the environment. (See page 4.) The designer therefore, has an enormous responsibility to consider very carefully the potential effects of any new design. These will include:

**health and safety factors, noise, smell, aesthetic qualities,
pollution** etc.

Where to obtain the information

Research can involve reading, listening, talking, and of course observing.

General background information can be obtained from **reading** magazines, data sheets and other written material. Your teacher will be able to suggest suitable books etc., and of course you can ask at your school and local libraries.

If more detailed information is required you may need to **write a letter** to a particular industry, government department or research establishment, for example.

Looking at similar products is a useful form of research. You can quickly learn about the different methods and techniques used. You will then be in a good position to start thinking about your own product, and ways of improving on current designs. However, it is important not to allow other people's solutions to become a barrier to your own creativity.

A valuable area of research is often within your own community. Sources of information can include industries, museums, shops and of course parents and friends.

Factors which affect peoples' lives are sometimes described as the **social implications of technology**. School subjects like Humanities and Politics for example, can often provide information and ideas related to this area of your research.

Conclusion

Having carefully researched the topic, you should identify the information which is most likely to be of use to you. At this stage you should also be able to identify the **design limits** which will affect what can ultimately be produced. These will vary between school and industry but can include for example, costs. In industry the costs will include research, design, materials and processing costs, wages etc. In school, material costs are probably the most limiting factor. Time imposes limits too. It is no use developing a solution if the time is not available to produce it. In school, the time allocated to project work can significantly affect what can be achieved. Your personal skills and your school's facilities will also limit what you can achieve, and so on. It is important therefore, to consider these factors before writing the specification.

Specification

A **specification** is a detailed description of the problem to be solved. It should 'spell out' exactly what the design must achieve, whilst taking into account the design limits which will affect the final solution. It can be in the form of a list or a written statement.

The specification written by Pauline and Nick is shown here.

Note   A specification should only state that which is required to solve the problem – not how to solve it, this comes later.

SPECIFICATION.

a) The device must either carry, or assist the person, up and down the stairs

b) It must be very easy to use, and not have any complicated controls.

c) It must be completely safe for the user, and any persons or animals standing nearby.

d) It must not obstruct the normal use of the stairs.

e) It must be neat and attractive.

f) It must be cheap to operate.

g) The cost of the equipment should not exceed £350.

Possible solutions

This is the stage in the design process when you need to be really **imaginative** – to think up, and draw, lots of really good ideas for solving the problem set out in the brief.

Use your research notes to help you to make decisions about: how the product will **function** (including any maintenance facilities), what it will look like (its **aesthetic qualities**), the most suitable **materials** and components to use, how it might be **manufactured** and assembled, and don't forget to consider the effects of its manufacture, use and final disposal on people and the natural environment.

You should ideally think of at least three different ways of solving the problem before you concentrate on any one in particular. Quick sketches and notes are all that is really needed at this stage.

The chosen solution

When you feel ready to make a choice from your range of possible solutions, the first step should be to **look back at the specification**.

Then, by comparing what the specification '**asks for**', to what each of your designs **can provide**, you should be able to choose the one which will '**do the job best**'. Alternatively, you might decide that a combination of your ideas will provide the best solution. Before a final decision is made it may be necessary to make some simple models to test and compare the different designs.

Note It is important to realise that you may **not** actually be able to use the best solution. You must ask the questions: Do I have the **time** to complete the work? Can I, or the school **afford** the materials and components required? And, do I have, or can I acquire, the necessary **skills** to complete the project?

'Which one shall we choose?'

Working drawings

Once you have decided which design to develop, the next stage is to produce some working drawings. It is from these drawings that the prototype, or final product, will be made.

The type of drawings you produce will depend upon your own particular skills. You might choose to produce a **detailed** freehand drawing. Alternatively, you may prefer to make a 'technical drawing', using a drawing board and instruments. If you enjoy using a computer, you could produce a 'print out' from diagrams developed on the VDU.

Whichever method you use, the aim is to produce a detailed drawing containing all the information needed to allow the design to be made. This will include: dimensions, angles, technical data (component values etc.), materials and so on.

Prepare working drawings

Planning

Before any practical work can begin, it is very important to **plan out** the work ahead. It is important for a number of reasons:

a) Planning should help you to get the work finished on time.

   Your teacher will tell you how much time is available. With this information you should draw up a **timetable** showing how much time you expect to spend on each part of the design. As the work progresses, changes may have to be made to this timetable if jobs take less time, or longer than expected.

b) Planning should also ensure that you have the necessary materials, components and equipment available when you need them.

   Make a **list** of these requirements and check with your teacher that they are available. If something needs ordering, for example, you may need to rearrange your work timetable to fit in with these changes. Your work plan will also help you to decide 'what to do next' if, for example, equipment, materials or components are not available when you need them.

Construction work

Having worked out a timetable, and collected some of the materials and components you need, construction work can begin. The construction of a prototype, or final product, can involve a great deal of skilful activity. This can include: taking measurements and marking out, cutting, moulding, casting and fabricating. Fabricating can include: brazing, welding, pinning and jointing, the use of adhesives, and not least, the use of nuts and bolts. In addition, projects which have electrical circuitry can involve circuit construction techniques such as etching, soldering and wiring. All these activities are potentially dangerous.

It is important therefore:

- **never to use tools, equipment or machinery without your teacher's permission,**
- **always to wear protective clothing and goggles where appropriate,**
- **to observe the safety regulations in your school.**

The pictures and captions which follow also give some guidance on how to work safely.

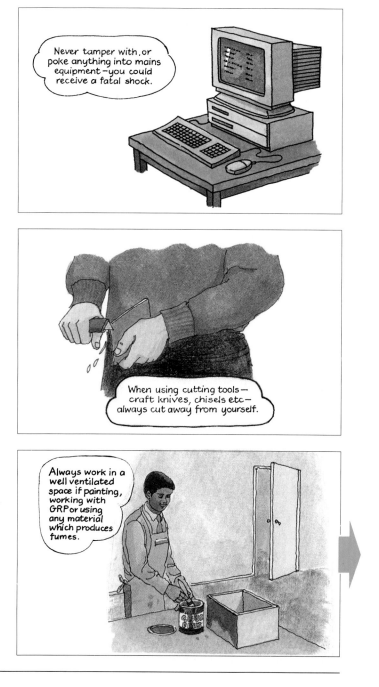

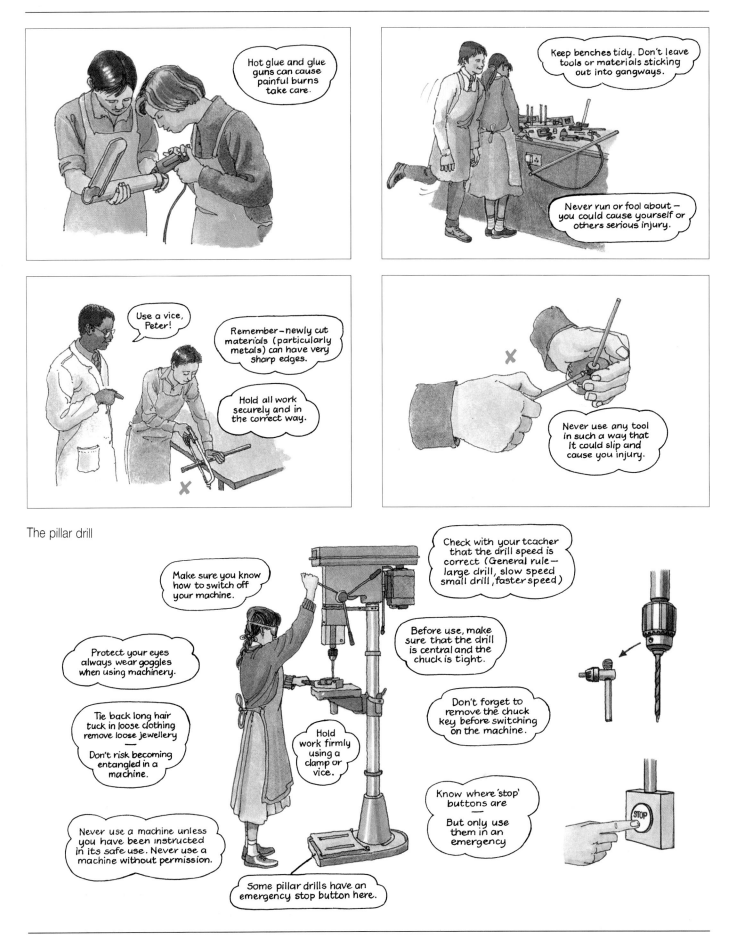

The pillar drill

Construction work – continued

Tests and modifications

As construction work progresses, and the design begins to 'take shape', you will automatically carry out **tests** on the design. You might test the strength of a joint, the operation of a mechanism, the working of an electrical circuit etc. In addition to these 'ongoing' tests, **complete systems** will need to be tested at various stages. It is important to make these tests to check that the product satisfies the specification. If as a result of testing you feel that the design does not perform as required, you might have to change part of the design. Whenever you make a change to the original design, you have made what designers call a **modification**. Sometimes however, a problem cannot be overcome with a modification. In such cases an alternative solution would have to be considered. Where part of a project has to be re-designed, a number of alternative solutions should be considered in the normal way.

If you were designing in industry, it would be necessary to consider how a proposed modification, or change of design, would affect the design's production. This would depend, for example, on the staff, materials, equipment and resources available to the industry. In addition, it would be necessary to consider how any increased costs would be met. For these reasons, a **written report** would have to be prepared.

Reporting on tests and modifications in school technology projects

Because of the importance of carrying out tests, making modifications, or re-designing, most examination boards will expect you to write about these in your final **project report**. (See page 18.) It is therefore important to keep a note of these activities to ensure that you do not forget about them.

Final test and evaluation

When construction work is complete, the product must be **tested** *to see if it does the job for which it was designed*. It will be necessary to look back at the specification and check each requirement carefully.

An **evaluation** can then be written. This should be a statement outlining the strengths and weaknesses in the design of the product itself, the choice of materials and processes used to make the product, and the way *you* tackled the project.

Here is a list of questions which will help you to prepare this statement.

1 How well does the design function?
2 Does it meet the needs of the user?
3 Does it work reliably and efficiently?
4 Is the design safe to use?
5 Can it be maintained easily (if required)?
6 Does the design look good?
7 Did I find the manufacture of the product straightforward or difficult? (Did I use the most appropriate method of manufacture?)
8 Did I use the most suitable materials with regard to the design's appearance, safety, reliability, durability and overall quality?
9 Did it cost more or less than expected?
10 What social and environmental factors did I consider when designing the product?
11 How could I have improved on my design?

The report

The purpose of a school project report is to provide your teacher and the examiner with **evidence** of your ability to analyse, design, plan, carry out practical work, evaluate and communicate.

What should a project report contain?

This will depend upon the type of course you are following, and the examination board which your school is using. Your teacher will tell you exactly what is required. As a general rule however, you can assume that the **evidence** listed above will be required in almost all types of reports. A guide to help you present this information is given below.

How to present your report

Your report should begin with a 'title page' upon which is written your **name**, **school**, **date** and the **project title**.

The second page should list the **contents** of your report giving page numbers. (All pages in your report should be numbered.)

Situation – Begin your report with an explanation of how you identified the need for the product which you have designed and made. This should include notes on the investigations you carried out and how you planned them. Include here any questionnaires, notes from interviews, etc., which you made use of. Next, show why you considered your project a worthwhile thing to do. You should 'back up' this **evaluation** with evidence gathered during your investigations. This should include your own opinions and observations and those of others, including potential users. Show also that you considered relevant moral, economic, social, cultural, environmental and technological factors before proceeding with your project.

Brief – Your project **brief** (which states the need you identified) should be written next.

Research – Give a brief account of how you began to tackle the problem. This should include details of **research** carried out to help you develop your ideas. Next describe *how* this information helped you. Include here reference to potential users of the product, function, appearance, materials, methods of construction and social and environmental factors and so on.

Specification – The **specification** should be given next. The quality of this specification will demonstrate your ability to analyse a problem in detail and show your understanding of the limitations imposed on the design.

Possible solutions – The next step is to describe the range of **possible solutions** you considered. The **sketches** and **notes** which you made at this stage are the ones which should be included here. If you explored ideas used in existing products, explain this, and show how you used them to develop your own ideas. Describe any models you made, and any tests you carried out, and explain how this work helped you to improve and refine your ideas and to recognise the restrictions imposed on the design by materials, methods of manufacture, costs etc.

Chosen solution – Next you should outline how you arrived at the **chosen solution**. This will have required you to **evaluate** each of the possible solutions with regard to the specification. In other words, you will have considered the strengths and weaknesses in each design, and have chosen the one design (or combination of designs) which best satisfied the specification. Include this evaluation here and show that you also considered your own skills, your school's facilities and the availability and cost of materials and components.

Working drawings – Here you should include the **working drawings** which you prepared. They should be neat and clear. They should be easy for the teacher, the examiner and indeed anyone who sees them, to understand.

Realisation – Planning is essential for successful project work. Show that you planned the stages in the manufacture of your project, and considered the constraints of time, materials and labour by including your **timetable** and **materials list** here.

Details of the **construction work** can now be given. The kind of information required here will include: notes on **how the work progressed**, the **test** you carried out, the kind of **problems** you faced with materials, tools, processes, methods of manufacture etc., and the **decisions** you had to make to overcome these problems. Include here any sketches, notes and plans you produced to assist you during the making of the product. If you had to review the original design proposal in the light of problems encountered, explain this. Any **modifications** made as a result should be fully explained using sketches, diagrams and notes. If part of the project was **re-designed**, rather than modified, the possible solutions you considered must be described and the reasons for the chosen solution given.

Final tests and evaluation – Now you must describe how successful your project has been – that is, you must **evaluate** it. Your evaluation should outline the **strengths** and **weaknesses** in (1) the design of the product itself, (2) the choice of materials and processes used to make the product and (3) the way *you* tackled the task.

Product – Begin by describing the **tests** made on the completed product and outline the results of these tests. Use these results to show where you have **succeeded** and where you have **failed** to satisfy the specification. For example, if you designed a drinks dispenser and it failed to dispense the required quantity of liquid, then you would have failed to achieve one of the design's **functions**. This must be reported and explained. But equally, of course, your successes must be reported too. *All of the design's functions* must be evaluated in this way. Similarly, a detailed evaluation of the product's **aesthetic** qualities must be made. Where possible, the evaluation should take into account the views and reactions of potential users of the product and show the extent to which you have met the needs of others.

An often difficult, but important, area for evaluation is **economics**. Where appropriate, you should comment on your product's sales potential, production costs, profitability and so on.

Because people's lives can be affected by the things we make, the possible **social** and **environmental** effects of the product must be evaluated.

Finally, you should mention **how you could improve your design**. This might include a description of further modifications or developments you considered, but did not have time to carry out. Alternatively, you might conclude that further development of the product would not be worthwhile, and you should say why.

Materials and processes – This part of the evaluation concerns **production** matters. If you feel that you made the right choices of materials and components for your product, say so and explain why. Alternatively, if you think that the product could have functioned better, looked better, been cheaper to make, safer to use and so on, using different materials or components, explain this too. Similarly, you should evaluate the techniques and processes used to make the product, either justifying those used or suggesting alternative approaches.

The task – The final part of the report should be an evaluation of 'how *you* tackle the task'. Include here a review of your initial investigations, research, design work, and your planning and making activities. In each case, comment on the way you went about the tasks and the decisions you made. Describe what you think you did well, and what you did less well, and suggest how you might do better in the future.

CHAPTER TWO

Aesthetics

Chapter 1 described the *stages in the design process*. This, and the following chapters contain information and ideas to help you progress through those stages.

Function

The most important reason for designing something is to solve a problem to satisfy a need. A successful design therefore must **function** properly – that is, it must do the job for which it was designed. A lot of information which may help you with the **functional** aspects of your designs can be found in chapters 3–9 in this book.

Appearance and aesthetics

Whilst it is essential that a design functions properly, because we have feelings and emotions and are surrounded by the things we make, it is important that it also 'looks good'. The qualities which make a design attractive to look at or pleasing to experience, determine its **aesthetic** appeal. It is through the senses of sight, touch, hearing, smell and taste that these qualities can be appreciated.

However, one person's ideas about what 'looks good' can be very different from another's. This is because our aesthetic judgement is conditioned by so many different factors – not least the many **influences** upon us in our everyday lives. Some of these influences can be identified in the photographs shown here, and are discussed further at the end of this chapter.

For economic reasons, designers try to make sure that their designs appeal to a large number of people. As a consumer, you have to decide if they look good to you and will function properly. As a designer and maker, you have to make the same decisions. This chapter will help you to make decisions about a design's **appearance**.

Elements of visual design

When thinking about the appearance of a design, it is useful to 'break down' the visual form into elements which can be easily examined. This will help you to understand and develop your own feelings about **appearance**.

Line

Lines are the basic elements used to organise a visual form. They can exist in their own right, but are usually joined together to create shapes and forms and to organise space and structure.

Lines can also be used to apply decoration, provide information, evoke feeling, etc.

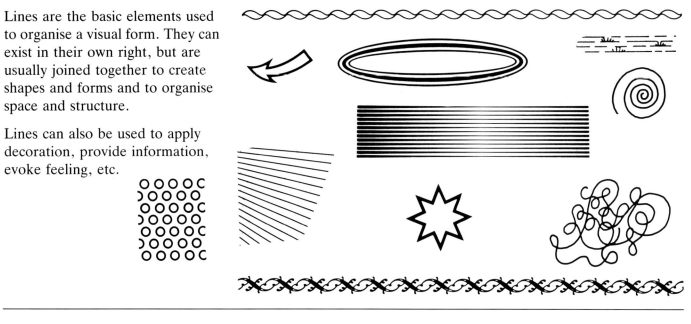

Shape and form

A **shape** is an area enclosed by lines. As you can imagine, numerous different shapes are possible. Shapes are two dimensional – they have length and width, but no depth.

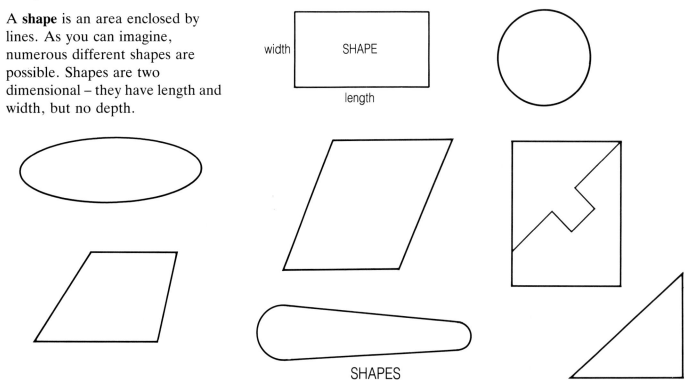

SHAPES

Forms have depth as well as length and width and are described as three dimensional. Many designs are 'built up' from a number of different component parts which make up the whole. The combination, arrangement and proportion of these parts creates the **form** of the overall design.

Geometric shapes and forms are regular and precise and usually arise out of the purpose for which the design is being made. They are fundamental to the appearance of most manufactured products and structures and indeed are often dictated by the choice of manufacturing process.

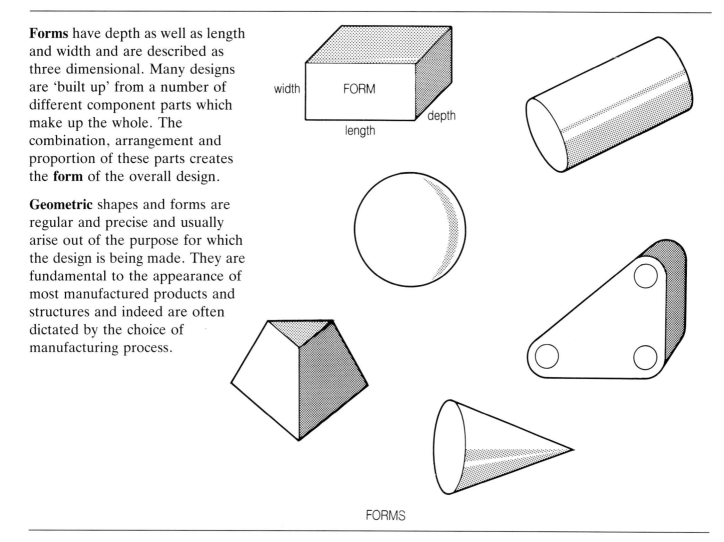

FORMS

Free shapes and forms are very much less precise and have greater application in the 'decorative' aspects of a design and in craft based products. Their variety is limitless and numerous variations can be derived from natural objects.

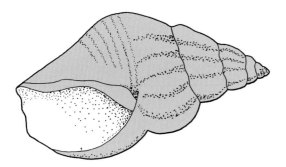

Look at the products and structures pictured here. Try to visualise their 'make up' in terms of line, shape and form. Think about how the particular materials used, and the method of manufacture, have determined or dictated certain aspects of the design's appearance. Think also about your own 'feelings' related to the design's shape and form. Some of the words which can be used to describe the **aesthetic** qualities associated with shape and form include: 'stylish', 'functional', 'elegant', 'strong', 'tasteful', 'interesting', 'beautiful', 'sleek', – but can also include words such as 'repulsive', 'yuk', 'weak', 'boring'. Can you think of any more?

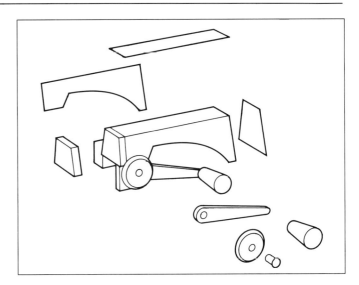

Clock/radio

Lead guitar

Vacuum cleaner

Patio furniture

Concorde

Greenhouse

Trolley jack

Texture

In addition to variations of shape and form, a designer can alter the design's appearance through the use of texture.

Texture is the 'surface finish' on a material. It is both **visual** and **tactile** – that is, we can both **see** and **feel** texture.

All materials have their own particular texture, and it is this which helps us to identify them. Even so, a material's texture will vary depending upon the way it was worked, or the manufacturing process used. For example, carved wood and planed wood have very different textures. Similarly, die cast aluminium can have a very different texture from sand cast aluminium. In the case of plastics, numerous different textures are possible depending on the nature of the polymer and the surface of the mould, and so on. Some examples of both natural and 'manufactured' textures are illustrated in the photographs.

We see texture when light strikes, and is reflected from, a material's surface. On a material which has surface relief, little shadows are cast which help to produce the particular visual effect. The brighter the light, the 'rougher' the surface appears.

Rough, smooth, hard, soft, warm, cold – these are just some of the **tactile** qualities associated with texture which we experience by touching and handling products. These qualities can be important to a design's function. For example, whilst a kitchen work surface should be smooth for reasons of hygiene (it must be easy to clean), paving slabs should ideally be rough for reasons of safety (they should prevent us from slipping in the wet).

Some of the words which can be used to describe the **aesthetic** qualities associated with texture include: 'functional', 'warm', 'pretty', 'attractive', 'hygienic', 'cold', 'clinical'. Can you think of any more?

Multi-textured baby's star toy

Ceramic tile

Hessian fabric

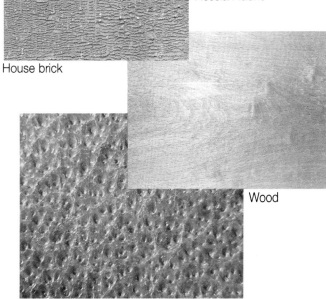

House brick

Wood

Leather

Colour

Just for a moment look around and study some of the things which surround you (or even just the objects in the picture shown here). Notice how your attention switches from one part of an object to another, and how certain details 'stand out' or attract you. Imagine how dreadfully dull and uninteresting the same objects would be if you saw them in just one colour and against the same coloured background.

Whilst shape, form and texture provide the basic characteristics of an object's appearance, it is through **colour** that we see *detail* and *variation* in these features, as our attention is drawn from one part of the design to another. But this is not all, as you will see later.

The colour wheel

When thinking about colour and how to use it to change or affect a design's appearance, a useful aid is the 'colour wheel'.

In the mixing of inks, dyes and paints, there are three basic colours from which all the other colours (on the colour wheel) can be made – red, yellow and blue. These are called **primary colours** and are shown on diagram 1.

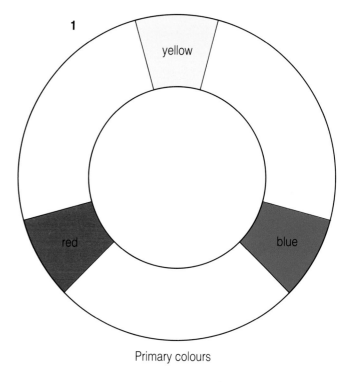

Primary colours

When two primary colours are mixed in equal amounts, a **secondary colour** is produced. There are three secondary colours – green, violet and orange. Diagram 2 shows that mixing yellow and blue produces green, blue and red produces violet and red and yellow produces orange.

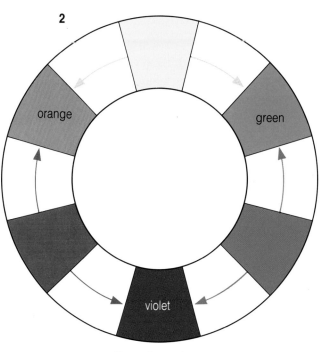

Secondary colours

Finally, when a primary and secondary colour are mixed a **tertiary colour** is produced, as shown in diagram 3. There are six tertiary colours, as shown in the complete colour wheel in diagram 4.

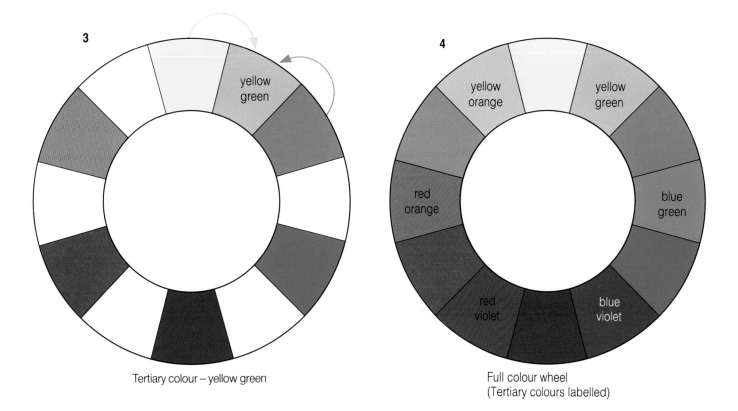

Tertiary colour – yellow green

Full colour wheel
(Tertiary colours labelled)

Note The colours produced when mixing coloured **light** are different to the above. For an explanation of this you should refer to a good physics or science book.

Colour tone

By adding either **black** or **white** to a colour, we can change its **tone**. The addition of white makes the colour lighter (or paler), black makes it darker. The tonal range of red is shown here as an example.

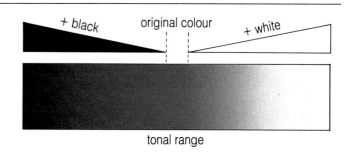

tonal range

Although black and white are not actually colours, they can of course be used in their own right in our designs, as we use real colours. A tone chart between black and white is shown opposite.

tone chart

Harmony and contrast

Colours can be used to create a sense of harmony or contrast in a design. Colours which are closest together on the colour wheel relate **harmoniously**. Diagram 1 shows a colour wheel (containing only the primary and secondary colours) divided into semi-circular arcs. Each arc shows a family of colours which are harmonious. Three other families could have been shown. If yellow, green and blue is one of them, what are the other two?

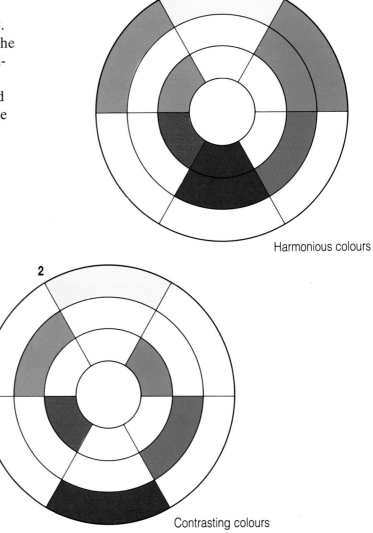

Harmonious colours

Colours which are opposite on the colour wheel (diagram 2) are those which have the greatest **contrast** and are known as complementary colours.

Choosing colours for a design which harmonise can make parts of the design look closely related. Alternatively, contrasting colours can be used to emphasise the difference between parts of a design or make something stand out, for example.

Contrasting colours

To help you understand the use of colour harmony and contrast in designs, look at the things which surround you at school, in the home, outdoors, in shops, etc. Look at them carefully and think about how colour harmony and contrast has been used in each design and for what *purpose*. You can begin by looking at the products pictured here. You might like to note down some of your ideas.

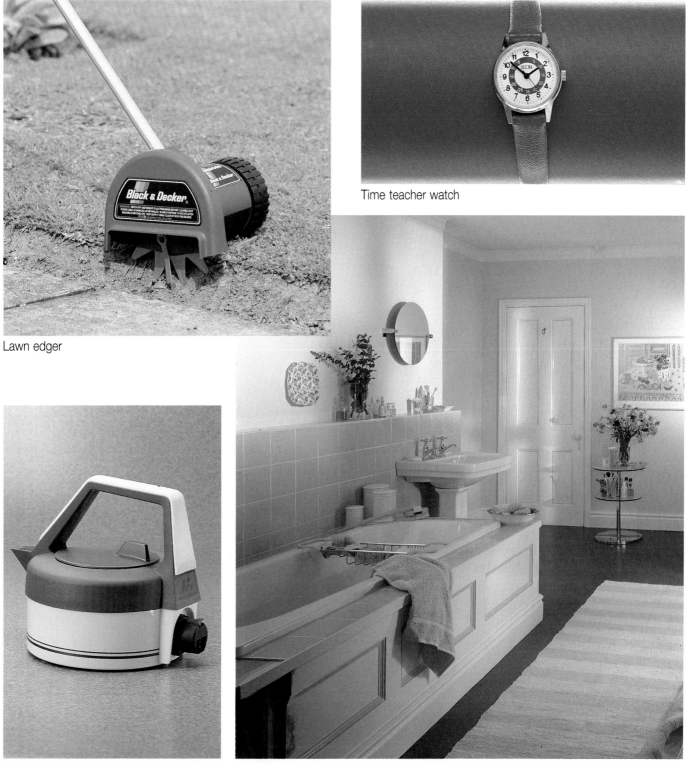

Lawn edger

Time teacher watch

Automatic kettle

Bathroom

Size and weight

Colour can be used to create all sorts of different illusions which can affect our feelings about a design. For example, an object (or part of an object) can be made to look smaller by the use of a dark colour, or larger using a lighter colour.

Similarly, dark colours can be used to make things look heavier (or stronger) whilst lighter colours can make them look lighter in weight.

See if you can identify some designs in which light or dark colours have been used for the purposes described.

Colour and emotions

The way a design makes us feel has a lot to do with its aesthetic appeal, and through the use of colour our very moods can be affected. For example, yellow is supposed to have a soothing effect upon us, whilst red (in large areas) can be oppressive. Colours also can give a sense of **warmth** or **coldness**. The warm colours include red, orange and yellow, while the cool colours include violet, blue and green. Not least of course, colour can make things look bright or dull, exciting or boring.

With the above in mind, write down some of your feelings and thoughts about the room in the picture.

Colour association

Through our experiences as we grow up we come to associate different colours with particular situations, products or designs. Red for danger and green for safety is an obvious example. White for cleanliness is another. Do you think that people would buy brown nappies or black washing powder, for example?

See if you can think of any other colour associations and examples of how they are exploited in product design, packaging, advertising, etc.

Finally, remember to take colour association into account in your own designs.

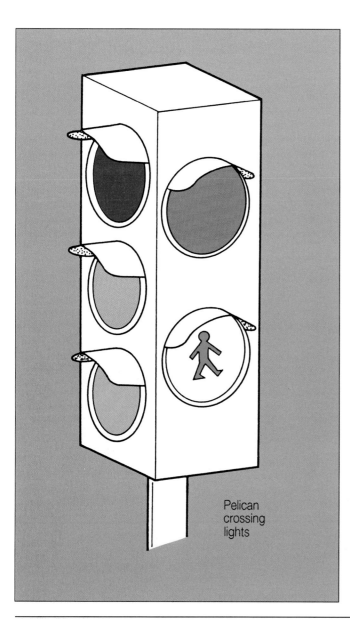

Pelican crossing lights

Principles of visual design

There are certain ways of arranging and combining the *visual elements* of a design which most people accept and feel comfortable with. As a consumer you make decisions all the time about whether things 'look right'. As a designer and maker you have to make the same decisions.

Some of the ways of *arranging* the visual elements are discussed below.

Proportion

Most of the things we design and make are made up of a number of different parts. When a design is in **proportion**, the relative size and arrangement of these parts, and the dimensions of the design as a whole, will 'look right', but of course this is a matter of personal taste.

Which of the cups and saucers shown here do *you* think has good proportions?

As well as being in proportion 'themselves', designs should also be in proportion to the environment in which they will be used and the people who will use them (see 'Ergonomics' chapter 3). If a design is suited to its purpose, and functions well, its dimensions will be right and its proportions should look good.

Maclaren buggy – a well proportioned design

Nature is very good at producing good proportions and can be a rich source of reference for designers. Take flowers and plants for example, they always seem to be 'just the right size' for their particular growing environment.

People through the ages have also striven to produce 'pleasing' proportions in their designs, and therefore the built environment is a valuable reference source. The ancient Greeks felt that the dimensions of a *rectangle* with the most pleasing proportions, had sides in a ratio of 1 to 1.6 (1 : 1.6) and they exploited this in the construction of the famous Parthenon. Many designers have since exploited this so called 'golden mean proportion' in their designs.

Balance

When the elements of visual design (shape, form, texture, colour, etc), are the 'same' on either side of an imaginary central line (one side being a mirror image of the other), the design is said to be **symmetrical**. Symmetry is one way of creating **balance** in a design, giving it a sense of stability.

Taj Mahal, India

Visual balance can also be created **asymmetrically**. This means that the visual elements on either side of the 'central line' may be different, but because of their differing proportions balance is maintained. It is not uncommon for a design to be symmetrical in one plane, and asymmetrical in another. The kettle shown here is an example.

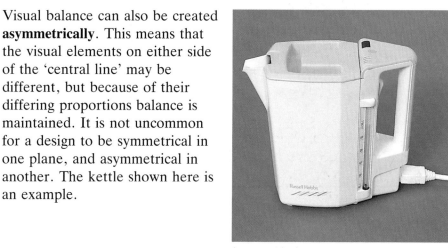

Asymmetrical

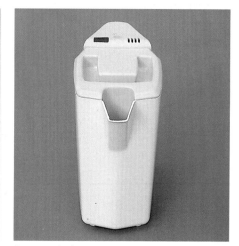

Symmetrical

Nature provides many examples of another kind of balance – **radial balance**, where elements of the design radiate in a uniform manner from a central point.

As a designer, an awareness of visual balance is very important, since a sense of stability in a design is more readily 'accepted' by the human mind than instability.

Radial balance

Radial balance in a light fitting

Harmony and contrast

The elements of visual design can be arranged to create either a sense of harmony or contrast within a design. The way in which colour can be used for this purpose was discussed on page 28.

When elements are in **harmony**, they make parts of the design look closely related and generally give a feeling of uniformity.

Contrast is often used when you wish to attract attention, or emphasise some aspect of a design, or create a feeling of 'liveliness' for example. Interestingly, contrast can actually be used to enhance harmony. This can be achieved for example by contrasting some aspects of a design's appearance – colour or texture perhaps – to emphasise the harmonising features.

Table lamp with harmonising hexagonal features

Table with contrasting geometrical forms

Pattern

An artistic decoration made up of repeated shapes, is probably the first thing you think of when you hear the word **pattern**. But patterns can be both two and three dimensional. They may be designed for a purpose, or occur naturally within the design's structure.

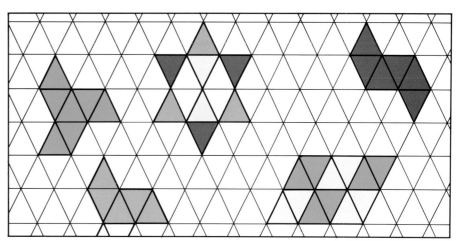

Triangular grid-patterns

Pattern is formed by the repeated use of lines, shapes, forms, texture, colour etc. The 'element' which is repeated to form the pattern is called a **motif**. Two dimensional patterns can be worked out on a grid, or drawn using a stencil, for example.

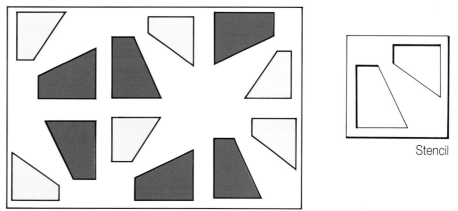

Pattern drawn with stencil

Stencil

The idea of repetition can be developed into **tessellations**, which are shapes or forms which 'interlock' within the design.

Patterns are usually designed to make something look more attractive or to disguise an unwanted feature. They are often applied to surfaces which have little decorative character of their own.

Tesselated pattern

Patterns which occur naturally within a design often arise out of **function**. The familiar pattern created by bricks in a wall arises out of the need to make the bricks 'key' together for strength. Even the pattern of holes in a pair of training shoes arises partly from the need to keep the feet cool.

An example of pattern in three dimensional design is in the repeated use of **standardised units**. This can be seen in designs ranging from kitchen equipment to buildings.

As a designer, an understanding of pattern is very important – not only as a decorative feature, but because the human eye is more comfortable with pattern than irregularity.

Vegetable rack

Conclusions

Some of the factors which can affect a design's **appearance** and its **aesthetic** appeal have been discussed in this chapter. However, aesthetics is a complex subject. In addition to our personal psychological 'make up' there are many different **influences** in our lives which can affect our aesthetic judgement. The photographs on pages 20 and 21 and those shown here illustrate some of these influences, and some are described below.

Environmental influences – the effects upon us resulting from how and where we have grown up.

Personal experiences – what we have done, seen and felt in our lives, including our physical and psychological interactions with objects, systems and environments.

Peer group influences – what our friends like or dislike.

Media influences – the effects of radio, television, magazines, etc, upon us.

Fashion – 'accepted' styles influenced by some peoples' ideas of what is 'good design'.

Travel – visiting other countries and experiencing different cultures.

Education – thinking about design and gaining experience of materials through their use in designing and making.

If you think about the above factors you will probably agree that most of them (if not all) will have some effect upon our thoughts, feelings, expectations and actions during our lives. It is not surprising therefore, that they can affect our **aesthetic** judgement.

With the above in mind, you might agree that as designers, makers and consumers, we should take every opportunity to observe, analyse and discuss designs both old and contemporary, and within nature, in the hope of 'broadening our minds' and developing our design skills.

CHAPTER THREE

Ergonomics

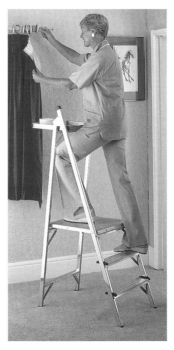

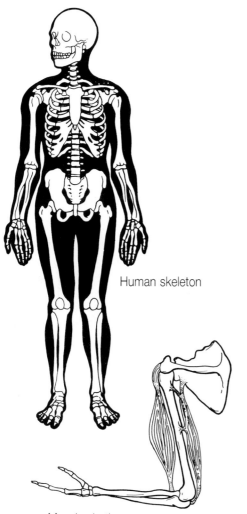

Human skeleton

Muscles in the upper arm

Most of the things we design and make are used by people. We may **touch** or **hold** them, **lift** or **carry** them, **manipulate**, **operate** or **control** them, **stand**, **sit** or **lie** on (or in) them, **wear** them, **look** at them and so on. Our **health** and **safety** and **comfort** therefore depend on them being **well designed and constructed**.

The study of the design of objects, systems and environments for their safe and efficient use by people is called **ergonomics**.

When designing for people, three main factors will require investigating:

the **size** of the people who will use the designs,
the **movements** they will make, and
the reactions of the body to the design through the **senses**.

People of course vary considerably in **size**. Some are tall, others short, some are plump, some thin. Some have large hands, some small, some can reach further than others and so on. Of course, these 'sizes' change throughout our lives. The skeleton is largely responsible for a person's size, although muscle and other body tissue plays an important part in a person's physical make up.

The structure of the skeleton, and the way in which the bones connect and articulate, enables human beings to perform a wide range of complex and intricate **movements**. The movements are produced by the contraction and relaxation of muscles (attached to the skeleton) under the control of the brain.

All human activity relies on the feedback of information from the **senses** to the brain (via the nervous system) to allow us to control our bodily movements and functions. In addition to these 'control messages', the senses of touch, sight, hearing, taste and smell also transmit 'sensation messages' (pain, irritation etc) and communicate information, and hence protect us from harm or warn us of danger.

When designing for people, therefore, all of these factors must be taken into account as we strive to mould the design to provide the greatest safety, comfort and advantage to the user.

Designing for people

Introduction

All design must begin with an understanding of the product's **functions** which should be listed in the specification (see page 12).

For example, the specification for a personal alarm might be as shown here, but in this case a vital piece of information is missing. It is essential to know **who** will use the design – their **age** and **sex** and whether they are **able-bodied** or **handicapped** and so on. Only then can the **ergonomic** factors be fully investigated.

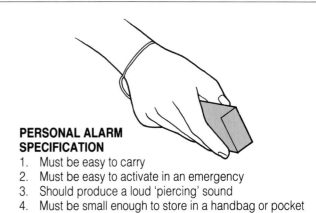

PERSONAL ALARM SPECIFICATION
1. Must be easy to carry
2. Must be easy to activate in an emergency
3. Should produce a loud 'piercing' sound
4. Must be small enough to store in a handbag or pocket
5. Should be available in a range of colours
6. Maximum cost – £10

Total design

Some of a design's functions will relate directly to the *use of the product by the person*. Others will concern aspects of the design which have no direct 'contact' with the user. However, a designer must be concerned with the **total design**. For example, it would be of no use to design a powerful audio system for the personal alarm, if the components were too big to fit into a case of the appropriate size and shape.

Size

When designing for people you must take into account all the '**measurements**' which are important for the *safe and comfortable use* of the design. However, the shape and size of human beings vary greatly. Designing for an individual therefore, is very different from designing for a group of people. In the case of a group, the average measurements may have to be calculated, but this is not always a satisfactory solution. The science of measuring people is called **anthropometrics**.

Some measurements which might need investigating include:

hand (and other limb) dimensions – these will be important if the design is to be pushed, lifted, held, carried, operated, controlled, manipulated, etc.

body proportions – these are important to ensure that a design is appropriate to the 'size and shape' of the user.

design's overall dimensions – these are important to the convenience and safety of the design in relation to the user, other people and the environment in which the design will be used.

Movements

The human body is capable of a wide range of complex and intricate movements which enable us to carry out numerous different tasks and activities. If in normal use a design causes discomfort, pain or injury, it is a poor design.

Some of the factors to address when designing for movement include:

natural body movements – avoid designs which cause the body to make unnatural movements. *Observe and measure* the limits of the bodily movements in relation to your proposed design, to ensure that the body is protected from having to turn, reach, stretch, bend, lean, stoop, etc. too far.

restricted movements – some movements can prove difficult or painful for some elderly people. These should be taken into account in your designs as should the restricted movements of handicapped users.

body fatigue – human beings work most efficiently when the body feels warm and comfortable. Designs should therefore ensure that all movements and operations can be carried out in comfort and without causing excessive muscle strain. The age and sex of the user must of course be taken into account, since these factors affect a person's strength, stamina, agility, etc.

Dashboard and controls – Ford

balance – the body must remain in balance when moving (otherwise we would fall over). All designs should therefore satisfy or allow for this requirement.

A surfboard's design allows for the continuous adjustment of balance

space – it is important that the space in, on, under, and around a design is sufficient to allow the body to function normally, without limiting the natural movements or causing discomfort.

A tight squeeze – or just enough space?

Senses

Designs can 'come into contact' with the body in a number of ways. They can make physical contact, which we experience through the sense of touch, or 'contact' via the senses of sight, hearing, smell or taste. All of these forms of contact can cause irritation, discomfort or pain (as well as pleasurable sensations of course – see chapter 2).

Some important design factors therefore include:

size, shape and form – make sure that the design fits the part of the body which will come into contact with it, the hand, posterior, back, etc. and avoids uncomfortable or painful pressure points.

surface finishes – avoid sharp edges, dangerous corners and rough surfaces, but remember that texture can be important to good 'grip' in some designs.

supporting surfaces – whilst providing adequate support, these should be soft enough to be comfortable.

For maximum comfort, surfaces should also be designed to minimise sweating. This can be achieved through the appropriate use of materials and good ventilation, for example.

heat and cold – where necessary insulate against heat or cold for the protection and comfort of the user.

noise and vibration – in excess these can be very distressing and damaging to health, therefore observe British Standards.

visual elements – designs which communicate information through sight, using letters, words, symbols etc, should be of an appropriate size, be correctly positioned, use the most effective colour schemes, be well illuminated, display good contrast in colour, shape and form, and so on.

weight – designs which have to be lifted or carried should be designed for minimum weight and ease of use.

Terminal 4 check-in, Heathrow Airport

Design exercise

Pick up your own **pen** and *look at it carefully* as you hold it in the normal writing position. Now write something with it.

Does it write well? Is it easy to use? Does it feel comfortable? Could you use it for a long period without discomfort? If you can answer '**yes**' to these questions, it would appear that your pen has been well designed for its main function.

Now put your pen down on the table. Does it 'stay' where you put it? Now put it in your pocket, pencil case or bag. Is it convenient to store there, and carry? Does it stay where you put it? Does it stay clean? These are just a few more questions to which you should ideally be able to answer '**yes**'.

Exercise

1 List and *describe in detail* all the **ergonomic** factors which you feel are important to the safe, comfortable and efficient use of a pen.

2 Outline the **anthropometric** data which you feel would be required to produce a successful design and describe how you might obtain some of this data in the classroom.

3 Write a specification for a pen for a particular market, and on paper, produce a range of possible designs.

The diagram opposite will remind you of the areas which need to be addressed. If necessary read this chapter again before you begin, or just scan the **bold headings**.

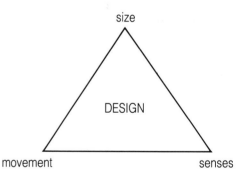

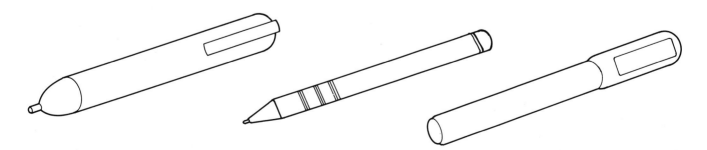

Note   With regard to the **safe** use of a pen, there has been a case of a boy who tragically died at school when a pen **top** became stuck in his throat.

CHAPTER FOUR

Structures

The Potteries shopping centre

The Forth bridges, Port Edgar, Scotland

BAe 748

A circus tent

A house under construction

Wherever you look you see examples of **structures**. They occur in nature, and in the things which people make to solve problems to satisfy needs.

What do structures do?

There are many different kinds of structures, each designed to perform a particular job. A few examples are given here. To be successful, all structures however, must:

1 Be capable of carrying the load for which they were designed without toppling over or collapsing, and,
2 Support the various parts of the object in the correct relative position.

Types of structures

The crane and the electricity pylon are examples of **frame structures**. Frames are made from bars joined together to form a 'framework'. This is one of the most economical ways of building structures. Some modern buildings have a frame structure which can only be seen during construction. Others are designed to make the 'frame' a feature of the design. How many different frame structures can you see in these pictures?

Other structures are formed in quite a different way. The body of a motor car, for example, is assembled from shaped panels and is called a **shell** structure.

Structural failure

From time to time something goes wrong with a design and a structure collapses or fails to do its job. There are many causes of structural failure and these can include: poor design, fatigue, and the failure of a material or joint.

Failure occurs because of **forces** acting on the structure. These can be **static** forces (stationary forces) due to the structure's own weight or the load being carried, OR **dynamic** forces (moving forces) produced by the wind, sea, vehicles, people etc.

This chapter looks at the design of structures through an understanding of the forces which act upon them.

A tower crane

An electricity pylon

Car body shells

The Lloyd's building, London

The design of frame structures

If you examine some pictures of familiar frame structures, you may notice a similarity between the structures, as well as obvious differences. In the illustration, Carmel has noticed a very important similarity.

Making structures rigid

Andrew is correct. A 'criss-cross' structure does make a framework rigid.

When **forces** are applied to a simple four-sided structure as shown here, it can be forced out of shape. A structure which behaves in this way is said to be **non-rigid**.

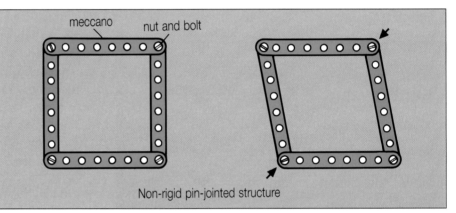

Non-rigid pin-jointed structure

By adding an extra bar (or member) however, corners **A** and **B** are prevented from moving apart. The structure therefore can no longer be forced out of shape, and is said to be **rigid**. Notice that the additional member has formed **triangles** in the structure. The effect is known as **triangulation**. The triangle is the most rigid frame structure.

Alternatively, a frame structure can be made rigid by the use of **gusset** plates. A gusset is simply a piece of material used to brace and join the members in a structure. Triangular gusset plates have been used in this structure.

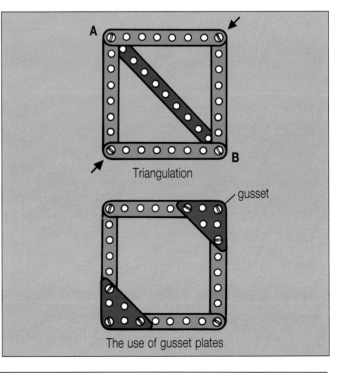

Triangulation

The use of gusset plates

Question

1 Some simple meccano structures are shown. Draw them on a piece of paper and label them R for rigid, and NR for non-rigid.

Stability

A structure which will not topple over easily when acted upon by a force is said to be **stable**.

Carmel has applied a force to her model tower by pulling on it with a piece of thread.

When the force is removed, the tower will fall back to its original position. This is the behaviour of a **stable** structure.

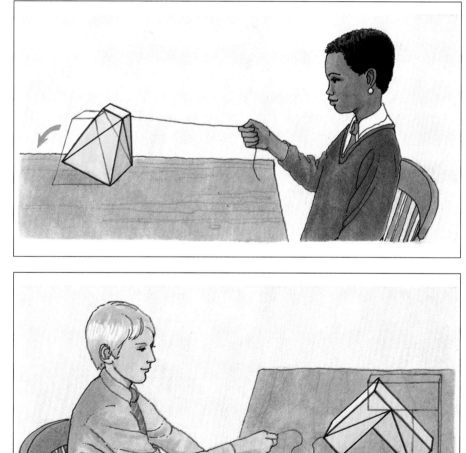

When a similar force is applied to this structure however, it tilts and topples over. This is the behaviour of an **unstable** structure.

To gain a better understanding of stability, it is necessary to understand **centre of gravity**.

Stability and centre of gravity

If you try to balance a ruler on your finger – as shown – the ruler topples and falls off.

It does this because the pull of gravity on the material to the right and to the left of your finger is not equal. It is the 'pull of gravity' acting on a substance which gives it its **weight**. (Weight is a **force** which we measure in newtons.)

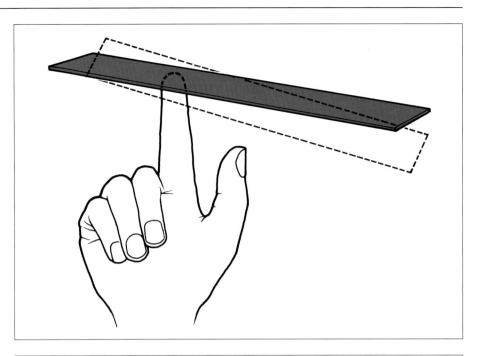

To balance the ruler you must find the point at which the pull of gravity (or weight) acting to the right and to the left of your finger is equal. When you have done this you have found the **centre of gravity**.

You can use this principle to find the centre of gravity of an irregular shaped object, too.

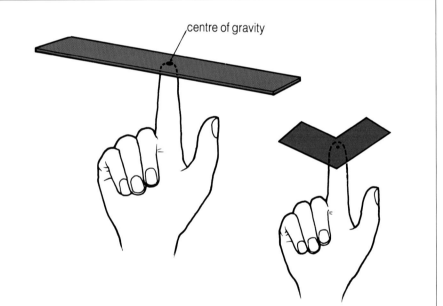

centre of gravity

Question

2 Where do you think the centres of gravity of these shapes are?

Draw the shapes on a piece of paper and mark the C of G with a dot.

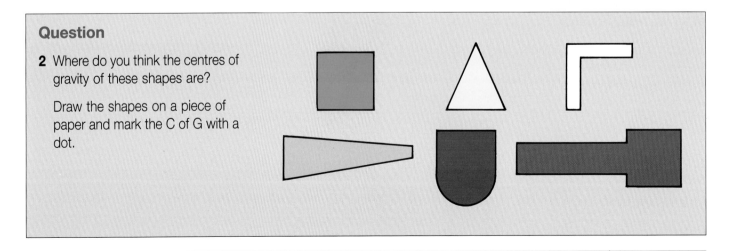

Finding the centre of gravity by experiment

You can check your answers to the above question by doing a simple experiment.

Using thick cardboard, cut out one of the shapes shown above. Hang the 'shape' and a **plumb line** from a nail or large pin. Then draw a pencil line directly underneath the plumb line.

Now hang the 'shape' and the plumb line from a different position. Again draw a pencil line underneath the plumb line. Where the two lines cross is the centre of gravity of the 'shape'.

Try this experiment with other shapes from Question 2.

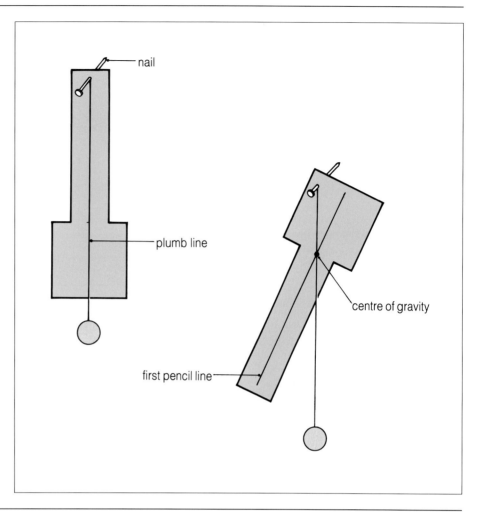

Stable and unstable structures

The **position** of a structure's centre of gravity has a lot to do with its stability.

When an stable structure is tilted, its centre of gravity **rises**. This is important because when the tilting force is removed, gravity pulls the structure back to its original position.

When an unstable structure is tilted however, its centre of gravity moves downwards.

If the centre of gravity moves outside the base area, gravity will make the structure topple over.

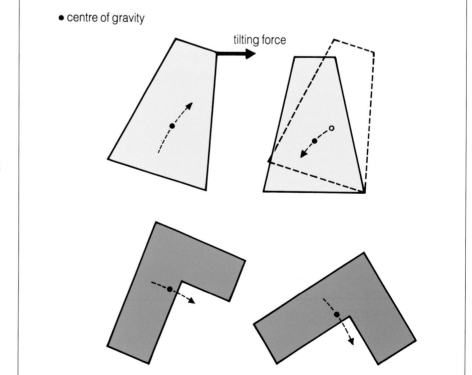

Some general rules about structural stability

The **lower** the centre of gravity of a structure, the more difficult it is to make it topple over. The lower the centre of gravity therefore, the more stable the structure.

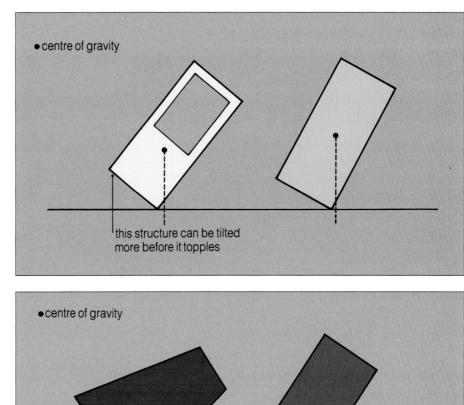

• centre of gravity

this structure can be tilted more before it topples

It is more difficult to make a structure with a **wide base** topple over. The wider the base therefore, the more stable the structure.

• centre of gravity

this structure can be tilted more before it topples

Question

3 Draw the structures shown on a piece of paper. Label them S for stable, and US for unstable.

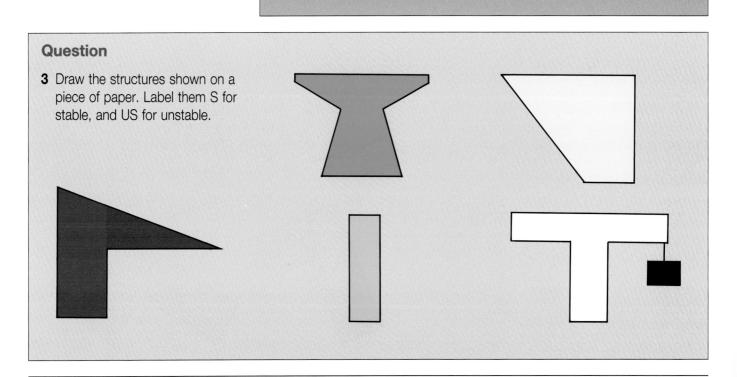

Forces in frame structures

A 'successful' structure must be able to withstand all the forces it will experience without toppling over or collapsing. An understanding of the kinds of forces which can act **on** and **within** a structure is therefore important to a designer. Five different kinds of forces are described below.

Tension forces

Forces which can cause a member to 'stretch' are called **tension** forces.

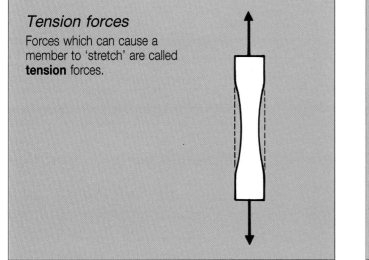

Compression forces

Forces which can cause a member to be 'squashed' or buckled are called **compression** forces.

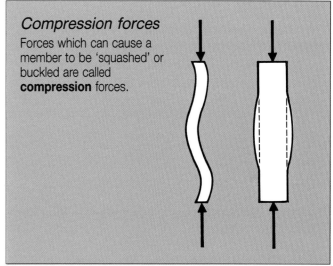

Shear forces

Shear forces act 'across' a material in such a way that one part of the structure can be forced to slide over another.

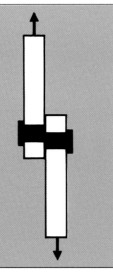

Torsional forces

When a turning force (or **torque**) is applied to a member, the member may twist. The member shown below is said to be in a state of **torsion**.

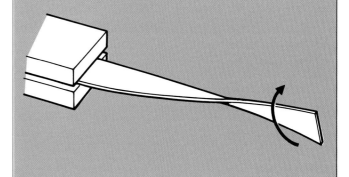

Bending forces

Forces which act at an angle to a member, tend to make it bend. These are called **bending** forces.

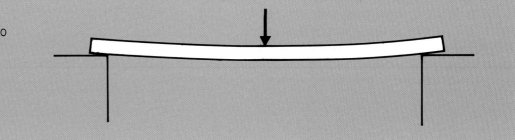

Structural analysis

When designing your first frame structure you may be uncertain about the types of forces acting in each member.

After designing and building this bridge, Carmel asked her teacher to explain how she could work out which forces were acting. The teacher began the explanation like this:

A structure always changes shape when a force is applied to it. In a straw model like this, you can actually watch this happening. The members may be stretched, compressed, bent etc, and in this way internal forces are set up which push back against the external forces produced by the load.

Analysing for tension and compression

In a simple structure it is easy to work out what kind of forces are acting.

In this structure for example, member **AB**, is being stretched by the load and therefore it feels a **tension** force.

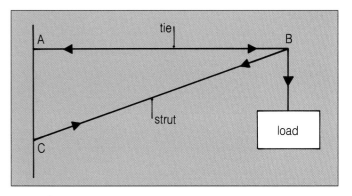

This must be true because if **AB** were to break (as shown), the points **x x** would **move apart**. This could only happen if the member was under tension. A member under tension is called a **tie**.

Member **CB** however, is being squashed. It therefore feels a **compression** force.

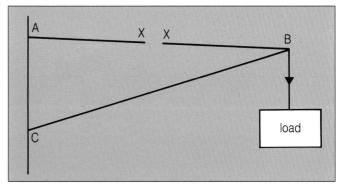

This must be true because if member **CB** were to break, points **x x** would **cross over** one another. This could only happen if the member was under compression. A member under compression is called a **strut**.

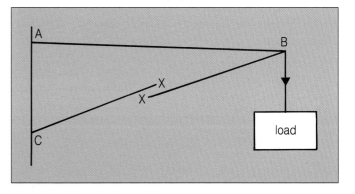

When designing a frame structure therefore, you can check for tension or compression by simply asking yourself this question: 'What would happen to the member if it broke – would the two ends move apart, or would they cross over one another?'

The identification of shear and torsion forces is usually fairly easy, and bending is likely to occur if a force is seen to be acting at an angle to a member.

Pupils building and testing a straw bridge

Questions

4 a Using the above ideas, analyse these structures for tension, compression and bending.

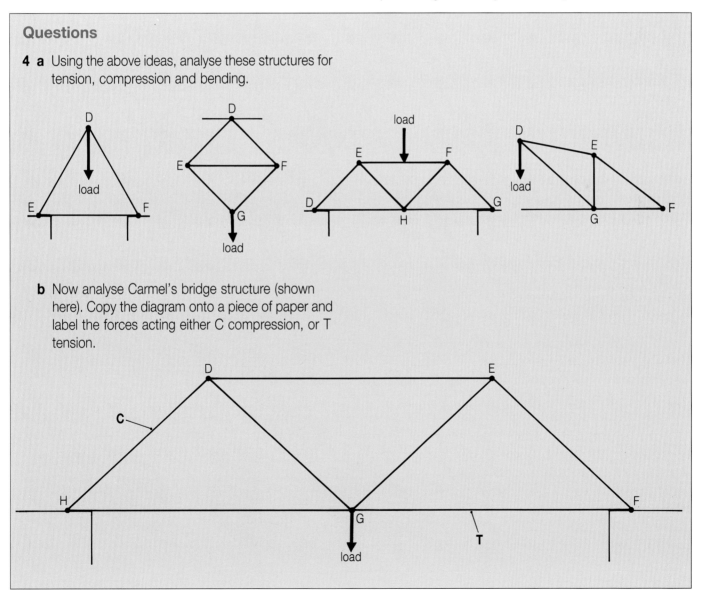

b Now analyse Carmel's bridge structure (shown here). Copy the diagram onto a piece of paper and label the forces acting either C compression, or T tension.

Types of members and their uses

As you have seen above, different members within a structure have to resist different kinds of forces. It is important therefore to choose the most suitable member for the job. In addition to its ability to resist forces however, weight, cost and appearance can be important factors in the choice of a member.

Structural sections

When a member is required to resist **tension forces**, flat strip, cable, or wire can be used successfully. However, all of these 'shapes' or **sections** are poor in compression.

When **compression forces** are present, angle girder, **I** girder and other similar sections must be used.

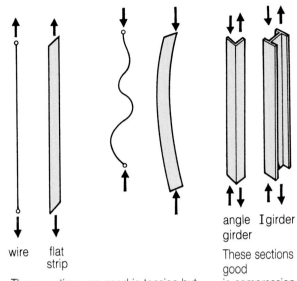

wire flat strip

These sections are good in tension but poor in compression

angle girder I girder

These sections are good in compression and tension

Beams

Any member which has to resist **bending** is called a **beam**. Beams are used a great deal in bridge construction and in buildings where we need to span a gap and carry a load.

The **stiffness** of a beam – its ability to resist bending – depends upon the material from which the beam is made, and the **section** of the beam.

For a given material, the stiffness of a simple beam is proportional to its breadth $\times$ depth^3 (b $\times$ d^3).

SURVIVAL COURSE STARTS HERE

HELP!

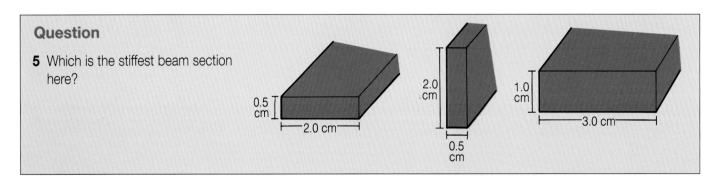

Question

5 Which is the stiffest beam section here?

0.5 cm   2.0 cm

2.0 cm   0.5 cm

1.0 cm   3.0 cm

The design of beams

When a beam is loaded as shown, the upper surface 'feels' compression and the lower surface 'feels' tension. However, along an imaginary centre line called the neutral axis, the tension and compression forces cancel out, and the 'resultant' force is zero.

Originally, all beams were made of solid material which made them heavy and expensive. Today, however, many different beam sections are available which can be just as strong as a solid beam, but much lighter, thus giving them a better **strength to weight ratio**.

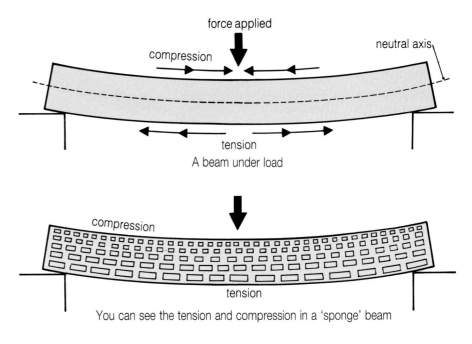

A beam under load

You can see the tension and compression in a 'sponge' beam

Questions

Designers aim to produce beams that are strong enough to do the required job, but at minimum cost and weight. Some good examples are shown here.

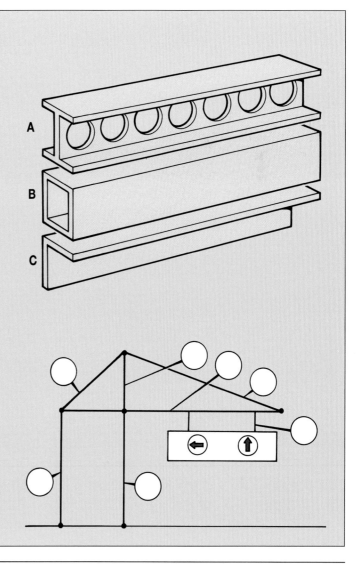

6 Use your understanding of structural sections, and a beam under load, to explain why beam **A** is a particularly good design.

7 The diagram shows the plans for a model road sign gantry (shown in two dimensions). It will be constructed from meccano flat strip and angle. Angle is almost twice the cost of flat strip.
  a Choose the most suitable members to make the structure rigid and strong, but at the same time, as light as possible and at minimum cost.
  b Copy the diagram onto a piece of paper and fill in the circles. Use A to indicate the use of angle, and FS for flat strip. Explain your choice of member in each case.

Questions

8 Many large modern buildings are constructed 'around' a framework of **concrete** beams and pillars. Concrete is good in compression, but poor in tension. A 'pure' concrete beam therefore has a certain weakness.

A hospital building under construction

a With your understanding of a beam under load, explain what this weakness is.

b Explain how the steel-reinforced concrete beam shown reduces this problem.

Reinforced concrete beam

9 If wire were used to make this structure rigid, a single member would not do the job.

a Explain why, and show where a second member would have to be fitted.

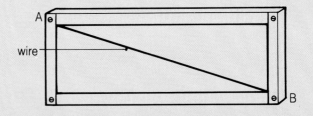

10 If member **AB** in the above structure was an **I** girder or angle girder for example, a second member would **not** be needed to make the structure rigid.

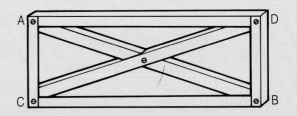

CD in the structure shown can therefore be removed without affecting its rigidity. Any member which can be removed from a frame structure without affecting its rigidity is called a **redundant member**.

Identify redundant members in the structures shown. (All members are good in compression.)

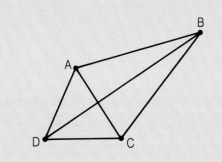

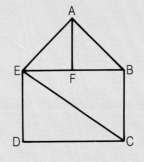

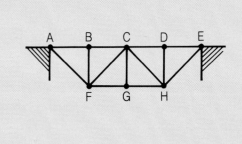

Moments

Have you ever been to a circus and watched a 'high-wire act'? The artist is able to perform balancing tricks, by using the **principle of moments**.

Moments is the strange name given to a simple idea. We can begin to explain moments by thinking about children on a see-saw.

Derrico-Alazanas high-wire act

The see-saw

It's not much fun playing on a see-saw when your big brother or sister does this.

To use the see-saw properly, the heavier person must sit closest to the pivot. You can work out exactly where each child should sit using the principle of moments.

Moments explained

The 'turning effect' produced by each child on the see-saw is called a moment, and it is dependent upon two factors:

1 The **force** produced as a result of the child's weight, and
2 the 'leverage' gained by the **length** of the beam (the **distance** from pivot to child).

The **force** multiplied by the **distance** is called the **moment** of the force.

$$\textbf{moment} = \textbf{force} \times \textbf{distance}$$

In the see-saw shown, the 600 N force is trying to turn the beam clockwise. Its moment about the pivot is

$600 \times 1 = 600$ Nm (clockwise moments).

The 300 N force however, is trying to turn the beam anticlockwise. Its moment about the pivot is

$300 \times 2 = 600$ Nm (anti-clockwise moments).

Only when the 'clockwise moments' equal the 'anti-clockwise moments' (as in this example) will the beam balance.

Since the unit of force is the newton, and the unit of distance is the metre, you will notice that the unit of moment is the newton metre, Nm.

A see-saw in equilibrium

Questions

11 To test your understanding of moments, answer the questions below. (Assume, in each case, that the beam has no weight.)

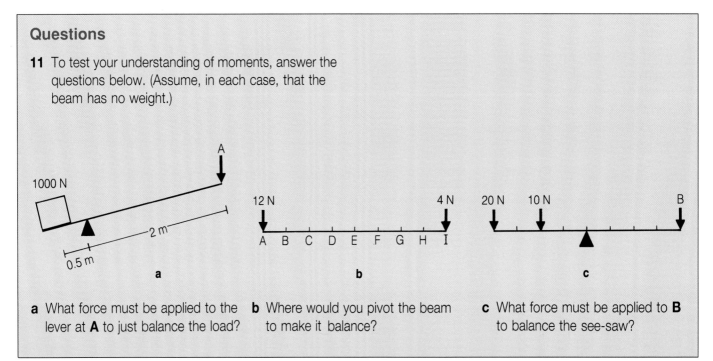

a

b

c

a What force must be applied to the lever at **A** to just balance the load?

b Where would you pivot the beam to make it balance?

c What force must be applied to **B** to balance the see-saw?

Structures mini-project – Bridge

What to do first

1 Find a piece of cardboard and cut a strip 400 mm long by 90 mm wide. This will be used for the 'roadway' of your bridge.
2 Using two tables, or two blocks of wood, create a 'gorge' 360 mm wide.
3 Span the gorge with the cardboard, and load it with a 1 N weight. The card should sag 'badly'. If it doesn't, add more weight until it does. **Remember this weight**.

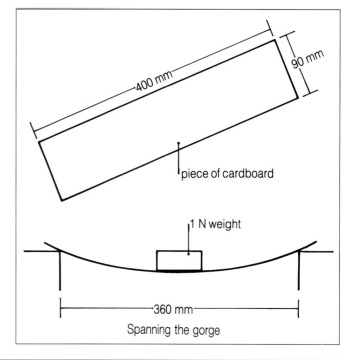

piece of cardboard

1 N weight

360 mm

Spanning the gorge

Brief

Using the card as the 'roadway', and Artstraws for the remaining structure, **design** (on paper) a bridge. The bridge must carry up to twenty times the original load on the card. No straws must be positioned below the 'roadway'.

Useful information

Before you begin designing, examine the straws from which your bridge will be constructed.

Try stretching one of the straws – in other words, put it in **tension**.

Then put a straw under **compression**. You will discover that straws are much stronger in tension than under compression.

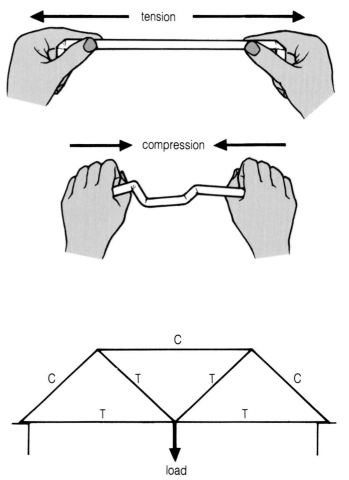

tension

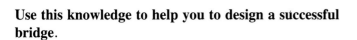

compression

Use this knowledge to help you to design a successful bridge.

Analyse the designs for tension and compression and see if each straw member is 'up to' the job you are giving it. If not, modify the design.

Note   When you have considered several designs, **choose** the one which you think will best satisfy the brief. You will then be ready to begin construction work.

C

C   T   T   C

T   T

load

Construction work

For this project you will need:
  1 piece of thin card –
      400 mm × 90 mm
  15–20 Artstraws
      (420 mm length)
  1 glue gun and glue stick
  20–30 1 N (100 g) slotted
      weights
  Paper, pen, pencil and ruler.

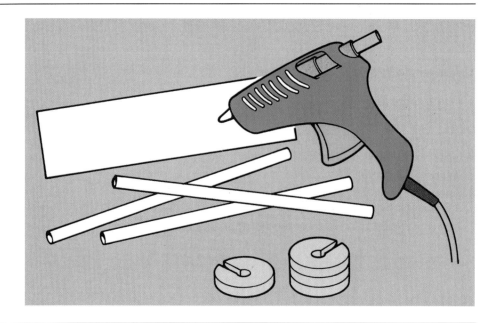

Learning from the project

Test your bridge at several stages as the work progresses.

Gently load it as shown, and notice **how** and **where** it begins to fail – but don't allow members to become damaged.

Final test

When the bridge is complete, load it until it eventually fails. Take careful note of how and where it fails.

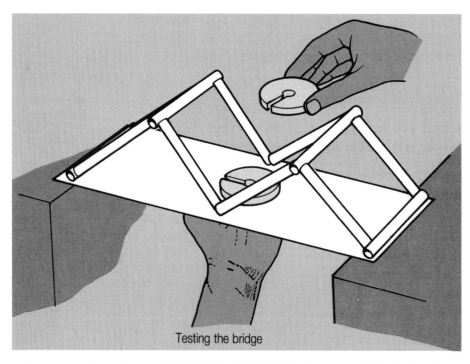

Testing the bridge

The report

You should now write a report containing the following:

1 The project brief.
2 Any information on frame structures which you made use of.
3 Sketches showing several possible designs which you considered.
4 Notes explaining your choice of design.
5 Any important information concerning the construction work.

6 Notes concerning the tests you made, and any modifications made as a result of these tests.
7 Notes concerning the final test – describe how the various parts of the structure failed, and under what kind of loading.
8 An evaluation of the project – identifying successful and unsuccessful features in the design.

Project briefs

A number of project briefs are given below. Follow the design process (outlined in Chapter 1) as you try to satisfy the briefs. Any suitable materials can be used to realize the projects including wood strips, Artstraws and cardboard.

1 Playframe – activity centre

A local authority has provided a safe 'woodchip' play area in a city centre park.

Design and build a scale model of a playframe–activity centre to be positioned on the site. The structure should provide for a range of play activities and can include moving structures (swings etc.) providing that they do not endanger other users.

woodchip play area

2 Pop group's mobile stage

A local pop group requires a stage and canopy for use on a summer tour of open air concerts.

Design and construct a scale model of a suitable design. The design should be made from lightweight sections which can be erected, dismantled, stored and transported easily.

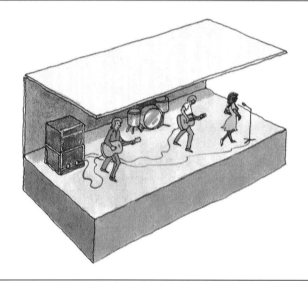

3 Water storage tank

A water storage tank is required for an industrial plant. The tank will contain 50 000 litres of water (mass 50 000 kg) and be positioned 8 metres above the ground.

Design and construct a model of the tower using Artstraws. The model should be 25 cm high, and support a mass of 1.5 kg.

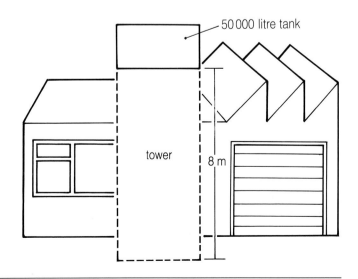
50 000 litre tank

tower

8 m

4 Footbridge

An additional car park is to be provided for a 'superstore' to cater for peak hour shopping periods. The car park will be situated across a busy road from the store and will therefore require an access bridge. The store is situated on raised ground 4 metres above the car park level.

Design and build a scale model of a footbridge suitable for pedestrians, pushchairs, wheelchairs and shopping trolleys.

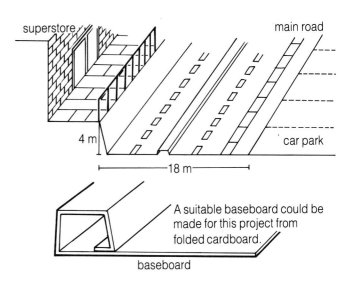

A suitable baseboard could be made for this project from folded cardboard.

baseboard

5 Rapid assembly shelter

Famine and disaster relief agencies are often required to provide emergency shelter for homeless families.

Design and construct a 1/10 scale model of a quick-assembly shelter from suitable materials. The shelter should enable four adults to stand comfortably and sleep a family of six. It must be constructed from sections which can be fitted together easily, **or** be in the form of a 'fold-down' assembly. The shelter must protect the occupants from wind, rain, and sub-zero temperatures.

Shelters in use: Leninakan after the earthquake, 1988

6 Cantilever grandstand

A cantilever type grandstand canopy is required for a football stadium.

Design a 1/100 scale model of the canopy which will provide adequate protection from the weather, and construct a 1/4 length section of the model.

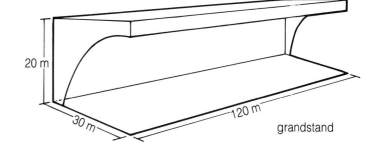

20 m

30 m

120 m

grandstand

Further ideas for projects

- Baby's play pen
- Model kit car chassis and body shell
- Suspension bridge

- Collapsible child's play house
- Novel style greenhouse
- Dry ski slope.

Lightweight pushchair
(Caroline Cunningham – year 10)

Brief   I enjoy working with children in the school creche. My idea is to design and make a light pushchair which can be folded easily.

Solution

Cantilever (Teacher's brief)

Brief   Design and construct a cantilever using Artstraws. It must be capable of supporting a mass of 2 kg (20 N), at a distance of 35 cm from the bench.

One pupil's solution

Road-bridge (Teacher's brief)

Design and construct a road bridge to cross a (model) gorge 80 cm wide. The structure should be made from 6 mm square wooden strips, hardboard, and glue. The island in the river at the bottom of the gorge can be used to support the structure if required. The maximum length of any one member must not exceed 45 cm. The bridge must not be attached to the gorge.

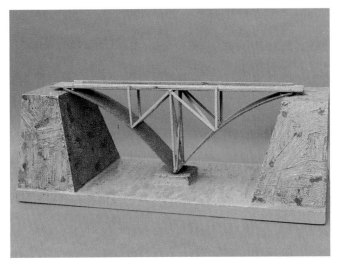

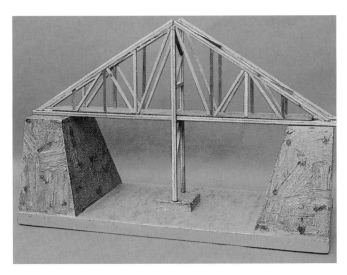

Two pupils' solutions

Fairground ride (Teacher's brief)

Brief   Design and construct a 'fairground ride' toy using any suitable materials. The toy can have moving parts, but must be safe for young children to use.

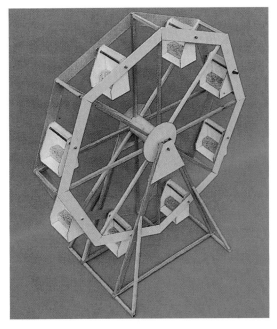

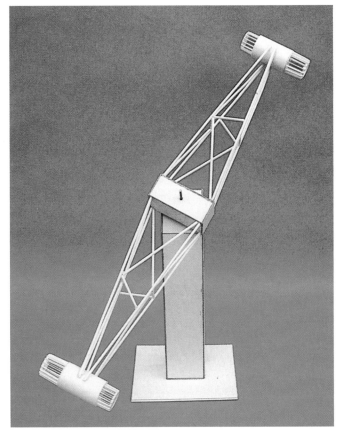

Two pupils' solutions

Systems and control – an introduction to chapters 5–7

In the following three chapters, we examine the use of a range of mechanical, electrical, electronic and pneumatic components. **When designing products which use this kind of technology**, it can sometimes be useful to use a method of design known as the **systems approach**.

Systems approach explained

If you examine any technical product and then ask yourself these questions: **What does it do? How does it do it? What makes it do it?** your answers will explain (albeit in simple terms) how that product works.

Look carefully at the example shown here, and read the answers to the questions.

Can you see that the answer to question 1 describes the **output** of the product – what it does? The answer to question 2 describes the action or **process** which takes place to make the output happen, and the answer to question 3 describes the **input** needed to make the process take place.

Instead of asking the three questions, therefore, we could simply ask, what is the **output**, **process** and **input** of the product – and this is exactly what you do when designing using the **systems approach**. When you see these words written in a systems diagram, however, they are usually written in this order: **input – process – output**.

We have just used the systems approach to analyse an existing product and to recognise the input, process and output. This is something you will be expected to do for a range of products, including products you make yourself, as you progress through your design and technology course. In addition, you will be required to use this process (where appropriate) to help you to **design new products**. To demonstrate its use, let's imagine for a moment that a **hole punch** *hasn't yet been invented*.

The first question we usually ask when designing anything is: what is the **need**, or, what must the product do? The brief for this product is shown here.

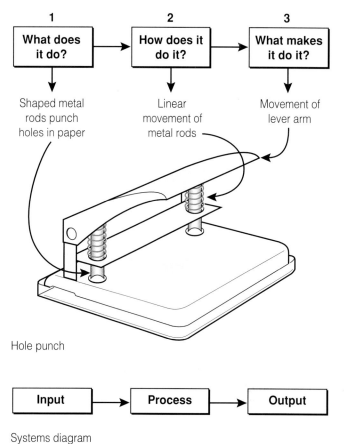

Hole punch

Systems diagram

BRIEF

To design a device for making two 6mm diameter holes, 8cm apart, 1cm from the edge of a sheet of paper.

Systems approach in action

When designing using the systems approach, *the detail of **how** the product will function* (the **process**) is not important in the first instance. The systems designer is more concerned with what the product must do (the **output**) and what **inputs** will be present. Only later will they, or a specialist designer, consider how the process will be performed. When working at school, you will act as both the systems and specialist designer. A simple way for you to use the systems approach, therefore, is as follows. First **draw a systems diagram** and then use it as a starting point for creating a web diagram. Knowing the required output function of the product, and the nature of the input, a range of possible input, output and process **devices** can then be added as ideas come to mind. The diagram below shows some ideas for the hole-making product.

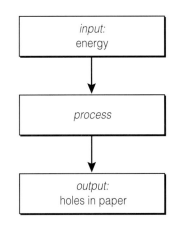

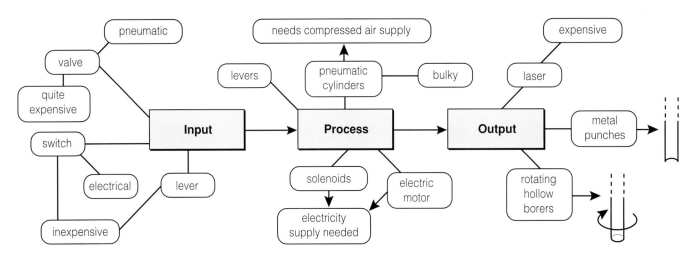

Possible solutions

Having researched the above ideas, a range of possible solutions should be considered before a final choice is made. The diagram here and the notes below illustrate one possible solution.

Output – nylon rods (machined to have cutting edge).
Process – two solenoids. These convert electrical energy into kinetic energy necessary to force the rods through the paper.
Input – low voltage electricity supply activated by a switch. Solenoids require electrical energy to make them operate.

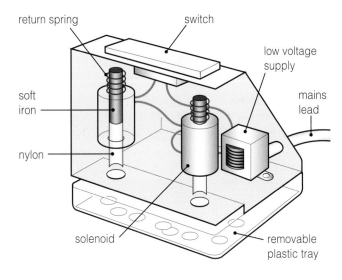

Note the word **'system'** can be used to describe any collection of 'things' which work together to perform a function of some kind. Technical products are just one example of systems. Use the systems 'design process', therefore, whenever you feel that it is useful and appropriate.

Control

In chapters 5–7 you will learn about a wide range of components used to **control** mechanical, electronic and pneumatic devices. Control is about 'making things happen and keeping them working correctly'.

An example of control is shown here. It is a door which opens and closes automatically. This kind of control system is given a special name – it is called **open loop**. Open loop describes a system where a particular input produces a particular output. In this example, when the infra-red sensor is activated (input) the door opens, and then closes (output) and nothing will change this behaviour.

Closed loop is the name given to another kind of control system – a system which has **feedback**. Feedback can best be explained by looking at an example of its use. Look at the diagram of the **water bath** shown here. It is the kind used in some science laboratories to keep things warm and at a constant temperature. Notice that it has **two** input devices. One is a **temperature selector**. Its job is to **set the required temperature** of the water. The **output device** is a **heater**. Its job is to **heat the water**. The process, or **control device**, is an **electronic circuit** – its job is to **control the heater** (switch it on and off). The second input device is a **temperature sensor**. Its job is to **feed back** information (in the form of an electrical signal) to the control device. The control device **compares** this signal with the signal from the temperature selector. When the two signals are the same, the control device 'knows' that the water has reached the required temperature and it **turns the heater off**. If the water temperature falls, however, the control device **turns the heater back on again** and in this way the water can be kept at a constant temperature. Can you see that it is the **feedback** which enables this to happen?

In conclusion, a closed loop system has a means of checking what is happening at the output, and, if necessary, changing what is happening. An open loop system, however, cannot do this.

Look out for **feedback** in other manufactured products and consider how it might be used to ensure the correct functioning of *products you make* as you progress through your design and technology course.

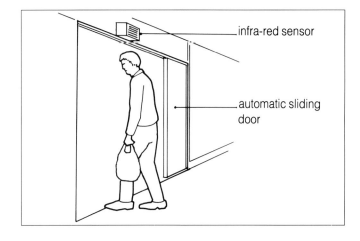

Systems diagram for automatic sliding door

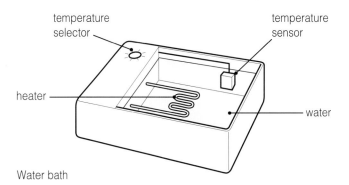

Water bath

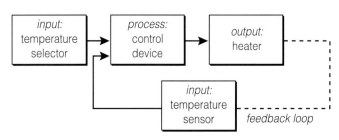

Systems diagram with feedback

CHAPTER FIVE

Mechanisms

Logging machinery

Aerogenerator

Water wheel

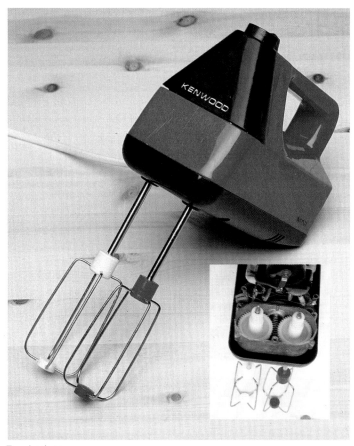

Food mixer

Tractor and plough

Oil derrick

Scissor jack

Forklift truck

The technological advances made by people through the ages have been closely linked with their ability to harness energy. The beauty of energy is that it can be transferred from one form into another. For example, the kinetic energy (or motion energy) of rushing water can be transferred, by a water wheel, into rotary kinetic energy. Similarly, a modern aerogenerator transfers the kinetic energy of the wind into electrical energy in the wires of the generator. These, and all the other 'energy converters' shown on this page are of course examples of **machines**.

Mechanisms

All machines, however basic or complex, are made up of simple **mechanisms**. A mechanism is a device which changes an input motion and force, into a desired output motion and force.

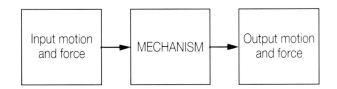

The car jack shown uses a **screw** and **nut mechanism**. This changes the 'round and round' motion (or **rotary motion**) at the screw into a straight line motion (or **linear motion**) at the nut, and changes a **small force** at the screw into a **large force** at the nut. In this way, only a small effort is required by the motorist, to raise the heavy load through the action of the scissor mechanism.

Unlike the scissor jack, most machines today have their mechanisms hidden from view within the body of the machine or behind panels. For aesthetic, ergonomic and safety reasons therefore, we rarely see them. You can be sure however, that wherever **movement** takes place, whether in a simple device like a door handle or a complex technological system, mechanisms will be found.

This chapter is all about different mechanisms, how they work, and how they can be used.

Pulley systems

Rotary motion is the most common type of motion to be found in machines.

In many machines, rotary motion must be **transmitted** from one shaft to another. On the pillar drill shown, for example, rotary motion is transmitted from the motor shaft to the output shaft or spindle. A pulley system is one kind of mechanism which can do this. In the illustration Jill is examining the drill's pulley system with her teacher.

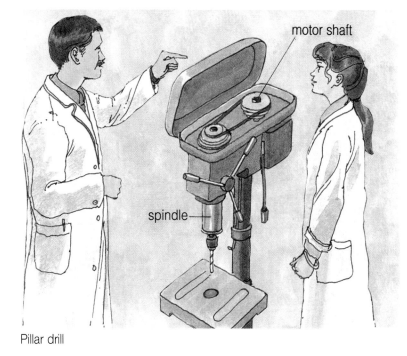

Pillar drill

Pulleys explained

A **pulley** is simply a wheel with a groove in its rim.

Using two pulleys and a flexible drive belt (to link the pulleys together), rotary motion and **torque** can be transmitted from one shaft to another. Torque, which can be described as the **turning force**, is explained fully on pages 100 and 101.

Features of belt and pulley transmission systems

The main advantages of belt and pulley transmission systems are that they are: **quiet** in operation, require **no lubrication**, and are **relatively cheap** to produce. They are used in domestic appliances for these reasons.

The main disadvantage is that slip can occur. They should only be used therefore where slip will not affect the operation of the machine.

In certain circumstances, slip can actually be useful. For example, if a machine like a pillar drill jams, the drive belt can slip. This could protect the user from injury, and protect the drive motor from damage.

Some examples of the use of belt and pulley transmission systems are shown.

Appliances using pulley systems

Washing machine – rear panel removed

Lawnmower

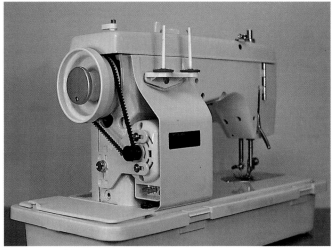

Sewing machine

Motor car engine

Shop window display project

The photograph shows one pupil's solution to the following **brief**:

Design a kinetic shop window display to attract the attention of the public and advertise a product.

The display is belt and pulley driven and uses a crank and slider mechanism to operate the saw. The crank and slider is described on page 90.

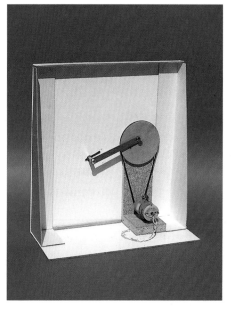

Speed ratio

The speed at which a machine's output shaft rotates, will depend upon the function of that machine. In the case of a record player for example, the output shaft must rotate at 45 rpm (45 revolutions per minute) and 33 rpm.

The rotary speed of the output shaft depends upon the **speed ratio** of the pulley system, and the speed at which the motor shaft rotates.

Record deck

Speed ratio explained

When a small pulley is used to drive a large pulley, the large pulley rotates **more slowly** than the small pulley. This can be explained by looking at the diagram of the transmission of motion by a pulley system.

If the 'driver' pulley has a circumference of say 8 cm, and the driven pulley a circumference of 24 cm, then for **one complete turn** of the driver pulley, 8 cm of drive belt is 'moved along'. The driven pulley therefore will only rotate through **one third of a turn**, as 8 cm of drive belt moves along.

Now, since the driven pulley only rotates through one third of a turn for each complete turn of the driver pulley, the driven pulley will only rotate at one third of the speed of the driver pulley.

The **ratio** between the rotary speed of the **driver** pulley and the **driven** pulley is known as the **speed ratio**. In the example above, the speed ratio is 3 : 1.

one complete revolution

8 cm

8 cm

1/3 revolution

drive belt

driver pulley 8 cm circumference

driven pulley 24 cm circumference

The transmission of motion by a pulley system

Calculating speed ratio – pulley system

A quick way of working out the speed ratio of a pulley system is to use this equation.

$$\text{speed ratio} = \frac{\textbf{circumference of driven pulley}}{\textbf{circumference of driver pulley}}$$

A more convenient way of working out speed ratio (or **velocity ratio** as it is usually called), is to use the equation shown here. The answer will be the same.

In above example,

$$\text{speed ratio} = \frac{24}{8} = \frac{3}{1} \text{ or } 3 : 1$$

$$\textbf{Velocity ratio} = \frac{\textbf{diameter of driven pulley}}{\textbf{diameter of driver pulley}}$$

Rotary shaft speeds

Once the velocity ratio of a system is known, the rotary speed (or **rotary velocity**) of a given shaft can be calculated.

The pulley system shown has a velocity ratio of 2 : 1. If you could rotate the input shaft at exactly 60 rpm, the output shaft would rotate at half this speed, i.e. 30 rpm.

The equation for calculating the rpm of the driven shaft is given below.

$$\text{RPM} = \frac{\text{RPM of driver shaft} \times \text{diameter of driver pulley}}{\text{diameter of driven pulley}}$$

(of driven shaft)

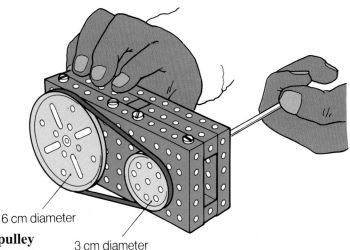

6 cm diameter

3 cm diameter

Pulley system made from Meccano

No-slip belt and pulley system

Where a quiet, no-slip drive is required, a special toothed belt and pulleys can be used.

Some motor car engine timing mechanisms use this system. In a car engine it is essential that the crankshaft and camshaft rotate 'in step' with one another. Any slip would cause serious damage to the engine.

Motor car engine timing mechanism

Questions

1 The air compressor below is driven via a pulley system from a motor running at 300 rpm as shown.
   a What is the velocity ratio of the pulley system?
   b At what speed does the compressor shaft rotate?

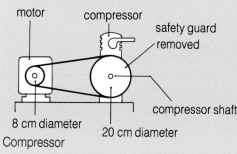

motor compressor
safety guard
removed

compressor shaft

8 cm diameter
20 cm diameter
Compressor

2 The diagram shows a stepped cone pulley system as used on some pillar drills. By changing the position of the V belt, three different shaft speeds can be obtained.
   a In which position must the belt be engaged to provide the highest drill speed?
   b If the drive motor runs at 1400 rpm, what is the highest drill speed?
   c What is the slowest speed at which the drill will run?

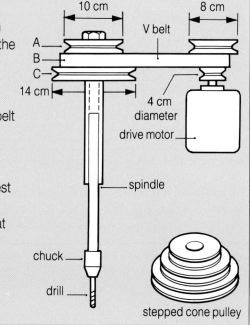

10 cm
8 cm
V belt
A
B
C
14 cm
4 cm diameter
drive motor
spindle
chuck
drill
stepped cone pulley

Chain and sprocket systems

Where it is essential to have no slip, but also a very **strong** drive linkage, a **chain and sprocket** system can be used.

Probably the most familiar use for this system is on the bicycle.

Milk race cyclists

Chain and sprocket explained

A **sprocket** is a toothed wheel, and a **chain** is a length of loosely jointed links.

Rotary motion and torque is transmitted between shafts by the traction between the chain and sprockets.

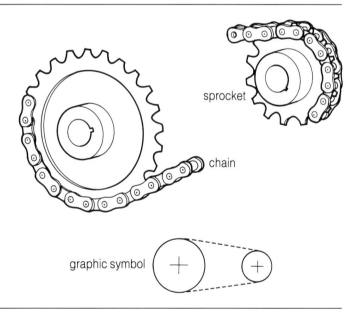

sprocket

chain

graphic symbol

Features of chain and sprocket transmission systems

The main advantage of a chain and sprocket transmission system is the positive, **no-slip drive**. This is essential in machinery where the relative position of the moving parts must not change.

The disadvantages include: the relatively high **cost**, the need for **lubrication** to reduce wear, 'backlash' between chain and sprockets, and **noisy** operation.

Some applications of the chain and sprocket transmission are shown.

Appliances using chain and sprocket systems

Motorcycle

Motor mower

Small printing machine

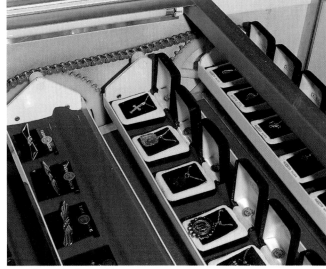

Jewellery display cabinet

Conveyor belt project

The photograph shows a pupil's idea for a sand quarry conveyor system. Sprockets and chain are used to link the conveyors providing a positive drive. This system also allows the position and angle of the belts to be changed to suit most conditions.

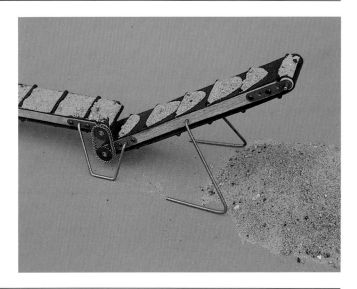

Velocity ratio

The velocity ratio of a chain and sprocket transmission system depends upon the **number of teeth** on the driven and the driver sprockets.

When a small sprocket is used to drive a large sprocket, the large sprocket rotates more slowly than the small sprocket. This can be explained by looking at the diagram of transmission of motion by the chain and sprocket.

If the driver sprocket has say 12 teeth, and the driven sprocket has 24 teeth, then for one **complete turn** of the driver sprocket, 12 links of chain are moved along. The driven sprocket therefore, will only rotate through **half a turn** as 12 links move along.

Now, since the driven sprocket only rotates through **half** a turn for each complete turn of the driver sprocket, the driven sprocket will only rotate at **half the speed** (or velocity) of the driver sprocket.

The **velocity ratio** of the above system therefore is 2 : 1.

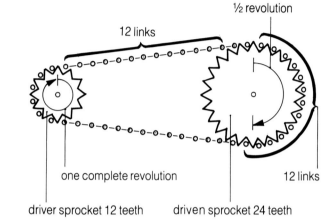

The transmission of motion by the chain and sprocket

Calculating velocity ratio – chain and sprocket

A quick way of working out the **velocity ratio** of a chain and sprocket transmission system is to use this equation,

$$\text{velocity ratio} = \frac{\textbf{number of teeth on the driven sprocket}}{\textbf{number of teeth on the driver sprocket}}$$

In above example,

$$\text{velocity ratio} = \frac{24}{12} = \frac{2}{1} \text{ or } 2 : 1$$

Question

4 A racing cycle uses the chain and sprocket system shown in the diagram.
   a What is the velocity ratio of the system?
   b If the cyclist pedals at 30 rpm, what is the road speed of the cycle?

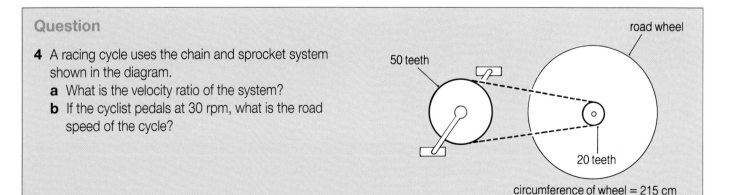

Gear systems

The **gear train** is another mechanism for transmitting rotary motion and torque. Unlike a belt and pulley, or chain and sprocket, no **linking device** (**belt** or **chain**) is required. Gears have **teeth** which interlock (or **mesh**) directly with one another.

Neena has used gears in this simple winch model.

These are called **spur gears**. The name probably originates from their resemblance to spurs worn by horse riders in olden days.

When spur gears of different sizes are meshed, the smaller gear is called the **pinion**, and the larger gear is called the **wheel**. Two or more gears meshed in this way is called a **gear train**.

pinion

wheel

Winch – using simple gear train

Spur gears explained

The diagram shows a simple gear train where **A** is the driver gear, and **B** is the driven gear.

When A makes one complete turn, its 15 teeth move past point **X** on the diagram. Since the gears are meshed (and cannot slip), 15 teeth on the driven gear also pass point **X**. For **each complete turn** of the driver gear therefore, the driven gear only rotates through a **quarter of a turn**.

Now, since the driven gear only rotates through a quarter of a turn for each complete turn of the driver gear, the driven gear will only rotate at a quarter of the speed (or velocity) of the driver gear.

The velocity ratio of the above system therefore (and **gear ratio**) is 4 : 1.

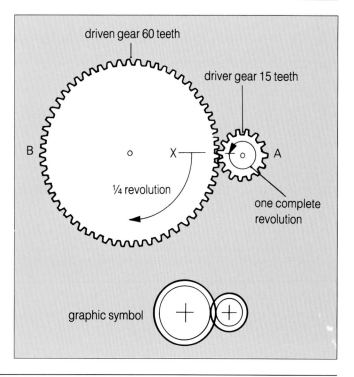

driven gear 60 teeth

driver gear 15 teeth

B

X

A

¼ revolution

one complete revolution

graphic symbol

Calculating gear ratio – simple gear train

To calculate the gear ratio of a simple gear train, use the equation shown here.

$$\text{Gear ratio} = \frac{\textbf{number of teeth on driven gear}}{\textbf{number of teeth on driver gear}}$$

For previous example,

$$\text{Gear ratio} = \frac{60}{15}$$

$$= \frac{4}{1} \text{ or } 4 : 1$$

Compound gear train

Sometimes a simple gear train cannot provide a big enough gear ratio.

In the picture, Julie is testing one of her designs for a cot mobile. It was important to make the mobile's arms rotate slowly to relax and calm the baby. On this prototype she experimented with a compound gear train.

The compound gear train explained

The diagram shows the compound gear train used for the cot mobile. Notice that four gears are used and that gears **B** and **C** are **fixed together** on the same shaft.

When the driver gear **A** makes one complete turn, gear **B** will rotate through a quarter of a turn. Now, since gear **C** is fixed to the same shaft as gear **B**, it too makes a quarter of a turn. Gear **D** therefore will only rotate through a $\frac{1}{4}$ of a $\frac{1}{4}$ of a turn, i.e. $\frac{1}{16}$ of a turn. The gear ratio of this compound gear train therefore, is 16 : 1.

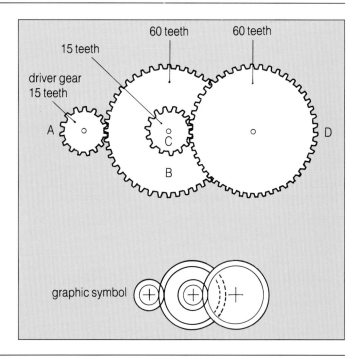

Calculating gear ratio – compound gear train

To calculate the gear ratio of a compound gear train, use the equation shown here.

$$\textbf{Gear ratio} = \frac{\textbf{no. of teeth on B}}{\textbf{no. of teeth on A}} \times \frac{\textbf{no. of teeth on D}}{\textbf{no. of teeth on C}}$$

In previous example,

$$\text{gear ratio} = \frac{60}{15} \times \frac{60}{15}$$

$$= \frac{4}{1} \times \frac{4}{1}$$

$$= \frac{16}{1} \text{ or } 16 : 1$$

Idler gear

When two spur gears are meshed in the normal way, the driver gear and the driven gear **rotate in opposite directions** to one another.

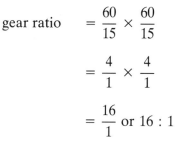

Direction of rotation of gears

However, by making use of an extra gear, called an **idler**, the driver and the driven gears can be made to rotate in the **same direction**.

Note It is important to understand that an idler gear does **not** alter the gear ratio of a system, neither does it change the velocity ratio.

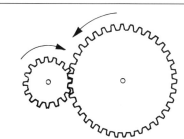

idler gear

Simple gear train with idler gear

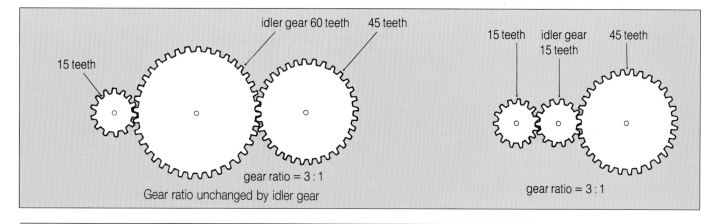

idler gear 60 teeth 45 teeth
15 teeth
gear ratio = 3 : 1
Gear ratio unchanged by idler gear

15 teeth idler gear 15 teeth 45 teeth
gear ratio = 3 : 1

Features of spur gear transmission systems

The main advantage of a spur gear transmission system is its **compactness**. Another important feature is the **minimal backlash** between gears.

The main disadvantage (of machined metal gears) is **high cost**. Inefficiency due to friction is another problem – this can be reduced by lubrication.

Some examples of the applications of spur gear transmission systems are shown.

Appliances using gear systems

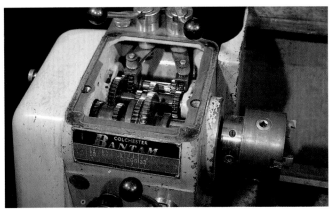

Lathe gearbox

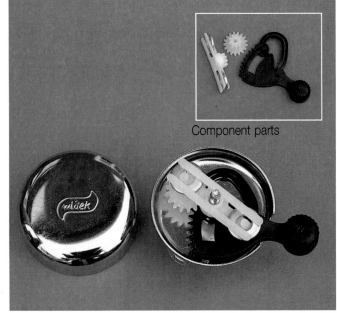

Component parts

Cycle bell

Gearbox from washing machine programme timer

Cassette tape head cleaner

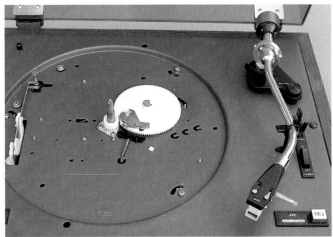

Semi-automatic record deck

Printing machine project

The photograph shows a pupil's hand-operated fabric printing machine. The print roller is driven through spur gears, and the pressure roller and ink roller are driven by friction.

The print design is cut into a piece of cycle inner tube which slides onto the print roller.

Questions

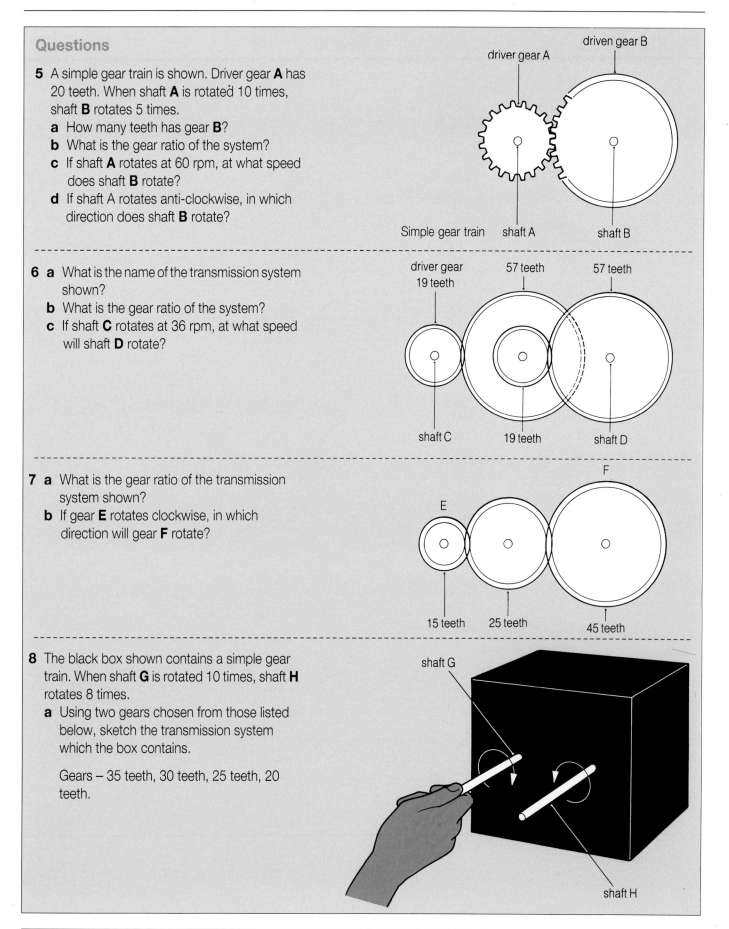

5 A simple gear train is shown. Driver gear **A** has 20 teeth. When shaft **A** is rotated 10 times, shaft **B** rotates 5 times.

  a How many teeth has gear **B**?

  b What is the gear ratio of the system?

  c If shaft **A** rotates at 60 rpm, at what speed does shaft **B** rotate?

  d If shaft A rotates anti-clockwise, in which direction does shaft **B** rotate?

driver gear A

driven gear B

Simple gear train   shaft A   shaft B

---

6 a What is the name of the transmission system shown?

  b What is the gear ratio of the system?

  c If shaft **C** rotates at 36 rpm, at what speed will shaft **D** rotate?

driver gear 19 teeth   57 teeth   57 teeth

shaft C   19 teeth   shaft D

---

7 a What is the gear ratio of the transmission system shown?

  b If gear **E** rotates clockwise, in which direction will gear **F** rotate?

E   F

15 teeth   25 teeth   45 teeth

---

8 The black box shown contains a simple gear train. When shaft **G** is rotated 10 times, shaft **H** rotates 8 times.

  a Using two gears chosen from those listed below, sketch the transmission system which the box contains.

  Gears – 35 teeth, 30 teeth, 25 teeth, 20 teeth.

shaft G

shaft H

Worm and wormwheel

All the rotary mechanisms described so far transmit motion between **parallel** shafts. The **worm** and **wormwheel** however, transmit motion between shafts which are at **right angles**.

The worm and wormwheel explained

A worm gear has just **one tooth** in the form of a screw thread, or spiral.

Each time the worm makes one complete revolution, just one tooth on the wormwheel moves past point **X** on the diagram.

To make the wormwheel make one complete revolution therefore, the worm must rotate 60 times (in the example shown).

Now, since the worm must rotate 60 times for each complete revolution of the wormwheel, the worm must rotate 60 times faster than the wormwheel. The velocity ratio (and gear ratio) of the above system therefore is 60 : 1.

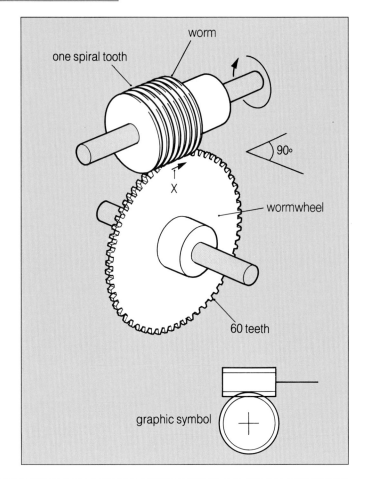

Calculating gear ratio – wormwheel

To calculate the gear ratio of a worm and wormwheel, use the equation shown here.

$$\textbf{Gear ratio} = \frac{\textbf{number of teeth on wormwheel}}{\textbf{number of teeth on worm}}$$

In previous example,

$$\text{Gear ratio} = \frac{60}{1} \text{ or } 60 : 1$$

Features of the worm and wormwheel transmission system

Probably the most important characteristic of a worm and wormwheel is the very **high gear ratios** which are possible. The ability to transmit motion through right angles, and the very quiet operation of the gears, is also important.

The main disadvantage (of metal gears) is their high cost. Plastic gears however can be produced more cheaply, especially if injection moulded in large quantities.

Some applications of the worm and wormwheel are shown.

Appliances using the worm and wormwheel

Guitar machine heads

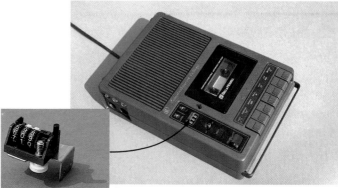

Cassette recorder

Motor car windscreen wiper mechanism

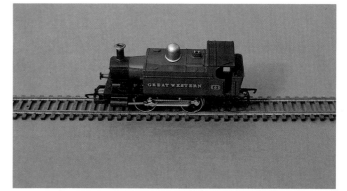

Model railway engine

Industrial motor unit

Dockside crane project

The photograph shows a pupil's dockside crane model. It was made using a variety of constructional materials and components.

A worm and wormwheel has been used to advantage in this model. A very useful feature of a worm and wormwheel is that the gears can only be driven by turning the worm shaft. If you try to turn the wormwheel shaft, the system 'locks up'. This makes the crane safe to use because when the drive motor is switched off, the load will not come crashing down.

Dockside crane project

The conversion of rotary motion into linear motion

Many technological problems involve movement in a straight line (or **linear motion**). Linear motion can be produced by the **conversion** of rotary motion using a **rack** and **pinion**.

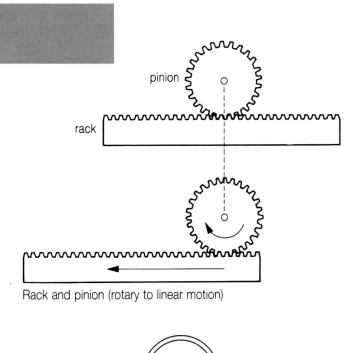

Rack and pinion (rotary to linear motion)

The rack and pinion explained

A **rack** is a '**flat**' **gear** whose teeth mesh with the teeth of a pinion.

If the pinion is rotated about a fixed centre, the rack will move 'sideways' in a straight line.

Linear to rotary motion

A rack and pinion can also be used to convert linear motion into rotary motion.

If the pinion is free to rotate – but cannot move sideways – linear motion of the rack will produce rotary motion in the pinion.

Rack and pinion (linear to rotary motion)

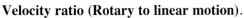

Velocity ratio (Rotary to linear motion).
The ratio between the pinion speed and the linear rack speed for a rack and pinion depends upon three factors.

1 The rotary speed of the pinion,
2 the number of teeth on the pinion,
3 the number of teeth per centimetre on the rack. This can be explained by looking at the diagram shown.

If the pinion has say 20 teeth, then for each complete revolution it makes, 20 pinion teeth will move past point **X** on the diagram. Now since the rack and pinion are meshed, 20 rack teeth must also move past point **X**. If the rack has 5 teeth per centimetre, then for each rotation of the pinion, $20 \div 5 = 4.0$ cm of rack will move past point **X**.

If the pinion rotates at say 10 rpm therefore, the rack will move at a linear speed of 40 cm per minute.

Some applications of the rack and pinion are shown.

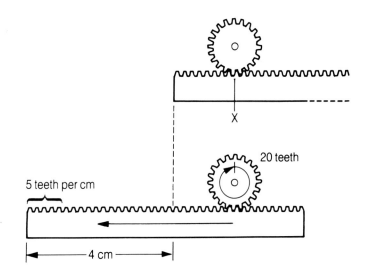

Rack movement during one revolution of the pinion

Appliances using rack and pinion systems

Sluice gate at lock

Corkscrew

Pillar drill

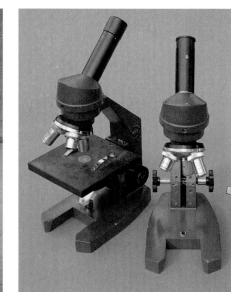

Microscope

Camera tripod

Sliding door project

The photograph shows a pupil's sliding door model. The door is driven by a rack and pinion. You can read about the electrical circuit used to control the door in Chapter 6.

Sliding door project (Fraser Campbell – Year 11)

Question

9 If the pinion has 20 teeth and the rack has 5 teeth per centimetre, how long would it take for the door to open (or close) if the pinion shaft rotates at 24 revolutions per minute? The door must move 8 cm to fully open (or close).

Screw mechanisms

The **screw mechanism** is another device which converts rotary motion into linear motion.

The screw mechanism explained

A screw is simply a spiral groove cut into the surface of a round bar.

When threaded into a tapped hole, or nut, the screw's rotary motion produces linear motion as one thread 'climbs' into the other.

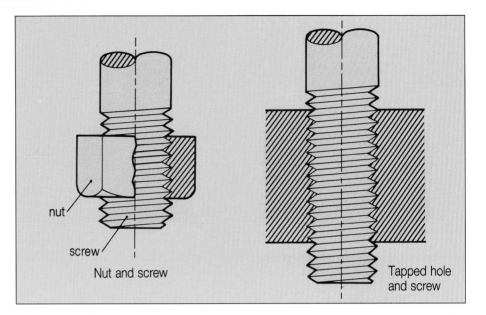

Nut and screw

Tapped hole and screw

Rotary to linear motion

The linear movement produced by the rotation of the screw is determined by the **pitch** of the thread. For each complete rotation of the thread, a nut (for example) will move a distance equal to the pitch of the thread.

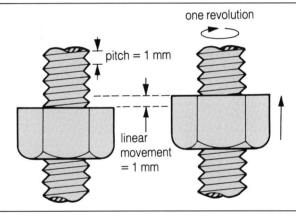

one revolution

pitch = 1 mm

linear movement = 1 mm

Types of thread

Two basic thread types are produced, the **'V' thread** and the **square thread**.

'V' threads are most commonly used for nuts and bolts, set screws and other fastening devices. The large amount of friction between the threads is used to advantage to prevent the devices from coming unscrewed.

Much less friction occurs with the square thread. These are used to advantage therefore for the moving parts of machines and tools.

Some applications of the screw mechanism are shown. Notice that in each case, a rotary motion input produces a linear motion output.

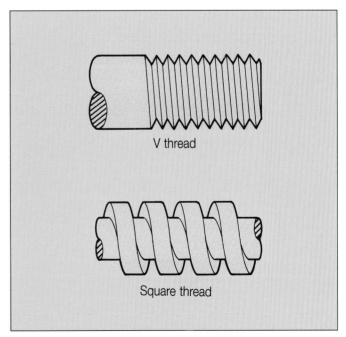

V thread

Square thread

Appliances using screw mechanisms

Playdough extruder

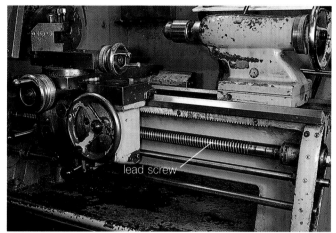

Lead screw on lathe

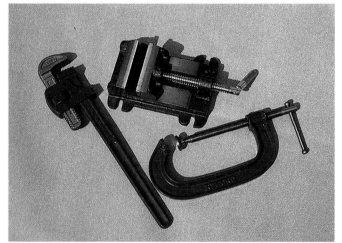

G cramp, machine vice and Stillson mole wrench

Corkscrew

Horse jump project

Claire has a pony and enjoys amateur show jumping. When practising alone however, she finds it a nuisance having to keep dismounting to raise (or lower) the rail. She decided therefore, to try to solve the problem. This is the solution she developed.

The horse jump model was designed to allow the rail to be raised or lowered by turning a crank handle. The handle is set at the correct height to be operated from horseback. The system uses two screw mechanisms, and other mechanisms described earlier.

Horse jump project

The crank mechanism

A crank is a device through which **rotary motion** and **torque** can be applied to a shaft. The simplest device is a **crank handle**.

When a number of cranks are incorporated into a shaft, it is called a **crankshaft**.

The most common application of the crankshaft is in the motor car engine.

A *crankshaft*, *connecting rod* and *piston*, is one example of a **crank and slider** mechanism (described below).

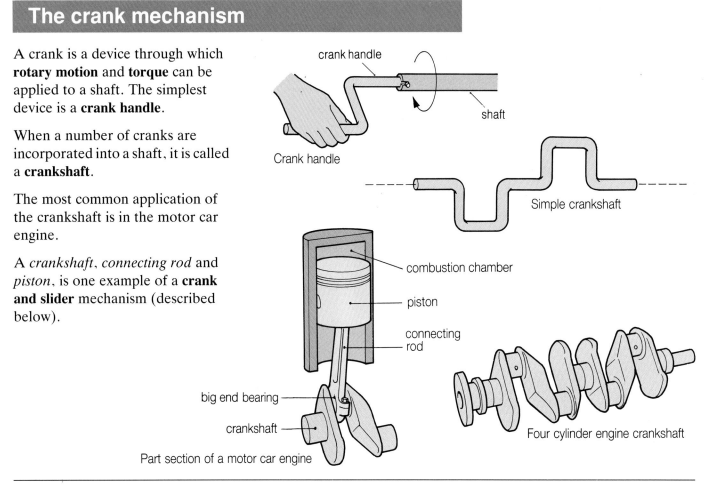

crank handle

shaft

Crank handle

Simple crankshaft

combustion chamber

piston

connecting rod

big end bearing

crankshaft

Part section of a motor car engine

Four cylinder engine crankshaft

Crank and slider mechanism

The **crank and slider** is another mechanism which can convert rotary motion into linear motion.

By rotating the crank, the slider is forced to move backwards and forwards as shown. This backwards and forwards motion is called **reciprocating motion**.

Alternatively, if the slider produces the input motion (as in the case of a piston in a motor car engine) the crank is forced to rotate.

The **distance moved** by the slider, is dependent upon the **length of the crank**.

As the crank rotates through 180°, the slider moves a distance equal to **twice** the length of the crank.

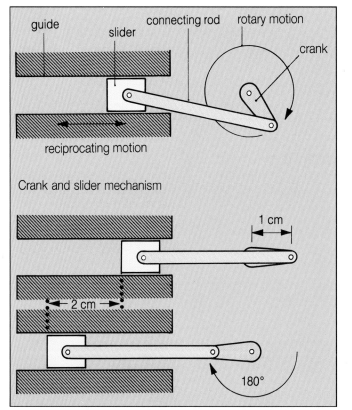

guide   slider   connecting rod   rotary motion

crank

reciprocating motion

Crank and slider mechanism

1 cm

2 cm

180°

Questions

10 The photograph shows a power hacksaw as used in some school workshops. The sketch outlines the crank and slider mechanisms which it uses.

If the **stroke** of the hacksaw blade is 12 cm, what is the length of the crank?

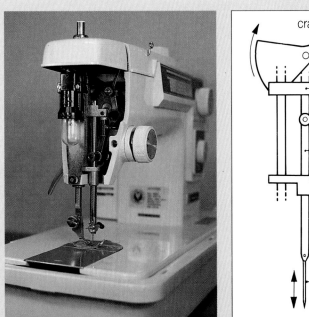

Power hacksaw

11 The photograph shows a domestic sewing machine. The sketch outlines the crank and slider mechanism which it uses to produce reciprocating motion at the needle.

At its slowest operating speed, the needle moves down 120 times per minute. At what speed does the crank rotate?

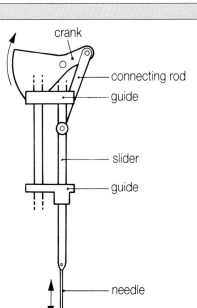

Sewing machine

12 Design a mechanism for a simple **machine press**. The mechanism must be driven from an electric motor whose output shaft rotates at 120 rpm.

The press head must move up and down continuously and make two 'down strokes' per minute. The head must rise and fall a distance of 3 cm.

The block diagram should help you to solve this problem.

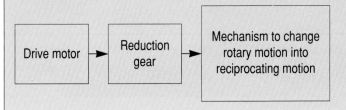

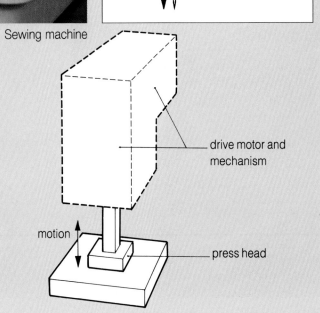

drive motor and mechanism

motion

press head

Cams

Yet another mechanism which can convert rotary motion into linear motion (and reciprocating motion) is the **cam** and **follower**.

Cam and follower explained

A **cam** is a specially shaped piece of metal (or other suitable material) which is fixed to an axle or shaft.

A **follower** is a device designed to move up and down as it follows the shape, or **profile** of the rotating cam. The follower may be held firmly against the cam profile by gravity, or more often by the action of a spring.

The **profile** of a cam determines the distance travelled by its follower. For the **pear-shaped** cam shown, the distance moved by the follower is equal to d_2 minus d_1 ($d_2 - d_1$).

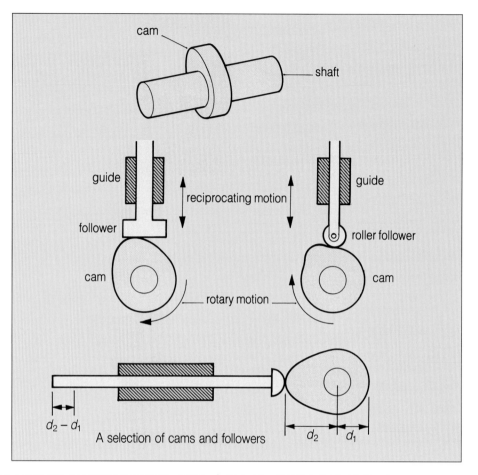

A selection of cams and followers

Appliances using cam and follower systems

Motor car engine

Gear cutting machine (shaper)

Appliances using cam and follower systems

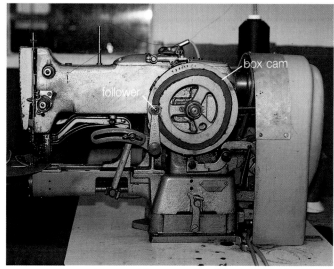

Staying machine (old machine–once used in shoe making)

Washing machine program timer

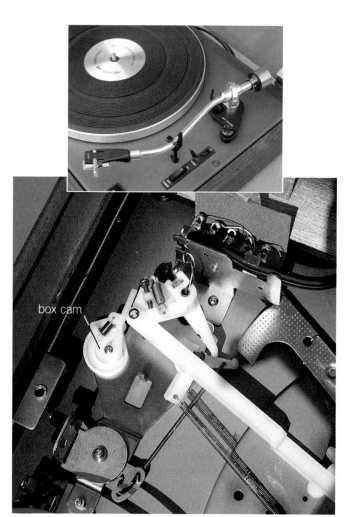

Record deck – anti-skating mechanism

Ram mechanism

Cams are used to **operate microswitches** in many different kinds of machines. The photograph shows a teacher's demonstration 'ram mechanism'. This is controlled by microswitches and a cam. You can read about the application of a ram mechanism, and how it is controlled, on page 162.

Levers and linkages

Levers

A simple **lever** is a rigid bar which pivots at a point called the **fulcrum**. A lever changes an input motion and force into a desired output motion and force.

A screwdriver, for example, acts as a lever when used to open a tin of paint. The input force is called the **effort**, and the output force is called the **load**.

Many kinds of tools contain lever systems, but sometimes they are disguised. See if you can identify the **fulcrum**, **effort** and **load** in the tools shown.

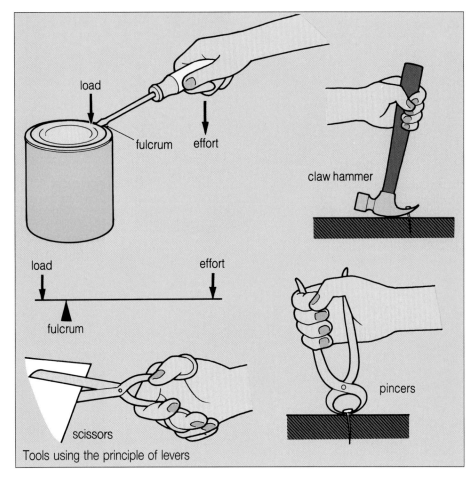

Tools using the principle of levers

Velocity ratio – levers

Velocity ratio can be explained by examining a lever in use.

Using this lever, Jack can move a load over a distance of 20 cm by exerting an effort over a distance of 80 cm.

The ratio of the distance moved by the effort to the distance moved by the load is called the velocity ratio.

To calculate velocity ratio, use this equation.

$$\textbf{Velocity ratio} = \frac{\textbf{distance moved by effort}}{\textbf{distance moved by load}}$$

In this example,

$$\text{Velocity ratio} = \frac{80}{20} = \frac{4}{1} \text{ or } 4:1$$

The larger the velocity ratio of a lever, the larger the load which can be moved for a given effort. This is explained below.

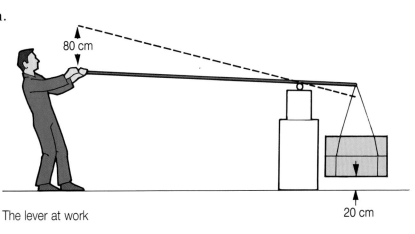

The lever at work

Mechanical advantage

Using this lever, Jack can raise a load of 1200 newtons using an effort of just 300 newtons.

If he wasn't using the lever, four times this effort would be required. We say therefore, that the lever has a **mechanical advantage** of 4.

To calculate mechanical advantage, use the equation shown here.

Mechanical advantage $= \dfrac{\textbf{load}}{\textbf{effort}}$

In this example,

Mechanical advantage $= \dfrac{1200}{300}$

$= 4$

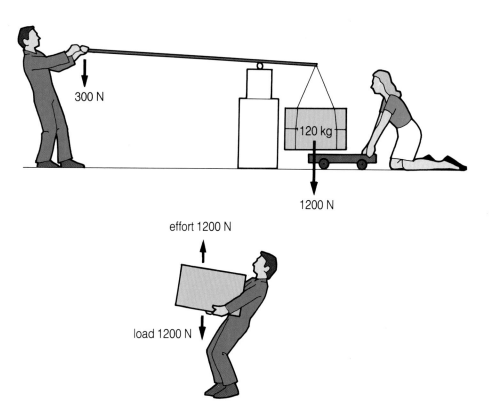

Moments

The mechanical advantage gained by a lever can be explained by the principle of **moments**.

When the effort force is applied to a lever, the lever rotates about the fulcrum. The 'turning effect' produced is called a **moment**. The moment depends upon the **force**, and the **distance** at which the force acts from the fulcrum.

moment = force × distance

When a lever is in **equilibrium** – that is, when the effort force just 'balances' the load force – the moments to the right and the left of the fulcrum are equal. (See diagram.)

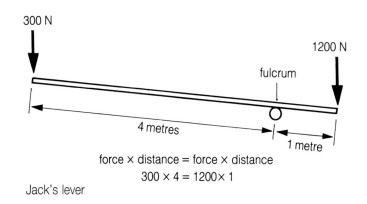

force × distance = force × distance
300 × 4 = 1200 × 1

Jack's lever

Question

13 What effort would be required to raise the load in the previous example if the long arm of the lever was 6 metres long?

Types of lever

There are three different types, or **classes** of lever – each with the effort, load and fulcrum arranged in different ways.

A crowbar is one example of a **class 1 lever**. To increase the mechanical advantage of a class 1 lever the fulcrum must be moved closer to the load. However, we 'pay' for this increased mechanical advantage by having to move the effort over a greater distance.

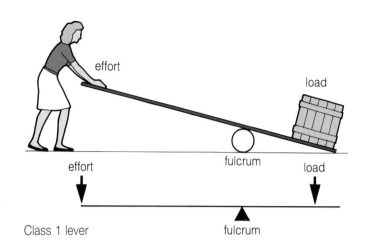

Class 1 lever

The bottle opener is an example of a **class 2 lever**.

The mechanical advantage of a class 2 lever is increased by moving the load nearer to the fulcrum. However, the 'cost' is the same as described for the class 1 lever.

To calculate the turning forces at the effort and load, the principle of moments is applied as shown in the diagram.

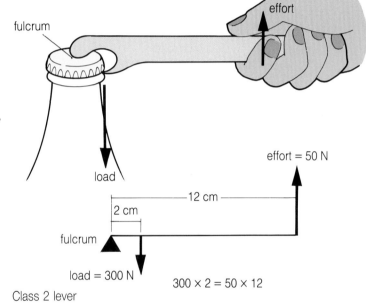

$300 \times 2 = 50 \times 12$

Class 2 lever

The arm provides a good example of a **class 3 lever**.

Unlike the class 1 and 2 levers, a class 3 lever has a **mechanical disadvantage**. The input force (the effort) is greater than the force produced at the load. However, the distance moved by the load is greater than the distance moved by the effort.

When a mechanical system requires a large output movement for a small input movement, we have to 'pay' by providing a large effort.

To calculate the turning forces at the effort and load, the principle of moments is applied as shown in the diagram.

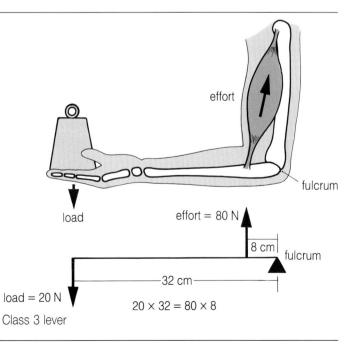

$20 \times 32 = 80 \times 8$

Class 3 lever

Linkages

Many machines and other devices use link mechanisms to make them operate. Sonal has used a fairly complex link mechanism in her 'crazy snake' project.

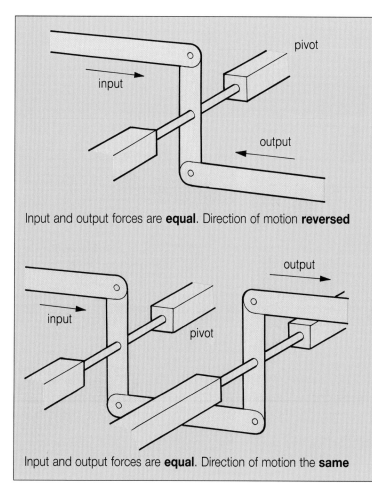

Crazy snake project

Linkages explained

A linkage is simply an assembly of levers designed to transmit motion and force.

By carefully designing the linkage, a given input motion and force can be transferred into the required output motion and force. Some examples are shown here.

Input and output forces are **equal**. Direction of motion **reversed**

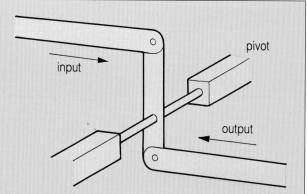

Output force **greater** than input force. Direction of motion **reversed**

Input and output forces are **equal**. Direction of motion the **same**

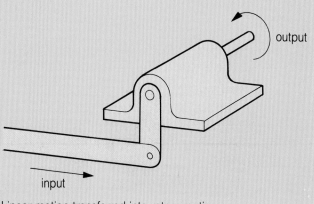

Linear motion transferred into rotary motion

Appliances using link mechanisms

Motor car windscreen wiper mechanism

Small printing machine

Semi-automatic record deck

Motor car steering linkage

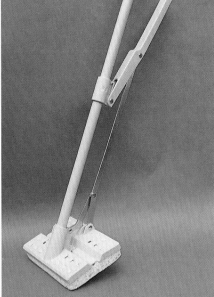

Refuse lorry – lifting and crushing mechanism

Squeeze mop

Buggy brake mechanism

Questions

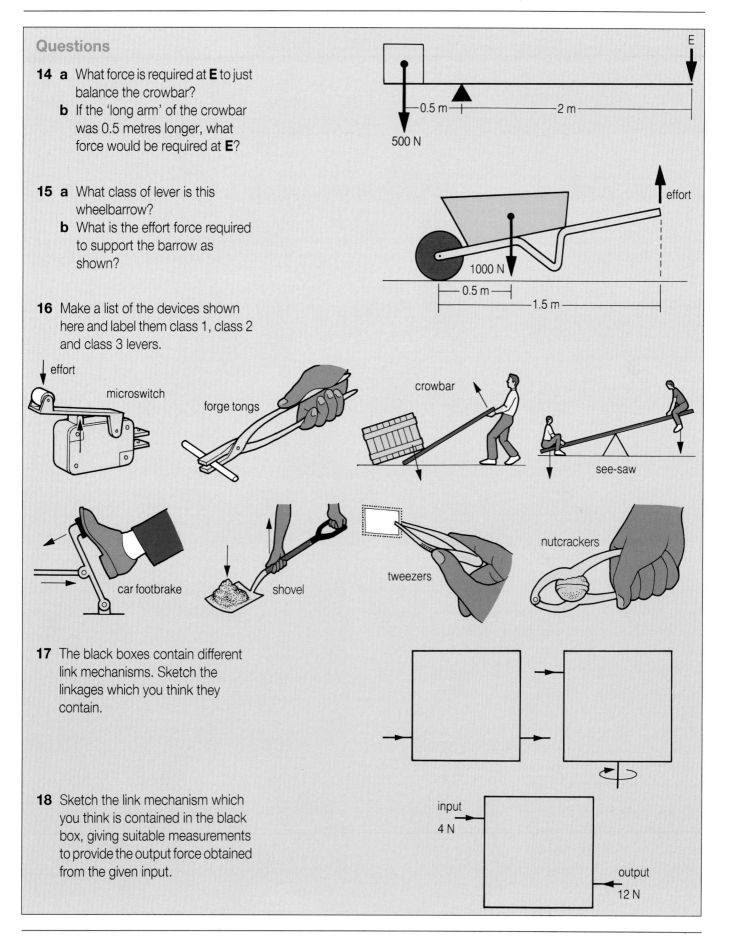

14 a What force is required at **E** to just balance the crowbar?

b If the 'long arm' of the crowbar was 0.5 metres longer, what force would be required at **E**?

15 a What class of lever is this wheelbarrow?

b What is the effort force required to support the barrow as shown?

16 Make a list of the devices shown here and label them class 1, class 2 and class 3 levers.

17 The black boxes contain different link mechanisms. Sketch the linkages which you think they contain.

18 Sketch the link mechanism which you think is contained in the black box, giving suitable measurements to provide the output force obtained from the given input.

The transmission of force

Many examples of the transmission of movement (or **motion**) have been given in this chapter. However, machines do **work**, and therefore mechanisms must transmit **force** as well as motion. (Work = force × distance moved.)

John's teacher has set up a simple experiment to demonstrate the transmission of force. A heavy load is attached to a piece of string, which is wrapped around an axle, and John has to try to 'wind it up'.

John finds it difficult because such a large **turning force** is required.

By using a second axle and a transmission system however (a gear train in this example), a much smaller turning force is required. John can now raise the load very easily.

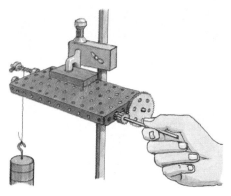

The explanation

Imagine how easy it would be to turn the axle in the first experiment if there was an 'arm' attached to it as shown in the diagram. The action is rather like a lever. In fact, just like a lever, the longer the arm, the easier it would be to produce a turning motion. The 'arm' in fact multiplies the turning force applied to the axle. We call the turning moment (or force $F \times$ distance r) a **torque**.

Now, when two gears are meshed, as shown, they act rather like levers. Each gear tooth can be regarded as the end of a lever. When shaft **A** is turned, 'lever **A**' applies a force to the end of 'lever **B**'. The **longer** lever '**B**' is made therefore, the greater the **torque** which is applied to the shaft **B**.

We can make 'lever **B**' longer of course, by using a gear with a greater number of teeth. Further, the smaller we make gear **A**, the greater the force which appears at the end of 'lever **A**'. A gear system therefore, not only transmits motion, but also transmits and converts torque.

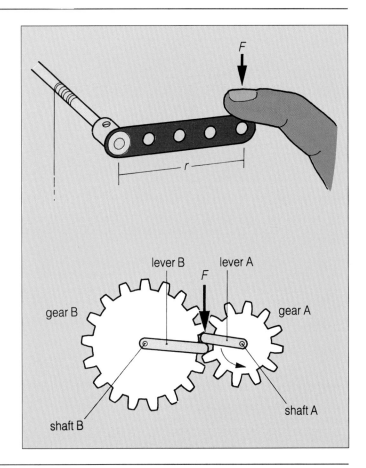

The importance of torque conversion

Motors used in school technology projects tend to be small, low-powered types. The shaft usually turns fairly quickly, and with very little torque.

If you tried to use such a motor to drive directly to the wheel of a small vehicle, for example, the motor just wouldn't cope, and would possibly 'burn out'.

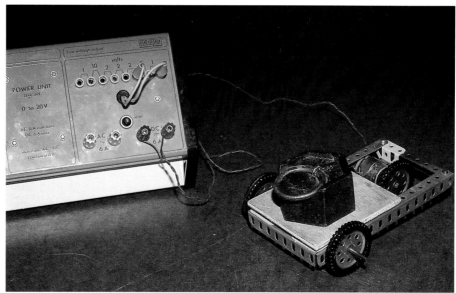

Motor provides insufficient torque to drive the loaded vehicle

You can feel just how much torque is required to drive a small vehicle, by turning the axle with your fingers.

To successfully drive this vehicle from its motor, the high-speed low-torque output must be converted into a **low-speed**, **high-torque** output. To do this, a transmission system will be needed.

By using a suitable transmission system, both models and full-size machines can be made to operate at the correct speed and with enough torque to do the job.

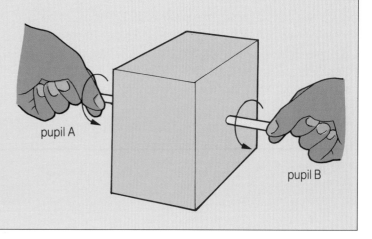

By turning the axle by hand, you can feel just how much torque is required

Questions

19 The black box shown contains a transmission system. Two pupils use the box in a 'test of strength' by applying turning forces as shown. Pupil A finds it very easy to beat pupil B.
   a Sketch two different transmission systems which would give pupil A the best possible chance of winning.
   b Explain why pupil A can win so easily using your chosen systems.

pupil A

pupil B

Project briefs

A number of project briefs are given below. Follow the design process (outlined in Chapter 1) as you try to satisfy the briefs. Any suitable materials and construction kits – Lego, meccano, etc. – can be used to realize the projects.

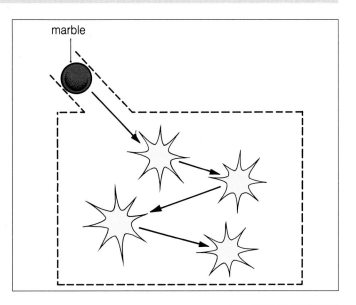

1 Mechanical toy

Design and construct a mechanical toy which is 'driven' by the energy of a moving marble. As the marble moves, it should trigger all sorts of interesting visual and sound effects.

2 Alternative energy vehicle

Energy can be stored in a stretched spring or elastic band. This is sometimes called strain energy.

Design and construct a small vehicle which is driven by strain energy. Test the completed vehicle for maximum speed, hill climbing ability, and maximum distance travelled.

$$\text{speed} = \frac{\text{distance covered (m)}}{\text{time taken (s)}}$$

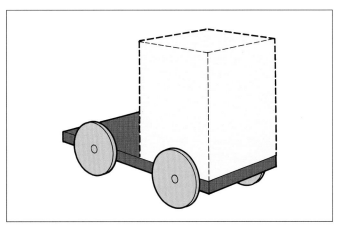

3 Builder's lift

A small building firm requires a lift to carry bricks, mortar and other building materials up the scaffolding.

Design and build a model of a suitable lift. The lift must be simple in operation and easy to install. It can be either hand-operated, or driven by an electric motor. The lift must be completely safe in its operation – for example, if the driving force is removed the lift must not be able to 'crash' to the ground.

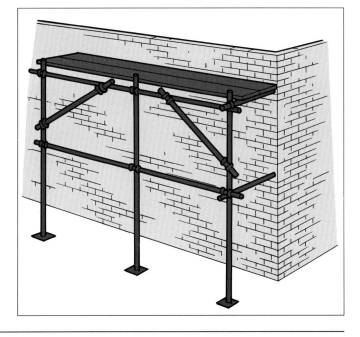

4 Shop window display

A shopkeeper requires a window display unit for a jeweller's shop. The purpose of the unit is to display watches in a novel way to attract the attention of passers by.

Design and construct a display unit which makes use of movement to attract attention. The unit can display either a number of watches, or a single watch.

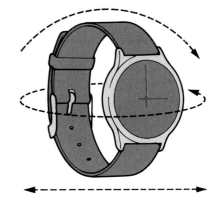

5 Coin sorter

'Mixed up' 1p and 2p coins require sorting into separate containers.

Design and construct a device which will accept the mixed up coins, separate them and store them separately.

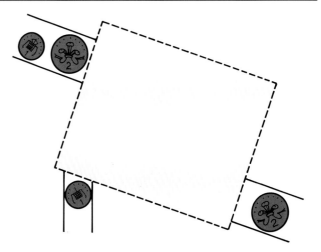

6 Fun park cable car

With the hope of attracting more visitors, a local 'fun park' wishes to install a cable car ride.

Design and construct a scale model of one section of the ride. This should include towers, winding gear and cars. For the purpose of the model, the winding gear can be driven using a crank handle. The system must be designed for maximum safety and the cars must provide protection against the wind, rain and snow.

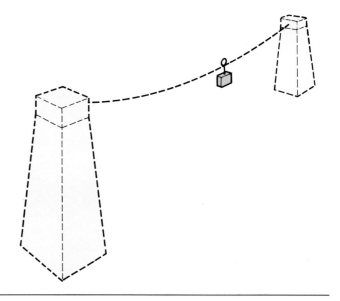

Further ideas for projects

- Swing bridge
- Fairground ride
- Slow-moving rough terrain vehicle

- Pull-along toy
- Walking robot
- Gardening aid for the elderly

- Mechanical game
- Child's pedal toy
- Automatic aluminium/steel drinks can sorter

Examples of school technology projects

Energy converters (Teacher's brief – year 10)

Brief – Unlike the fossil fuels which will eventually run out, some energy sources can be used over and over again. These are called **renewable** energy sources and include the wind, waves, tide and solar energy (energy from the sun). Design and construct a machine which can harness one of these energy sources to do useful work.

Some solutions

Water turbine which can raise a load.
Nikki Berridge year 10.

Wind turbine which can both raise and lower a load. Adrian Horsburgh and Michael Freeman year 10.

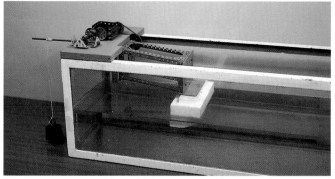

A wave energy machine which can raise a load. (Teacher's demonstration model).

A water turbine which can generate electricity. Samantha Veitch – year 10

Log sorting machine (Philip Beasley – year 11)

Brief – When I was on holiday in Canada I went to a Timber Mill where I got the idea for my project. I want to design and make a machine which will separate long logs from short logs and scraps.

Solution

Sorting device (Susan Riley – year 10)

Whilst visiting a local industrial complex, I became fascinated with the machine used for sorting and packaging.

Brief – I would like to test my ingenuity by designing a device for sorting out discs or ball bearings of different diameters, or cotton reels of different colour.

Solution – Ball bearing sorter

Robot arm (David Cox – year 10)

After watching the TV reports of the Chernobyl nuclear accident I began to understand some of the dangers of nuclear energy, particularly for those who had to work on the site of the power station.

Brief – To design and construct a remote-controlled robot arm for use in a dangerous environment.

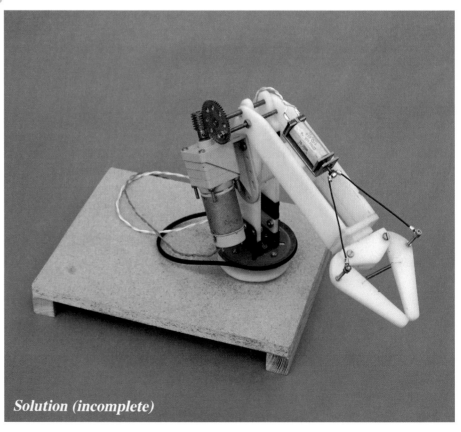

Solution (incomplete)

Railway level-crossing barrier (Leslie Hind – year 11)

My hobby is model railways.
I have an O gauge layout which I
am gradually adding to, but the
accessories are very expensive.
I would like to buy a level crossing
but I cannot afford one.

Brief – To design and make a
suitable level crossing using cheap
materials and components, and to
produce a set of plans for its
construction which I could sell to
other enthusiasts.

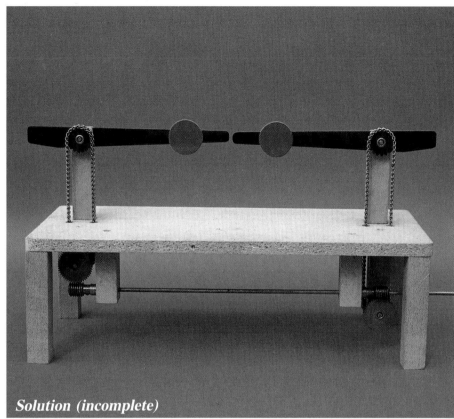

Solution (incomplete)

Car park barrier (Matthew Lock – year 10)

My neighbour works as a gateman
at a small inner city company. His
job is to operate a car park barrier
by hand when employees' cars
arrive and leave. This can be a
very miserable job, especially
when it is cold and wet.

Brief – Design a semi-automatic
car park barrier which can be
controlled from inside the
gateman's hut.

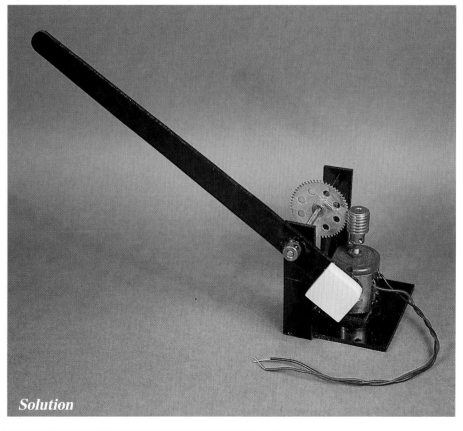

Solution

CHAPTER SIX

Control electrics and electronics

Automatic sliding door

Payphone in use

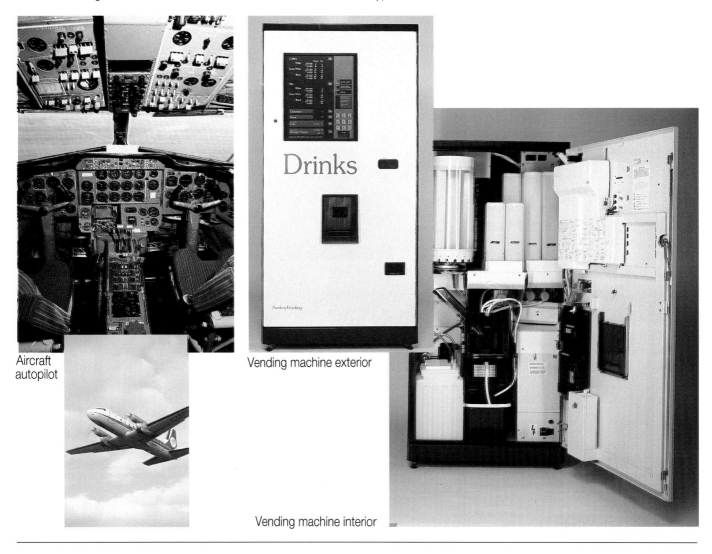

Aircraft
autopilot

Vending machine exterior

Vending machine interior

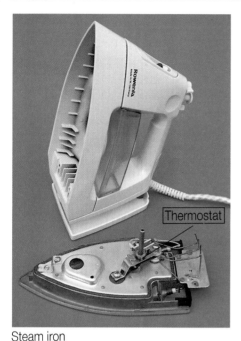

Thermostat

Steam iron

Automatic washing machine

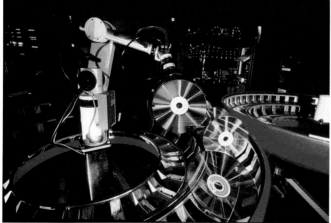

Factory robots

There is hardly any area of present day human activity that does not depend in some way on **electrical** or **electronic devices**.

Most of the devices in these pictures will be very familiar to you. Without these, and numerous other electrical 'servants', our lives would be very different.

All the devices shown here contain electrical or electronic **control systems** – that is, circuits which control the way the device operates.

A steam iron for example, uses electricity to heat an element which applies heat to the clothes. The temperature of that element however, must be controlled. The circuit which does this contains a special component called a thermostat. This is an example of a very simple control system.

An automatic washing machine is much more complex. It controls the flow of water into and out of itself, the temperature of the water, the speed of rotation of the drum, and so on – in other words, the complete 'wash cycle'.

Some of the most sophisticated control systems however, belong to the 'robots'. One example of a robotic device is the robot arm. These are increasingly taking over production processes in factories. Robots can work much faster than a human operator, performing a wide variety of tasks. They can work in dangerous environments, rarely make mistakes, and never get bored.

A true robot has an 'electronic brain'. This is used to store and process the information which controls the actions of the robot. If the robot is required to do a new job, it can have its 'memory' rubbed clean and a new set of instructions given – this is called programming.

Many interesting control projects can be built at school. Before learning about control circuitry however, it will be useful to revise some basic electrical theory.

Basic electrics – revision

Voltage and current

A battery is a source of electrical energy – it provides the 'pressure' which causes electricity to flow. We measure this electrical pressure in **volts, V**. The higher the **voltage**, the greater the pressure.

The flow of electricity is called **current** and is measured in **amps, A**

If a single battery makes a bulb glow dimly, two batteries connected in **series** as in circuit 2 will make it glow brighter. This happens because when batteries are connected in **series** their voltages **'add up'**. Two similar batteries connected in series produce twice the electrical pressure. The greater the electrical pressure (in a given circuit) the higher the current.

1)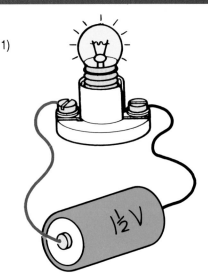

2)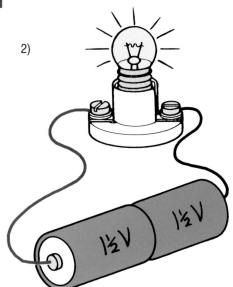

batteries connected in series

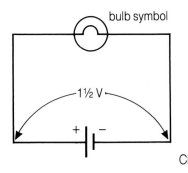

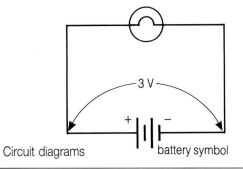

bulb symbol

Circuit diagrams

battery symbol

When batteries are connected in **parallel** however, their voltages do **not** 'add up'. The voltage provided by the two batteries in circuit 3 is the same as by the single battery in circuit 1.

Even so, there are reasons for connecting batteries in parallel: two batteries last longer than one, and can supply a higher current, should it be required.

3)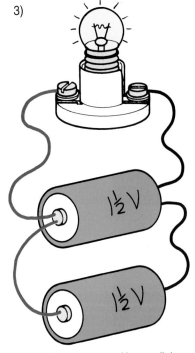

batteries connected in parallel

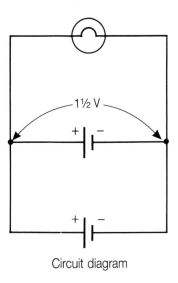

Circuit diagram

Resistance

Anything which opposes the flow of current in a circuit is said to offer **resistance**. We measure resistance in **ohms** Ω.

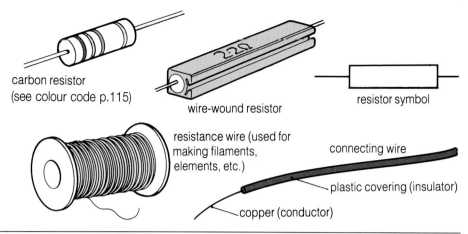

carbon resistor
(see colour code p.115)

wire-wound resistor

resistor symbol

Resistance wire, and components called **resistors** are specially made to resist the flow of electricity. Connecting wire however, has a very, very low resistance – it allows electricity to flow freely.

resistance wire (used for making filaments, elements, etc.)

connecting wire

plastic covering (insulator)

copper (conductor)

All electrical components offer some resistance to the flow of electricity. The filament in a bulb is a resistor which glows and gives off light.

The brightness of a bulb gives an indication of how much current is flowing in a circuit. Use this knowledge to decide which of the circuits shown offers least resistance and which offers the most.

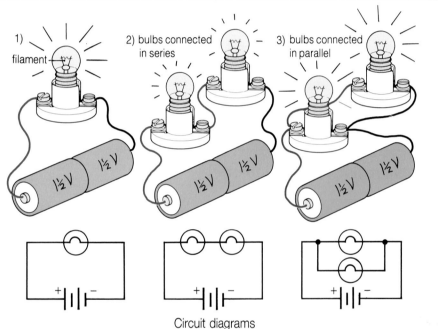

1) filament

2) bulbs connected in series

3) bulbs connected in parallel

Circuit diagrams

When resistors or resistive components are connected in **series**, the effect is to add more resistance to the circuit. The total resistance can be found by simply adding up all the resistance values.

To calculate the value of resistors in series, we use the equation:

$$R_T = R_1 + R_2 + R_3 \text{ etc}$$
(total)   (resistor values)

What is the effective resistance of R_1 and R_2 connected like this?

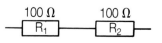

100 Ω   100 Ω
R_1 R_2

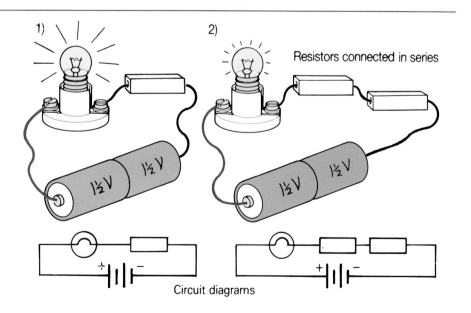

1)   2)

Resistors connected in series

Circuit diagrams

When resistors, or resistive components, are connected in **parallel**, the effect is to **reduce** the resistance in the circuit. That is why the bulb in circuit 5 is brighter than the bulb in circuit 4.

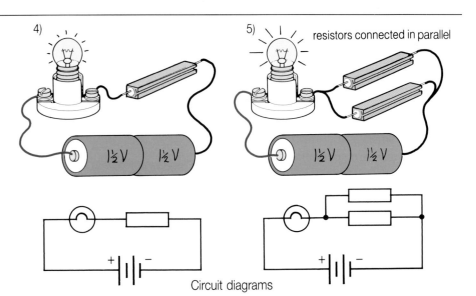

resistors connected in parallel

Circuit diagrams

To calculate the value of resistors in parallel, we use the equation:

$$\frac{1}{R_T} = \frac{1}{R_1} + \frac{1}{R_2} + \frac{1}{R_3}$$

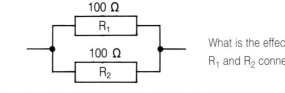

100 Ω
R₁

100 Ω
R₂

What is the effective resistance of R_1 and R_2 connected like this?

Variable resistor (potentiometer)

A variable resistor can be used to adjust the flow of current in a circuit.

When the resistor's spindle is rotated, a sliding contact puts more or less resistance material in series with the circuit.

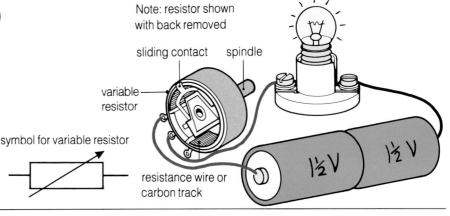

Note: resistor shown with back removed

sliding contact   spindle

variable resistor

symbol for variable resistor

resistance wire or carbon track

Other resistive components

Light dependent resistor (or LDR)

An LDR is a component whose resistance depends upon the amount of **light** falling on it.

When the LDR in this circuit is slowly covered up, the bulb gets dimmer and finally goes out. What does this tell you about how the resistance of an LDR varies? Try to complete this sentence:

As the light falling on an LDR decreases, the resistance of the LDR ....

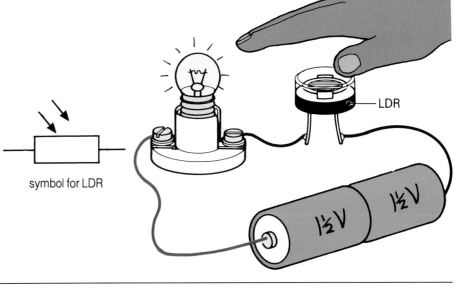

symbol for LDR

LDR

Thermistors

A thermistor is a component whose resistance varies with **temperature**.

Two types of thermistor are made: those whose resistance increases with increasing temperature (these are said to have a positive temperature coefficient +t), and those whose resistance decreases with increasing temperature (these are said to have a negative temperature coefficient –t).

Which type of thermistor is being used in the experiment illustrated?

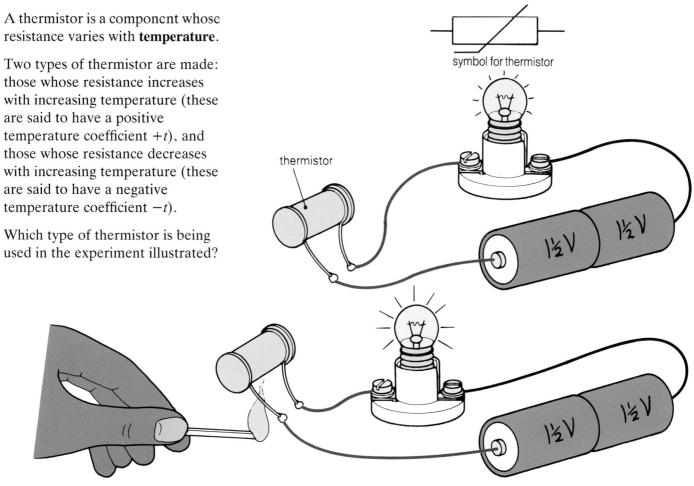

symbol for thermistor

thermistor

Ohm's law

Earlier in this chapter we saw that we could increase the current flowing in a circuit by increasing the electrical pressure (or voltage). We also saw that by **increasing** the resistance in a circuit we could **reduce** the flow of current.

In 1826 George Ohm understood this, and went on to discover a special relationship between **voltage, current** and **resistance**. He discovered that the current passing through a resistor was proportional to the voltage across it. In other words, if the voltage across a resistor was doubled, the current flowing through that resistor would double, and if the voltage was trebled, the current would treble, and so on. This became known as Ohm's Law.

From the above knowledge, Ohm derived this equation:

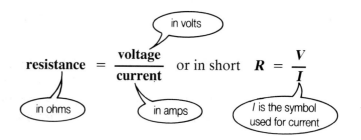

$$\text{resistance} = \frac{\text{voltage}}{\text{current}} \quad \text{or in short} \quad R = \frac{V}{I}$$

in volts

in ohms

in amps

I is the symbol used for current

Measuring current, voltage and resistance

Ammeters are used to measure the flow of **current** in a circuit. They must be connected in **series** with the circuit components. In this way, the current flowing in the circuit also flows through the ammeter and therefore can be measured.

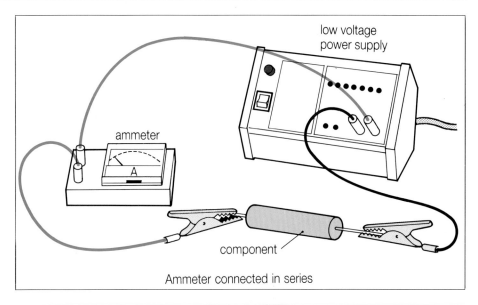

Ammeter connected in series

Voltmeters however, must be connected across (or in **parallel** with) circuit components. They are connected in this way because their job is to measure the electrical pressure (or voltage) across a component.

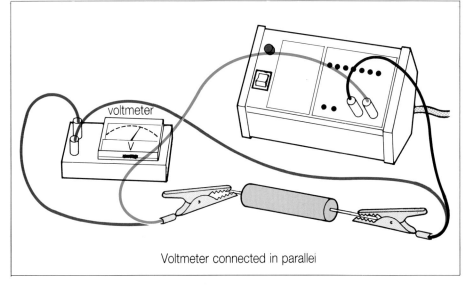

Voltmeter connected in parallel

The resistance of a component can be found using the Ohm's Law equation. First we must measure the current passing through the component, and the voltage across it.

For the carbon resistor in the diagram:

$$R = \frac{V}{I}$$

$$= \frac{10}{0.1}$$

$$= 100\,\Omega$$

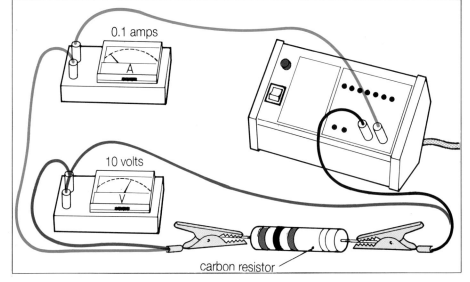

carbon resistor

Simple Ohm's Law calculations

The teacher is explaining that $R = \dfrac{V}{I}$ can be used not only for calculating resistance, but **voltage** and **current** too. She has shown that the equation can be rearranged for this purpose, and also how to use it in calculations.

If you have difficulty with rearranging the equation, ask your teacher for help.

Resistor colour codes

Some resistors have their resistance value shown using numbers. These tend to be the lower value types.

Most resistors are coded using coloured bands. The first three bands (closest together) give the value of the resistor in ohms Ω.

The fourth band indicates how accurate the given value is. The most expensive resistors carry a red 4th band. A red fourth band means that the resistor's value will be within 2% of the stated value, gold 5%, and silver 10%.

Example

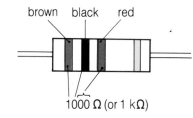

brown   black   red

1000 Ω (or 1 kΩ)

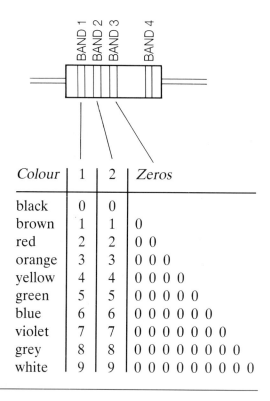

Colour	1	2	Zeros
black	0	0	
brown	1	1	0
red	2	2	0 0
orange	3	3	0 0 0
yellow	4	4	0 0 0 0
green	5	5	0 0 0 0 0
blue	6	6	0 0 0 0 0 0
violet	7	7	0 0 0 0 0 0 0
grey	8	8	0 0 0 0 0 0 0 0
white	9	9	0 0 0 0 0 0 0 0 0

Questions

1 a Calculate the value of resistor R in this circuit.
b How much current would flow if the value of R was doubled?

2 a Calculate the current flowing in this circuit.
b What would be the ammeter reading if the resistor's value was halved?

3 a Calculate the voltage across R in this circuit.
b How much current would flow if the voltage across R was doubled?

4 a Calculate the current flowing through R_1.
b Calculate the current flowing through R_2.
c What will be the reading on the ammeter?
d What is the **total** resistance in this circuit?
(Note – an ideal ammeter has no resistance.)
Use the equation $R_T = R_1 + R_2$

5 When 12 V is applied across a 10 Ω resistor, a current of 1.2 A flows.

When two 10 Ω resistors are connected in **parallel**, twice as much current flows (2.4 A). The total effective resistance of R_1 and R_2 in parallel therefore must be less than 10 Ω.

What will this value be? You can check your answer by using the equation:

$$\frac{1}{R_T} = \frac{1}{R_1} + \frac{1}{R_2} \cdots \cdots$$

You may need your teacher's help with this calculation.

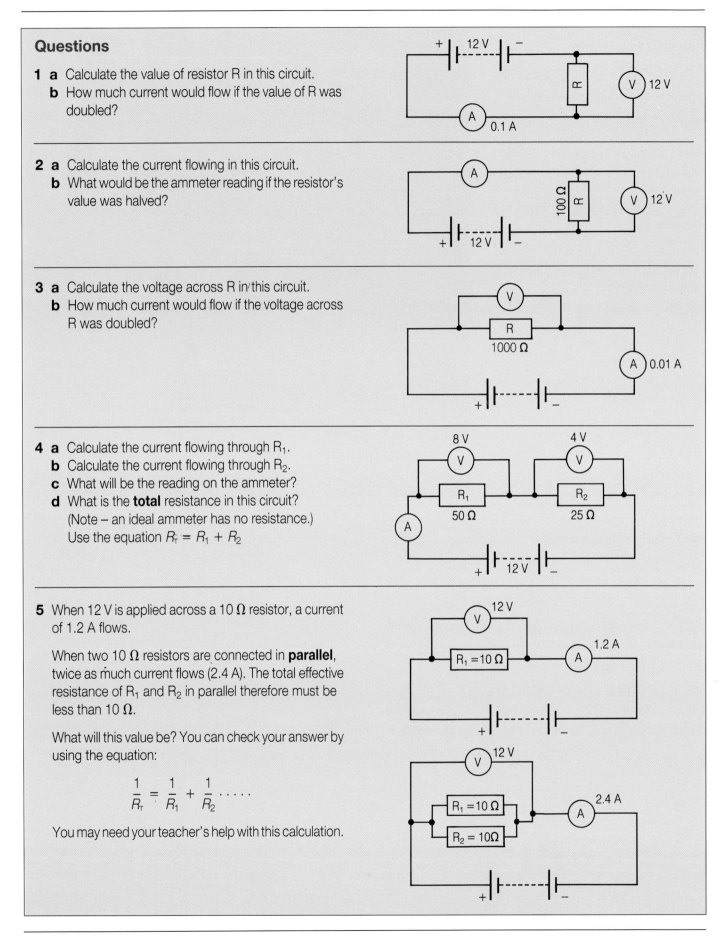

Control electrics

The switch

We all make use of switches every day. We use them to turn on lights, radios, hairdriers and numerous other devices. A switch is used for making and breaking an electrical circuit. Only when the circuit is 'made', by switching on, will current flow.

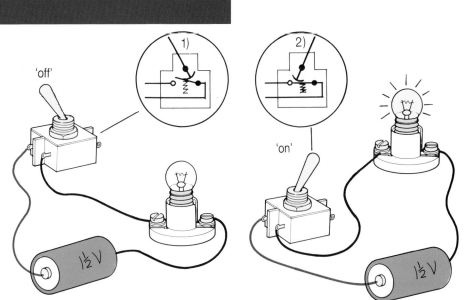

Switch names and symbols

The simplest type of switch is represented by the symbol shown here. Notice that it has two parts, a **pole** and a **contact**. It is called a **single pole single throw** switch (SPST).

It is given this name because its single pole can be 'thrown into contact' in one position only.

Three more switch symbols are shown here. Can you work out how they got their names?

All sorts of switches are available. Some of the more common types are shown below.

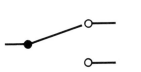

Symbol for single pole single throw (SPST) switch

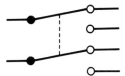

Symbol for single pole double throw (SPDT) switch

Symbol for double pole single throw (DPST) switch

Symbol for double pole double throw (DPDT) switch

Toggle switch

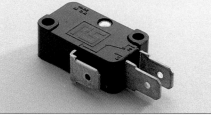

Microswitch

Slide switch

Push button switch

Reed switch

Rotary switch

Note Some switches return to their 'unswitched', state after the operating force has been removed. Microswitches, reed switches and some press switches do this.

The contacts on these switches are often labelled **N/C** or **N/O**. **N/C** stands for 'normally closed'. This is the contact which is connected to the pole when the switch is not activated. The **N/O**, or 'normally open' contact, connects to the pole when the switch is activated.

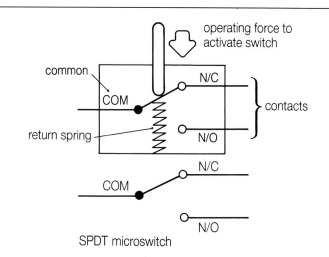

SPDT microswitch

Questions

6 The control of electric motors is common in technology. Sometimes this simply involves turning them on and off. The circuit shown here is designed to operate in this way.

Using the circuit symbols given, draw the circuit diagram for this control circuit.

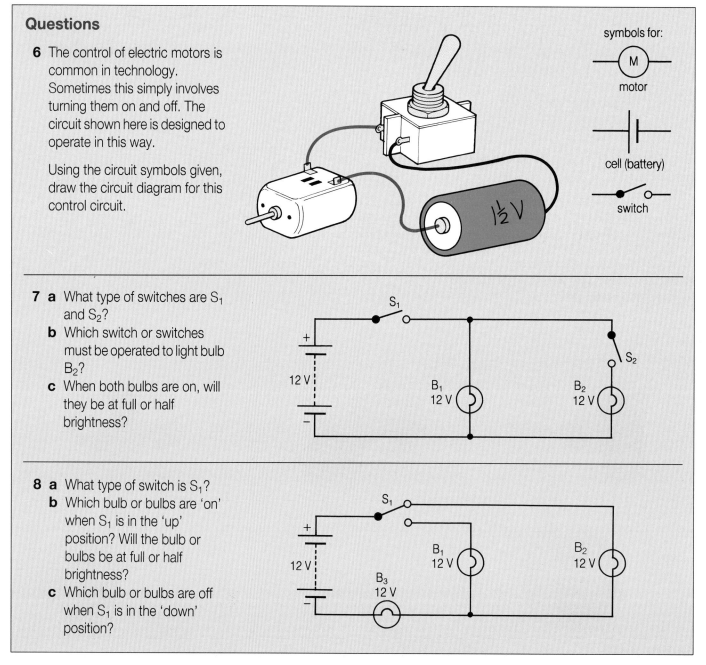

7 a What type of switches are S_1 and S_2?
  b Which switch or switches must be operated to light bulb B_2?
  c When both bulbs are on, will they be at full or half brightness?

8 a What type of switch is S_1?
  b Which bulb or bulbs are 'on' when S_1 is in the 'up' position? Will the bulb or bulbs be at full or half brightness?
  c Which bulb or bulbs are off when S_1 is in the 'down' position?

9 The landing light in most houses is controlled by a circuit similar to that shown. When S_1 and S_2 are in the 'up' position, the light is on.

a What other switch positions will turn the light on?

b What positions will turn the light off?

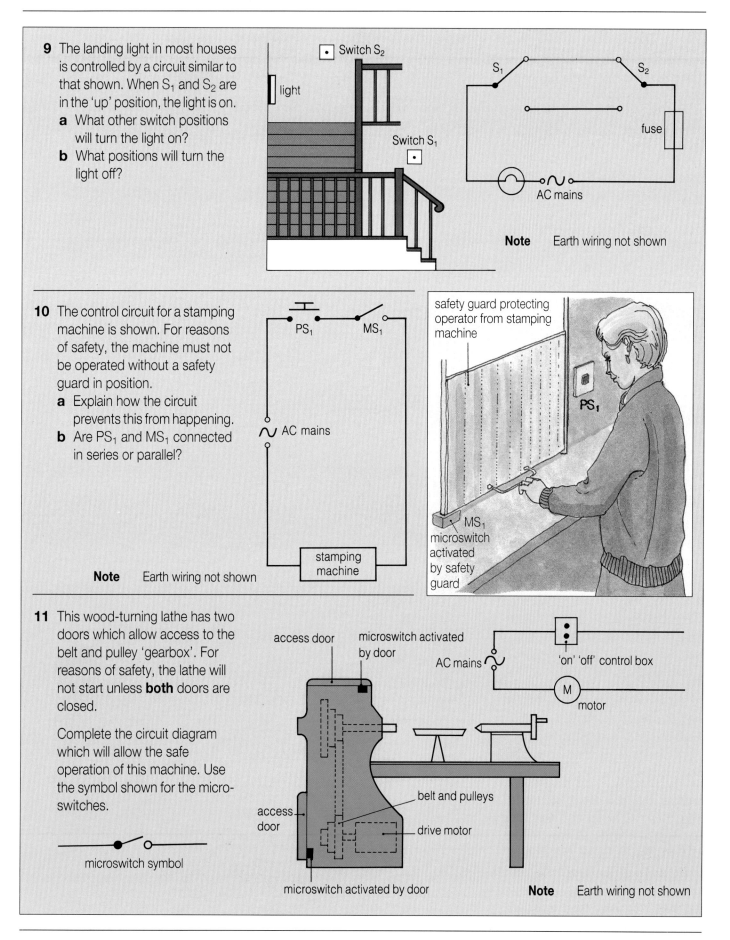

Switch S_2

light

Switch S_1

S_1 S_2

fuse

AC mains

Note Earth wiring not shown

10 The control circuit for a stamping machine is shown. For reasons of safety, the machine must not be operated without a safety guard in position.

a Explain how the circuit prevents this from happening.

b Are PS_1 and MS_1 connected in series or parallel?

Note Earth wiring not shown

PS_1 MS_1

AC mains

stamping machine

safety guard protecting operator from stamping machine

PS_1

MS_1 microswitch activated by safety guard

11 This wood-turning lathe has two doors which allow access to the belt and pulley 'gearbox'. For reasons of safety, the lathe will not start unless **both** doors are closed.

Complete the circuit diagram which will allow the safe operation of this machine. Use the symbol shown for the microswitches.

microswitch symbol

access door

microswitch activated by door

AC mains

'on' 'off' control box

M motor

belt and pulleys

access door

drive motor

microswitch activated by door

Note Earth wiring not shown

More advanced switching circuits

It is often necessary to change the direction of rotation of a motor shaft. This is so in the case of lifts and automatic sliding doors for example.

Joanne is working on a vehicle project which requires its motor to be reversible. Her teacher explains that a **DC motor** can be reversed by changing the direction in which the current flows through the motor. This can be done by reversing the wires to the battery. (See circuit diagrams.) A more convenient way however, is to use a switch.

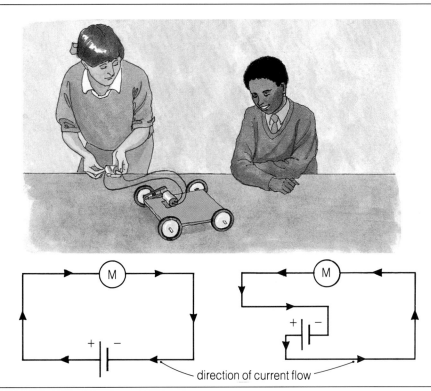

direction of current flow

Switched reversing circuit

If a double pole double throw (DPDT) switch is connected to a motor as shown here, you can **change the direction** of current flow through a motor at the 'flick of the switch'.

Circuit explained

With the switch in the 'up' position, current flows through the motor from right to left as shown. Let us assume that this causes the motor to run clockwise.

When the switch is flicked to the 'down' position, the current flows through the motor from left to right, causing the motor to run anti-clockwise.

Joanne used the above circuit to control her vehicle, but also added two microswitches as shown. She added these to make the vehicle stop if it bumped into a wall or other object. Switches which operate in this way are called **limit switches**.

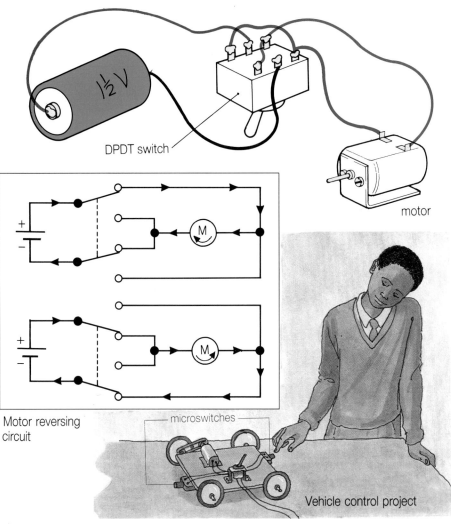

DPDT switch

motor

Motor reversing circuit

microswitches

Vehicle control project

Question

12 Joanne's vehicle moves backwards when the switch is in the down position. Which microswitch would stop the vehicle if it bumped into something when travelling forwards?

MS₁

limit switches to break circuit when vehicle bumps into an obstruction

+

−

M

MS₂

Reversing circuit (with limit switches)

Control using relays

Fraser has built a model sliding door, and has learnt to control it using a reversing circuit and limit switches. The limit switches stop the motor when the door is in the open and closed positions.

However, he really wanted the movement of the door to be fully automatic. His teacher explained that he could do this if he learnt about relays.

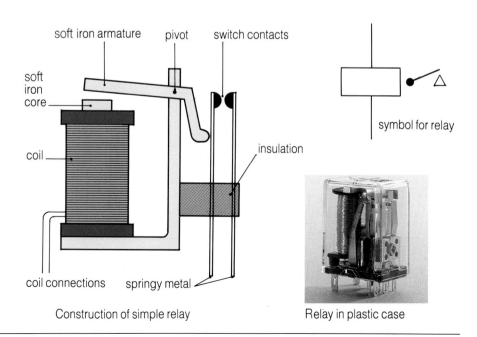

DPDT switch

limit switches

Sliding door project

The relay

A relay is a switch which is turned on and off by an electromagnet.

Look at the diagram of the construction of a relay. When a small current flows through the coil it produces a magnetic field which magnetizes an iron core. This attracts the armature which forces the switch contacts to touch. When the current is turned off, the switch contacts open again.

A relay is a very useful type of switch because it can be turned on and off in all sorts of different ways. This is illustrated in the following questions.

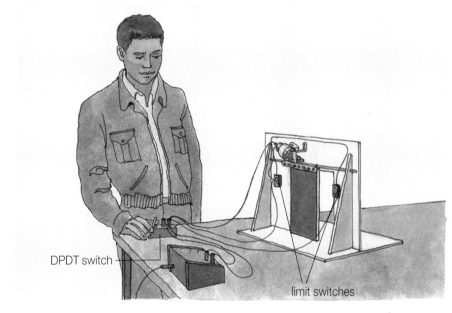

soft iron armature   pivot   switch contacts

soft iron core

coil

insulation

symbol for relay

coil connections   springy metal

Construction of simple relay

Relay in plastic case

Questions

13 The relay in this circuit can be turned on and off by light using an LDR. (See LDRs page 112.)

If light is shone onto the LDR, does the motor turn on or off?

14 The relay in this circuit can be turned on and off by heat using a thermistor. (See thermistors page 113.)

Will a rise or fall in temperature cause bulb B1 to turn on?

15 The relay in this circuit can be turned on and off by magnetism using a reed switch. (See reed switches page 118.)

  a Will the alarm be on or off when the magnet is moved away from the reed switch?

  b Can you suggest a use for this circuit?

Note This circuit shows an important property of a relay. It enables a safe low voltage circuit to operate a high voltage or high current circuit – the two circuits are completely separate.

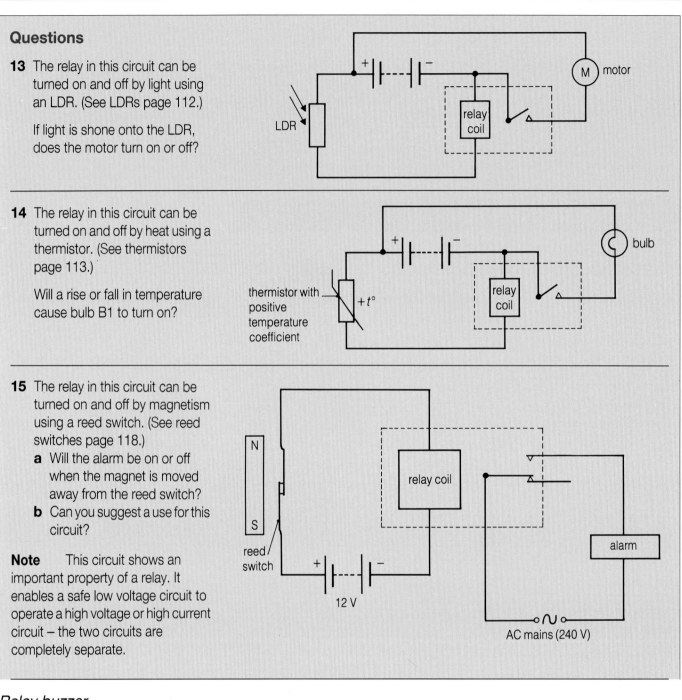

Relay buzzer

The relay coil in this circuit has been connected in series with its own switch. When operating, the relay switches on and off very rapidly, producing a buzzing sound. A relay can therefore be used to make a crude buzzer.

Question

16 Why does the relay in this circuit switch on and off continuously?

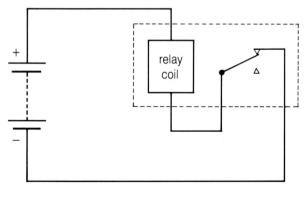

A project – using relays

The 'fast reaction' game

Using the circuit shown, design and make a 'fast reaction' game.

The game

Three people are involved in the game – two players and an operator. The operator (whose hand must be hidden from view) presses switch S_1 to light bulb L_1. The players (with their fingers poised 2 cm above their press switches) watch and wait for the light to come on. On seeing the light, they press their own switch as quickly as possible. The person whose reaction is faster wins because their light and relay switch on. At the same time, their relay disconnects the opponent's circuit.

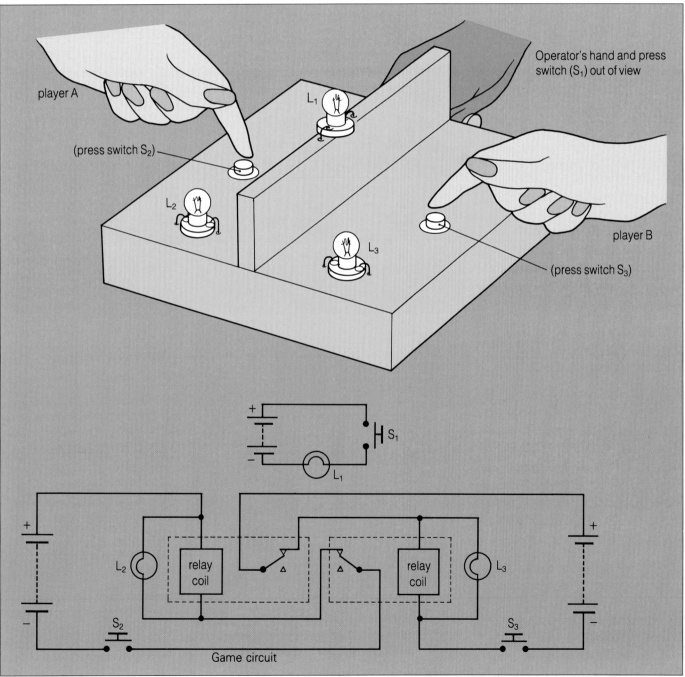

More complex relay circuits

The relay reversing circuit

The standard switch-operated motor reversing circuit is shown on page 120. This of course is a manually operated circuit (operated by the finger). When semi-automatic, or automatic control is required, the **relay** reversing circuit can be used.

The diagrams show two useful relays for school technology projects.

Two-pole changeover relay

Four-pole changeover relay

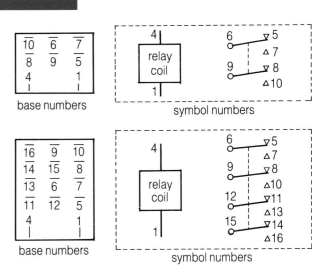

base numbers

symbol numbers

RS Components 'Continental' series (185 Ω) relays

The circuit

The relay reversing circuit is very similar to the switch reversing circuit. The motor must be connected to the relay's switch contacts, and the poles must be connected to the power supply, in the normal way. In addition, the relay coil is connected to the power supply via a switch, PS$_1$.

When PS$_1$ is **not** pressed (Fig. 1), current flows to the motor causing it to run – say clockwise.

When PS$_1$ is pressed however (Fig. 2), the relay 'flicks over' (energizes) and current is directed in the opposite direction through the motor. Hence, the motor runs anti-clockwise. When PS$_1$ is released the relay 'flicks back' (de-energizes) and the motor once again runs clockwise.

On its own, the above circuit doesn't appear to have any advantages over the normal circuit. As you read on however, you will learn how it can be built up into a very useful control circuit.

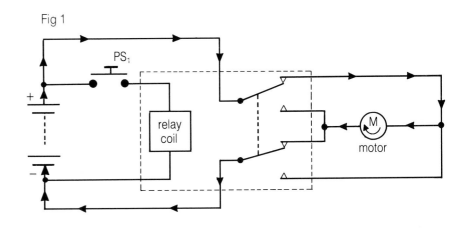
Fig 1

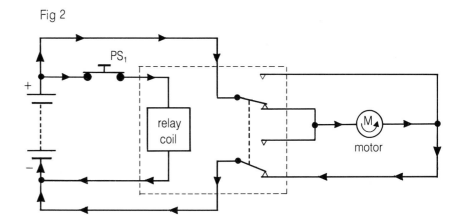
Fig 2

Relay reversing circuit

The relay latch

When a relay is operated via a press switch, the relay will only remain energized whilst your finger is on the button. In some control circuits however, it is necessary for the relay to remain energized after the button is released. This can be achieved using the relay **latch** circuit described below.

Relay latch explained

In the relay latch circuit, two extra wires are connected in a special way. We will call these wires XX. (See diagram.)

When PS_1 is pressed, current flows to the relay coil in the normal way via PS_1. However, current also flows via wires XX, and through part of the relay's own switch.

When PS_1 is released therefore, although current can no longer flow to the relay coil via PS_1, it continues to get there via wires XX. The relay therefore cannot switch off. It is said to be 'latched'.

Below, you can see how Fraser used the relay reversing circuit **and** the relay latch to control his automatic sliding door.

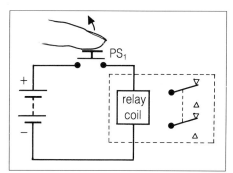

Relay de-energizes when PS_1 is released

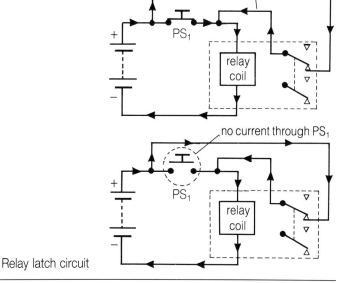

Relay latch circuit

Fraser's sliding door project – continued from page 121

The control circuit explained

Note The relay used in this circuit is a 4 pole changeover type.

Microswitch MS_1 is a limit switch which stops the motor when the door is in the closed position. When either pressure pad PP_1 or PP_2 is pressed, the relay energizes and latches. The motor now drives the door open until it hits a second limit switch – microswitch MS_2 – which forms part of the latch circuit. When MS_2 opens, the latch is 'broken' and the relay de-energizes. The motor therefore runs in the reverse direction, closing the door. When the door is fully closed, MS_1 is 'opened' and the motor stops again.

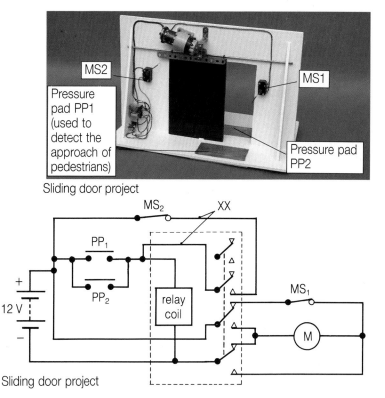

Sliding door project

Sliding door project

Projects using the relay latch

'Steady hand' game

The diagram here shows the traditional 'steady hand' game.

Re-design the circuit to include a latch. This will ensure that the buzzer remains on after the first contact is made.

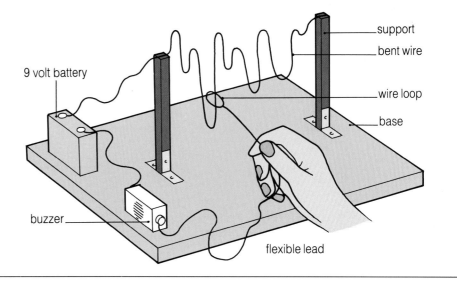

support
bent wire
9 volt battery
wire loop
base
buzzer
flexible lead

Simon's money box project

Simon challenged Fraser to steal his special money box. However, the project had a design fault.

Using Fraser's suggestion, re-design the circuit so that the alarm remains on even if the thief does press the switch.

THE TROUBLE IS FRAZER, IF YOU PRESS THE SWITCH, THE ALARM STOPS.

YOU COULD SOLVE THAT PROBLEM WITH A LATCHING RELAY.

normally open contact
MS₁ N/C
N/O
+
9 V
buzzer
Alarm circuit

A commercial relay latch circuit

Workshop power supplies

Factory and school workshops must be fitted with emergency stop buttons by law. The circuit shown here illustrates how this can be done using a relay latch circuit.

To switch on the power, a key switch is turned on momentarily, and then turned off – this causes the relay to latch. 'Stop' buttons are connected in series in the latch 'wires'.

If either stop button is pressed, the latch is broken and the relay de-energizes – cutting the power to the machinery.

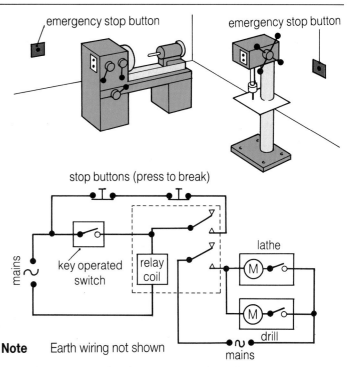

emergency stop button
emergency stop button
stop buttons (press to break)
lathe
mains
key operated switch
relay coil
drill
Note Earth wiring not shown
mains

Control electronics

The diode

A diode is a component which allows current to flow in **one direction only**. It creates a kind of 'one way street' in an electrical circuit.

The most common diodes consist of a junction of 'p-type' and 'n-type' silicon **semiconductor** materials.

The diagrams here show the 'one way street' effect of a diode.

A diode has two leads known as the 'anode' and 'cathode'. Only when the anode is connected to the positive side of a power supply, and the cathode to the negative side of the power supply, will current flow. When connected in this way a diode is said to be **forward biased**.

Some common silicon diodes

symbol for diode

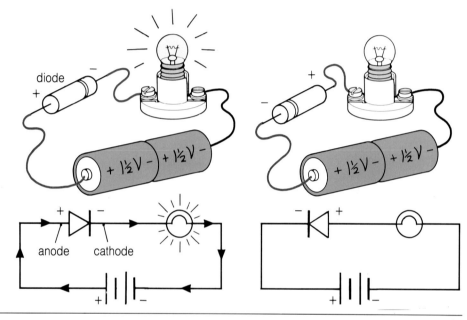

Light emitting diodes

Special diodes are made which emit light. These are called light emitting diodes (or LEDs).

LEDs are used mainly as visual indicators that a circuit is working or an appliance is 'on'. Like ordinary diodes, LEDs allow current to flow in one direction only.

LEDs normally work at around 2 volts. In order to obtain the correct working voltage for the LED in a circuit, a resistor is normally placed in series with the LED. Ohm's Law can be used to calculate the value of this resistor.

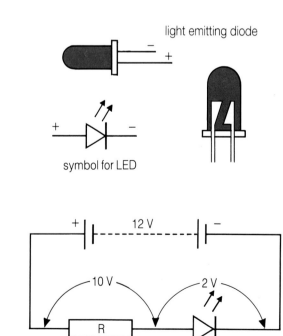

light emitting diode

symbol for LED

Calculating resistance value

When two or more components are connected across a power supply in this way, they are said to form a **potential divider**. The components divide the power supply voltage between them. If the LED requires 2 V across it, 10 V must be 'dropped' across the resistor.

If the LED requires say 10 mA (1000 mA = 1 A) to operate it, the value of R can be calculated as shown here:

$$R = \frac{V}{I}$$
$$= \frac{10}{0.01}$$
$$= 1000 \ \Omega.$$

'Game of chance' project – using diodes

Susan and Steven have designed and made a 'game of chance' which uses diodes.

Both players gamble by pressing either button A or B. The player whose turn it is spins the disc. The player whose light remains on after the disc has stopped is the winner.

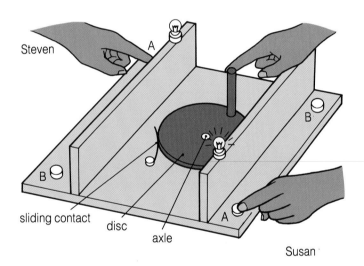

Game of chance explained

Look closely at the game circuit. Steven has gambled with button A. Susan has gambled with button A and has spun the disc. The disc has stopped as shown. Susan's light is on – she wins 2 points.

Trace the circuits to see why Susan's light is on whilst Steven's is off. Remember, a diode only allows current to flow in one direction.

There are three other possible results for this gamble: Susan could win 1 point, if both her and Steven's lights stayed on, OR Steven could win 1 point if his light stayed on but Susan's went off, OR neither player would gain a point if both lights went off.

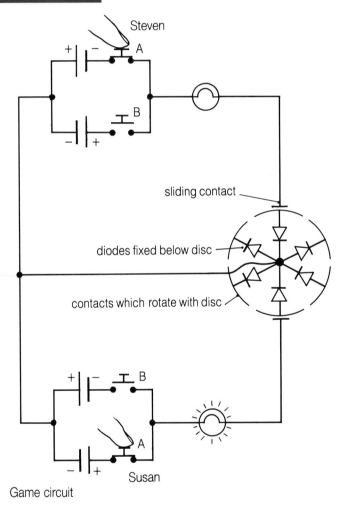

Game circuit

Questions

17 a Which position must the diodes be in to give Susan a 1 point win for this gamble?

  b Which position must they be in to give Steven a 1 point win?

Transistors

Tom's dilemma

Tom asked his teacher for some help with a design problem. He was working on an aid for the disabled – a bathwater level alarm for the blind.

The purpose of the alarm was to allow a blind person to leave a 'running bath' unattended until the alarm signalled that the bath was ready.

Tom discovers a problem

low voltage power supply

Water conducts electricity doesn't it? So why doesn't my alarm work?

probes
water
buzzer

Tom's problem explained

Although Tom was correct – water does conduct electricity – the **resistance** of water is very high. The current flowing in Tom's circuit was too small to operate the buzzer.

Tom measured the current – it was only 0.001 A (1 mA).

When he measured the current needed to operate the buzzer, he discovered that 0.025 A (25 mA) was required.

His teacher explained that a **transistor** could solve his problem.

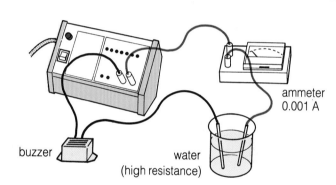

buzzer
water
(high resistance)
ammeter
0.001 A

Measuring the circuit current

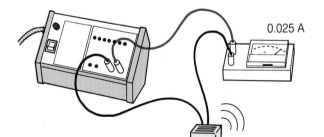

0.025 A

buzzer

Measuring the buzzer current

Transistors explained

A transistor is another **semiconductor** device. It is made of three layers of n- and p-type semiconductor material.

The three layers are called the **emitter, base** and **collector**.

Transistors are available in a wide variety of shapes and sizes, but there are only two basic types. (Only npn-types will be used in this book.)

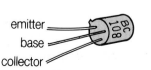

emitter
base
collector

BC108 transistor
(actual size)

b c e

transistor symbol
(npn type)

What do transistors do?

We can begin to answer this question by looking at a simple transistor circuit.

In diagram 1, switch S1 is open and in this condition current will **not** flow in any part of the circuit.

When S1 is closed however, a **very small** current flows through the base of the transistor via resistor R. When this happens the transistor 'turns on' allowing a **larger** current to flow through its collector, via the bulb. (See diagram 2.)

Can you see that the transistor has used a small current to turn on a large current?

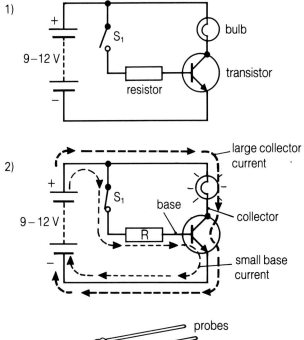

Tom's problem solved

Using the above knowledge, Tom designed and built this experimental bathwater level alarm circuit.

He connected the probes in the transistor's base circuit, and the buzzer in the transistor's collector circuit.

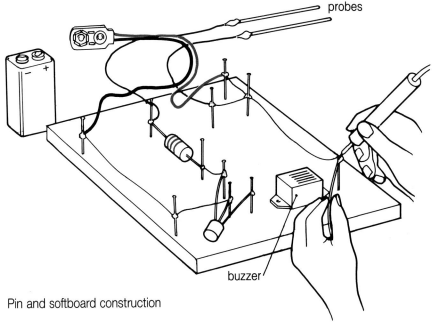

Pin and softboard construction

How the circuit operates

The tiny current passing through the water (between the probes) provides the base current to turn the transistor 'on'. The buzzer is then driven by the transistor's larger collector current.

Note   Resistor R is included in this circuit to protect the transistor. If the base current became too large, the transistor would be damaged.

Project note   Caution – transistors will be damaged if they, or the power supply, are connected the wrong way round.

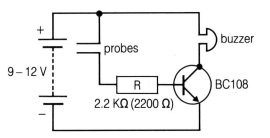

Electronic systems

In the introduction to chapters 5–7 (pages 67–69) the **systems approach** was discussed and the idea of **input**, **process** and **output** was explained. In the next few pages, you will see how this approach can apply to the design of electronic circuits.

Introduction

As you know, human beings have five **senses**: sight, hearing, touch, taste and smell. As we live our lives, the body takes in information, via the senses, and the brain **processes** this information. The brain may then respond and cause the body to move, produce sound, 'remember', etc. An electronic system operates in a similar way. It has an **input** device, to sense changes in the environment, a **processor** (or control device), to make a response to these changes, and an **output** device, to perform whatever function is required.

An example of an electronic system is shown here. You will be asked to look at it again later.

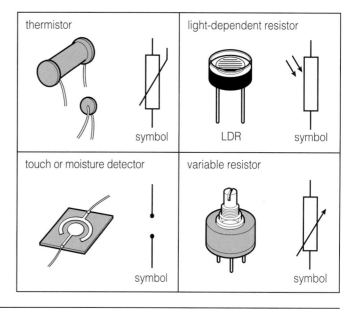

Input devices

In this chapter we have looked at a range of components which can be used to **control the flow of electricity**. Those shown here can be incorporated into a special electronic circuit called a **sensor**. A sensor **detects changes in the environment** – a change of temperature, light intensity, moisture level, movement, etc., and responds by **producing a change of voltage**.

Sensors are important **input devices** in electronic systems. Let's investigate how they work.

Sensors explained

An interesting sensor, which is often used in school technology projects, is a **light sensor**. Let's investigate how it works. In the explanation, a 'water circuit' has been used to help you to understand the circuit's operation.

Look at the **electrical circuit** shown here (circuit 1). It contains an LDR and a resistor connected in series across a power supply. The two components make up the **sensor** circuit.

You will remember that an LDR is a component whose **resistance** depends upon **the amount of light falling on it**. In the dark its resistance is high, and in bright light its resistance is low. In this circuit, the LDR is in bright light – its resistance is low. In the equivalent water circuit (circuit 1a) we can represent a low LDR resistance by **not** squeezing the water pipe very much. Water will flow easily through the 'LDR', therefore, but its flow will still be restricted by the 'resistor' below it. The result will be a **high water pressure** across this 'resistor'. Using a device called a 'U' tube manometer, this pressure can be measured as shown. In the electrical circuit, of course, **electricity is flowing**, not water, and the pressure across resistor R is an electrical pressure or **voltage** which can be measured using a voltmeter. Notice the **high** voltage reading.

Now look at circuit 2. The LDR is in darkness and therefore its resistance is high. In the equivalent water circuit (circuit 2a) we can represent this high LDR resistance by **squeezing the pipe** a lot. This would result in a reduced flow of water through the whole circuit and therefore the **water pressure** across the 'resistor' would fall – as indicated by the manometer. Now, in the electrical circuit, a high LDR resistance would result in a **reduced** flow of **current** through the circuit, and the **voltage** across resistor R would be low – as shown.

Can you see, therefore, that the **voltage at the output terminal** (the voltage across R) depends on **how much light is reaching the LDR**? In other words, the sensor detects changes in the environment and responds by producing a change of voltage at the output terminal.

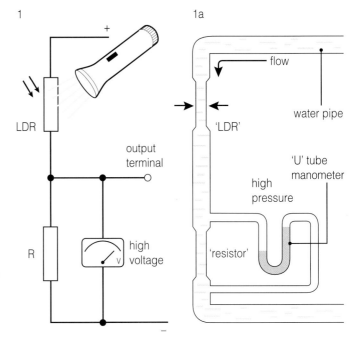

1   sensor circuit   1a   'water circuit'

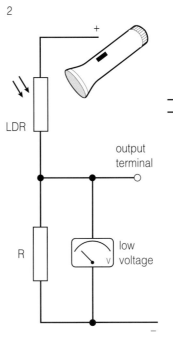

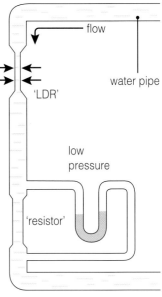

2   sensor circuit   2a   'water circuit'

> **Note** – To set up a successful water circuit, the 'resistor' would have to lie horizontally to prevent water from leaking into the manometer.

Control systems

You have just seen an example of how an input device responds to changes in the environment and how its output 'reflects' these changes. It is the job of the system's **processor** (or control device) to respond to these changes. The **transistor** (explained earlier) is an example of a processor device. It has the ability to **detect voltage changes** (as at the output of a sensor, for example) and respond by controlling the current which flows in other devices – in output devices, for example.

Tom's bathwater level alarm (page 130) contains **input**, **process** and **output** devices. Let's identify them.

The input device in this system is a **moisture sensor**. It reacts to the presence of water in the bath at the required level. You will notice that the sensor is **correctly drawn** in this circuit. The resistor was omitted in Tom's circuit because it made the circuit's operation easier to explain.

The **processor** (or control device) in this circuit is a **transistor** (and protective resistor). It responds to changes at the input and reacts by controlling current in the output.

The output device is a **buzzer**. It is turned on by the processor (the transistor) to produce an audible warning indicating that the bath has filled to the required level. A **buzzer** is an example of an output transducer. All **output transducers** convert electrical energy into some other form of energy – in this case, sound energy.

In your design and technology course you will be required to **identify** input, process and output devices in **existing products** and in the **products _you make_**. Use the information above to help you to do this. Use it also to help to identify input, process and output devices **in the circuits contained in this chapter**.

Turn back to page 131 now, and see if you can identify the input, process and output devices in the system shown.

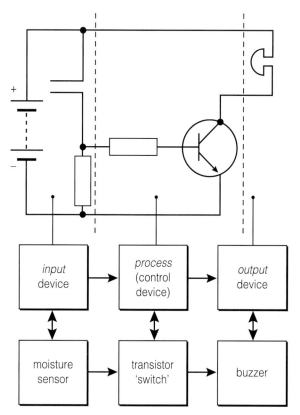

Systems diagram for bath water level alarm

Transistor circuits – continued

By making a number of simple changes to Tom's circuit shown on page 130, a wide range of control problems can be solved.

Lorna has designed a **water pollution indicator** for rivers and canals. In her circuit, the input device is a light sensor and the output device is a bulb.

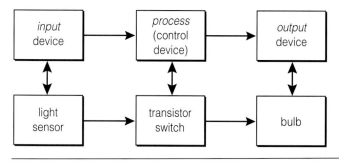

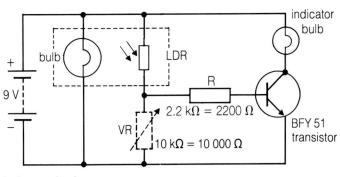

Water pollution indicator

How the indicator works

Polluted water often contains suspended particles, which affect the passage of light. When light is shone through the water towards the LDR therefore, the amount of light reaching the LDR will depend upon the level of pollution. (See diagrams.)

The resistance of an LDR depends upon the amount of light falling on it. (See page 112.) As the light level increases, so the resistance decreases. The ORP12 LDR has a resistance of 10 million ohms (10 MΩ) in the dark, and as little as 130 Ω in bright light.

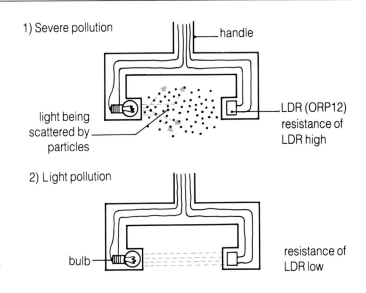

How the circuit works

If you ignore the variable resistor (VR) for a moment, the operation of the circuit can be explained as follows.

When the LDR is in darkness (in polluted water) its resistance is high. Insufficient base current flows to turn on the transistor, and the indicator bulb is off.

In less polluted water however, the resistance of the LDR falls. This allows sufficient base current to flow to turn the transistor on. The transistor's collector current passes through the indicator bulb, making it glow.

Indicator circuit

What does the variable resistor do?

In the actual circuit, current flowing through the LDR 'splits' taking the two routes shown.

Now, the current flowing in the base circuit depends upon the voltage across VR, which in turn depends upon the resistance of VR and of the LDR – see **Sensors explained** (page 132). By adjusting the variable resistor, therefore, we can set the circuit to operate at a particular light level (and therefore at a particular level of pollution).

Project note   See page 137.

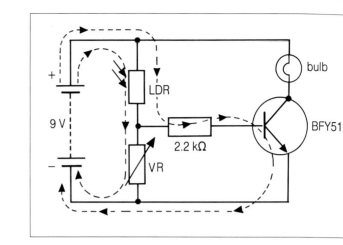

Circuit design information

Collector current

For each kind of transistor, there is a maximum collector current which must not be exceeded. A BC108 transistor, for example, has a maximum collector current (or I_c) of 100 mA.

If the device to be 'turned on' requires more current than the transistor can provide, a **relay** can be utilised.

The circuit shown here, for example, enables a fan motor (which draws 2 A) to be switched on when a preset temperature is reached.

Note   When a relay de-energizes it releases a surge of electrical energy which could destroy a transistor. By connecting a diode across the transistor (as shown in the diagram), the energy is diverted away from the transistor which is thus protected from damage.

A relay is an example of an interface device. An interface provides a control link between two circuit functions, but keeps the circuitry separate.

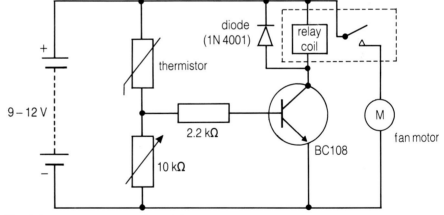

Circuit for a temperature activated fan

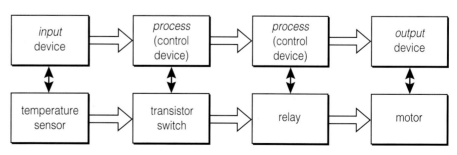

Systems diagram for a temperature activated fan

Transistor gain

We have seen that a small current flowing in the base of a transistor will 'turn on' a larger collector current. This is known as current amplification.

The ratio $\dfrac{I_c}{I_b}$ collector current / base current

is a measure of this amplification which we call the transistor's current **gain**. The symbol for transistor current gain is h_{FE}.

$$h_{FE} = \frac{I_c}{I_b}$$

$$= \frac{0.05}{0.00025}$$

$$= 200$$

for the transistor in the circuit shown.

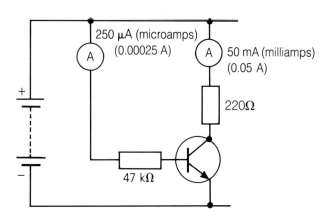

The Darlington Pair amplifier

The amplification of a single transistor is often not sufficient in a circuit. If the amplified current of one transistor is fed into the base of a second transistor however, the amplification can be increased many times.

If the gain of each transistor shown here is 100, for example, then the combined gain of the two transistors is in excess of 10 000. Can you see why?

This method of connecting transistors is known as a Darlington Pair.

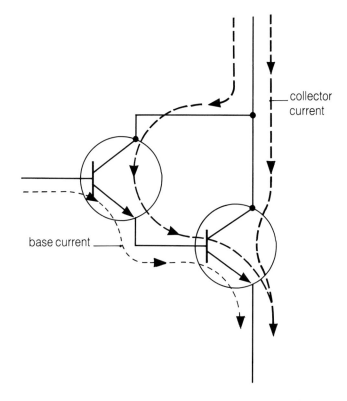

Coupling of two transistors – known as a Darlington pair

Project notes

Lorna's Water Pollution Indicator, shown on page 134, did work using a single transistor. However, the circuit was far more **sensitive** (could detect smaller changes of light intensity) using the Darlington Pair circuit shown here.

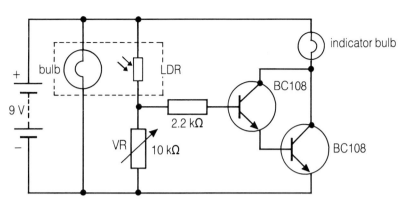

Indicator circuit

A printed circuit board construction was used for this project.

A note for teachers – printed circuit board, etch resist pens, chemicals, trays etc. can be obtained from component suppliers.

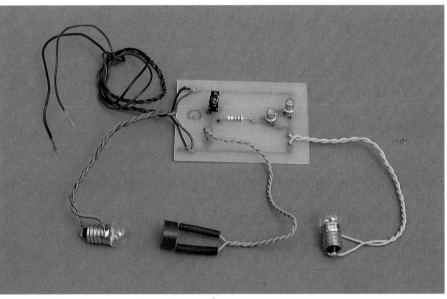

Water pollution indicator (PCB construction)

Light activated switch

The circuit shown here is a modification of the Water Pollution Indicator circuit.

By replacing the indicator bulb with a relay (and protective diode) the circuit may be used to control other devices in response to changing light levels. Further modifications include the replacement of the LDR with a thermistor – to produce a temperature activated switch; or metal probes or plates – to produce a moisture activated switch.

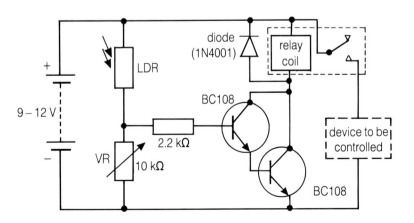

Projects

Touch sensitive switch

The circuit shown can be used in any project which requires something to be switched on by the touch of a finger. The circuit can be used to turn on a lamp or buzzer for example, or control an electric motor.

How the circuit works

The finger is used to 'connect' the touch plates. The tiny current which flows through the finger-tip becomes the base current which turns the transistor on. The transistor's collector current is used to energize a relay, which in turn can be used to switch on other devices.

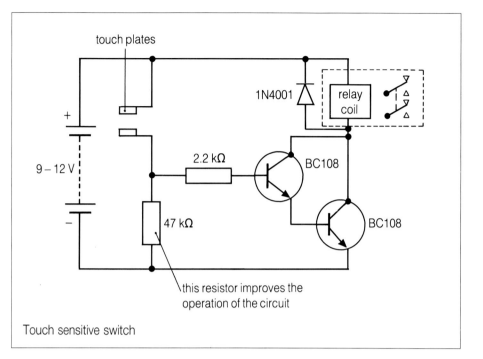

Touch sensitive switch

Circuit modification

In the above circuit, the relay will de-energize the moment the finger is removed from the touch plates. If you require the relay to remain on however, the modification shown here can be used.

This is another example of a **latching circuit**. Can you see why the relay remains on?

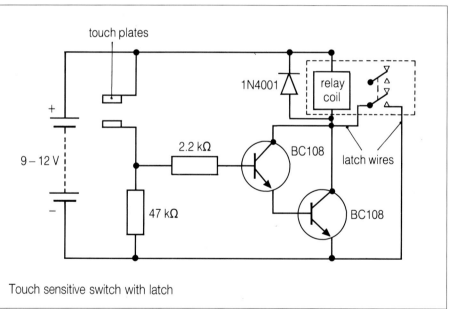

Touch sensitive switch with latch

Note   You can use a second touch-sensitive switch as an 'off' switch to work in conjunction with the above circuit. To do this, wire the second relay's contacts **in series** with the first relay's 'latch wires'. When the second circuit is activated therefore, the latch in the first circuit will be broken.

'Fast reaction' game (alternative circuit)

The diagram shows an alternative circuit for the 'fast reaction' game described on page 123.

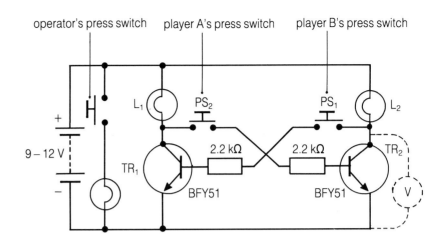

operator's press switch   player A's press switch   player B's press switch

How the circuit works

If PS_2 is pressed **first** (by player A), TR_2 turns on – due to the connection of its base circuit, and L_2 lights. Now, when TR_2 switches on, the voltage at its collector falls to zero (you can check this using a voltmeter). If PS_1 is pressed a fraction of a second later therefore, TR_1 will **not** turn on, since there is no voltage available to produce a base current. The reverse applies of course, if PS_1 is pressed first.

Reaction trainer

Think of a situation in which a person's 'fast reaction' is important. This could be whilst driving a car or taking part in a sport, for example.

Briefs

Either
1 Design and construct a simulator which could be used to **compare** the reactions of two people in your chosen situation.

Or
2 Design and construct a simulator which could be used to **improve** the reaction of an individual in your chosen situation.

Note

For brief number 2, you might find it useful to refer to the section on timing circuits in this chapter (pages 145–150).

Integrated circuits

The circuits discussed so far have been made up from **discrete** (or separate) components such as resistors, transistors etc. Integrated circuits (or ICs) however, are complete circuits in themselves. ICs contain very small 'chips' of silicon, into which numerous components have been formed. Each silicon chip is mounted in a plastic case and is connected to pins set in the side of the case.

The 741 operational amplifier, or **op amp**, is a particularly useful IC for school technology projects. Its basic operation is described below.

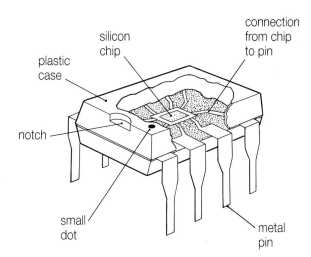

741 operational amplifier IC

The 741 operational amplifier

The op amp chip contains a complex circuit. We can neither see it, nor could we repair it if it went wrong. It is only necessary therefore to understand what it can do, not how it does it.

On page 136, we mentioned the amplification of a transistor and learnt about **current gain**. In the case of the op amp, however, it is more appropriate to consider **voltage gain**.

The standard symbol for an amplifier is a triangle. It has an input (into which the 'signal' is sent) and an output (from which the amplified signal is obtained).

If the amplifier had a gain of say 10, and the voltage at the input was +0.5 volts, we would expect the output to be +5 volts (0.5 × 10 = 5).

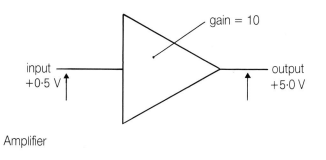

Amplifier

Unlike the amplifier described above, an op amp has **two** inputs. These are called the **inverting**, and **non-inverting** inputs. The amplifier uses these inputs in a special way. It amplifies **the difference** between the two input voltages.

For example, if +0.5 volts was applied to the non-inverting input, and +0.1 volts was applied to the inverting input, the op amp would amplify 0.4 volts (the difference) to give an output of +4 volts.

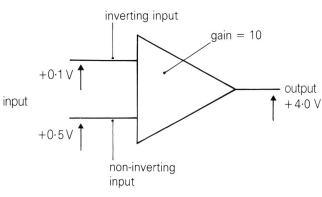

Operational amplifier

If the input voltages were reversed however, i.e. +0.1 volts on the non-inverting input and +0.5 volts on the inverting input, the op amp would still amplify the difference between the two input voltages, but the output would be −4 volts (**minus** 4 volts).

The effect of applying the larger voltage to the **inverting** input therefore, is to **invert** the output (make it go negative).

Note For the purpose of the explanation, the op amp described above was said to have a gain of 10. In reality however, an op amp's gain can be in excess of 100 000.

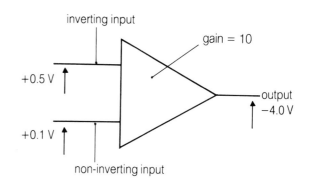

Experimental op amp circuit

The circuit described below can be used to investigate and experiment with the 741 op amp. For ease of understanding, the circuit has been explained in several stages.

The power supply

The diagram shows an op amp connected to its power supply. Notice that two batteries have been connected in a special way. Three terminals are provided: a common (0 volts), a positive supply (+9 volts) and a negative supply (−9 volts). This is called a **dual rail power supply**.

Notice that the inputs have been labelled '+' and '−'. This has nothing to do with the power supply. '+' is the symbol used to indicate the non-inverting input, and '−' indicates the inverting input.

Inputs and outputs

In the diagram, three resistors have been added to form a potential divider – 'dividing up' the +9 V supply as shown. These will be used to provide the inputs.

Two LEDs have been connected across the output (in series with a resistor). These will be used to indicate the 'state' of the output.

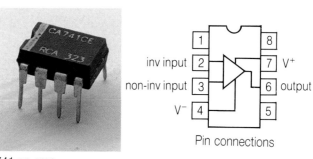

741 op amp

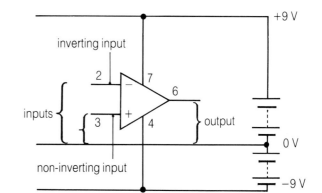

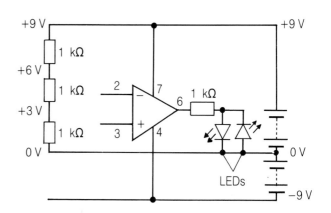

The experiment

'Flyleads' can be used to connect the non-inverting input to +6 volts, and the inverting input to +3 volts, as shown.

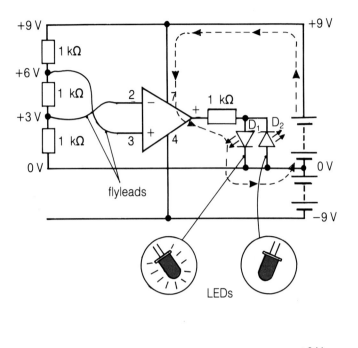

With this arrangement, the difference between the two voltages will be amplified, and the output will go **positive**. Current will therefore flow in the output as shown, and D_1 will pass current and 'glow'. D_2 however, will **not** pass current, because its anode is not connected to the positive supply. (See diodes page 127.)

Note   As we have stated, the gain of an op amp is typically 100 000. However, the 3.0 volts difference between the two inputs can only be amplified up to the maximum supply voltage (9 volts in this case) and not 300 000 volts, as you might expect.

If the flyleads are reversed as shown (connecting the non-inverting input to +3 volts and the inverting input to +6 volts), the output goes to −9 volts. Current will therefore flow in the output as shown, and D_2 will pass current and 'glow', but D_1 of course will not.

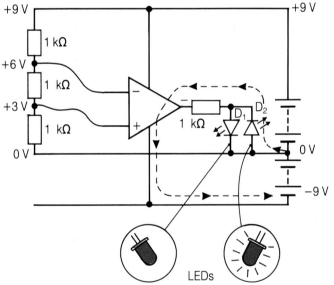

Conclusions

Because of the very large gain of an op amp we can assume that the output voltage will **either**,

1 be close to the positive supply voltage (when the non-inverting input is at a higher potential than the inverting input) **or**,
2 close to the negative supply voltage (if the inverting input is at a higher potential than the non-inverting input).

A useful op amp circuit

This circuit can be used as a very sensitive 'light activated switch'. It operates as follows:

When the LDR is illuminated its resistance is low and the voltage across it is low. When voltage V_1 is lower than V_2, the output of the op amp is negative. The transistor will therefore be off and the relay will not energize. When the LDR is in shadow however, its resistance rises and the voltage across it rises. If V_1 rises above V_2 the output of the op amp goes positive, the transistor turns on, and the relay energizes. The use of VR_1 enables the circuit to be adjusted to operate at a particular light level.

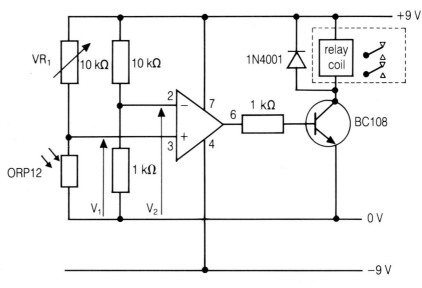

Light activated switch circuit

Projects

Car park exit barrier

Design an exit barrier system for a car park. The barrier must open when a vehicle breaks a light beam, and must remain open until the vehicle is clear of the barrier.

Note   If you use the op amp circuit for this project, the relay could be used to operate a motor reversing circuit to control the position of the barrier. (See page 124.)

Weighing machine

The photograph shows an experimental weighing machine which uses two 741 op amps.

The machine was designed to sense a 2 N weight, a 1 N weight and zero weight. Two LEDs light when 2 N are present, one LED lights when 1 N is present, and when the scale pan is empty, neither LED lights.

Notice that variable resistor VR_1 has a small pulley attached to its spindle, around which is wound the thread. When weights are placed on the scale pan, the spring extends and the spindle of VR_1 is rotated.

How the circuit works

R_3, R_4 and R_5 form a potential divider to which the inverting inputs of op amps 1 and 2 are connected. The voltages at these inputs are approximately 4.0 volts and 4.8 volts as shown. R_1, R_2 and VR_1 form a second potential divider to which the op amp's non-inverting inputs are connected.

When the scale pan is empty, VR_1 is at its lowest resistance value and the voltage across VR_1 and R_2 is less than 4 volts. Hence the outputs of both op amps are negative, and neither LED lights. When a 1 N weight is placed on the scale pan however, the spindle of VR_1 is made to rotate, and its resistance rises. This causes the voltage across VR_1 and R_2 to rise above 4.0 volts (but to less than 4.8 volts). The output of op amp 1 therefore goes positive and LED 1 lights. With two 1 N weights on the scale pan, the spindle of VR_1 is further rotated, again increasing its resistance. The voltage across VR_1 and R_2 now goes above 4.8 volts and the output of op amp 2 goes positive – hence LED 2 also lights.

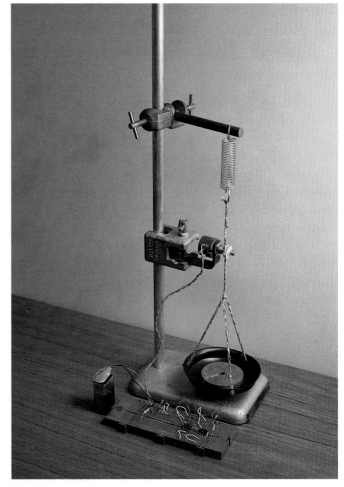

Weighing machine

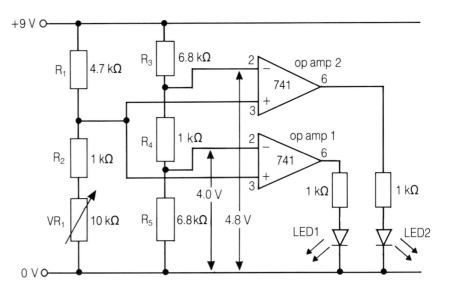

Note   This circuit does **not** require a dual rail power supply. For each op amp, pin 7 is connected to +9 volts (in the normal way) and pin 4 connected to 0 volts. (These connections have not been shown on the circuit diagram.)

Timing circuits

In addition to simple 'timing' applications such as photographic timers, egg timers, cooker timers etc, **time delay** circuits are used to produce time delay sequences in control processes. The traffic lights at this Pelican crossing for example, operate using time delay circuits.

A number of useful timing circuits for school technology projects are described below. To understand how they work however, requires an understanding of **capacitors**.

Pelican crossing

Capacitors

A capacitor is a component which can store and release electrical energy. This can be demonstrated by doing the simple experiment described overleaf.

Capacitance is measured in farads, but the smaller values – microfarads (μF), nanofarads (nF) and picofarads (pF) are more convenient for our purposes.

There are two basic types of capacitor:

Polarized   which tend to be the higher value types. These have a positive (+) and negative (−) lead which **must** be connected the correct way round in a circuit (+ to + and − to −).

Non-polarized   which are low value types. These can be connected either way round in a circuit.

All capacitors have a maximum working voltage. This is shown using either numbers or a colour code.

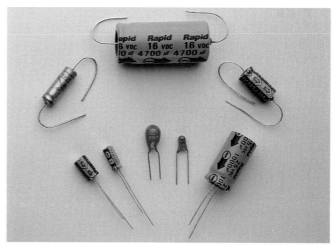

Polarized capacitors

symbol for polarized capacitor

symbol for non-polarized capacitor

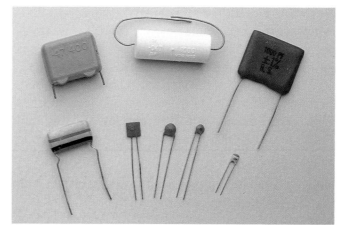

Non-polarized capacitors

The experiment

Connect a fairly large value capacitor across a 12 volt power supply as shown. This will cause the capacitor to 'charge up'. Remember to connect the positive side of the capacitor to the positive side of the power supply, and so on.

Then remove the charged capacitor and connect it across a 12 volt bulb. The stored energy will be released from the capacitor, causing the bulb to glow.

Within a few seconds, all the stored energy will be released and the bulb will go out.

Now repeat the experiment using **two** similar capacitors connected in **parallel**. What effect does this have? Discuss this with your teacher. Experiment with capacitors of other values too.

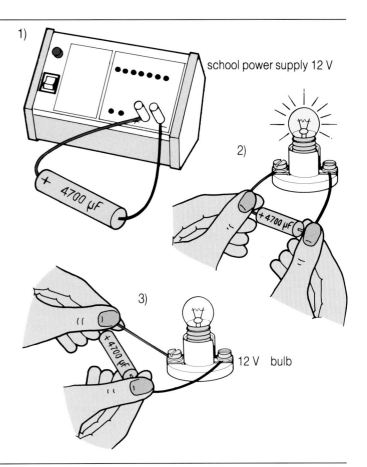

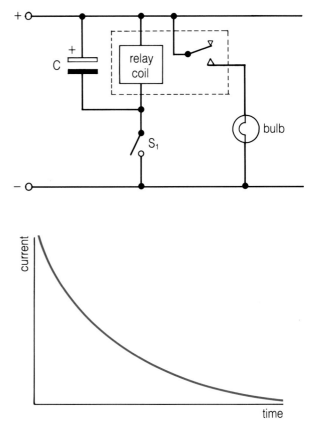

Time delay circuits

Circuit 1

This circuit is designed to keep a device turned on for a few seconds, after you have used the switch to turn it off.

The circuit explained

Notice that a capacitor has been connected in **parallel** with the relay coil in this circuit.

When S_1 is closed, the relay energizes and the bulb is switched on. At the same time the capacitor becomes charged. When S_1 is opened therefore, the relay does **not** turn off. It remains on for a few seconds as the capacitor discharges through the relay coil. The bulb therefore also remains on. As a capacitor discharges however, the current it delivers gets less and less until it is no longer sufficient to keep the relay energized. (See graph.)

Note   The bulb in this circuit can be replaced with any device which you wish to control.

Graph of current against time for a discharging capacitor

Circuit 2

The operation of this timing circuit is quite different from Circuit 1. It can be used to turn a bulb on (or other device) for a short period of time, and then automatically turn it off. Notice that a capacitor has been connected in **series** with the relay coil in this circuit.

The circuit explained

When S_1 is closed, the capacitor charges via the relay coil. The charging current is high at first, but gradually decreases, until it is finally zero when the capacitor is fully charged. (See graph.)

When S_1 is first closed therefore, the relay energizes. It then remains energized until the capacitor's charging current falls below the minimum required to operate the relay. At this point the relay de-energizes. The larger the value of the capacitor, the longer the time delay.

Note To re-set the circuit, first open S_1, then press PS_1 (this will discharge the capacitor). When S_1 is closed again the circuit will operate as above.

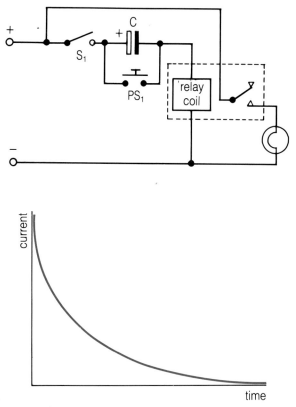

Graph of current against time for a charging capacitor

Circuit 3

This circuit produces yet another time delay sequence. When the circuit is activated, a delay occurs **before** the relay is energized and the bulb (or other device) is switched on.

The circuit explained

The operation of this circuit will be described in two stages.

1 When S_1 is closed, capacitor C charges via resistor R. As the capacitor charges up, the voltage across it rises (as shown by the graph). As the voltage across C rises however, the voltage across R falls. The total voltage across C and R will always equal the supply voltage.

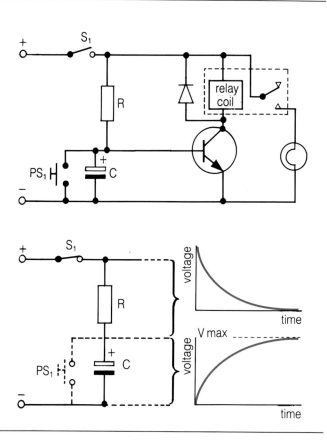

2 It has been shown that a small current flowing in the base of a transistor will turn the transistor on. However, a transistor will only begin to turn on when the voltage across its base emitter junction equals about 0.6 volts.

When S_1 is first closed therefore, the voltage across the capacitor (and therefore across the base emitter junction) is zero – the transistor will be 'off'. As the capacitor charges however, the voltage across it rises. When the voltage equals about 0.6 volts, the transistor will begin to turn on and at 0.7 volts will be fully on and the relay will have energized.

3 To re-set the circuit, first open S_1, then press PS_1 (this will discharge the capacitor). When S_1 is closed again, the circuit will operate as above.

Note It is important to be aware that when a capacitor is charging (or discharging) **no current** flows between the capacitor's plates. Electricity is **stored** on the plates when the capacitor is charging, and is **released** on discharge. For a fuller explanation, you will need to read a more specialized electronics book.

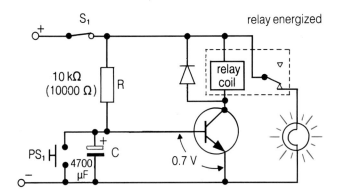

How quickly does a capacitor charge up?

R.C. time constants

When a capacitor charges via a resistor, the time it takes for the voltage across the capacitor to reach about $\frac{2}{3}$ of the supply voltage is known as the **time constant**.

To calculate the time constant for a given R.C. circuit, use the equation

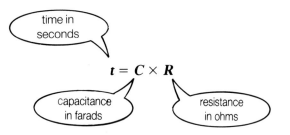

$$t = C \times R$$

In the diagram,

$$t = 0.0047 \times 10\ 000$$

$$t = 47 \text{ seconds}$$

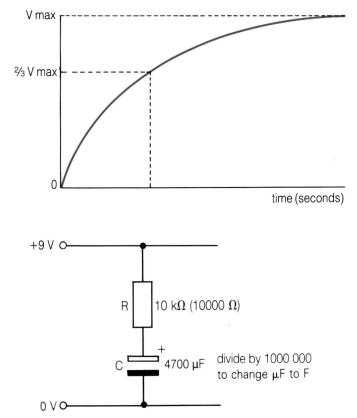

Voltage across C reaches 6 V ($\frac{2}{3}$ of 9 V) in about 47 seconds

Time constants and timing circuits

As we have said, in the timing circuit shown here, the transistor will begin to turn on when the base–emitter voltage equals about 0.6 V.

Now, since it takes $C \times R$ seconds (47 seconds) for the voltage across the capacitor to reach 6.0 V ($\frac{2}{3}$ of the supply voltage), it will take (approximately) $\frac{1}{10}$ of this time (4.7 seconds) to reach 0.6 V. The transistor therefore will begin to turn on after this time period.

Note   To increase the time period, increase the value of C. If you increase the value of R very much, the circuit will fail to operate.

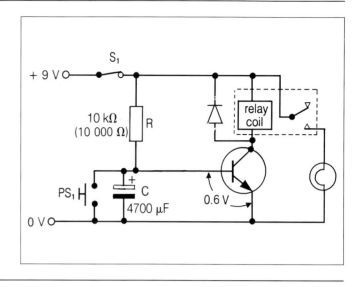

555 timer – integrated circuit

One of the disadvantages of circuits 2 and 3 described on the previous pages, is that they must be re-set manually (by pressing a switch) after each timing sequence. Further, only relatively short time delays can be produced by any of the circuits. These problems can be overcome by the use of the 555 timer IC.

As with the 741 op amp, we will only describe the operation of the IC, and not how its complex circuitry works.

555 timer IC

555 timing circuit explained (monostable operation)

The 555 timer circuit is designed to switch on a device for a pre-set period of time, and then switch it off (as in circuit 2).

To start the timing sequence, PS_1 is pressed momentarily.

Now, pin 3 (which is normally at 0 volts) immediately goes to +9 volts and the relay energizes. The relay then remains on for the period determined by the timing components R and C – it then turns off (as pin 3 goes back to 0 volts).

The graphs show the voltages on pins 2, 3 and 7 during the above sequence. At the same instant that the relay switches off, the capacitor is automatically discharged by the IC's internal circuitry. Hence the circuit is immediately made ready for the next timing sequence.

Note   The device to be controlled (a bulb in this example) is turned on and off by the relay in the normal way.

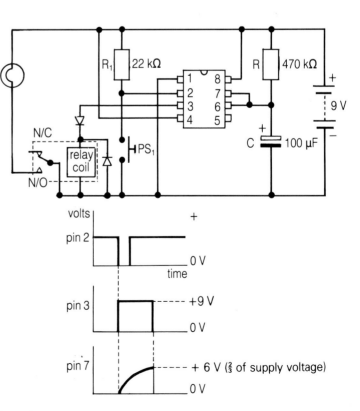

Calculating delay time

For the 555 timer IC the delay time is given by the equation:

$$t = 1.1 \times C \times R$$

time in seconds

capacitance in farads

resistance in ohms

For $R = 470 \text{ k}\Omega$ and $C = 100 \text{ }\mu\text{F}$
      $= 470\ 000\ \Omega$ $= 0.0001 \text{ F}$

      $t = 1.1 \times 470\ 000 \times 0.0001$
      $t = 51.7 \text{ seconds}$

Project note R can be replaced by a 3 MΩ (3 000 000 Ω) variable resistor to give **variable** time delays of several minutes.

Project

Automatic porch light

Design an automatic porch light. The light must be activated by a **pressure pad**. After a short delay, the light must switch off.

This project could be made more sophisticated by adding a **light activated switch** circuit. This circuit would control the porch light – only allowing it to operate in the dark. Light activated switch circuits are shown on pages 122, 134 and 137.

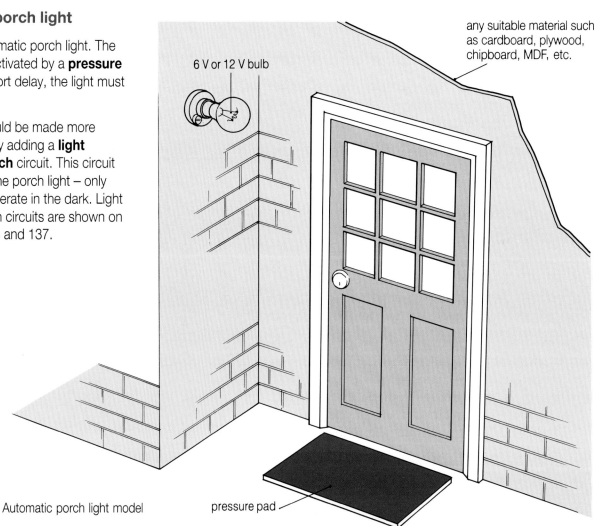

6 V or 12 V bulb

any suitable material such as cardboard, plywood, chipboard, MDF, etc.

Automatic porch light model   pressure pad

555 timer (astable operation)

The monostable operation of the 555 timer was described on page 149. **Monostable** means that the output of the IC (the voltage at pin 3) has *one* stable state (0 V). Although the output can be made to change to +9 V (for example), it always goes back to 0 V (its stable state) after a pre-determined period of time.

Astable refers to a system which has no stable state. The output of the 555 circuit shown here does not have a stable state – it changes between 0 V and +9 V continuously. The LED, therefore, flashes on and off continuously.

The **frequency** of an astable timer can be calculated as shown here.

Note 1   If you wish to adjust the frequency of the astable, replace R_2 with a variable resistor as shown 'dotted'.

Note 2   If you require *two* LEDs to flash on and off alternately, include a second LED (and resistor), where shown dotted.

Tone generator

By making a number of changes to the above circuit, a tone generator can be constructed. This has applications in alarms, musical instruments, Pelican crossing bleepers, and so on.

The note produced by the speaker can be changed by adjusting the 10 K variable resistor.

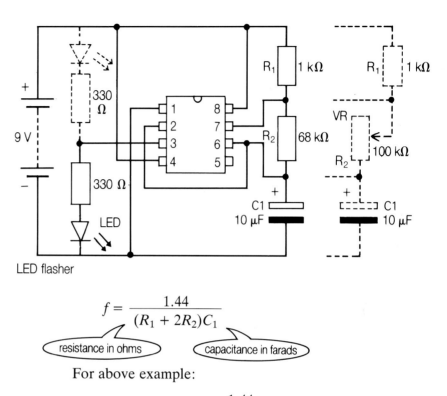

LED flasher

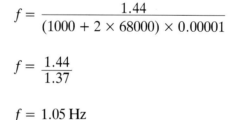

$$f = \frac{1.44}{(R_1 + 2R_2)C_1}$$

resistance in ohms   capacitance in farads

For above example:

$$f = \frac{1.44}{(1000 + 2 \times 68000) \times 0.00001}$$

$$f = \frac{1.44}{1.37}$$

$$f = 1.05 \text{ Hz}$$
(Approximately one flash per second.)

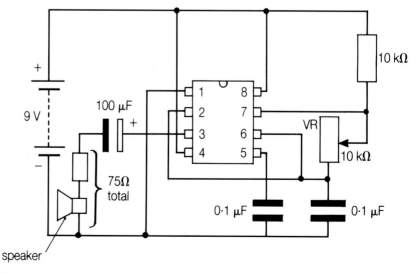

speaker

Tone generator

An introduction to control logic

The cartoon characters **Eyeball, Sensation** and **Muscles** will be used to explain **control logic**.

In these demonstrations, control logic will be used to help solve some design problems.

Eyeball

Sensation

Muscles

Brief To design a system which will automatically take washing under cover when it rains **OR** when night falls.

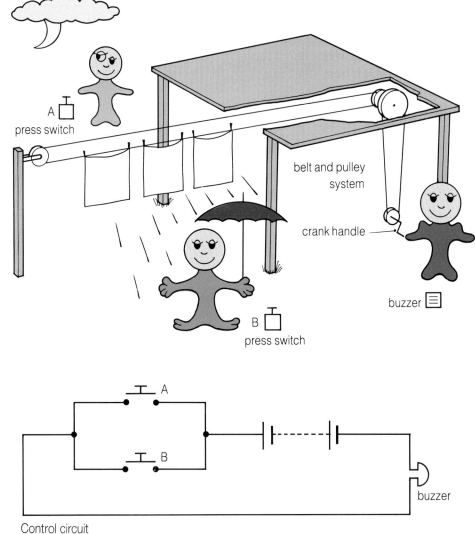

belt and pulley system

crank handle

buzzer

Possible solution
(See diagram.) **Muscles** will be used to control the position of the washing and will be in charge of the crank handle. **Sensation** will be responsible for detecting rainfall, and **Eyeball** will keep a look out for nightfall.

Notice that Sensation and Eyeball each have a press switch. These are connected into a buzzer circuit which is used to tell Muscles when to wind in the washing. Muscles will hear the buzzer if either switch A **OR** B (or both) is pressed.

In logic, a circuit which behaves like these switches is called an **OR gate**. An OR gate gives an output when input A **OR** B (or both) is present – in this case, when switch A OR B is closed.

Control circuit

Using this simple control circuit, the three characters are able to control the washing line to ensure that the washing is taken under cover at night, OR when it rains, or both.

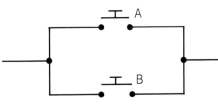

Logic OR gate

The language of logic

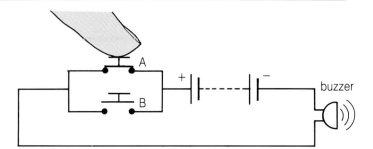

In the language of logic, when a switch is closed it is said to be at logic state **1**. In the circuit shown, switch A is at logic state **1**. An open switch is said to be at logic state **0**. Similarly, when a logic gate produces an output, the output is said to be at logic state **1**. No output, logic state **0**.

Most logic gates however, are electronic devices, not switches, and the inputs are in the form of **electrical pulses**. The inputs and output can only have two states (or voltage levels), 'high' or 'low'. 'High' (say +5 V) is referred to as logic **1**, 'low' (0 V) as logic **0**. The **OR** gate IC shown here operates in this way.

OR gate integrated circuit

Any OR gate can be represented with a block diagram. The block diagram for a two input OR gate is shown here.

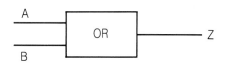

Truth table

We can represent the state of the inputs and output of a logic gate in a special table called a **truth table**.

The truth table for a (two input) OR gate is shown. Notice that the letter **Z** has been used to indicate the output. (Other letters are sometimes used.)

inputs		output
A	B	Z
0	0	0
0	1	1
1	0	1
1	1	1

Automating the washing line

Automation often involves replacing a human operator (or operators) with mechanical or electrical systems. In deciding what system to use therefore, it is useful to examine the operators' 'jobs'.

Sensation was responsible for detecting rainfall and therefore could be replaced by a **moisture sensing circuit**.

Eyeball detected changing light levels and therefore could be replaced by a **light activated switch**.

Finally, Muscles did the heavy work and could be replaced by a **motor reversing circuit** and a **transmission system**.

Demonstration 2

Brief   To design a system to automatically open a garage door when the car headlights are flashed. To add security to the system, the car must also be standing in a particular position when the lights are flashed.

Possible solution (See diagram.)   Muscles will be used to control the movement of the door and will be in charge of the winch. Sensation will be responsible for detecting the position of the car, and Eyeball will keep a look out for the car's headlights.

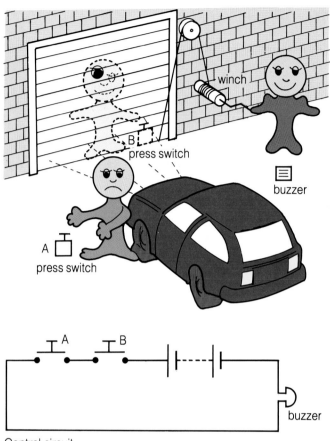

Again, both operators have press switches connected into a buzzer circuit. These are used to tell Muscles when to open the door. However, the buzzer will only sound when switches A **AND** B are pressed together.

In logic, a circuit which behaves like these switches is called an **AND gate**. An AND gate only gives an output when both inputs A **AND** B are present – in this case, when switches A AND B are closed.

Control circuit

Using this simple control circuit, the three characters are able to control the garage door and ensure that it will only open when the car headlights are flashed AND it is parked in the correct position.

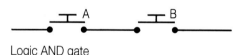

Logic AND gate

Truth table

The truth table for a (two input) AND gate is shown here.

inputs		output
A	B	Z
0	0	0
0	1	0
1	0	0
1	1	1

Automating the garage door

Once again, Eyeball was responsible for detecting a change in light level, and therefore could be replaced by a light activated switch.

Sensation however, acted as a position sensor, and in this situation could be replaced by a **pressure pad**.

Finally, Muscles did the heavy work again and could be replaced by a motor reversing circuit and a transmission system.

The NOT gate

Now that you understand the principle of logic gates, and how they can be used in control circuits, the **NOT gate** can be explained in brief.

A **NOT gate** can be represented with the block diagram shown. Notice that a NOT gate has a single input and a single output. The operation of a NOT gate is as follows:

When the input is at logic **1**, the output goes to logic **0**, and when the input is at logic **0**, the output goes to logic **1**.

The truth table for a NOT gate is shown here.

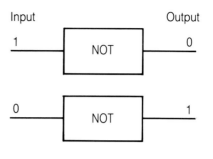

input	output
A	Z
0	1
1	0

The operation of a NOT gate can be illustrated using a simple switching circuit. When the input is at logic **0** (switch not pressed) the output goes to logic **1** (and the bulb is lit).

When the input is at logic **1** however, most of the current takes the path of least resistance (through the switch), the output goes to logic **0** (and the bulb goes out).

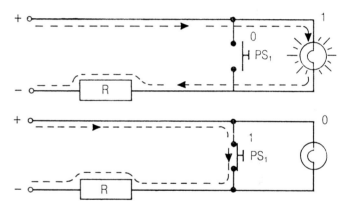

Logic NOT gate (using switches)

The NOT gate in a control circuit

A block diagram for an automatic watering system is shown. The design of the system ensures that the moisture content of the soil is constantly monitored.

However, because seedlings can be damaged if watered in bright (hot) sunlight, watering only takes place at night.

Trace the block diagram and see how the NOT gate prevents the AND gate from turning on the sprinkler during the daytime.

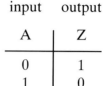

Automatic watering system

Circuit construction techniques

Tom's bathwater level alarm (shown on page 130 in this chapter) was built using a pin and board construction. This is one example of **modelling** – a method of construction which allows you to test and develop an idea quickly and easily.

More permanent, but still quite fast, methods of construction include the use of **matrix board** and **strip board**. With matrix board, small rigid pins are pressed into pre-drilled holes in the board and the components and connecting wires are soldered to these. Strip board looks similar to matrix board, but on one side it has strips of copper which join parallel lines of holes. The circuit is built up using these copper strips as connectors.

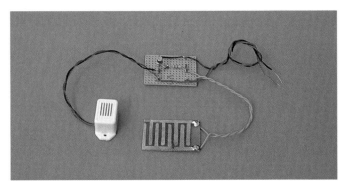

Matrix board circuit with PCB sensor pad

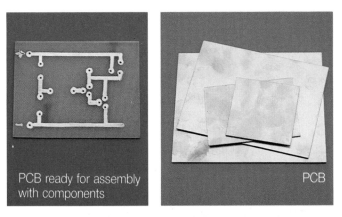

Strip board circuit

Printed circuit board (PCB)

Printed circuit board can be used to produce a permanent circuit when you are satisfied with a design after modelling.

PCB is clad with a thin coat of copper (sometimes on both sides) and does not contain any pre-drilled holes. One method of transforming this material into a **printed circuit**, ready for final assembly with circuit components is described below.

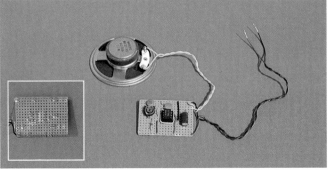

PCB ready for assembly with components

PCB

1 First collect a full set of components for your circuit.

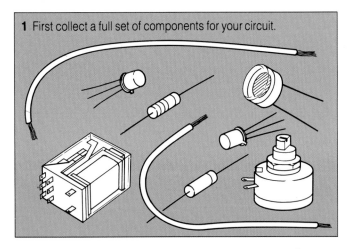

2 Begin to draw the circuit into which your components will fit on a piece of plain paper.
Use the actual components to work out spacing between the 'blobs'

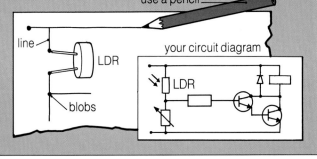

use a pencil

line

LDR

your circuit diagram

blobs

LDR

3 After completing the circuit, attach it to a piece of PCB using Sellotape

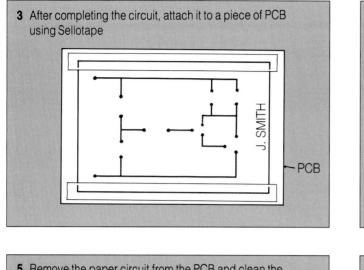

4 Now drill through each of the 'blobs' using a 1 mm drill whilst holding the work firmly over a piece of scrap wood.

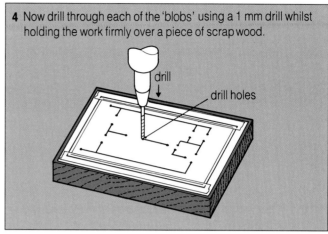

5 Remove the paper circuit from the PCB and clean the surface of the board using wire wool.
Now re-draw the circuit on the PCB using an **etch resist pen.**

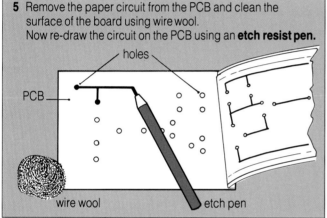

6 The circuit can now be etched in iron (III) chloride either in a tray, or preferably in a special etching bath.
Only do this with your teacher's supervision.

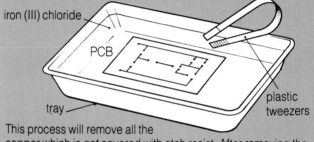

This process will remove all the copper which is *not* covered with etch resist. After removing the board with tweezers, wash it thoroughly with water.

Assembling the circuit

1 When you are ready to complete your circuit rub off the etch resist from the copper strips using wire wool.

2 Next insert the components in the correct position, from the underside of the board.

3 Using a soldering iron with a **clean** bit, heat up a joint, wait for a moment and then apply the solder to the joint. Remove the iron and solder and allow the joint to cool. Repeat for all the connections.

Note Any movement of a joint before it sets will create a **dry joint** having a poor electrical connection.

4 When soldering transistors and diodes, or other components which can be damaged by heat, always use a **heatsink** – a pair of pointed pliers can be used for this purpose.

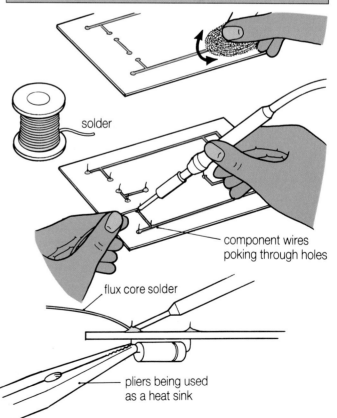

Questions

18 The block diagram of a fish tank environment alarm is shown here. The system is designed to monitor both water temperature and water level. If either are below a pre-set value, the system displays a visible warning.

Complete the block diagram by filling in the empty boxes.

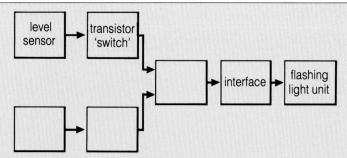

Block diagram – fish tank environment alarm

19 A stamping machine is loaded by hand with metal blanks. A light sensor detects the presence of the operator's arm. The machine 'stamps' when PS_1 is pressed, but only if the operator's arm has been withdrawn.

If the light sensor gives an output of **0** when the beam is interrupted, and the press switch gives an output of **1** when closed, what type of logic gate should be in the box X to allow the machine to operate safely?

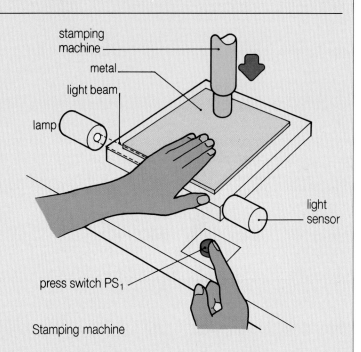

Stamping machine

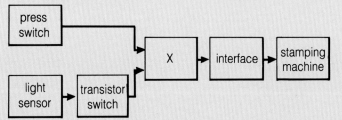

Block diagram – stamping machine

20 The block diagram of a control system is shown. If the input at A is logic **1** and at B is logic **0**, what are the values at C, D and E?

A	B	C	D	E
1	0			

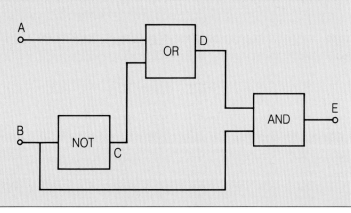

Projects

A number of project briefs are given below. Follow the design process (outlined in Chapter 1) as you try to satisfy the briefs. A wide range of materials and components can be used in the realization of these projects, including construction kits.

1 Transistor tester

A transistor tester is a very useful device to have available when building electronic circuits.

Design and construct a transistor tester using the circuit shown in the diagram.

If you have read Chapter 6 you should understand how the circuit works.

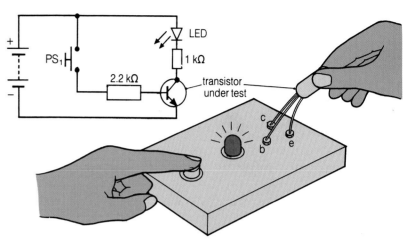

Transistor tester

2 Burglar alarm

Many people feel anxious about leaving their homes unattended at night and during holidays, because of the risk of being burgled.

Design and construct a burglar alarm system for a (model) room containing a window and a door. The alarm (a buzzer or bell) should be activated if either the window or door is opened. The alarm should continue to sound even if the window or door is closed again.

3 Motor car courtesy light delay

A car's courtesy light is operated by microswitches activated by the car doors. The light automatically swiches on when a door is opened, and off when it is closed. It would be much more useful however, if the light remained on for a short time after the door was closed.

Design and construct a circuit to do this, and a model to demonstrate its operation.

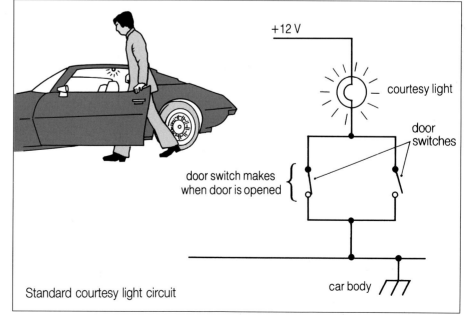

Standard courtesy light circuit

4 Goods transporter

Design and construct a scale model of a goods transporter vehicle for use in a warehouse. The flow chart below describes how the vehicle must operate.

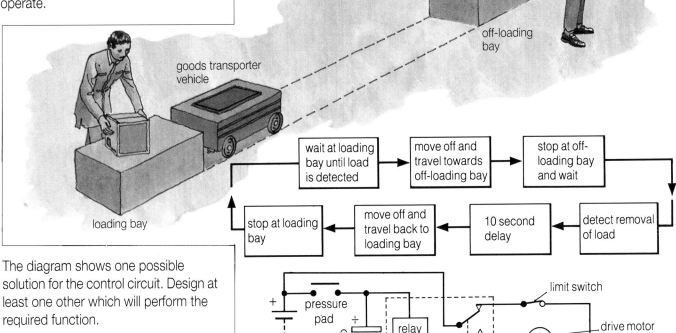

The warehouse

off-loading bay

goods transporter vehicle

loading bay

wait at loading bay until load is detected → move off and travel towards off-loading bay → stop at off-loading bay and wait

stop at loading bay ← move off and travel back to loading bay ← 10 second delay ← detect removal of load

The diagram shows one possible solution for the control circuit. Design at least one other which will perform the required function.

Vehicle control circuit

pressure pad · C · relay coil · limit switch · drive motor · M · limit switch

5 Noughts and crosses

Design and construct an electronic noughts and crosses game.

One idea would be to use different coloured LEDs to represent the noughts and crosses. See if you can think of a more ingenious idea.

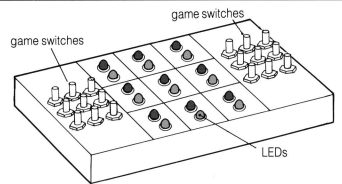

game switches

game switches

LEDs

6 Self-balancing crane

Design and construct a model of a tower crane with a self-balancing jib.

The crane should be fitted with sensors which detect when the jib is out of balance, and a control system which automatically adjusts the position of the counterweight to re-balance the jib.

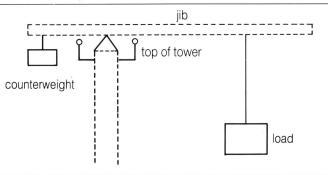

jib

top of tower

counterweight

load

7 Damp detector

Young people buying their first houses often buy older properties. Damp can be a problem in some of these houses.

Design and construct a small, hand-held damp detector which could be marketed at around £10.

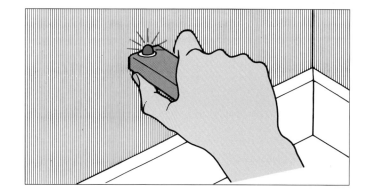

8 Personal safe

Design and construct a small safe with a combination lock, for keeping your private possessions secure.

One solution could include the use of rotary switches, connected in series, to form part of the control circuit, and a solenoid activated bolt.

To make the project more sophisticated, you could add a 'wrong combination' alarm, which once activated could not be switched off by the thief.

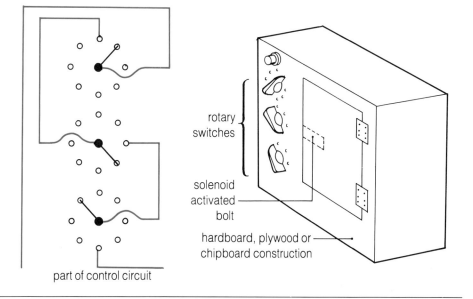

part of control circuit

rotary switches

solenoid activated bolt

hardboard, plywood or chipboard construction

9 Electronic ruler

Design and construct an electronic ruler which can be used to check the dimensions of small components.

The diagram should give you a clue to one possible solution. The control circuit can be similar to that used for the electronic weighing machine (page 144).

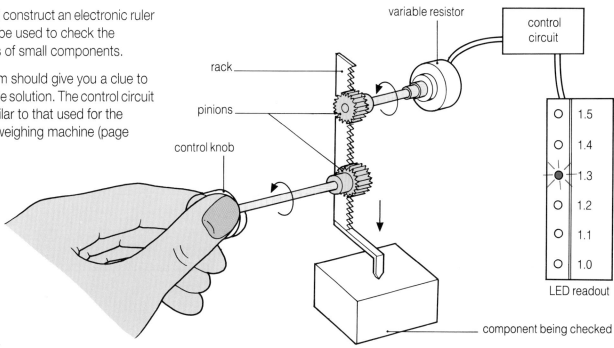

variable resistor

control circuit

rack

pinions

control knob

1.5
1.4
1.3
1.2
1.1
1.0

LED readout

component being checked

10 Automatic box-sorter

The diagram shows an idea for an automatic box-sorter. Tall boxes are detected by the light beam, but short boxes pass underneath undetected.

The circuit shown could be used to control the ram mechanism to push the tall boxes off the conveyor belt.

How the circuit works

When the light beam is broken, the relay contacts close, the motor runs, and the ram begins to move. When the drive shaft has rotated through a few degrees, the cam 'releases' MS_1, allowing its contacts to make. When the box is pushed out of the light beam therefore, and the relay de-energizes, the motor can continue to run until the cam once again opens MS_1.

The project

Using the above, or similar ideas, design and make an automatic box-sorter which will separate tall and short boxes and store them in two separate containers.

Ram control circuit

11 Personal alarm

Many people feel anxious about going out at night in some areas because of the fear of being attacked.

Design and construct a low cost personal alarm to help allay some of these fears. It must be easy to carry, and quick to activate in the case of an emergency.

Further ideas for projects

- Food or drink dispenser
- Cycle theft alarm
- Disco effects unit
- Automatic garage door
- Automatic watering system for a greenhouse
- Low-temperature alarm for the elderly
- Remote controlled robot arm
- Flashing shop sign

- Reaction timer
- Line following vehicle
- Electronic key
- Musical game
- Household aids for the handicapped
- Sports timer
- Baby alarm.

Examples of school technology projects

Some examples of year 10 and 11 technology projects are shown below. They may give you some ideas for your own projects. Try the **exercises** too – you will see just how easy it is to design quite complex circuits.

Stair-lift project

These photographs show the completed stair-lift project made by Pauline and Nick (as illustrated in Chapter 1).

See project brief and specification on pages 10 and 12.

Exercise Design a circuit suitable for controlling the stair-lift.

Plant care system (John Richardson – year 11)

Brief Some greenhouse plants cannot tolerate very bright light. I wish to design a system which prevents light above a certain intensity reaching the plants.

Solution A light-activated switch circuit which controls a motor-driven gauze blind.

Exercise Complete the circuit diagram by including a light-activated switch circuit.

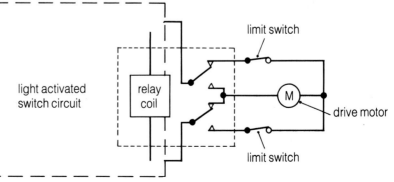

light activated switch circuit — relay coil — limit switch — M — drive motor — limit switch

Fun robot (Jeremy Rooke – year 11)

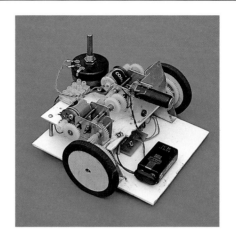

Brief   To design and construct a light-seeking robot toy. The robot should 'search' for a light beam (from a torch), lock on to it, and travel towards it. If the light beam is moved or interrupted, the robot must stop travelling forwards and begin to search for the light again.

Solution   A two wheel drive vehicle. The right wheel is driven continuously, but the left wheel is driven only when light from a torch falls on the LDR. See the circuit diagram shown.

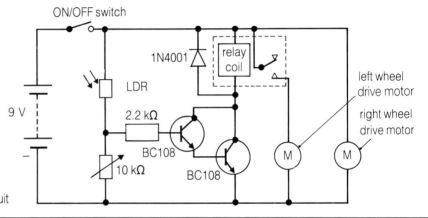

Robot control circuit

Factory lift (Andrew Timms – year 11)

Brief   Design and make a passenger lift for use in a busy factory. The lift must work between two floors and does not need to have any doors. It must be possible to 'call' the lift from either floor.

Solution   See photograph and circuit diagram.

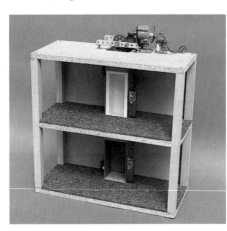

Exercise   Explain why the ground floor 'up' button and the first floor 'call' button are connected in parallel, whilst the first floor 'down' button and the ground floor 'call' button are connected in series.

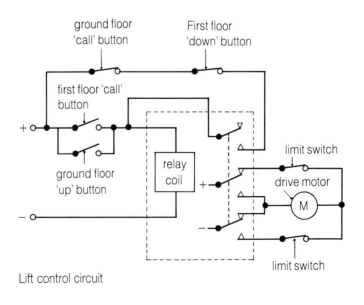

Lift control circuit

Fork lift truck (Robert Timson – year 10)

Brief I want to design a remote-controlled fork lift truck. It will be used in a yard where dangerous chemicals are stored. The truck must be controlled by a hand-held control box.

Solution (See photograph and circuit diagram.)

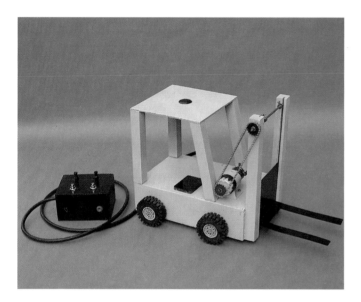

Exercise The teacher suggested that limit switches could have been fitted to protect the fork lift motor from damage.

Explain this, and re-draw the circuit with the limit switches included.

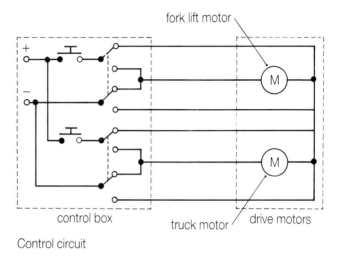

Control circuit

A warehouse lift (Neil Denny – year 11)

Brief Goods which are delivered to the ground floor of a warehouse are off-loaded from lorries by hand. These must be transported to other floors in the warehouse to be stored.

Design and construct a convenient transport system to help with this work.

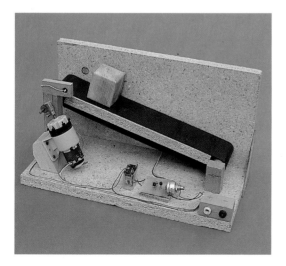

Solution A conveyor belt system which operates as outlined in the flow chart.

Exercise Design a circuit which could be used to operate the conveyor belt as outlined in the flowchart.

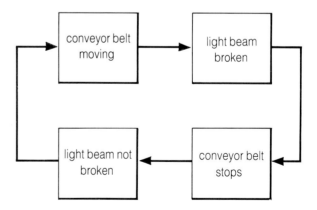

IN/OUT cat flap (Alex Burton – year 10)

Brief I like to make sure that my cat is indoors at night. I want to make a cat flap which tells me when my cat is IN and when she is OUT.

Solution (See photograph and circuit diagram.)

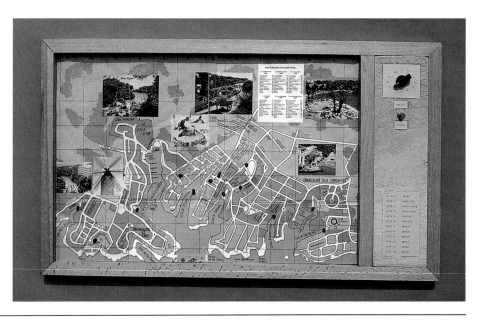

Information The control circuit used for this project is called a bistable multivibrator. (You may like to build a similar circuit and experiment with it.) When RS_1 is closed momentarily, TR_2 turns off. (Can you see why?) When TR_2 turns off, the voltage at its collector rises (you can check this with a voltmeter). A small current therefore flows in the base of TR_1 causing it (and L_1) to turn on. TR_1 remains on until RS_2 is closed momentarily. This causes the circuit to 'flip' turning L_2 on and L_1 off.

Tourist information map (Andrew Bruce – year 11)

Brief I went on holiday to Majorca where I got lost several times. This gave me the idea for a useful project – to design and make an information map which helps you to locate places of interest.

Solution LEDs which flash at the required location for a pre-set period of time. The location is selected using a rotary switch. A press switch is used to activate the sequence.

Dispensing machine (Adrian Horsburgh – year 11)

Brief To design a **gob-stopper dispenser** which uses a novelty theme and operates automatically when triggered by the customer.

Solution See photographs.

When a coin is inserted in the slot and the press button operated, the snooker player pots a gob-stopper into the collecting tray.

Notice the use of the large **cam** to operate the snooker player's arm.

Note The motor used to drive this cam is controlled by a circuit similar to that shown on page 162 (automatic box sorter project).

Burglar deterrent (Jonathan Munton – year 11)

Brief To design a burglar deterrent for Mr Jones. He is a shift worker whose flat is unoccupied until he returns home each night at 10 o'clock. He lives in an area where burglaries are becoming fairly regular.

Solution A system which detects nightfall and responds by turning on the living room light and closing the curtains.

Exercise Design a circuit which could be used in this project.

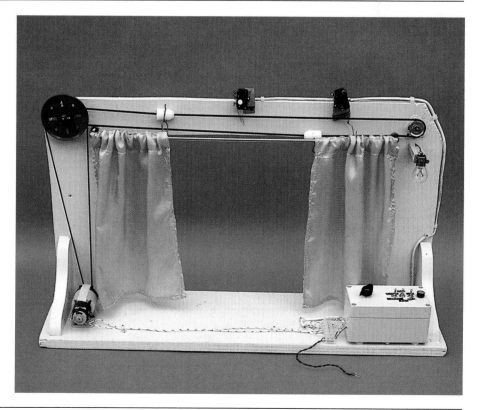

CHAPTER SEVEN

Pneumatics

Bus with pneumatically operated doors

Pneumatic screwdriver

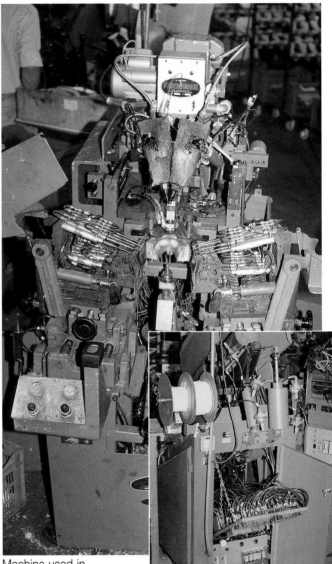

Machine used in shoe-making

Tyre bay equipment

Compressor and receiver

Pneumatic road drill

Air tanks on lorry

Example of pneumatically operated fairground ride

Pneumatics is all about using **compressed air** to 'make things happen'.

Compressed air is ordinary air which has been forced under pressure into a small space. Air under pressure possesses **energy** which can be released to do useful work.

For example, the doors on some buses and trains are operated using compressed air, and some lorries, buses and other large vehicles have air operated brakes. You can actually hear the air being used as these systems are operated.

Many different kinds of pneumatic tools are in use today, including the dentist's drill and the very familiar (and noisy) pneumatic road drill.

In industry, pneumatic systems have many applications. They are commonly used, for example, on automated production lines. This can involve, for example, moving materials, assembling products and packaging.

All the above systems rely for their operation on a constant supply of compressed air. This is usually provided by a **compressor**. A compressor is an 'air pump' driven by an electric motor or an internal combustion engine. The compressed air is usually stored in a strong metal tank called a **receiver**. The air is passed on to where it is needed along narrow plastic or metal pipes.

Understanding pneumatics is really very simple. All you have to do is to learn about the operation of a few basic components.

Understanding pneumatics

Jo has used two of the most basic pneumatic components, a **three port valve** and a **single acting cylinder**, in her stamping machine. The machine is designed to stamp dome shaped discs for use in the manufacture of medallions.

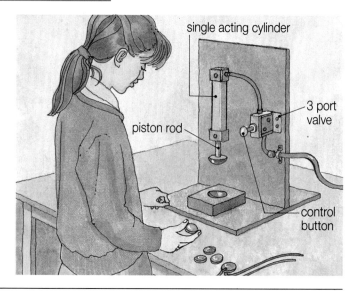

How the machine operates

A three port valve is a switch used to control the flow of air. The type shown here contains a component called a **spool** which moves inside the valve when the button is pressed or released. Its job is **to direct the flow of air** through the valve. Look at the picture of the valve and notice that when the button is pressed, compressed air from the supply is allowed to pass out of pipe 1 and into pipe 2 (which is connected to the cylinder).

Note The 'airways' into and out of the valve, which we have called pipes, are actually called **ports**. This is why the valve is called a three port valve.

A **single acting cylinder** uses compressed air to produce motion and **force**. It contains a piston which can slide 'up and down'. The piston is normally pushed 'up' into the cylinder by a spring. However, when the valve is operated as shown, compressed air enters the cylinder and forces the piston down. The air on the 'spring side' of the piston escapes through the vent hole.

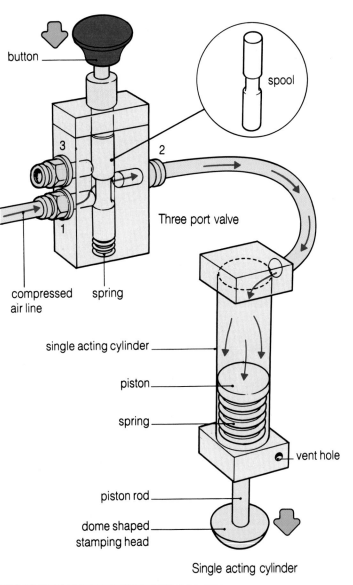

When the button is released, a small spring inside the valve pushes the spool back up. Notice that in this position, compressed air can no longer get from the supply to the cylinder. In fact the valve now allows the compressed air **in the cylinder** to escape down the pipe and out into the atmosphere through port 3. At the same time the spring in the cylinder pushes the piston back up. So by pressing and releasing the button, Jo is able to control her stamping machine.

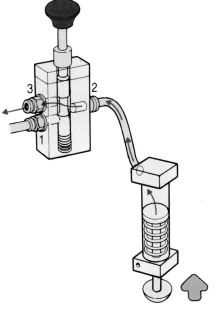

Component symbols

The above pictures make it very easy to understand how Jo's pneumatic circuit operates.

However, when drawing pneumatic circuits yourself it will be much easier to use **symbols** rather than pictures – although at first sight some pneumatic symbols look rather complicated. The symbol for the push button three port valve is shown here.

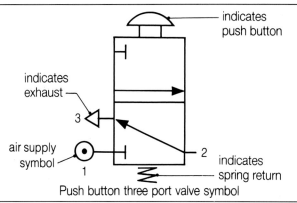

Push button three port valve symbol

The three port valve symbol explained

Just for a moment, look at the bottom half of the symbol, and ignore the top. Notice that the symbol shows port 1 'blocked off' (but ports 2 and 3 connected) just like in the real valve.

Now ignore the bottom half of the symbol and imagine that when the button is pressed the top part of the symbol slides over the bottom half as shown. This shows how the ports in the real valve are connected when the button is pressed.

So you can see that the bottom half of the symbol shows the connections inside the valve when the button is not pressed, and the top half shows the connections when the button is pressed.

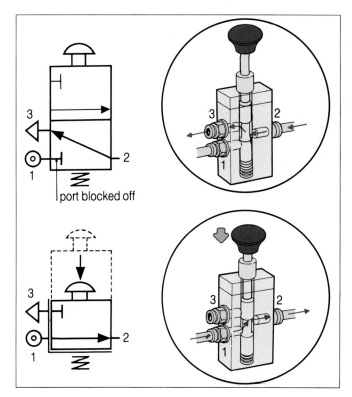

Single acting cylinder symbol

The symbol for a single acting cylinder really does not need any explanation. However, it is important to know that when the piston rod is 'out', the piston is said to be **positive**, and when it is 'in', it is said to be **negative**.

Note   Single acting cylinders are used mainly where relatively small forces are required and where the linear motion is small. The piston's movement (or stroke) is actually restricted by the spring.

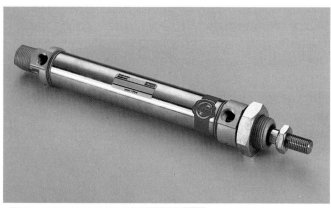

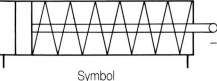

Symbol

Jo's pneumatic circuit

The diagram here shows the complete pneumatic circuit used in Jo's project drawn using circuit symbols.

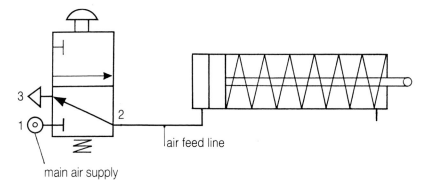

3

1

2

air feed line

main air supply

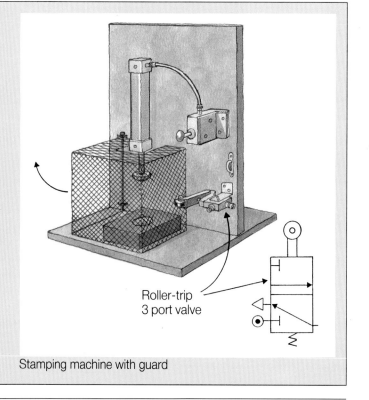

Question

1 Jo realised that operating her stamping machine **without a safety guard** was **dangerous**. She therefore redesigned the equipment to include a guard as shown here. By adding an additional valve she also made it impossible for the machine to be operated **unless the guard was in position**.

  a Using the correct symbols, draw a circuit which would only allow the machine to be operated with the safety guard in position.

  b What kind of **logic gate** do the valves in the above circuit form? Look back at *An introduction to control logic* (pages 152 to 155) if necessary.

Roller-trip
3 port valve

Stamping machine with guard

Dual control

Sometimes it is necessary to be able to operate a machine from more than one position. The circuit shown here works in this way. The single acting cylinder can be activated by pressing either button A *or* B. The circuit, however, must contain a **shuttle valve**. This 'new' component is explained below.

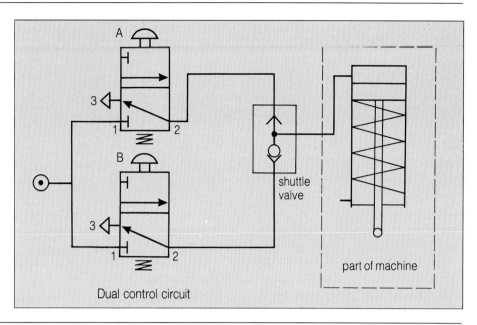

Dual control circuit

The shuttle valve explained

A shuttle valve is a very simple component, as you can see.

It has three ports, and contains a small rubber piston which is free to move between A and B within the valve. If air enters port 1A, the piston is pushed into position B. The air therefore, has to flow out of the valve through port 2. Similarly, if air enters the valve through port 1B, the piston is pushed into position A and once again the air can only 'escape' through port 2. If air enters both ports 1A and 1B at the same time, the piston 'floats' between A and B and again the air escapes through port 2.

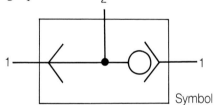

Symbol

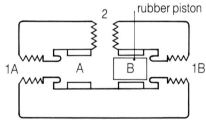

Question

2 The shuttle valve in the 'dual control' circuit is included for a good reason. If it was replaced with a simple 'T' connector, the circuit would not work. Neither valve A nor valve B could be used to activate the cylinder. Explain why.

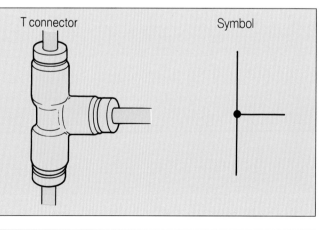

T connector   Symbol

Forces at work

Air under pressure can be released to do useful work, as explained in the introduction, and as we saw in Jo's stamping machine (page 170).

The single acting cylinder in Jo's machine produces a **force** (and does work) because air exerts a **pressure** upon the piston. The force which a piston produces depends on two factors: the **air pressure**, and the **surface area** of the piston.

If the air pressure was 0.5 N/mm^2 then the air would exert a force of 0.5 newtons on each square millimetre of piston, as you can see on the diagram. So if the piston had a total area of 300 mm^2, then the total force on the piston would be 0.5×300 newtons. Can you see that:

force = pressure × area?

Note   The force produced by a single acting cylinder as it goes negative, does *not* depend upon the air pressure or piston area. The force comes from the spring inside the cylinder.

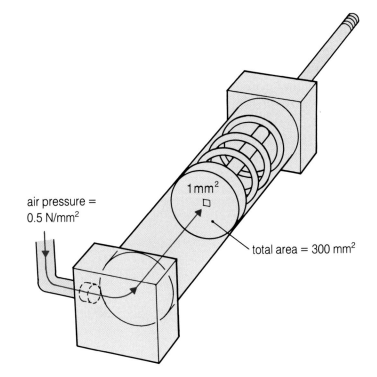

air pressure = 0.5 N/mm^2

1 mm^2

total area = 300 mm^2

Force = pressure × area
Force = 0.5 × 300 (for above example)
        = 150 N

Questions

3 What force is produced by the piston shown here if the air pressure is 0.3 N/mm^2?

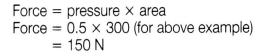

Diameter = 20 mm

air pressure = 0.3 N/mm^2

4 The diagrams show two methods of using a single acting cylinder to apply a compression force via a lever. Which method would you use, and why?

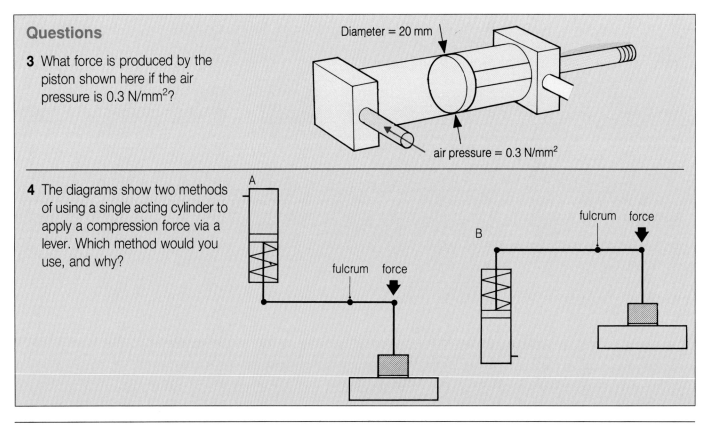

A

fulcrum   force

B

fulcrum   force

The double acting cylinder

A double acting cylinder and its symbol are shown here.

Notice that unlike a single acting cylinder, it does *not* contain a 'return' spring. Its movement *in both directions* is powered by compressed air.

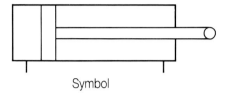

Symbol

Forces in a double acting cylinder

The force produced by a double acting cylinder as it goes positive, is **not** equal to the force it produces when going negative.

This can be explained by looking at the piston in the cylinder, and remembering that

force = pressure × area

Notice that the areas of the 'front' and 'back' faces of the piston are *not* equal. The piston rod reduces the area of the 'back' face. So although the air pressure on either side of the piston may be exactly the same the force produced will be less for a piston going negative.

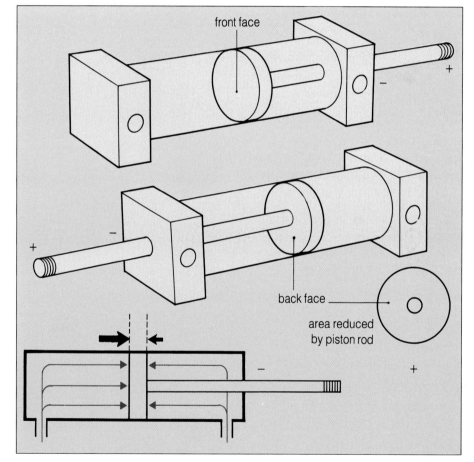

front face

back face

area reduced by piston rod

Questions

The pressure available to operate the piston shown here is 0.4 N/mm^2.

5 What force does the positive-going piston produce?

6 What force does the negative-going piston produce?

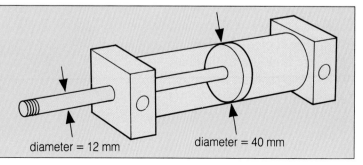

diameter = 12 mm

diameter = 40 mm

Controlling double acting cylinders

One method of controlling a double acting cylinder is illustrated in the project shown here. It was one pupil's solution to the following brief.

Brief   Design a 'pneumatic grab' which can grip a heavy round bar, lift it vertically and drop it when required.

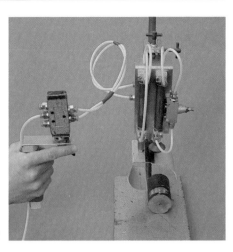

Pneumatic grab project

How the circuit operates

In addition to two double acting cylinders, two 'new' components are used in this project: a **five port valve** and a **flow regulator**.

The five port valve explained

As the name implies, this valve has five ports. This particular one is lever operated.

When the spool is in the position shown in diagram 1, compressed air from the supply passes through the valve between ports 1 and 2, and the air causes the pistons to move 'down'. Air trapped below the pistons is forced down the pipes and through the valve, escaping into the atmosphere through port 5.

When the lever is moved to its other position the spool moves up as shown in diagram 2.

Now follow the air flow on the diagram, and you will see that the pistons are forced to move 'up'. Also note how the trapped air above the pistons is forced out of the system.

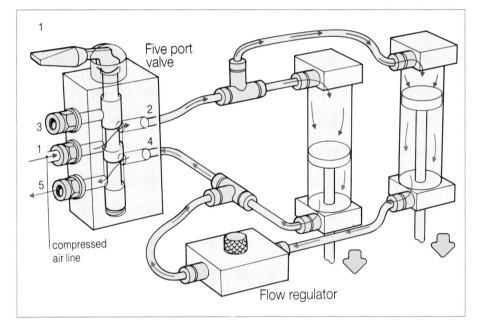

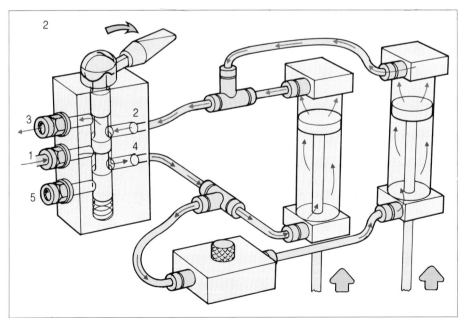

The five port valve symbol explained

Note Make sure that you understand the three port valve symbol (explained on page 171) before you read the following.

Ignore the top half of the symbol for a moment, The bottom half shows the connections inside the valve when the lever is in one particular position.

Now ignore the bottom half of the symbol, and imagine that when the lever is moved to the other position the top half of the symbol slides over the bottom half. This shows the connections inside the valve now.

Notice that a 'lever' symbol appears on both ends of the five port valve symbol. This is rather confusing – there is, of course, only *one* lever on the real valve.

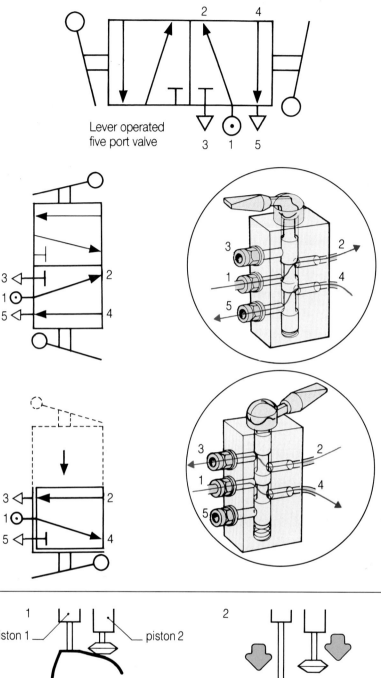

Lever operated
five port valve

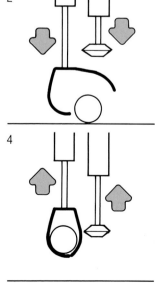

Piston speed control

It is often necessary to control the *speed* of a piston's movement.

For example, in the pneumatic grab project, piston 2 needs to move more slowly than piston 1.

Piston 1 positions the grab, and a few seconds later, piston 2 closes it as shown in the diagram. In the project a **flow regulator** was used for this purpose.

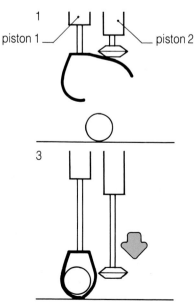

piston 1   piston 2

The flow regulator explained

Several different types of flow regulator are available. One example is shown here.

Air can pass through the regulator in either direction. When air enters port 1, however, a rubber piston is pushed into position A so that air can only pass through the regulator down the central pipe. The flow of air through this pipe can be controlled by turning a finger screw.

If air enters the regulator through port 2, however, the piston is pushed into position B and the air can flow through the valve unrestricted.

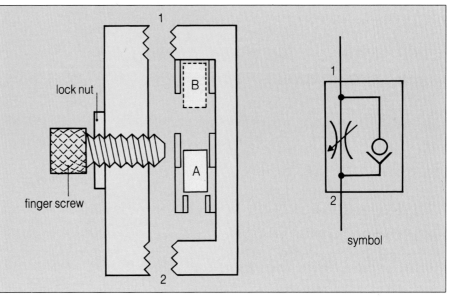

Pneumatic grab circuit

The diagram shows the circuit for the pneumatic grab project illustrated on page 176.

Can you see that the flow regulator makes piston 2 move down more slowly than piston 1? However, when the pistons are rising both pistons move at the same speed.

Note   Piston speed control is achieved, in this circuit, by regulating the rate at which **exhausting air** can leave the cylinder. This produces a much smoother control than regulating air flow into a cylinder.

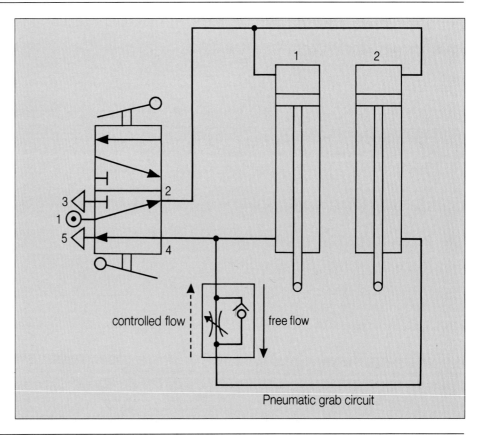

Pneumatic grab circuit

More flow regulator applications

The diagrams show part of a labelling machine and its control circuit.

When button A is pressed, the roller advances *slowly*, and labels the box. When A is released the piston rapidly returns the roller to its rest position.

Note For light applications, regulating air flow into a cylinder is acceptable.

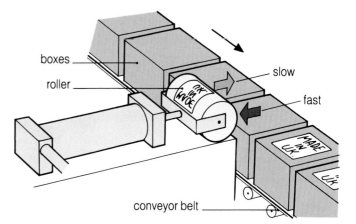

Questions

7 It was found that the rapid return of the label roller often caused the printing on the label to smudge.

Using the same components (but including a second flow regulator) draw a circuit which would control piston speed going both forwards and backwards, for this machine.

8 Wherever it is dangerous to move something at full piston speed, or where a sudden jerky movement could cause damage to a product or device, piston speed must be controlled.

Choose one of the processes pictured here and design a control circuit for its safe operation. You may use any of the pneumatic components described in this chapter so far.

Labelling machine control circuit

1 End of production line

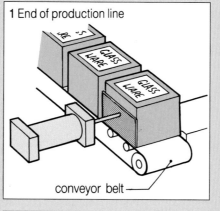

conveyor belt

2 Tipper trolley

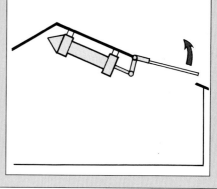

3 Sliding door

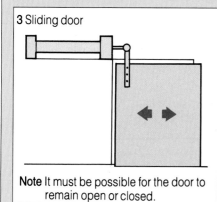

Note It must be possible for the door to remain open or closed.

4 Paper guillotine

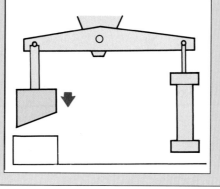

5 Factory window

Air operated valves

In the valves described so far, the spool (which controls the flow of air through the valve) has been moved either by a button or lever. In air operated valves, the spool is moved by air pressure.

Three different air operated valves, and their symbols, are shown here. Notice that **arrowheads** and **dashed lines** are used to indicate that they are air operated.

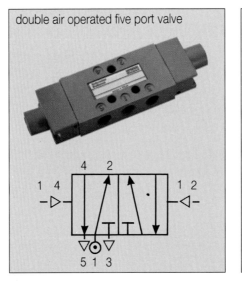

double air operated five port valve

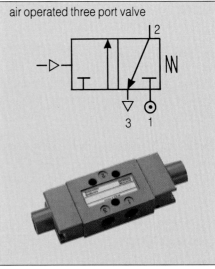

air operated three port valve

diaphragm operated three port valve

Double air operated five port valve – DAO5PV

One of the dangers associated with pneumatic equipment is the very high pressures which are sometimes used. For example, high pressure air escaping from a loose pipe causes the pipe to 'lash about' violently. This can cause serious injury.

In industry, where high pressure systems are common, it is essential to keep employees well away from danger. The system shown here allows you to do this.

In the circuit, the DAO5PV is being used to control a cylinder at very high pressure. However, the air pressure required to control the valve itself (the signal) only needs to be small. Hence the operator can work in safety.

Notice that the symbol for the pipe supplying the air signals to control the DAO5PV is shown dashed and that the valves used to provide the signal are called **pilot valves**.

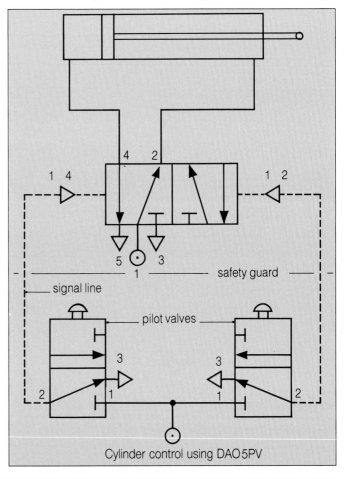

Cylinder control using DAO5PV

The DAO5PV symbol explained

The internal structure of this valve is very similar to the five port valve described on page 176.

When the signal is applied to the DAO5PV as shown here, the spool moves and connects port 1 to port 2 (and 4 to 5). This is why the numbers 1 2 are written on the symbol.

Similarly, when the signal is applied to the valve, as shown here, the spool moves and connects port 1 to port 4 (and 2 to 3). This is why the numbers 1 4 are written on the symbol.

Note If a DAO5PV receives a signal from both ends (and at the same pressure) the spool does not move.

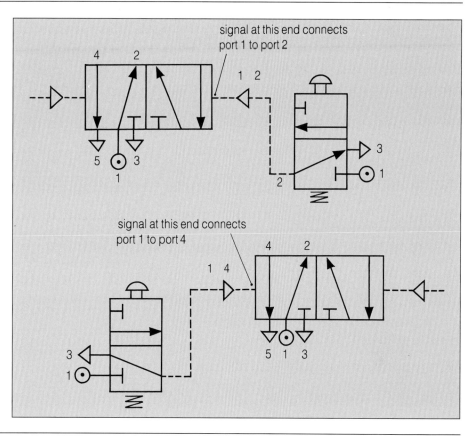

Diaphragm operated three port valve

For some applications, it is necessary to use a valve which will operate at *very low* signal pressures. The diaphragm operated valve is designed to do this.

Now **Force = pressure × area**. Therefore, if only a tiny pressure is available to operate a valve, then to provide enough force to move the spool the area upon which the air signal acts must be large. This is the purpose of the diaphragm in this valve.

Note Sometimes it is necessary to operate a valve by an air signal *below* normal air pressure. For this purpose the signal is connected to the vacuum port on the valve.

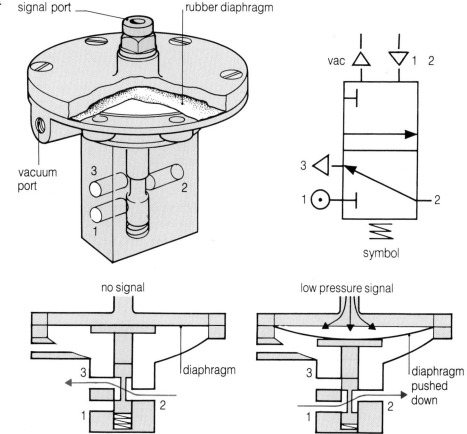

Diaphragm operated valve applications

One application of a diaphragm operated valve is shown here. It is a system used in some garages to indicate to the attendant that a vehicle has driven onto the forecourt. It uses what is called an **air bleed circuit**.

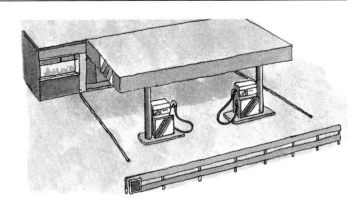

How the system operates

Air from the supply is fed into a flow regulator. This emits a controlled flow of air into a T-junction. One pipe from this junction is connected to the diaphragm operated valve and the other is left open to bleed air into the atmosphere. This is why the circuit is called an air bleed circuit.

When the air bleed pipe is 'blocked off' by a vehicle's wheel, pressure builds up in the pipe and the diaphragm operated valve is activated (connecting port 1 to port 2). This allows compressed air to activate the piston, making it go positive and hit the gong.

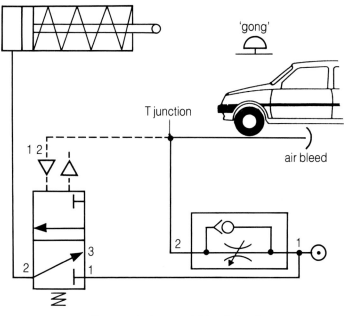

Forecourt alarm – air bleed circuit

Piston position sensor

Another application of the diaphragm operated valve is as a **sensor** to detect when a piston is at the end of its stroke (either fully in or fully out).

Here is an example of its use. This picture shows part of a semi-automatic assembly line. When the worker is ready to receive a component, the worker taps the foot operated valve. This activates a circuit, causing a piston to push the next component to the worker. When the piston reaches the end of its stroke, the circuit detects this, and automatically returns the piston to its rest position ready to supply the next component.

The complete control circuit is described below.

Control circuit operation

First notice that the air supply to the diaphragm operated valve is connected in an unusual way. It is connected to port 3 instead of port 1.

Now, when the piston is held negative (by the connection of port 1 to port 2 in the DAO5PV), the pressure at X also supplies an air signal to activate the diaphragm operated valve (connecting port 1 to port 2). In this state, no signal reaches the DAO5PV from this valve.

However, when the button of the foot operated 3 port valve is pressed an air signal is sent to the DAO5PV, the valve is activated, and ports 1 and 4 are connected. So the piston begins to go slowly positive (controlled by the flow regulator) and at the same time the regulator helps to maintain the pressure at X. At the end of the stroke (when all the air is exhausted) the signal pressure to the diaphragm operated valve drops. This valve then returns to its normal off position allowing an air signal to be sent to the DAO5PV. The valve is activated, and ports 1 and 2 are connected, causing the piston to go negative automatically.

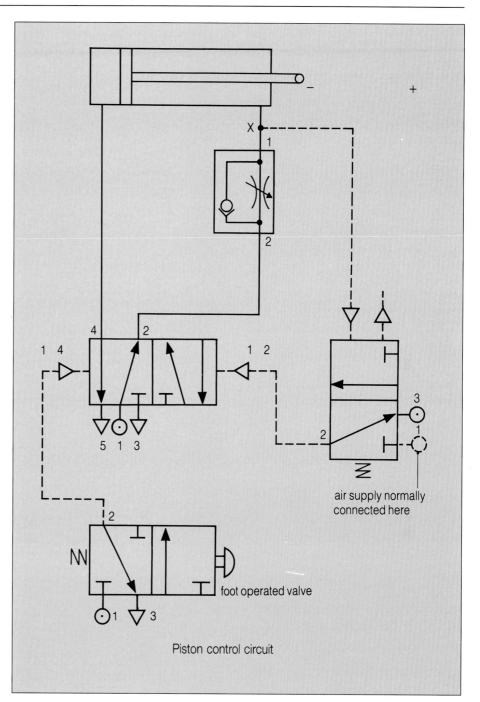

Piston control circuit

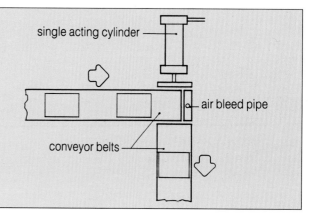

Question

9 The diagram shows a junction between two conveyor belts in a factory. Boxes (containing delicate components) are transferred from one belt to the other by the action of a single acting cylinder. An air bleed pipe is used to detect when a box is in position for transfer.

Design a control circuit for this equipment.

Time delays

Sometimes it is necessary to introduce a **time delay** at some stage in the operation of a pneumatic circuit.

For example, here is a machine used in the production of laminated table mats. The operator loads the machine with a mat base and a decorative surface lamina (both coated with impact adhesive). After the button is pressed momentarily, the piston (and pressure pad) go positive, and the table mat is held under pressure for a few seconds before the piston automatically goes negative again. This allows the impact adhesive *time* to grip.

To produce a time delay of this kind you need to understand another pneumatic component called a **reservoir**, see below.

push button

Time delays explained

Time delays in a pneumatic circuit can be created using the components shown here. The only component new to you is the reservoir. A reservoir is simply a container for air.

A flow of air (controlled by the flow regulator) enters the reservoir, slowly 'filling it up'. When the pressure in the reservoir reaches about 0.2 N/mm², the DAO5PV is activated. The delay time depends upon the adjustment of the flow regulator and the **volume** of the reservoir.

The complete circuit diagram for the pneumatic press is shown here.

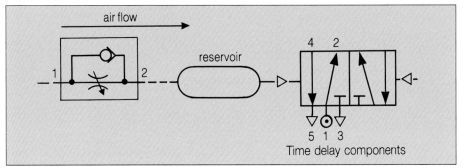

air flow

reservoir

4 2

5 1 3
Time delay components

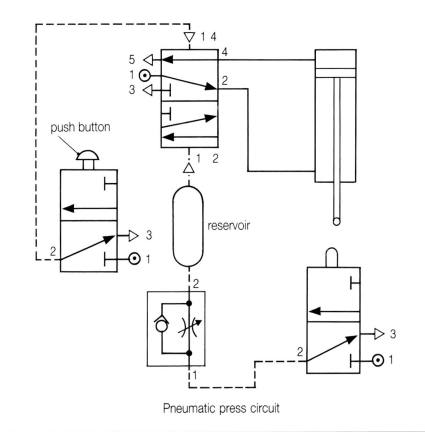

push button

reservoir

Pneumatic press circuit

Question

10 Describe the operation of the pneumatic press and its circuit. Begin your description like this. *When the push button is pressed, an air signal is sent to the . . .*

Automatic control

All the pneumatic circuits described so far have needed an **input** from the outside world to make them operate: a button being pressed, or a pipe being blocked off, for example. A fully automatic circuit however, controls itself.

The pictures here show a pupil's idea for a technology project which uses a fully automatic circuit.

The brief was to design a moving advertising board to attract attention to a discount tyre centre. A pneumatic system was chosen because compressed air would be readily available.

The piston in this device goes positive–negative, positive–negative continuously (**reciprocates**) and this action is used to drive the mechanism which makes the mechanic's arm move. The control circuit is explained below.

rear view of drive mechanism

The automatic control circuit explained

This circuit works automatically because the piston operates its own control valve (C) by activating pilot valves A and B at each end of its movement.

Look at the circuit and imagine that at this moment the piston is going positive. When fully positive, the piston activates valve A, which sends an air signal to activate valve C (connecting port 1 to port 2). Therefore, the piston immediately begins to go negative until valve B is activated. Valve B then sends an air signal to activate valve C (connecting port 1 to port 4) and the piston begins to go positive again . . . and so the cycle repeats continuously as long as the air supply is maintained.

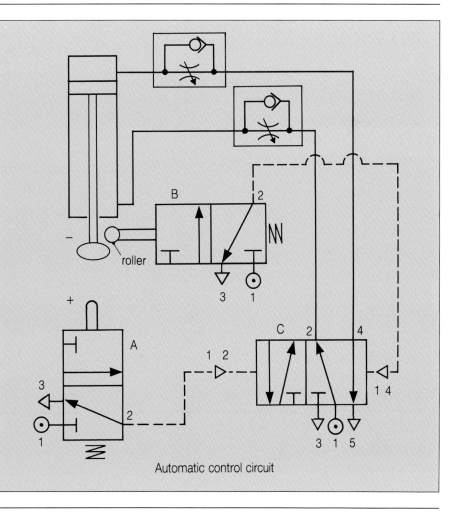

Automatic control circuit

Questions

11 For some industrial applications it is not practicable to control an automatic circuit using mechanical valves (as above); the valves get in the way of the work being done. The circuit shown here, avoids this by using **air bleeds**.

Explain the full operation of this circuit.

12 Sometimes it is necessary for the piston, in an automatic circuit, to return and stop in the negative (or positive) position, when the circuit is switched off.

Where would you connect a valve to make this circuit stop automatically with the piston in the negative position only?

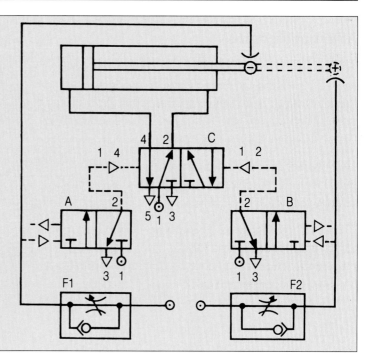

Sequential control

Sometimes, two or more pistons in a pneumatic circuit, are required to operate in a particular order to carry out a job. An example is shown here.

This machine is designed to stamp triangles on to wooden blocks in a continuous process. The blocks are fed into the machine at point X, and are ejected at point Z. To carry out this job, pistons A and B must go positive and negative in a particular sequence.

If you follow the diagrams in order from **1** to **4**, you will see that the sequence is as follows.

1 Piston A goes positive.
2 Piston B goes positive.
3 Piston A goes negative.
4 Piston B goes negative.

The above can be written as

Sequence = A+, B+, A−, B−

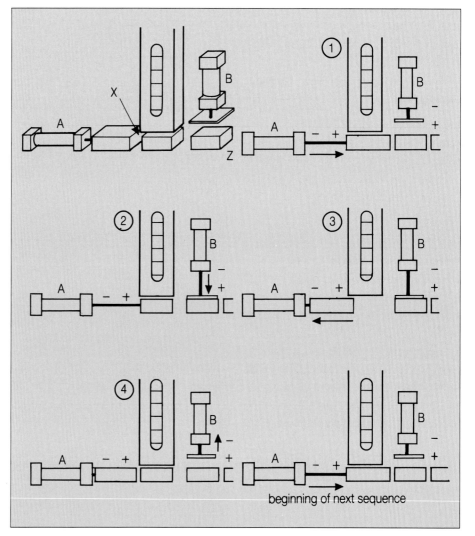

beginning of next sequence

Sequential control circuit explained

Look at the circuit and imagine that at this moment piston A is going positive.

When fully positive, pilot valve A2 is activated. An air signal is therefore sent to control valve C1 (connecting port 1 to port 4).

Therefore, piston B goes positive (and stamps the triangle). When fully positive, piston B activates pilot valve B2. An air signal is therefore sent to control valve C2 (connecting port 1 to port 4).

Therefore, piston A goes negative. When fully negative, piston A activates pilot valve A1. An air signal is therefore sent to control valve C1 (connecting port 1 to port 2).

Therefore, piston B goes negative. When fully negative, piston B activates pilot valve B1. An air signal is therefore sent to control valve C2 (connecting port 1 to port 2) . . . and so the sequence is repeated continuously until the air supply is switched off.

Questions

13 Where would you position an 'on/off' valve in this circuit so that when the circuit was switched off, both pistons would return and stop in their negative positions?

14 Describe how this system could be made to switch off automatically when the supply of wooden blocks runs out.

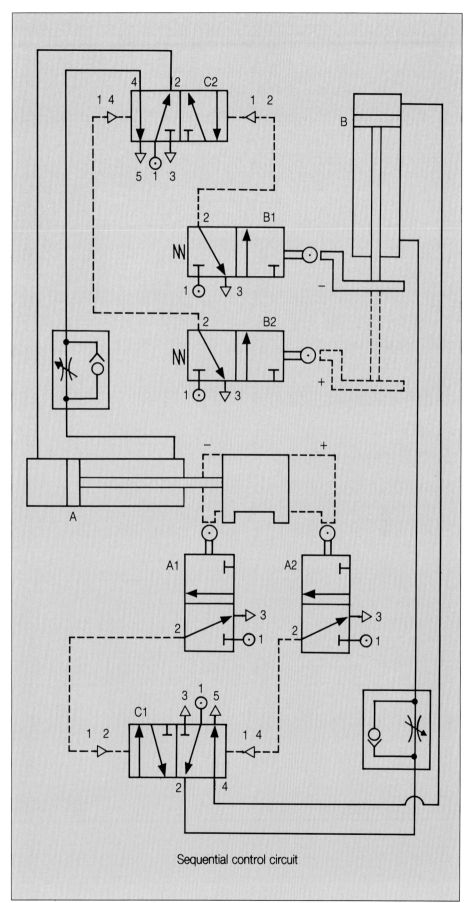

Sequential control circuit

Hydraulics

Look at the pictures of the mechanical digger and the refuse lorry here. Notice that both vehicles have mechanisms which make use of **cylinders**.

You might be surprised to know that the cylinders and pipes on these vehicles do not contain air (as in a pneumatic system) but oil.

In a hydraulic system, oil replaces compressed air as the means of transmitting motion and force.

Mechanical digger

Refuse lorry

Hydraulics explained

A simple hydraulic system is shown here. It consists of two cylinders of different diameters connected together by a pipe and containing oil.

When a force is applied to piston A, oil is forced to move along the pipe and into cylinder B. Piston B therefore rises. The force exerted by piston A creates a pressure which is transmitted through the liquid in all directions.

Pressure is a measure of force over a given area. If the area of piston A is 100 mm², and the force exerted by the piston equals 50 N then the pressure exerted by the piston equals 0.5 N/mm².

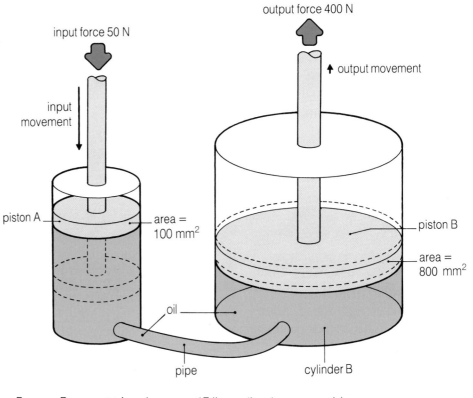

Force = Pressure × Area (see page 174)

$\therefore$ Pressure $= \dfrac{\text{Force}}{\text{Area}}$

(for above example)

Pressure $= \dfrac{50}{100} = 0.5$ N/mm²

Now, pressure is transmitted through the liquid in all directions, so the pressure exerted on piston B is also 0.5 N/mm². However, because the area of piston B is 800 mm², the force produced at piston B becomes 400 N – eight times greater than the input force. (See opposite.)

It might appear that you are getting 'something for nothing', but in fact you are not because for each 1 centimetre moved by piston B, piston A has to be moved 8 cm.

Hydraulic jack

Oil has a major advantage over compressed air: *it cannot be compressed*. The hydraulic jack illustrates this advantage.

Because oil cannot be compressed it is possible to jack up a vehicle safely. The large piston can be stopped at any point in its movement and will stay there whatever happens to the load. This is not possible with compressed air.

How the jack works

A piston (connected to the jack handle) moves up and down as the handle is moved up and down. This piston, which has a small diameter, forces oil from a reservoir through a one-way valve into a cylinder of larger diameter. So only a small force is required by the operator to raise the heavy load. To lower the vehicle, the one way valve is released and the vehicle's weight forces the oil back into the reservoir.

$$\text{Force} = \text{Pressure} \times \text{Area}$$

$$\begin{aligned}\text{Therefore force}\atop\text{on piston B} &= 0.5 \times 800 \\ &= 400\ \text{N}\end{aligned}$$

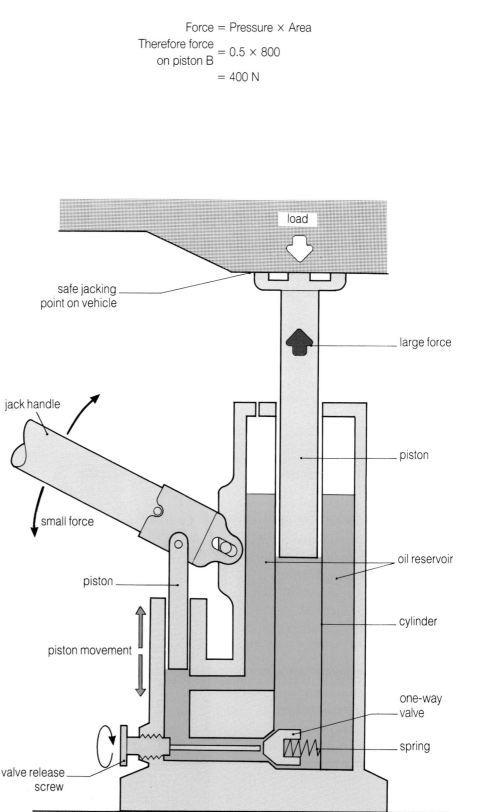

Hydraulic jack

Hydraulic brakes

The brakes on most vehicles today are hydraulically operated. The diagram shows part of a motor car's braking system.

When the brake pedal is pressed, a small piston in the **master cylinder** creates a pressure in the brake fluid which is transmitted to the **wheel cylinders** (at each of the four wheels). The pistons in the wheel cylinders exert a force on the **brake pads** which rub against the rotating **disc**. This slows down, and eventually stops the vehicle.

Although some cars have disc brakes on all four wheels, most use **drum brakes** on the rear (and disc brakes at the front).

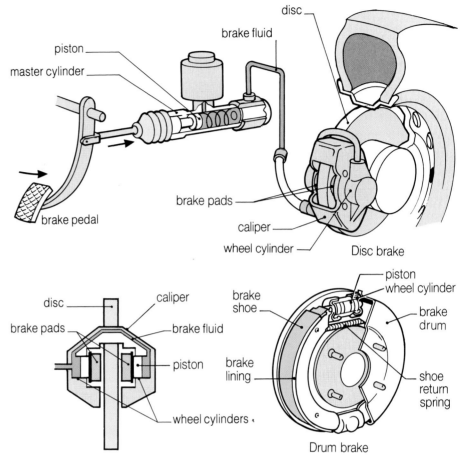

Disc brake

Drum brake

Other hydraulic systems

The jack and the car brakes (described above) rely on the human body to provide the force to create the pressure in the hydraulic system. For most applications however, a **pump** (driven by an electric motor or internal combustion engine) creates the pressure.

The mechanical digger and the refuse lorry (pictured on page 188) and the machines shown here, illustrate just a few of the numerous applications of pump driven hydraulic systems.

Close up of aircraft undercarriage

Bulldozer

Extending mobile crane

Lorry mounted crane

Pump driven hydraulics explained

The diagram shows a basic pump driven hydraulic system for a single **ram**.

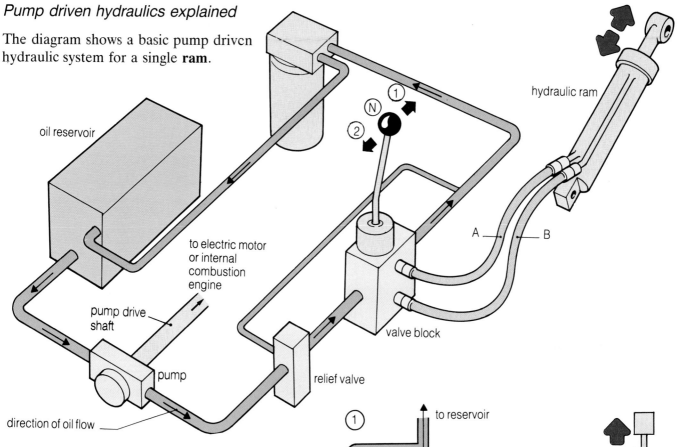

oil reservoir

hydraulic ram

to electric motor
or internal
combustion
engine

pump drive
shaft

pump

relief valve

valve block

A   B

direction of oil flow

How the system operates

When the control lever is in the 'neutral' position (diagram 1), oil is pumped straight through the valve block and back to the reservoir.

With the lever in position 1 (diagram 2), a spool (in the valve block) *stops* the oil flowing straight through the valve, and directs it into pipe A – sending the ram positive. Oil on the 'top' side of the piston is forced out of the cylinder, through pipe B and back into the main circuit through the valve block.

When the ram is fully positive, the oil flow to the valve block stops completely, but the **relief valve** opens to allow oil to continue to flow around the main circuit (as in diagram 3).

To drive the ram negative, the lever is moved into position 2 and the valve block redirects the oil accordingly.

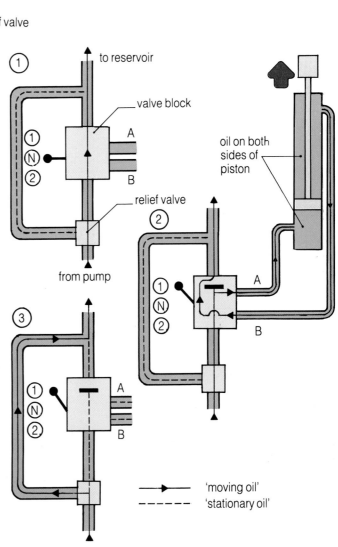

to reservoir

valve block

oil on both
sides of
piston

relief valve

from pump

A

B

'moving oil'

- - - - - 'stationary oil'

Projects

A number of project briefs are given below. Follow the design process (outlined in Chapter 1) as you try to satisfy the briefs.

1 Walking machine

The sketches show an idea for a novel 'walking machine'.

Either develop the idea and construct a working model, or design and construct a totally new system.

The machine must walk slowly and safely without falling over. It can be either automatically or manually controlled.

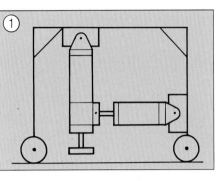
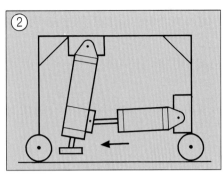

2 Clay extruder

Design and construct a pneumatically operated 'miniature' clay extruder for use in a school ceramics department.

The machine must be capable of producing a range of useful extrusions, and must be very easy to operate and clean.

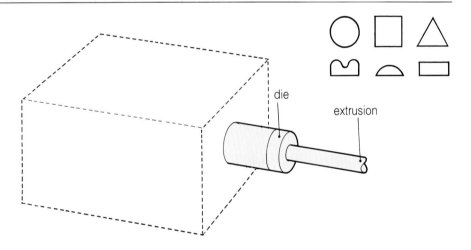

die

extrusion

3 Car park barrier

Design a **coin-operated** car park barrier. The barrier should rise when the correct coinage is deposited, and allow the vehicle to pass through safely before closing automatically.

Note The information on page 193 may be useful for your design.

£1 ALL DAY

Information

Sometimes it is necessary to control a pneumatic circuit with an **electrical signal** instead of an air signal. For this purpose a **solenoid-operated valve** may be used.

A solenoid is simply a coil of wire. When an electric current is passed through the wire, it produces a magnetic field around the coil. A piece of soft iron called an armature, placed just inside the coil, will be attracted into the coil whilst the current is flowing. A spring can be used to push the armature out again when the current is switched off.

The diagrams show how these principles are used to operate a pneumatic valve.

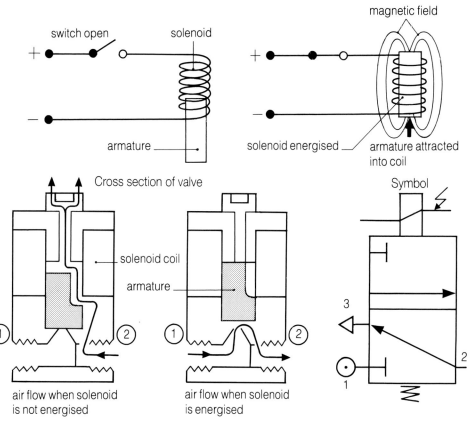

switch open   solenoid

armature

magnetic field

solenoid energised   armature attracted into coil

Cross section of valve

solenoid coil

armature

air flow when solenoid is not energised

air flow when solenoid is energised

Symbol

3

1

2

4 Automatic door

To cut down on heating costs, the owners of a large garage wish to install an automatic door to reduce heat loss from the garage workshop area.

Design and construct a model of a working system which makes use of the garage's compressed air supply.

The door should open automatically when a vehicle approaches, and close when the vehicle is safely 'in' or 'out'. The system must be completely safe – it must not be possible for the door to trap or injure any person standing in the doorway or nearby.

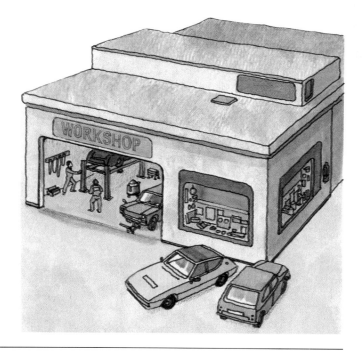

Further ideas for project work

– Pneumatic road drill
– Automatic self-levelling suspension for trailer used on very steep farmland

– Labelling machine
– Polishing machine
– Metal bending machine

Examples of school technology projects

Automatic stamping machine
(Andrew Wilson – year 11)

Brief   To investigate an automatic production process for my project using pneumatic equipment.

I shall try to design and make a model of a machine which stamps triangles onto blocks of wood in a continuous process.

Solution   See photograph and **sequential control** information on pages 186 and 187 of this chapter.

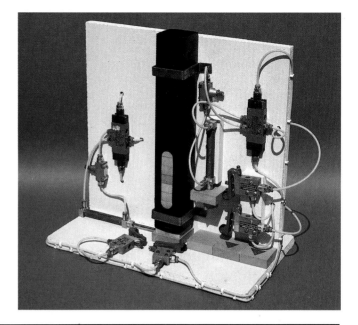

Belt strap manufacturing machine
(John Hollingsworth – year 11)

Brief   To design and make a machine which will produce belt straps from a continuous roll of leather. The machine must stamp out the holes, cut the tongue and produce belts of any length.

Solution   See photograph.

Exercise   Design an electro-pneumatic control circuit for this project.

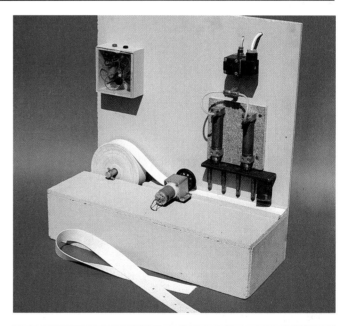

Car park barrier
(Nick Geeson – year 11)

Brief   To design and make a model of a car park barrier for use in a hospital car park. The barrier will be operated by a car park attendant who will charge patients and visitors for entry but allow hospital staff to enter without paying.

Solution   See photograph.

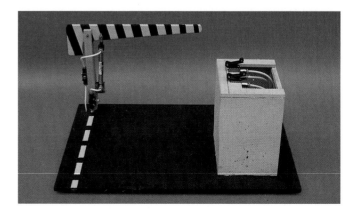

Bus step aid
(Neal Hillier – year 11)

Brief   Some buses have high steps which make it difficult for some elderly people, and small children, to get onto the bus. The problem is made worse when the bus parks next to a low kerb, or when there is no kerb at all.

Design and make a model of a pneumatically-operated step which could be moved into position when the bus stops, and be retracted before the bus moves off.

Solution   See photograph.

Exercise   Design a control circuit for this project.

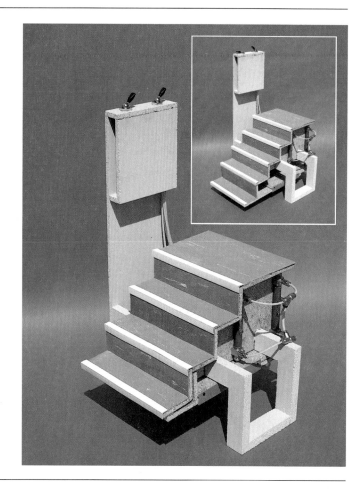

Remote-controlled hoist
(Louise Roe – year 11)

Brief   When I was on 'work experience' in a factory I saw the need for a simple hoist to raise boxes of fabric from one floor to the next.

Design a safe, remote-controlled hoist, which could make use of the factory's compressed air supply.

Solution   See photograph.

To understand how the hoist operates, you will need to be familiar with a simple 'block and tackle' pulley system. You will then notice that the **effort** force is being applied at the point *where the load normally hangs* and that the load is suspended on the rope where the effort is normally applied. In this way a large lifting movement is produced for a short piston movement.

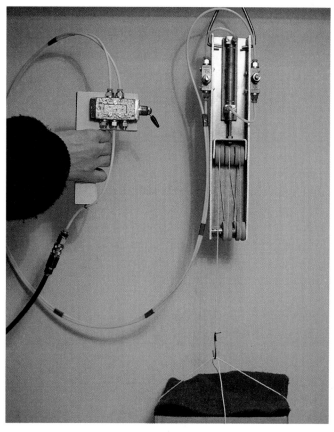

CHAPTER EIGHT

Materials

Think for a moment about all the different kinds of materials which are in use today, and their many different forms. We have an enormous range at our disposal and new materials are being developed all the time.

Anyone involved in designing and making needs to know what materials are available, how they behave, and how to use them. This chapter provides a useful introduction.

Selecting materials

When selecting a material for a particular product, the first question you need to ask is: what materials are **suitable** for the product?

A material which melts at a low temperature, for example, would not be suitable for making a saucepan. Similarly, a material which absorbs water, would be unsuitable for making wellington boots.

It is essential therefore, to choose a material with the appropriate **properties**. In the case of the saucepan body, the material must be capable of withstanding a high temperature, be a good conductor of heat, be light in weight, and so on. In the case of the wellington boots, the material must be waterproof, have good heat insulating properties, and be flexible for example.

The **aesthetic** qualities are important too. These will include colour, surface texture, pattern etc.

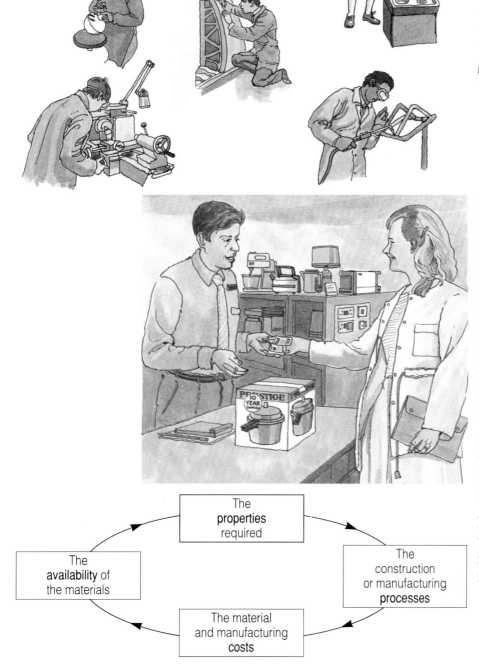

The way the product will be made – the **method of construction or manufacture** – is another essential factor in the choice of materials. Some materials can only be 'worked' in a limited number of ways. Others are more versatile. You will need, therefore, to consider the range of tools, equipment and machinery available to you, and the methods of working. Your own skills (or the skills of the workforce in a factory) are essential considerations too.

Cost is another vital element. In school the cost of the materials used is your main concern. In industry however, many different factors are involved. For example, quality of product, type of market, projected life etc, will all affect 'spending' on materials. Manufacturing costs are also affected by the chosen material because the material dictates the processes used, which in turn affects profitability.

Finally, both the short and long term **availability** of a material will affect its selection for use. This must be investigated carefully.

In conclusion therefore we can see that there are four **inter-related** factors which affect the choice of material.

The
properties
required

The
construction
or manufacturing
processes

The
availability of
the materials

The material
and manufacturing
costs

The properties of materials

Strength

Strength is a measure of how good a material is at resisting being misshapen, or deformed, when acted upon by a force.

Tensile strength

This is the ability of a material to withstand pulling forces or **tension forces**.

A material which deforms easily under tension has a low tensile strength.

Which of these materials has the lowest tensile strength?

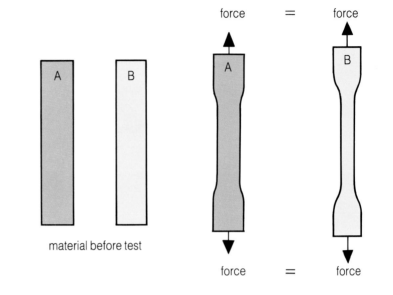

Compressive strength

This is the ability of a material to withstand 'squeezing' forces or **compression forces**.

A material which can resist a large compression force with little deformation, is said to have a high compressive strength.

Which of these materials has the highest compressive strength?

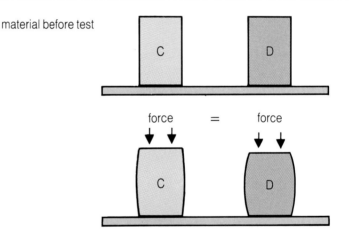

Torsional properties

Another test of a material's strength is its ability to withstand twisting forces, or **torsion**.

Which of these materials has the highest torsional strength?

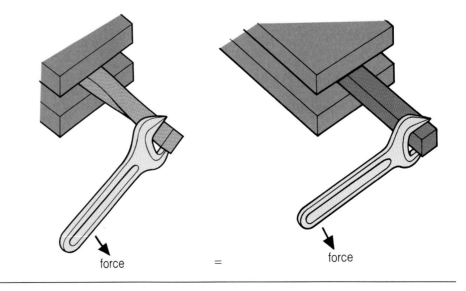

Question

1 For each of the products shown here, state whether the structure indicated needs to be strong in **tension**, **compression** or **torsion**.

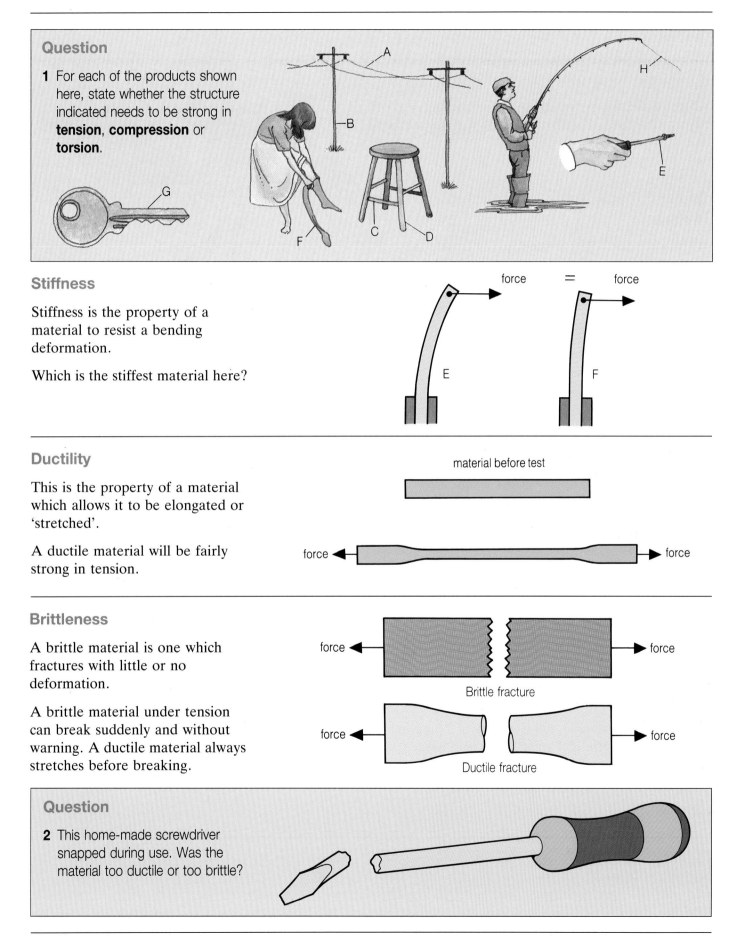

Stiffness

Stiffness is the property of a material to resist a bending deformation.

Which is the stiffest material here?

Ductility

This is the property of a material which allows it to be elongated or 'stretched'.

A ductile material will be fairly strong in tension.

material before test

Brittleness

A brittle material is one which fractures with little or no deformation.

A brittle material under tension can break suddenly and without warning. A ductile material always stretches before breaking.

Brittle fracture

Ductile fracture

Question

2 This home-made screwdriver snapped during use. Was the material too ductile or too brittle?

Hardness

The hardness of a material is a measure of its ability to withstand being scratched, cut or dented.

Which of the two materials shown here is the hardest? (Assume that equal pressure was applied to both scribers.)

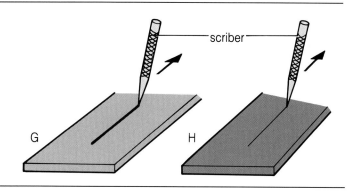

Toughness

This is a measure of **how much energy is required to break a material**. The energy of a 'swinging hammer' can be used to compare the toughness of different materials, as shown here.

Potential energy is given to the hammer as it is raised to position **1** in the diagram.

When the hammer is released, its potential energy is transferred into motion energy or kinetic energy. At position **2**, the hammer has maximum kinetic energy.

If a material is clamped into the vice, the energy of the swinging hammer can be used to break it.

By experimenting with the 'release height', the energy required to break a material can be found.

Which of these materials was the toughest?

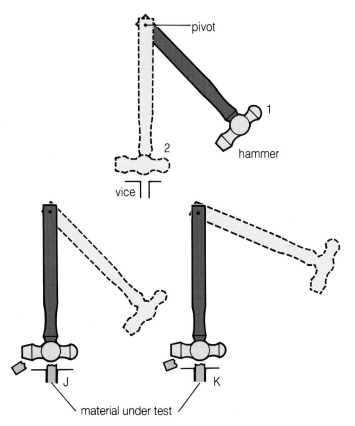

Density

Density is the **mass of 1 cubic centimetre** of a substance.

Aluminium for example, has a density of 2.7 grams per cubic centimetre (2.7 g/cm³), and lead has a density of 11.3 g/cm³.

To calculate a material's density we use the equation:

$$\text{density} = \frac{\text{mass}}{\text{volume}}$$

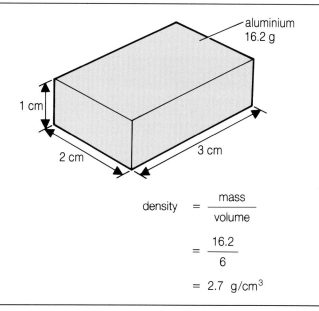

$$\text{density} = \frac{\text{mass}}{\text{volume}}$$
$$= \frac{16.2}{6}$$
$$= 2.7 \ \text{g/cm}^3$$

Questions

3 Bumpers are made from plastic on many modern cars.

Why is it necessary to choose a material which is very tough?

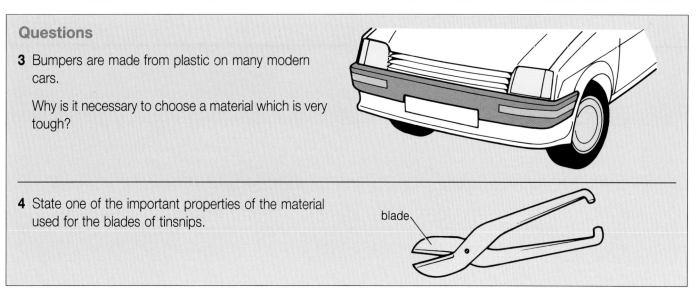

4 State one of the important properties of the material used for the blades of tinsnips.

blade

Thermal conductivity

'Therm' is an ancient Greek word meaning heat. **Thermal conductivity** relates to **how heat travels**, or is **conducted** through a material.

This simple apparatus, can be used to **compare** the thermal conductivity of different materials.

The heat is conducted along the material until it 'reaches' the candle wax. The wax melts and the ballbearing falls off.

Metals are good conductors of heat. Most non-metals have a low thermal conductivity.

materials under test

candle wax

ball-bearing

hot water

Thermal expansion

Most materials 'get bigger', or **expand** when heated, and 'shrink', or **contract** as they cool down. This property can be demonstrated using the jaws and T-bar apparatus.

When cold, the T-bar will just slide between the metal jaws.

During heating however, the bar **expands** and will no longer fit. Only after the bar has cooled to its original temperature will it again slide between the jaws.

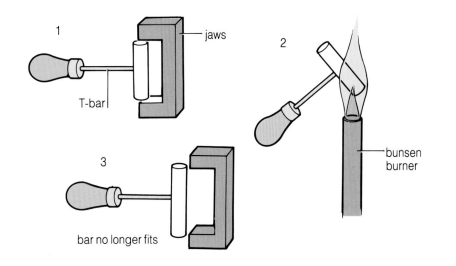

1   jaws

T-bar

2

bunsen burner

3

bar no longer fits

Questions

5 Which part of this saucepan needs to have a low thermal conductivity? Explain your answer.

6 Why is it necessary for the tip of a soldering iron to be a good conductor of heat?

7 One of the components in this automatic electric kettle makes use of the thermal expansion. Try to find out what it is, and what its function is.

Can you think of any other examples of where this property is used to advantage, and where it can be a disadvantage?

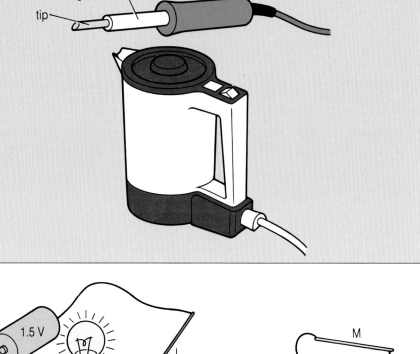

Electrical properties

The best known electrical property is **resistance**. This is what affects a material's ability to **conduct** electricity. A material with a low resistance will conduct electricity well. If it has a high resistance it will be a poor conductor of electricity.

Using a simple battery and bulb circuit the conductivity of materials can be **compared**.

Which material here has the lowest resistance, and which has the highest? Explain your answer.

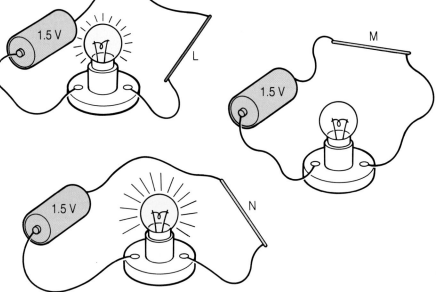

Question

8 Should the body of this electrical plug have a very high or very low resistance? Explain your answer.

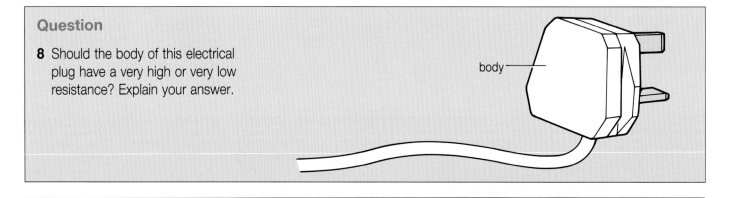

Magnetic properties

Have you ever used a magnet to pick up or attract other materials? It is this ability of a material to **exert a force** upon certain other materials which we call **magnetism**.

Materials which can be attracted by a magnet are those which themselves possess magnetic properties. These include **iron**, (the most magnetic), cobalt, nickel and steel.

The first magnetic material to be used was **magnetite** – a naturally occurring ore known as lodestone. Today, magnets are 'manufactured' using electricity.

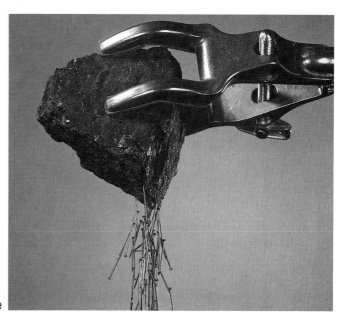

Lodestone

When electricity is passed through a coil of wire, a magnetic field 'appears' around that coil. If a piece of steel is placed inside the coil for a few minutes, it will become magnetised. The 'new' magnet can then be removed, after first switching off the electricity.

If a **soft iron** core is permanently fixed inside the coil we have an **electromagnet** which can be switched on and off. Soft iron is used because it loses most of the induced magnetism when the current is switched off, whereas steel does not.

invisible magnetic field

+ −

steel rod

Making a magnet

soft iron

Electromagnet

low voltage power supply

Alternatively, if the core is free to move in and out of the coil we have what is called a **solenoid**. A solenoid produces linear motion in the core when electricity is passed through the coil. The core can only be made to 'move in' however – reversing the current will not make it move out.

connecting wire

core

coil

Commercial solenoid

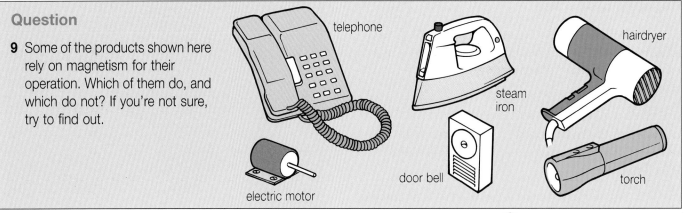

Question

9 Some of the products shown here rely on magnetism for their operation. Which of them do, and which do not? If you're not sure, try to find out.

telephone

steam iron

hairdryer

electric motor

door bell

torch

Optical properties

The optical properties of a material relate to the way in which it reacts to light.

The most obvious optical property is **transparency**. A transparent material allows light rays to pass through it, which in turn allows us to see images through it. A **translucent** material however, passes some light, but not enough to allow us to see through it.

Some products are shown here which make use of these properties. Can you think of any more?

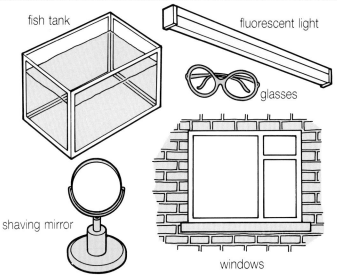

fish tank

fluorescent light

glasses

shaving mirror

windows

Reflection

Everyone knows that light 'bounces' off shiny surfaces – this is the property of **reflection**. Whilst some materials have particularly good reflective properties – like the surface of a mirror – **all materials** do of course reflect light. It is the reflection of light from objects which allows us to **see** them.

The **colour** we see is dependent on reflection too. The light from the sun appears to be 'white', but in fact it is made up of the colours of the rainbow – the spectrum.

The reason why grass, for example, looks green, is because it reflects **green** light into our eyes and absorbs the other spectrum colours. Similarly, a **red** object looks red because it reflects red light and absorbs the others, and so on.

Radiation and absorption

The colour of a material also affects its ability to **absorb** (take in) and **radiate** (give out) **heat**. This can be demonstrated with a simple experiment.

In experiment **1**, metal cans containing **cold** water (and thermometers) are placed in direct sunlight.

In experiment **2**, similar cans containing **hot** water (and thermometers) are placed in a cool place.

The results show that a **black** surface not only absorbs heat more readily than a shiny surface, but also radiates heat more readily. In fact, a matt **black** surface is the best absorber and radiator of heat.

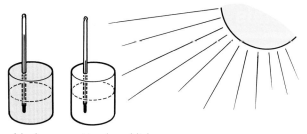

black surface   shiny (or white) surface

black surface   shiny (or white) surface

Questions

10 Clothes viewed under artificial light in a shop, appear to have a slightly different colour when viewed outside.

Think about this and try to explain why.

11 Why do you think that houses in very hot countries are often painted white?

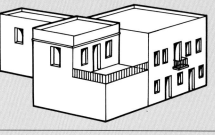

12 Solar panels work best when painted one particular colour. What is that colour and why is it the best colour to use?

Metals

Iron ore mining in Western Australia

When the earth was formed the molten mass contained the many different metals which today we extract and use in huge quantities.

Most of the metals combined with rock when molten, to form **metallic ores**. The most common of these are **bauxite**, from which **aluminium** is extracted, and **iron ore** from which **iron** is extracted. More than seventy different metals are extracted and used in the manufacturing industries today. Some,

like copper and lead for example, can be used in their pure state, to take advantage of their natural properties. But often, we combine different metals, or metals with other materials to form **alloys**. By making alloys, we can **change the properties** of a metal to suit our particular needs.

Metals can be divided into two main groups: **ferrous metals** – those which contain **iron**, and **non-ferrous metals** – those which contain **no** iron.

Ferrous metals

Iron

Pure iron is of little use as an engineering material because it is too soft and **ductile**.

When iron cools and changes from a liquid to a solid, most of the atoms in the metal pack tightly together in orderly layers. Some, however, become misaligned, creating areas of weaknesses called **dislocations**.

When a piece of iron is put under stress, layers of atoms in these areas 'slip' over one another and the metal deforms. This begins to explain the ductility of soft iron.

By adding **carbon** to the iron however, we can produce a range of **alloys** with quite different properties. We call these the **carbon steels**.

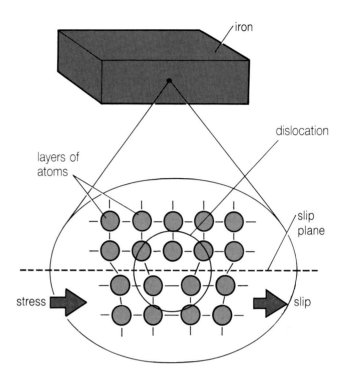

Carbon steels – their properties and uses

Mild steel

Steels produced with a carbon content between 0.1% and 0.3% are classified as mild steels.

When carbon is added to iron in a furnace, the carbon atoms 'enter' the material changing both its structure and properties. The resulting **steel** is much less ductile because the carbon helps to reduce slip between layers of atoms by 'interfering' with the slip planes. It is also harder, and tougher than iron, and has a higher **tensile strength**. Mild steel has a density of 7.8 g/cm^3, and its melting point is around 1600°C. It corrodes by rusting, it can be magnetised, and its colour is grey.

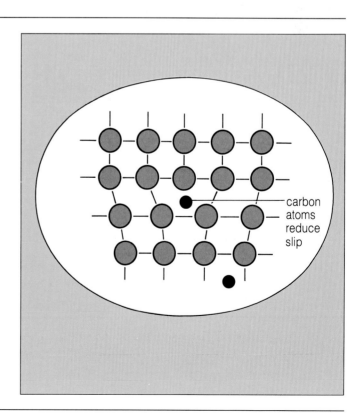

Mild steel is produced in many different forms – some examples of which are shown here. Most will undergo further processing before emerging as products, but some, such as **I** girders and channel for example, are ready for immediate use in buildings, bridges and other structures.

Mild steel can be cut and machined easily, and can be soldered, brazed and welded. The ductility and tensile strength of mild steel allows it to be 'cold' pressed into deep, complex sections. However, pressing and bending changes the 'internal structure' of the steel, making it stronger and harder. This is known as **work hardening**. In many manufacturing processes this effect is welcomed. Work hardened steel however, is less ductile and more brittle. If these properties are not desired, the steel can be returned to its original state by a process known as **annealing**. The metal is heated to red heat, and then allowed to cool down slowly.

Mild steel is the most common type of steel in use today. Some examples of the many products made from this material are shown above.

Medium carbon steel

The medium carbon steels contain between 0.3% and 0.7% carbon. These steels are therefore harder and less ductile than the mild steels. They are very **tough** and have a **high tensile strength**.

Steels with a carbon content of 0.3% and above can be further hardened by **heat treatment**. The medium carbon steels therefore, are more specialised in their use.

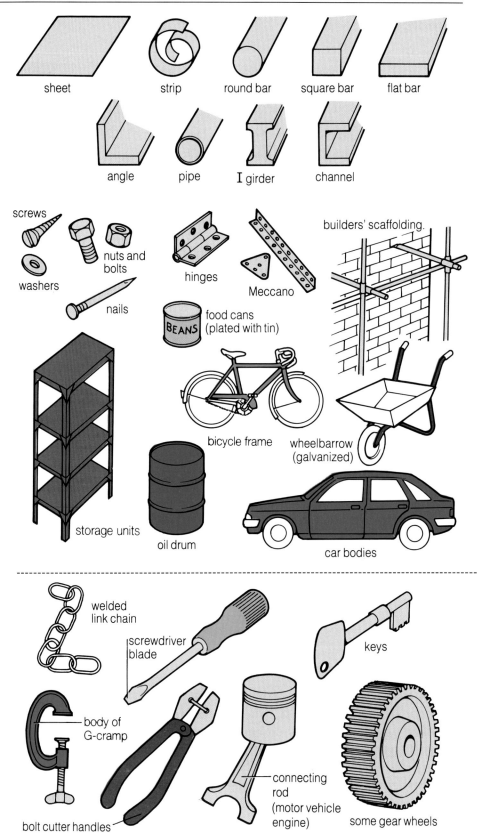

sheet strip round bar square bar flat bar

angle pipe I girder channel

screws

washers nuts and bolts

nails

hinges

Meccano

food cans (plated with tin)

builders' scaffolding.

storage units

oil drum

bicycle frame

wheelbarrow (galvanized)

car bodies

welded link chain

screwdriver blade

keys

body of G-cramp

bolt cutter handles

connecting rod (motor vehicle engine)

some gear wheels

They are used for the manufacture of products which have to be tough and hard wearing.

Some examples of products made from medium carbon steel are shown here.

High carbon steel

The high carbon steels have a carbon content ranging from 0.7% to 1.3%. These are very **hard** and **brittle** materials. The maximum hardness produced by heat treatment is achieved with steels containing about 0.7% carbon.

High carbon steels are used mainly for **cutting** tools and products which have to withstand **wear**. Some examples of such products are shown here.

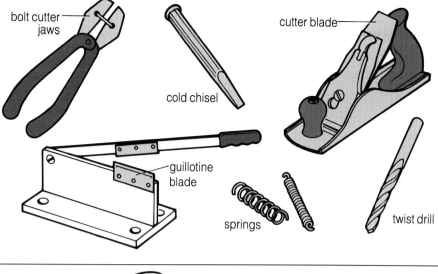

Stainless steel

Stainless steels are **iron/chromium** alloys. A wide range of steels are available with a chromium content between 13% and 27%. Some contain only iron, carbon and chromium, whilst others contain nickel and other alloying elements also.

The effect of the chromium is to create an oxide film which prevents rusting. Paints and other surface treatments are not therefore necessary. The degree of protection depends upon the percentage of chromium present. Other properties such as ductility, hardness and tensile strength are dependent upon the percentage of the other alloying elements.

Stainless steel is a shiny attractive metal (but should not be confused with chromium-plated steel). This, combined with its other properties, makes it a very versatile material.

Some examples of the many products made from stainless steel are shown here.

Grey cast iron

Cast iron is an alloy of iron (94%), carbon (3%), silicon (2%) and traces of magnesium, sulphur and phosphorus.

It is a very **brittle** metal with a hard skin. It has a high compressive strength, but low tensile strength, and will fracture if struck with a heavy blow. It corrodes by rusting.

Whilst all metals can be cast (melted and poured into a mould), cast iron is particularly suited to casting – hence its name. It can be poured at a relatively low temperature (between 1400°C and 1500°C) and will cast into complex shapes. After casting, it can be machined easily (if necessary) into the finished article.

Some examples of products made from cast iron are shown here.

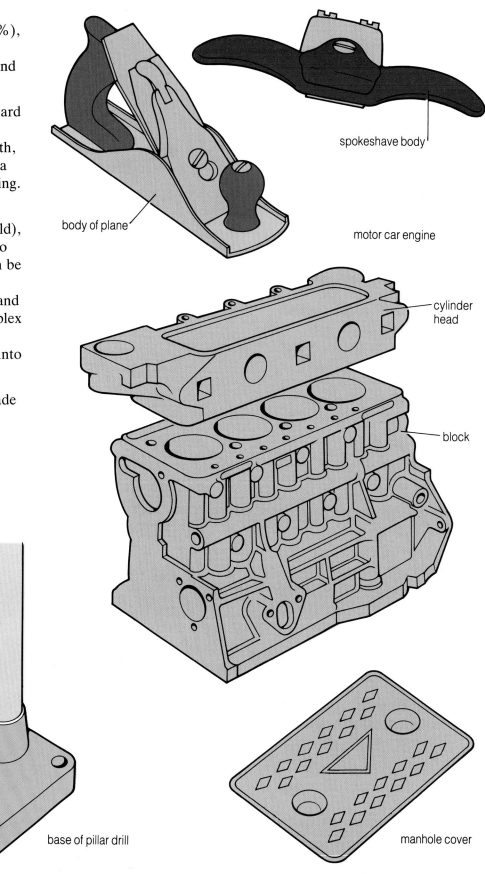

spokeshave body

body of plane

motor car engine

cylinder head

block

base of pillar drill

manhole cover

Non-ferrous metals – their properties and uses

Aluminium

Aluminium is the most abundant metal in the earth's crust and, after steel, is the most widely used of all the metals today.

Pure aluminium is **soft** and **ductile** and has a low tensile strength. Even so, it has a high strength to weight ratio. Its density is 2.7 g/cm^3, ($\frac{1}{3}$ of the density of mild steel). Its melting point is 660°C (compared to 1600°C for steel). It has a shiny silver-grey appearance.

Due to the natural formation of a **surface oxide film**, aluminium has good resistance to corrosion. It is a good conductor of both electricity and heat (next to copper in this respect). It cannot be magnetised. It cuts and machines easily, and can be polished to a bright finish.

Aluminium alloys

Because aluminium is light and resists corrosion, it is an 'attractive' material for engineering purposes. Unfortunately it is soft and has a low tensile strength. To impart hardness and strength and to produce other desirable properties, a wide range of **alloys** are manufactured. The alloying elements include copper, magnesium, chromium, silicon and tin.

Some examples of the numerous products made from aluminium and its alloys are shown here.

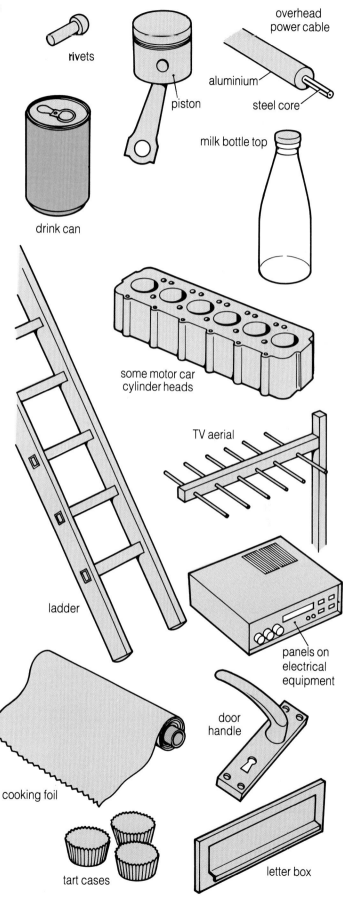

rivets

piston

overhead power cable

aluminium

steel core

drink can

milk bottle top

some motor car cylinder heads

TV aerial

ladder

panels on electrical equipment

door handle

cooking foil

tart cases

letter box

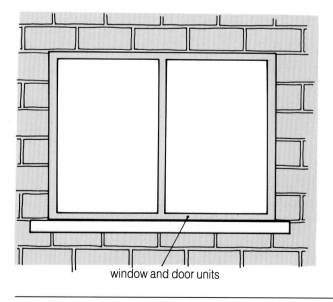

window and door units

Copper

Copper is a **pure metal**. It is the world's third most important metal, in terms of volume of consumption.

It is a fairly **ductile** material and is moderately strong. Its melting point is around 1080°C. It is quite a heavy metal, having a density of 8·9 g/cm³. A naturally forming oxide film (having a greenish colour) gives it good anti-corrosion properties. Copper is a very good conductor of electricity (second only to silver in this respect) and is a good conductor of heat. It cannot be magnetised. It will cut, saw, file and machine easily.

Copper is a reddish-brown metal which will polish to a beautiful deep shine. Some examples of the many products made from copper are shown here.

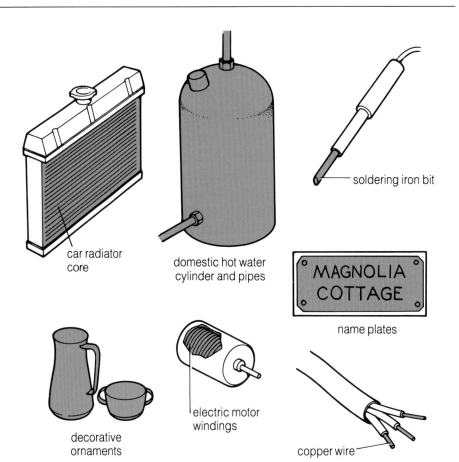

car radiator core

domestic hot water cylinder and pipes

soldering iron bit

MAGNOLIA COTTAGE

name plates

decorative ornaments

electric motor windings

copper wire

Brass

The term 'brass' covers a wide range of **copper–zinc alloys**. The amounts of copper and zinc present are varied to obtain the desired properties.

The melting point of brass is lower than copper, and its density is around 8·4 g/cm³. It has good electrical conductivity (although lower than copper) and good anticorrosive properties. It is gold in colour and, like copper, can be polished to give a deep shine.

Some examples of the many products made from brass are shown here.

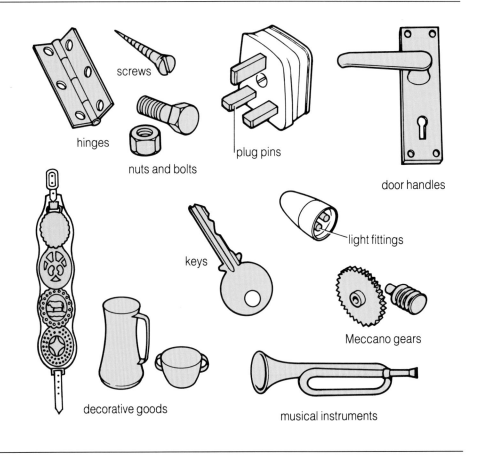

hinges

screws

nuts and bolts

plug pins

door handles

keys

light fittings

Meccano gears

decorative goods

musical instruments

Industrial manufacturing with metals

The manufacture of **metal products**, or **components** for assembly into products, takes many forms. Some of the more common industrial processes are described below.

Blanking

This is one of the simplest 'pressing' operations.

A hardened **punch** is used to stamp sheet metal through a **die**. The metal is stamped **cold**. 'Blanks' of almost any shape can be produced in this way.

Simple components like washers for example, are produced by blanking alone. For many products however, this is just one of a series of production operations. Blanking is often followed by press forming or bending for example.

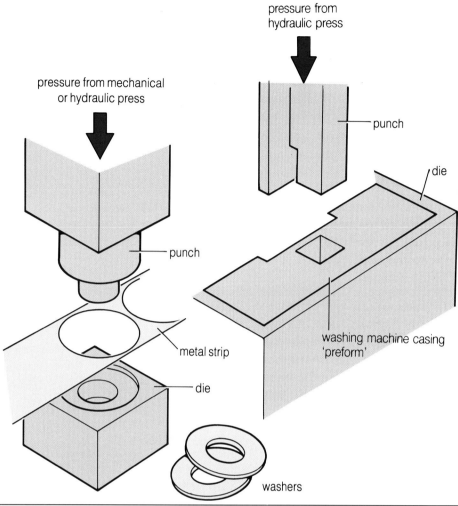

Press forming

This is the shaping of components from **sheet** metal between a punch and a die. The metal blank (or preform) is pressed **cold**. Components made in this way have consistently accurate dimensions and **work hardening** imparts strength and rigidity. The process is also very fast and produces very little waste.

Most sheet metals are suited to this process, but mild steel is the most widely used.

Motor car panels (wings, doors, roofs, etc.) are amongst the numerous components which are press formed.

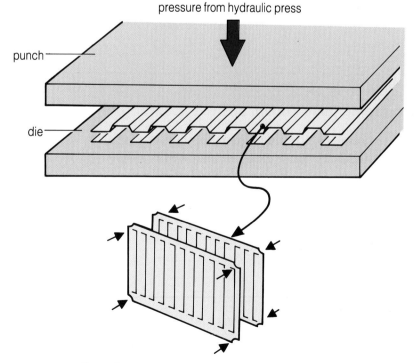

Press-formed panels for domestic radiator

Forging

Forging is the shaping of metal using compression forces. The force may be applied by hammer, press or rollers. The metal is usually **hot**, but some operations are carried out cold. (See cold heading for example.) Forging at temperature increases the plasticity of a metal, and reduces the forces needed to work it. Many different forging operations are carried out, but we will only discuss drop forging here.

Drop forging

This is the forming of a component from a metal bar or billet between two 'half' dies. The **hot** metal is placed on the lower die, and is forced into the cavity between the upper and lower die by the blow of a machine hammer.

Parts made in this way cannot usually be formed by the single hammer blow in a single die. A drop forged component is usually moved from one die impression to the next until the final shape is produced. Forgings can be made to very close tolerances, hence very little **finishing** is required.

Materials used in drop forging include: mild and medium carbon steel, aluminium and copper alloys.

Motor car crankshafts, some G-cramps, and other tools, door handles, and other 'hardware' items are amongst the numerous products which are drop forged.

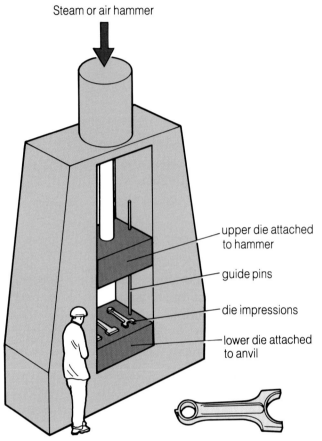

Steam or air hammer

upper die attached to hammer

guide pins

die impressions

lower die attached to anvil

product – forged connecting rod (motor car)

Cold heading (also known as cold upsetting)

This is the process of forming **cold** metal slugs or wire into components by 'squeezing' the metal into a die cavity. This is a quick and cheap method of changing the shape and diameter of a metal bar to produce products.

Brass, stainless steel, mild steel and medium carbon steel are the materials commonly used in this process.

The largest single use of this process is in the manufacture of bolts, screws, rivets and nails.

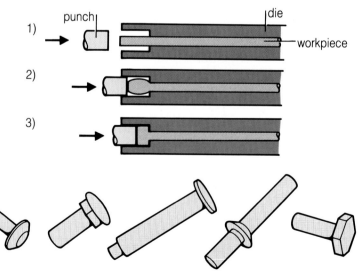

Examples of cold-headed components

Thread rolling

This is one method of applying a **thread** to machine bolts produced by cold heading. Other parallel-sided components can be threaded in this way too.

Knurled patterns, splines and worm gears are just a few of the many other forms which can be produced by **roll forming**.

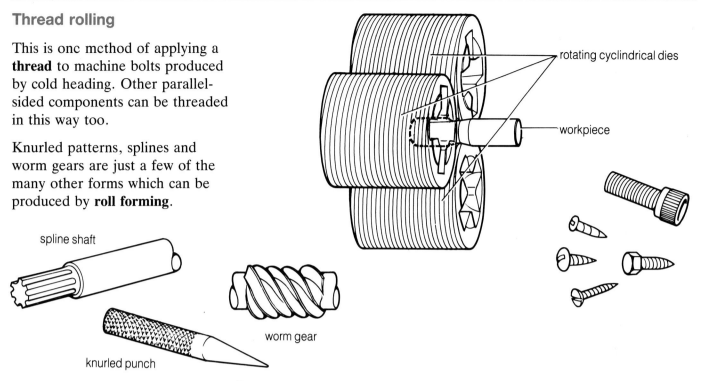

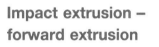

Examples of roll-formed components

Impact extrusion – forward extrusion

This process consists of forcing a **hot** billet of metal through an extrusion die using a hydraulic ram.

The product is a continuous length of metal whose shape corresponds to the die orifice.

An almost infinite number of solid cross-sections can be produced in this way, as well as tubing. Extrusion produces complex sections which could otherwise only be manufactured by expensive machining operations.

Products made from extruded sections include: door and window frames, hinges, components for locks, edging strips etc.

By far the largest number of sections produced are made from aluminium and brass.

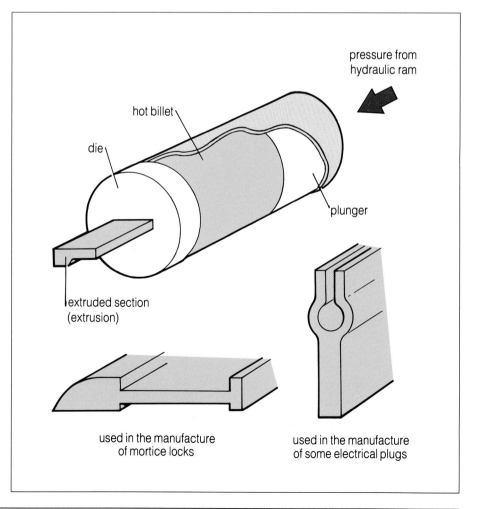

Sand casting

This is the shaping of metal by 'pouring' **molten** metal into a **mould**. A mould is a cavity which has the shape of the required object.

Sand is a particularly good material for making moulds. It can withstand very high temperatures and can be moulded into complex shapes. It is particularly suitable for the high melting point metals.

Sand casting is a quick method of producing complex shapes, but a new mould is required for each new casting. The more common casting metals include: cast iron, steel, aluminium alloys, and brass.

Motor car engine blocks and cylinder heads, bases for heavy machinery, manhole covers, and the body of a mechanic's vice (found in the school workshops) are examples of sand cast products.

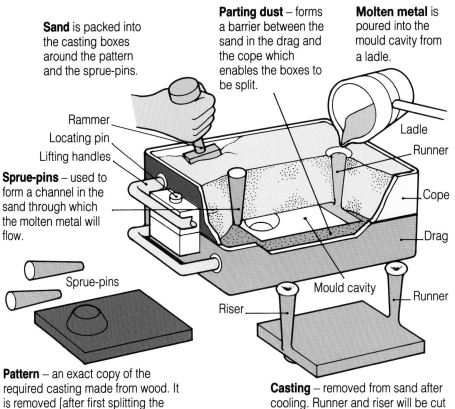

Sand is packed into the casting boxes around the pattern and the sprue-pins.

Parting dust – forms a barrier between the sand in the drag and the cope which enables the boxes to be split.

Molten metal is poured into the mould cavity from a ladle.

Rammer
Locating pin
Lifting handles
Sprue-pins – used to form a channel in the sand through which the molten metal will flow.

Sprue-pins

Pattern – an exact copy of the required casting made from wood. It is removed [after first splitting the moulding box] to leave the mould cavity.

Ladle
Runner
Cope
Drag
Mould cavity
Runner
Riser

Casting – removed from sand after cooling. Runner and riser will be cut off and re-used.

Die casting

Where many items of the same form are to be manufactured, die casting is employed. In this process, molten metal is forced into the cavity between dies under high pressure. After the metal has been injected, the pressure is held for a short time whilst the metal solidifies. The die blocks are then opened and the casting is ejected automatically.

Die casting is a very fast production method which can produce extremely complex precision parts due to the injection of metal under pressure. The products have a high quality surface requiring very little secondary finishing.

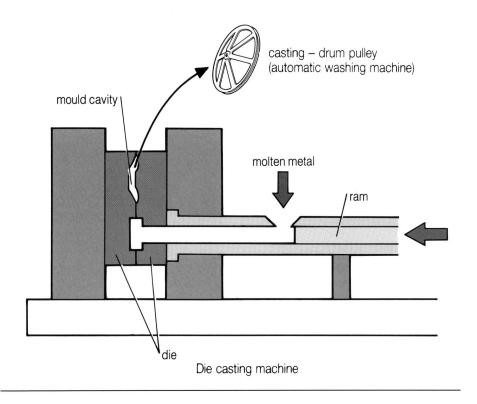

casting – drum pulley (automatic washing machine)

mould cavity

molten metal

ram

die

Die casting machine

Many thousands of different die cast products are manufactured. These include: the cases of some electric hand tools (drills, jig-saws, sanders, etc.), chassis for record players, tape decks and other similar products, component parts for washing machines, food mixers and lawn mowers, and, not least, many motor car components including, fuel pump and carburettor parts, fans and grills, body trim and door handles.

Die casting is limited to non-ferrous metals whose molten temperatures will not damage the dies.

Machining

Some components can be shaped into their final form in just one operation, such as in die casting. Many however, have to be **machined** into their final form. The machining processes which include **drilling**, **cutting** and **grinding** are carried out on **machine-tools**. Some of the more common machining operations are described below.

Lathework

Turning is the most basic operation to be carried out on a lathe. The metal workpiece is shaped as it is rotated in contact with a cutting tool.

The tool (which will be shaped according to its purpose), can be moved across, along, and at an angle to the workpiece. (See diagrams **1**, **2** and **3**.)

Other lathe operations include drilling, thread cutting, and boring. (See diagrams **4**, **5** and **6**.)

The centre lathe is only suitable for 'one off' or short production runs. By replacing the tailstock with a **turret** however, and automating the lathe feed mechanisms, mass production can be achieved.

The **CNC** (**c**omputer **n**umerically **c**ontrolled lathe) can be programmed for fully automatic production.

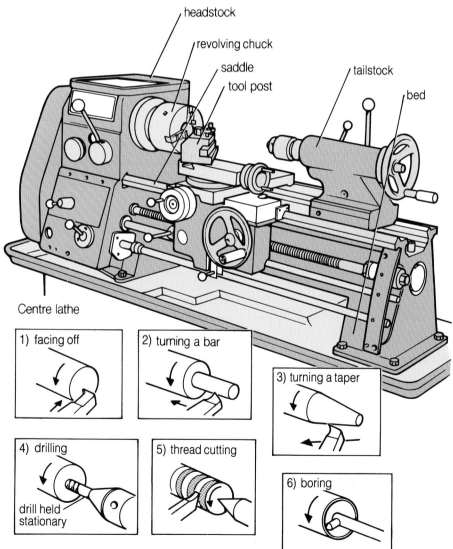

Centre lathe

1) facing off

2) turning a bar

3) turning a taper

4) drilling
drill held stationary

5) thread cutting

6) boring

Milling

Milling is the use of a rotating cutter to shape a metal workpiece. The workpiece is fixed to a table which can be moved in relation to the cutter.

Just a few of the numerous types of milling cutters are shown in operation here

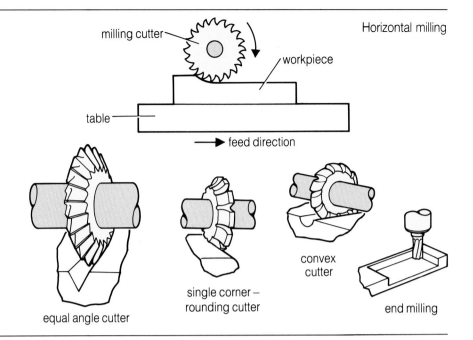

Horizontal milling

milling cutter

workpiece

table

feed direction

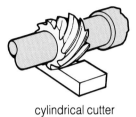

cylindrical cutter

equal angle cutter

single corner – rounding cutter

convex cutter

end milling

Grinding

This is the process in which metal is removed by the 'rubbing' contact of an abrasive material such as **carborundum**. Most grinding operations are carried out using grinding **wheels**, but rotating belts and other machines are also used.

Unlike 'heavy' cutting with a metal tool, grinding applies only a tiny force to the workpiece. As a result there is very little deformation of the workpiece and an accurate and very smooth finish can be obtained.

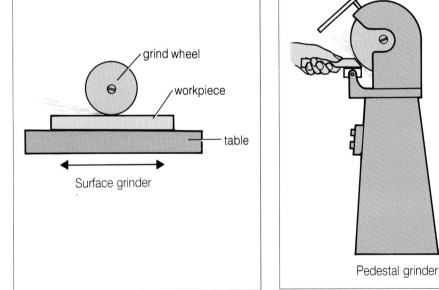

grind wheel

workpiece

table

Surface grinder

Pedestal grinder

Drilling

Drilling a circular hole is one of the most common metal cutting operations. The cutting tool is usually a twist drill.

In industry, multi-head drilling machines are common. The photograph shows part of an adjustable multi-head machine.

Question

13 To choose the most suitable material for a particular product requires you to have a good knowledge of materials. See how much you know about **metals** by using the chart below. **Copy it** on to a piece of paper and 'fill in' the empty boxes (and also add to the other boxes if you can). Some of the information you require can be found in this chapter. For more detailed information you will need to use a more specialist book.

Material	Ferrous	Non-ferrous	Composition	Colour	Properties	Common uses
mild steel	✔		iron + 0.1% to 0.3% carbon		fairly high tensile strength heavy metal (density = 7.8 g/km³ high melting point (1600°C) corrodes by rusting	
		✔			soft and ductile low tensile strength lightweight (density = 2.7 g/km³) melting point 660°C	milk bottle tops cooking foil ladders door and window frames
			iron + 0.3% to 0.7% carbon	siver-grey		
			pure metal	reddish-brown	heavy metal (density = 8.9 g/cm³) good conductor of electricity and heat cannot be magnetised	
	✔				properties vary depending upon percentage of chromium	
	✔				brittle high compressive strength low tensile strength corrodes by rusting	machine bases manhole covers motor car engine blocks
			copper-zinc	yellow		

Questions

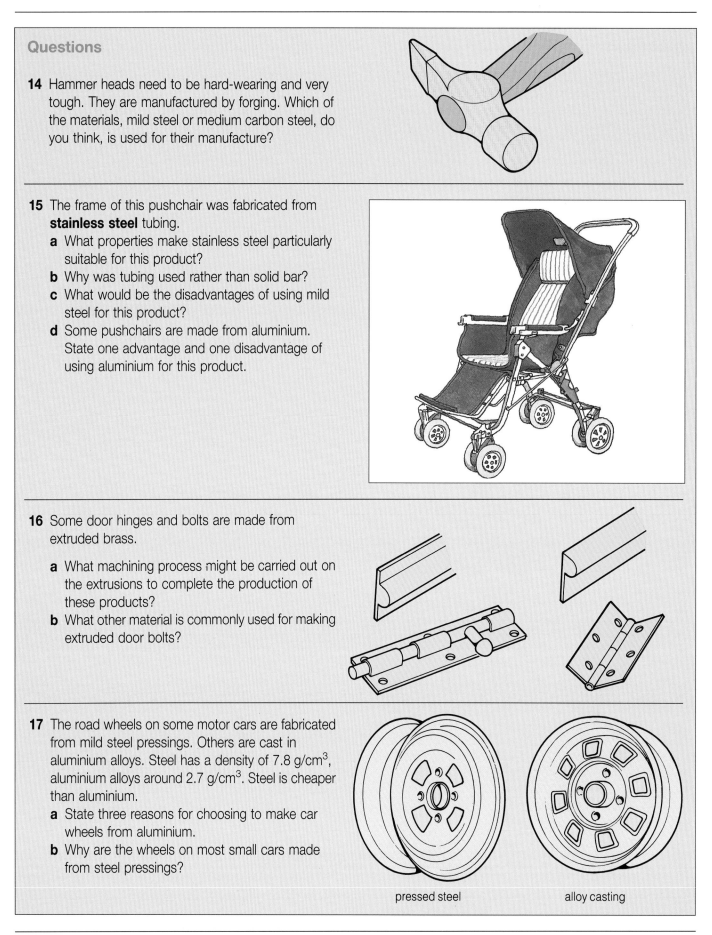

14 Hammer heads need to be hard-wearing and very tough. They are manufactured by forging. Which of the materials, mild steel or medium carbon steel, do you think, is used for their manufacture?

15 The frame of this pushchair was fabricated from **stainless steel** tubing.
  a What properties make stainless steel particularly suitable for this product?
  b Why was tubing used rather than solid bar?
  c What would be the disadvantages of using mild steel for this product?
  d Some pushchairs are made from aluminium. State one advantage and one disadvantage of using aluminium for this product.

16 Some door hinges and bolts are made from extruded brass.

  a What machining process might be carried out on the extrusions to complete the production of these products?
  b What other material is commonly used for making extruded door bolts?

17 The road wheels on some motor cars are fabricated from mild steel pressings. Others are cast in aluminium alloys. Steel has a density of 7.8 g/cm^3, aluminium alloys around 2.7 g/cm^3. Steel is cheaper than aluminium.
  a State three reasons for choosing to make car wheels from aluminium.
  b Why are the wheels on most small cars made from steel pressings?

pressed steel   alloy casting

18 This mortice key was fabricated from three components: the shank, bit and bow. The shank was manufactured on an automatic lathe.
   a How do you think the bow was manufactured?
   b What materials would be suitable for this product?

19 The door handles shown were pressure die cast.
   a What materials are suited to this method of production, and why?
   b Why is pressure die casting unlikely to be used for short production runs?

20 The 'high tensile' bolt cutters shown here were assembled from several component parts.
   a Which parts do you think were drop forged?
   b Which components would be made from high carbon steel, and why?
   c Why might an engineer smear oil on the jaws?

21 Some greenhouse frames are assembled from complex aluminium sections.
   a What method of manufacture do you think was used to produce these sections?
   b What property of aluminium makes it unnecessary for the frame to be painted?

22 Domestic washing machines and refrigerators are usually housed in steel casings. These are fabricated from mild steel pressings.

What is the name of the 'effect', produced by pressing, which imparts hardness to the steel and helps to add rigidity to the product?

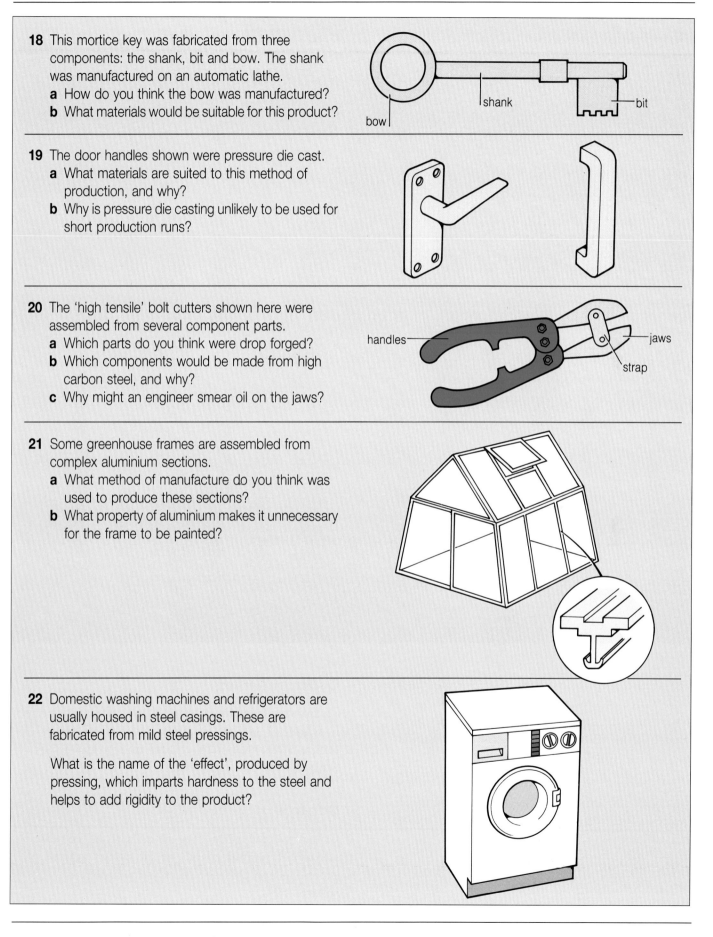

Wood

Wood collection in Finnish forest

For thousands of years, **trees** have provided us with a wide range of products including food stuffs, medicines, paper and fuel. Not least, they have provided one of the most versatile construction materials – **wood**.

Large areas of the earth, including much of Britain, were once covered with forests. Today however, Britain produces only limited amounts of timber, most of our wood is imported.

Although there are hundreds of different kinds of trees, there are just two types: deciduous trees and conifers.

Deciduous trees

Deciduous trees have broad leaves which they shed in winter. They grow mainly in the warmer temperate regions of the earth and produce the timber known as **hardwood**.

Conifers

Conifers are usually 'evergreen' with needle-like leaves. They grow mainly in the cooler regions of the earth and produce the timber known as **softwood**.

The structure of wood

Trees are living structures. They grow by producing hollow tube-like cells composed mainly of cellulose.

During the growing season (from spring through to autumn) a tree increases its girth by producing new cells in the cambium layer. In some trees, the cells produced in spring and summer are quite different in diameter. It is this difference which shows up as the 'annual rings' at the end of a sawn log. In other trees, the difference between spring and summer growth is not obvious. Even so, in most trees the cells produced during the drier summer months have thicker cell walls. It is this summer growth which is responsible for much of the mechanical strength in wood.

Softwoods are composed almost entirely of tube-like cells, but hardwoods have a more complex structure. Some contain a great deal of fibrous material which adds mechanical strength to the wood and also makes it harder.

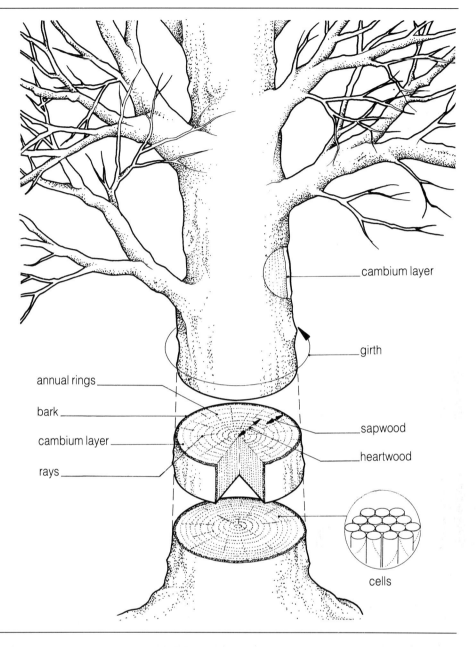

The properties of wood

From an engineering point of view, all wood can be thought of as bundles of parallel tubes, rather like bundles of drinking straws. Further, in all wood these tubes are made essentially from the same material, but with varying wall thicknesses. As you might imagine therefore, the **denser** the wood, the stronger the wood. (See density page 200.)

However, it is important to remember that wood is a **natural** material and that climate and soil conditions will affect its growth. We can only therefore describe the general properties of wood, since even pieces of wood from the same tree will have different characteristics.

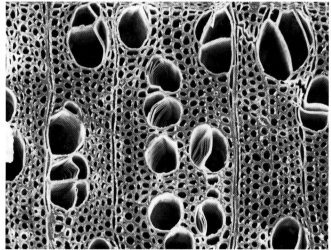

Magnified section of wood – tube cells

The strength of wood

A bundle of drinking straws, glued together, will demonstrate fairly accurately the mechanical properties of wood.

The tensile strength of wood is in general fairly high. Some woods have a tensile strength greater than that of mild steel (weight for weight).

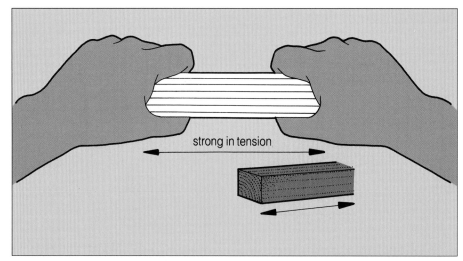

strong in tension

The compressive strength of wood however, is much lower. Wood is also very weak in both tension and compression across the grain.

Hardwoods tend to be **stiffer** than the softwoods and because of their fibre content are usually harder. Even so, it is important to realise that the terms 'hardwood' and 'softwood' are botanical classifications – they are **not** descriptions of the mechanical properties of wood. As you will discover with use, some hardwoods are very soft and easy to work whilst some softwoods are tough and difficult to work. Balsa wood and jelutong are notable examples. They are both hardwoods and yet are soft and can be worked easily. Most softwoods cut easily, but the majority of hardwoods will machine better. The **decorative finish** of most hardwoods is also superior to the softwoods.

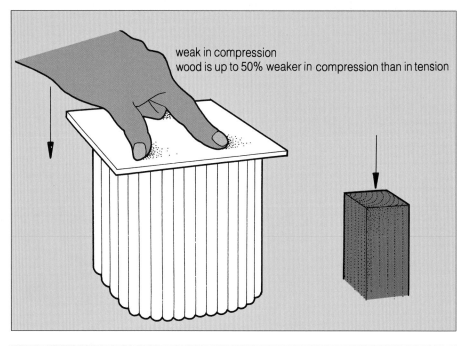

weak in compression
wood is up to 50% weaker in compression than in tension

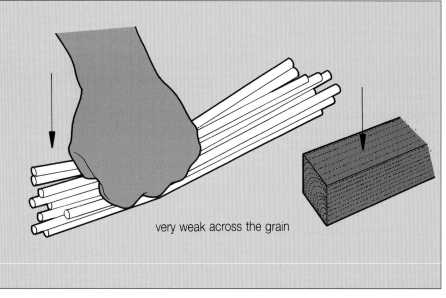

very weak across the grain

The conversion of timber

After a tree has been felled, its logs are sawn up into boards or planks. This is known as **conversion**.

There are two general methods of doing this: **plain sawing** (sometimes known as through and through) and **quarter sawing** (or radial sawing).

Often a combination of the two methods is used to avoid waste and therefore provide the most **economical** conversion.

Plain sawing is the cheapest way of converting a log but the outer planks or boards tend to warp. Quarter sawing is far more expensive because it requires more time and labour, and produces more waste. However, quarter sawn logs are far more **stable** (less likely to warp).

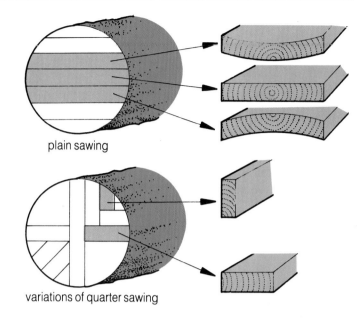

plain sawing

variations of quarter sawing

The effects of water content on wood

Timber contains a great deal of moisture when felled, which makes it almost impossible to work. It also shrinks as it dries out and often cracks. To reduce these problems, the wood must be **seasoned**. Seasoning involves stacking the wood for long periods in dry air to allow the moisture to evaporate. Alternatively the wood can be dried under controlled conditions in a kiln.

Even after seasoning however, wood can still **warp** and **twist** when in use. This happens because wood is **hygroscopic** – that is, it absorbs water from a moist atmosphere (causing it to expand) and loses water in a dry atmosphere (causing it to contract). A timber which is prone to this problem is said to be **unstable**. Paints and other surface treatment reduce this effect, but do not eliminate it.

A low water content is also important for durability. Dry wood resists decay, and is less likely to be infested by woodworm and beetle.

Wood drying kiln

Some examples of softwoods

Pine (Red Baltic pine, Scots pine)

Pine, which is commonly known as **deal**, is probably the most common softwood and is one of the most durable. Its colour varies from a pale yellowy cream to reddy brown.

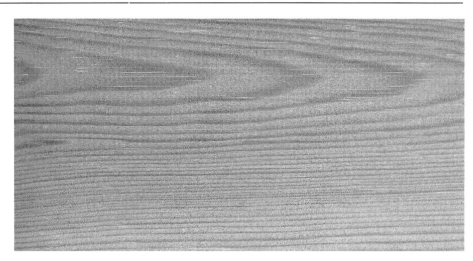

The best quality pine is almost knot free. The lower quality materials, whilst containing some knots, will contain mainly 'live' or sound knots which do not fall out after shrinking.

When dry, pine can be cut and machined easily, and planed to a bright shiny finish. Whilst it contains some resinous material, it can be glued without difficulty. It can be nailed without splitting and takes screws well.

Pine is a fairly hard, durable material and is quite stable. It is often used unprotected indoors, but is commonly painted or varnished.

Some examples of its uses are shown here.

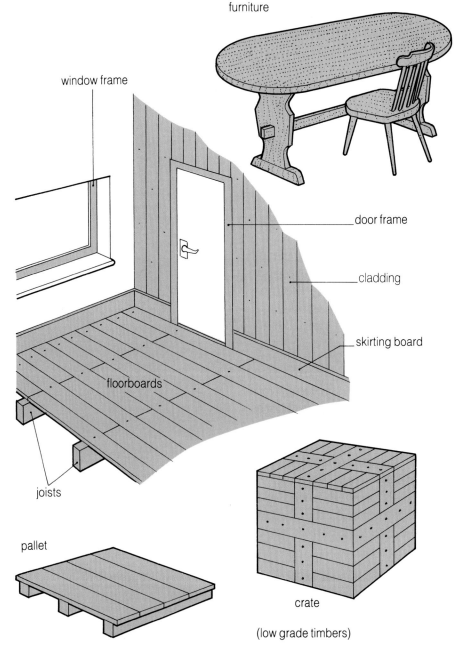

furniture

window frame

door frame

cladding

skirting board

floorboards

joists

gate

pallet

crate

(low grade timbers)

Spruce

Spruce, which is commonly known as whitewood, has a similar colour to deal but never quite as dark. It grows in Canada and the British Isles.

Unlike deal, it contains a lot of very hard 'dead' knots which often fall out. Resin pockets may also be present – these should be cut out before use.

Spruce is a very tough material, and is fairly hard and durable. Even so, it is not very stable and therefore is not suitable for outdoor use.

Some examples of its uses are shown here.

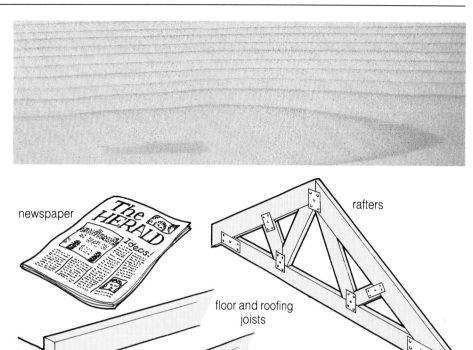

newspaper

rafters

floor and roofing joists

pit props

Parana pine

Parana pine has a fine even texture, and is a pale creamy brown colour. It is available in long wide boards and often without knots. It grows mainly in South America.

It is a fairly heavy, tough timber which is very prone to twisting. For this reason it is commonly used for structures which are securely jointed, or where it can be securely fixed to battens. It is most commonly used for staircases and window boards (sills).

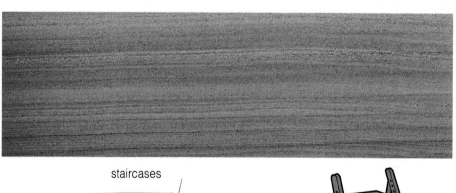

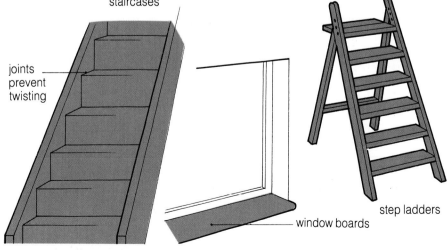

staircases

joints prevent twisting

window boards

step ladders

Some examples of hardwoods

Ash (European)

The colour of ash varies from creamy white to light brown.

It is a long-grained timber which is tough and **flexible**. It also has good resistance to shock – hence its use in sports equipment.

Ash is a stable timber, and therefore can be used outdoors.

Some examples of products made from ash are shown here.

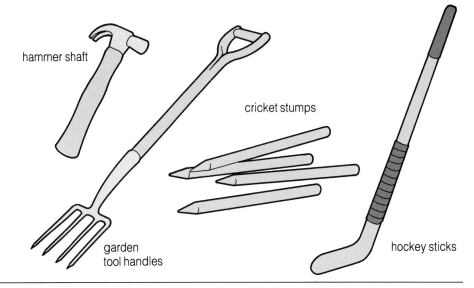

hammer shaft

cricket stumps

garden
tool handles

hockey sticks

Beech (European)

Beech is a very light brown wood with very characteristic 'speckles'.

It has a close even grain and is very tough. It is a fairly heavy wood and is quite hard.

It is **not** prone to splitting, and it has no taste or odour. These properties make it particularly suitable for childrens toys and kitchen utensils.

Some examples of the many products made from beech are shown here.

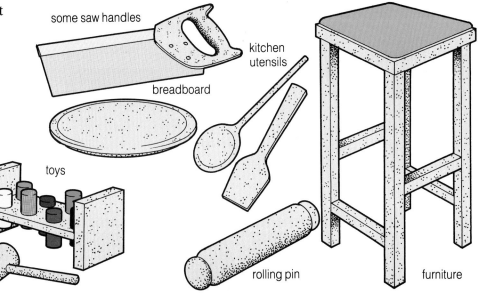

some saw handles

kitchen
utensils

breadboard

toys

rolling pin

furniture

Mahogany

Mahogany is the name used to describe a number of reddish-brown timbers whose properties can be quite different. Gaboon, sapele and utile are three common examples. These all grow in Africa.

Sapele is well known for its attractive striped grain, which has made it popular for furniture making. It is a strong, medium weight timber but the nature of its grain makes it difficult to work. The alternate grain stripes 'lift' when it is planed. Ideally it should be finished by machine sanding.

Utile is a denser timber than sapele but it is easier to work. It is a particularly stable and durable timber.

Gaboon is a lightweight timber of fairly low strength. It has little decorative character and because it is fairly cheap is used in the making of plywood.

For many applications, mahogany veneers (thin layers of wood) are applied to a base material (often chipboard or plywood) to make maximum use of the timber.

Some examples of products made from mahogany are shown here.

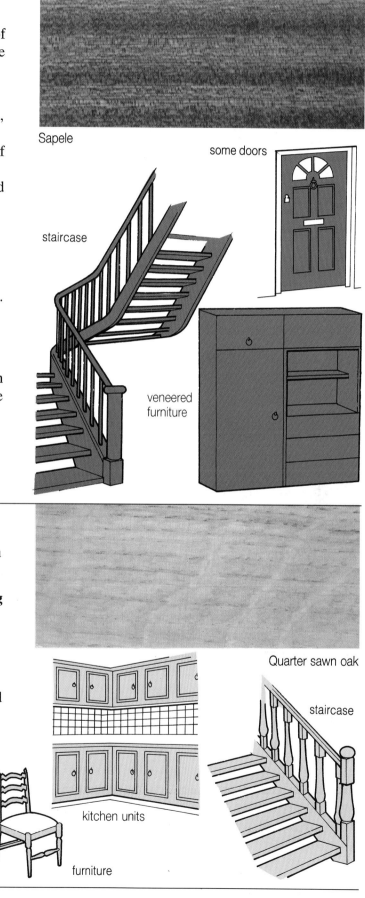

Sapele

some doors

staircase

veneered furniture

Oak (English)

Freshly planed oak has a beige-brown colour which changes to a rich deep brown with time.

Quarter sawn oak is noted for its decorative **figuring** which shows a silver fleck effect.

It is a very hard, strong and durable timber and is quite heavy. Trees which have grown quickly tend to produce long straight-grained timber which is ideal for furniture making. The harder short-grained timbers from slow growing trees are more suitable for outdoor use.

Some examples of products made from oak are shown here.

Quarter sawn oak

staircase

kitchen units

furniture

Manufactured boards

Some of the disadvantages of natural wood can be overcome by using manufactured boards. These include: plywood, chipboard and hardboard. These are essentially **sheet** materials.

Plywood and its properties

Plywood is made up of three or more thin layers (or veneers) of wood, glued together. The veneers are arranged so that their grains run in alternate directions. Since wood is much stronger along the grain than across it, this gives the material **uniform strength**. This can be demonstrated with a straw model.

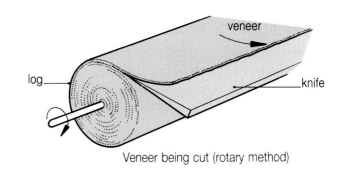

Veneer being cut (rotary method)

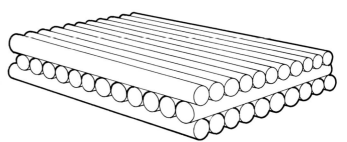

straw model

Because of this construction, plywood is less likely to warp or split than natural woods. It is always made with an odd number of veneers 3, 5, 7 etc. The greater the number, the stronger the plywood.

Although very 'stable', plywood is not immune to warping, since the tensions in the veneers are never equal. Further, if one side of the board gets wet, or is heated, the board will warp as the outer veneers expand or contract.

A major advantage of plywood over natural timber is that it is relatively cheap and is available in much larger sheets than natural woods, and in a wide range of thicknesses. Decorative hardwood veneers can also be attached to a cheaper core or base material. This allows for the economic use of rare woods, and provides wide boards which otherwise might not be available. Plastic coatings are also used to provide water-resistant surfaces. Another advantage of plywood is that it is flexible and can be 'formed' into curves.

If individual veneers are glued together between formers a **permanent** curved shape can be produced. These are known as **laminated forms**.

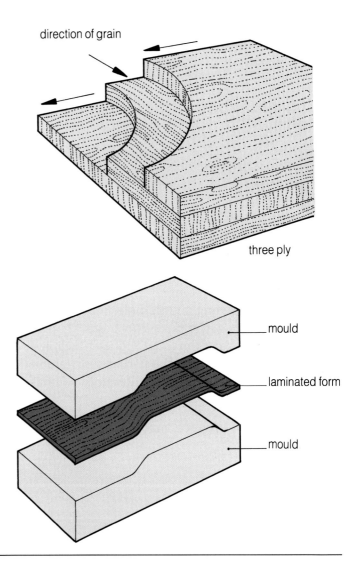

Types of plywood

A range of plywoods is available, made from different woods, and each having its own particular properties. Birch ply for example, is one of the strongest and most rigid plywoods. It will cut easily, and its edge can be planed to a good quality finish. Douglas fir however, is a much coarser grained plywood. It snags badly when sawn, and is difficult to plane to a good finish.

The type of **glue** used in the manufacture of the plywood will determine its use. Plywood suitable for exterior use or boat building must have waterproof glue.

Some examples of products made from plywood are shown here.

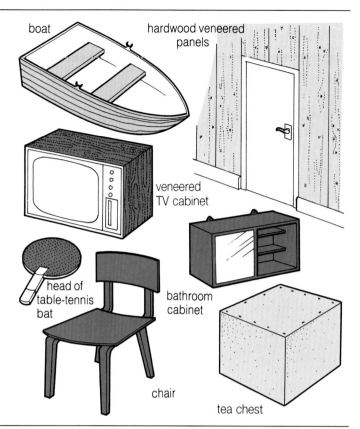

boat

hardwood veneered panels

veneered TV cabinet

head of table-tennis bat

bathroom cabinet

chair

tea chest

Chipboard (particle board)

Chipboard is made from chips (or particles) of wood, mixed with a synthetic glue. The mixture is squeezed between rollers and then dried between metal plates under high pressure and heat.

Because the particles criss-cross, chipboard has similar strength properties in both directions. Even so, it is a relatively weak material and will break under fairly low bending forces. However, the material is given considerable strength when its surface is covered with a veneer. Hardwood veneers and plastic coatings are common.

Chipboard will cut and machine easily, but it wears saw teeth and cutters quickly because of the high glue content. It can be jointed similarly to natural wood, but fixings should not be made into the edge – they will pull out easily. A hardwood edging strip (or lipping) should be fitted before attaching hinges and other fittings.

Some examples of products made from chipboard are shown here.

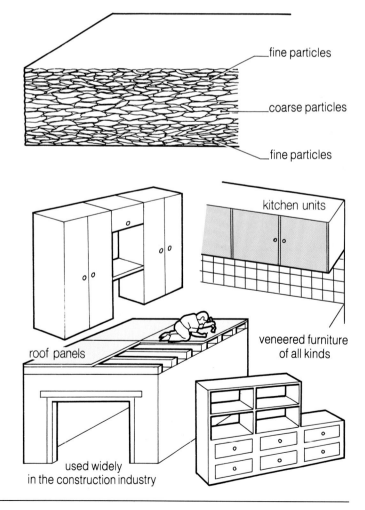

fine particles

coarse particles

fine particles

kitchen units

roof panels

veneered furniture of all kinds

used widely in the construction industry

Hardboard and its properties

Hardboard is made from softwood pulp which is formed into sheets under high pressure. **Standard hardboard** is smooth on one face whilst the reverse side has a rough mesh-like texture.

A variety of other forms are available including: double faced (smooth on both faces), perforated (pegboard for example), embossed (having a raised patterned surface) and so on. **Medium hardboard** (of which Sundeala is a well known example) is a softer and thicker board.

Although hardboard is a versatile sheet material, it has very little rigidity and must therefore be fixed to battens, or a solid surface, to prevent buckling. Untreated hardboard absorbs water readily, and is particularly susceptible to buckling.

Some examples of products made from hardboard are shown here.

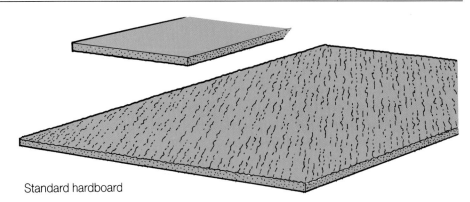

Standard hardboard

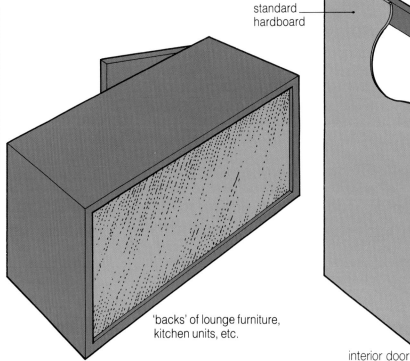

pegboard storage rack

standard hardboard

deal frame

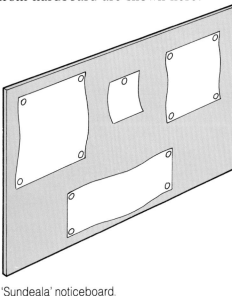

'Sundeala' noticeboard.

'backs' of lounge furniture, kitchen units, etc.

interior door

Industrial manufacturing with wood

Of all the construction materials, wood is the one most commonly used by the home DIY enthusiast. This is because wood can be worked and formed using relatively simple, inexpensive tools. In mass production however, most of the hand tool operations are carried out on specialist machines. Some of the more common industrial wood working processes are described below.

Sawing

Nearly every woodwork job begins with sawing. After sawing, some timbers are ready for assembly into finished products. Most however, are passed on for further processing on other machines.

Circular saws are used for 'through cutting', 'cross cutting' and 'trenching' for example.

Band saws are used mainly for 'through' and 'cross cutting'.

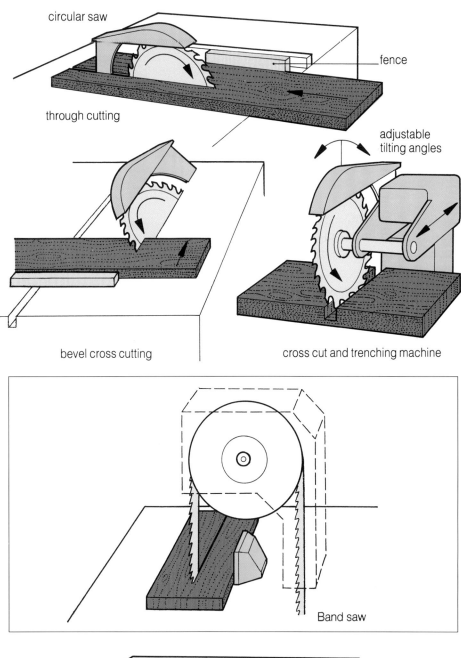

circular saw

fence

through cutting

adjustable tilting angles

bevel cross cutting

cross cut and trenching machine

Band saw

Planing

Planing is the process which most often follows sawing. Planing reduces the wood to **exact dimensions** leaving it flat and smooth.

Surface planers are used to prepare the 'face side' and 'face edges' of the timber. Thicknessers can then be used to plane the timber to an exact thickness. After planing, the next stage of production is often **moulding** or **joint cutting**.

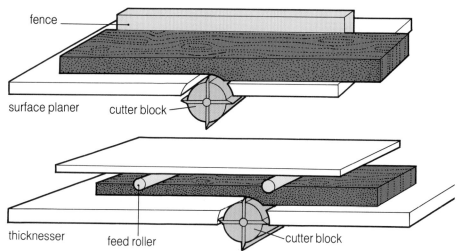

fence

surface planer   cutter block

thicknesser   feed roller   cutter block

Moulding

Moulding machines are used to produce a wide range of 'shaped' timbers called **mouldings**. These are then used in the manufacture of numerous other products.

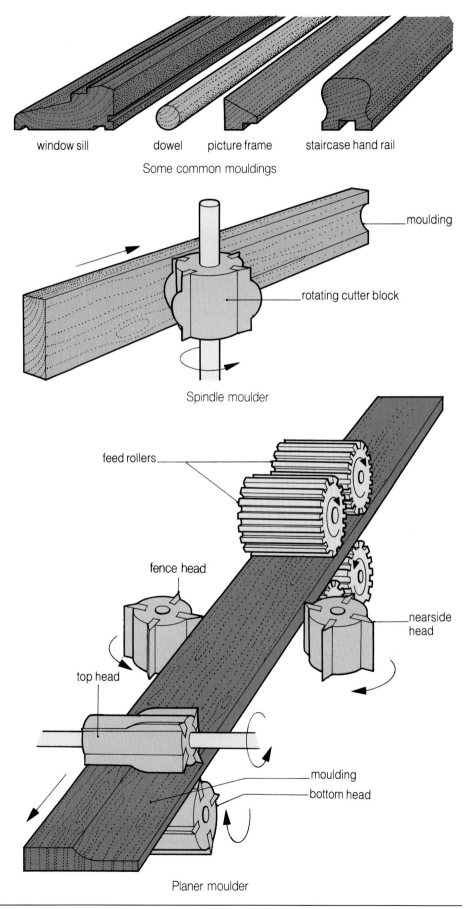

window sill   dowel   picture frame   staircase hand rail

Some common mouldings

Spindle moulders These are used to machine a single face or edge on a previously planed timber.

moulding

rotating cutter block

Spindle moulder

Planer moulders These machines first plane, and then produce a moulding in **one** through cutting operation. All four surfaces can be machined in one pass. Although moulding machines are very expensive, the products (the moulding) can be produced very rapidly and to very close tolerances. Further, a moulded section (such as a window sill) is a much more stable and durable product compared to a 'constructed' section.

feed rollers

fence head

top head

nearside head

moulding

bottom head

Planer moulder

Joint cutting

The construction of a product from wood nearly always involves some form of jointing.

Many different types of joint are used which fall into the categories: **T** joints, **L** joints and **+** joints. The choice of joint will be dependent upon:
1 the task which the joint has to fulfil,
2 the nature of the material,
3 the appearance of the joint.

Some joint cutting machinery is shown here.

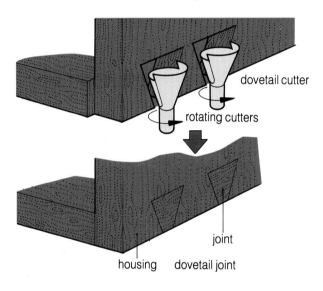

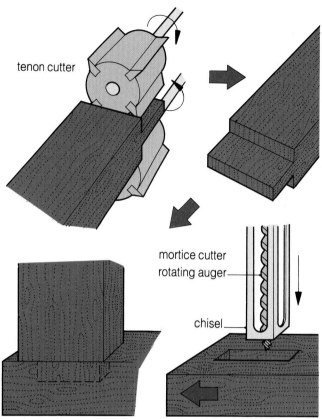

Routers

A router is a cutting tool whose operation can best be understood by looking at some of the many forms which can be manufactured.

A router's cutting tool (or profile cutter), is 'guided' (on the latest machines), by a computer.

CNC or **C**omputer **N**umerical **C**ontrolled machines can be fully automated. This increases both the speed of production and the accuracy of the product.

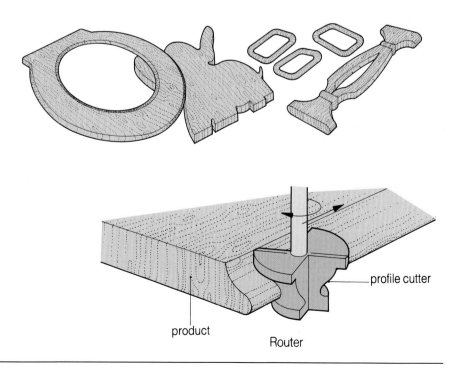

Sanding

After assembly, most products are 'cleaned up' and given a very smooth surface by sanding. Disc, bobbin and belt sanders are all used for this purpose.

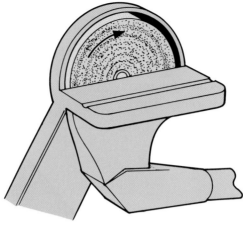

disc sander (used for small items)

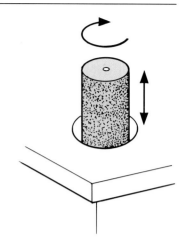

bobbin sander (used for curved edges)

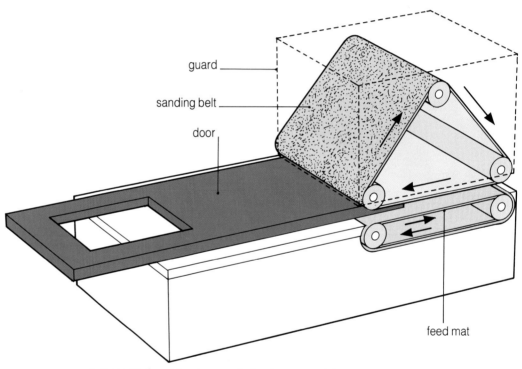

guard

sanding belt

door

feed mat

belt sander (used for doors and other large panels)

Finishing

After sanding the product may be 'finished' with a surface coating. The type of finish will depend upon: the type of wood, the required effect, and the function of the product.

Oil, varnish, paint and wax polish are some of the many types of finishes used on wood.

Questions

23 To choose the most suitable material for a particular product requires you to have a good knowledge of materials. See how much you know about **wood** by using the chart below. **Copy it** on to a piece of paper and 'fill in' the empty boxes (and also add to the other boxes if you can). Some of the information you require can be found in this chapter. For more detailed information you will need to use a more specialist book.

Name	Natural	Manu-factured	Colour	Properties	Common uses
pine (deal)	✔			fairly hard durable and quite stable cuts and machines easily finishes well	
			creamy white to light brown		hockey sticks garden tool handles hammer shafts
				fine even texture tough prone to twisting	staircases window boards step ladders
beech				close even grain very tough quite heavy and hard doesn't split easily no taste and odour	
			reddish-brown		veneered furniture solid furniture window and door frames
				some very stable available in large sheets of various thicknesses	cabinets small boats wall panels tea chests
			creamy and 'speckled'		roofing and flooring base material for knock down furniture

Questions

24 This 'peg basher' toy is made from **beech.**

What properties make beech particularly suitable for this product?

25 Some saw handles are made from **ash**.
  a What method of manufacture do you think was used to produce this handle?
  b What other wood might be suitable for making saw handles?

26 This picnic bench is made from **Scotch pine**. Would quarter sawn or plain sawn timbers be more suitable for this product? Explain your answer.

27 This exterior door is fitted with a weather board. How do you think this product was manufactured?

weather board

28 a What kind of wood might this pick-axe handle be made of?
  b What properties make your chosen material particularly suitable for this product?

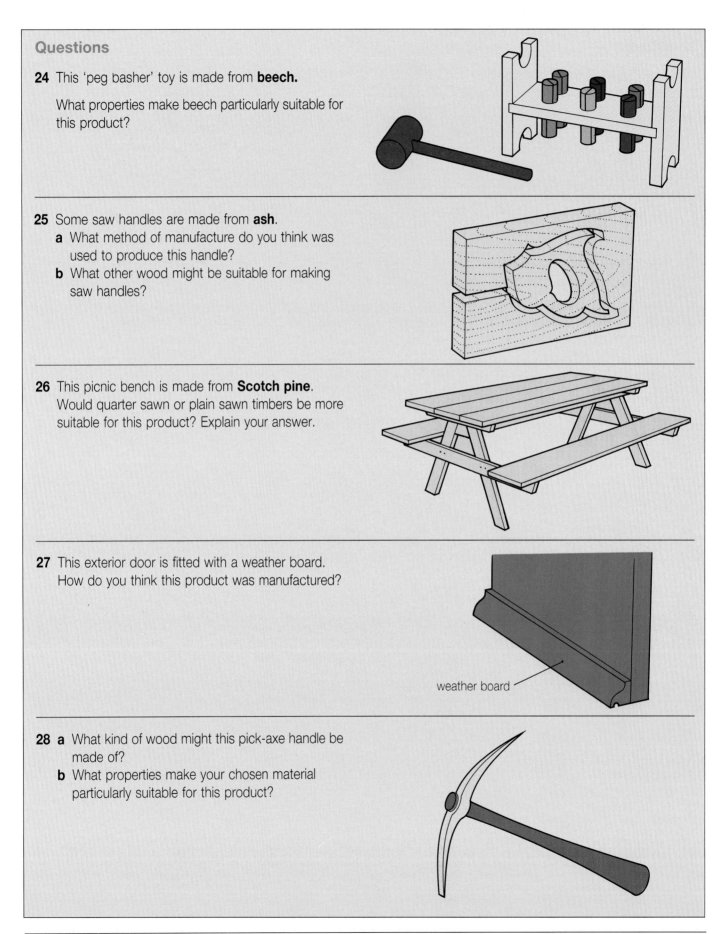

29 This gate is made from **red baltic pine**.
Why is parana pine unsuitable for this product?

30 a What would be a suitable wood from which to make these kitchen utensils?
   b What properties make your chosen material particularly suitable for these products?

Salad servers

31 Half of the world's tropical rainforests have been destroyed in the past 40 years. As well as timber, the rainforests are the main sources of chemical compounds for medicines and are home to half of the world's species. Britain is the largest European importer of tropical timber, of which 5% is from well-managed forests, where the amount of timber felled is carefully controlled. Uses of tropical hardwoods include some chipboards and plywoods, veneers, doors, furniture, window frames, coffins and salad bowls.

As a consumer, what steps can you take to preserve the tropical rainforests?

Amazon rain forest

Plastics

ICI plastics division, Wilton, Cleveland

'Plastic-like' materials were first used thousands of years ago. These were the plastics which occurred in nature. **Amber** for example (a resinous substance from trees), was used by the Egyptians and other civilisations to make jewellery. Similarly, the **horns** of animals were used to make drinking vessels and simple instruments.

Today of course, numerous different plastics are available. Some are still made from natural materials (such as cellulose from plants), but most are made entirely from chemicals obtained from crude **oil** and, to a much lesser extent, coal.

It is the job of the plastics manufacturer to convert these chemicals into plastics. Product manufacturers then use these materials to produce goods.

The structure of plastics

One of the chemicals obtained from crude oil is the gas **ethene**. This can be used to make the well known plastic **polythene**.

If we look at how polythene is made, we can learn about the general structure of plastics and begin to understand their properties.

A simple explanation must begin with the understanding that all substances are made up of tiny units called **molecules**, and that each molecule is made up of minute particles called **atoms**. The ethene molecule is described here.

The ethene molecule

Molecules of course are invisible to the naked eye, but we can build models or make drawings to represent them.

A scientist might draw an ethene molecule like this. Notice that it is made up of two **carbon** atoms and four **hydrogen** atoms. In the drawing the lines (—) represent the chemical bonds which hold the atoms of the molecule together.

Ethene gas is made up of millions of these molecules which 'move around' quite freely, and with very little attraction for one another.

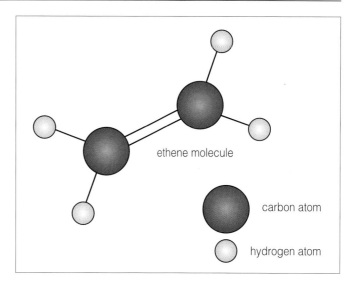

ethene molecule

carbon atom

hydrogen atom

How polythene is made

Polythene is made, by 'persuading' the free roaming ethene gas molecules to join together to form long chain polythene molecules. The persuasion is provided by chemicals known as **catalysts** or **initiators**. During the process many thousands of ethene molecules join together to form each molecule of polythene.

Now, although ethene gas molecules have very little attraction for one another, the newly formed polythene molecules **do attract one another** and become tangled and twisted together to form the **solid** – high density **polythene**.

Small molecules such as ethene, which can link together in this way, are called **monomers**. The process of joining molecules is called **polymerization**, and the products of polymerization – such as polythene – are called **polymers**.

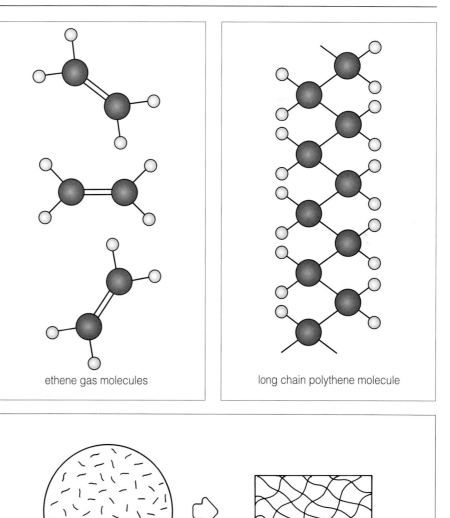

ethene gas molecules

long chain polythene molecule

ethene – gas

polythene – solid

Types of polymerization

When a polymer is made as described above, the process is known as **addition polymerization** because molecules of the monomer 'join together' to form the long chain molecules.

Condensation polymerization is a different process which usually involves the joining of two different kinds of monomers.

By starting with different **monomers** therefore, and using different polymerization processes, a whole range of polymers (plastics) can be made. Even so, in each case the polymer formed will be made up of **long chain molecules**, and it is these molecules which give plastics the properties which we find so useful.

Plastics and their properties

The name 'plastic' describes a material which, at some point in its manufacture, behaves in a plastic or putty-like way. In other words, it will deform under pressure, and retain the 'new shape' when the pressure is removed.

Although there are many different kinds of plastic, there are just two main types: **thermoplastics** and **thermosetting plastics**.

Thermoplastics

Polythene, PVC and polystyrene are examples of thermoplastics. They soften on heating and can be moulded into shape. On cooling they harden again.

On heating, the molecules are given the energy to move apart. As a result the forces between the molecules become weaker. This allows them the freedom to slip over one another to form a new shape when under pressure. This process of softening and hardening can be repeated over and over again because the molecules in a thermoplastic are always free to behave in this way.

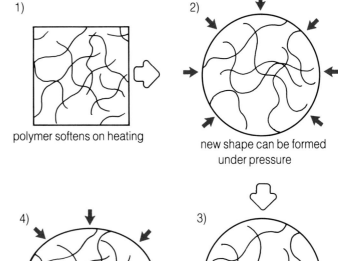

1) polymer softens on heating

2) new shape can be formed under pressure

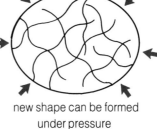

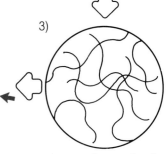

4) new shape can be formed under pressure

3) polymer softens on heating

Thermosetting plastics

Phenol formaldehyde (Bakelite) and urea formaldehyde are examples of **thermosetting** plastics. These behave quite differently to the thermoplastics.

On first heating, the polymer softens and can be moulded into shape under pressure. However, the heat triggers a **chemical reaction** in which the molecules become permanently locked together. The reaction is known as **cross linking**. As a result the polymer becomes permanently 'set' and cannot be softened again by heating.

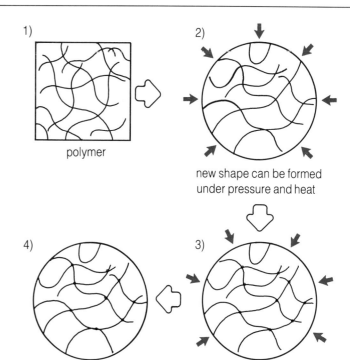

1) polymer

2) new shape can be formed under pressure and heat

3) as heating continues, chains become 'cross linked'

4) the links are permanent and the polymer cannot be softened by heating

Some examples of thermoplastics

Polythene (high density)

High density polythene is made in such a way that the chains are 'straight'. This allows the molecules to **pack close together** to produce a high density material. (See density, page 200). Because the chains lie close together, they attract one another firmly and have less freedom to move.

The result is a fairly stiff, strong plastic which is also quite tough. It softens at a fairly high temperature (around 120–130°C), and is resistant to chemical attack.

Some examples of the many products made from high density polythene are shown here.

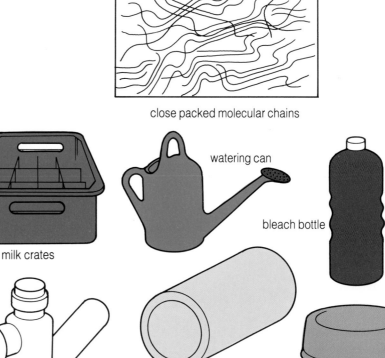

close packed molecular chains

watering can

bleach bottle

milk crates

yellow gas pipe

plumbing components

decorative chain

large water container

Polythene (low density)

Low density polythene is made by a process which produces **side branches** on the chains. These branches prevent the chains from packing close together. As a result, they are less firmly attracted to one another, and the polymer is weaker, softer and more flexible than high density polythene. Less energy is required to separate the chains and therefore the polymer softens at a lower temperature (around 85°C). The polymer can be transparent or opaque. It is a very good electrical insulator.

We 'consume' more low density polythene than any other polymer.

Some of its many uses are shown here.

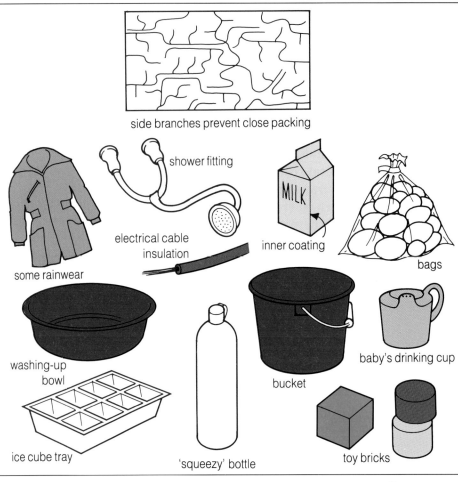

side branches prevent close packing

shower fitting

electrical cable insulation

some rainwear

inner coating

MILK

bags

washing-up bowl

bucket

baby's drinking cup

ice cube tray

'squeezy' bottle

toy bricks

Polypropylene

Polypropylene belongs to the same family of plastics as the polythenes. It is tougher however, and more rigid than high density polythene. It also has a greater resistance to heat – it softens at around 150°C. Polypropylene has the lowest density of the thermoplastics, and yet it has a very high impact strength. Its ability to be flexed many thousands of times without breaking is another valuable characteristic.

Some examples of the many products made from polypropylene are shown here.

cotton reel

mixing bowl

stackable chairs (seat)

cutlery

'flexible' hinge

push toy

box with strip hinge

rawl plugs

snap-on re-sealable lids

plumbing components

bottles

BABY LOTION

safety helmet

BABY MILK FOOD

Polyvinyl chloride (PVC)

PVC can be produced to give a range of properties. The stiff, hard wearing PVC used to make drain pipes and guttering is one example. A more flexible and rubbery material can be produced by adding a **plasticiser** to the PVC.

The plasticiser chemical has molecules which are much smaller than those of the polymer. Their effect is to **separate the polymer chains** making them attract each other less strongly. As a result they slide more easily over one another and the polymer becomes more soft and pliable. PVC is used in its softer forms as an insulator for electrical cables, and in the manufacture of some rainwear. PVC containing a higher proportion of plasticiser is used to coat cloth in the production of 'leathercloth'. This tough, flexible material is used to cover some motor car seats, and in the manufacture of furniture and handbags for example.

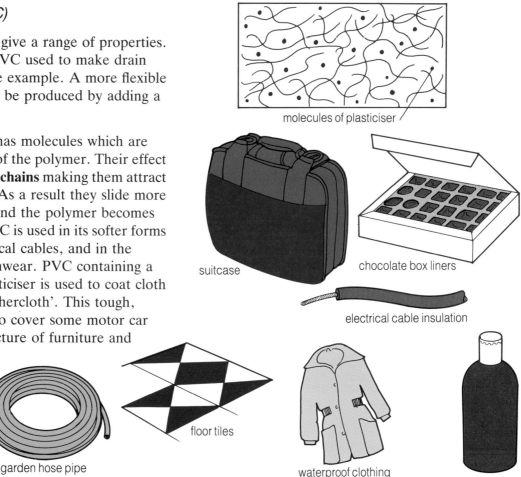

molecules of plasticiser

suitcase

chocolate box liners

electrical cable insulation

garden hose pipe

floor tiles

waterproof clothing

bottles

Acrylics

Probably the most familiar acrylic plastic is the sheet material known by its trade name **Perspex**. The polymer is called polymethyl methacrylate. It can have a glass-like transparency or be opaque. Both forms can be coloured with pigments. It is fairly hard wearing and will not shatter. However, it can crack and is fairly easily scratched. It can be formed, bent and twisted when heated to temperatures between 165 and 175°C. In its cold state Perspex is quite brittle and care must be taken to avoid cracking when it is cut or drilled.

Acrylic is also produced in granule form for use in injection moulding machines. (See page 250.) For this purpose the methyl methacrylate is polymerized in a different way from that used for Perspex. The polymer obtained softens more readily, and in this form is known as **acrylic moulding powder**.

Some examples of the uses of acrylic are shown here.

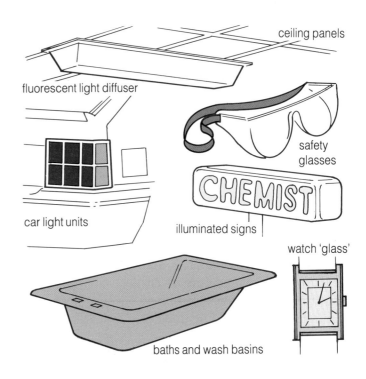

ceiling panels

fluorescent light diffuser

safety glasses

CHEMIST

car light units

illuminated signs

watch 'glass'

baths and wash basins

Nylon

Many different types of nylon are produced, which are identified with a number: type 6.6 and type 6.10 for example.

Nylon is probably best known in the form of a **fibre** and is widely used in the manufacture of clothing, carpets and brushes for example. It is a fairly hard material with a good resistance to wear and a high degree of resistance to chemical attack.

'Solid' nylon is widely used for engineering purposes. It is particularly useful for making fast moving parts such as gcars and bearings. It wears well, has low frictional properties, and has a fairly high melting point. In this form it is usually a creamy white colour.

Some examples of the many products made from nylon are shown here.

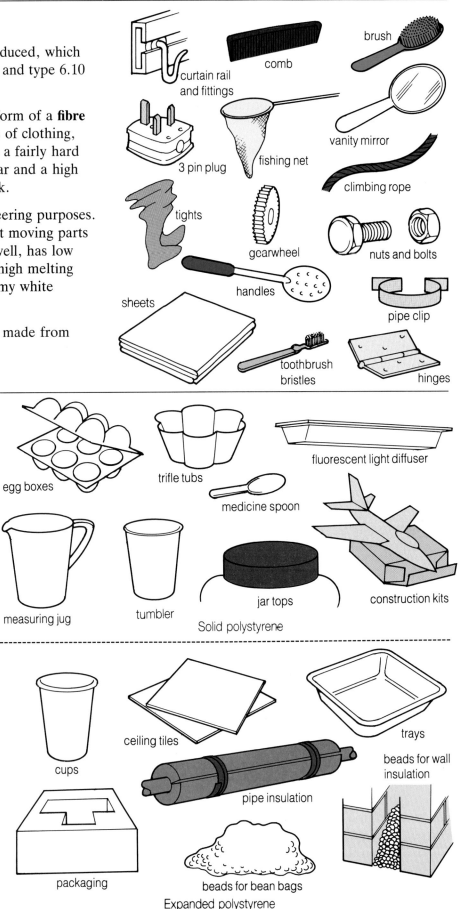

curtain rail and fittings

comb

brush

3 pin plug

fishing net

vanity mirror

climbing rope

tights

gcarwheel

nuts and bolts

handles

sheets

pipe clip

toothbrush bristles

hinges

Polystyrene

Polystyrene is available in several forms but is most common as a crystal clear solid, and a 'foamed' plastic known as expanded polystyrene.

In its 'solid' form it is very brittle and can be identified by the metallic ring it makes when dropped. In this form it is used to make a wide range of products, including containers and packaging.

Expanded polystyrene is soft and spongy. During manufacture a gas is produced which becomes trapped within its honeycomb structure. This gives the material good heat insulating properties. It is a very low density material, and because of its spongy nature is very good at absorbing shock. It is used a great deal in the building trade as an insulating material, and is widely used in packaging.

egg boxes

trifle tubs

fluorescent light diffuser

medicine spoon

measuring jug

tumbler

jar tops

construction kits

Solid polystyrene

cups

ceiling tiles

trays

beads for wall insulation

pipe insulation

packaging

beads for bean bags

Expanded polystyrene

Some thermosetting plastics

Phenol formaldehyde (Bakelite)

The first plastic to be made artificially from chemicals was **Bakelite** (named after the man who first made it in 1909 – Leo Baekeland).

It is a hard, brittle plastic with a natural **dark** glossy colour. As it is a 'thermoset' plastic it resists heat without softening (see page 243) and is a good thermal insulator. However, at very high temperatures it will char and decompose. Bakelite is a good electrical insulator.

Phenol formaldehyde is not used extensively these days but many products made from this material are still in use. Some examples are shown here.

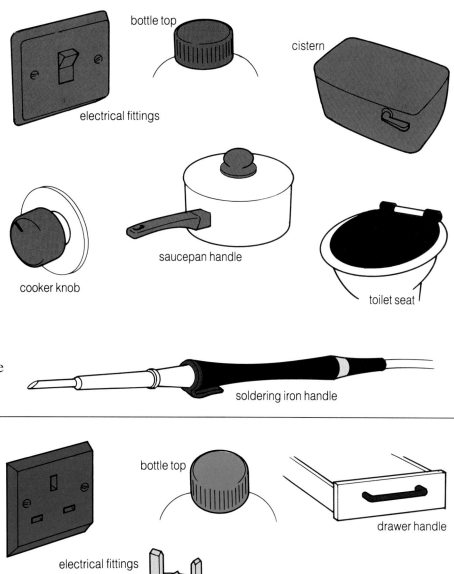

bottle top

cistern

electrical fittings

cooker knob

saucepan handle

toilet seat

soldering iron handle

Urea formaldehyde

Unlike Bakelite, urea formaldehyde is a colourless polymer. It can therefore be coloured artificially with pigments to produce articles in a wide range of colours. It is harder than Bakelite and has no taste or odour. It is a good thermal and electrical insulator.

Some examples of products made from this material are shown here.

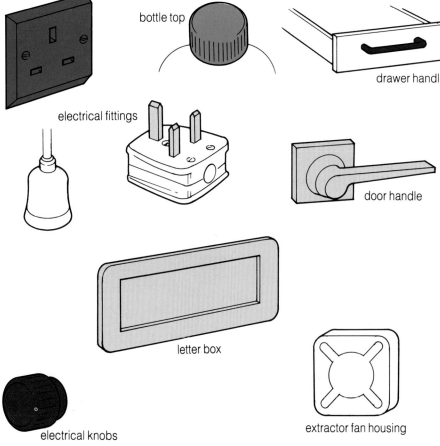

bottle top

drawer handle

electrical fittings

door handle

letter box

electrical knobs

extractor fan housing

Melamine formaldehyde

This polymer has similar properties to urea formaldehyde and is used in the manufacture of high quality tableware. Its heat resistant properties make it particularly suitable for the surfaces of laminated kitchen worktops.

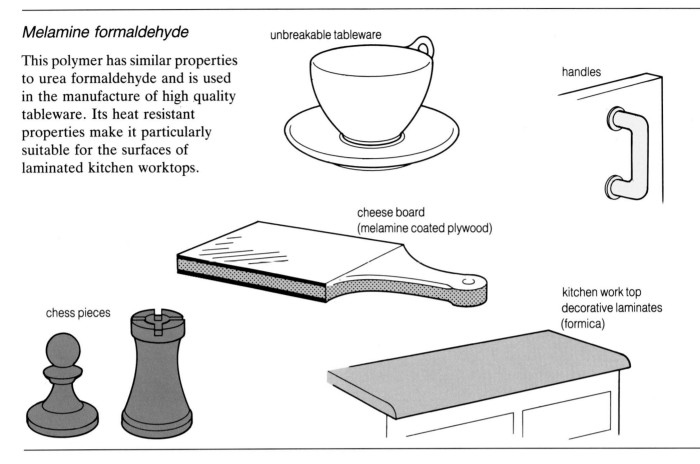

unbreakable tableware

handles

cheese board
(melamine coated plywood)

kitchen work top
decorative laminates
(formica)

chess pieces

Polyester resin

Polyester resin is one example of a thermosetting plastic which **polymerizes at room temperature**.

The resin, (a treacle-like substance) and a chemical known as a hardener, are mixed just before use. When set the plastic is stiff, hard and brittle. To add strength and bulk, it is often reinforced with **glass fibre** to make glass reinforced plastic (GRP).

Some examples of its uses are shown here.

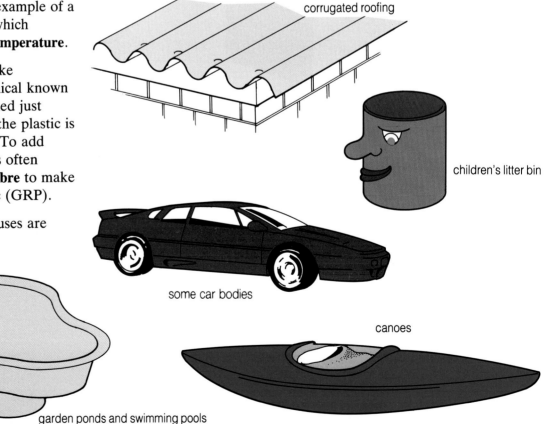

corrugated roofing

children's litter bin

some car bodies

canoes

garden ponds and swimming pools

Manufacturing with plastics

Plastic raw materials are available in a variety of forms including powders, viscous fluids, pellets and granules. Product manufacturers use a wide range of processing machinery to convert these materials into components and products. Some of this machinery is described below.

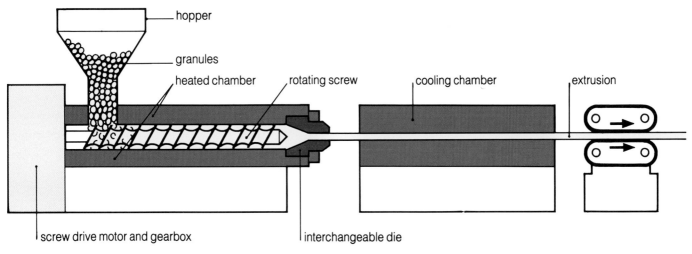

Extrusion

This is the process used to make 'long' products like drain-pipes and curtain rails. Plastic granules are fed from a hopper on to a rotating screw. The screw forces the plastic through a heated tube where it becomes molten before being forced under pressure through a die. The die contains a hole whose shape corresponds to that of the required article. As it leaves the die, the 'extrusion' is cooled in a water bath or in jets of air. The hardened extrusion is then cut into lengths or coiled, depending on the product. Thermoplastics such as polythene, PVC and nylon are commonly used in extrusion.

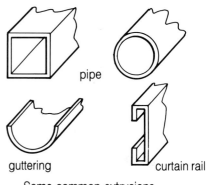

Some common extrusions

Extrusion blow-moulding

This process is used for making articles like bottles and hollow toys.

Air is blown into a section of extruded plastic tube, causing it to expand and take up the shape of the mould. The mould is then opened and the product removed.

PVC, polythene and polypropylene are common blow-moulding materials.

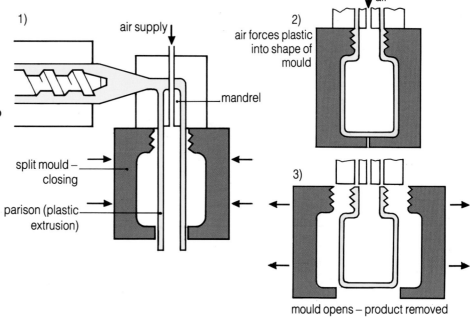

Injection moulding

This is the process of forming articles by injecting **molten** plastic into a mould. An injection moulding machine is similar to that used for extrusion, the difference being that the feed screw (in addition to feeding plastic from the hopper) is used as a ram. The screw is moved backwards, as it rotates, until a measured quantity of plastic is at position **A** in the diagram. The screw is then driven forwards by a hydraulic ram, forcing the molten plastic into the mould.

The mould consists of two or more parts which fit together forming a cavity of the required shape. Cold water is circulated through the body of the mould to reduce the cooling time of the moulding. After a short time the mould can be opened and the moulding removed. The complete cycle can then be repeated.

Injection moulding produces components and products which have consistently accurate dimensions and a high quality finish. A wide range of complex forms can be produced which could otherwise only be manufactured by expensive machining processes. Production is fast and the process produces very little waste.

An enormous range of products are manufactured in this way. These include:

- kitchenware – pedal bins, bowls, buckets, jugs, cutlery and containers;
- cases for electrical appliances – hairdryers, vacuum cleaners, food mixers etc;
- toys and games;
- products for the car industry;
- component parts for many other products.

Polythene, polystyrene, polypropylene and nylon are typical injection moulding materials.

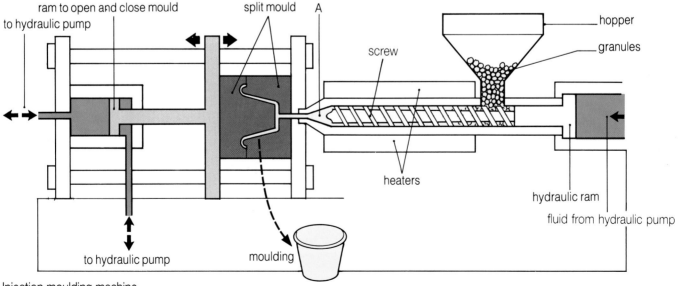

Injection moulding machine

Compression moulding

In compression moulding, huge forces are used to squeeze a measured quantity of polymer into shape between **heated** moulds.

The polymer can be in the form of a powder or 'slug'. A slug is simply powder which has been compressed into a cube shape. Slugs can be handled more easily than powder, and can be pre-heated in a high frequency oven. This reduces the 'cycle time' in the moulding machine.

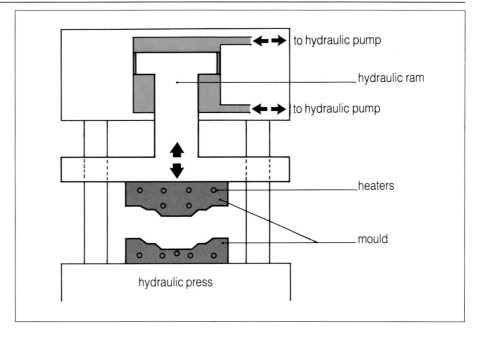

Compression moulding is used for **thermosetting** plastics. The heat from the mould triggers the chemical reaction known as 'cross-linking' (see page 243).

After a short period of time (known as the curing time), the cross-linking is complete and the mould can be opened and the moulding removed. The mouldings have a high quality finish requiring only the removal of 'flash'.

Electrical fittings (plugs and sockets for example), saucepan and cutlery handles, bottle tops and toilet seats are just a few of the many products which are manufactured in this way.

Phenol, urea, and melamine formaldehyde are typical compression moulding materials.

1)

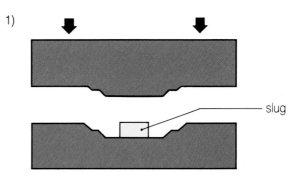

2)

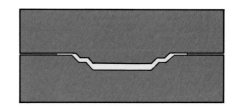

3)

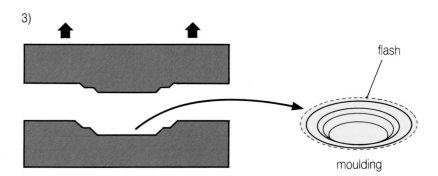

Vacuum forming

This is one of the processes used to make articles from **thermoplastic sheet**. The sheet is first cut to size and clamped above a mould. A heater then raises the temperature of the sheet until it becomes soft and rubbery.

Finally, air is evacuated from beneath the sheet. This allows the normal 'outside' air pressure to push down on the softened sheet, forcing it to take up the shape of the mould.

After a suitable cooling period, the hardened moulding can be removed from the mould.

The process described above is used mainly for shallow products made from thin sheet. When large or complex mouldings are produced using thicker sheet, a pressure chamber may also be used above the sheet. Vacuum forming enables **large** irregular shaped mouldings to be produced which could not be manufactured by any other plastic forming process. Further, the equipment is relatively cheap and requires the use of only one mould.

Products manufactured in this way include

- egg boxes, chocolate box liners and numerous other food and confectionery packaging
- seed trays
- shop signs and fittings
- some motor car dashboards
- wash basins and baths.

Acrylic, polystyrene, and PVC are typical vacuum forming materials.

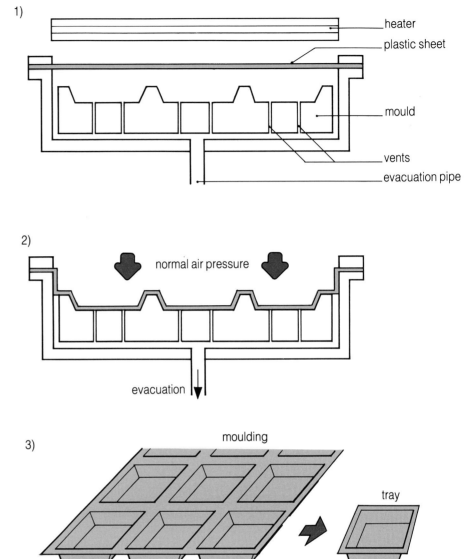

Questions

32 To choose the most suitable material for a particular product requires you to have a good knowledge of materials. See how much you know about **plastics** by using the chart below. **Copy it** on to a piece of paper and 'fill in' the empty boxes (and also add to the other boxes if you can). Some of the information you require can be found in this chapter. For more detailed information you will need to use a more specialist book.

Name	Thermo-plastic	Thermo-setting plastic	Properties	Common uses
high density polythene	✓		hard and stiff quite tough softens at around 120–130°C	
				garden hose electrical cable insulation waterproof clothing floor tiles door and window frames
		✓	very hard and brittle good thermal insulator dark glossy colour	
			rigid high impact strength softens at around 150°C has the lowest density of the thermoplastics can be flexed many times without breaking	
	✓			plastic bags and sheets squeezy bottles hollow toys buckets and bowls
	✓		available in fibre and 'solid' form hard and tough good resistance to chemical attack low frictional properties hard wearing	
acrylic				
			stiff, hard and brittle	(when reinforced with glass fibre) canoes, garden ponds some car bodies

Questions

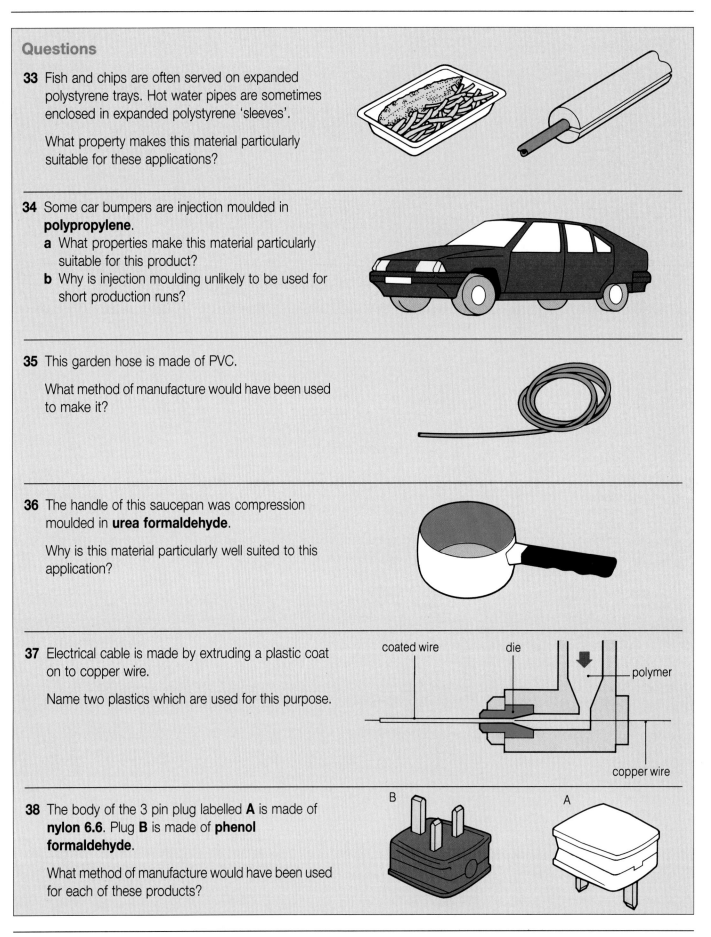

33 Fish and chips are often served on expanded polystyrene trays. Hot water pipes are sometimes enclosed in expanded polystyrene 'sleeves'.

What property makes this material particularly suitable for these applications?

34 Some car bumpers are injection moulded in **polypropylene**.
  a What properties make this material particularly suitable for this product?
  b Why is injection moulding unlikely to be used for short production runs?

35 This garden hose is made of PVC.

What method of manufacture would have been used to make it?

36 The handle of this saucepan was compression moulded in **urea formaldehyde**.

Why is this material particularly well suited to this application?

37 Electrical cable is made by extruding a plastic coat on to copper wire.

Name two plastics which are used for this purpose.

coated wire   die   polymer

copper wire

38 The body of the 3 pin plug labelled **A** is made of **nylon 6.6**. Plug **B** is made of **phenol formaldehyde**.

What method of manufacture would have been used for each of these products?

B   A

39 This washing-up bowl is made of **low density polythene**.

How do you think it was manufactured?

40 This 'squeezy' tomato ketchup bottle is made of **polythene**.

a From which kind of polythene would it be made?
b What method of manufacture do you think was used to produce this product?

41 This patio door unit was fabricated from a very stiff **PVC** called uPVC. A cross section of part of the door unit is shown inset.

a What do you think the 'u' stands for?
b What method of manufacture do you think was used to produce the plastic members?

42 **Expanded polystyrene** is a very versatile material. Some of the many products made from this material are listed below. For each product, describe the properties which make polystyrene particularly suitable for the application.

a Lagging for hot water pipes.
b Packaging for electrical equipment.
c Swimming floats.
d Egg boxes.
e Cycle safety helmets.
f Take-away food boxes and trays.

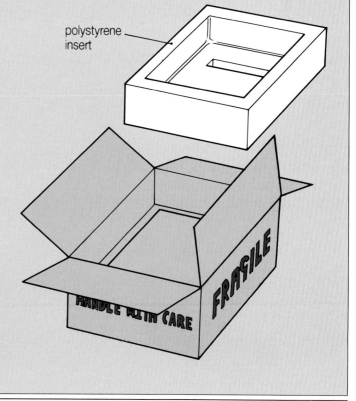

polystyrene insert

Working with materials at school

Marking out

When you have decided which material, or materials to use for a particular 'job', those materials will need **marking out**.

Accurate marking out is very important. It helps to ensure that the different parts fit together correctly and that the final product looks good.

Refer to your working drawings when marking out

Straight edges

Marking out usually starts from a straight edge.

If the material doesn't have one, you will need to make one using a file, plane or disc sander for example.

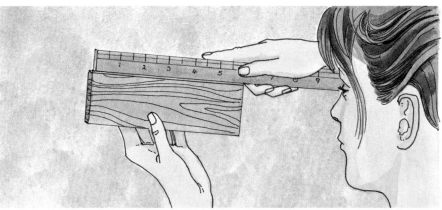
Testing for a straight edge

Right angles and parallel lines

Lines which need to be at 90° to the straight edge can be marked out using a **try square** and a scriber, marking knife or pencil.

Parallel lines can be made using a **marking gauge** on wood and with **odd leg callipers** on metal and plastic.

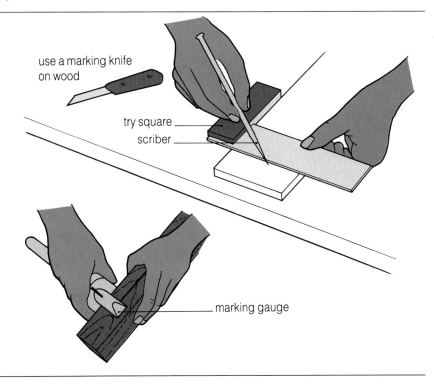

use a marking knife on wood

try square

scriber

marking gauge

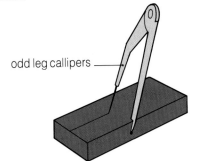

odd leg callipers

Circles

Circles, or parts of circles can be marked out using a pair of **compasses** or **dividers**.

To prevent the dividers slipping on metal and plastics, a small dent should be made at the 'centre' of the curve using a centre punch.

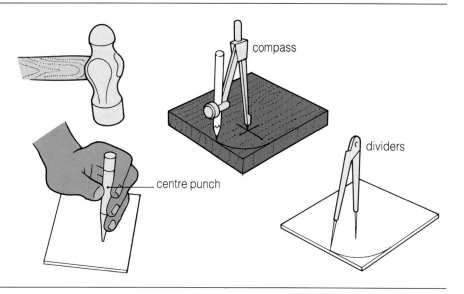

compass

dividers

centre punch

Centres

When preparing to drill a hole, you will need to mark out the hole's centre using a ruler.

The centre of the end of a round bar can be found using a **centre square**. On the end of a square or rectangular bar the centre can be found using diagonal lines.

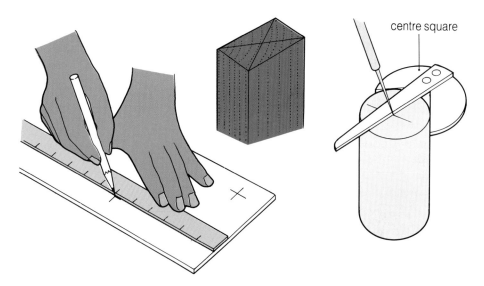

centre square

Irregular shapes

When you need to mark out an irregular shape, it is sometimes useful to use a **template**.

A template can be made from cardboard for example, around which you can **draw** the shape. Alternatively a paper template can be 'stuck' onto the material to act as the guide when cutting.

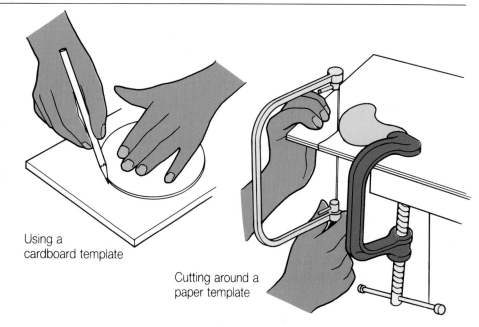

Using a cardboard template

Cutting around a paper template

Shaping materials

Shaping metal

Sawing

This is often the first process to be used when shaping metal. A **hacksaw** with the appropriate number of teeth on its blade should be selected. (See diagrams.)

For very fine work a **junior hacksaw** can be used. **Abrafiles** are used for cutting curves. The blade is actually a very fine round file.

Always hold the material firmly in a vice (or using a G cramp) and position it so that you cut as close to the vice as possible. This reduces vibration.

Sawing produces a rough surface, so cut on the waste side of the line and finally smooth down to the line by filing.

hold the hacksaw like this and make long steady strokes

junior hacksaw

abrafile

for hard materials

for soft materials

for cutting 'thin' materials

Filing

Cross-filing and **draw-filing** are the two basic operations used to produce a straight edge on a piece of metal.

Cross-filing is used to remove waste material. Draw-filing produces a final smooth finish.

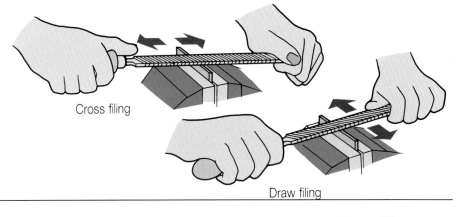

Cross filing

Draw filing

Types of files and their uses

A range of different files are available. Some of the more common types are shown here.

You should always select the most suitable file for the job. For example, when removing a lot of waste material use a coarse file (a file with large teeth). Use a fine file for smoothing and finishing. When filing a long edge, use a broad file, and so on. Small shapes can be produced using a round, square, or 'triangular' file as required.

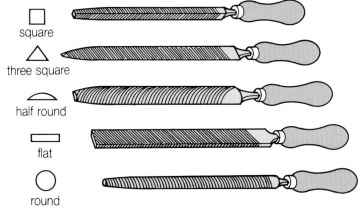

square

three square

half round

flat

round

Shearing

Shears (or tinsnips) can be used for cutting and shaping thin metals.

Note Take care – sheared metals can be very sharp. They usually require finishing by filing.

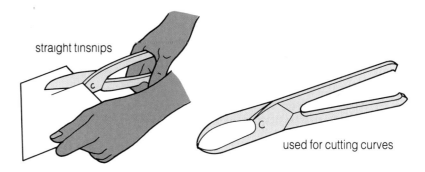

straight tinsnips

used for cutting curves

Bending

After marking out, sheet metal can be shaped by folding. This can be done using a special folding bar (or alternatively, pieces of strong metal) clamped in a vice.

The bending force can be applied using a heavy mallet. To prevent damage to the metal, use a piece of scrap wood as shown.

Note If a piece of metal is to be bent in several places, the **order** in which the bends are made is often important – so check!

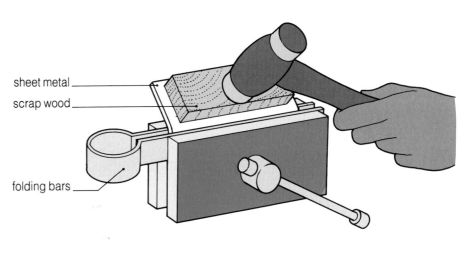

sheet metal

scrap wood

folding bars

Drilling

Drills are used to produce round holes in a material. After marking out the hole's centre, use a centre punch to make a small dent in the metal – this will prevent the drill from slipping.

Whether using a drilling machine or hand drill, always clamp work securely using a hand vice, machine vice or G cramp.

Safety note **If you fail to do this, and the drill jams (when using a drilling machine), the metal will spin and this could cause you serious injury.**

Other metal shaping and forming operations include **lathework** (see page 217) and **casting** (see page 216).

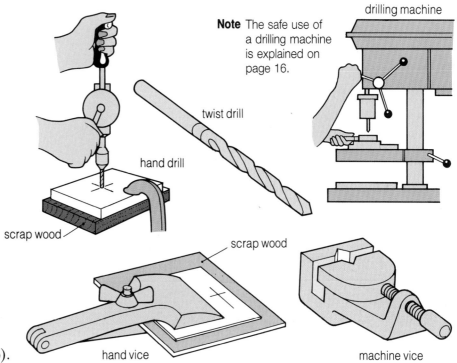

Note The safe use of a drilling machine is explained on page 16.

drilling machine

twist drill

hand drill

scrap wood

scrap wood

hand vice

machine vice

Shaping wood

Sawing

This is usually the first process to be used when shaping wood. A range of different wood cutting saws are available.

A **tenon** saw is used for making short straight cuts – it has a stiff metal back which holds the blade straight and firm.

Hand saws are used for cutting long lengths or sheets of wood. Small curves can be cut with a **coping saw** whose blade can be turned in the frame to allow access to awkward places.

Always hold the work firmly using a vice, bench hook, or G cramp.

Sawing always produces a rough surface, so cut on the waste side of the line and, where required, plane to a smooth finish.

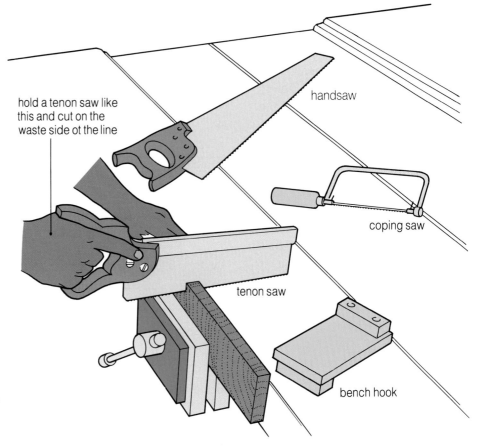

hold a tenon saw like this and cut on the waste side of the line

handsaw

coping saw

tenon saw

bench hook

Planing

Planing is carried out to remove excess wood and to produce a smooth surface finish.

The two most common planes are shown here.

The **jack plane** is heavier and longer than the smoothing plane. It is used for removing excess wood and for producing a smooth surface on **longer** pieces of timber. The **smoothing** plane is a general purpose plane and, as its name suggests, is used for smoothing – particularly on smaller pieces of work.

jack plane

smoothing plane

at the end of the cut, raise the plane like this whilst holding the back pressed down

press

push

Use a plane like this

Useful tips for planing

1 The surface of some types of wood 'roughs up' when planing. When this happens, try planing in the opposite direction.

2 Planing **end grain** often causes the wood to split (as shown). To prevent this, either plane from both ends towards the centre, or clamp pieces of scrap wood to the work as shown.

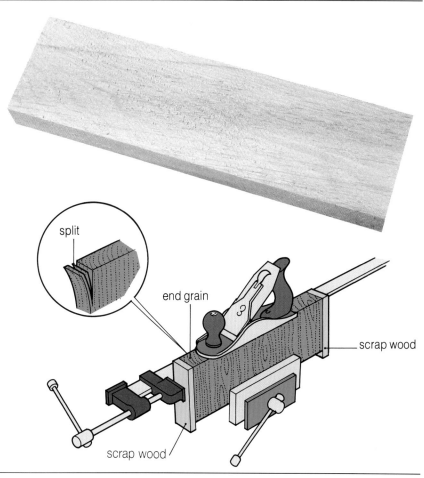

split

end grain

scrap wood

scrap wood

Chisels and their uses

Chisels are used for removing small amounts of wood, often between saw cuts. A chisel can be 'pushed' by hand for fine controlled chiselling, or hit with a wooden mallet.

Two basic types of chisel are used, the **firmer chisel** and the **bevel-edged chisel**. The bevel-edged chisel is the weaker of the two, but its shape allows it to be used in difficult corners.

Safety note   **Keep both hands *behind* the chisel's cutting edge at all times.**

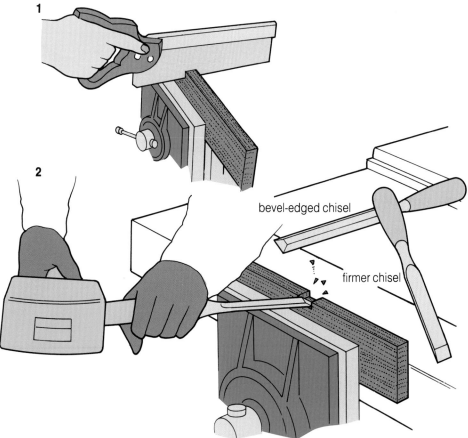

1

2

bevel-edged chisel

firmer chisel

Shaping plastics

Sawing

Acrylic (e.g. Perspex) is probably the most common plastic used in schools, although nylon and other plastics find many uses.

Any of the saws shown here can be used for cutting acrylic. To prevent breaking however, it is important to hold the material firmly, and to regularly move the work so that it is always being gripped in the area of cutting.

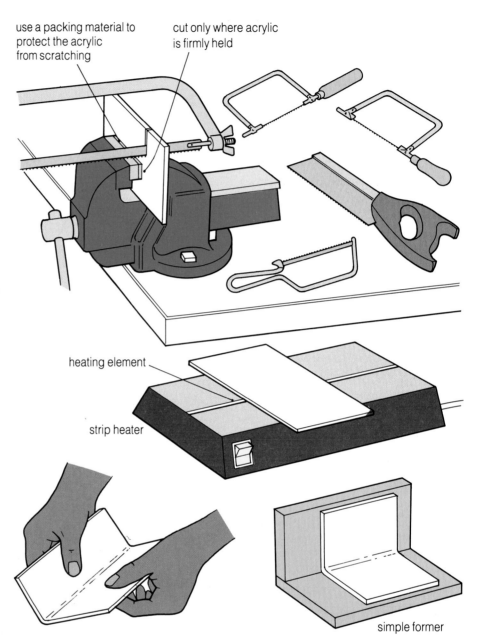

use a packing material to protect the acrylic from scratching

cut only where acrylic is firmly held

Bending

Acrylic sheet is ideally suited to bending because it is a thermoplastic and softens on heating.

After marking out, acrylic can be prepared for bending using a strip heater. This consists of an electric heating element mounted below a narrow opening in a heat resistant material.

The plastic should be turned frequently to ensure even heating and to prevent burning. When the plastic is soft enough it can be bent into the required shape 'freehand' or using a former.

heating element

strip heater

simple former

Vacuum forming

This is a common industrial process which can be carried out in school using relatively inexpensive equipment. The process is used to produce 'hollow' shapes from sheet plastic (see page 252).

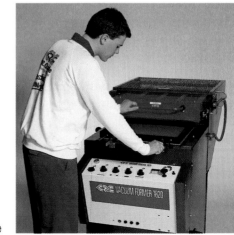

School vacuum-forming machine

Fabrication

Fabrication is the 'putting together' of materials and components to make structures or products.

There are basically three different types of **joint** used for 'fixing' things together. These are **permanent joints, temporary joints** and **moveable joints**.

Some examples of each are shown here.

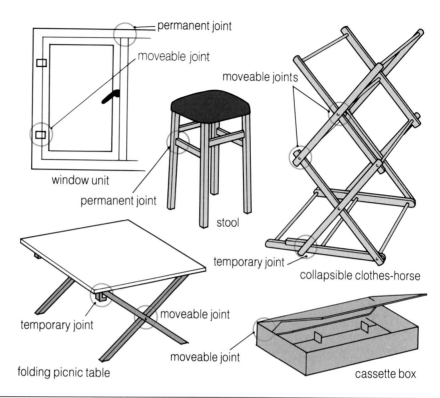

window unit

permanent joint

moveable joint

moveable joints

permanent joint

stool

temporary joint

collapsible clothes-horse

temporary joint

moveable joint

moveable joint

folding picnic table

cassette box

Permanent joints in wood

Many products made from wood are in the form of a **box** structure. These include book cases, drawer units, wardrobes, cabinets etc.

Some examples of the **joints** used in box structures are shown here.

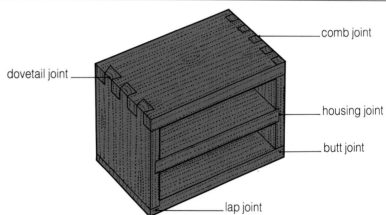

dovetail joint

comb joint

housing joint

butt joint

lap joint

Other products such as chairs, doors, step ladders, stools etc, are examples of **frame** structures.

The diagram shows some examples of frame joints.

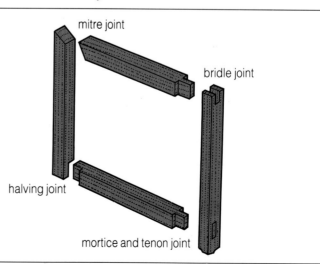

mitre joint

bridle joint

halving joint

mortice and tenon joint

Gluing wood

Most wooden joints are assembled with glue. Glue of course produces a **permanent joint**.

Some joints rely on glue alone and these must be held together firmly until the glue has set.

Other joints are a combination of glue and nails or screws. These do not require clamping but must be left undisturbed until the glue has set.

Nails are produced in many shapes and sizes and are usually made from mild steel. Some examples are shown here.

Screws produce a stronger joint than nails because they 'pull' the joint together. They all have the same basic shape but have different heads. They are most commonly available in mild steel and brass (which may be plated).

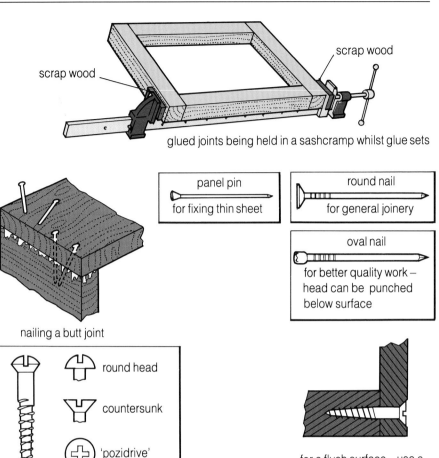

glued joints being held in a sashcramp whilst glue sets

nailing a butt joint

panel pin — for fixing thin sheet

round nail — for general joinery

oval nail — for better quality work – head can be punched below surface

round head

countersunk

'pozidrive'

for a flush surface – use a countersunk head screw

Wood glues

PVA (polyvinylacetate) is a very convenient wood glue. It can be used straight out of the container, but requires 3 to 4 hours to dry. The 'original' PVA is not waterproof and therefore cannot be used for products which come into contact with water. However, a waterproof PVA is now available.

Cascamite is a long established waterproof glue. It is a synthetic resin used where greater strength and water resistance are required. However, it is less convenient to use – it requires mixing with water, but dries within 1 to 2 hours.

Hot glue, delivered by an electrically heated glue gun, is a useful adhesive although not terribly strong. The glue sets very quickly and therefore is only practical for small areas.

mix to a thick paste

gluestick

gluegun

Permanent joints in metal

Soldering

This is the joining of metals with melted solder. A permanent joint is formed on cooling – the strength of the joint being determined by the type of solder used.

Soft soldering

Soft solders are tin–lead alloys. A general purpose solder for use in a school metalwork shop would have a melting point around 230°C. Being a relatively soft substance, it is used mainly for joining thin metals and only produces a relatively weak joint. Most metals can be soldered – but not aluminium.

It is essential that the materials to be joined are thoroughly cleaned. A flux is then applied to keep the materials clean and to help the solder flow into the joint. The complete soldering process (using a gas torch) is illustrated here. For very thin metals a process using a soldering bit would be used.

1 Clean the surfaces to be joined with wire wool or emery cloth.

2 Apply flux to the cleaned surfaces.

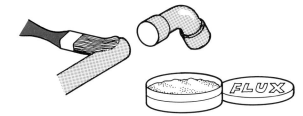

3 Heat the joint. When the metal is hot enough, the solder can be touched on to the joint where it will melt and flow on to the fluxed metal.

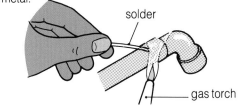

4 Allow the joint to cool.

Soft soldering a pipe fitting

Silver soldering and brazing

Silver solders are alloys of copper, zinc and silver having a melting point between 600 and 800°C. They are used for producing strong, ductile joints in copper, brass and in jewellery work.

Brazing (or hard soldering) makes use of copper–zinc alloys. They are melted at temperatures between 850 and 900°C and produce very strong joints. The process is usually confined to ferrous metals in school but can be successfully used for copper.

Both the above processes follow the stages described opposite.

1 Make sure that the surfaces to be joined are a good fit and are clean.
2 Apply a suitable flux.
3 Where necessary, 'wire' materials together to prevent movement.
4 Position the job on a brazing hearth surrounded by bricks.
5 Bring the joint quickly up to red heat, after first warming up the surrounding metal.
6 Apply solder or brazing rod until the joint is made.
7 Allow the job to cool – then dip into cold water.

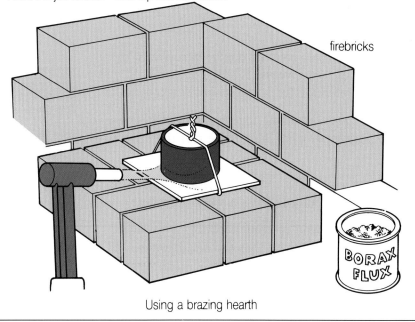

Using a brazing hearth

Welding

When metals are welded, the pieces to be joined are raised to a high temperature and are **fused** together.

Oxyacetylene welding uses burning gases to produce the heat needed for welding. A mixture of acetylene and oxygen in equal quantities produces a temperature around 3150°C. Welding rod is used to provide the extra metal needed to produce a good joint.

Gas welding

In **arc welding** an electric current is made to 'jump' a gap between an **electrode** and the metal being welded, producing a temperature in the region of 3600°C. The heat of the arc melts the electrode and droplets of metal are forced across the arc and onto the metal, forming a weld.

Safety note   **When welding, special goggles, or masks (having 'coloured' glass) *must be worn* to protect the eyes from the glare from the flame or arc. A leather apron and gloves should also be worn to protect against molten metal and flying sparks.**

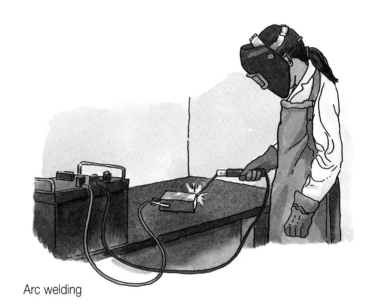

Arc welding

Riveting

Although large scale riveting has been replaced by welding in industry, riveting is still a useful fabrication technique for some school work.

Riveting involves 'trapping together' the pieces of metal to be joined, using metal rivets of the same material.

Countersunk riveting is used when a flush surface is required. The riveting process is illustrated here.

Round or **'snap' head riveting** produces a stronger join than countersunk, but has the disadvantage of leaving the heads protruding above the work surface. Additional simple tools are also required for this process.

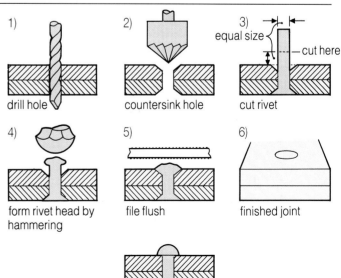

1) drill hole
2) countersink hole
3) equal size — cut here
cut rivet
4) form rivet head by hammering
5) file flush
6) finished joint

snap head rivet in position

Pop riveting is a much quicker and easier process than normal riveting. It uses a special riveting tool and rivets. The resulting joint however, is weaker and less neat.

The riveting process is illustrated here.

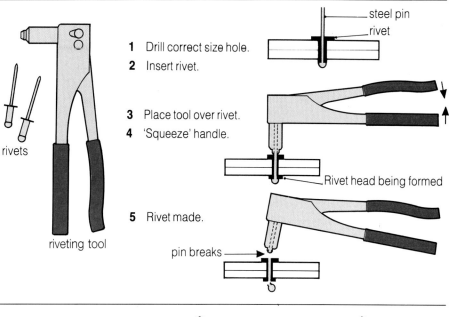

rivets

riveting tool

1 Drill correct size hole.
2 Insert rivet.

3 Place tool over rivet.
4 'Squeeze' handle.

5 Rivet made.

steel pin
rivet

Rivet head being formed

pin breaks

Gluing

Glues are used when other joining methods cannot be used, for example when different kinds of metals are to be joined or when heat would distort the metal, or rivets would spoil the appearance etc. The epoxy resin *Araldite* can be used successfully for joining metals if the surfaces are first roughened using sandpaper.

Rapid Araldite sets in ten minutes, and is quite hard within an hour. 'Standard' *Araldite* requires at least 16 hours to harden.

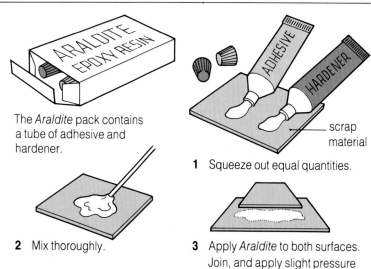

The *Araldite* pack contains a tube of adhesive and hardener.

scrap material

1 Squeeze out equal quantities.

2 Mix thoroughly.

3 Apply *Araldite* to both surfaces. Join, and apply slight pressure until set.

Permanent joints in plastic

Gluing

The most common method (in schools) of producing a permanent joint in plastic is the use of adhesives. If you use the wrong glue for a particular plastic however, it is likely that the plastic will 'break down' or melt.

For acrylic, although *Araldite* can be used successfully, special acrylic glues are better. *Tensol cement* (the trade name of acrylic cements manufactured by ICI) is probably the best known.

To produce a successful joint follow the stages described opposite.

For good results:

1 the joint must be a good fit.
2 the surfaces of the joint must be clean.
3 only use just enough cement for the job.
4 hold the joint securely, applying slight pressure until the cement has set.

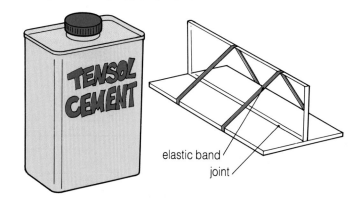

elastic band
joint

Caution Always work in a well ventilated space and avoid inhaling fumes.

Temporary joints

Joints which have to be disconnected, or 'undone' at some time, can be described as **temporary joints**.

Temporary joints are used, for example:

- on devices which have to be erected and dismantled;
- where access is required for maintenance or repair or simply access;
- where a temporary connection has to be made, and so on.

Although '**nuts and bolts**' are widely used in temporary fixings, numerous other devices and components are utilised. Some examples are shown here.

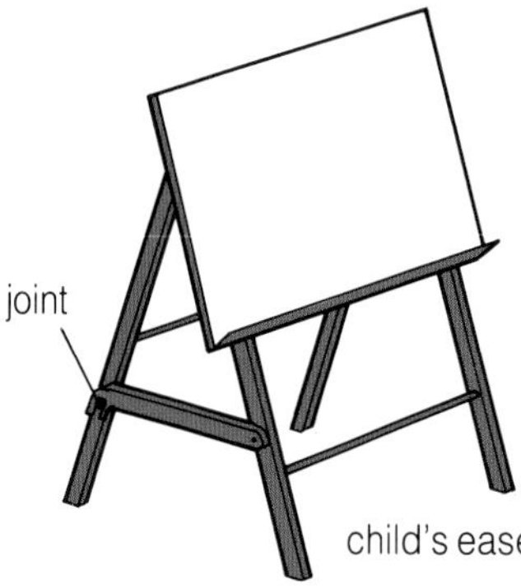

child's easel

gearbox inspection plate
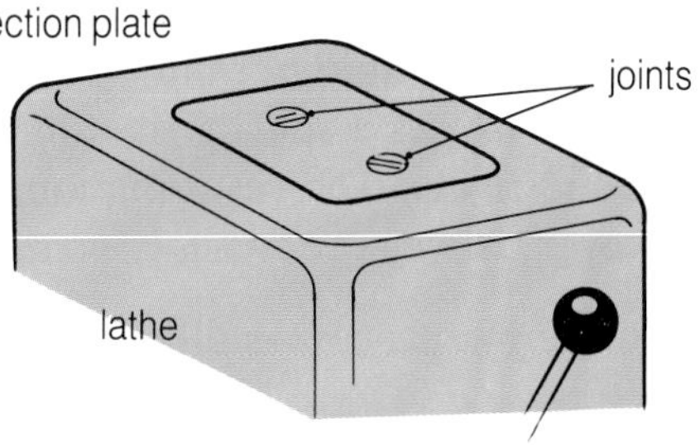

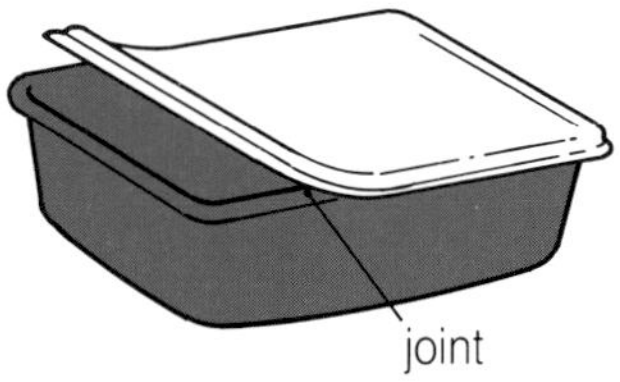

re-sealable margarine tub

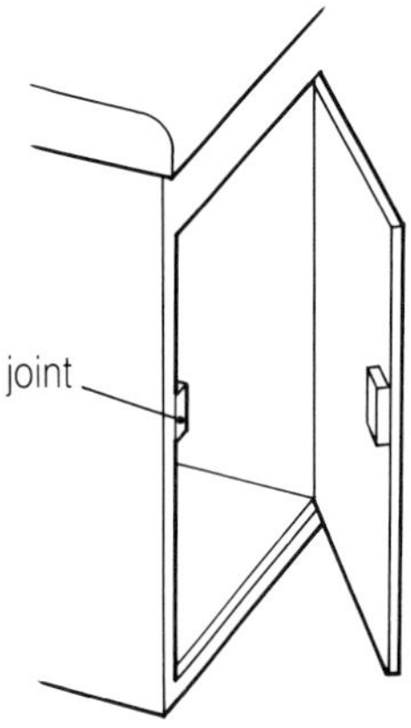

magnetic door latch

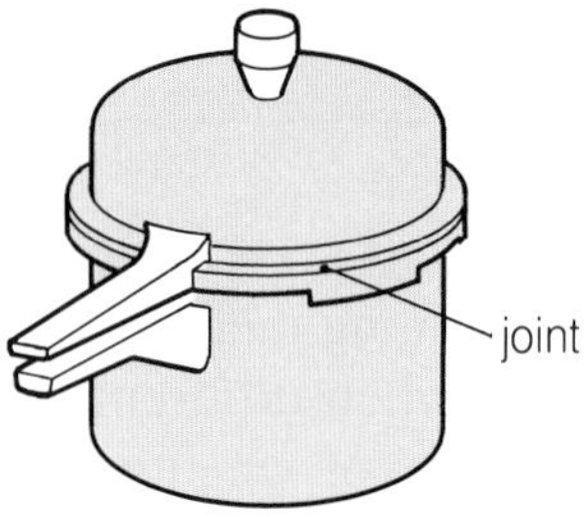

pressure cooker

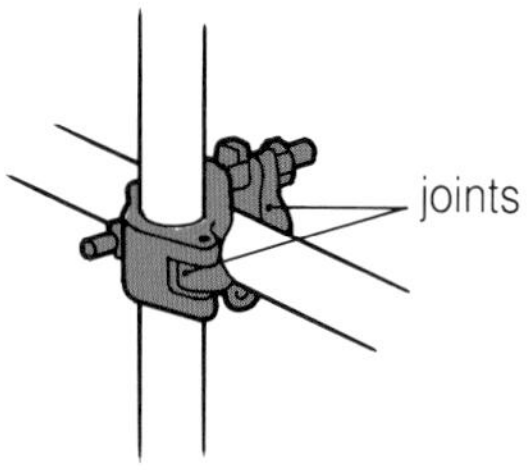

builders' scaffolding

Construction kits

For school technology, a variety of construction kits are available for the temporary assembly of entire projects. These kits of course contain numerous components specially made to form **temporary joints**.

Components from these kits may also be used in conjunction with 'real' materials to manufacture projects.

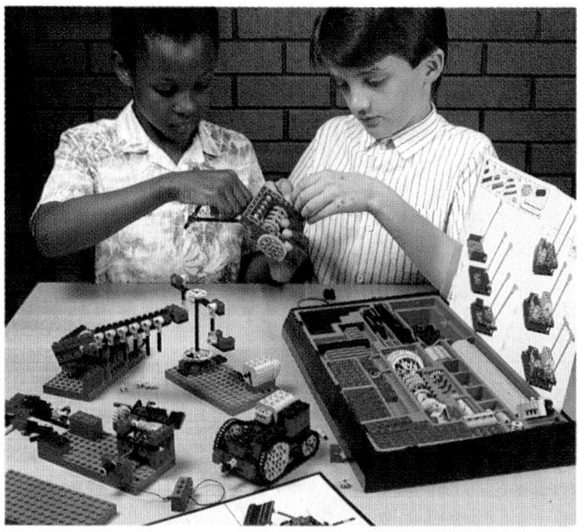
Legotechnic

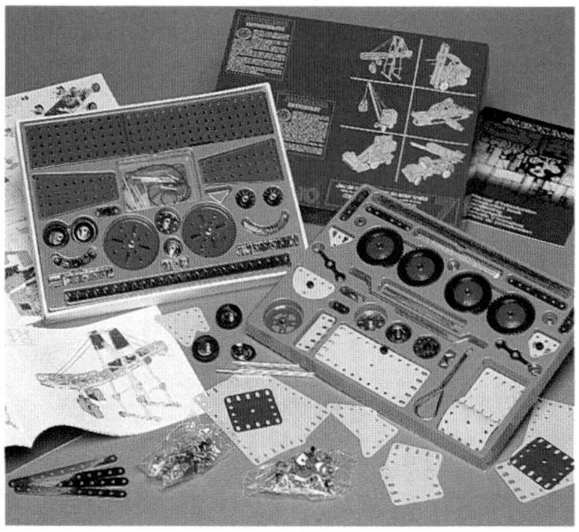
Meccano

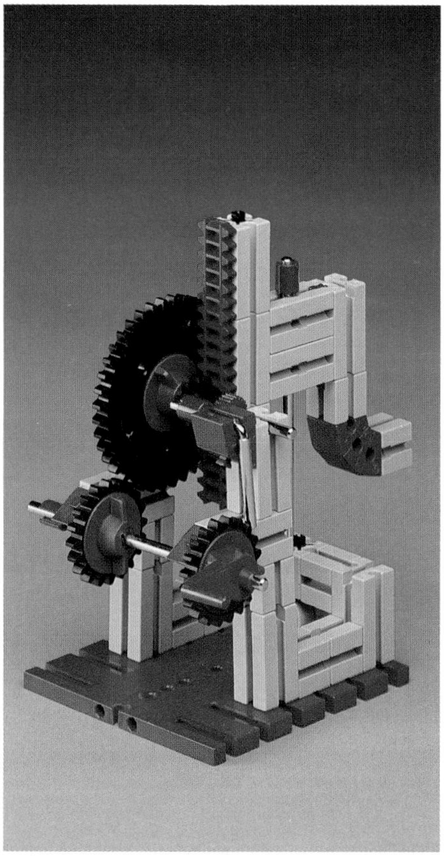
Fischertechnik

Moveable joints

Many devices rely for their operation on moveable joints. The movement may be linear (in a straight line) or rotary (round and round).

Many types of joint rely simply on one material sliding or rotating in contact with another. Others make use of a material's flexibility, and some rely on one material rolling in contact with another. Where prolonged movement is experienced (as in a bearing) lubrication may be required.

Some examples of moveable joints are shown here.

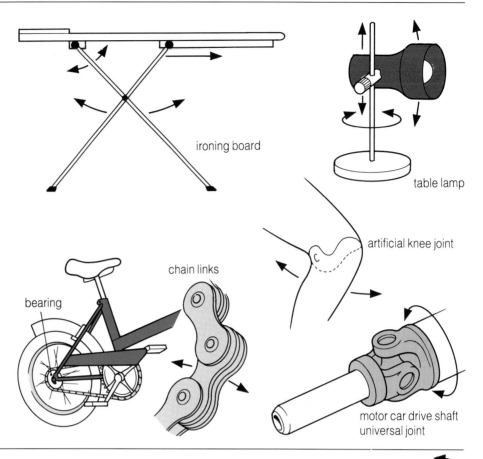

ironing board

table lamp

artificial knee joint

chain links

bearing

motor car drive shaft universal joint

School project work

Construction kits contain a range of specialist moveable joints.

In addition however, ordinary materials and components can be used in all sorts of different ways to form moveable joints in project work.

Some examples are shown here.

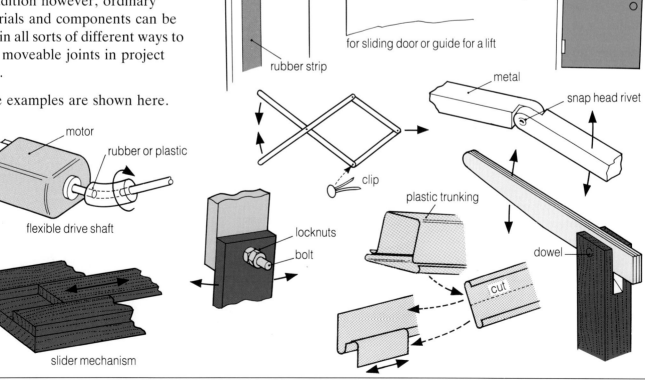

simple hinge

eye   4 mm axle

hinge

rubber strip

for sliding door or guide for a lift

metal

snap head rivet

motor

rubber or plastic

clip

plastic trunking

flexible drive shaft

locknuts

bolt

cut

dowel

slider mechanism

Finishing materials

Surface finishes are used to **protect** a material and to improve or change the way it looks and even the way it feels.

Finishing metals

Some metals need to be protected against the effects of moisture. Ferrous metals, like the carbon steels for example, **rust** if unprotected. Non-ferrous metals however, including copper, brass, and aluminium, do not. Even so, if unprotected these materials eventually lose their shine.

Some common finishes

Oil is sometimes used to provide a temporary protection against rusting.

Paint provides a long term protection providing the surface is well prepared. Cellulose and 'hammer finish' paints are just two types suitable for metals – but don't use emulsion paints on ferrous metals – they contain water. **Always read the instructions** on the tin or can before you begin.

Lacquer can be used on copper and brass for example, to prevent tarnishing. Several different types are available. Cellulose lacquer is just one example – it can be applied successfully using a soft brush whilst working in a warm, dust-free atmosphere.

A **plastic** coat can be applied to a metal to protect it, change its appearance and change the way it feels to the touch. The metal (which must first be heated) is coated by being dipped into a fluidised plastic powder. Many schools have dip coating equipment.

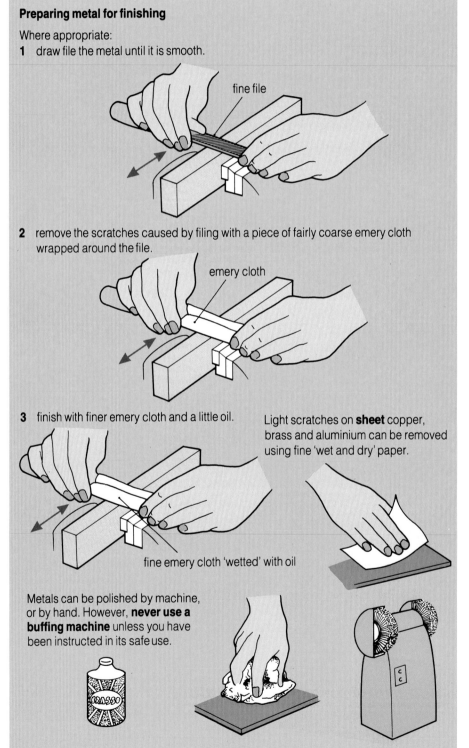

Preparing metal for finishing

Where appropriate:
1 draw file the metal until it is smooth.

fine file

2 remove the scratches caused by filing with a piece of fairly coarse emery cloth wrapped around the file.

emery cloth

3 finish with finer emery cloth and a little oil.

fine emery cloth 'wetted' with oil

Light scratches on **sheet** copper, brass and aluminium can be removed using fine 'wet and dry' paper.

Metals can be polished by machine, or by hand. However, **never use a buffing machine** unless you have been instructed in its safe use.

Finishing wood

Most types of wood require a surface finish to protect them from the effects of moisture (see page 225). In some cases, the finish may also be used to enhance the natural beauty of the wood. Alternatively, a less attractive wood can have its appearance changed by the application of a surface finish.

Some common finishes

Stains are used to change the colour of wood whilst leaving the grain still visible. Numerous different colours and shades are available, but stains **do not** protect the wood against moisture.

Oil finishes (of which linseed is one of the best known) provide a water-resistant, non-gloss finish. All types darken the wood, but leave the grain visible. A liberal quantity should be applied across the grain, left to soak in for an hour or so, and then the surplus wiped off with a soft non-fluffy cloth.

Varnish provides a clear tough surface and can provide a high degree of protection against moisture. Various types and finishes are available. If varnish is applied by brush, first brush across the grain, but finish off by brushing out along the grain.

Paints are used to apply surface colour and to protect against moisture, but they also, of course, provide a different surface texture. Polyurethane gloss paint for example, produces a very smooth shiny surface on wood. Brushing techniques vary for different paints and surfaces – these will be learnt with experience.

To prepare wood for finishing, follow the stages described opposite.

Preparing wood for finishing

1   Sanding should be kept to a minimum (especially on hardwoods) so plane to the best possible finish before sanding.

2   Sand with moderate pressure and always in the direction of the grain. One scratch across the grain takes 'a lot of getting out'.

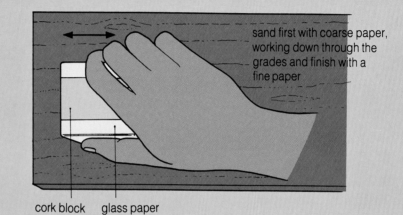

sand first with coarse paper, working down through the grades and finish with a fine paper

cork block   glass paper

3   Use a fine brush to remove dust after sanding – always brush in the direction of the grain.

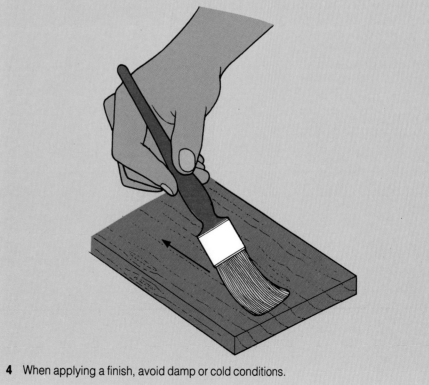

4   When applying a finish, avoid damp or cold conditions.

Finishing plastics

The manufacturing process leaves most plastics with a high quality surface which does not require any kind of surface finish. After cutting and shaping however, the edges (of acrylic for example) will require smoothing. See the illustration opposite.

Some plastics, including acrylic, are supplied with a protective paper covering. This should be 'kept on' for as long as possible during working.

Finishing an edge on acrylic

1 Draw file the edge whilst holding the work firmly in a vice – using a suitable material to protect the surfaces.

2 Carefully smooth the edge using 'wet and dry' – keep the paper moist with clean water.

3 Finally, polish the edge using a special acrylic polish or Brasso.

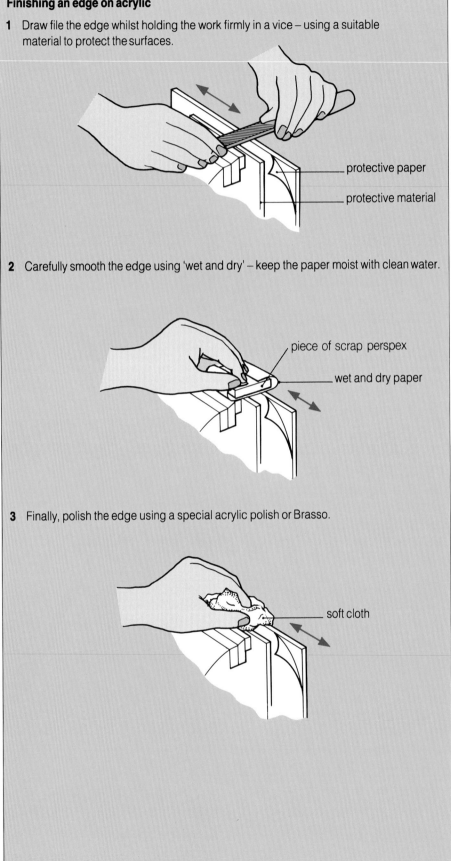

protective paper

protective material

piece of scrap perspex

wet and dry paper

soft cloth

Manufactured products

Modern shopping centres can be exciting places with creative displays of every kind of product. People can spend hours looking for things they need and comparing similar products which are available in different shops.

Many of the products we buy and enjoy using, however, are not designed and made in this country. Some people think that this is an issue of real concern. Indeed, many jobs, our way of life and our prosperity are dependent, to a large extent, on the design and manufacture of products. Increasingly, as trade becomes more international, countries are importing goods they would previously have made themselves, and exporting their own products.

As trade becomes more competitive, product design becomes more important, and many countries have formed organisations to encourage good design. In Britain, for example, this role is carried out by the Design Council. Good design is reflected in the performance of the product, its appearance, finish, ease of use, safety and overall quality. All of this adds value to the product and makes it more competitive.

In this chapter, we are going to look at some of the factors which influence and affect the design and manufacture of consumer products. Use this information to help you when designing at school as you strive to consider an increasing number of users for the products you make and to improve the quality of the design and manufacture of your products.

Product design

If you could **list** all the different **products** which are available in the shops – including toothbrush, jumper, hairdryer, suitcase, telephone, chair, lampshade, teddy bear, CD player, ice lolly, door handle, and so on – your list would be enormous. Now, although these products may all be very different, they all have one thing in common – *they all have 'a job to do'*. In other words, they all have a particular **function** or range of functions to perform.

Different 'makes' of most products are often available of course, like the toothbrushes shown here. As a consumer you have to decide which of the competing brands you prefer. When you do this, you are making a decision about the product's **design**.

What makes a 'good design'?

You will probably agree that a well-designed product is one that **successfully does the job for which it was designed.** Let's investigate this by looking at the design of toothbrushes.

The main function of a toothbrush is to clean teeth. This can be described as its **primary function.** However, it is also important that a toothbrush is easy to use, safe to use, easy to clean, attractive to look at and so on. These functions, *which enhance its use*, are called **secondary functions.**

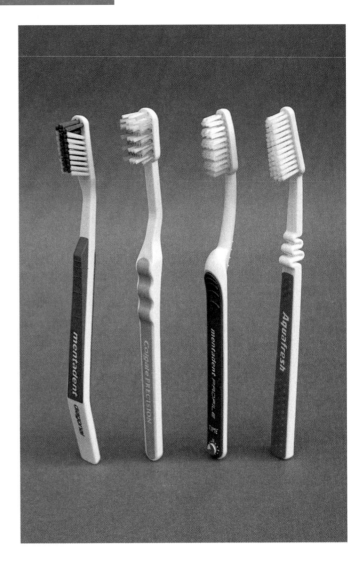

Questions

1 a Using sketches and notes, describe the **parts** of a toothbrush which perform the **primary function** and explain **how** they perform this function.

  b Describe some of the ways in which the design of these parts varies between toothbrushes. Suggest some possible reasons for these variations.

  Before answering the following question, read it carefully, **then** scan pages 21–37, **Aesthetics**, and pages 39–44, **Ergonomics,** picking out relevant information.

  c Look at the toothbrush **handles** above. Describe some of their design features – shape, form, texture, colour, etc., and explain how you think these features help to satisfy some of the **secondary functions** of a toothbrush.

Quality of design

You have just analysed and described the functions of a toothbrush. For some of this analysis you used your knowledge of **scientific** and **technical** principles. The branch of design concerned with these principles is called **engineering design**, or product design.

Other functions required you to understand the characteristics which made the product **'user friendly'** and **aesthetically** pleasing. The branch of design concerned with these principles is called **industrial design**.

When engineering and industrial design are brought together in a creative way, the result *should* be products which work well, look good, are safe to use, are environmentally friendly and can be manufactured easily. Products which satisfy these requirements to a high standard can be said to have a **quality of design**. Let's investigate some of the factors which reflect quality of design.

Function and reliability

Products must be designed to perform to the highest possible standards and work reliably. It is important that the designs also **meet the needs** of the user – not only with regard to their functions, but also as a **design** which will form part of the user's environment.

Fly sheet   Inner tent   Poles

Ground sheet   Guy lines

Steering mechanism

Chassis

Brake   Pedal

Questions

2 a List all the **functions** of a video recorder which must work reliably to ensure complete user satisfaction. In each case, explain how a malfunction would affect the product's performance.

b Explain the **functions** of the labelled parts of the touring dome tent shown, and

c Outline the **properties** of each of the materials used for these parts, which are important for the tent's **reliability**.

d Describe a **range of factors** which are important to the successful **functioning** and **reliability** of the child's go-kart shown.

e Name one product, which in your experience did **not work reliably**. Describe how its unreliability affected its use throughout its life.

Function and reliability – continued

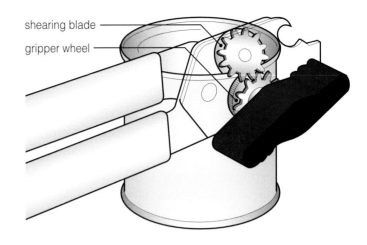

shearing blade
gripper wheel

Questions

3 There is 'nothing worse' than a can opener which is unreliable. Faults can include poor grip of the can and failure to produce a continuous cut.

The primary function of a can opener is usually performed by a **gripper wheel**, which grips and rotates the can, and a **shearing blade**, which cuts the metal to remove the lid. Several different designs are available.

The mechanism on the can opener shown here is a particularly good design. It produces good grip and can rotation with a resulting accurate continuous cut. This is partly achieved by the use of a **rotating** shearing blade.

Before you answer the questions below, read page 79 – **Gear systems**.

a The gripper wheel rotates when the can opener is operated. What mechanism ensures that the shearing blade also rotates and does not slip?

b Is it necessary for the two gears to have the same number of teeth? Explain your answer.

c What changes would have to be made to make the shearing blade **rotate faster** than the gripper wheel? Can you foresee any advantages or disadvantages of such a design?

d The two gears rotate in **opposite directions** to one another. Why is this important to the successful operation of the can opener?

e To aid **reliability**, can openers should be maintained (cleaned and lubricated) regularly. Does the design of the can opener enable this to be carried out easily? Explain your answer.

f This can opener also has a bottle opener facility. Draw a simple diagram to show how it works. What kind of **lever** system is it? Use the index to look up levers and check your answer.

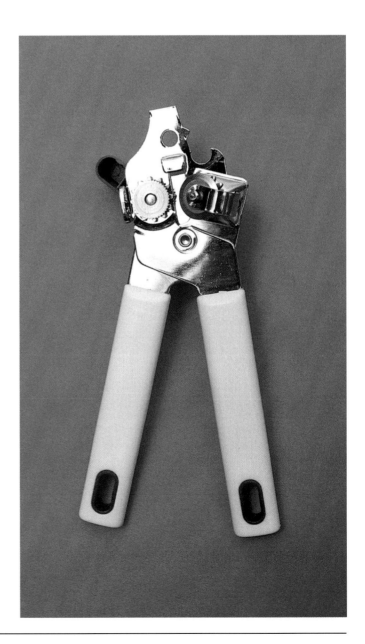

Safety and efficiency

Products should be designed to provide the greatest safety, comfort and advantage to the user. They should be **ergonomically safe** and **technically safe**.

Question

4 Before answering the following question, read it carefully, **then** read pages 39–44, **Ergonomics**, picking out relevant information.

Vacuum cleaners are in frequent use and do a demanding job. In addition to their technical function – 'vacuuming' – they have to be pushed and pulled, carried, switched on and off, have their dust bags emptied, and so on.

Describe all the factors which must be taken into consideration in the design of an 'upright cleaner' to ensure: (1) **user safety**, (2) **user comfort** and (3) **ease of use**.

Safety – continued

In addition to making products safe to use through good ergonomic design, they should also be technically safe.

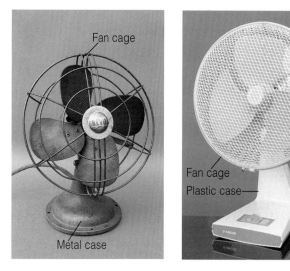

Fan cage

Metal case

Fan cage
Plastic case

Questions

5 a Two domestic fans are shown opposite. One is a very old product and the other is modern. Explain in detail why the modern design is so much safer.

b Safety plugs were introduced several years ago. Which of the two plugs shown *is* a safety plug? Describe why the old style plug was potentially dangerous and how the new design has overcome the problem.

Activity 1

Many electrical appliances are made safer by being **double insulated**. Find out what this means by speaking to your local electrical dealer.

Safety – use and misuse

All products should be designed to meet the highest possible safety standards which *anticipate* both the dangers of normal use, and misuse, throughout the life of the product.

Question

A young child could be seriously injured if it fell down the stairs. **Stair gates** are a very effective way of helping to prevent this.

6 A stair gate could be made from solid panels – but most are not. Describe and explain all the factors which are important to the safe design of a stair gate made from **bars**.

Activity 2

a Whilst it should be impossible for a young child to open a stair gate, it should be easy for an adult or an older child to do so. Design (on paper) a 'locking system' which would fulfil this requirement.

b A stair gate **left open** by mistake is an example of the product's misuse. In anticipation of this problem, design an electronic warning system which would sound an alarm after 15 seconds if the stair gate were left open. If you need help, read about timing circuits on pages 145–150.

Stair gate

Risk assessment

As a designer and maker at school, you should be constantly alert to health and safety hazards in the working environment and hazards associated with workshop activities. As a consumer, you should also be concerned about health and safety factors associated with the products you buy.

Question

7 Look carefully at the Baby Walker shown here and: Describe a range of factors which you consider are important to the safe use of this kind of product, by a very young child. Include in your answer reference to: ergonomic factors, mechanical functions, component parts and materials.

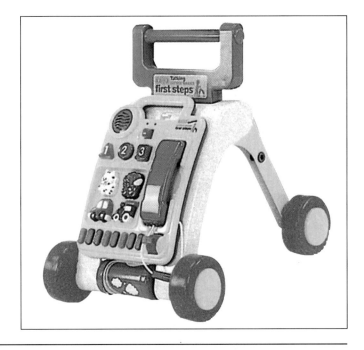

Maintenance

Products should be designed to require very little maintenance – but where it is necessary, it should be easy to carry out. This will include the removal and exchange of component parts and batteries, adjustment, lubrication, and the most basic maintenance – cleaning.

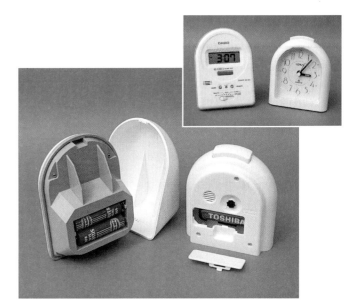

Question

8 Two different products requiring **access** for maintenance are shown here. The clocks require access to their batteries and the electric shaver requires access for cleaning.

   a Explain and compare the **means of access** in the two clocks with reference to **function** and **aesthetics**.

   b When the shaver is in use, the three shaving heads are rotated by three drive shafts driven by an electric motor contained in the body of the shaver.

   What technical problem had to be overcome in the design of the **drive shafts** to allow the shaving head to be removed and replaced?

   c Name and draw two other products which require access for technical maintenance, and two products which require access for cleaning. In each case, explain why the access is required.

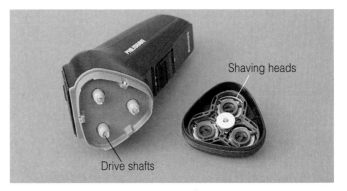

Shaving heads

Drive shafts

Activity 3

Maintenance is not the only reason for access to the 'inside' of a product. **Containers** of every kind require access, of course, to do their jobs as 'containers'.

Collect a range of plastic bottles with **different closures** (different tops). Study the closure designs carefully and in each case:

a Describe the nature of the product which is stored in the container – viscous liquid, powder, etc.

b Describe the **design** of the closure and explain in detail how it retains the product and how it allows the product to be dispensed.

Aesthetic qualities

Whilst it is essential that products function properly and safely, because we are surrounded by manufactured products and because we have feelings and emotions, **it is also important** that the designs 'look good'. The qualities which make a design attractive to look at or pleasing to experience determine its **aesthetic** appeal.

Through **quality of design**, products can have a 'pleasing appearance' and that appearance can have a big impact on consumer choice.

Questions

Read pages 22–24 and 32–34, **Aesthetics**, before answering the following questions.

9 Look carefully at the products on this page and for each design:

  a Describe what you like and what you dislike about their **shape** and **form**, and

  b Describe your feeling about **proportion**, **symmetry** and other **visual elements** in the designs.

Read page 25, **Aesthetics**, before answering the following question.

10 For each design, describe the use of surface texture and its affect on the product's **appearance** and **use**.

Read pages 26–31, **Aesthetics**, before answering the following questions.

11 For each design:

  a Describe in detail how **colour** has been used **and to what effect**, and

  b Explain how the choice of material for the product has affected or dictated the finished colour of the product.

People and 'the market'

If you asked lots of different people to answer questions 9–11a (page 280) you would almost certainly receive lots of different answers. They would be different because people's **tastes** are different – and they are different for many reasons. For example, people belong to different **age groups**, different **cultures**, have different **interests** and **life styles**. In addition, they have different **incomes**. All of these factors can affect which products a person chooses to buy. All of these factors, therefore, and many others (not least fashion) must be taken into consideration by designers as they consider *the market for which the product is intended*.

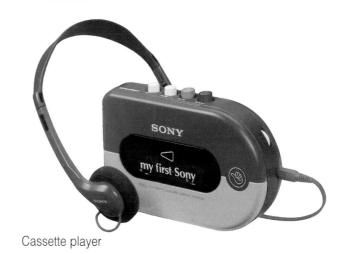

Cassette player

Questions

12 A **cassette player** is shown above. Think about its use and the *market for which it was intended*. A simple market analysis sheet is shown opposite.

  a Do you agree with this analysis? If not, what would you change? Explain your answer.

  b Complete a similar market analysis sheet for any three products of your choice. Choose products which are very different.

Market analysis – cassette player

Need – musical entertainment
Age group – 5–8
Gender – male or female
Culture – non specific
Life style – play
Income bracket – not directly applicable
Fashion considerations – young modern image

---

13 Taste is concerned with **how people perceive things aesthetically**. You should have a fair understanding of this having read the **Aesthetics** chapter and answered questions 9, 10 and 11.

Look at the photographs of the different styles of jug kettle shown here. Which style do you prefer, **which is to your taste?**

In answering the above question, refer to shape, form, texture, colour, proportion, etc., and explain why you feel the way you do about these features in each design.

Society and the environment

The manufacture, use and disposal of any product can have both beneficial and detrimental effects upon people, wildlife and the environment. All products, therefore, should be designed to minimise the detrimental effects.

Product manufacture

Modern shopping centres are exciting places full of enticing products often in a spotless environment. It is important to remember, however, that many of the processes used to make these products, or the materials from which the products are made, produce **waste**. All waste is unsightly; some waste can be dangerous. **Toxic waste** is very dangerous – it can damage the health of people and wildlife. About 90% of toxic waste comes from industry and it is essential that this is kept away from living things. This can be done by **burying**, **burning** and **dumping**, but these methods are not always successful. Leaks from containers, seepage from landfill sites and air pollution from incinerators, for example, all contribute towards environmental pollution. In addition, some industries discharge their waste into rivers, and waste has, for hundreds of years, been dumped at sea.

In addition to pollution caused by waste materials, huge quantities of **energy** are used by the manufacturing industries, and energy production itself causes pollution.

Many industries have responded to pressure from governments, pressure groups and consumers to reduce toxic waste by (a) developing alternative methods of waste disposal, and (b) designing products and using processes which avoid producing toxic waste in the first place.

Product use

We all have a responsibility for pollution, because **we all demand products** – but the problem doesn't stop at manufacturing. People, wildlife and the environment can be put at risk when we simply **use** products. Motor cars, for example, kill thousands of people every year and their exhaust fumes pollute the atmosphere. Some aerosol cans still use CFCs as propellant gases, which damage the ozone layer. Many products use electricity and the burning of fossil fuels in power stations produces sulphur dioxide which helps to make acid rain, and so on.

Some people believe that consumers need to **modify their behaviour** with regard to product use with the aim of reducing environmental damage and providing a healthier environment for people to live in. We could, for example, use products more **efficiently**, take greater **care** of products and the built environment to make them last longer, choose products which **waste less energy** and **use less materials**, and we could **reduce our demand** for products.

Product disposal

Discarded products, along with household and industrial refuse, are collected in huge quantities from dustbins every week. Some of this waste is sorted and the materials recycled, some is incinerated or compressed to reduce its volume, but the majority is disposed of untreated in landfill sites. The decomposition of waste produces many pollutants. Some can dissolve in water and if these get into ground water or rivers they can kill plants and animals and make the water unfit for drinking. Good **siting**, good **design** and good **management** of landfill sites are therefore very important. Clearly, good waste management of all kinds is essential in a high technology society to reduce to a minimum the detrimental effects of consumerism.

Questions

Some manufacturers have introduced new products which they claim are better for the environment. Labels such as 'ozone friendly', 'recyclable', 'biodegradable', and so on, appear on product packaging. But are these claims always completely true?

14 Work with a group of friends and collect from home a range of different products which make similar claims and, to the best of your ability, investigate them and write a short report on your findings.

15 Giving **party bags** to children at the end of a birthday party is now commonplace. In addition to sweets and cake, parents often include **plastic toys and novelties** of which a huge range is available. Plastic is made from chemicals obtained from crude oil, and to a much lesser extent, coal. These are **non-renewable resources** – they will eventually run out. It could be argued, therefore, that consumers should modify their behaviour with regard to the use of these products.

a What are your views on the value of party bags to children's enjoyment and on the consumption of raw materials and energy to produce the bags and their contents?

b Describe any areas in which you think consumers could modify their buying habits and of what benefit this would be.

16 Manufacturing processes used to make everyday products sometimes produce waste which can be dangerous if mismanaged. **But consumers can also mismanage waste**. We all use products and therefore have a responsibility to dispose of the waste safely. Poisons like weedkiller (left in the bottom of the container) and disposed of in the dustbin, and old motor oil poured down the drain, are two examples of waste mismanagement by consumers.

State two other examples of waste mismanagement and suggest some measures which could be taken to **ensure** that it **could not** happen in the future.

Refuse tip

Questions

17 Energy is consumed during the manufacture of every kind of product and it is important, therefore, that manufacturers continually strive to reduce energy use and wastage. In addition, of course, many products consume energy throughout their working life – and this includes all types of electrical appliances. No appliance is 100% efficient – they all waste some energy, but some waste more energy than others. In 1995 the European Union introduced an **Energy Labelling** scheme for household appliances. All refrigerators and freezers must now display the label shown here. The 'A–G' coloured scale shows the consumer, at a glance, the **efficiency** of the appliance (to which the label is attached) compared to other appliances in the same category. An 'A' rated appliance would use less than half the energy of a 'G' rated appliance of the same type.

a In what ways does a more efficient refrigerator benefit (a) the consumer, and (b) the environment?

b Will the labelling scheme affect consumer buying habits, in your opinion? Explain your answer.

c In what ways do you think the labelling scheme might affect manufacturers?

18 All products have an impact beyond the purpose for which they were designed. All designers, therefore, have a responsibility to design products which will:

a use less energy,
b use less materials,
c be safer in use,
d be less environmentally damaging during their manufacture, use and disposal.

Choose any product with which you are familiar and try to **redesign** it to improve on the requirements in list **a–d**.

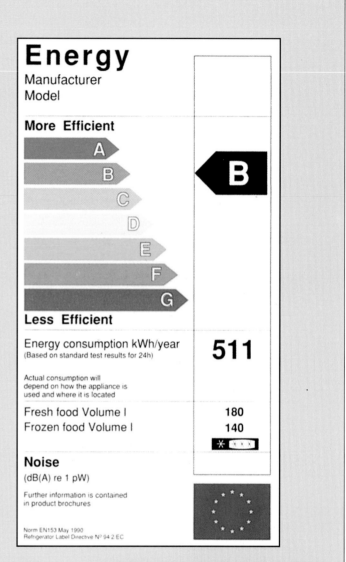

Trevor Baylis, the inventor, with his clockwork radio designed for use in countries where batteries are prohibitively expensive

Materials, components and manufacturing

It is not enough to design products which work well and look good, they should also be **designed for ease of manufacture**. However, because the method of manufacture is largely dictated by the materials used, both **materials** and **manufacturing processes** must be considered together.

Look at the cassette carousel here. Like all products its **functions**, **appearance**, **safety**, **reliability**, **durability**, and overall **quality**, are all affected by the materials used. It is the materials' **properties** which determine their suitability for the product. We investigate the materials used for the cassette carousel below, and on page 286 we will look at its manufacture.

The primary function of a cassette carousel is to provide storage and access for cassette tapes. But it also has to satisfy a range of secondary functions. Some of the **material requirements** for this product are suggested here. Think about these requirements as you answer the questions below.

Cassette carousel

Material requirements

- rigid
- medium strength
- medium density
- scratch resistant
- transparent
- quality finish

Question

19 Many of the component parts for the above product are made from the plastic known as acrylic. Read about acrylic now on page 245, and then using the information gained, and your own experience of using acrylic at school, answer the following questions.

  a Does acrylic **meet the material requirements** for the cassette carousel as outlined above? Explain your answer.

  b How suitable do you think acrylic is for this product with regard to **durability**? Durability is concerned with how well something wears and lasts. Remember to consider the kind of use the product will experience.

  c Describe your feelings about the use of acrylic in this product with particular reference to its **appearance**. Remember to consider the **environment** in which the product is likely to be used.

Methods of manufacture

The way a product is manufactured is largely dictated by the materials used. In the case of the cassette carousel, the component parts were **injection moulded**. This process was used because (a) thermoplastics were used for its manufacture, and (b) it would be difficult to manufacture the component parts using any other plastic moulding or forming technique. Read about injection moulding **now** on page 250.

Look again at the cassette carousel on page 285 and look at the component parts shown here.

Can you see that the **transparent acrylic section** is **made up of many small standard parts**? This is a clever design which keeps the cost of production to a minimum, since only **one small mould** is required to provide the components for this large section of the product. This is reflected in the final cost of the product (less than £5 in 1996).

Cassette carousel – component parts

Questions

You may need to refer to page 250 again when answering questions 20 and 21.

20 Some of the factors which can affect the **quality of appearance** of a product are listed opposite.

Which of these factors **benefits directly** from the use of the **injection moulding** process? Explain your answer.

Shape and form
Style
Surface detail
Texture
Colour
Surface finish

21 The cassette carousel is assembled from **20 component parts**. Which factors listed opposite are important to the satisfactory **assembly** and **performance** of the product? Explain your answer.

Style
Texture
Accurate dimensions
Colour
Surface detail

22 Name one other **non plastic** material which could have been used to make a similar cassette carousel and describe how it might be manufactured.

Methods of manufacture – continued

Look at the picture **frames** below. They all have the same basic
function – to protect and display pictures – but they all have very
different styles and appearances. The differences arise by 'design' and
by the use of different materials and components and different
manufacturing processes.

Questions

23 Before answering the questions below: (a) read pages 213 – **Press forming**, 216 – **Sand casting** and
Die casting, 234 – **Moulding**, and 252 – **Vacuum forming**, and (b) read the descriptions of the picture
frames below.

A Plastic – thin, flimsy, no joints
B Metal – thick, heavy, accurate surface detail, no joints
C Wood – light, rigid, mitred joints
D Metal – thin, rigid, no joints
E Metal – heavy, poor surface detail, no joints

a State which method of manufacture you think was used to produce frames A to E and explain your
reasoning in each case.

b Frame F is made from a fast-setting **resin** (see **Polyester resin**, page 248). How do you think it
was manufactured?

c **Protection and display** is the **primary function** of picture frames. One of their **secondary functions** is
to look good themselves. Describe the appearance of picture frames A to F and say how the choice of
materials and manufacturing processes has influenced their style and overall appearance.

Methods of manufacture – continued

Questions

Two ice cream scoops, designed to perform the same basic function, **but manufactured in different materials**, are shown opposite. The component parts from which they were assembled are shown below. Notice that one is constructed mainly from metal components and the other is constructed mainly from plastic components.

Before answering the questions below, read page 213 – **Industrial manufacturing with metals**, and page 250 – **Injection moulding**.

24 Look at the component parts for the **metal** ice cream scoop.

   a How do you think the **scoop head** and **handle components** were manufactured?

   b Explain briefly the **processes used** and the **stages of manufacture**.

   c Read about **Permanent joints in metal** (pages 265–266) and then state (with reasons) which method you think was used to attach the scoop head to the handle.

25 Look at the component parts for the **plastic** ice cream scoop.

   a How do you think the **scoop head** and **handle** components were manufactured?

   b Explain briefly the **manufacturing process**.

Functions question

26 Squeezing the handles (in both products) operates a **mechanism** which rotates a 'blade' in the scoop head to release the ice cream.

   a Read page 86 and then explain (using a labelled diagram) how you think this mechanism works.

   b When the handles are released, the blade returns to its normal position. In the plastic product, it is the springiness of the plastic which drives the mechanism in reverse. How is the mechanism in the metal product driven in reverse? Use a diagram in your explanation.

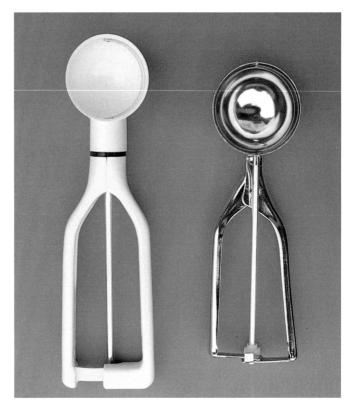

Ice cream scoops

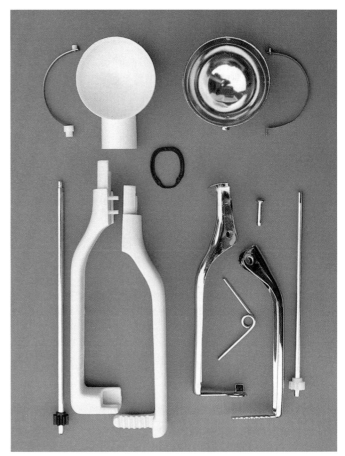

Component parts

Team activity – production line simulation

In this section on manufacturing, you have read about a range of **individual** production processes. In the manufacture of many products, however, a **range** of processes and operations are often required to produce the finished product, and these are often carried out on a **production line**.

In recent years, many industrial production processes have been redesigned to reduce the amount of energy they use and the quantity of material they waste. In addition, **quality control** has been improved to ensure that products are produced to a consistently high standard. In the past, quality control often meant inspecting a product **after it had come off the production line** to check that it had been made to a satisfactory standard, and if it had not, it was discarded. This system, of course, was very wasteful of energy and resources, and made products less competitive. Today, quality control relies on a system of management which aims to ensure that **everything which contributes to the production of a product operates to high standards** with the aim of **preventing** errors, such as poor quality products, from happening. This will include:

a   continuously **monitoring** people, processes and materials at every stage in the chain of production (including outside suppliers of materials and components) to identify where problems have arisen or could arise (in relation to quality and performance) and to introduce procedures to correct them;

b   **checking the quality** of component parts and products **throughout** the manufacturing process, recording the results for future reference, and taking action to correct any problems which arise;

c   encouraging every department and individual to take **responsibility** for quality at all times, and to feed back relevant information to management.
This approach is sometimes called TQM – Total Quality Management.

Activity 4

Your task is to simulate a highly efficient production line which uses TQM. Work with a group of friends to manufacture 10 **high quality door wedges** using the materials and design shown here. Decide on the most **efficient** way to make the product – and who will do what. Then choose someone to be the **production manager** to keep control of the activity. You should try to ensure that:

● the product can be completed in a specified **time** period;
● materials, tools and equipment are in the **correct place** at all times, and that their **quality** is of a consistently high standard;
● all processes are constantly **monitored** and **tests carried out** to check that (a) they are operating efficiently, and (b) that the parts produced are being manufactured to a high standard – and if not, this can be corrected;
● everyone is encouraged to take **responsibility** for quality control;
● material and energy usage is monitored and measures taken to **keep its use to a minimum**.

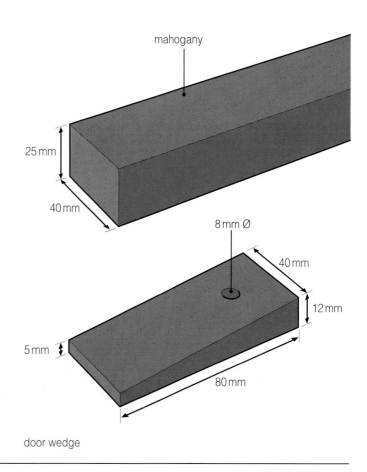

mahogany

25 mm

40 mm

8 mm Ø

40 mm

12 mm

5 mm

80 mm

door wedge

Production manager's report

When production is complete, evaluate (a) the **quality** of the product itself (consistency of size, quality of finish, etc.), and (b) the **processes** used to make the product. Finally, suggest any modifications which you could make to (a) improve the product's **quality**, (b) improve the **efficiency** of the production method, and (c) reduce the amount of waste material produced.

Quality assurance

If you were a real business, which manufactured door wedges, how would you convince a prospective buyer that you were capable of producing large quantities of the product **to a consistently high standard?**

Some businesses do this by obtaining a **BSI Registered Firm** certificate. BSI Quality Assurance sets down *rigorous standards concerning the procedures needed* [within a given business] *to produce high quality products that will meet customer requirements*. Achieving a certificate is a lengthy procedure but the result will be a highly organised, documented quality management system which should:

● improve customer perception of the firm's performance,
● improve consistency of product performance resulting in greater customer satisfaction, and
● improve productivity and efficiency resulting in improved competitiveness.

Computer aided manufacture

Many products which were once made by people are now manufactured by machines controlled by computers. This is called **Computer Aided Manufacture, CAM**. Often, the products are first designed on a **CAD** system. CAD (Computer Aided Design) uses an electronic drawing board, a powerful computer and a high resolution monitor, and allows the designer to design products on a computer screen – rather than on paper. With some systems, the designer can even **test** the performance of the design on screen. All the information related to the design (the **data**) is then stored in a data base. This data can then be used to control the machines and equipment used to manufacture the products. These will include: conveyor systems, lathes, milling machines, presses and robot arms which can manipulate all sorts of tools, welding equipment, and so on. A product, therefore, can be designed, tested and manufactured with the aid of a computer. This is the CAD/CAM system.

Computer-aided manufacture at Saab Automobile AB

Industrial production methods

Products are manufactured in a variety of different ways. Where **large quantities** of a product are to be manufactured, and over a long period of time, **flow production** is most often used. Car manufacture in a modern factory is an example of flow production.

Production is organised so that **different** operations are carried out, **one after the other**, in a **continuous sequence** until the product is complete.

In many industries, flow production is highly automated and controlled by computers (**CAM**). A number of linked computers will co-ordinate and control the many thousands of operations needed to complete a complex product. This can include the movement of raw materials, the manufacture of component parts, assembly of the parts, inspection, and so on.

A Rover 400 in the robotic glazing cell

Another method of production called **batch production** is used mainly for the manufacture of smaller products and component parts in **smaller quantities** or batches. Batch production is often organised so that **one operation** is completed on a **whole batch** of components (usually transported on a pallet), and then the batch is moved on to the next stage of manufacture where the next process is completed. The batch continues along the production line in this way until all stages in the product's manufacture are complete. Computer controlled machines, used in batch production, are often so versatile that they can be programmed to manufacture a particular product or component on one day, and a totally different product or component the next day.

Batch production at Cadbury

Consumer choice

For most purchases, consumers can choose from *a range of alternative products* in the same market 'slot'. Products, therefore, have to compete against the opposition for sales.

One very powerful opponent is **brand name**. Names like 'Coca Cola', 'Sony', 'Rover', 'Panasonic', etc., are just a few examples. They identify the product to the purchaser and differentiate it from the competitors – but that's not all. The brand name says a lot about the product itself. It says something about its quality, reputation, history, cost and so on.

Activity 5

Look at the brand name logos for the cameras shown here. Even though you may never have bought a camera yourself, you will almost certainly have an opinion on which is the 'best make'.

Draw a 'tick chart' similar to the one shown opposite and use it to give each brand a **score**. The scores should be between 1 and 10 and should indicate how highly *you* 'rate' each brand in terms of **quality** and **reputation**.

Score	1	2	3	4	5	6	7	8	9	10
OLYMPUS										
Canon										
SAMSUNG										
PENTAX®										
Vivitar										

Questions

27 If all the above manufacturers produced a camera of the **same quality**, with **identical features** and **performance** and at the **same price** (£125):

a Which camera would you buy? Explain your answer.

b Would you buy the camera at the bottom of your list if the manufacturer's recommended price was £105? Explain your answer.

28 What does the above tell you about the importance of brand names and their effect on consumer choice?

Advertising

Many companies spend millions of pounds each year on advertising their products. Advertising, of course, **makes people aware of the existence of different products** – but that's not all. Some advertising aims to persuade the consumer that a particular product is **better or more desirable** than similar products on the market. Through the media of advertising, therefore, products have to compete against the opposition.

Questions

29 Persuasive advertising – the kind which stresses that one product is better or more desirable than another – can, it is argued, persuade consumers to buy products which they might otherwise not have bought. To avoid disappointment, therefore, consumers should always try to **become fully informed *themselves*** about the quality and performance of competing products before they buy. Several ways to do this are suggested here.

Write an account giving your opinion about the usefulness of each method in obtaining **correct information**, and describe the advantages and disadvantages of each approach.

a Talk to friends who own similar products.

b Examine and appraise the products yourself.

c Question shop assistants.

d Read consumer magazines (*Which?*, for example)

Fitness for purpose

When choosing products from the range of alternatives available, it is *you* who must make the final choice. You must decide if the product *meets your needs, is fit for the purpose for which it was designed* and *is value for money*. The more informed you become about how products function, and the more alert you are to design characteristics, the more likely you will be to choose products which will function to your satisfaction and be to your liking.

See how much you know, and what you can learn about products, by completing the work in this chapter. You will find **questions** to answer, and **activities** and **investigations** to carry out.

See also the **Product design summary and questions** on pages 304 and 305 to help you. Guidance and information on disassembling products is also given at the end of the chapter (pages 306–309).

Questions

A **stubby** POZIDRIV **screwdriver** is shown here.

A range of information related to its use is displayed on the packaging and is quoted below.

Other information to help you to answer question 31 is also given below.

a 'Ergonomically designed grip combines torque power and user comfort'

b 'Hexagonal lower handle designed for easy finger tip control when required'

c 'Chrome vanadium blade hardened and tempered'

d 'Magnetised tip is precisely machined for accurate working'

Information for question 31 – heat treatment

Steel can be **hardened** by first heating it to a high temperature, and then cooling it rapidly in a suitable liquid. The resulting steel is **very hard** and **brittle**. This, however, is not a good combination of properties for steel used for tools. However, a second heating, in which the steel is raised to a lower temperature and then cooled, results in a slight **decrease of hardness** and an **increase of toughness**. This is called **tempering**. The whole process is called hardening and tempering.

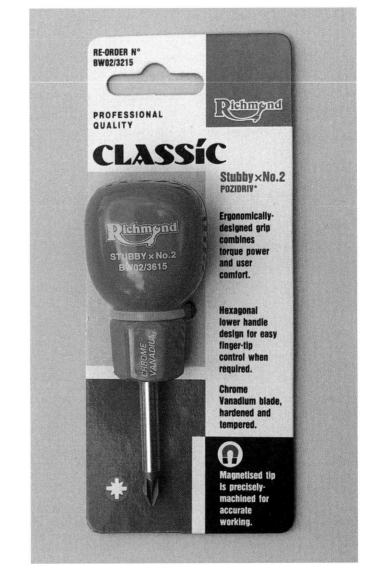

30	Before answering the question opposite, read about **Senses** on page 43, and about **torque** on page 100 (paragraphs 1–5).	From your observations of the stubby screwdriver, describe in detail the design features which, in your opinion, justify statements **a** and **b** above.
31	Read the information related to this question above, then read about **Brittleness**, **Hardness** and **Toughness** on pages 199 and 200 before answering the question opposite.	Why does the manufacturer stress that the blade has been hardened and tempered? Use the words **hard**, **brittle** and **tough** in your answer.
32	Screws sometimes have to be located into awkward places where it is difficult or impossible to hold the screw in position by hand.	What feature, or features, mentioned in **d** above, enables the screwdriver to operate more efficiently in this connection? Explain your answer.

Pencil cases

Millions of pupils take pencil cases to school every day. Many different designs are available. A few examples are shown here.

Activity 6

Work with a group of friends who own a range of **different** pencil cases. Study the pencil cases carefully and:

a Copy and complete the web diagram below to gather as much information as you can about the design of pencil cases.

b Sketch several different pencil cases, and **for each one**:

- Describe how well its design satisfies the **primary function**.

- Describe how well its design satisfies the **secondary functions**.

c Which design **best** satisfies the primary function, in your opinion? Explain your answer.

d Which design **best** satisfies the secondary functions, in your opinion? Explain your answer.

e Which **material** makes the most **durable** product? Explain your answer.

f How does the choice of material affect the product's **design** and the **method of manufacture**?

g **Design a pencil case** to satisfy, to a high standard, both the primary and secondary functions, as identified in your web diagram. Illustrate your design using a three-dimensional drawing or sketch and label all the important design features. Label also the materials used and any special fixtures, etc.

h Carry out a survey amongst pupils other than those you have worked with to see how popular your design is. Use the product analysis guide on page 305 to help you to write an appropriate questionnaire.

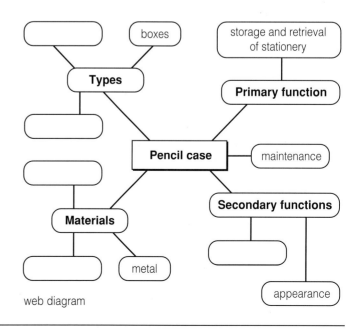

web diagram

Spectacle designs

Spectacles were originally designed as a medical aid and this, of course, is still their primary function today. However, people want to look good in their spectacles and, in response, designers have developed them into a high fashion product.

It is often said that 'first impressions' determine the success or failure of a friendship and since the first contact between people is usually **eye contact**, the design of spectacles, for those who wear them, can be as important as the design of their clothes and other accessories. To create the most positive first impression, therefore, everything must be 'just right'. For *some* people this means that their hair, make-up (if worn), clothes, spectacles and other accessories, should **harmonise**. Read about **colour**, **harmony** and **contrast** on pages 28 and 29. Read also about the **Principles of visual design** on pages 32–34.

Spectacle design is influenced by a number of factors. **Fashionable trends**; hair, face and eye **pigmentation**; and **face shapes** (illustrated on the opposite page) are three of these factors. Spectacles are produced in a range of colours and shapes designed to harmonise with the colour and shape of a person's individual features. This is important of

course, because not only should designs look good themselves, but they should also look good in the surroundings in which they will be used. In the case of spectacles, the 'surroundings' is the face.

The activity below is designed to allow you to investigate in a fun way the designs and colours of spectacles, and their suitability for different face types.

Activity 7

- **Photo-copy page 297** and, if possible, enlarge it to A3 size.
- Carefully **cut out the spectacles** (cutting just above the dotted line).
- Try each pair of spectacles on the four different faces and choose the design which, in your opinion, best suits each face.
- **Glue** the chosen spectacles onto the faces.
- Using **coloured pencils**, colour the hair, eyes and lips (using the guidance notes opposite) and finally colour the spectacles to harmonise with these features.
- **Write a short report** in which you explain **why** you chose the particular pair of spectacles for each face type and the particular **colour** for the spectacles.

Skin: Ivory coloured, peach coloured, pink
Eyes: Light to dark blue, light brown
Hair: Blond, brown, red

Skin: Ivory coloured, peach coloured, pink
Eyes: Light to dark brown, green, green/blue
Hair: Honey coloured, brown, reddish brown

Skin: Brown, dark brown, black
Eyes: Light to dark brown, black
Hair: Dark brown, black

Pigmentation guide

Skin: Light pink, dark pink
Eyes: Blue, grey/blue, green/blue, light brown
Hair: Ash blond, medium blond

Skin: White, beige, olive coloured
Eyes: Light to dark brown, grey/blue, grey/green, dark blue, yellow/brown
Hair: Brown, chestnut coloured, black/brown, black

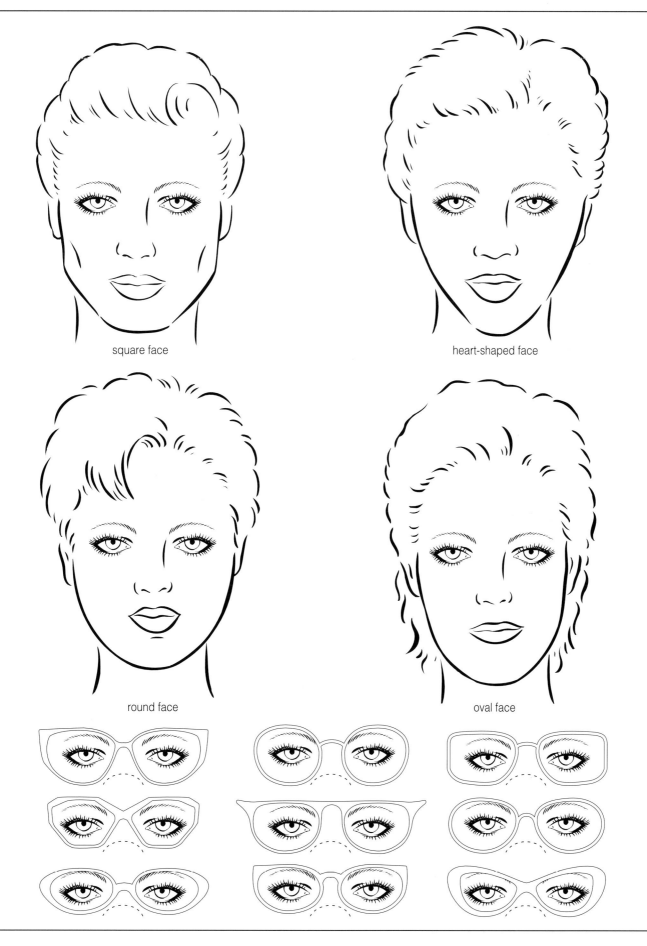

square face

heart-shaped face

round face

oval face

Investigation

The products we buy are sometimes a 'disappointment' to us – they do not always perform as well as we had hoped. *Which?* and other consumer magazines help people to make informed choices about the products they buy.

In your design and technology course, *you* will be expected to **test** products yourself and to write an **evaluation** of their performance. Below is an activity in which you can investigate and evaluate the performance of **pegs**.

Pegs investigation

The primary function of a peg is **to secure washing on a washing-line**. On a good drying day (a warm **windy** day) they have a tough job to do. The wind exerts a force on the washing, which in turn 'pulls' on the pegs. In this investigation you will examine the **design** of a range of pegs and **test** them to see how good they are at their job. A number of pegs, of different **design**, are shown here. See how many different designs you can collect for your investigation.

What to do

Set up a test rig similar to that shown here.

Attach a piece of **damp** cloth to the line using a single peg, and then attach a newton meter (spring balance) to the end of the cloth. Gently pull on the newton meter to exert a force on the cloth. Watch the reading gradually increase and **note the force** at which the peg 'fails' to hold the cloth. Repeat this test on several pegs of different design.

Write a report in which you:

a describe the investigation,
b record the test **results** in a table,
c describe in detail the **design** of each peg and write an evaluation in which you explain **why** you think each peg performed in the way it did.

Note You might like to test the pegs using different cloth samples and different types of clothes-line.

Consumer magazines

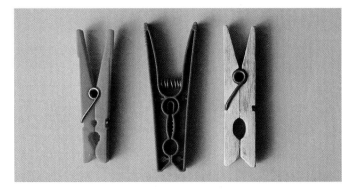

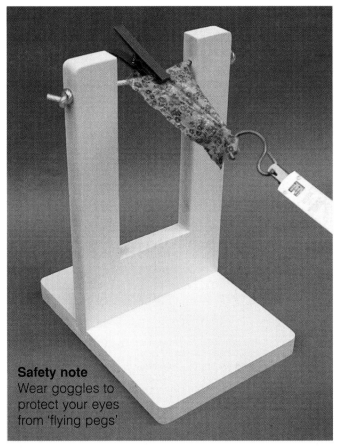
Safety note
Wear goggles to protect your eyes from 'flying pegs'

Test rig

Questions

33 Some products have to be bought on trust. That is, we are expected to trust that they *will function correctly* and be to our liking, but we are only able to confirm this when we get them home. This situation can arise as a result of modern packaging methods.

    a State clearly the primary and secondary functions of a **pair of scissors**.

    b For the scissors shown here, which functions are we expected to take on trust and which are we given the opportunity to 'test'? Explain your answer.

The information on the back of the scissors' packaging describes the product as having **'ergonomic handles and surgical steel blades'**.

The blades are made of **stainless steel**. The scissors cost £9.25 (in 1996).

    c From your observations of the product and the information given above, would you expect the scissors to perform their primary and secondary functions to a high standard? Explain your answer.

Activity 8

Collect a piece of cloth and several pairs of general purpose scissors of **different design**.

With each pair of scissors in turn, cut a strip of cloth and:

a take careful note of the **positions** of your thumb and fingers,

b notice any **pressure points** which cause discomfort during use,

c notice how your fingers and thumb **move** whilst cutting and note any **discomfort** caused by this action.

For each pair of scissors, describe the results of your tests, making reference to **a**, **b** and **c** above. Finally, write a short report evaluating each pair of scissors in terms of **ease of use**, **comfort** and **overall performance**.

Questions

An understanding of scientific and technical principles is needed when investigating 'technical' products. The questions below will help you to develop some knowledge in these areas.

A Bostic glue gun, with part of its case removed, is shown on page 301. Look carefully at its **component parts**. The primary function of a glue gun is to deliver hot liquid glue. It works as follows. When the trigger is squeezed, a series of levers operates first to grip the glue stick, and then force it forward into a heater chamber where it melts before being ejected as a hot viscous fluid at the nozzle.

Before answering question 34 below, read pages 94–97 – **Levers and linkages**.

34 a Explain in detail (using a labelled diagram) how the lever system operates. A cross-section of the gripper mechanism is shown here for clarity.

  b What is the **velocity ratio** of lever 'a', and why do you think this velocity ratio was chosen?

A **heating element** is a device which gets hot when electricity is passed through it. The glue gun's element is shown here.

35 a The element is made from a special kind of wire. Should it have a high or a low resistance, and what is this kind of wire called? Find out by reading (and looking at the diagrams) at the top of page 111 – **Resistance**.

  b Name **five** other electrical appliances which use elements. In each case, draw a diagram of the appliance and show where its element is positioned. State also the purpose of the element in each case.

  c The glue gun uses a small **neon** bulb to indicate when it is 'on'. What other electrical component is commonly used for this purpose in other electrical appliances? Find out on page 127, if necessary.

  d Describe and explain, in detail, all the **design features** in this product which help to make it electrically and physically **safe**.

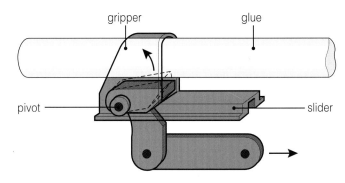

gripper mechanism

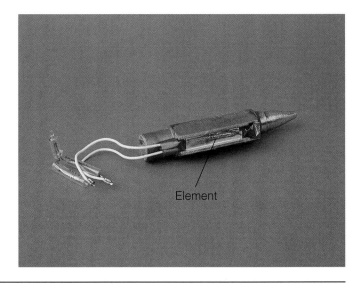

Element

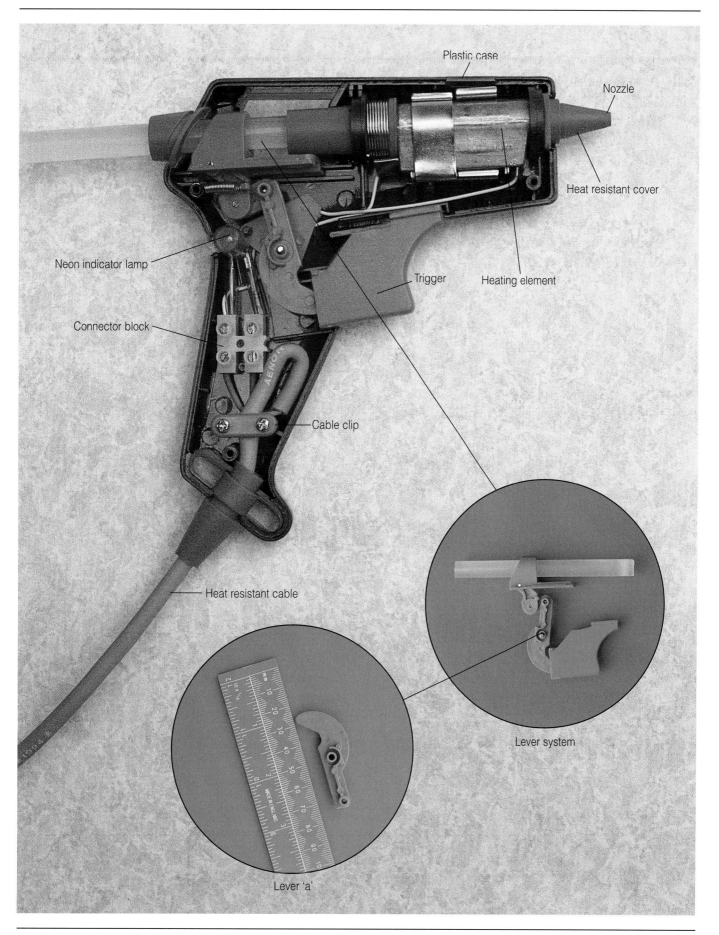

Plastic case

Nozzle

Heat resistant cover

Neon indicator lamp

Trigger

Heating element

Connector block

Cable clip

Heat resistant cable

Lever system

Lever 'a'

Table lamps

Good lighting is a vital ingredient in any room. It would be a shame, after spending time and money on decoration, furniture and furnishings, to ignore lighting. Lights can be used to great effect to change both the 'mood' and the 'look' of a room. One of the many forms of lighting available are **table lamps**. These are often used in the background to provide a warm intimate glow. They can also be used for reading or for illuminating favourite objects, if their shades provide enough 'down light'. Table lamps with open-top shades can also be used for bouncing light off walls or ceiling to create interesting lighting effects, and for illuminating pictures, and so on.

Bases and shades come in a variety of styles which can be bought separately or together. A few examples are shown on page 303. The **style** of the **base** and the **shade** should be **compatible**, and of course, the table lamp as a whole should complement the style and colour scheme of the room.

Activity 9 asks you to make some decisions about compatibility. To help you do this, read pages 32–34, **Principles of visual design**, before you begin.

Activity 9

- **Photo–copy** page 303 and carefully cut out all the shades and bases.
- Try different shades with different bases.
- Select a base and shade which, in your opinion, suits the bedroom. Do the same for the lounge.
- Glue your chosen bases and shades in position.

Now read pages 26–30, **Colour**, and, using coloured pencils, colour the bedroom and lounge to your taste. Finally, colour the lamp shades and bases to complement the colour schemes of the rooms.

Write a report giving:

a detailed reasons for your choice of base and shade for each room, and

b explain your choice of colour for the table lamps' shades and bases.

Questions

Tungsten filament bulbs get very **hot** in use and this heat can be transferred to the fittings and shade. For this reason, light fittings and shades are usually **power rated**. That is, the maximum recommended **wattage** of bulb for the product is stated (usually on a label or tag).

36 Size of shade, **shape** of shade, **material** and **ventilation**, can all affect the power rating of a shade. Explain (using drawings and notes) **how** each factor might affect the power rating.

Note Shades are commonly made from fabric, cane, plastic and glass.

The wrong combination of base and shade can make a table lamp **unstable**. An unstable table lamp can be dangerous since it could easily get knocked over. Read about **Stability** on pages 49–51, and then answer the question below.

37 Select a base and shade which would produce an **unstable** table lamp. Draw the table lamp, and using your knowledge of centre of gravity and stability, explain **why** the lamp is unstable.

Note Assume that all bases are ceramic and hollow.

bedroom

position
lamp
here

lounge

position
lamp
here

Product design – summary

The word PRODUCTS has been used below in a fun way to help you to **remember** the factors (covered in this chapter) related to the design, manufacture and use of products. The eight factors are **P**eople, **R**esources, **O**pposition, **D**esign, **U**se, **C**onstruction, **T**echnology and **S**ociety. The information in the 'boxes' summarises these factors, and on page 305 these summaries have been broken down into 15 questions which you can ask when carrying out a full product analysis.

People

Resources

Opposition

Design

Use

Construction

Technology

Society

The market for which the product is intended People belong to different age groups and different cultures, they have different incomes and life styles. All of these factors can affect a person's tastes and therefore can have an influence on what they buy.	7f
Whether it is an appropriate use of resources (materials) The function, appearance, safety, reliability, durability and overall quality of a product are all affected by the materials used. It is the material's properties which determine its suitability for the product.	8c
The range of alternative products and solutions Most products have to compete against a range of alternative products in the same market slot – the opposition. Brand name, advertising and not least price, will all affect a product's competitiveness.	7g
The intended purpose of the product A well-designed product should successfully do the job for which it was designed. It must fulfil, to a high standard, both the primary function and the range of secondary functions which enhance its use, and it should meet the needs of the user.	7a 8a 8e
Its fitness for purpose Products must be designed to the highest possible standards and work reliably, safely and efficiently. Quality of design, quality of manufacture and the appropriate use of components and materials should ensure 'fitness for purpose'.	8b
The choice of materials and components, the way in which they have been used and the manufacturing requirements All products should be designed for ease of construction and manufacture. This requires a clear understanding of materials, available components and manufacturing processes.	7b 7c 7d
The application of scientific principles The design of technical products relies on the application of scientific principles. The type of technology incorporated will depend upon the functions of the product.	7e
Its impact beyond the purpose for which it was designed The product should be designed to reduce to the minimum the detrimental effects which could be caused to people, wildlife and the environment by its manufacture, use and final disposal.	8d

Teacher's note – National Curriculum references (KS4)

By analysing products (using the questions below) you can learn a lot about product design, manufacture and use, and this can help **you** to become a better designer and maker at school. It can also help you to become a more aware consumer. **Use these pages to help you when investigating and evaluating products in the classroom.**

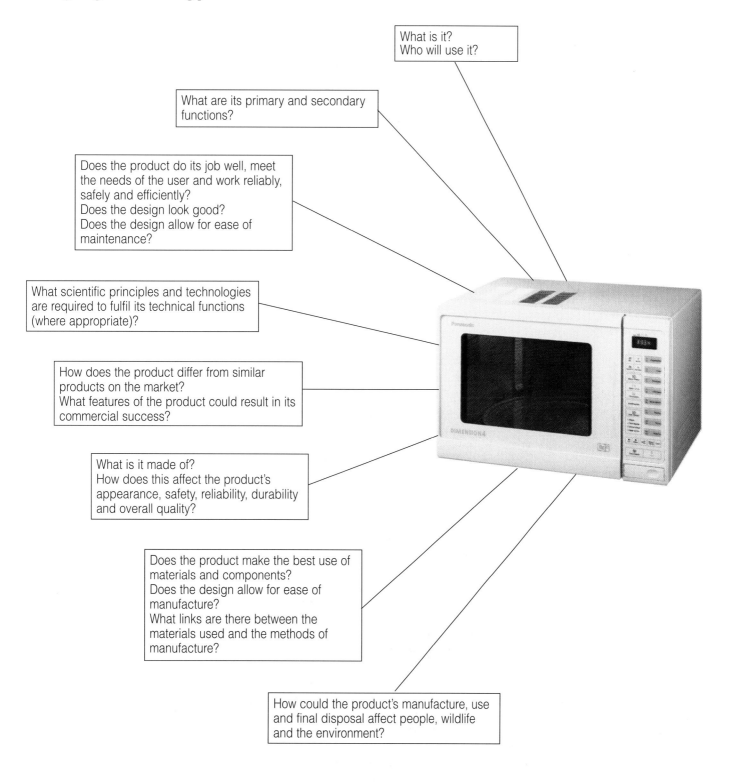

What is it?
Who will use it?

What are its primary and secondary functions?

Does the product do its job well, meet the needs of the user and work reliably, safely and efficiently?
Does the design look good?
Does the design allow for ease of maintenance?

What scientific principles and technologies are required to fulfil its technical functions (where appropriate)?

How does the product differ from similar products on the market?
What features of the product could result in its commercial success?

What is it made of?
How does this affect the product's appearance, safety, reliability, durability and overall quality?

Does the product make the best use of materials and components?
Does the design allow for ease of manufacture?
What links are there between the materials used and the methods of manufacture?

How could the product's manufacture, use and final disposal affect people, wildlife and the environment?

Disassembling products

Taking products to pieces can be a very enjoyable and useful activity – but it must be done **safely**, so:

Always check with your teacher before taking any product to pieces.

Never take products to pieces at home.

Never work on an electrical appliance which has a plug on it. <u>Ask your teacher to remove it for you.</u>

Never use any tool in such a way that it could cause you injury. If in doubt – check with your teacher.

Pupils disassembling an electrical product

Teacher's note – removing plugs

For conventional plugs, disconnect the plug from the power cable, and then **tape up** the bare wires. After the product has been disassembled, remove the cable from the appliance completely and do not refit.

For moulded plugs, **destroy the plug whilst it is still attached to the cable**, then cut it off the cable and tape up the wires. If a plug with part of its cable attached was plugged into a mains socket, this could result in a **fatal shock.** Do not throw away moulded plugs until they have been destroyed. After the product has been disassembled, remove the cable completely and do not refit.

1 Remove fuse
2 Cut off earth pin to prevent the plug from being inserted into a socket

Moulded plug

Tools and equipment

Products are assembled and held together in many different ways. For example, they may be clipped together, glued, screwed or bolted together. They may be soldered, riveted or stitched, and so on. Most of the tools you will require for disassembling them can be found in the school workshop. A useful selection is shown here.

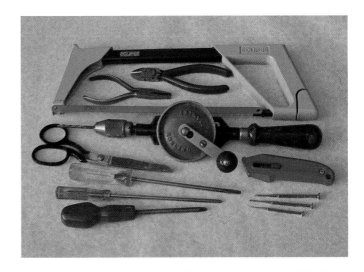

Disassembling products – continued

To gain maximum benefit from disassembling any product, it is recommended that you **analyse it first**, using the questions on page 305.

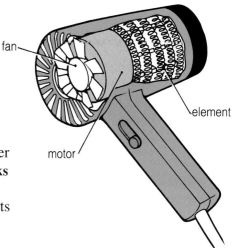

You may then like to predict **what the product is like inside** and what component parts it contains. You could, for example, draw a 'cut away' diagram similar to the one shown here for a hair-dryer.

As you disassemble a product, **take careful note** of where screws and other components come from. **Only disassemble it sufficiently to see how it works and how it is put together** – a pile of components on the table is of little value. To enable you to put the product back together again, keep the parts safe by storing them in suitable containers.

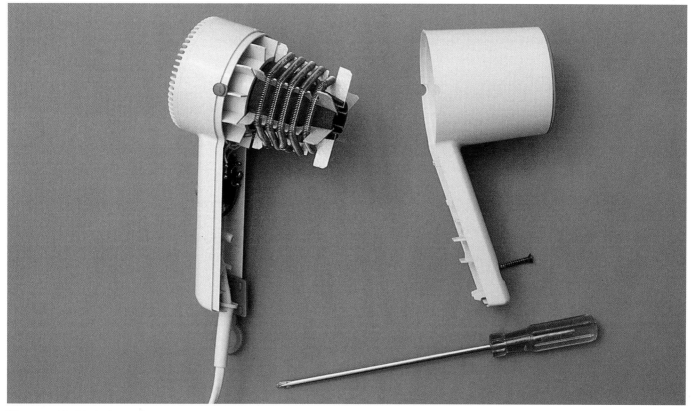

Disassembled hair-dryer

Analysis – look carefully at the disassembled product and

- try to identify all the **different parts** from which the product is constructed,
- notice how these parts are **fitted together**,
- try to work out the **function** of each of these parts,
- try to identify the **materials** from which these parts are made,
- think about the **manufacturing processes** used to make the various component parts,
- notice any **special design features** which might be unique to the product.

Write a report which includes your answers to the questions on page 305 and all additional information gained having disassembled the product.

Disassembling a water pistol

Some products are more difficult to take to pieces than others. The water pistol shown here was firmly **glued together**. To separate the two halves, it was necessary to use a hacksaw. It took about 15 minutes to do this and great care was needed to ensure that the plastic did not crack and that the internal parts were not damaged.

Look at the disassembled water pistol below and answer the questions.

Water pistol

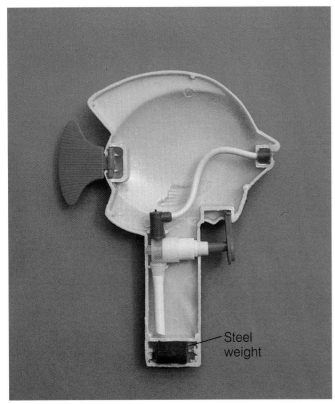

Water pistol with side removed

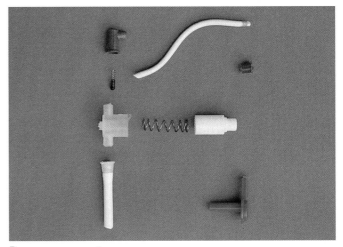

Pump components

Questions

38 a Most of the plastic parts for the water pistol were **injection moulded**. How many **different** moulds were required to produce all the parts for this product?

b Which of the following materials could **not** have been used for the injection moulded components: polythene, acrylic, urea formaldehyde, polypropylene? Explain your answer. See pages 240–251 if necessary.

c The handle and the body of the 'fish' form the 'water tank' for the water pistol. Explain, therefore, why the two halves had to be glued together.

d Notice that a steel weight is fitted in the **bottom** of the handle. What do you think its purpose is? Here's a clue – **C of G**.

Comparing products

It can be very interesting to disassemble **similar** products and to **compare** them – like the two different clocks shown here, for example.

You could begin by asking the **analysis questions** listed on page 305. You might then like to compare in more detail particular aspects of their designs. For example, in the case of the clocks you could compare **the way they work** – the technologies they use. You would discover that one contains some moving parts – gears and so on – whilst the other contains only electronic components and no moving parts. You could compare the way that they **'communicate'** with us – tell us the time. One, of course, is a digital clock and uses a liquid crystal display, whilst the other is an analogue clock and uses hands and numbers, and you could compare the **appearance** of the clocks – and so on.

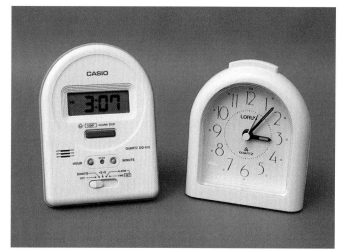

Digital and analogue clocks

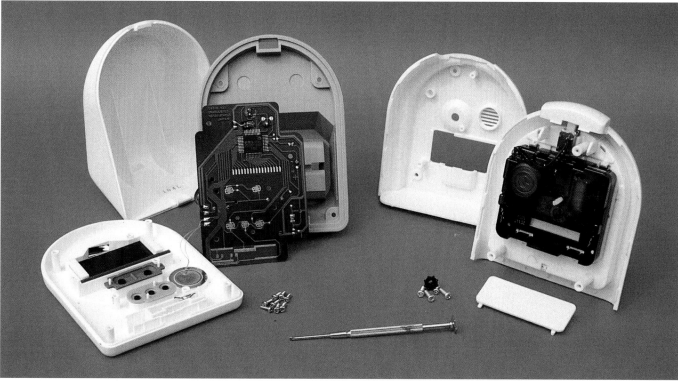

Disassembled clocks

Conclusion

Disassembling products can be good fun and very rewarding – but remember to **take care** and **keep yourself safe**. If you are in doubt about any procedure, **ask your teacher for help**.

Numerical answers

Structures

11   **a**   250 N
       c   25 N

Mechanisms

1   **a**   2.5:1
    b   120 rpm

2   **b**   1120 rpm
    c   400 rpm

4   **a**   0.4:1
    b   161.25 metres per minute

5   **a**   40 teeth
    b   2:1
    c   30 rpm

6   **b**   9:1
    c   4

7   **a**   3:1

9   5 s

10   6 cm

11   120 rpm

13   200 N

14   **a**   125 N
     b   100 N

15   **b**   333.3 N

Control electrics and electronics

1   **a**   120 Ω
    b   0.05 A

2   **a**   0.12 A
    b   0.24 A

3   **a**   10 V
    b   0.02 A

4   **a**   0.16 A
    b   0.16 A
    c   0.16 A
    d   75 Ω

5   5 Ω

Pneumatics

3   94.2 N

5   502.6 N

6   457.4 N

List of suppliers

RS Components
PO Box 99
Corby
Northants
NN17 9RS

Rapid Electronics
Heckworth Close
Severalls Industrial Estate
Colchester
Essex
CO4 4TB

Technology Supplies
Phoenix Bank
Market Drayton
Shropshire
TF9 1JS

Technology Teaching Systems
Unit 4
Park Road
Homewood
Chesterfield
S42 5UY

Economatics (Education) Ltd
Epic House
Darnall Road
Attercliffe
Sheffield
S9 5AA

Testbed Technology Ltd
The Science Park
Hutton Street
Blackburn
Lancashire
BB1 3BY

EMA Model Supplies Ltd
58–60 The Centre
Feltham
TW13 4BH

Your local S.A.T.R.O

Project index

Pupil's note

More than 80 projects have been included in this book. Nearly half are project briefs which identify needs or opportunities for design and technological activities. These could be used as a starting point for your own design and making activities, or as a stimulus for identifying needs and opportunities yourself. The others are examples of completed projects which may also serve to stimulate your own ideas.

The text which follows the project index gives further guidance on how to begin to identify needs and opportunities for design and technological activities yourself.

Briefs

Examples of completed projects

Identifying needs – further guidance

Situation analysis

Situation analysis was described briefly on page 10. It is likely that within the area around your school and home there will be many places where this kind of study can take place, including shops, parks, banks, car parks, schools, factories and so on.

Observing peoples' actions and reactions in a given situation is an excellent way of identifying needs. If possible, talk to people in a given situation, ask them questions and ask for their opinions; but don't forget to explain 'what you are doing' and why you need the information.

Safety note – It is advisable never to talk to strangers if you are alone.

Design analysis

Design analysis, in which you study existing designs, is another useful way of identifying needs – see chapter 9. This involves examining designs and asking questions about them, such as

What is it?
Who will use it?
What are its primary and secondary functions?
Does the product do its job well?
Does the product look good?
Does the product make the best use of materials and components?
Is the product 'environmentally friendly'?
How does the product differ from similar products on the market?
In what ways could it be improved?

A close examination of this kind often reveals weaknesses in a design. Using this information you could possibly improve on the design or even produce a new design to perform the required function.

Questionnaires

When designing for people it is important to take account of their differing needs, tastes and opinions. To find out what people 'think', therefore, you need to ask them questions. One way of doing this **for a large group of people** is to use a questionnaire. A questionnaire is simply a list of questions designed to obtain the information you require quickly and efficiently.

Writing a questionnaire

1 Use a web diagram to help you 'think up' questions.
2 Give your questionnaire a title.
3 Write some questions with 'yes' or 'no' answers or multi-choice answers. (Use boxes for these 'tick' answers.)
4 Include questions which ask people for their opinions. (Leave space for these answers.)
5 Check your questionnaire carefully to make sure that it will provide the information you require.

Keywords

One very effective way of identifying needs and opportunities for design and technological activity is shown here. This method relies solely on your imagination and creativity.

Begin by writing a **keyword** or words (shown here in red). Then build up a web diagram by adding **link words** – words which relate to the keyword/s (shown here in blue). Finally, use the link words to identify needs. (Some examples are shown here in black.)

Almost any word can be used, but obviously words like 'it', 'the', 'big', 'down' etc., should be avoided. You could choose, for example, words related to **activities** (e.g. swimming, sitting, laughing, etc.), **objects** (e.g. chair, shirt, pencil, etc.), **people** (e.g. child, pensioner, tourist, etc.), **environments** (e.g. kitchen, bus shelter, classroom, etc.) and so on.

Note – This activity can be performed in a slightly different way with a number of people sitting together and spontaneously stating their thoughts and ideas about 'something'. The starting point can be specific (as above) or can begin with the first word which someone says. Everything should be recorded, however silly it might sound, using a web diagram or notes. This approach is called brainstorming.

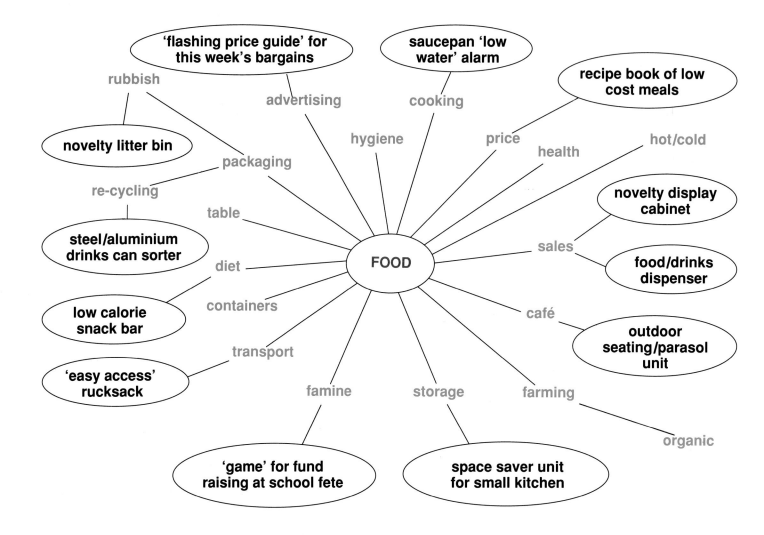

Index

Acknowledgments

The author and publishers would like to thank the following for permission to reproduce their photographs (by page):

4 (tractor) Massey Ferguson; (packaging) Shell; (truck) Sally & Richard Greenhill; (intensive care) Science Photo Library; 5 (car bodies) Science Photo Library; (power station) National Power Plc; (intercontinental flight) The Aviation Picture Library; (records department) Hertfordshire Constabulary; 20 (pop concert) Elliot Landy / Redferns Music Picture Library; (woodland) Spectrum Colour Library; (watching tv) J Bradbury / Spectrum Colour Library; (children playing, Asian family) Sally & Richard Greenhill; (restaurant) zefa pictures; 21 (garden) Spectrum Colour Library; (students) courtesy Anglia Polytechnic University; 24 (guitar, vacuum cleaner, patio furniture, greenhouse, trolley jack) Littlewoods plc; (Concorde) zefa pictures; (clock radio) courtesy Sony Transparency Library; 25 (leather) British Leather Confederation; 26 ICI Paints; 29 (lawn edger, automatic kettle, time teacher watch) Littlewoods plc; (bathroom) Crown Paints; 30 Crown Paints; 32 Maclaren; 33 (pool) W. F. Davidson / zefa pictures; (Taj Mahal) W. R. Davis / Spectrum Colour Library; 34 (flower) J. Pfaff / zefa pictures; (light fitting, table lamp, table) Littlewoods plc; 36 (shoe, vegetable rack) Littlewoods plc; 37 (design exhibit) The Design Council; (students) Sally & Richard Greenhill; (Ubudiah Mosque) zefa pictures; 38 (multiflash photo, toddler, woman on ladder, skateboard, woman with tv) Littlewoods plc; (in kitchen) Sally & Richard Greenhill; (woman in chair) Richard Nichalas / Science Photo Library; (man with machine) Sheila Terry / Science Photo Library; 39 (rucksack) Littlewoods plc; 42 (dashboard) Ford Motor Co Ltd; (surfboard) Allsport; (ticket barriers) zefa pictures; 43 (mixer, camera) Littlewoods plc; (car seat) Volvo Car UK Ltd; 44 (saucepans) Littlewoods plc; (Heathrow) W. R. Davis / Spectrum Colour Library; 46 (shopping centre) British Gas plc; (jet) Aviation Picture Library; (Forth bridges) Still Moving Picture Company; 47 (car body shells) courtesy Saab Automobile AB; 59 Spectrum Colour Library; 64 Novosti / Frank Spooner Pictures; 70 (logging machinery) Forest Life Picture Library; (water wheel) Barnaby's Picture Library; (tractor) Massey Ferguson; (aerogenerator) Wind Energy Group Ltd; 71 (derrick) British Petroleum p.l.c.; 73 (car engine) Practical Motorist; 76 Havlicek / zefa pictures; 87 (tripod) Trevor Scotcher / Stenton Associates; 92 (car engine) Ford Motor Co Ltd; 108 (telephones) BT Corporate Pictures, a BT photograph; (aircraft & autopilot) Aviation Picture Library; (vending machine exterior & interior) Sankey Vending; 109 (robots) Philippe Plailly / Science Photo Library; 117, 121, 124, 127 (diodes) Graham Portlock; 131 Trevor Scotcher / Stenton Associates, courtesy Chew & Osborne Ltd, Saffron Walden;

139 Allsport UK Ltd; 141 (amp), 145 (capacitors), 149 (timer), 153 (circuit) Graham Portlock; 168 (bus) London Transport Museum; (tyre bay) courtesy KWIK-FIT (G.B.) Limited; 172; 173; 175, 178, 180, Parker Hannifin plc; 190 (aircraft undercarriage) Aviation Picture Library; 203 The Natural History Museum; 206 Barnaby's Picture Library; 218 Fredk. Pollard & Co Ltd; 222 Barnaby's Picture Library; 223 Biophoto Associates; 225 Cubbage Bollmann Ltd; 226, 227, 228 (ash) Construction Research Communications Ltd; 228 (beech), 229 Timber Research & Development Association; 239 The Hutchinson Library; 240 ICI Chemicals & Polymers Ltd; 262 C.R. Clarke & Co (UK) Ltd; 268 (Lego) Premier Educational Supplies Ltd; (Fischertechnik) Economatics (Education) Ltd; (Meccano) Atlascraft; 273 (shopping centre) courtesy Lakeside Shopping Centre, West Thurrock; (shop) courtesy Argos Distributors Limited; 275 (video recorder) courtesy Sony Transparency Library; (tent) courtesy John James Hawley (Speciality Works) Ltd.; (go-kart) courtesy Barval Toys UK Ltd; 277 (vacuum cleaner) courtesy Panasonic Consumer Electronics U.K.; (modern fan) courtesy Amcor (Appliances) Ltd; 278 (stair gate) courtesy Mothercare; (baby walker) courtesy Vtech Electronics UK plc; 280 (bathroon cabinet, chair) courtesy Grattan plc; (scales) the Academy 100 personal scale, designed, manufactured and marketed worldwide by Salter Housewares Limited, Tonbridge, Kent; (lawn mower) courtesy Flymo; 281 (cassette player) courtesy Sony Transparency Library; (kettles) courtesy Pifco Limited; courtesy Moulinex Swan Holdings Ltd.; 284 (energy label) courtesy Department of Energy, Environmental and Energy Awareness Division; (radio) courtesy Baygen Power (Europe) Ltd; 290 courtesy Saab Automobile AB; 291 (flow production) courtesy Rover Group Ltd; (batch production) courtesy Cabdury Limited; 292 logos courtesy Canon UK; Cheil Communications Inc.; Clarks International; Olympus Optical Co. (U.K.) Limited; Pentax U.K. Limited; Philips Consumer Electronics; Sony Consumer Products Company UK; Moulinex Swan Holdings Ltd, Vivitar (Europe) Ltd; Wrangler; 293 courtesy Grafton Centre, Cambridge; 298 (magazines) Trevor Scotcher / Stenton Associates, courtesy Essex County Council Libraries, Saffron Walden Library.

Every effort has been made to reach copyright holders; the publishers would be very pleased to hear from anyone whose rights have been unwittingly infringed.

AS & A2
Biology

Exam Board: OCR

Complete Revision
and Practice

AS-Level Contents

A2-Level Contents

Published by CGP

From original material by Richard Parsons.

Editors:
Claire Boulter, Ellen Bowness, Katie Braid, Joe Brazier, Charlotte Burrows, Katherine Craig, Rosie Gillham, Murray Hamilton, Jane Towle, Karen Wells, Dawn Wright.

Contributors:
Gloria Barnett, Jessica Egan, Mark Ellingham, James Foster, Barbara Green, Julian Hardwick, Derek Harvey, Liz Masters, Stephen Phillips, Adrian Schmit, Sophie Watkins, Anna-fe Williamson.

Proofreaders:
Sue Hocking, Glenn Rogers.

ISBN: 978 1 84762 424 6

With thanks to Laura Stoney for the copyright research.
With thanks to Science Photo Library for permission to reproduce the photograph used on page 21.
Data used to construct the graph on page 87 from R. Doll, R. Peto, J. Boreham, I Sutherland.
Mortality in relation to smoking: 50 years' observations on male British doctors. BMJ 2004; 328:1519.
Exam question graph on page 91 © 2006 WWF (panda.org). Some rights reserved.

Groovy website: www.cgpbooks.co.uk
Jolly bits of clipart from CorelDRAW®
Printed by Elanders Ltd, Newcastle upon Tyne.

The Scientific Process

'How Science Works' is all about the scientific process — how we develop and test scientific ideas.
It's what scientists do all day, every day (well, except at coffee time — never come between a scientist and their coffee).

Scientists Come Up with **Theories** — Then **Test Them**...

Science tries to explain **how** and **why** things happen — it **answers questions**. It's all about seeking and gaining **knowledge** about the world around us. Scientists do this by **asking** questions and **suggesting** answers and then **testing** them, to see if they're correct — this is the **scientific process**.

1) **Ask** a question — make an **observation** and ask **why or how** it happens. E.g. why is trypsin (an enzyme) found in the small intestine but not in the stomach?

2) **Suggest** an answer, or part of an answer, by forming a **theory** (a possible **explanation** of the observations) e.g. pH affects the activity of enzymes. (Scientists also sometimes form a **model** too — a **simplified picture** of what's physically going on.)

3) Make a **prediction** or **hypothesis** — a **specific testable statement**, based on the theory, about what will happen in a test situation. E.g. trypsin will be active at pH 8 (the pH of the small intestine) but inactive at pH 2 (the pH of the stomach).

4) Carry out a **test** — to provide **evidence** that will support the prediction (or help to disprove it). E.g. measure the rate of reaction of trypsin at various pH levels.

The evidence supported Quentin's Theory of Flammable Burps.

A theory is only scientific if it can be tested.

...Then They **Tell** Everyone About Their **Results**...

The results are **published** — scientists need to let others know about their work. Scientists publish their results in **scientific journals**. These are just like normal magazines, only they contain **scientific reports** (called papers) instead of the latest celebrity gossip.

1) Scientific reports are similar to the **lab write-ups** you do in school. And just as a lab write-up is **reviewed** (marked) by your teacher, reports in scientific journals undergo **peer review** before they're published.

2) The report is sent out to **peers** — other scientists that are experts in the **same area**. They examine the data and results, and if they think that the conclusion is reasonable it's **published**. This makes sure that work published in scientific journals is of a **good standard**.

3) But peer review **can't guarantee** the science is **correct** — other scientists still need to **reproduce** it.

4) Sometimes **mistakes** are made and bad work is published. Peer review **isn't perfect** but it's probably the best way for scientists to self-regulate their work and to publish **quality reports**.

...Then **Other Scientists** Will **Test** the Theory Too

Other scientists read the published theories and results, and try to **test the theory** themselves. This involves:

• Repeating the **exact same experiments**.

• Using the theory to make **new predictions** and then testing them with **new experiments**.

If the **Evidence** Supports a Theory, It's **Accepted** — for Now

1) If all the experiments in all the world provide good evidence to back it up, the theory is thought of as **scientific 'fact'** (for now).

2) But it will never become **totally indisputable** fact. Scientific **breakthroughs or advances** could provide new ways to question and test the theory, which could lead to **new evidence** that **conflicts** with the current evidence. Then the testing starts all over again...

And this, my friend, is the **tentative nature of scientific knowledge** — it's always **changing** and **evolving**.

The Scientific Process

So scientists need evidence to back up their theories. They get it by carrying out experiments, and when that's not possible they carry out studies. But why bother with science at all? We want to know as much as possible so we can use it to try and improve our lives (and because we're nosy).

Evidence Comes from Lab Experiments...

1) Results from **controlled experiments** in **laboratories** are **great**.
2) A lab is the easiest place to **control variables** so that they're all **kept constant** (except for the one you're investigating).
3) This means you can draw meaningful **conclusions**.

See pages 106-107 and 220-222 for more on experiment design and interpreting data.

For example, if you're investigating how temperature affects the rate of an enzyme-controlled reaction you need to keep everything but the temperature constant, e.g. the pH of the solution, the concentration of the solution etc.

...and Well-Designed Studies

1) There are things you **can't** investigate in a lab, e.g. whether stress causes heart attacks. You have to do a study instead.
2) You still need to try and make the study as controlled as possible to make it **more reliable**. But in reality it's **very hard** to control **all the variables** that **might** be having an effect.
3) You can do things to help, e.g. have **matched groups** — **choose two groups** of people (those who have quite stressful jobs and those who don't) who are **as similar as possible** (same mix of ages, same mix of diets etc.). But you can't easily rule out every possibility.

Samantha thought her study was very well designed — especially the fitted bookshelf.

Society Makes Decisions Based on Scientific Evidence

1) Lots of scientific work eventually leads to **important discoveries** or breakthroughs that could **benefit humankind**.
2) These results are **used by society** (that's you, me and everyone else) to **make decisions** — about the way we live, what we eat, what we drive, etc.
3) All sections of society use scientific evidence to make decisions, e.g. politicians use it to devise policies and individuals use science to make decisions about their own lives.

Other factors can **influence** decisions about science or the way science is used:

Economic factors
- Society has to consider the **cost** of implementing changes based on scientific conclusions — e.g. the **NHS** can't afford the most expensive drugs without **sacrificing** something else.
- Scientific research is **expensive** so companies won't always develop new ideas — e.g. developing new drugs is costly, so pharmaceutical companies often only invest in drugs that are likely to make them **money**.

Social factors
- **Decisions** affect **people's lives** — E.g. scientists may suggest **banning smoking** and **alcohol** to prevent health problems, but shouldn't **we** be able to **choose** whether **we** want to smoke and drink or not?

Environmental factors
- Scientists believe **unexplored regions** like remote parts of rainforests might contain **untapped drug** resources. But some people think we shouldn't **exploit** these regions because any interesting finds may lead to **deforestation** and **reduced biodiversity** in these areas.

So there you have it — how science works...

Hopefully these pages have given you a nice intro to how science works, e.g. what scientists do to provide you with 'facts'. You need to understand this, as you're expected to know how science works — for the exam and for life.

AS-Level

Biology

Exam Board: OCR

Eukaryotic Cells and Organelles

Cells — what an original way to start a biology book... Oh well. There are two types of cell — prokaryotic and eukaryotic. Eukaryotic cells are stuffed full of organelles (all the tiny bits and bobs that you can only see in detail with a fancy microscope), and you need to know about all of them...

Organisms can be **Prokaryotes** or **Eukaryotes**

1) Prokaryotic organisms are **prokaryotic cells** (i.e. they're single-celled organisms) and eukaryotic organisms are made up of **eukaryotic cells**.

2) Both types of cells contain **organelles**. Organelles are **parts** of cells — each one has a **specific function**.

⟹

1) Eukaryotic cells are **complex** and include all **animal** and **plant cells**.

2) Prokaryotic cells are **smaller** and **simpler**, e.g. bacteria.

Plant and **Animal** Cells are Both **Eukaryotic**

Eukaryotic cells are generally a **bit more complicated** than prokaryotic cells. You've probably been looking at **animal** and **plant cell** diagrams for years, so hopefully you'll be familiar with some of the bits and pieces...

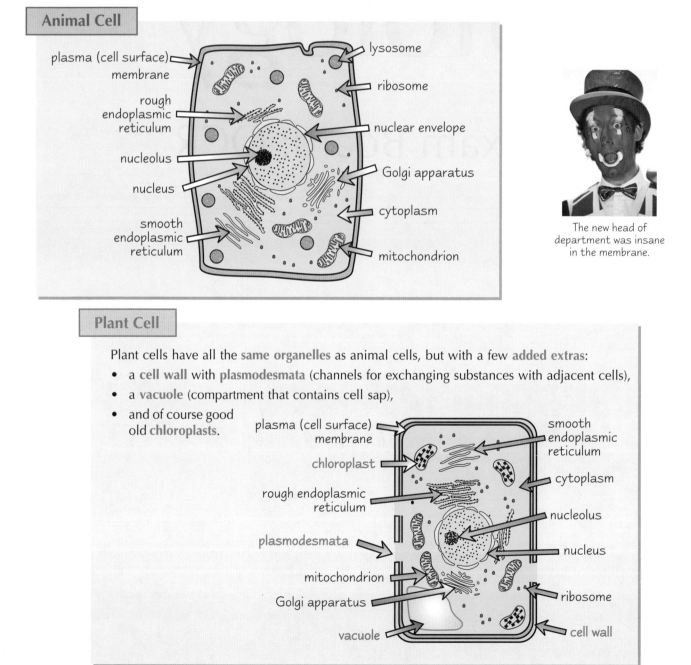

Animal Cell

plasma (cell surface) membrane
rough endoplasmic reticulum
nucleolus
nucleus
smooth endoplasmic reticulum

lysosome
ribosome
nuclear envelope
Golgi apparatus
cytoplasm
mitochondrion

The new head of department was insane in the membrane.

Plant Cell

Plant cells have all the **same organelles** as animal cells, but with a few **added extras**:

• a **cell wall** with **plasmodesmata** (channels for exchanging substances with adjacent cells),

• a **vacuole** (compartment that contains cell sap),

• and of course good old **chloroplasts**.

plasma (cell surface) membrane
chloroplast
rough endoplasmic reticulum
plasmodesmata
mitochondrion
Golgi apparatus
vacuole

smooth endoplasmic reticulum
cytoplasm
nucleolus
nucleus
ribosome
cell wall

Eukaryotic Cells and Organelles

Different Organelles have *Different Functions*

This giant table contains a big list of organelles — you need to know the **structure** and **function** of them all. Sorry.
Most organelles are surrounded by **membranes**, which sometimes causes confusion — don't make
the mistake of thinking that a diagram of an organelle is a diagram of a whole cell.
They're not cells — they're **parts of** cells.

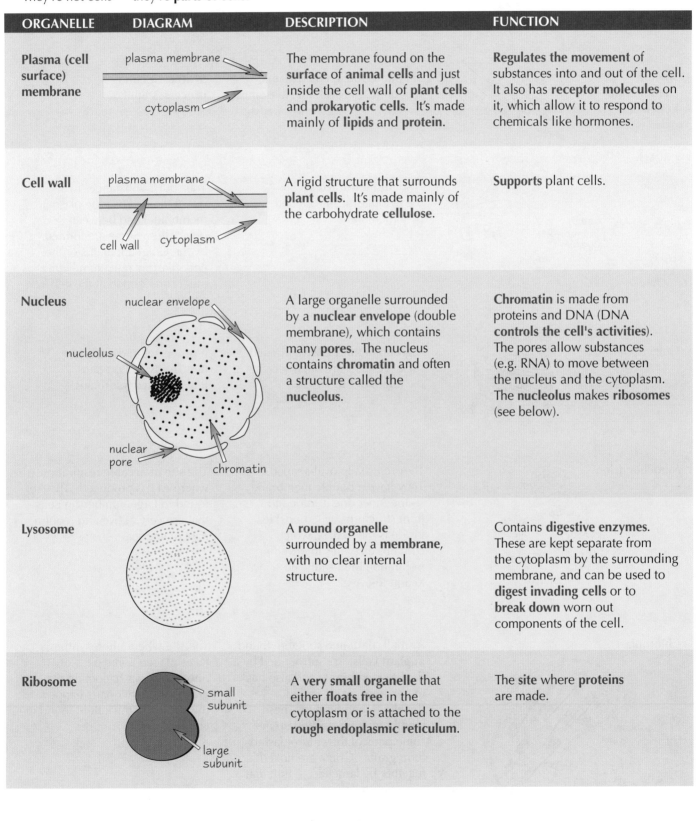

ORGANELLE	DIAGRAM	DESCRIPTION	FUNCTION
Plasma (cell surface) membrane	plasma membrane cytoplasm	The membrane found on the **surface** of **animal cells** and just inside the cell wall of **plant cells** and **prokaryotic cells**. It's made mainly of **lipids** and **protein**.	**Regulates the movement** of substances into and out of the cell. It also has **receptor molecules** on it, which allow it to respond to chemicals like hormones.
Cell wall	plasma membrane cell wall cytoplasm	A rigid structure that surrounds **plant cells**. It's made mainly of the carbohydrate **cellulose**.	**Supports** plant cells.
Nucleus	nuclear envelope nucleolus nuclear pore chromatin	A large organelle surrounded by a **nuclear envelope** (double membrane), which contains many **pores**. The nucleus contains **chromatin** and often a structure called the **nucleolus**.	**Chromatin** is made from proteins and DNA (DNA **controls the cell's activities**). The pores allow substances (e.g. RNA) to move between the nucleus and the cytoplasm. The **nucleolus** makes **ribosomes** (see below).
Lysosome		A **round organelle** surrounded by a **membrane**, with no clear internal structure.	Contains **digestive enzymes**. These are kept separate from the cytoplasm by the surrounding membrane, and can be used to **digest invading cells** or to **break down** worn out components of the cell.
Ribosome	small subunit large subunit	A **very small organelle** that either **floats free** in the cytoplasm or is attached to the **rough endoplasmic reticulum**.	The **site** where **proteins** are made.

Eukaryotic Cells and Organelles

ORGANELLE	DIAGRAM	DESCRIPTION	FUNCTION
Rough Endoplasmic Reticulum (RER)	ribosome / fluid	A system of membranes enclosing a fluid-filled space. The surface is **covered with ribosomes**.	**Folds** and **processes proteins** that have been made at the ribosomes.
Smooth Endoplasmic Reticulum		Similar to rough endoplasmic reticulum, but with no **ribosomes**.	**Synthesises** and **processes lipids**.
Vesicle	cell's plasma membrane / vesicle	A small **fluid-filled sac** in the cytoplasm, surrounded by a membrane.	**Transports substances** in and out of the cell (via the plasma membrane) and between organelles. Some are formed by the Golgi apparatus or the endoplasmic reticulum, while others are formed at the cell surface.
Golgi Apparatus	vesicle	A group of fluid-filled **flattened sacs**. Vesicles are often seen at the edges of the sacs.	It **processes** and **packages** new lipids and proteins. It also **makes lysosomes**.
Mitochondrion	outer membrane / inner membrane / crista / matrix	They're usually oval-shaped. They have a **double membrane** — the inner one is folded to form structures called **cristae**. Inside is the **matrix**, which contains enzymes involved in respiration (but, sadly, no Keanu Reeves).	The **site of aerobic respiration**, where **ATP** is produced. They're found in large numbers in cells that are very **active** and require a lot of **energy**.
Chloroplast	stroma / two membranes / granum (plural = grana) / lamella (plural = lamellae)	A small, **flattened** structure found in **plant cells**. It's surrounded by a **double membrane**, and also has membranes inside called **thylakoid membranes**. These membranes are stacked up in some parts of the chloroplast to form **grana**. Grana are linked together by lamellae — thin, flat pieces of thylakoid membrane.	The **site** where **photosynthesis** takes place. Some parts of photosynthesis happen in the **grana**, and other parts happen in the **stroma** (a thick fluid found in chloroplasts).

Eukaryotic Cells and Organelles

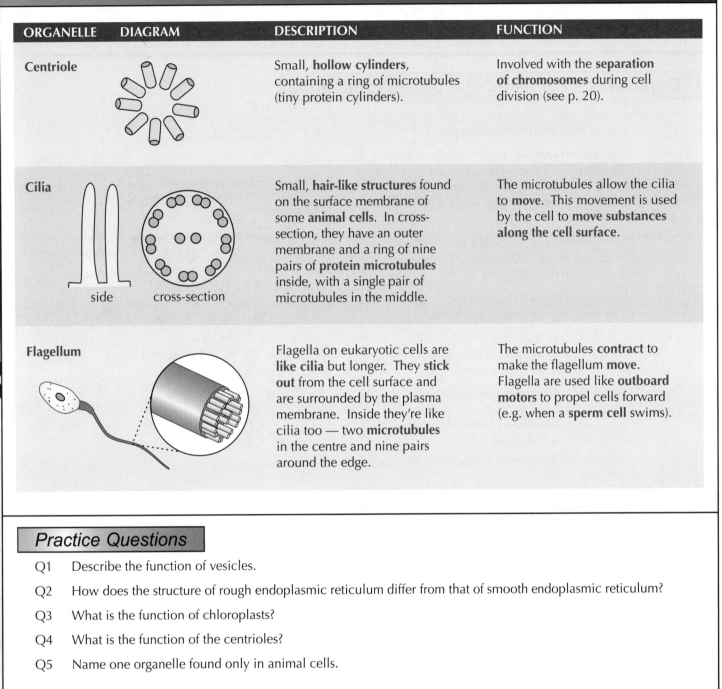

ORGANELLE	DIAGRAM	DESCRIPTION	FUNCTION
Centriole		Small, **hollow cylinders**, containing a ring of microtubules (tiny protein cylinders).	Involved with the **separation of chromosomes** during cell division (see p. 20).
Cilia	side / cross-section	Small, **hair-like structures** found on the surface membrane of some **animal cells**. In cross-section, they have an outer membrane and a ring of nine pairs of **protein microtubules** inside, with a single pair of microtubules in the middle.	The microtubules allow the cilia to **move**. This movement is used by the cell to **move substances along the cell surface**.
Flagellum		Flagella on eukaryotic cells are **like cilia** but longer. They **stick out** from the cell surface and are surrounded by the plasma membrane. Inside they're like cilia too — two **microtubules** in the centre and nine pairs around the edge.	The microtubules **contract** to make the flagellum **move**. Flagella are used like **outboard motors** to propel cells forward (e.g. when a **sperm cell** swims).

Practice Questions

Q1 Describe the function of vesicles.

Q2 How does the structure of rough endoplasmic reticulum differ from that of smooth endoplasmic reticulum?

Q3 What is the function of chloroplasts?

Q4 What is the function of the centrioles?

Q5 Name one organelle found only in animal cells.

Exam Questions

Q1 Give four things commonly found in plant cells but not in animal cells. [4 marks]

Q2 a) Identify these two organelles from their descriptions as seen in an electron micrograph.

i) An oval-shaped organelle surrounded by a double membrane. The inner membrane is folded and projects into the inner space, which is filled with a grainy material. [1 mark]

ii) A collection of flattened membrane 'sacs' arranged roughly parallel to one another. Small, circular structures are seen at the edges of these 'sacs'. [1 mark]

b) State the function of the two organelles that you have identified. [2 marks]

That's enough talk of fluid-filled sacs for my liking. Scientists these days...

'Organelle' is a very pretty-sounding name for all those blobs. Actually, under a microscope some of them are really quite fetching — well I think so anyway, but then my mate finds sheep fetching, so there's no accounting for taste. Anyway, you need to know the names and functions of all the organelles and also what they look like.

Organelles Working Together

After that endless list of organelles, you might need a few minutes to regain consciousness... Then you can read this lovely page about how they work together to produce proteins. And there's some stuff on cytoskeletons too... Whoop!

Organelles are Involved in Protein Production

1) Proteins are made at the **ribosomes**.

2) The ribosomes on the **rough endoplasmic reticulum (ER)** make proteins that are **excreted** or attached to the **cell membrane**. The free ribosomes in the **cytoplasm** make proteins that **stay in the cytoplasm**.

3) New proteins produced at the rough ER are **folded** and **processed** (e.g. sugar chains are added) in the rough ER.

4) Then they're **transported** from the ER to the **Golgi apparatus** in **vesicles**.

5) At the Golgi apparatus, the proteins may undergo **further processing** (e.g. sugar chains are trimmed or more are added).

6) The proteins enter more **vesicles** to be transported around the cell.
E.g. glycoproteins (found in **mucus**) move to the cell surface and are **secreted**.

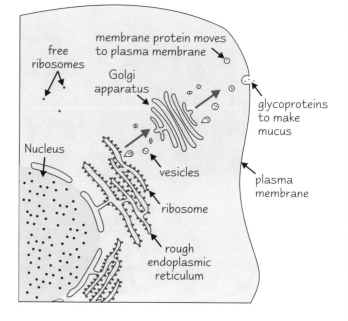

The Cytoskeleton has Several Functions

1) The organelles in cells are surrounded by the **cytoplasm**. The cytoplasm is more than just a solution of chemicals though — it's got a **network of protein threads** running through it. These protein threads are called the **cytoskeleton**.

2) In eukaryotic cells the protein threads are arranged as **microfilaments** (small solid strands) and **microtubules** (tiny protein cylinders).

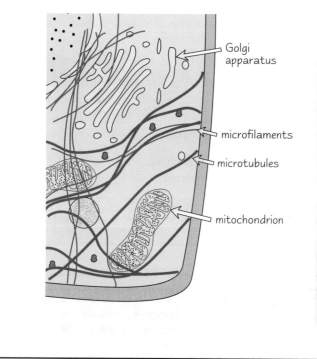

The cytoskeleton has **four main functions**:

1) The microtubules and microfilaments **support** the cell's organelles, keeping them **in position**.

2) They also help to **strengthen** the cell and **maintain its shape**.

3) As well as this, they're responsible for the **transport of materials** within the cell. For example, the movement of **chromosomes** when they separate during cell division depends on contraction of microtubules in the spindle (see page 20 for more on cell division).

4) The proteins of the cytoskeleton can also cause the cell to **move**. For example, the movement of **cilia** and **flagella** is caused by the cytoskeletal protein filaments that run through them. So in the case of single cells that have a flagellum (e.g. sperm cells), the cytoskeleton propels the **whole cell**.

Prokaryotic Cells

Prokaryotes are a Different Kind of Cell

You need to be able to compare and contrast prokaryotic and eukaryotic cells. This big orange table should help...

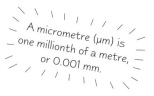

A micrometre (µm) is one millionth of a metre, or 0.001 mm.

PROKARYOTES	EUKARYOTES
Extremely small cells (less than 2 µm diameter)	Larger cells (2-200 µm diameter)
DNA is circular	DNA is linear
No nucleus — DNA free in cytoplasm	Nucleus present — DNA is inside nucleus
Cell wall made of a polysaccharide, but not cellulose or chitin	No cell wall (in animals), cellulose cell wall (in plants) or chitin cell wall (in fungi)
Few organelles, no mitochondria	Many organelles, mitochondria present
Small ribosomes	Larger ribosomes
Example: *E. coli* bacterium	**Example:** Human liver cell

Bacterial Cells are Prokaryotic

1) Prokaryotes like bacteria are roughly a **tenth the size** of eukaryotic cells.

2) This means that normal microscopes aren't really powerful enough to look at their **internal structure**.

3) The diagram shows a bacterial cell as seen under an **electron microscope** (see next page).

flagellum (tail used to propel the cell)

DNA (bacterial chromosome)

plasma (cell surface) membrane

cell wall

ribosome

plasmid (ring of DNA)

Practice Questions

Q1 Give two structures that you might find in a prokaryotic cell but not in an animal cell.

Q2 An unidentified cell is found to contain mitochondria. Is it prokaryotic or eukaryotic?

Exam Questions

Q1 Some mucus-secreting cells were immersed in a solution of radioactive amino acids. Every five seconds, some of the cells were removed and their organelles were separated and analysed. The radioactivity in the different organelles was measured for each five second interval.

When answering the first two questions below, use organelles from this list —
Golgi apparatus, ribosomes, rough endoplasmic reticulum, vesicles.

a) In which of these organelles would you expect radioactivity to appear first? Explain your answer. [2 marks]

b) After 5 minutes, the Golgi apparatus had become radioactive.
Which other organelle(s) would be radioactive by this time? [3 marks]

c) The researchers were particularly interested in the cells' vesicles. What is the function of vesicles? [1 mark]

Q2 Give three functions of a cell's cytoskeleton. [3 marks]

A cell without a nucleus — that can't be right... it's like Posh without Becks...

Prokaryotes are way, way older than eukaryotes. In fact, most cellular biologists think that mitochondria and chloroplasts are remnants of ancient prokaryotes that lived inside the first eukaryotes and eventually just became part of them... Mad.

Studying Cells — Microscopes

If you were born over a century ago then you wouldn't have had to learn all this stuff about organelles because people wouldn't have known anything about them. But then better microscopes were invented and here we are. Unlucky.

Magnification is Size, Resolution is Detail

We all know that microscopes produce a **magnified image** of a sample, but **resolution** is just as important...

1) MAGNIFICATION is how much **bigger** the image is than the specimen (the sample you're looking at). It's calculated using this formula:

$$\text{magnification} = \frac{\text{length of image}}{\text{length of specimen}}$$

2) RESOLUTION is how **detailed** the image is. More specifically, it's how well a microscope **distinguishes** between **two points** that are **close together**. If a microscope lens can't separate two objects, then increasing the magnification won't help.

You Need to be Able to Calculate the Linear Magnification of an Image

In the exam, you might be told the actual and magnified size of an object and then be asked to calculate the **magnification**. You can do this by using the **formula** above. Here's an example...

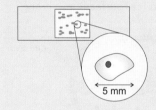

You have a magnified image that's 5 mm wide.
Your specimen is 0.05 mm wide.
magnification = 5 ÷ 0.05
= **× 100**.

Georgina didn't believe in the need for microscopes — she had her trusty varifocals.

There are Two Main Types of Microscope — Light and Electron

Light microscopes

1) **Light microscopes** use light (no surprises there).
2) They have a **lower resolution** than electron microscopes — they have a maximum resolution of about **0.2 micrometres** (µm).
3) The maximum useful **magnification** of a light microscope is about × **1500**.

Electron microscopes

Electron microscopes use **electrons** instead of light to form an image. They have a **higher resolution** than light microscopes so give **more detailed images**. There are two kinds of electron microscope:

1) **Transmission electron microscope (TEM)** — use **electromagnets** to focus a **beam of electrons**, which is then transmitted **through** the specimen. **Denser** parts of the specimen absorb **more electrons**, which makes them look **darker** on the image you end up with. TEMs are good because they provide **high resolution images**, but they can only be used on **thin specimens**.

2) **Scanning electron microscope (SEM)** — scan a beam of electrons across the specimen. This **knocks off** electrons from the specimen, which are gathered in a **cathode ray tube** to form an **image**. The images produced show the **surface** of the specimen and can be **3-D**. But they give **lower resolution images** than TEMs.

There are quite a lot of facts and figures about microscopes here. You need to know about the **magnification** and **resolution** of light microscopes and both types of electron microscope. So I've put all the important numbers in this box 'cos I'm nice like that.

	light microscope	TEM	SEM
maximum resolution	0.2 µm	0.0001 µm	0.005 µm
maximum magnification	× 1500	more than × 1 000 000	less than × 1 000 000

Studying Cells — Microscopes

You Need to Stain Your Samples

1) In light microscopes and TEMs, the beam of light (or electrons) **passes through the object** being viewed. An image is produced because some parts of the object **absorb more light** (or electrons) than others.

2) Sometimes the object being viewed is completely **transparent**. This makes the whole thing look **white** because the light rays (or electrons) just pass **straight through**.

3) To get round this, the object can be **stained**:

- For the light microscope, this means using some kind of **dye**. Common stains are **methylene blue** and **eosin**. The stain is taken up by some parts of the object more than others — the **contrast** makes the different parts show up. →

- For the electron microscope, objects are dipped in a solution of **heavy metals** (like **lead**). The metal ions scatter the electrons, again creating contrast.

Either way, an image is produced because some parts of the object show up **darker** than others.

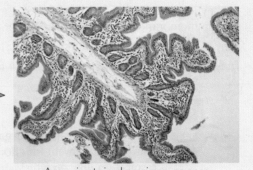

An eosin stained specimen, as seen through a light microscope.

Practice Questions

Q1 What is the formula for calculating the magnification of an image?

Q2 What is meant by a microscope's resolution?

Q3 Why is it sometimes necessary to stain an object before viewing it through a microscope?

Exam Questions

Q1 An insect is 0.5 mm long. In a book, a picture of the insect is 8 cm long.
Calculate the magnification of the image. [2 marks]

Q2 The table shows the dimensions of some different organelles found in animal cells.

organelle	diameter / μm
lysosome	0.1
mitochondrion	2
nucleus	5
ribosome	0.02
vesicle	0.05

a) Name those organelles in the table that would be visible using a good quality light microscope.
Explain your answer. [3 marks]

b) Which organelles would be visible using an SEM? Explain your answer. [2 marks]

'Staining your samples' — a common problem at the start of exams...

OK, there's quite a bit of info on these pages, but the whole magnification thing isn't all that bad once you've given it a go. Make sure you can define resolution — that's a bit trickier. You also need to have a good grasp of what TEMs and SEMs are, and how the resolution of their images compare to each other and to those of light microscopes. Happy memorising...

Cell Membranes — The Basics

You might remember a bit about cell membranes from that giant pink table of fun back in Section 1. Well now it's time to delve a little deeper and see exactly what they do — lucky you.

Membranes Control What Passes Through Them

Cells, and many of the **organelles** inside them, are surrounded by **membranes**, which have a **range of functions**:

Membranes at the surface of cells (PLASMA membranes)

1) They control **which substances enter and leave** the cell. They're **partially permeable** — they let some molecules through but not others. Substances can move across the plasma membrane by **diffusion, osmosis** or **active transport** (see pages 16-19).

2) They allow **recognition** by other cells, e.g. the cells of the **immune system** (see p. 81).

3) They allow **cell communication** (see p. 14 for more).

Partially permeable membranes can be useful at sea

Membranes within cells

1) The membranes around **organelles divide** the cell into different **compartments**. This makes different **functions more efficient**, e.g. the substances needed for **respiration** (like enzymes) are kept together inside **mitochondria**.

2) The membranes of some organelles are folded, increasing their **surface area** and making **chemical reactions more efficient**. E.g. the **inner membrane** of a mitochondrion contains **enzymes** needed for **respiration**. It has a large surface area, which **increases** the **number** of enzymes present and makes respiration more efficient.

3) They can form **vesicles** to **transport** substances between different areas of the cell (see p. 6).

4) They control **which substances enter and leave** the organelle, e.g. RNA (see p. 63) leaves the nucleus via the nuclear membrane. They are also **partially permeable**.

Cell Membranes have a 'Fluid Mosaic' Structure

The **structure** of all membranes is basically the same. They're composed of **lipids** (mainly phospholipids), **proteins** and **carbohydrates** (usually attached to proteins or lipids).

1) In 1972, the **fluid mosaic model** was suggested to describe the **arrangement** of **molecules** in the membrane.

2) In the model, **phospholipid molecules** form a continuous, double layer (**bilayer**).

3) This bilayer is '**fluid**' because the phospholipids are **constantly moving**.

4) **Cholesterol** molecules are present within the bilayer (see next page).

5) **Protein molecules** are scattered through the bilayer, like tiles in a **mosaic**.

6) Some **proteins** have a **polysaccharide** (carbohydrate) **chain** attached — these are called **glycoproteins**.

7) Some **lipids** also have a **polysaccharide chain** attached — these are called **glycolipids**.

The phospholipid bilayer is about 7 nm thick.

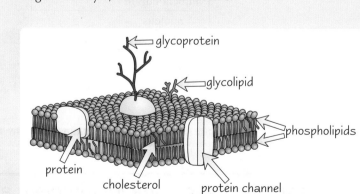

Cell Membranes — The Basics

The **Different Components** of Cell Membranes have **Different Roles**

Phospholipids Form a Barrier to Dissolved Substances

1) **Phospholipid molecules** have a 'head' and a 'tail'.
2) The **head** is **hydrophilic** — it **attracts water**.
3) The **tail** is **hydrophobic** — it **repels water**.
4) The molecules automatically **arrange** themselves into a **bilayer** — the **heads face out** towards the water on either side of the membrane.
5) The **centre** of the bilayer is **hydrophobic** so the membrane **doesn't** allow **water-soluble substances** (like ions) through it — it acts as a **barrier** to these dissolved substances.

phospholipid head

phospholipid tail

phospholipid bilayer

See p. 59 for more on phospholipids and cholesterol.

Cholesterol Gives the Membrane Stability

1) **Cholesterol** is a type of lipid (fat).
2) It's present in **all** cell membranes (except bacterial cell membranes).
3) Cholesterol molecules fit **between** the phospholipids. They bind to the hydrophobic tails of the phospholipids, causing them to pack **more closely together**. This makes the membrane **less fluid** and **more rigid**.

phospholipid

cholesterol

Proteins Control What Enters and Leaves the Cell

1) Some proteins form **channels** in the membrane (see p. 18) — these allow **small** or **charged** particles **through**.
2) Other proteins (called **carrier proteins**) **transport molecules** and **ions** across the membrane by **active transport** and **facilitated diffusion** (see page 18).
3) Proteins also act as **receptors** for molecules (e.g. hormones) in **cell signalling** (see next page). When a molecule **binds** to the protein, a **chemical reaction** is triggered inside the cell.

Glycolipids and Glycoproteins act as Receptors for Messenger Molecules

1) Glycolipids and glycoproteins **stabilise** the membrane by forming **hydrogen bonds** with surrounding **water molecules**.
2) They're also sites where **drugs**, **hormones** and **antibodies** bind.
3) They act as **receptors** for **cell signalling** (see next page).
4) They're also **antigens** — cell surface molecules involved in the immune response (see p. 80).

Practice Questions

Q1   Give two functions of membranes within the cell and two functions of membranes at the cell surface.

Q2   Give three molecules, other than proteins and cholesterol, that are present in animal cell membranes.

Exam Questions

Q1   Explain why the plasma membrane can be described as having a fluid-mosaic structure.   [2 marks]

Q2   Describe the role of cholesterol in cell membranes.   [1 mark]

Fluid Mosaic Model — think I saw one being sold at a craft fair...

It's weird to think that cells are surrounded by a layer that's 'fluid' — it's a good job it is though, 'cause if cell membranes were rigid a cell wouldn't be able to change shape or stretch without bursting, and that wouldn't be a pretty sight. It's also a good job that the membrane's partially permeable — so that it can let oxygen and carbon dioxide in and out of the cell.

Cell Membranes — The Basics

Cells like to have a good chat with one another every once in a while to make sure everything's going OK. To do this they use a process called cell signalling. The cell membrane is pretty important in cell signalling.

Cell Signalling is How Cells Communicate with Each Other

Cells need to communicate with each other to **control processes** inside the body and to **respond** to **changes** in the **environment**.

> Cells communicate with each other using **messenger molecules**:
> 1) One cell **releases** a messenger molecule (e.g. a **hormone**).
> 2) This molecule **travels** to another cell (e.g. in the blood).
> 3) The messenger molecule is detected by the cell because it **binds** to a **receptor** on its **cell membrane**.

Emma was learning that communication with the opposite sex wasn't always easy...

Cell Membrane Receptors Play an Important Role in Cell Signalling

The **cell membrane** is **important** in the signalling process.
1) Membrane-bound **proteins** act as **receptors** for messenger molecules.
2) Receptor proteins have **specific shapes** — only **messenger molecules** with a **complementary shape** can **bind** to them.
3) **Different cells** have **different types** of receptors — they respond to **different messenger molecules**.
4) A cell that responds to a particular messenger molecule is called a **target cell**.

The diagram below shows how messenger molecules bind to target cells.

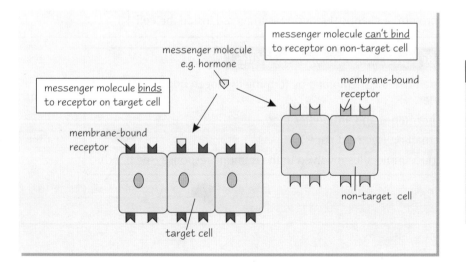

messenger molecule can't bind to receptor on non-target cell

messenger molecule e.g. hormone

messenger molecule binds to receptor on target cell

membrane-bound receptor

membrane-bound receptor

target cell

non-target cell

EXAMPLE: GLUCAGON

Glucagon is a **hormone** that's **released** when there **isn't enough glucose** in the **blood**. It **binds** to **receptors** on **liver cells**, causing the liver cells to **break down** stores of **glycogen** to glucose.

Drugs Also Bind to Cell Membrane Receptors

1) Many **drugs** work by **binding** to **receptors** in cell membranes.
2) They either to **trigger** a **response** in the cell, or **block** the receptor and **prevent** it from **working**.

EXAMPLE: ANTIHISTAMINES

Cell damage causes the release of **histamine**. Histamine binds to receptors on the surface of other cells and causes **inflammation**. **Antihistamines** work by **blocking histamine receptors** on cell surfaces. This **prevents** histamine from binding to the cell and **stops inflammation**.

Cell Membranes — The Basics

Membranes are Affected by Temperature

Temperature affects how much the phospholipids in the bilayer can move, which affects membrane structure.

(1) **Temperatures below 0 °C**
The phospholipids don't have much energy, so they can't move very much. They're **packed closely together** and the membrane is **rigid**. But **channel proteins** and **carrier proteins** in the membrane **denature** (see p. 68), increasing the **permeability** of the membrane. **Ice crystals** may form and **pierce** the membrane, making it **highly permeable** when it thaws.

(2) **Temperatures between 0 and 45 °C**
The phospholipids can **move around** and **aren't** packed as tightly together — the membrane is **partially permeable**. As the temperature **increases** the phospholipids **move more** because they have more energy — this **increases** the **permeability** of the membrane.

(3) **Temperatures above 45 °C**
The phospholipid bilayer starts to **melt** (break down) and the membrane becomes more **permeable**. **Water** inside the cell **expands**, putting pressure on the membrane. **Channel proteins** and **carrier proteins** in the membrane **denature** so they can't control what enters or leaves the cell — this increases the **permeability** of the membrane.

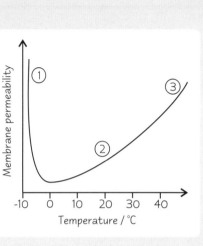

Practice Questions

Q1 What is cell signalling?

Q2 What do messenger molecules bind to?

Exam Questions

Q1 Nicotine has an effect on nerve cells, but not on other types of cell in the body.
Use your knowledge of cell membrane structure to explain why. [3 marks]

Q2 Beetroot cells contain a red pigment. In an experiment, four identical cubes of beetroot were washed and placed in four different test tubes of water. Each test tube was placed in a water bath at a different temperature, for 10 minutes. The water from each test tube was then placed in a colorimeter, to measure the concentration of pigment. A large absorbance value indicates a high concentration of pigment. The results are shown in the table on the right.

Tube number	Temperature / °C	Absorbance
1	10	1
2	30	5
3	50	43
4	70	56

a) Which tube contained the greatest concentration of beetroot pigment? [1 mark]

b) Describe and explain the difference between the results for tubes 1 and 2. [4 marks]

c) Describe and explain the difference between the results for tubes 2 and 3. [4 marks]

d) The experiment was repeated, with a test tube placed in the freezer for 10 minutes.
The test tube was left to thaw before the absorbance reading was taken.
Suggest whether the absorbance reading would have been high or low, and explain your answer. [4 marks]

Perm-eability — it's definitely decreased since the 80s...

Hopefully the mystery of cell signalling should now seem a bit clearer. At any one time, there are loads of messenger molecules being released by different cells in your body — travelling round and binding to receptors on other cells, causing some kind of response or another. This signalling fine-tunes all the body's processes and keeps us working properly.

Transport Across Cell Membranes

The beauty of cell membranes is that they're partially permeable — they'll only let certain substances enter and leave. Some substances move across cell membranes by passive transport, which means no energy is involved in the process. Passive transport processes include diffusion, osmosis and facilitated diffusion (see p. 18).

Diffusion *is the* Passive Movement *of* Particles

1) Diffusion is the net movement of particles (molecules or ions) from an area of **higher concentration** to an area of **lower concentration**.

2) Molecules will diffuse **both ways**, but the **net movement** will be to the area of **lower concentration**. This continues until particles are **evenly distributed** throughout the liquid or gas.

3) The **concentration gradient** is the path from an area of higher concentration to an area of lower concentration. Particles diffuse **down** a concentration gradient.

4) Diffusion is a **passive process** — **no energy** is needed for it to happen.

5) Particles can diffuse **across plasma membranes**, as long as they can **move freely** through the membrane. E.g. oxygen and carbon dioxide molecules are **small enough** to pass easily through spaces between phospholipids.

Diffusion — not good in a swimming pool.

The Rate of Diffusion *Depends on* Several Factors

1) The **concentration gradient** — the **higher** it is, the **faster** the rate of diffusion.

2) The **thickness** of the **exchange surface** — the **thinner** the exchange surface (i.e. the **shorter** the **distance** the particles have to travel), the **faster** the rate of diffusion.

3) The **surface area** — the **larger** the surface area (e.g. of a cell membrane), the **faster** the rate of diffusion.

Osmosis *is* Diffusion *of* Water Molecules

1) Osmosis is the **diffusion of water molecules** across a **partially permeable membrane**, from an area of **higher water potential** (i.e. higher concentration of water molecules) to an area of **lower water potential** (i.e. lower concentration of water molecules).

2) **Water potential** is the potential (likelihood) of water molecules to diffuse out of or into a solution.

3) **Pure water** has the **highest water potential**. All solutions have a **lower** water potential than pure water.

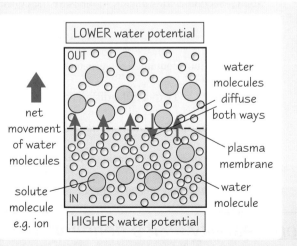

Transport Across Cell Membranes

Cells are Affected by the Water Potential of the Surrounding Solution

Water moves **in** or **out** of a cell by osmosis. **How much** moves in or out depends on the **water potential** of the **surrounding solution**. Animal and plant cells behave differently in different solutions.

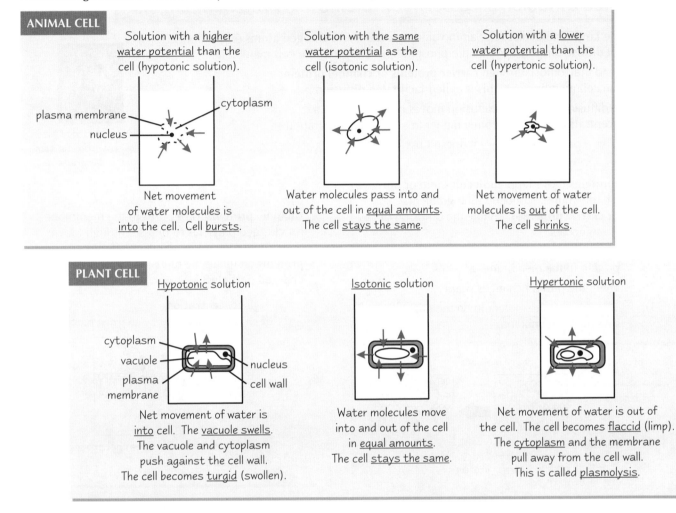

ANIMAL CELL

Solution with a <u>higher</u> <u>water potential</u> than the cell (hypotonic solution).

Solution with the <u>same</u> <u>water potential</u> as the cell (isotonic solution).

Solution with a <u>lower</u> <u>water potential</u> than the cell (hypertonic solution).

plasma membrane
nucleus
cytoplasm

Net movement of water molecules is <u>into</u> the cell. Cell <u>bursts</u>.

Water molecules pass into and out of the cell in <u>equal amounts</u>. The cell <u>stays the same</u>.

Net movement of water molecules is <u>out</u> of the cell. The cell <u>shrinks</u>.

PLANT CELL

<u>Hypotonic</u> solution

<u>Isotonic</u> solution

<u>Hypertonic</u> solution

cytoplasm
vacuole
plasma membrane
nucleus
cell wall

Net movement of water is <u>into</u> cell. The <u>vacuole swells</u>. The vacuole and cytoplasm push against the cell wall. The cell becomes <u>turgid</u> (swollen).

Water molecules move into and out of the cell in <u>equal amounts</u>. The cell <u>stays the same</u>.

Net movement of water is out of the cell. The cell becomes <u>flaccid</u> (limp). The <u>cytoplasm</u> and the membrane pull away from the cell wall. This is called <u>plasmolysis</u>.

Practice Questions

Q1 Diffusion is a passive transport process. What does this mean?

Q2 What happens to an animal cell if it is placed in a solution with the same water potential as the cell?

Q3 What happens to a plant cell if it is placed in a solution with a higher water potential than the cell?

Exam Question

Q1 Pieces of potato of equal mass were put into different concentrations of sucrose solution for three days. The difference in mass for each is recorded in the table.

Concentration of sucrose / %	1	2	3	4
Mass difference / g	0.4	0.2	0	− 0.2

a) Explain why the pieces of potato in 1% and 2% sucrose solutions gained mass. [3 marks]

b) Suggest a reason why the mass of the piece of potato in 3% sucrose solution stayed the same. [1 mark]

c) What would you expect the mass difference for a potato in a 5% solution to be? Explain your answer. [4 marks]

Ginantonic solution — my gran's favourite...

Osmosis is just a fancy name for the diffusion of water molecules. But whether water moves in or out of a cell depends on the water potential of the surrounding solution. Water potential can be pretty confusing — if you can't make head nor tail of an exam question about it try replacing the word 'potential' with 'concentration' and it'll become clearer.

Transport Across Cell Membranes

Facilitated diffusion is another passive transport process, but there's also an active transport process, which is imaginatively named 'active transport'. Facilitated diffusion and active transport are actually quite similar though — they both involve proteins.

Facilitated Diffusion uses Carrier Proteins and Protein Channels

1) Some **larger molecules** (e.g. amino acids, glucose) and **charged atoms** (e.g. chloride ions) **can't diffuse directly through** the phospholipid bilayer of the cell membrane.

2) Instead they diffuse through **carrier proteins** or **channel proteins** in the cell membrane — this is called **facilitated diffusion**.

3) Like diffusion, facilitated diffusion moves particles **down** a **concentration gradient**, from a higher to a lower concentration.

4) It's also a passive process — it **doesn't** use **energy**.

Andy needed all his concentration for this particular gradient...

Carrier proteins move **large molecules** into or out of the cell, down their concentration gradient. **Different carrier proteins** facilitate the diffusion of **different molecules**.

1) First, a large molecule **attaches** to a carrier protein in the membrane.

2) Then, the protein **changes shape**.

3) This **releases** the molecule on the **opposite side** of the membrane.

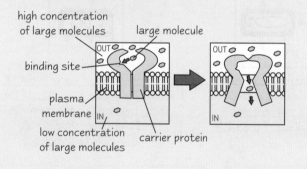

Channel proteins form **pores** in the membrane for **charged particles** to diffuse through (down their concentration gradient). **Different channel proteins** facilitate the diffusion of **different charged particles**.

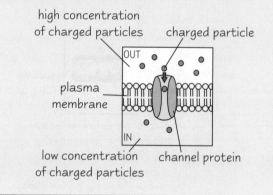

Active Transport Moves Substances Against a Concentration Gradient

Active transport uses **energy** to move **molecules** and **ions** across plasma membranes, **against** a **concentration gradient**. This process involves **carrier proteins**.

1) The process is pretty similar to facilitated diffusion — a molecule **attaches** to the carrier protein, the protein **changes shape** and this moves the molecule **across** the membrane, **releasing it** on the other side.

2) The only difference is that **energy** is used (from **ATP** — a common source of energy used in the cell), to move the solute against its concentration gradient.

3) The diagram on the right shows the active transport of **calcium**.

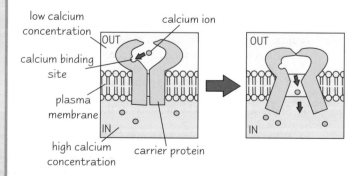

Transport Across Cell Membranes

Cells can **Take in** Substances by **Endocytosis**

1) Some molecules are way too **large** to be taken into a cell by carrier proteins, e.g. proteins, lipids and some carbohydrates.

2) Instead a cell can **surround** a substance with a **section** of its **plasma membrane**.

3) The membrane then **pinches off** to form a **vesicle** inside the cell containing the **ingested substance** — this is **endocytosis**.

4) Some cells also take in much **larger objects** by endocytosis — for example, some **white blood cells** (mainly phagocytes, see p. 80) use endocytosis to take in things like **microorganisms** and **dead cells** so that they can destroy them.

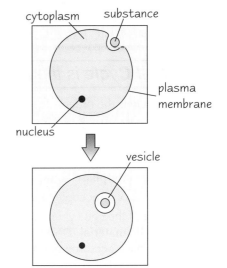

Cells can **Secrete** Substances by **Exocytosis**

1) Some substances **produced** by the cell (e.g. **digestive enzymes**, **hormones**, **lipids**) need to be **released** from the cell — this is done by **exocytosis**.

2) **Vesicles** containing these substances **pinch off** from the sacs of the **Golgi apparatus** (see p. 6) and **move towards** the plasma membrane.

3) The vesicles **fuse** with the **plasma membrane** and **release** their contents **outside** the cell.

4) Some substances (like membrane proteins) **aren't** released outside the cell — instead they are **inserted** straight into the plasma membrane.

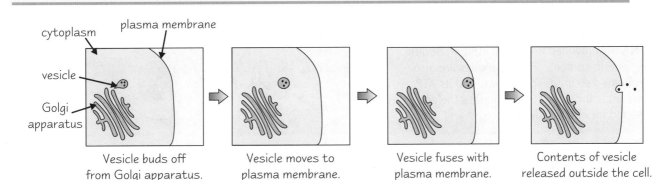

| Vesicle buds off from Golgi apparatus. | Vesicle moves to plasma membrane. | Vesicle fuses with plasma membrane. | Contents of vesicle released outside the cell. |

Practice Questions

Q1 What is active transport?

Q2 Which molecule provides the energy for active transport?

Exam Questions

Q1 Describe the role of membrane proteins in facilitated diffusion. [6 marks]

Q2 Explain the difference between endocytosis and exocytosis. [4 marks]

Revision — like working against a concentration gradient...

Wouldn't it be great if you could revise by endocytosis — you could just stick this book on your head and your brain would slowly surround it and take it in... actually when I put it like that it sounds a bit gross. Maybe just stick to good old 'closing the book and scribbling down the diagrams till you know them off by heart'.

Cell Division — Mitosis

I don't like cell division. There, I've said it. It's unfair of me, because if it wasn't for cell division I'd still only be one cell big. It's all those diagrams that look like worms nailed to bits of string that put me off.

The **Cell Cycle** is the Process of **Cell Growth** and **Division**

The **cell cycle** is the process that all body cells from **multicellular organisms** use to **grow** and **divide**.

1) The cell cycle **starts** when a cell has been produced by cell division and **ends** with the cell dividing to produce two identical cells.

2) The cell cycle consists of a period of **cell growth**, called **interphase**, and a period of **cell division**, called **mitosis**. →

3) Mitosis only occupies a **small percentage** of the cell cycle.

4) Most of the cell cycle is taken up by **interphase**, during which the **genetic material** (DNA) is **copied** and **checked** for any errors that may have occurred during copying.

5) If errors in the genetic material are detected at this stage, the cell may **kill itself**. This prevents any **mutations** (errors) in the DNA from being passed on.

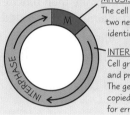

MITOSIS
The cell divides to produce two new genetically identical cells.

INTERPHASE
Cell grows — new organelles and proteins are made. The genetic material is copied and checked for errors.

Mitosis has **Four Division Stages**

1) Mitosis is needed for the **growth** of multicellular organisms (like us) and for **repairing damaged tissues**.

2) Mitosis is really one **continuous process**, but it's described as a series of **division stages** — prophase, metaphase, anaphase and telophase.

3) **Interphase** comes **before** mitosis in the cell cycle — it's when cells grow and replicate their DNA ready for division.

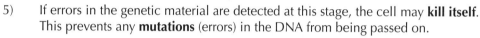

Interphase — The cell carries out normal functions, but also prepares to divide. The cell's **DNA** is unravelled and **replicated**, to double its genetic content. The **organelles** are also **replicated** so it has spare ones, and its ATP content is increased (ATP provides the energy needed for cell division).

Homologous pair   Interphase
Cell
Chromosome
Cytoplasm
Nucleus
Centriole
Unravelled DNA containing two copies of each chromosome

1) <u>Prophase</u> — The **chromosomes condense**, getting shorter and fatter. Tiny bundles of protein called **centrioles** start moving to opposite ends of the cell, forming a network of protein fibres across it called the **spindle**. The **nuclear envelope** (the membrane around the nucleus) **breaks down** and chromosomes lie free in the cytoplasm.

Nuclear envelope starts to break down
Centrioles move to opposite ends of the cell
Centromere

As mitosis begins, the chromosomes are made of two strands joined in the middle by a <u>centromere</u>. The separate strands are called <u>chromatids</u>.

One chromatid   Centromere
Sister chromatids

There are two strands because each chromosome has already made an <u>identical copy</u> of itself during <u>interphase</u>. When mitosis is over, the chromatids end up as one-strand chromosomes in the new daughter cells.

2) <u>Metaphase</u> — The chromosomes (each with two chromatids) **line up** along the middle of the cell and become **attached** to the **spindle** by their **centromere**.

Spindle fibres
Centromeres on spindle equator

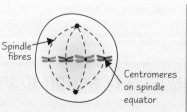

Cell Division — Mitosis

3) <u>Anaphase</u> — The centromeres divide, **separating** each pair of sister **chromatids**. The spindles contract, pulling chromatids to opposite ends of the cell, centromere first.

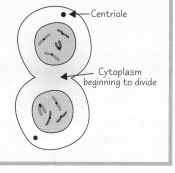

Sister chromatids moving to opposite ends of the cell

So long and thanks for all the organelles!

It's so hard letting go of my baby girls. It feels like a part of me has gone with them.

There, there love — it's all part of the cycle of life.

Mitosis can be a moving time.

4) <u>Telophase</u> — The chromatids reach the **opposite poles** on the spindle. They uncoil and become long and thin again. They're now called **chromosomes** again. A **nuclear envelope** forms around each group of chromosomes, so there are now **two nuclei**. The **cytoplasm divides** and there are now **two daughter cells** that are **genetically identical** to the original cell and to each other. Mitosis is finished and each daughter cell starts the **interphase** part of the cell cycle to get ready for the next round of mitosis.

Centriole

Cytoplasm beginning to divide

You can **Observe Mitosis** by **Staining Chromosomes**

You can **stain chromosomes** so you can see them under a **microscope**. This means you can watch what happens to them **during mitosis** — and it makes high-adrenaline viewing, I can tell you. You need to be able to **recognise** each stage in mitosis from diagrams and **photographs** — lucky you. You've seen the diagrams, now enjoy the photos:

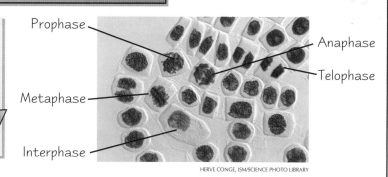

Prophase

Anaphase

Telophase

Metaphase

Interphase

HERVE CONGE, ISM/SCIENCE PHOTO LIBRARY

Practice Questions

Q1   What happens during interphase?

Q2   List in order the four stages of mitosis.

Q3   At what stage in mitosis does the nuclear envelope break down?

Exam Question

Q1   The diagrams show cells at different stages of mitosis.

a) For each of the cells A, B and C state the stage of mitosis, giving a reason for your answer.

[6 marks]

b) Name the structures labelled X, Y and Z in cell B.

[3 marks]

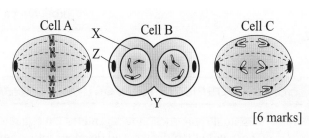

Cell A   X   Cell B   Cell C

Z

Y

Doctor, Doctor, I'm getting short and fat — don't worry, it's just a phase...

Quite a lot to learn in this topic — but it's all dead important stuff, so no slacking. Most body cells undergo mitosis — it's how they multiply and how organisms like us grow and develop. Remember that chromosomes during mitosis are made up of two sister chromatids joined by a centromere. Nice to know family values are important to genetic material too.

Cell Division and Reproduction

And now on to the exciting topic of cell division in reproduction — well, on to a topic slightly more exciting than the workings of mitosis, but not quite as exciting as I've led you to believe... sorry...

Some Organisms **Reproduce Asexually** Using **Mitosis**

Some organisms (e.g. some **plants** and **fungi**) **reproduce asexually** (without sex) using mitosis. This means any new organisms produced are **genetically identical** to the original, parent organism.

Yeast Cells Reproduce Asexually by **Budding**

1) Yeast are single-celled **microorganisms**. They're a type of fungi.
2) Yeast cells are **eukaryotic**, with all the usual **organelles** in the cytoplasm (see pages 5-7) and a **nucleus** containing chromosomes (DNA).
3) Yeast can reproduce **asexually** by a process called **budding**.
4) Budding involves **mitosis**.
5) This means the offspring produced are **genetically identical** to the parent cell.

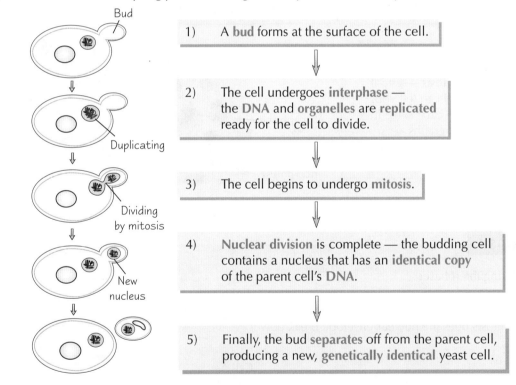

1) A **bud** forms at the surface of the cell.

2) The cell undergoes **interphase** — the DNA and organelles are **replicated** ready for the cell to divide.

3) The cell begins to undergo **mitosis**.

4) **Nuclear division** is complete — the budding cell contains a nucleus that has an **identical copy** of the parent cell's DNA.

5) Finally, the bud **separates** off from the parent cell, producing a new, **genetically identical** yeast cell.

Some Organisms **Reproduce Sexually** Using **Meiosis**

1) In sexual reproduction two **gametes** (an egg and a sperm) join together at **fertilisation** to form a **zygote**. The zygote then divides and develops into a **new organism**.
2) **Meiosis** is a type of **cell division** that happens in the reproductive organs to **produce gametes**.
3) Cells that divide by meiosis have the **full number** of chromosomes to start with, but the cells that are formed from meiosis have **half the number**.
4) Cells formed by meiosis are all **genetically different** because each new cell ends up with a **different combination** of chromosomes.

Cell Division and Reproduction

Cell Division by **Meiosis** Creates **Genetically Different Cells**

You don't need to learn the details of meiosis, just understand that it produces genetically different cells. Here's how it happens:

1) The DNA **replicates** and coils up to form **chromosomes**.

•2) The chromosomes **arrange** themselves into **homologous pairs**.

3) The chromosome pairs then **swap bits** with each other.

Chromatids of one chromosome | Bits of chromatids swap over | Chromatids now have a new combination of alleles

4) In the first division, these homologous pairs **split up**. Any one chromosome from **each pair** can go into **either cell**, as long as each cell gets one number 1, one number 2, etc.

5) In the second division, each chromosome **splits in half**. Any half can go into **any cell**.

6) **Four** new **genetically different** cells are produced.

7) They're genetically different from each other because the chromosomes **swap bits** during meiosis and each gamete gets a **combination of half** of them, at **random**.

Humans have **46 chromosomes** in total — **23 pairs**. **One chromosome** in each pair came from mum and one from dad, e.g. there are two number 1s (1 from mum and 1 from dad), two number 2s, etc. The chromosomes that make up each pair are the same size and have the **same genes**, although they could have **different versions** of those genes (called **alleles**). These pairs of chromosomes are called **homologous pairs**.

You do need to learn what a homologous chromosome is.

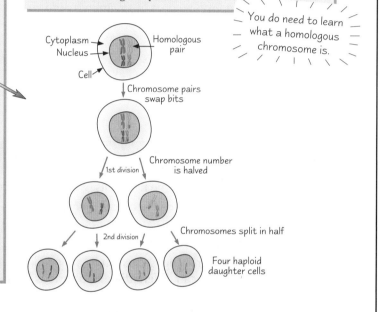

Practice Questions

Q1 Does asexual reproduction in yeast produce genetically identical cells or genetically different ones?

Q2 Which form of cell division, meiosis or mitosis, leads to the production of genetically different cells?

Exam Questions

Q1 The diagram opposite shows three stages of budding in a yeast cell.

   a) Describe what has happened between stages A and B.   [3 marks]

   b) Describe what has happened between stages B and C.   [2 marks]

Q2 Explain the meaning of the term 'homologous pair of chromosomes'.   [2 marks]

Reproduction isn't as exciting as some people would have you believe...

This stuff can take a while to sink in — but that's no excuse to sit there staring at the page muttering things like "I don't get it" and "guinea pigs don't have to learn this stuff — I wish I was a guinea pig". Use the diagrams to help you understand — they look evil, but they really help. And remember, mitosis produces genetically identical cells and meiosis genetically different cells.

Stem Cells and Differentiation

Life's pretty easy for single-celled organisms like yeast. One minute they're a little bud on the side of their parent cell and the next they're a fully grown organism, ready to face the exciting world of brewing or baking (or anything else a young yeast likes to do). But things aren't quite so easy for multicellular organisms like us — we have to grow and develop.

Stem Cells are Unspecialised Cells

1) **Multicellular organisms** are made up from many **different** cell types that are **specialised** for their function, e.g. liver cells, muscle cells, white blood cells.

2) **All** these specialised cell types originally came from **stem cells**.

3) Stem cells are **unspecialised** cells — they can develop into **any** type of cell.

4) **All** multicellular organisms have some form of **stem cell**.

5) In **humans**, stem cells are found in **early embryos** and in a few places in **adults**.

- In the first few days of an embryo's life, **any** of its cells can **develop** into **any** type of human cell — they're **all** stem cells.
- In adults, stem cells are found in a few places (e.g. **bone marrow**), but they're **not as flexible** — they can only develop into a **limited range** of cells (see below).

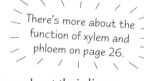

Joe knew his cells were specialised — specialised to look good.

Stem Cells Differentiate into Specialised Cells

1) Stem cells **divide** to become **new cells**, which then become **specialised**.

2) The process by which a cell becomes specialised for its job is called **differentiation**.

3) In animals, adult stem cells are used to replace **damaged cells**, e.g. to make **new skin** or **blood cells** (see below).

4) **Plants** are always growing, so stem cells are needed to make **new shoots** and **roots** throughout their lives. Stem cells in plants can **differentiate** into various plant tissues including **xylem and phloem** (see below).

There's more about the function of xylem and phloem on page 26.

Cells in the Bone Marrow Differentiate into Blood Cells

1) **Bones** are living organs, containing nerves and **blood vessels**.

2) The main bones of the body have **marrow** in the **centres**.

3) Here, **adult stem cells** divide and **differentiate** to replace worn out blood cells — **erythrocytes** (red blood cells) and **neutrophils** (white blood cells that help to fight infection).

Neutrophil (white blood cell)

DIFFERENTIATION

Undifferentiated stem cell

Erythrocyte (red blood cell)

Cells in the Cambium Differentiate into Xylem and Phloem

1) In plants, **stem cells** are found in the **cambium**.

2) In the root and stem, stem cells of the **vascular cambium** divide and **differentiate** to become **xylem** and **phloem**.

3) The vascular cambium forms a **ring** inside the root and shoots.

4) The cells **divide** and grow out from the ring, **differentiating** as they **move away** from the cambium.

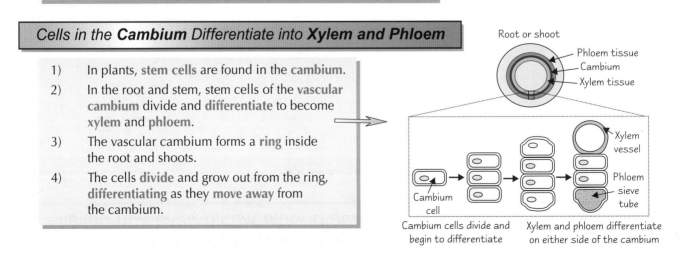

Root or shoot

Phloem tissue
Cambium
Xylem tissue

Xylem vessel

Phloem sieve tube

Cambium cell

Cambium cells divide and begin to differentiate

Xylem and phloem differentiate on either side of the cambium

Stem Cells and Differentiation

Cells are **Specialised** for their Particular Function

Once cells **differentiate**, they have a **specific function**. Their **structure** is **adapted** to perform that function. You need to **know** how the following cell types are specialised for their functions:

Animal cells

1) **Neutrophils** (white blood cells, e.g. phagocytes) defend the body against disease. Their **flexible shape** allows them to **engulf** foreign particles or pathogens (see p. 80). The many **lysosomes** in their cytoplasm contain **digestive enzymes** to **break down** the engulfed particles.

2) **Erythrocytes** (red blood cells) carry oxygen in the blood. The **biconcave** disc shape provides a **large surface area** for gas exchange. They have **no nucleus** so there's more room for **haemoglobin** (see p. 42), the protein that carries oxygen.

3) **Epithelial cells** cover the surfaces of organs. The cells are **joined** by **interlinking** cell membranes and a membrane at their base. Some epithelia (e.g. in the **lungs**) have **cilia** that beat to move particles away. Other epithelia (e.g. in the **small intestine**) have **microvilli** — folds in the cell membrane that increase the cell's **surface area**.

4) **Sperm cells** (male sex cells) have a **flagellum** (tail) so they can **swim** to the egg (female sex cell). They also have lots of **mitochondria** to provide the **energy** to swim. The **acrosome** contains **digestive enzymes** to enable the sperm to **penetrate** the surface of the egg.

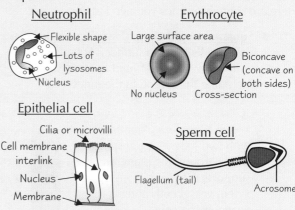

Plant cells

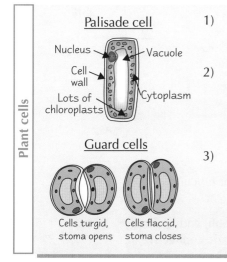

1) **Palisade mesophyll cells** in leaves do most of the **photosynthesis**. They contain **many chloroplasts**, so they can absorb a lot of sunlight. The walls are **thin**, so carbon dioxide can **easily diffuse** into the cell.

2) **Root hair cells** absorb water and mineral ions from the soil. They have a **large surface area** for absorption and a **thin**, permeable cell wall, for entry of water and ions. The cytoplasm contains **extra mitochondria** to provide the **energy** needed for **active transport** (see p. 18).

3) **Guard cells** line the **stomata** — the tiny pores in the surface of the leaf used for **gas exchange**. In the **light**, guard cells **take up water** and become **turgid**. Their **thin outer walls** and **thickened inner walls** force them to bend outwards, **opening** the stomata. This allows the leaf to exchange gases for photosynthesis.

Root hair cell — Nucleus, Thin cell wall

Practice Questions

Q1 What are stem cells?

Q2 Stem cells in bone marrow can differentiate into other cell types. Name two of these cell types.

Exam Questions

Q1 Describe how a palisade cell is adapted for its role in photosynthesis. [4 marks]

Q2 Describe, with examples, the role of stem cells in adult animals and plants. [5 marks]

And you thought differentiation was just boring maths stuff...

Stem cells are pretty amazing when you think about it — they can differentiate to become any cell in the whole body. Scientists are excited about them because they could be used to repair damaged cells, like muscle cells after a heart attack.

Tissues, Organs and Systems

Multicellular organisms are made up of lots of different cell types, which are organised to work together — cells that carry out the same job are organised into tissues (e.g. epithelium), different tissues are organised into organs (e.g. the lungs) and organs work together as organ systems (e.g. the respiratory system).

Similar Cells are Organised into Tissues

A **tissue** is a group of cells (plus any **extracellular material** secreted by them) that are specialised to **work together** to carry out a **particular function**. A tissue can contain **more than one** cell type. Here are some examples you need to know:

1) **Squamous epithelium tissue** is a **single layer** of **flat cells** lining a surface. Squamous epithelium tissue is found in many places including the alveoli in the lungs.

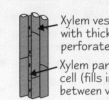

Nucleus

Basement membrane

Epithelium is a tissue that forms a covering or a lining.

2) **Xylem tissue** is a plant tissue with two jobs — it **transports water** around the plant, and it **supports** the plant. It contains **xylem vessel cells** and **parenchyma cells**.

Xylem vessel cell with thickened wall perforated by pits

Xylem parenchyma cell (fills in gaps between vessels)

3) **Ciliated epithelium** is a layer of cells covered in **cilia** (see p. 7). It's found on surfaces where things need to be **moved** — in the trachea for instance, where the cilia waft mucus along.

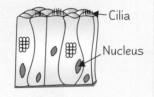

Cilia

Nucleus

4) **Phloem tissue** transports **sugars** around the plant. It's arranged in **tubes** and is made up of **sieve cells**, **companion cells**, and some **ordinary** plant cells. Each sieve cell has end walls with **holes** in them, so that sap can move easily through them. These end walls are called **sieve plates**.

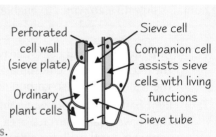

Perforated cell wall (sieve plate)

Ordinary plant cells

Sieve cell

Companion cell assists sieve cells with living functions

Sieve tube

Different Tissues Make up an Organ

An **organ** is a group of different tissues that **work together** to perform a particular function. Examples include:

- The **lungs** — they contain **squamous epithelium** tissue (in the alveoli) and **ciliated epithelium** tissue (in the bronchi etc.). They also have **elastic connective tissue** and **vascular tissue** (in the blood vessels).
- **Leaves** — they contain **palisade tissue** for photosynthesis, as well as **epidermal** tissue, and **xylem** and **phloem** tissues in the veins.

Different Organs Make up an Organ System

Organs work together to form **organ systems** — each system has a **particular function**.
Yup, you've guessed it, more examples:

1) The **respiratory system** is made up of all the organs, tissues and cells involved in **breathing**. The lungs, trachea, larynx, nose, mouth and diaphragm are all part of the respiratory system.

2) The **circulatory system** is made up of the organs involved in **blood supply**. The heart, arteries, veins and capillaries are all parts of this system.

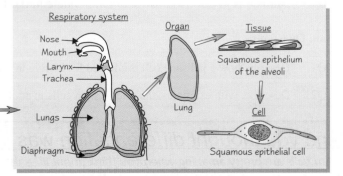

Respiratory system

Nose
Mouth
Larynx
Trachea

Lungs

Diaphragm

Organ

Lung

Tissue

Squamous epithelium of the alveoli

Cell

Squamous epithelial cell

Tissues, Organs and Systems

Different Tissues, Organs and Systems **Cooperate Together**

1) Multicellular organisms work **efficiently** because they have **different cells** specialised for **different functions**.

2) It's **advantageous** because **each** different cell type can carry out its specialised function **more effectively** than an **unspecialised** cell could.

3) Specialised cells can't do everything on their own though.

4) Each cell type **depends** on other cells for the functions it **can't** carry out.

5) This means the **cells**, **tissues and organs** within multicellular organisms must **cooperate** with each other to keep the organism **alive** and **running**.

Cooperation, that's what got Hugo and Cuthbert to where they are today — National Wheel-of-Cheese-Carrying Champions.

6) For example:

- A **palisade cell** (see p. 25) is good at **photosynthesising**, but it's **no good** at absorbing water and minerals from the soil. It **depends** on **root hair cells** (see p. 25) for this. And vice versa.

- **Muscles cells** are great for getting you where you want to go, but to do this they need **oxygen**. They **depend** on **erythrocytes** (red blood cells) to carry oxygen to them from the **lungs**.

7) Multicellular organisms have developed different **systems of cooperation** between different cells:

> **1) Transport systems**
>
> These are used to **carry substances** between the different cells. For example, **xylem cells** carry water and minerals from the root hair cells to the palisade cells, and **phloem cells** carry sugars around the plant. In humans, the **circulatory system** helps to move substances around the body in the **blood**.

> **2) Communication systems**
>
> These allow communication **between** cells in different **parts** of the organism. Both plants and animals have **chemical** communication systems that use **messenger molecules** such as **hormones** (see p. 14). Animals also have a **nervous system** for communication, sending **electrical signals** to different tissues and organs.

Practice Questions

Q1 Define what is meant by a tissue.

Q2 Briefly describe squamous epithelium tissue.

Q3 What is the difference between the functions of xylem and phloem tissues?

Q4 Name one organ found in plants and one organ found in animals.

Exam Questions

Q1 The liver is made of hepatocyte cells that form the main tissue, blood vessels to provide nutrients and oxygen, and connective tissue that holds the organ together. Discuss whether the liver is best described as a tissue or an organ. [2 marks]

Q2 Name one organ system and list the organs it contains. [3 marks]

<u>Soft and quilted — the best kind of tissues...</u>

There's a bit to get through on these pages, but it's all important stuff. If the cells of multicellular animals like you and me didn't cooperate we'd never get anything done. Still, it's better than being a lazy-boned yeast cell — well, to be fair, not lazy-boned as they don't have bones. Obviously I've not been paying attention properly to this section. Oh, dear...

Gas Exchange

Exchanging things with the environment is pretty easy if you're a single-celled organism, but if you're multicellular it all gets a bit more complicated... and it's all down to this 'surface area to volume ratio' malarkey.

Organisms Need to **Exchange Substances** with their **Environment**

Every organism, whatever its size, needs to exchange things with its environment.

1) Cells need to take in oxygen (for aerobic respiration) and **nutrients**.
2) They also need to excrete **waste products** like **carbon dioxide** and **urea**.

How easy the exchange of substances is depends on the organism's **surface area to volume ratio**.

Raj was glad he'd exchanged his canoe for a bigger boat.

Smaller Animals have Higher **Surface Area : Volume Ratios**

A mouse has a bigger surface area **relative to its volume** than a hippo. This can be hard to imagine, but you can prove it mathematically. Imagine these animals as cubes:

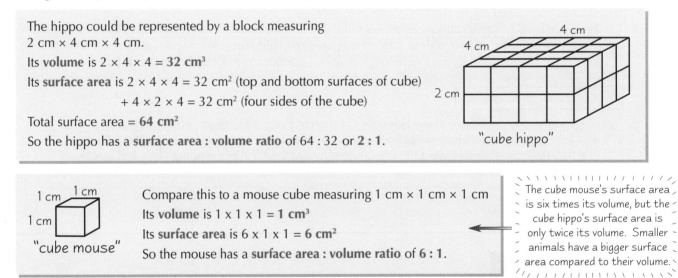

The hippo could be represented by a block measuring
2 cm × 4 cm × 4 cm.
Its **volume** is 2 × 4 × 4 = **32 cm³**
Its **surface area** is 2 × 4 × 4 = 32 cm² (top and bottom surfaces of cube)
    + 4 × 2 × 4 = 32 cm² (four sides of the cube)
Total surface area = **64 cm²**
So the hippo has a **surface area : volume ratio** of 64 : 32 or **2 : 1**.

"cube hippo"

Compare this to a mouse cube measuring 1 cm × 1 cm × 1 cm
Its **volume** is 1 x 1 x 1 = **1 cm³**
Its **surface area** is 6 x 1 x 1 = **6 cm²**
So the mouse has a **surface area : volume ratio** of **6 : 1**.

"cube mouse"

The cube mouse's surface area is six times its volume, but the cube hippo's surface area is only twice its volume. Smaller animals have a bigger surface area compared to their volume.

To calculate the surface area to volume ratio you just **divide** the **surface area** by the **volume**. Easy.

Multicellular Organisms need **Exchange Organs**

An organism needs to supply **every one of its cells** with substances like **glucose** and **oxygen** (for respiration). It also needs to **remove waste products** from every cell to avoid damaging itself.

1) In **single-celled** organisms, these substances can **diffuse directly** into (or out of) the cell across the cell surface membrane. The diffusion rate is quick because of the small distances the substances have to travel (see p. 16).

2) In **multicellular** animals, diffusion across the outer membrane is **too slow**, for two reasons:

- Some cells are deep **within the body** — there's a big distance between them and the **outside environment**.

- Larger animals have a **low surface area to volume ratio** — it's difficult to exchange **enough** substances to supply a **large volume of animal** through a relatively **small outer surface**.

So rather than using straightforward diffusion to absorb and excrete substances, multicellular animals need specialised **exchange organs** like **lungs**...

Gas Exchange

In Mammals the Lungs are Exchange Organs

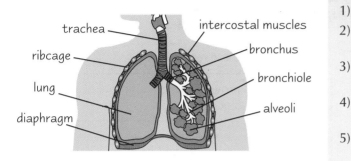

1) As you breathe in, air enters the **trachea** (windpipe).
2) The trachea splits into two **bronchi** — one **bronchus** leading to each lung.
3) Each bronchus then branches off into smaller tubes called **bronchioles**.
4) The bronchioles end in small 'air sacs' called **alveoli** — this is where gases are exchanged.
5) The **ribcage**, **intercostal muscles** and **diaphragm** all work together to move air in and out (see page 32).

Gas Exchange Happens in the Alveoli

Lungs contain millions of **alveoli** — the gas **exchange surface**.
Each alveolus is made from a single layer of thin, flat cells called the **alveolar epithelium**.

1) Alveoli are arranged in **bunches** at the end of bronchioles.
2) They're surrounded by a network of **capillaries**, giving each alveolus its **own blood supply**.

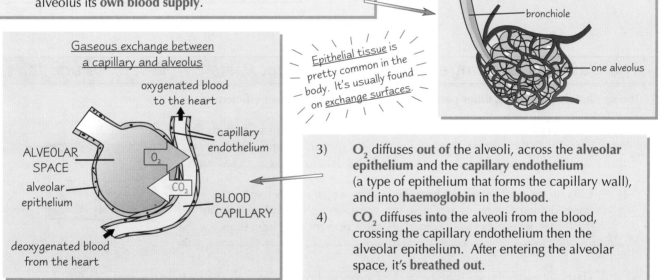

Epithelial tissue is pretty common in the body. It's usually found on exchange surfaces.

3) **O$_2$** diffuses **out of** the alveoli, across the **alveolar epithelium** and the **capillary endothelium** (a type of epithelium that forms the capillary wall), and into **haemoglobin** in the **blood**.
4) **CO$_2$** diffuses **into** the alveoli from the blood, crossing the capillary endothelium then the alveolar epithelium. After entering the alveolar space, it's **breathed out**.

Practice Questions

Q1 Name four substances an organism needs to exchange with its environment.

Q2 How do the surface area to volume ratios of large and small organisms differ?

Q3 Describe the passage of air from the mouth to the alveoli.

Exam Questions

Q1 Explain why humans have a specialised gas exchange system. [5 marks]

Q2 Describe gaseous exchange in the alveoli. [4 marks]

Cube hippos... very Picasso...

I know you've just got to the end of a page, but it would be a pretty smart idea to have another look at diffusion on page 16. Not the most thrilling prospect I realise, but it'll help these pages make more sense — all I can think about at the moment is cube hippos. You need to understand why large multicellular organisms need exchange organs, so get learnin'.

The Gaseous Exchange System

Lungs aren't just a couple of bags full of gas... probably a good thing too, since breathing's kind of important...

The **Lungs** are **Adapted** for **Efficient Gaseous Exchange**

See page 16 for more on diffusion.

Most **gas exchange surfaces** have two things in common:

The lungs have these features:

1) They have a **large surface area**, which **increases** the **rate of diffusion**.

→ **Many alveoli** provide a **large surface area** for diffusion to occur across.

2) They're **thin** (often just one layer of epithelial cells) — this provides a **short diffusion pathway** across the gas exchange surface, which **increases** the **rate of diffusion**.

→ The **alveolar epithelium** and **capillary endothelium** are each only **one cell thick**, giving a **short diffusion pathway**.

The organism also maintains a **steep concentration gradient** of gases across the exchange surface, which **increases** the **rate of diffusion**.

→ All the alveoli have a **good blood supply** from capillaries — they constantly **take away oxygen** and **bring more carbon dioxide**, maintaining the **concentration gradient**.

Breathing in and out refreshes the air in the alveoli, keeping the **concentration gradients** high.

The **Gaseous Exchange System** has Different **Parts** with Different **Functions**

The respiratory system has **other parts** that help it to exchange gases **efficiently**.

1) **Goblet cells** secrete **mucus**. The mucus **traps** microorganisms and dust particles in the inhaled air, stopping them from reaching the alveoli.

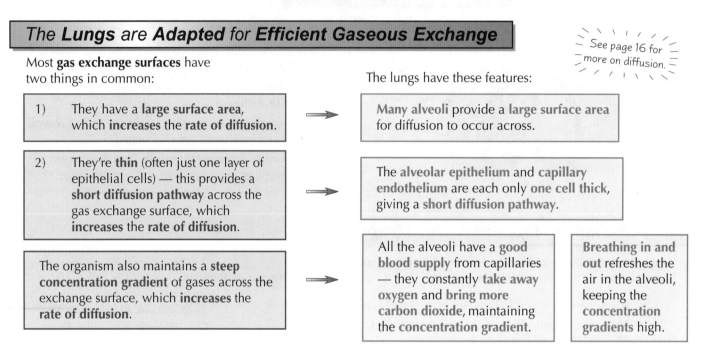
cilia
goblet cell

2) **Cilia** on the surface of cells **beat** the mucus, which **moves** it (plus the trapped microorganisms and dust) upward away from the alveoli towards the throat, where it's swallowed. This helps **prevent lung infections**.

3) **Elastic fibres** in the walls of the trachea, bronchi, bronchioles and alveoli help the process of **breathing out** (see p. 32). On breathing in, the lungs inflate and the elastic fibres are **stretched**. Then, the fibres **recoil** to help push the air out when exhaling.

4) **Smooth muscle** in the walls of the trachea, bronchi and bronchioles allows their **diameter to be controlled**. During exercise the smooth muscle **relaxes**, making the tubes **wider**. This means there's **less resistance** to airflow and air can move in and out of the lungs more easily.

5) **Rings of cartilage** in the walls of the trachea and bronchi **provide support**. It's strong but flexible — it stops the trachea and bronchi **collapsing** when you breathe in and the pressure drops (see p. 32).

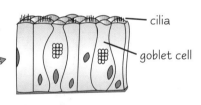
trachea

rings of cartilage

Derek was quickly mastering efficient gaseous exchange.

The Gaseous Exchange System

The Different **Parts** are Found in **Different Places** in the System

Part of the lung	Cross section	Cartilage	Smooth muscle	Elastic fibres	Goblet cells	Epithelium
trachea	smooth muscle / elastic fibres / c-shaped cartilage / ciliated epithelium	large C-shaped pieces	✓	✓	✓	ciliated
bronchi	smooth muscle / small cartilage pieces / elastic fibres / ciliated epithelium	smaller pieces	✓	✓	✓	ciliated
larger bronchiole	smooth muscle and elastic fibres	none	✓	✓	✓	ciliated
smaller bronchiole		none	✓	✓	✗	ciliated
smallest bronchiole	ciliated epithelium	none	✗	✓	✗	no cilia
alveoli	blood capillary / elastic fibres / alveolar epithelium	none	✗	✓	✗	no cilia

Practice Questions

Q1   Describe the distribution of cartilage in the mammalian gas exchange system.

Q2   Describe the distribution of elastic fibres in the mammalian gas exchange system.

Q3   How does the structure of the trachea differ from the structure of the bronchi?

Exam Questions

Q1   Efficient gas exchange surfaces have the following characteristics:

- large surface area
- short diffusion pathway
- high concentration gradient

Explain how these characteristics apply to human lungs.   [5 marks]

Q2   Name five tissues, cells or cell structures found in the mammalian gas exchange system
and explain the function of each.   [10 marks]

Rings of cartilage — I prefer mine in gold... with diamonds...

There's a lot to learn on these two pages. Copying out my beautiful blue table will help — and then you can write out what the function of each part is. Make sure you understand what makes a good exchange surface and how the lungs are adapted to efficient gas exchange too. You won't be coughing and spluttering in the exam once you know this lot.

Breathing

If you're in need of inspiration then there's plenty on this page... sadly I'm only talking about the kind of inspiration that gets air into your lungs — if you want the other sort head over to the Grand Canyon.

Ventilation is Breathing In and Out

Ventilation consists of **inspiration** (breathing in) and **expiration** (breathing out).
It's controlled by the movements of the **diaphragm**, **intercostal muscles** and **ribcage**.

Inspiration

1) The **intercostal** and **diaphragm muscles contract**.

2) This causes the **ribcage** to move **upwards and outwards** and the **diaphragm** to **flatten**, **increasing the volume** of the thorax (the space where the lungs are).

3) As the volume of the thorax increases the lung pressure **decreases** (to below atmospheric pressure).

4) This causes air to flow **into the lungs**.

5) Inspiration is an **active process** — it requires **energy**.

air flows in

volume increases, air pressure decreases

intercostal muscles contract, causing ribs to move outwards and upwards

diaphragm muscles contract, causing diaphragm to move downwards and flatten

Expiration

air is forced out

volume reduces, air pressure increases

intercostal muscles relax, causing ribs to move inwards and downwards

diaphragm muscles relax, causing diaphragm to become curved again

1) The **intercostal** and **diaphragm muscles relax**.

2) The **ribcage** moves **downwards and inwards** and the **diaphragm** becomes **curved** again.

3) The thorax volume **decreases**, causing the air pressure to **increase** (to above atmospheric pressure).

4) Air is forced **out of the lungs**.

5) Expiration is a **passive process** — it **doesn't** require energy.

Tidal Volume is the Volume of Air in a Normal Breath

Here are some terms that you need to know about breathing:

1) **Tidal volume (TV)** — the volume of air in **each breath** — usually about **0.4 dm³**.

2) **Vital capacity** — the **maximum** volume of air that can be breathed **in** or **out**.

3) **Breathing rate** — **how many** breaths are taken — usually in a minute.

4) **Oxygen uptake** — the rate at which a person **uses up** oxygen (e.g. the number of dm³ used per minute).

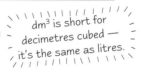
dm³ is short for decimetres cubed — it's the same as litres.

Jane couldn't maintain her breathing rate when she saw all those TVs.

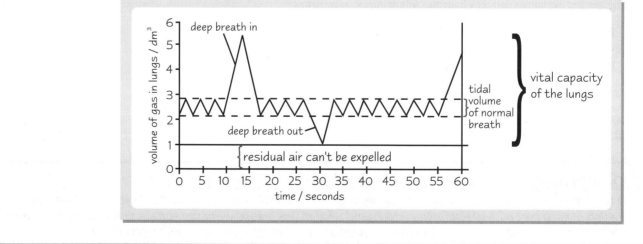

volume of gas in lungs / dm³

deep breath in

deep breath out

tidal volume of normal breath

vital capacity of the lungs

residual air can't be expelled

time / seconds

Breathing

Spirometers Can be Used to *Investigate Breathing*

A spirometer is a machine that can give readings of **tidal volume**, **vital capacity**, **breathing rate** and **oxygen uptake**.

1) A spirometer has an **oxygen-filled** chamber with a **movable lid.**

2) The person breathes through a **tube** connected to the oxygen chamber.

3) As the person breathes in and out, the lid of the chamber moves **up and down.**

4) These movements are recorded by a **pen** attached to the lid of the chamber — this writes on a **rotating drum**, creating a **spirometer trace.**

5) The **soda lime** in the tube the subject breathes into absorbs **carbon dioxide.**

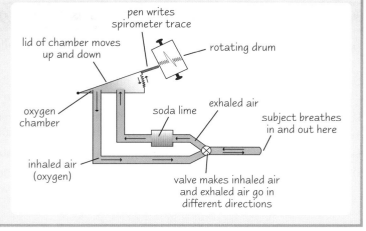

The **total volume of gas** in the chamber **decreases** over time. This is because the air that's breathed out is a **mixture** of oxygen and carbon dioxide. The carbon dioxide is absorbed by the **soda lime** — so there's **only oxygen** in the chamber which the subject inhales from. As this oxygen gets used up by respiration, the total volume decreases.

You Need to be Able to *Analyse* Data from a *Spirometer*

In the exam, you might have to work out **breathing rate**, **tidal volume**, **vital capacity** and **oxygen consumption** from a spirometer trace. For example:

This graph looks different to the one on the previous page because it shows the volume of air in the spirometer, not in the lungs.

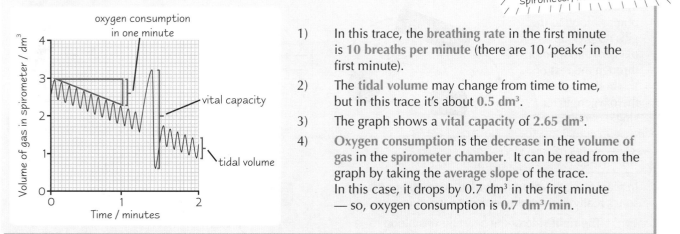

1) In this trace, the **breathing rate** in the first minute is **10 breaths per minute** (there are 10 'peaks' in the first minute).

2) The **tidal volume** may change from time to time, but in this trace it's about **0.5 dm³.**

3) The graph shows a **vital capacity** of **2.65 dm³.**

4) **Oxygen consumption** is the **decrease** in the **volume of gas** in the **spirometer chamber.** It can be read from the graph by taking the **average slope** of the trace. In this case, it drops by 0.7 dm³ in the first minute — so, oxygen consumption is **0.7 dm³/min.**

Practice Questions

Q1 What is meant by tidal volume and vital capacity?

Q2 Describe how a spirometer can be used to measure oxygen uptake.

Exam Question

Q1 Describe the changes that take place in the human thorax during inspiration. [5 marks]

Investigate someone's breathing — make sure they've had a mint first...

I thought spirometers were those circular plastic things you draw crazy patterns with... apparently not. I know the graphs don't look that approachable, but it's important you understand what the squiggly lines show, and the four terms used when investigating breathing — I'd bet my right lung there'll be a question on spirometer graphs in the exam.

The Circulatory System

Right then, this section's all about blood and hearts and veins and things, so if you're a bit squeamish then it's not gonna float your boat. Unfortunately for you, it's all really important for the exams. And besides, without a circulatory system you'd probably have some issues when it comes to things like... ooh I dunno... living.

Multicellular Organisms need Transport Systems

1) As you saw on page 28, **single-celled** organisms can get all the substances they need by **diffusion** across their outer membrane.

2) If you're **multicellular** though, it's a bit **harder** to supply all your cells with everything they need — multicellular organisms are relatively **big** and they have a **low surface area to volume ratio**.

3) A lot of multicellular organisms (e.g. mammals) are also **very active**. This means that a **large number of cells** are all **respiring very quickly**, so they need a constant, rapid supply of glucose and oxygen.

4) To make sure that every cell has a good enough supply, multicellular organisms need a **transport system**.

5) In mammals, this is the **circulatory system**, which uses **blood** to carry glucose and oxygen around the body. It also carries hormones, antibodies (to fight disease) and waste (like CO_2).

Fish and Mammals have Different Circulatory Systems

Not all organisms have the same type of circulatory system
— **fish** have a **single circulatory system** and **mammals** have a **double circulatory system**.

1) In a **single** circulatory system, blood only passes through the heart **once** for each complete circuit of the body.

2) In a **double** circulatory system, the blood passes through the heart **twice** for each complete circuit of the body.

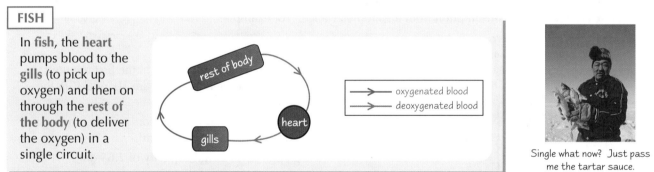

FISH

In **fish**, the **heart** pumps blood to the **gills** (to pick up oxygen) and then on through the **rest of the body** (to deliver the oxygen) in a single circuit.

→ oxygenated blood
→ deoxygenated blood

Single what now? Just pass me the tartar sauce.

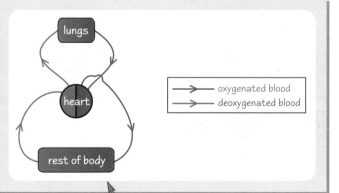

MAMMALS

In **mammals**, the heart is **divided** down the middle, so it's really like **two** hearts joined together.

1) The **right side** of the heart pumps blood to the **lungs** (to pick up oxygen).

2) From the lungs it travels to the **left side** of the heart, which pumps it to the rest of the **body**.

3) When blood **returns** to the heart, it enters the right side again.

→ oxygenated blood
→ deoxygenated blood

So, our circulatory system is really two linked loops. One sends blood to the lungs — this is called the **pulmonary** system, and the other sends blood to the rest of the body — this is called the **systemic** system.

The right and left sides of the heart are reversed in the diagram because it's the right and left of the person the heart belongs to.

The **advantage** of the mammalian double circulatory system is that the heart can give the blood an **extra push** between the lungs and the rest of the body. This makes the blood travel **faster**, so oxygen is delivered to the tissues **more quickly**.

The Circulatory System

Circulatory Systems can be **Open** or **Closed**

All vertebrates (e.g. fish and mammals) have **closed circulatory systems** — the blood is **enclosed** inside **blood vessels**.

1) The heart pumps blood into **arteries**. These **branch out** into millions of **capillaries** (see p. 40).

2) Substances like oxygen and glucose **diffuse** from the blood in the capillaries into the body cells, but the blood **stays inside** the blood vessels as it circulates.

3) **Veins** take the blood back to the heart.

Some invertebrates (e.g. insects) have an **open circulatory system** — blood **isn't enclosed** in blood vessels all the time. Instead, it flows freely through the **body cavity**.

1) The heart is **segmented**. It **contracts** in a **wave**, starting from the back, pumping the blood into a **single main artery**.

2) That artery **opens up** into the body cavity.

3) The blood flows around the insect's **organs**, gradually making its way back into the heart segments through a series of **valves**.

The circulatory system supplies the insect's cell with nutrients, and transports things like hormones around the body. It **doesn't supply** the insect's cells with **oxygen** though — this is done by a system of tubes called the **tracheal system** (see p. 102 for more).

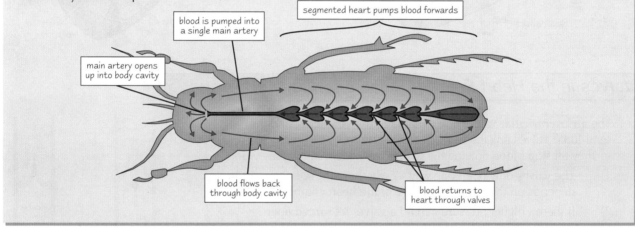

segmented heart pumps blood forwards

blood is pumped into a single main artery

main artery opens up into body cavity

blood flows back through body cavity

blood returns to heart through valves

Practice Questions

Q1 Give three reasons why multicellular organisms usually need a transport system, but unicellular organisms don't.

Q2 Explain why the mammalian circulatory system is described as a double circulatory system.

Q3 What is an open circulatory system?

Exam Questions

Q1 Explain why the circulatory system of a fish is described as being closed. [1 mark]

Q2 Briefly describe the circulatory system of an insect. [2 marks]

Q3 Describe one way in which the circulatory system of a fish is:

a) similar to that of a mammal. [1 mark]

b) different from that of a mammal. [1 mark]

OK, open circulatory systems are officially grim. Body cavities?! Bleurgh...

After reading this page, we can all finally put to rest the idea that the Earth will eventually be overrun by giant insects. Their circulatory system just isn't up to it you see... All the nutrients and stuff in their blood have to diffuse through the whole body cavity, so if they were giant they wouldn't be able to supply all their organs and bits and pieces properly. Phew.

The Heart

You saw on page 34 that mammals have a double circulatory system — well that means that our hearts have to be a bit more complicated than just a big old pump.

The **Heart** Consists of **Two Muscular Pumps**

The diagrams below show the **internal** and **external structure** of the heart. The **right side** of the heart pumps **deoxygenated blood** to the **lungs** and the **left side** pumps **oxygenated blood** to the **rest of the body**.

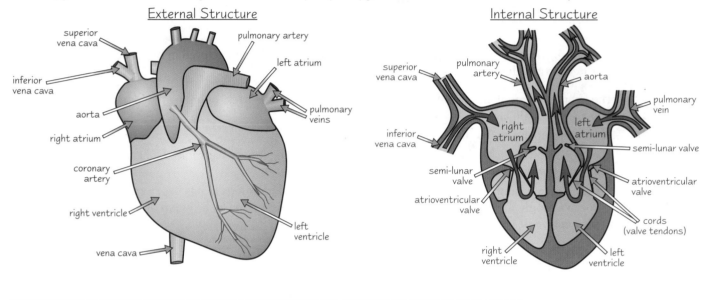

Valves in the Heart **Prevent** Blood Flowing the **Wrong Way**

The **atrioventricular valves** link the atria to the ventricles, and the **semi-lunar** valves link the ventricles to the pulmonary artery and aorta — they all stop blood flowing the **wrong way**. Here's how they work:

1) The **valves** only open one way — whether they're open or closed depends on the **relative pressure** of the heart chambers.

2) If there's higher pressure **behind** a valve, it's **forced open**.

3) If pressure is higher **in front** of the valve, it's **forced shut**.

The **Thickness** of the **Chamber Walls** Depends on Their **Function**

The heart is mainly **muscle**. When it contracts it creates **high pressure** — enough to force blood all the way around the body.

Each of the four **chambers** of the heart has a **different function**. The more **work** that a heart chamber has to do, the more **muscle** it needs — so, the **thicker** its wall is.

1) The **left ventricle** of the heart has **thicker**, more muscular walls than the **right ventricle**, because it needs to contract powerfully to pump blood all the way round the body. The right side only needs to get blood to the lungs, which are nearby.

2) The **ventricles** have **thicker walls** than the **atria**, because they have to push blood out of the heart whereas the atria just need to push blood a short distance into the ventricles.

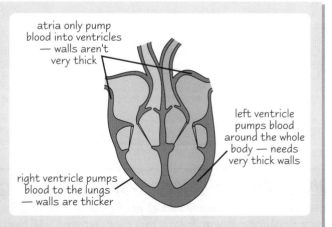

The Heart

The **Cardiac Cycle** Pumps Blood Round the Body

The cardiac cycle is an ongoing sequence of **contraction** and **relaxation** of the atria and ventricles that keeps blood **continuously circulating** round the body. The **volume** of the atria and ventricles **changes** as they contract and relax, altering the **pressure** in each chamber. This causes **valves** to open and close, which directs the **blood flow** through the heart. The cardiac cycle can be simplified into three stages:

① **Ventricles relax, atria contract**

The **ventricles are relaxed**. The atria fill with blood, which **decreases** their **volume** and **increases** the **pressure**. The **higher pressure** in the atria causes the **atrioventricular valves** to **open**, allowing the blood to flow into the **ventricles**. The atria then **contract**, **decreasing** their **volume** and **increasing** the **pressure** even further — forcing the remaining blood out.

② **Ventricles contract, atria relax**

The **ventricles contract** and the **atria relax**. The pressure is **higher** in the ventricles than the atria, so the atrioventricular valves **close** to prevent **backflow**. The high pressure in the ventricles **opens** the semilunar valves — blood is forced out into the **pulmonary artery** and aorta.

③ **Ventricles relax, atria relax**

The **ventricles and atria both relax**, increasing their volume and lowering the pressure in the heart chambers. The higher pressure in the pulmonary artery and aorta causes the semilunar valves to **close**, preventing backflow. Then the atria **fill with blood** again due to the higher pressure in the vena cava and pulmonary vein, and the cycle **starts over again**.

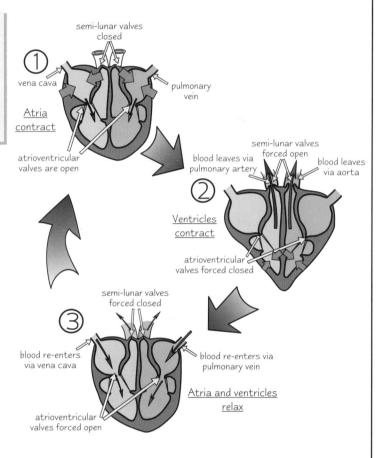

Practice Questions

Q1   Which chamber of the heart receives blood from the lungs?

Q2   Why does the left ventricle of the heart have such a thick wall?

Exam Questions

Q1   The graph shows the pressure changes in the left side of the heart during one heartbeat.

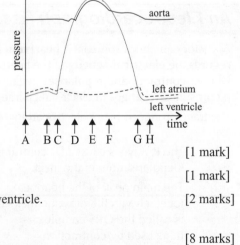

a)   At which labelled point (A-H) on the graph does:

i)   the semi-lunar valve open?   [1 mark]

ii)   the atrioventricular valve close?   [1 mark]

b)   On the diagram, sketch the graph that you would expect for the right ventricle.   [2 marks]

Q2   Describe the events that take place in one complete cardiac cycle, beginning with when the heart muscle is completely relaxed.   [8 marks]

Apparently an adult heart is the size of two fists. Two whole fists! That's huge!

It's not really surprising that your left ventricle wall is so much thicker than the other bits of your heart — just think about how far it has to pump all that blood. It's a good job we've got those valves to stop everything shooting backwards though...

The Heart

You don't have to think about making your heart beat — your body does it for you.
So you couldn't stop it beating even if for some strange reason you wanted to. Which is nice to know.

Cardiac Muscle Controls the Regular Beating of the Heart

Cardiac (heart) muscle is 'myogenic' — it can contract and relax without receiving signals from nerves.
This pattern of contractions controls the regular heartbeat.

1) The process starts in the sino-atrial node (SAN), which is in the wall of the right atrium.

2) The SAN is like a pacemaker — it sets the rhythm of the heartbeat by sending out regular waves of electrical activity to the atrial walls.

3) This causes the right and left atria to contract at the same time.

4) A band of non-conducting collagen tissue prevents the waves of electrical activity from being passed directly from the atria to the ventricles.

5) Instead, these waves of electrical activity are transferred from the SAN to the atrioventricular node (AVN).

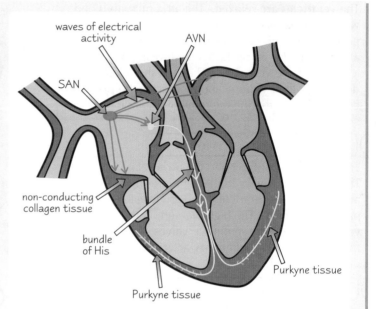

6) The AVN is responsible for passing the waves of electrical activity onto the bundle of His. But, there's a slight delay before the AVN reacts, to make sure the ventricles contract after the atria have emptied.

7) The bundle of His is a group of muscle fibres responsible for conducting the waves of electrical activity to the finer muscle fibres in the right and left ventricle walls, called the Purkyne tissue.

8) The Purkyne tissue carries the waves of electrical activity into the muscular walls of the right and left ventricles, causing them to contract simultaneously, from the bottom up.

An Electrocardiograph Records the Electrical Activity of the Heart

A doctor can check someone's heart function using an electrocardiograph — a machine that records the electrical activity of the heart. The heart muscle depolarises (loses electrical charge) when it contracts, and repolarises (regains charge) when it relaxes. An electrocardiograph records these changes in electrical charge using electrodes placed on the chest.

The trace produced by an electrocardiograph is called an electrocardiogram, or ECG. A normal ECG looks like this:

1) The P wave is caused by contraction (depolarisation) of the atria.

2) The main peak of the heartbeat, together with the dips at either side, is called the QRS complex — it's caused by contraction (depolarisation) of the ventricles.

3) The T wave is due to relaxation (repolarisation) of the ventricles.

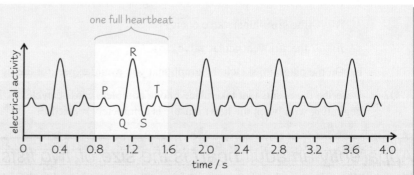

The Heart

Doctors use ECGs to Diagnose Heart Problems

Doctors **compare** their patients' ECGs with a **normal trace**. This helps them to diagnose any heart problems.

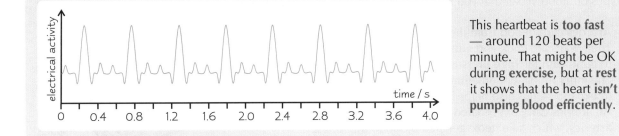

This heartbeat is **too fast** — around 120 beats per minute. That might be OK during **exercise**, but at **rest** it shows that the heart **isn't pumping blood efficiently**.

Here, the **atria** are contracting but sometimes the **ventricles** are **not** (some **P waves** aren't followed by a **QRS complex**). This might mean there's a problem with the **AVN** — impulses aren't travelling from the atria through to the ventricles.

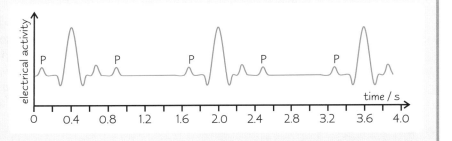

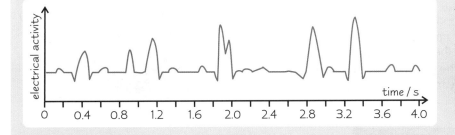

This is **fibrillation** — a really **irregular heartbeat**. The atria or ventricles completely **lose their rhythm** and **stop contracting properly**. It can result in anything from chest pain and fainting to lack of pulse and death.

Practice Questions

Q1 What prevents impulses from the atria travelling straight into the ventricles?

Q2 What is the name of the structure that picks up impulses from the atria and passes them on to the ventricles?

Q3 What causes the QRS part of an ECG trace?

Exam Questions

Q1 Describe the function of:

a) the sino-atrial node? [1 mark]

b) the Purkyne tissue? [1 mark]

Q2 Suggest the cause of an ECG which has a QRS complex that is smaller than normal. [2 marks]

Perhaps if I plug myself into the mains, my heart'll be supercharged...

It's pretty incredible that your heart manages to go through all those stages in the right order, at exactly the right time, without getting it even slightly wrong. It does it perfectly, about 70 times every minute. That's about 100 800 times a day. If only my brain was that efficient. I'd have all this revision done in five minutes, then I could go and watch TV...

Blood Vessels

So, provided all the electrical bits and pieces in your heart are working properly, it'll be pumping out about a litre of blood every 15 seconds. You'll be needing some vessels or something to put that in, otherwise it'll be all over the place...

Blood Vessels Transport Substances Round the Body

The three types of blood vessel that you need to know about are **arteries**, **capillaries** and **veins**:

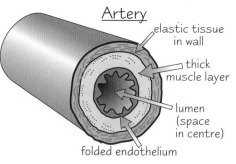

Artery
- elastic tissue in wall
- thick muscle layer
- lumen (space in centre)
- folded endothelium

1) **Arteries** carry blood **from** the heart **to** the rest of the body. Their walls are thick and **muscular** and have elastic tissue to cope with the **high pressure** produced by the heartbeat. The inner lining (**endothelium**) is **folded**, allowing the artery to **expand** — this also helps it to cope with high pressure. All arteries carry **oxygenated** blood except for the **pulmonary arteries**, which take deoxygenated blood to the lungs.

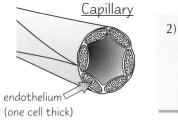

Capillary
- endothelium (one cell thick)

2) Arteries branch into **capillaries**, which are the **smallest** of the blood vessels. Substances like glucose and oxygen are exchanged between cells and capillaries, so they're adapted for **efficient diffusion**, e.g. their walls are only **one cell thick**. Capillaries connect to veins.

3) **Veins** take blood **back to the heart** under low pressure. They're **wider** than equivalent arteries, with very little elastic or muscle tissue. Veins contain **valves** to stop the blood flowing backwards (see p. 36). Blood flow through the veins is helped by contraction of the **body muscles** surrounding them. All veins carry **deoxygenated** blood (because oxygen has been used up by body cells), except for the **pulmonary veins**, which carry oxygenated blood to the heart from the lungs.

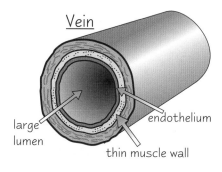

Vein
- large lumen
- endothelium
- thin muscle wall

Tissue Fluid is Formed from Blood

Tissue fluid is the fluid that **surrounds cells** in tissues. It's made from substances that leave the blood, e.g. oxygen, water and nutrients. Cells take in oxygen and nutrients from the tissue fluid, and release metabolic waste into it. In a **capillary bed** (the network of capillaries in an area of tissue), substances move out of the capillaries, into the tissue fluid, by **pressure filtration**:

1) At the **start** of the capillary bed, nearest the arteries, the pressure inside the capillaries is **greater** than the pressure in the tissue fluid. This difference in pressure **forces fluid out** of the **capillaries** and into the **spaces** around the cells, forming tissue fluid.

2) As fluid leaves, the pressure reduces in the capillaries — so the pressure is much **lower** at the **end** of the capillary bed that's nearest to the veins.

3) Due to the fluid loss, the **water potential** at the end of the capillaries nearest the veins is **lower** than the water potential in the **tissue fluid** — so some **water re-enters** the capillaries from the tissue fluid at the vein end by **osmosis** (see p. 16 for more on osmosis).

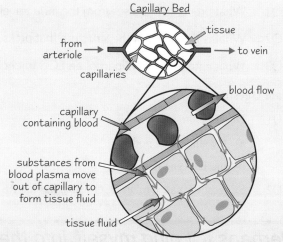

Capillary Bed
- from arteriole
- tissue
- to vein
- capillaries
- blood flow
- capillary containing blood
- substances from blood plasma move out of capillary to form tissue fluid
- tissue fluid

Unlike blood, tissue fluid **doesn't** contain **red blood cells** or **big proteins**, because they're **too large** to be pushed out through the capillary walls.

Blood Vessels

Excess Tissue Fluid Drains into the Lymph Vessels

Not all of the tissue fluid **re-enters** the capillaries at the vein end of the capillary bed —
some **excess tissue fluid** is left over. This extra fluid eventually gets returned to the blood
through the **lymphatic system** — a kind of **drainage** system, made up of **lymph vessels**.

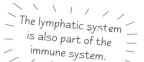
The lymphatic system is also part of the immune system.

1) The smallest lymph vessels are the **lymph capillaries**.

2) Excess tissue fluid passes into lymph vessels. Once inside, it's called **lymph**.

3) **Valves** in the lymph vessels stop the lymph going **backwards**.

4) Lymph gradually moves towards the main lymph vessels in the **thorax**. Here, it's returned to the **blood**, near the **heart**.

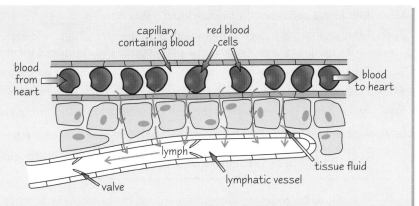

You Need to Know the Differences Between Blood, Tissue Fluid and Lymph

Blood, tissue fluid and lymph are all quite **similar** — **tissue fluid** is formed from **blood**, and **lymph** is formed from
tissue fluid. The main differences are shown in the table.

	blood	tissue fluid	lymph	comment
red blood cells	✓	✗	✗	Red blood cells are too big to get through capillary walls into tissue fluid.
white blood cells	✓	very few	✓	Most white blood cells are in the lymph system. They only enter tissue fluid when there's an infection.
platelets	✓	✗	✗	Only present in tissue fluid if the capillaries are damaged.
proteins	✓	very few	only antibodies	Most plasma proteins are too big to get through capillary walls.
water	✓	✓	✓	Tissue fluid and lymph have a higher water potential than blood.
dissolved solutes	✓	✓	✓	Solutes (e.g. salt) can move freely between blood, tissue fluid and lymph.

Practice Questions

Q1 Is the blood pressure highest in veins or arteries?

Q2 Explain the differences between blood, tissue fluid and lymph.

Exam Questions

Q1 Explain how the structure of each of the following blood vessels is adapted to its function:

    a) arteries   [2 marks]

    b) capillaries   [1 mark]

    c) veins   [1 mark]

Q2 Explain how tissue fluid is formed and how it is returned to the circulation.   [4 marks]

Tissue fluid... Imagine draining the fluid out of a used tissue. Urrrgh.

*That table looks a bit terrifying, but a lot of it's pretty obvious when you think about it — there can't be any red blood cells
floating around loose in your tissues, otherwise you'd be bright red. And platelets are the bits that cause blood clots,
so they're going to be in your blood... In fact, proteins and white blood cells are the only tricky bits.*

Haemoglobin

Aaagh, complicated topic alert. Don't worry though, because your poor, over-worked brain cells will recover from the brain-strain of these pages thanks to haemoglobin. So the least you can do is learn how it works.

Oxygen is Carried Round the Body as Oxyhaemoglobin

1) **Red blood cells** contain **haemoglobin** (Hb).
2) Haemoglobin is a large **protein** with a **quaternary** structure (see p. 54 for more) — it's made up of **more than one** polypeptide chain (**four** of them in fact).
3) Each chain has a **haem group** which contains **iron** and gives haemoglobin its **red** colour.
4) Haemoglobin has a **high affinity for oxygen** — each molecule can carry **four oxygen molecules**.
5) In the lungs, oxygen **joins** to the **iron** in haemoglobin to form **oxyhaemoglobin**.
6) This is a **reversible reaction** — when oxygen leaves oxyhaemoglobin (**dissociates** from it) near the body cells, it turns back to haemoglobin.

'Affinity' for oxygen means tendency to combine with oxygen.

$$Hb + 4O_2 \rightleftharpoons HbO_8$$
$$\text{haemoglobin} + \text{oxygen} \rightleftharpoons \text{oxyhaemoglobin}$$

Haemoglobin Saturation Depends on the Partial Pressure of Oxygen

1) The **partial pressure** of **oxygen** (pO_2) is a measure of **oxygen concentration**. The **greater** the concentration of dissolved oxygen in cells, the **higher** the partial pressure.
2) Similarly, the **partial pressure** of **carbon dioxide** (pCO_2) is a measure of the concentration of CO_2 in a cell.
3) Haemoglobin's **affinity** for oxygen **varies** depending on the **partial pressure** of **oxygen**:

> Oxygen **loads onto** haemoglobin to form oxyhaemoglobin where there's a **high** pO_2. Oxyhaemoglobin **unloads** its oxygen where there's a **lower** pO_2.

4) Oxygen enters blood capillaries at the **alveoli** in the **lungs**. Alveoli have a **high** pO_2 so oxygen **loads onto** haemoglobin to form oxyhaemoglobin.
5) When **cells respire**, they use up oxygen — this **lowers** the pO_2. Red blood cells deliver oxyhaemoglobin to respiring tissues, where it unloads its oxygen.
6) The haemoglobin then returns to the lungs to pick up more oxygen.

There was no use pretending — the pCH_4 had just increased, and Keith knew who was to blame.

Dissociation Curves Show How Affinity for Oxygen Varies

A **dissociation curve** shows how **saturated** the haemoglobin is with oxygen at any given partial pressure.

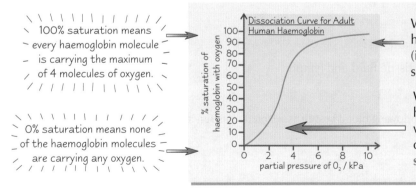

100% saturation means every haemoglobin molecule is carrying the maximum of 4 molecules of oxygen.

0% saturation means none of the haemoglobin molecules are carrying any oxygen.

Dissociation Curve for Adult Human Haemoglobin

% saturation of haemoglobin with oxygen
partial pressure of O_2 / kPa

Where pO_2 is high (e.g. in the lungs), haemoglobin has a **high affinity** for oxygen (i.e. it will **readily combine** with oxygen), so it has a **high saturation** of oxygen.

Where pO_2 is low (e.g. in respiring tissues), haemoglobin has a **low affinity** for oxygen, which means it **releases oxygen** rather than combines with it. That's why it has a **low saturation** of oxygen.

1) The graph is '**S-shaped**' because when haemoglobin (Hb) combines with the **first O_2 molecule**, its **shape alters** in a way that makes it **easier** for other molecules to join too.
2) But as the Hb starts to become saturated, it gets **harder** for more oxygen molecules to join.
3) As a result, the curve has a **steep** bit in the middle where it's really easy for oxygen molecules to join, and **shallow** bits at each end where it's harder. When the curve is steep, a **small change in** pO_2 causes a **big change** in the **amount of oxygen** carried by the Hb.

Haemoglobin

Fetal Haemoglobin has a Higher Affinity for Oxygen than Adult Haemoglobin

Adult haemoglobin and fetal haemoglobin have different affinities for oxygen. Fetal haemoglobin has a **higher affinity** for oxygen (the fetus's blood is **better at absorbing** oxygen than its mother's blood). This is really important:

1) The fetus gets oxygen from its **mother's blood** across the placenta.

2) By the time the mother's blood reaches the placenta, its oxygen saturation has **decreased** (because some has been used up by the mother's body).

3) For the fetus to get **enough oxygen** to survive its haemoglobin has to have a **higher affinity** for oxygen (so it takes up enough).

4) If its haemoglobin had the **same** affinity for oxygen as adult haemoglobin its blood **wouldn't** be **saturated enough**.

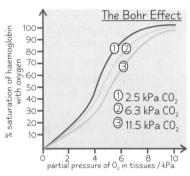

Carbon Dioxide Concentration Affects Oxygen Unloading

To complicate matters, haemoglobin gives up its oxygen **more readily** at **higher partial pressures of carbon dioxide** (pCO_2). It's a cunning way of getting more oxygen to cells during activity. When cells respire they produce carbon dioxide, which raises the pCO_2, increasing the rate of oxygen unloading. The reason for this is linked to how CO_2 affects blood pH.

1) Most of the CO_2 from respiring tissues diffuses into red blood cells and is converted to **carbonic acid** by the enzyme **carbonic anhydrase**. (The rest of the CO_2, around 10%, binds directly to haemoglobin and is carried to the lungs.)

2) The carbonic acid **splits up** to give **hydrogen ions** and **hydrogencarbonate ions**.

3) This increase in hydrogen ions causes oxyhaemoglobin to **unload** its oxygen so that haemoglobin can take up the hydrogen ions. This forms a compound called **haemoglobinic acid**. (This process also stops the hydrogen ions from increasing the cell's acidity).

4) The **hydrogencarbonate ions** diffuse out of the red blood cells and are **transported in the blood plasma**.

5) When the blood reaches the **lungs** the low pCO_2 causes the hydrogencarbonate and hydrogen ions to **recombine into CO_2**.

6) The CO_2 then diffuses into the **alveoli** and is breathed out.

When carbon dioxide levels increase, the dissociation curve 'shifts' down, showing that more oxygen is released from the blood (because the lower the saturation of haemoglobin with O_2, the more O_2 is released). This is called the Bohr effect.

Practice Questions

Q1 How many oxygen molecules can each haemoglobin molecule carry?

Q2 What effect does respiration have on a cell's pO_2?

Q3 What is carbon dioxide converted to in red blood cells?

Exam Questions

Q1 Explain why fetal haemoglobin is different from adult haemoglobin. [3 marks]

Q2 Describe how carbon dioxide from respiring tissues is transported to the lungs. [6 marks]

The Bore effect — it's happening right now...

Dissociation graphs can be a bit confusing — but basically, when tissues contain lots of oxygen (i.e. pO_2 is high), haemoglobin readily combines with the oxygen, so the blood has a high saturation of oxygen (and vice versa when pO_2 is low). Simple. Also, make sure you get the lingo right, like 'partial pressure' and 'affinity' — hey, I'm hip, I'm groovy. Honest.

Xylem and Phloem

A whole section on transport in plants... just what I always dreamed of... you too? Oh good, because you need to learn it all for your exam.

Multicellular Plants Need Transport Systems

1) Plant cells need substances like **water**, **minerals** and **sugars** to live.
    They also need to **get rid of waste substances**.

2) Like animals, plants are **multicellular** so have a **small surface area : volume ratio** (see page 28).

3) Plants could exchange substances by **direct diffusion** (from the outer surface to the cells),
    but that would be **too slow**.

4) So plants **need transport systems** to move substances to and from individual cells **quickly**.

> Plants also need <u>carbon dioxide</u>, but this enters at the leaves (where it's needed).

Two Types of Tissue are Involved in Transport in Plants

Xylem tissue transports **water** and **mineral ions**. **Phloem tissue** transports **dissolved substances**, like **sugars**. Xylem and phloem are found **throughout** a plant — they **transport materials** to all parts. **Where** they're found in each part is connected to the **xylem's** other function — **support**:

1) In a **root**, the xylem and phloem are in the **centre** to provide support for the root as it **pushes** through the soil.

2) In the **stems**, the xylem and phloem are **near the outside** to provide a sort of 'scaffolding' that reduces bending.

3) In a **leaf**, xylem and phloem make up a **network of veins** which support the thin leaves.

Emma had been through 12 rolls but she still couldn't find any phloem.

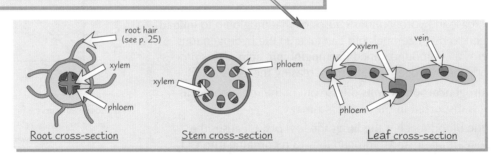

root hair
(see p. 25)

xylem

phloem

Root cross-section

xylem

phloem

Stem cross-section

xylem

vein

phloem

Leaf cross-section

Xylem Vessels are Adapted for Transporting Water and Mineral Ions

Xylem is a **tissue** made from several **different cell types** (see page 26).
You need to learn about **xylem vessels** — the part of xylem tissue that actually transports the water and ions. Xylem vessels are adapted for their **function**:

1) Xylem vessels are very **long**, **tube-like** structures formed from cells (**vessel elements**) joined end to end.

2) There are **no end walls** on these cells, making an **uninterrupted tube** that allows water to pass up through the middle easily.

3) The cells are **dead**, so they contain **no cytoplasm**.

4) Their walls are **thickened** with a **woody** substance called **lignin**, which helps to **support** the xylem vessels and stops them **collapsing inwards**.

5) The amount of lignin **increases** as the cell gets **older**.

6) **Water** and **ions** move **into** and **out of** the vessels through **small pits** in the walls where there's **no lignin**.

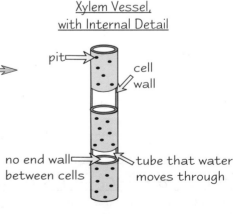

Xylem Vessel,
with Internal Detail

pit

cell
wall

no end wall
between cells

tube that water
moves through

Xylem and Phloem

Phloem Tissue is Adapted for Transporting Solutes

1) Phloem tissue transports **solutes** (dissolved substances), mainly sugars like sucrose, round plants.

2) Like xylem, phloem is formed from cells arranged in **tubes**.

3) But, unlike xylem, it's purely a **transport tissue** — it **isn't** used for support as well.

4) Phloem tissue contains **phloem fibres**, **phloem parenchyma**, **sieve tube elements** and **companion cells**.

5) **Sieve tube elements** and **companion cells** are the most important cell types in phloem for **transport**:

1 Sieve Tube Elements

1) These are **living cells** that form the tube for **transporting solutes** through the plant.

2) They are joined **end to end** to form **sieve tubes**.

3) The 'sieve' parts are the **end walls**, which have lots of **holes** in them to allow **solutes** to pass through.

4) Unusually for living cells, sieve tube elements have **no nucleus**, a **very thin** layer of **cytoplasm** and **few organelles**.

5) The cytoplasm of adjacent cells is **connected** through the holes in the sieve plates.

2 Companion Cells

1) The **lack** of a **nucleus** and **other organelles** in sieve tube elements means that they **can't survive** on their own.

2) So there's a **companion cell** for **every** sieve tube element.

3) Companion cells carry out the living functions for **both** themselves and their sieve cells. For example, they provide the **energy** for the **active transport** of solutes.

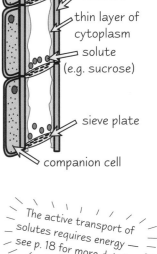

Phloem Tissue

- sieve tube element
- thin layer of cytoplasm
- solute (e.g. sucrose)
- sieve plate
- companion cell

The active transport of solutes requires energy — see p. 18 for more details.

Practice Questions

Q1 Why do multicellular plants need transport systems?

Q2 State two functions of xylem vessels in plants.

Q3 What is the name of the substance that thickens the walls of xylem vessels?

Q4 What is the function of phloem tissue?

Q5 What is the function of companion cells?

Exam Questions

Q1 Describe the distribution of the xylem and phloem tissue in stems, roots and leaves.
Explain how this distribution is linked to the support function of the xylem. [6 marks]

Q2 Describe how the structure of xylem vessels relates to their function. [8 marks]

Sieve tube — WLTM like-minded cell for companionship and maybe more...

Sieve tube elements sound a bit feeble to me — not being able to survive on their own, and all that. Anyway, it's vital your mind doesn't wander on this page, because the structures and functions of some of these cell types are quite similar. It can be easy to get mixed up if you haven't learnt it properly, so take the time now to sort out which cell type does what.

Water Transport

Water enters a plant through its roots and eventually, if it's not used, exits via the leaves. "Ah-ha", I hear you say, "but how does it flow upwards, against gravity?" Well that, my friends, is a mystery that's about to be explained...

Water *Enters a Plant through its* Root Hair Cells

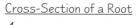
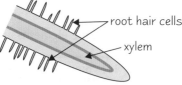

Cross-Section of a Root
- root hair cells
- xylem

1) Water has to get from the **soil**, through the **root** and into the **xylem** to be transported around the plant.

2) Water enters through **root hair cells** and then passes through **the root cortex**, including the **endodermis**, to reach the xylem (see below).

3) Water is drawn into the roots down a **water potential gradient**:

> Water always moves from areas of **higher water potential** to areas of **lower water potential** — it goes down a **water potential gradient**. The **soil** around roots generally has a **high water potential** (i.e. there's lots of water there) and **leaves** have a **lower water potential** (because water constantly **evaporates** from them). This creates a water potential gradient that keeps water moving through the plant in the right direction, **from roots (high)** to **leaves (low)**.

Water **Moves** *Through the* **Root** *into the* **Xylem**...

Water travels through the **roots** (via the **root cortex**) into the **xylem** by **two** different paths:

1) The **symplast pathway** — goes through the **living** parts of cells — the **cytoplasm**. The cytoplasm of neighbouring cells connect through **plasmodesmata** (small channels in the cell walls).

2) The **apoplast pathway** — goes through the **non-living** parts of the cells — the **cell walls**. The walls are very absorbent and water can simply **diffuse** through them, as well as passing through the spaces between them.

The prison had been strangely quiet ever since plasmodesmata were installed.

- When water in the **apoplast pathway** gets to the **endodermis** cells in the root, its path is blocked by a **waxy strip** in the cell walls, called the **Casparian strip**. Now the water has to take the **symplast pathway**.

- This is useful, because it means the water has to go through a **cell membrane**. Cell membranes are able to control whether or not substances in the water get through (see p. 12).

- Once past this barrier, the water moves into the **xylem**.

3) Both pathways are used, but the main one is the **apoplast pathway** because it provides the **least resistance**.

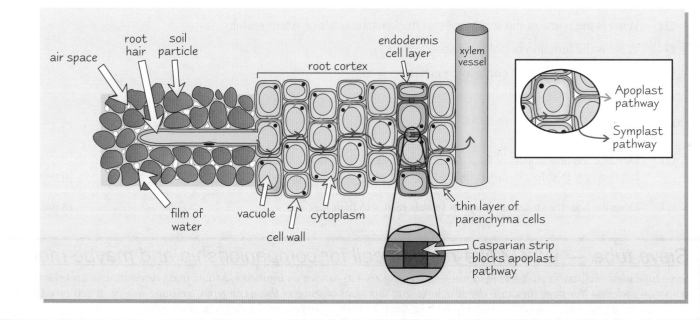

- air space
- root hair
- soil particle
- root cortex
- endodermis cell layer
- xylem vessel
- film of water
- vacuole
- cell wall
- cytoplasm
- thin layer of parenchyma cells
- Casparian strip blocks apoplast pathway
- Apoplast pathway
- Symplast pathway

Water Transport

...then *Up* the *Xylem* and *Out* at the *Leaves*

1) **Xylem vessels** transport the water **all around** the plant.

2) At the **leaves**, water leaves the xylem and moves into the cells mainly by the **apoplast pathway**.

3) Water **evaporates** from the cell walls into the **spaces** between cells in the leaf.

4) When the **stomata** (tiny pores in the surface of the leaf) open, the water moves out of the leaf (down the **water potential gradient**) into the **surrounding air**.

5) The loss of water from a plant's surface is called **transpiration** (see next page).

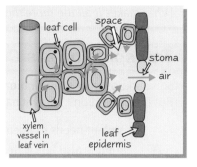

Water Moves *Up* a Plant *Against* the Force of *Gravity*

The movement of water from **roots to leaves** is called the **transpiration stream**. The **mechanisms** that **move** the water include **cohesion**, **tension** and **adhesion**.

Cohesion and **tension** help water move up plants, from roots to leaves, **against** the force of gravity.

1) Water **evaporates** from the **leaves** at the 'top' of the xylem (**transpiration**).

2) This creates a **tension** (**suction**), which pulls more water into the leaf.

3) Water molecules are **cohesive** (they **stick together**) so when some are pulled into the leaf others follow. This means the whole **column** of water in the **xylem**, from the leaves down to the roots, **moves upwards**.

4) **Water** enters the stem through the **root cortex cells**.

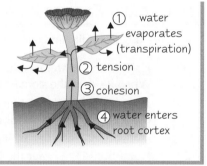

Adhesion is also partly responsible for the **movement of water**.

1) As well as being attracted to each other, water molecules are **attracted to** the **walls** of the xylem vessels.

2) This helps water to **rise up** through the xylem vessels.

Practice Questions

Q1 In terms of water potential, why does water move into the roots from the soil?

Q2 What is the Casparian strip?

Q3 What is cohesion?

Q4 How does adhesion help to move water through a plant?

Exam Questions

Q1 Explain why the movement of water in the xylem stops if the leaves of a plant are removed. [4 marks]

Q2 Water can take two different paths through the roots of a plant.

a) Describe the symplast pathway through the roots of a plant. [2 marks]

b) Describe the apoplast pathway through the roots of a plant. [4 marks]

So many routes through the roots...

As you've probably noticed, there are lots of impressive biological words on this page, to amaze your friends and confound your enemies. Go through the page again, and whenever you see a word like plasmodesmata, just stop and check you know exactly what it means. (Personally I think they should just call them cell wall gaps, but nobody ever listens to me.)

Transpiration

Plants can't sing, juggle or tap-dance (as you will hopefully be aware). But they can exchange gases — how exciting. What makes it all the more thrilling though is that they lose water vapour as they do it. Gripping stuff.

Transpiration *is a* Consequence *of* Gas Exchange

So you know that **transpiration** is the evaporation of **water** from a plant's surface, especially the **leaves**. But I bet you didn't know it happens as a result of **gas exchange**. Read on...

1) A plant needs to open its stomata to let in carbon dioxide so that it can produce glucose (by photosynthesis).

2) But this **also lets water out** — there's a **higher concentration** of water **inside** the leaf than in the air **outside**, so water moves **out** of the leaf down the **water potential gradient** when the stomata open.

3) So transpiration's really a **side effect** of the gas exchange needed for photosynthesis.

Four *Main Factors Affect* Transpiration Rate

Water moves from areas of higher water potential to areas of lower water potential — it moves down the water potential gradient.

Temperature, humidity and wind all alter the **water potential gradient**, but **light** is a bit different:

1) **Light** — the **lighter** it is the **faster** the **transpiration rate**. This is because the **stomata open** when it gets **light**. When it's **dark** the stomata are usually **closed**, so there's little transpiration.

2) **Temperature** — the **higher the temperature** the **faster** the **transpiration rate**. Warmer water molecules have more energy so they **evaporate** from the cells inside the leaf **faster**. This **increases** the **water potential gradient** between the inside and outside of the leaf, making water **diffuse** out of the leaf **faster**.

3) **Humidity** — the **lower** the **humidity**, the **faster** the **transpiration rate**. If the air around the plant is **dry**, the **water potential gradient** between the leaf and the air is **increased**, which increases transpiration.

4) **Wind** — the **windier** it is, the **faster** the **transpiration rate**. Lots of air movement **blows away** water molecules from around the stomata. This **increases** the water potential gradient, which increases the rate of transpiration.

A Potometer *can be Used to* Estimate Transpiration Rate

A **potometer** is a special piece of apparatus used to **estimate transpiration rates**. It actually measures **water uptake** by a plant, but it's **assumed** that water uptake by the plant is **directly related** to **water loss** by the **leaves**. You can use it to estimate how different factors **affect** the transpiration rate.

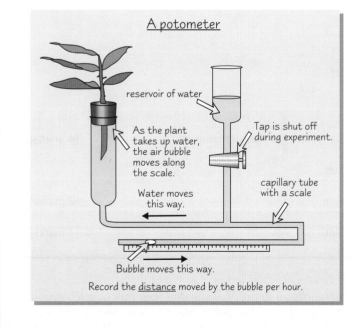

A potometer

reservoir of water

As the plant takes up water, the air bubble moves along the scale.

Tap is shut off during experiment.

Water moves this way.

capillary tube with a scale

Bubble moves this way.

Record the <u>distance</u> moved by the bubble per hour.

Here's what you'd do:

1) **Cut** a **shoot underwater** to prevent air from entering the xylem. Cut it at a **slant** to increase the surface area available for water uptake.

2) Check that the apparatus is **full of water** and that there are **no air bubbles**.

3) Insert the **shoot** into the apparatus **underwater**, so no air can enter.

4) Remove the potometer from the water and make sure it's **airtight** and **watertight**.

5) **Dry** the leaves, allow time for the shoot to **acclimatise** and then **shut the tap**.

6) Keep the **conditions constant** throughout the experiment, e.g. the temperature and the air humidity.

7) Record the **starting position** of the **air bubble**.

8) Start a **stopwatch** and record the **distance** moved by the bubble **per unit time**, e.g. per hour.

Transpiration

Xerophytic Plants are Adapted to Reduce Water Loss

Xerophytes are plants like **cacti**, **pine trees** and **prickly pears** (yes, the ones from the song).
They're **adapted** to live in **dry climates**. Their adaptations prevent them **losing too much water** by **transpiration**.
Examples of xerophytic adaptations include:

1) **Stomata** that are sunk in **pits** — so they're **sheltered from the wind**, which helps to slow transpiration down.

2) A layer of 'hairs' on the epidermis — this **traps moist air** round the stomata, which **reduces** the water potential gradient between the leaf and the air, **slowing** transpiration down.

3) **Curled** leaves — this **traps moist air**, slowing down transpiration. This also lowers the **exposed surface area** for losing water and protects the stomata from wind.

6) A reduced **number of stomata** — this means there are **fewer places** where water can be lost.

4) **Spines** instead of leaves (e.g. cactus) — this reduces the **surface area** for water loss.

5) **Thick, waxy layer** on the epidermis — this **reduces** water loss by evaporation because the layer is **waterproof** (water can't move through it).

Practice Questions

Q1   Explain why transpiration is a consequence of gaseous exchange.

Q2   What piece of apparatus is used to measure transpiration?

Q3   What is a xerophyte?

Q4   Suggest three ways that xerophyte leaves are adapted to reduce water loss by transpiration.

Exam Questions

Q1   Give four conditions that increase the rate of transpiration from a plant's leaves
and explain how each one increases transpiration.   [8 marks]

Q2   The diagram shows a section of a leaf of a xerophytic
plant. Describe and explain two ways, visible in the
picture, that this leaf is adapted to reduce water loss.   [4 marks]

Inside leaf   Stoma

Outside leaf

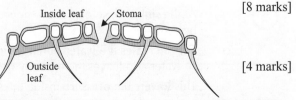

Xerophytes — an exciting word for a boring subject...

*Actually, that's unfair. It's taken millions of years for plants to evolve those adaptations, and here I am slagging them off.
When I've managed to develop a thicker waxy cuticle on my leaves and stems, then I can comment, and not before.
Oh, and learn the rest of the stuff on this page too. It may not be thrilling — but if you know it, it could earn you vital marks.*

Translocation

Translocation is the movement of solutes through a plant. Annoyingly, translocation sounds a lot like transpiration. Or is that just me? Make sure you don't get them confused.

Translocation is the Movement of Dissolved Substances

1) **Translocation** is the **movement** of dissolved substances (e.g. sugars like sucrose, and amino acids) to **where they're needed** in a plant. Dissolved substances are sometimes called **assimilates**.

2) It's an **energy-requiring** process that happens in the **phloem**.

3) Translocation moves substances from '**sources**' to '**sinks**'.
The **source** of a substance is **where it's made** (so it's at a **high concentration** there).
The **sink** is the area where it's **used up** (so it's at a **lower concentration** there).

See p. 45 for more on the phloem.

> **EXAMPLE**
>
> The **source** for **sucrose** is the **leaves** (where it's made), and the **sinks** are the **other parts** of the plant, especially the **food storage organs** and the **meristems** (areas of growth) in the roots, stems and leaves.

4) **Enzymes** maintain a **concentration gradient** from the source to the sink by **changing** the dissolved substances at the **sink** (e.g. by breaking them down or making them into something else). This makes sure there's always a **lower concentration** at the sink than at the source.

> **EXAMPLE**
>
> In **potatoes**, **sucrose** is converted to **starch** in the **sink** areas, so there's always a **lower concentration** of sucrose **at the sink** than inside the phloem. This makes sure a **constant supply** of new sucrose reaches the sink from the phloem.

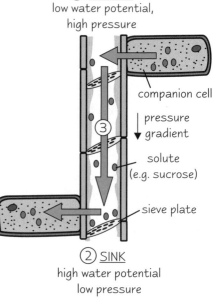

Howard liked a bit of translocation in his spare time.

The Mass Flow Hypothesis Best Explains Phloem Transport

Scientists still aren't certain **exactly how** the dissolved substances (solutes) are transported from source to sink by **translocation**. The best supported theory is the **mass flow hypothesis**:

①
1) Active transport (see p. 18) is used to **actively load** the dissolved solutes (e.g. sucrose from photosynthesis) into the **sieve tubes** of the phloem at the **source** (e.g. the **leaves**).
2) This **lowers the water potential** inside the sieve tubes, so water enters the tubes by **osmosis**.
3) This creates a **high pressure** inside the sieve tubes at the **source end** of the phloem.

②
1) At the **sink** end, **solutes** are removed from the phloem to be used up.
2) This **increases** the **water potential** inside the sieve tubes, so water also leaves the tubes by **osmosis**.
3) This **lowers the pressure** inside the sieve tubes.

③
1) The result is a **pressure gradient** from the **source** end to the **sink** end.
2) This gradient pushes solutes along the sieve tubes to where they're needed.

① SOURCE
low water potential, high pressure

companion cell

③

pressure gradient

solute (e.g. sucrose)

sieve plate

② SINK
high water potential low pressure

Translocation

There is **Evidence** Both For and Against **Mass Flow**

Supporting evidence

1) If you remove a **ring** of **bark** (which includes the phloem, but not the xylem) from a woody stem a **bulge forms above** the ring. If you analyse the fluid from the bulge, you'll find it has a **higher concentration** of sugars than the fluid from below the ring — this is evidence that there's a **downward flow** of sugars.

2) You can **investigate** pressure in the phloem using **aphids** (they pierce the phloem, then their bodies are removed leaving the mouthparts behind, which allows the sap to flow out... gruesome). The sap flows out **quicker nearer the leaves** than further down the stem — this is evidence that there's a **pressure gradient**.

3) If you put a **metabolic inhibitor** (which stops ATP production) into the **phloem** then **translocation stops** — this is evidence that **active transport** is involved.

4) There's an **experimental model** for mass flow (see below).

Objections

1) Sugar travels to **many different sinks**, not just to the one with the **highest water potential**, as the model would suggest.

2) The **sieve plates** would create a **barrier** to mass flow. A **lot** of **pressure** would be needed for the solutes to get through at a reasonable rate.

Mass Flow Hypothesis Can be **Demonstrated** in an **Experiment**

The hypothesis can be modelled in this experiment:

1) **A** and **B** are two containers, each lined with a **selectively permeable membrane** just like cells have.

2) The **top tube** connecting A and B represents the **phloem**, and the **bottom tube** represents the **xylem**.

3) **A** represents the **source** end and contains a **concentrated sugar solution**. **B** represents the **sink** end and contains a **weak sugar solution**.

4) Water enters **A** by **osmosis**, **increasing** the pressure, which causes the sugar solution to flow along the **top tube** (phloem).

5) **Pressure** increases in **B**, forcing water out and back through the **bottom tube** (xylem), which just transports water.

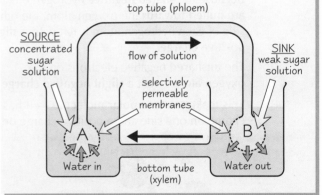

Experimental model for mass flow

Practice Questions

Q1 Explain the terms source and sink in connection with translocation.

Q2 State two pieces of evidence that support the mass flow hypothesis for translocation.

Exam Question

Q1 The mass flow hypothesis depends on a pressure difference in the phloem sieve tubes between the source and the sink. Explain how sugars cause the pressure to increase at the source end, according to the mass flow hypothesis.

[4 marks]

Human mass flow — running out of the hall at the end of an exam...

The mass flow hypothesis is just the best theory that scientists have come up with so far. If other evidence came along, a different theory could be developed based on the new findings (see p. 1). However, that doesn't mean that there's no point in learning about it — it could be in your exam. Don't look so sad — what else would you do with your time...

Water

Your body needs all sorts of different molecules to stay alive, and this section covers all the major groups. Life can't exist without water — in fact, everyday water is one of the most important substances on the planet. Funny old world.

Water is Vital to Living Organisms

Water makes up about 80% of a cell's contents. It has loads of important **functions**, inside and outside cells:

1) Water is a **reactant** in loads of important **chemical reactions**, like photosynthesis and **hydrolysis reactions** (see p. 54).

2) Water is a **solvent**, which means some substances **dissolve** in it. Most biological reactions take place **in solution**, so water's pretty essential.

3) Water **transports** substances. The fact that it's a **liquid** and a **solvent** means it can easily transport all sorts of materials, like glucose and oxygen, around plants and animals.

4) Water helps with **temperature control**. It carries away **heat energy** when it **evaporates** from a surface. This **cools** the surface and helps to **lower** the temperature.

Water Molecules have a Simple Structure

Examiners like asking you to relate **structure** to **properties** and **function**, so make sure you're clear on the structure of water.

1) A molecule of **water (H₂O)** is **one atom** of **oxygen (O)** joined to **two atoms** of **hydrogen (H₂)** by **shared electrons**.

2) Because the **shared negative** hydrogen electrons are **pulled towards** the oxygen atom, the other side of each hydrogen atom is left with a **slight positive charge**.

3) The **unshared** negative electrons on the oxygen atom give it a **slight negative charge**.

4) This makes water a **polar** molecule — it has a negative charge on one side and a positive charge on the other.

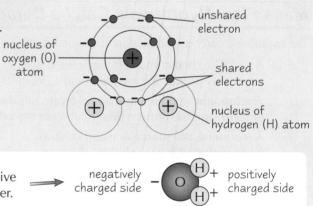

5) The **negatively charged oxygen atoms** of water **attract** the **positively charged hydrogen atoms** of other water molecules.

6) This attraction is called **hydrogen bonding** and it gives water some of its useful properties.

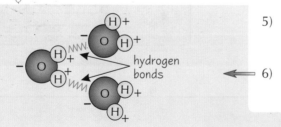

Water's Structure is Related to its Properties and Functions

The **structure of a water molecule** gives it some useful **properties**, and these help to explain many of its **functions**:

Hydrogen Bonds Give Water a High Specific Heat Capacity

1) Specific heat capacity is the **energy** needed to **raise the temperature** of 1 gram of a substance by 1 °C.

2) The **hydrogen bonds** between water molecules can **absorb** a **lot** of energy.

3) So water has a **high** specific heat capacity — it takes a lot of energy to heat it up.

4) This is useful for living organisms because it **stops rapid temperature changes**, allowing them to keep their temperature **fairly stable**.

Water

Hydrogen Bonds Also Give Water a High Latent Heat of Evaporation

1) It takes a lot of **energy** (**heat**) to **break** the hydrogen bonds between water molecules.

2) So water has a **high latent heat of evaporation** — a lot of energy is used up when water **evaporates**.

3) This is useful for living organisms because it means water's great for **cooling** things.

Water's Polarity Makes it Very Cohesive

1) Cohesion is the **attraction** between molecules of the same type (e.g. two water molecules). Water molecules are **very cohesive** (they tend to stick together) because they're **polar**.

2) This helps water to **flow**, making it great for **transporting substances**.

Water's Polarity Also Makes it a Good Solvent

1) A lot of important substances in biological reactions are **ionic** (like **salt**, for example). This means they're made from **one positively charged** atom or molecule and **one negatively charged** atom or molecule (e.g. salt is made from a positive sodium ion and a negative chloride ion).

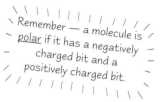

Remember — a molecule is polar if it has a negatively charged bit and a positively charged bit.

2) Because water is polar, the **positive end** of a water molecule will be attracted to the **negative ion**, and the **negative end** of a water molecule will be attracted to the **positive ion**.

3) This means the ions will get **totally surrounded** by water molecules — in other words, they'll **dissolve**.

4) So water's **polarity** makes it useful as a **solvent** for other polar molecules.

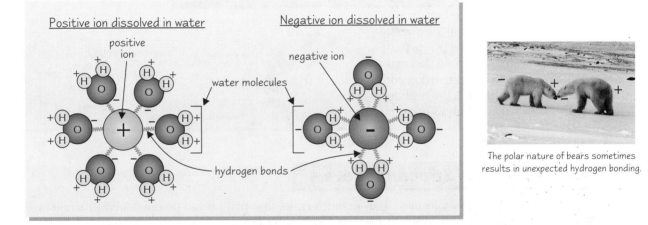

The polar nature of bears sometimes results in unexpected hydrogen bonding.

Practice Questions

Q1 State four functions of water in living organisms.

Q2 Briefly describe the structure of a water molecule.

Q3 Briefly describe what is meant by a polar molecule.

Q4 Why is water's high specific heat capacity useful for living organisms?

Exam Question

Q1 Relate the structure of the water molecule to its uses in living organisms. [15 marks]

Pssssssssssssssssssssssssssssssssssssssssssssss — need the loo yet?

Water is pretty darn useful really. It looks so, well, dull — but in fact it's scientifically amazing. It's essential for all kinds of jobs — keeping cool, transporting things, enabling reactions etc. You need to learn all of its properties and functions, and be able to say how they relate to its structure. Right, I'm off — when you gotta go, you gotta go.

Proteins

There are millions of different proteins. They're the most abundant molecules in cells, making up 50% or more of a cell's dry mass — now that's just plain greedy.

Proteins are Made from Long Chains of Amino Acids

1) A **dipeptide** is formed when two amino acids join together.
2) A **polypeptide** is formed when **more than two** amino acids join together.
3) **Proteins** are made up of **one or more polypeptides**.

Grant's cries of "die peptide, die" could be heard for miles around. He'd never forgiven it for sleeping with his wife.

Different Amino Acids Have Different Variable Groups

All amino acids have the same general structure — a **carboxyl group** (-COOH) and an **amino group** (-NH$_2$) attached to a **carbon** atom. The **difference** between different amino acids is the **variable** group (**R** on diagram) they contain.

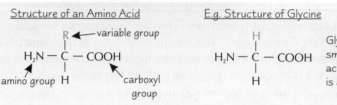

Glycine is the smallest amino acid — the R group is a hydrogen atom.

Amino Acids are Joined Together by Peptide Bonds

Amino acids are linked together by **peptide bonds** to form dipeptides and polypeptides. A molecule of **water** is **released** during the reaction. The **reverse** of this reaction **adds** a molecule of water to **break** the peptide bond. This is called a **hydrolysis** reaction.

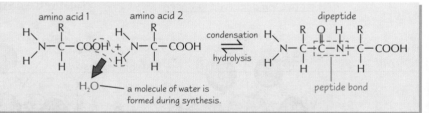

Proteins Have Four Structural Levels

Proteins are **big**, **complicated** molecules. They're much easier to explain if you describe their structure in four 'levels'. These levels are a protein's **primary**, **secondary**, **tertiary** and **quaternary** structures.

<u>Primary Structure</u> — this is the **sequence** of **amino acids** in the **polypeptide chain**.

<u>Secondary Structure</u> — the polypeptide chain doesn't remain flat and straight. **Hydrogen bonds** form between the amino acids in the chain. This makes it automatically **coil** into an **alpha (α) helix** or **fold** into a **beta (β) pleated sheet** — this is the secondary structure.

<u>Tertiary Structure</u> — the coiled or folded chain of amino acids is often **coiled** and **folded further**. **More bonds** form between different parts of the polypeptide chain. For proteins made from a **single** polypeptide chain, the tertiary structure forms their **final 3D structure**.

<u>Quaternary Structure</u> — some proteins are made of **several different polypeptide chains** held together by **bonds**. The **quaternary structure** is the way these polypeptide chains are assembled together. E.g. **haemoglobin** is made of **four** polypeptide chains, bonded together. For proteins made from **more than one** polypeptide chain, the quaternary structure is the protein's **final 3D structure**.

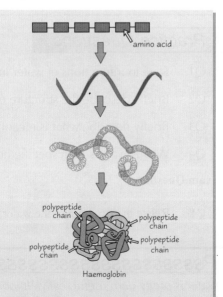

Proteins

Different Bonds Hold Different Structural Levels Together

The four structural levels of a protein are held together by **different kinds** of bonds:

1) **Primary structure** — held together by the **peptide bonds** between amino acids.

2) **Secondary structure** — held together by **hydrogen bonds** that form between nearby amino acids. These bonds create α-helix chains or β-pleated sheets.

3) **Tertiary structure** — this is affected by a few different kinds of bonds:
   - **Ionic interactions.** These are **weak attractions** between **negative** and **positive** charges on different parts of the molecule.
   - **Disulfide bonds.** Whenever two molecules of the amino acid **cysteine** come close together, the **sulfur atom** in one cysteine bonds to the sulfur in the other cysteine, forming a disulfide bond.
   - **Hydrophobic and hydrophilic interactions.** When **hydrophobic** (water-repelling) groups are close together in the protein, they tend to **clump together**. This means that **hydrophilic** (water-attracting) groups are more likely to be pushed to the **outside**, which affects how the protein **folds up** into its final structure.
   - **Hydrogen bonds.**

4) **Quaternary structure** — this tends to be determined by the **tertiary structure** of the individual polypeptide chains being bonded together. Because of this, it can be influenced by **all the bonds** mentioned above.

Hydrogen bonds are weak bonds between a positive hydrogen atom in one molecule and a negative atom or group in another molecule (see p. 52).

Protein Shape Relates to its Function

You need to learn these two **examples** of how proteins are **adapted** for their function:

1) **Collagen** is a **fibrous protein** that forms **supportive tissues** in animals, so it needs to be **strong**.
2) It's made of **three polypeptide chains** that are **tightly coiled** into a strong **triple helix**.
3) The chains are interlinked by strong **covalent bonds**.
4) **Minerals** can bind to the triple helix to **increase its rigidity**.

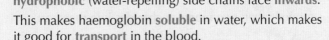

Fibrous proteins are tough and rope-shaped. They tend to be found in connective tissue — tendons and the like.

Globular proteins are round and compact. They're soluble, so they're easily transported in fluids.

1) **Haemoglobin** is a **globular protein** with an iron-containing **haem group** that binds to **oxygen**, **carrying it** around the body (see p. 42).
2) Its structure is curled up so that **hydrophilic** (water-attracting) side chains are on the **outside** of the molecule and **hydrophobic** (water-repelling) side chains face **inwards**.
3) This makes haemoglobin **soluble** in water, which makes it good for **transport** in the blood.

haem group

Practice Questions

Q1 Name the two groups found in all amino acid molecules.
Q2 Name the bond that joins amino acids together in proteins.
Q3 Name four types of bond that determine the structure of a protein.

Exam Questions

Q1 Describe the structure of proteins, explaining the terms primary, secondary, tertiary and quaternary structure. [9 marks]

Q2 Describe the structure of the collagen molecule and explain how this structure relates to its function in the body. [6 marks]

The name's Bond — Peptide Bond...

Quite a lot to learn on these pages — proteins are annoyingly complicated. Not happy with one, or even two structures, they've got four of the things — and you need to learn 'em all. Remember that synthesis and hydrolysis are the reverse of each other. And as for all that nasty stuff about disulfide bonds and ionic interactions... Urgh.

Carbohydrates

Carbohydrates are dead important chemicals — for a start they're the main energy supply in living organisms, and some of them (like cellulose) have an important structural role.

Carbohydrates are Made from Monosaccharides

1) Most carbohydrates are **large**, complex molecules composed of **long chains** of **monosaccharides** (e.g. starch is a large carbohydrate composed of long chains of glucose).
2) **Single** monosaccharides are also called carbohydrates though.
3) **Glucose** is a monosaccharide with **six carbon** atoms in each molecule.
4) There are **two forms** of glucose — **alpha** (α) and **beta** (β):

Remember, beta-glucose has the H on the bottom as you look at the structural diagram.

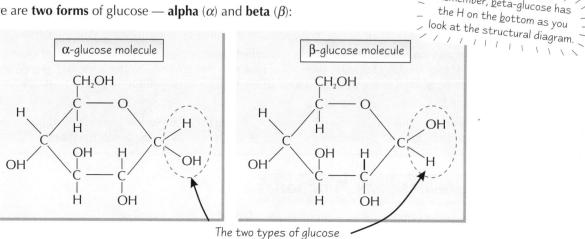

The two types of glucose have these groups reversed.

Glucose's **structure** is related to its **function** as the main **energy source** in animals and plants. Its structure makes it **soluble** so it can be **easily transported**. Its chemical bonds contain **lots of energy**.

Monosaccharides Join Together to Form Disaccharides and Polysaccharides

1) Monosaccharides are **joined together** by **glycosidic bonds**.
2) During **synthesis**, a **hydrogen** atom on one monosaccharide bonds to a **hydroxyl** (OH) group on the other, **releasing** a molecule of **water**.
3) Just like with the polypeptides on p. 54, the **reverse** of this synthesis reaction is **hydrolysis**. A molecule of water reacts with the glycosidic bond, **breaking it apart**.
4) A **disaccharide** is formed when **two monosaccharides** join together:

Sugar is a general term for monosaccharides and disaccharides.

Two α-glucose molecules are joined together by a **glycosidic bond** to form **maltose**.

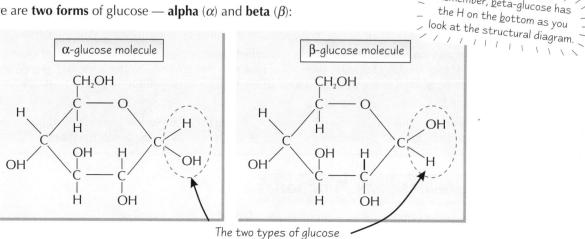

5) A **polysaccharide** is formed when **more than two** monosaccharides join together:

Lots of α-glucose molecules are joined together by **glycosidic bonds** to form **amylose**.

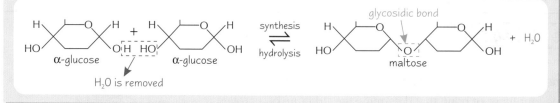

Extensive scientific research revealed an irreversible bond joining sugars to Pollyanna's gob.

Carbohydrates

You Need to Learn About **Three Polysaccharides**

You need to know about the relationship between the **structure** and **function** of three polysaccharides:

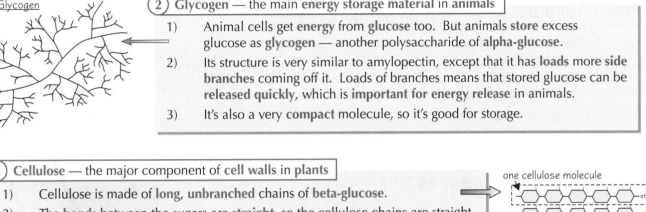

1 **Starch** — the main **energy storage material** in **plants**

1) Cells get **energy** from **glucose**. Plants **store** excess glucose as **starch** (when a plant **needs more glucose** for energy it **breaks down** starch to release the glucose).

2) Starch is a mixture of **two** polysaccharides of **alpha-glucose** — **amylose** and **amylopectin**:

- **Amylose** — a long, **unbranched chain** of α–glucose. The angles of the glycosidic bonds give it a **coiled structure**, almost like a cylinder. This makes it **compact**, so it's really **good for storage** because you can **fit more in** to a small space.

- **Amylopectin** — a long, **branched chain** of α–glucose. Its **side branches** allow the **enzymes** that break down the molecule to get at the **glycosidic bonds easily**. This means that the glucose can be **released quickly**.

3) Starch is **insoluble** in water, so it **doesn't** cause water to enter cells by **osmosis** (which would make them swell). This makes it good for **storage**.

Amylose

one alpha-glucose molecule

Amylopectin

Glycogen

2 Glycogen — the main **energy storage material** in **animals**

1) Animal cells get **energy** from **glucose** too. But animals **store** excess glucose as **glycogen** — another polysaccharide of **alpha-glucose**.

2) Its structure is very similar to amylopectin, except that it has **loads** more **side branches** coming off it. Loads of branches means that stored glucose can be **released quickly**, which is **important for energy release** in animals.

3) It's also a very **compact** molecule, so it's good for storage.

3 Cellulose — the major component of **cell walls** in **plants**

1) Cellulose is made of **long, unbranched** chains of **beta-glucose**.

2) The **bonds** between the sugars are **straight**, so the cellulose chains are straight.

3) The cellulose chains are linked together by **hydrogen bonds** to form strong fibres called **microfibrils**. The strong fibres mean cellulose provides **structural support** for cells (e.g. in plant cell walls).

one cellulose molecule

etc.

weak hydrogen bonds *one beta-glucose molecule*

Practice Questions

Q1 What type of bonds hold monosaccharide molecules together in polysaccharides?

Q2 Briefly describe the structure of amylose.

Q3 What is the function of glycogen?

Exam Questions

Q1 Describe, with the aid of a diagram, how glycosidic bonds are formed and broken in living organisms. [7 marks]

Q2 Compare and contrast the structures of starch and cellulose, describing how each molecule's structure is linked to its function. [12 marks]

*Mmmmm, starch... Tasty, tasty chips and beans... *dribble*. Ahem, sorry.*

Remember that synthesis and hydrolysis reactions are the reverse of each other. You need to learn how maltose and amylose are formed and broken down by these reactions. And don't forget that starch is composed of two different polysaccharides... and that glucose exists in two forms... so many reminders, so little space...

Lipids

Right, that's proteins and carbohydrates dealt with. There's only really one more important kind of molecule in biology, and that's lipids, or 'fatty oily things' to you and me. Some of them are just straightforward fats, but others have extra bits stuck to them — you need to know what they look like and how their structures relate to their functions...

Triglycerides are a Kind of Lipid

1) A triglyceride is made of **one** molecule of **glycerol** with **three fatty acids** attached to it.

2) Fatty acid molecules have long tails made of **hydrocarbons** (carbon chains with hydrogen atoms branching off).

3) The tails are **hydrophobic** (water-repelling).

4) These tails make lipids **insoluble** in water.

5) All **fatty acids** consist of the same basic structure, but the **hydrocarbon tail varies**. The tail is shown in the diagram with the letter **R**.

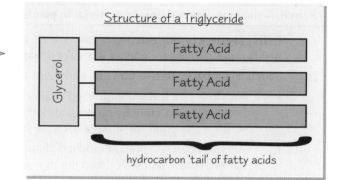

Structure of a Triglyceride

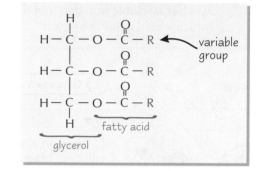

Phospholipids are Similar to Triglycerides

1) The lipids found in **cell membranes** aren't triglycerides — they're **phospholipids**.

2) Phospholipids are pretty similar to triglycerides except one of the fatty acid molecules is replaced by a **phosphate group**.

3) The phosphate group is **ionised** (electrically charged), which makes it **attract water** molecules (see p. 53).

4) So the phosphate part of the phospholipid molecule is **hydrophilic** (water-attracting) while the rest (the fatty acid **tails**) is **hydrophobic** (water-repelling).

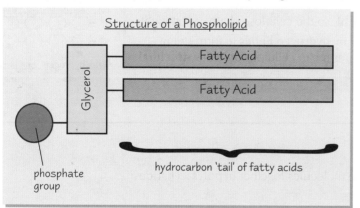

Structure of a Phospholipid

Contrary to popular belief, cows are actually hydrophilic.

Cholesterol has a Hydrocarbon Ring Structure

1) Cholesterol is a type of lipid often found in **cell membranes**. It's also used to make other things like **steroids**.

2) It has a **hydrocarbon ring** structure attached to a **hydrocarbon tail**.

3) The hydrocarbon ring has a **polar hydroxyl group** attached to it, which makes cholesterol slightly **soluble** in **water**. However, it's **insoluble** in **blood**, so it's carried around the body by proteins called **lipoproteins**.

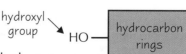

Lipids

The **Structures** of Lipids Relate to Their **Functions**

You need to know how the **structures** of triglycerides, phospholipids and cholesterol are related to their **functions**:

TRIGLYCERIDES

Triglycerides are mainly used as **energy storage molecules**. They're good for this because:

1) The **long hydrocarbon tails** of the fatty acids contain lots of **chemical energy** — a load of energy is **released** when they're **broken down**. Because of these tails, lipids contain about **twice** as much energy per gram as carbohydrates.

2) They're **insoluble**, so they don't cause water to enter the cells by **osmosis** (which would make them swell). The triglycerides bundle together as **insoluble droplets** in cells because the fatty acid tails are **hydrophobic** (water-repelling) — the tails **face inwards**, shielding themselves from water with their glycerol heads.

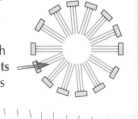

You learnt how the structure of phospholipids and cholesterol relate to their function in Unit 1: Section 2, but you need to know it for this unit too.

PHOSPHOLIPIDS

Phospholipids make up the **bilayer** of **cell membranes** (see p. 12). Cell membranes **control** what **enters and leaves a cell**.

1) Their heads are **hydrophilic** and their tails are **hydrophobic**, so they form a **double** layer with their heads facing **out** towards the water on either side.

2) The **centre** of the bilayer is **hydrophobic**, so water-soluble substances **can't** easily pass through it — the membrane acts as a **barrier** to those substances.

CHOLESTEROL

Cholesterol molecules help **strengthen** the cell membrane by **interacting** with the **phospholipid bilayer**.

The **small size** and **flattened shape** allows cholesterol to fit **in between** the phospholipid molecules in the membrane. They bind to the hydrophobic tails of the phospholipids, causing them to **pack more closely together**. This helps to make the membrane **less fluid** and **more rigid**.

Practice Questions

Q1 What are triglycerides composed of?

Q2 Sketch the structure of a phospholipid.

Exam Questions

Q1 a) In a phospholipid, which part of the molecule is hydrophilic and which is hydrophobic? [2 marks]

  b) Explain how phospholipid molecules arrange themselves in cell membranes and relate this to their structure. [3 marks]

Q2 Explain how each of these features of lipids is important for its function in living things:

  a) Cholesterol molecules have a flattened shape. [2 marks]

  b) Triglycerides have a hydrophobic tail. [2 marks]

Hydrocarbon tails, phospholipid bilayers... Whatever happened to plain old lard?

You don't get far in life without extensive lard knowledge, so learn all the details on this page good and proper. Lipids pop up in other sections, so make sure you know the basics about how their structure gives them some quite groovy properties. Right, all this lipids talk is making me hungry — chips time...

Biochemical Tests for Molecules

Here's a bit of light relief for you — two pages all about how you test for the different molecules you've just read about...

Use the **Benedict's Test** for **Sugars**

Sugar is a general term for **monosaccharides** and **disaccharides**. All sugars can be classified as **reducing** or **non-reducing**. To **test** for sugars you use the **Benedict's test**. The test **differs** depending on the **type** of sugar you are testing for.

REDUCING SUGARS

1) Reducing sugars include **all monosaccharides** (e.g. glucose) and **some disaccharides** (e.g. maltose).

2) You add **Benedict's reagent** (which is **blue**) to a sample and **heat it**. Make sure the solution **doesn't boil**. If the test's **positive** it will form a **coloured precipitate** (solid particles suspended in the solution).

The colour of the precipitate changes from: **blue** → **green** → **yellow** → **orange** → **brick red**

Always use an <u>excess</u> of Benedict's solution — this makes sure that <u>all</u> the sugar reacts.

3) The higher the concentration of reducing sugar, the further the colour change goes — you can use this to **compare** the amount of reducing sugar in different solutions. A more accurate way of doing this is to **filter** the solution and **weigh the precipitate**.

NON-REDUCING SUGARS

1) To test for **non-reducing sugars**, like sucrose, first you have to break them down into monosaccharides.

2) You do this by **boiling** the test solution with **dilute hydrochloric acid** and then **neutralising** it with **sodium hydrogencarbonate**. Then just carry out the **Benedict's test** as you would for a reducing sugar.

3) Annoyingly, if the result of this test is **positive** the sugar could be reducing **or** non-reducing. To **check** it's non-reducing you need to do the **reducing sugar test** too (to rule out it being a reducing sugar).

Use the **Iodine Test** for **Starch**

Make sure you always talk about <u>iodine in potassium iodide solution</u>, not just iodine.

Just add **iodine dissolved in potassium iodide solution** to the test sample.

- If starch **is present**, the sample changes from **browny-orange** to a dark, **blue-black** colour.
- If there's **no starch**, it stays browny-orange.

Use the **Biuret Test** for **Proteins**

test solution: sodium hydroxide solution and copper(II) sulfate solution

purple colour indicates protein

There are **two stages** to this test.

1) The test solution needs to be **alkaline**, so first you add a few drops of **sodium hydroxide solution**.

2) Then you add some **copper(II) sulfate solution**.

- If protein **is present** a **purple layer** forms.
- If there's **no protein**, the solution will **stay blue**. The colours are pale, so you need to look carefully.

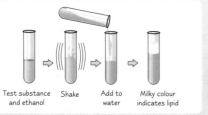

Carbohydrates are polar molecules. No wait, lipids are polar molecules. No wait, I know this, I know this...

Humphrey's revision for his starch test wasn't going so well.

Use the **Emulsion Test** for **Lipids**

Shake the test substance with **ethanol** for about a minute, then **pour** the solution into **water**.

- If lipid **is present**, the solution will turn **milky**.
- The **more lipid** there is, the **more noticeable** the milky colour will be.
- If there's **no lipid**, the solution will **stay clear**.

Test substance and ethanol → Shake → Add to water → Milky colour indicates lipid

Biochemical Tests for Molecules

Colorimetry is Used to Determine the Concentration of a Glucose Solution

1) A **quantitative** version of the **Benedict's test** allows you to estimate **how much** glucose (or other **reducing sugar**) there is in a solution.

2) It uses a **colorimeter** — a device that measures the **strength** of a **coloured solution** by seeing how much **light** passes through it.

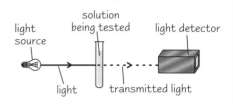

3) A colorimeter measures **absorbance** (the amount of light absorbed by the solution). The **more concentrated** the **colour** of the solution, the **higher** the absorbance is.

4) It's pretty difficult to measure the concentration of the coloured precipitate formed in the Benedict's test, so when you're estimating glucose concentration you measure the **concentration** of the **blue Benedict's solution** that's **left** after the test (the **paler** the solution left, the **more glucose** there was). So, the **higher** the glucose concentration, the **lower** the absorbance of the solution.

Here's how you do it:

First you need to make a **calibration curve**. To do this you need to:

1) Make up several glucose solutions of **different**, **known concentrations**, e.g. 10 mM, 20 mM and 30 mM. There should be the **same volume** of each.

2) Do a **Benedict's test** on each solution. Use the **same amount** of Benedict's solution in each case — it has to be a **large** enough volume to react with **all** the sugar in the strongest solution and still have some reagent **left over**.

3) **Remove** any **precipitate** from the solutions — either leave the test tubes for **24 hours** (so that the precipitate **settles out**) or **centrifuge** them.

4) Use a **colorimeter** to measure the **absorbance** of the Benedict's solution **remaining** in each tube.

5) Use the results to make the **calibration curve**, showing absorbance against glucose concentration.

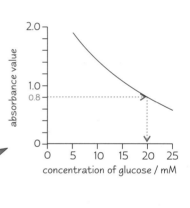

Then you can test the **unknown solution** in the same way as the known concentrations and use the calibration curve to find its concentration.

E.g. an **unknown solution** gives an absorbance value of **0.80**. Reading across the calibration graph from an absorbance value of 0.8 shows that the concentration of glucose in the unknown solution is **20 mM**.

Practice Questions

Q1 Describe how you would test a solution for starch. What result would you expect if:
a) starch was present; b) starch was not present?

Q2 Describe how you would test for lipids in a solution.

Exam Question

solution	absorbance
A	1.22
B	0.68
C	0.37

Q1 Equal volumes of three different sugar solutions (A, B and C) were each tested with the same large volume of Benedict's solution. Later, the concentrations of Benedict's solution in each test tube were compared, using a colorimeter. The table shows the absorbance of each solution.

a) Which original solution contained the highest concentration of reducing sugar? [1 mark]

b) Explain why a large volume of Benedict's solution had to be used. [1 mark]

c) Suggest two factors that should be kept constant when carrying out this test. [2 marks]

The Anger Test — annoy the test subject. If it goes red, anger is present...

A double page of biochemical tests... I literally can't think of anything worse. Well, maybe being slowly dissolved in a vat of vinegar would be worse, but it's a close one. Oh well, that's the end of this section, so good times must be on their way...

DNA and RNA

This section's all about nucleic acids — DNA and RNA. These molecules are needed to build proteins, which are required for the cells in living organisms to function. They're right handy little molecules.

DNA is Used to Store Genetic Information

1) Your DNA (**deoxyribonucleic acid**) contains your **genetic information** — that's **all the instructions** needed to **grow and develop** from a fertilised egg to a fully grown adult.

2) The DNA molecules are really **long** and are **coiled** up very tightly, so a lot of genetic information can fit into a **small space** in the cell nucleus.

3) DNA molecules have a **paired structure** (see below), which makes it much easier to **copy itself**. This is called **self-replication** (see p. 64). It's important for cell division (see p. 20) and for passing genetic information from **generation to generation** (see p. 23).

4) DNA contains **genes** — **sections of DNA** that code (contain the instructions) for a specific **sequence of amino acids** that forms a particular **protein**. See page 64.

5) The nucleic acid **RNA** (ribonucleic acid) is similar in structure to DNA. It's used to make **proteins** from the instructions contained within DNA (see next page).

DNA is Made of Nucleotides that Contain a Sugar, a Phosphate and a Base

1) DNA is a **polynucleotide** — it's made up of lots of **nucleotides** joined together.

2) Each nucleotide is made from a **deoxyribose sugar**, a **phosphate** group and a nitrogen-containing **base**.

3) Each nucleotide has the **same sugar and phosphate**. The **base** on each nucleotide can **vary** though.

4) There are **four** possible bases — adenine (**A**), thymine (**T**), cytosine (**C**) and guanine (**G**).

5) **A**denine and **g**uanine are a type of base called a **purine**. **C**ytosine and **t**hymine are **pyrimidines**.

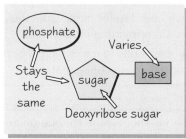

Two Polynucleotide Strands Join Together to Form a Double-Helix

1) DNA nucleotides join together to form **polynucleotide strands**.

2) The nucleotides join up between the **phosphate** group of one nucleotide and the **sugar** of another.

3) **Two** DNA polynucleotide strands join together by **hydrogen bonding** between the bases.

4) Each base can only join with one particular partner — this is called **complementary base pairing**.

5) **Adenine** always pairs with **thymine** (**A - T**) and **guanine** always pairs with **cytosine** (**G - C**). (A **purine** (A or G) always pairs with a **pyrimidine** (T or C).)

6) **Two** hydrogen bonds form between **A and T**, and **three** hydrogen bonds form between **C and G**.

7) Two **antiparallel** (running in opposite directions) polynucleotide strands **twist** to form the **DNA double-helix**.

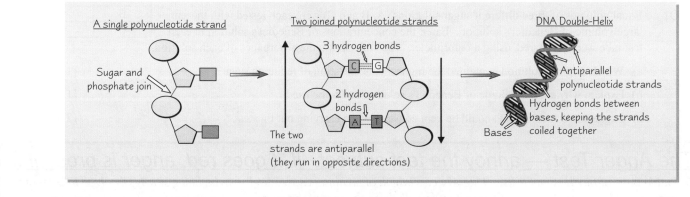

DNA and RNA

RNA is Very Similar to DNA

1) RNA and DNA are both made from nucleotides containing **sugar**, **nitrogen-containing bases** and **phosphate**.

2) Each nucleotide in both RNA and DNA contains one of **four** different bases.

3) Also, the nucleotides form a **polynucleotide strand** that is joined up between the sugar of one nucleotide and the phosphate of another.

4) But the structure of RNA **differs** from DNA in three main ways:

Mary didn't care if it was ribose or deoxyribose, she just wanted her cuppa.

1 The **sugar** in RNA nucleotides is a **ribose sugar** (not deoxyribose).

2 The nucleotides form a **single polynucleotide strand** (not a double one).

3 Uracil (a pyrimidine) replaces thymine as a base. Uracil **always pairs** with **adenine** in RNA.

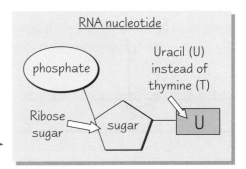

RNA nucleotide — phosphate — Ribose sugar — sugar — Uracil (U) instead of thymine (T) — U

Practice Questions

Q1 What are the three main components of nucleotides?

Q2 Which bases join together in a DNA molecule?

Q3 What sugar is found in DNA nucleotides?

Q4 What type of bonds join the bases in a DNA molecule together?

Q5 Which sugar do RNA nucleotides contain?

Exam Questions

Q1 Fill in the missing nucleotides on the diagram below.

A C C G T C A
T G   A   [1 mark]

Q2 a) Describe the structure of a DNA nucleotide.   [3 marks]

b) Describe the main differences between DNA and RNA molecules.   [3 marks]

Q3 Describe, using diagrams where appropriate, how nucleotides are joined together in DNA and how two single polynucleotide strands of DNA are joined.   [4 marks]

Give me a D, give me an N, give me an A! What do you get? — very confused...

*You need to learn the structure of DNA — the polynucleotide strands, the hydrogen bonds, and don't forget the complementary base pairing. And make sure you know the three main differences between RNA and DNA — **R**NA's got **r**ibose sugar, uracil bases and it's single-stranded. You need to learn all this before moving on, or you'll struggle later.*

DNA Replication and Protein Synthesis

Here comes some truly essential stuff — DNA replication, genes, and a wee bit on protein synthesis. I'm afraid it's all horribly complicated — all I can do is keep apologising. Sorry.

DNA can Copy Itself — Self-Replication

DNA **copies itself** before **cell division** (see page 20) so that each new cell has the full amount of DNA.

1) The **hydrogen bonds** between the two **polynucleotide** DNA strands **break**. The helix **unzips** to form two single strands.

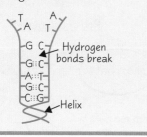

2) Each **original** single strand acts as a **template** for a new strand. Free-floating DNA nucleotides join to the **exposed bases** on each original template strand by **complementary base pairing** — A with T and C with G.

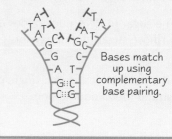

Bases match up using complementary base pairing.

3) The nucleotides on the new strand are **joined together** by the enzyme DNA polymerase. **Hydrogen bonds form** between the bases on the original and new strand.

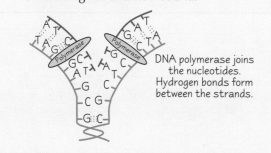

DNA polymerase joins the nucleotides. Hydrogen bonds form between the strands.

4) Each new DNA molecule contains **one strand** from the **original** DNA molecule and **one new strand**.

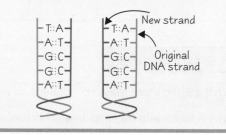

New strand
Original DNA strand

This type of copying is called **semi-conservative replication** because **half** of the strands in each new DNA molecule are from the **original** piece of DNA.

DNA Contains Genes Which are Instructions for Proteins

Polypeptide is just another word for a protein.

1) A **gene** is a **sequence** of DNA nucleotides that codes for a **protein** (polypeptide).
2) Proteins are made from **amino acids**.
3) Different proteins have a **different number** and **order** of amino acids.
4) It's the **order** of **nucleotide bases** in a gene that determines the **order of amino acids** in a particular **protein**.
5) Each amino acid is coded for by a sequence of **three bases** in a gene.
6) Different sequences of **bases** code for different **amino acids**. For example:

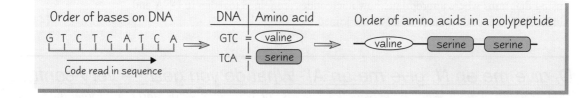

DNA Replication and Protein Synthesis

DNA is **Copied** into **RNA** for **Protein Synthesis**

1) All the reactions and **processes** in living organisms **need** proteins.

2) **DNA** carries the **instructions** to make **proteins** (as **genes**). It's found in the **nucleus**.

3) The organelles that make proteins (**ribosomes**, see p. 5) are found in the **cytoplasm**. But the DNA molecules are **too large** to move out of the nucleus.

4) Instead, sections of DNA are **copied** into **RNA**.

5) The RNA **leaves** the nucleus and joins with a ribosome in the cytoplasm, where it can be used to synthesise a protein.

6) So, DNA and RNA are **vital** for living organisms to produce proteins in order to **grow** and **develop**.

Mrs Thone knew how to synthesise some great tunes.

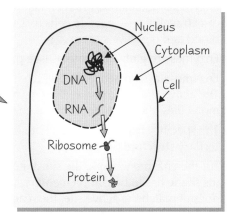

Practice Questions

Q1 Why is DNA copied before cell division?

Q2 What is the function of DNA polymerase in DNA replication?

Q3 Why is DNA replication described as semi-conservative?

Q4 Why is DNA copied into RNA?

Q5 Where is RNA formed?

Q6 Where are proteins synthesised?

Exam Questions

Q1 Describe the semi-conservative method of DNA replication.   [7 marks]

Q2 Write a definition of a gene.   [2 marks]

Q3 Describe the role of DNA and RNA in living organisms.   [3 marks]

Genes contain instructions — wash at 40 °C...

DNA self-replication can get a bit tricky, but you need to learn what's going on. Diagrams are handy for learning stuff like this, so get drawing. And don't go forgetting about RNA — it's a really important molecule. Without it we'd have no proteins. So remember — DNA is copied into RNA, which leaves the nucleus and is used to make a protein in the cytoplasm.

Action of Enzymes

Enzymes crop up loads in biology — they're really useful 'cos they make reactions work more quickly.
*So, whether you feel the need for some speed or not, read on — because you **really** need to know this*
basic stuff about enzymes.

Enzymes are Biological Catalysts

Enzymes **speed up chemical reactions** by acting as **biological catalysts**.

1) They catalyse **metabolic reactions** in your body, e.g. **digestion** and **respiration**.

2) Enzyme action can be **intracellular** — **within** cells, or **extracellular** — **outside** cells (e.g. in places like the blood and digestive system).

3) Enzymes are **globular proteins** (see p. 55).

4) Enzymes have an **active site**, which has a **specific shape**. The active site is the part of the enzyme where the **substrate** molecules (the substance that the enzyme interacts with) **bind to**.

5) The specific shape of the active site is determined by the enzyme's **tertiary structure** (see p. 54).

6) For the enzyme to work, the substrate has to **fit into** the **active site** (its shape has to be **complementary**). If the substrate shape doesn't match the active site, the reaction won't be catalysed. This means that enzymes work with very few substrates — usually only one.

A catalyst is a substance that speeds up a chemical reaction without being used up in the reaction itself.

Ahmed knew Sara was a lovely girl, but just couldn't get past the shape incompatibility thing.

Enzymes Reduce Activation Energy

In a chemical reaction, a certain amount of energy needs to be supplied to the chemicals before the reaction will start. This is called the **activation energy** — it's often provided as **heat**.

Enzymes **reduce** the amount of activation energy that's needed, often making reactions happen at a **lower temperature** than they could without an enzyme. This **speeds** up the **rate of reaction**.

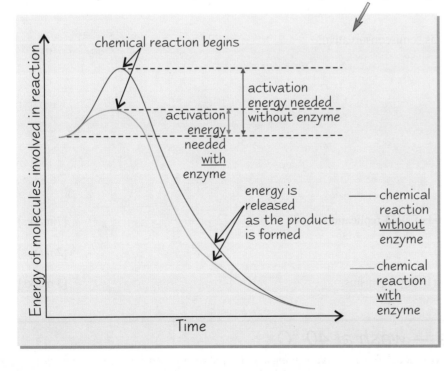

When a substance binds to an enzyme's active site, an **enzyme-substrate complex** is formed. It's the formation of the enzyme-substrate complex that **lowers** the **activation energy**. Here are two reasons why:

1) If two substrate molecules need to be **joined**, attaching to the enzyme holds them **close together**, **reducing** any **repulsion** between the molecules so they can bond more easily.

2) If the enzyme is catalysing a **breakdown reaction**, fitting into the active site puts a **strain** on bonds in the substrate. This strain means the substrate molecule **breaks up** more easily.

Action of Enzymes

The 'Lock and Key' Model is a Good Start...

Enzymes are a bit picky. They only work with **substrates** that fit their active site. Early scientists studying the action of enzymes came up with the 'lock and key' model. This is where the **substrate fits** into the **enzyme** in the same way that a **key fits** into a **lock**.

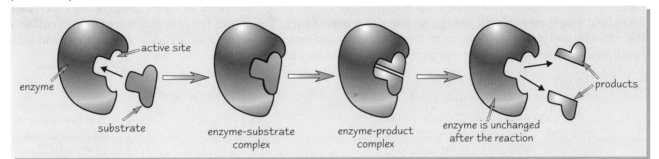

Scientists soon realised that the lock and key model didn't give the full story. The enzyme and substrate do have to fit together in the first place, but new evidence showed that the **enzyme-substrate complex changed shape** slightly to complete the fit. This **locks** the substrate even more tightly to the enzyme. Scientists modified the old lock and key model and came up with the 'induced fit' model.

...but the 'Induced Fit' Model is a Better Theory

The '**induced fit**' model helps to explain why enzymes are so **specific** and only bond to one particular substrate.

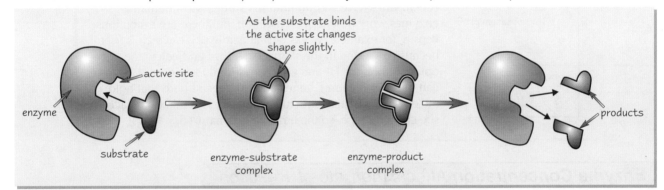

The substrate doesn't only have to be the right shape to fit the active site, it has to make the active site **change shape** in the right way as well. This is a prime example of how a widely accepted theory can **change** when **new evidence** comes along. The 'induced fit' model is still widely accepted — for now, anyway.

Practice Questions

Q1 What is an enzyme?

Q2 What is the name given to the amount of energy needed to start a reaction?

Q3 What is an enzyme-substrate complex?

Q4 Explain why enzymes are specific.

Exam Question

Q1 Describe the 'lock and key' model of enzyme action and explain how the 'induced fit' model is different. [7 marks]

But why is the enzyme-substrate complex?

OK, nothing too tricky here. The main thing to remember is that every enzyme has a specific shape, so it only works with specific substrates that fit the shape. The induced fit model is the new, trendy theory to explain this — the lock and key model is, like, so last year. Everyone who's anyone knows that.

Factors Affecting Enzyme Activity

Now you know what enzymes are and how they work, it's time to take a look at what makes them tick. Humans need things like money, caffeine and the newest mobile phone, but enzymes are quite content with the right temperature and pH.

Temperature has a Big Influence on Enzyme Activity

Like any chemical reaction, the **rate** of an enzyme-controlled reaction **increases** when the **temperature's increased**. More heat means **more kinetic energy**, so molecules **move faster**. This makes the enzymes **more likely** to **collide** with the substrate molecules. The **energy** of these collisions also **increases**, which means each collision is more likely to **result** in a **reaction**. But, if the temperature gets too high, the **reaction stops**.

1) The rise in temperature makes the enzyme's molecules **vibrate more**.

2) If the temperature goes above a certain level, this vibration **breaks** some of the **bonds** that hold the enzyme in shape.

3) The **active site changes shape** and the enzyme and substrate **no longer fit together**.

4) At this point, the enzyme is **denatured** — it no longer functions as a catalyst.

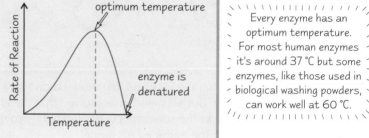

Every enzyme has an optimum temperature. For most human enzymes it's around 37 °C but some enzymes, like those used in biological washing powders, can work well at 60 °C.

pH Also Affects Enzyme Activity

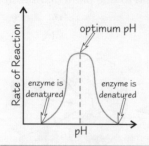

All enzymes have an **optimum pH value**. Most human enzymes work best at pH 7 (neutral), but there are exceptions. **Pepsin**, for example, works best at acidic pH 2, which is useful because it's found in the stomach. Above and below the optimum pH, the H^+ and OH^- ions found in acids and alkalis can mess up the **ionic bonds** and **hydrogen bonds** that hold the enzyme's tertiary structure in place. This makes the active site change shape, so the enzyme is **denatured**.

Enzyme Concentration Affects the Rate of Reaction

1) The **more enzyme molecules** there are in a solution, the more likely a substrate molecule is to **collide** with one and form an **enzyme-substrate complex**. So increasing the concentration of the enzyme **increases** the **rate of reaction**.

2) But, if the amount of **substrate** is **limited**, there comes a point when there's more than enough enzyme molecules to deal with all the available substrate, so adding more enzyme has **no further effect**.

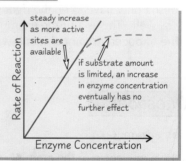

Substrate Concentration Affects the Rate of Reaction Up to a Point

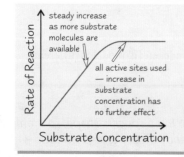

The **higher** the substrate concentration, the **faster** the reaction — more substrate molecules means a **collision** between substrate and enzyme is **more likely** and so more active sites will be used. This is only true up until a 'saturation' point though. After that, there are so many substrate molecules that the enzymes have about as much as they can cope with (all the **active sites are full**), and adding more **makes no difference**.

Factors Affecting Enzyme Activity

You can **Measure** the **Rate** of an **Enzyme-Controlled** Reaction

You need to be able to **describe** how the effects of pH, temperature, enzyme concentration and substrate concentration can be investigated **experimentally**. Here are two ways of measuring the **rate** of an enzyme-controlled reaction:

Example 1

You can measure **how fast** the **product of** the reaction **appears**. The diagram on the right shows how to measure this with the enzyme **catalase**. Catalase catalyses the **breakdown** of **hydrogen peroxide** into **water** and **oxygen**. It's easy to collect the oxygen produced and measure **how fast** it's given off.

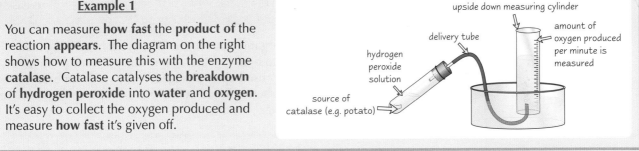

Example 2

You can also measure the **disappearance** of the **substrate** rather than the appearance of the product and use this to **compare the rate** of reaction under different conditions. For example, the enzyme **amylase** catalyses the breakdown of **starch** to **maltose** (see p. 57). It's easy to detect starch using a solution of potassium iodide and iodine. You can **time** how long it takes for the starch to disappear by **regularly** sampling the starch solution, and use the times to compare rates between different tests.

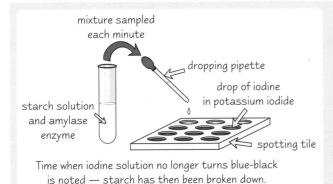

Time when iodine solution no longer turns blue-black is noted — starch has then been broken down.

Here are some general tips on what to include when describing an experiment:
1) Describe the **method** and the **apparatus** you'd use.
2) Say **what** you're **measuring** (the dependent variable), e.g. the volume of gas produced per minute.
3) Describe how you'd **vary** the **independent variable**, e.g. if your independent variable is **enzyme concentration** you might test **five different concentrations** of enzyme.
4) Describe what **variables** you're **keeping constant**, e.g. temperature, pH, volume of solution, substrate concentration etc.
5) Say that you need to **repeat** the experiment at least twice, to make the results **more reliable**.
6) Say that you need a **control**, e.g. a test tube containing the substrate solution but no enzyme.

Practice Questions

Q1 What does it mean if an enzyme is denatured?

Q2 Explain why increasing the concentration of an enzyme doesn't always increase the rate of reaction.

Q3 Explain the effect of increasing substrate concentration on the rate of an enzyme-catalysed reaction.

Q4 Suggest two methods of measuring the rate of an enzyme-catalysed reaction.

Exam Question

Q1 When doing an experiment on enzymes, explain why it is necessary to control the temperature and pH of the solutions involved. [8 marks]

This enzyme's not working very fast — he's out of shape...

Enzymes are pretty fussy — they'll only work best when they are nice and comfortable. So be like them — tell your teacher you'll need an optimum concentration of chocolate, a nice warm fire to sit by and... err... the right pH environment. Also, make sure you can describe how you'd investigate all those factors that affect enzyme activity.

Factors Affecting Enzyme Activity

Cofactors are substances that enzymes need to work. Enzyme inhibitors, yep you guessed it, inhibit their action. Some inhibitors are poisons, but they're not all bad — we use some of them as medicinal drugs.

Cofactors and Coenzymes are Essential for Enzymes to Work

Some enzymes will only work if there is another **non-protein** substance bound to them.
These non-protein substances are called **cofactors**.

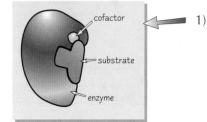

1) Some cofactors are **inorganic** molecules. They work by helping the enzyme and substrate to **bind together**. They don't directly participate in the reaction so aren't **used up** or **changed** in any way. For example, **manganese ions** are cofactors found in hydrolase (enzymes that catalyse the hydrolysis of chemical bonds).

2) Some cofactors are **organic** molecules — these are called **coenzymes**.
They participate in the reaction and are **changed** by it (they're just like a second substrate, but they aren't called that).
They often act as **carriers**, moving **chemical groups** between different enzymes. They're **continually recycled** during this process.

A is a coenzyme used by enzyme 1.

During the reaction A is changed to B.

B is a coenzyme used by enzyme 2.

enzyme 1

substrate 1

enzyme 2

substrate 2

During the reaction B is changed to A
(i.e. the coenzyme is recycled by enzyme 2).

Enzyme Activity can be Inhibited

Enzyme activity can be prevented by **enzyme inhibitors** — molecules that **bind to the enzyme** that they inhibit.
Inhibition can be **competitive** or **non-competitive**.

COMPETITIVE INHIBITION

1) **Competitive inhibitor** molecules have a **similar shape** to that of the **substrate** molecules.

2) They **compete** with the substrate molecules to **bind** to the **active site**, but **no reaction** takes place.

3) Instead they **block** the active site, so **no substrate** molecules can **fit** in it.

4) How much the enzyme is inhibited depends on the **relative concentrations** of the inhibitor and substrate.

5) If there's a **high concentration** of the **inhibitor**, it'll take up **nearly all** the **active sites** and hardly any of the substrate will get to the enzyme.

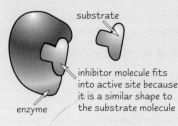

substrate

inhibitor molecule fits into active site because it is a similar shape to the substrate molecule

enzyme

NON-COMPETITIVE INHIBITION

1) **Non-competitive inhibitor** molecules bind to the enzyme **away from its active site**.

2) This causes the active site to **change shape** so the substrate molecules can **no longer bind** to it.

3) They **don't** 'compete' with the substrate molecules to bind to the active site because they are a **different shape**.

4) **Increasing** the concentration of **substrate won't** make any difference — enzyme activity will still be inhibited.

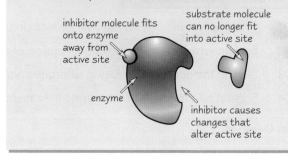

inhibitor molecule fits onto enzyme away from active site

substrate molecule can no longer fit into active site

enzyme

inhibitor causes changes that alter active site

Inhibitors can be **reversible** or **non-reversible**.
Which one they are depends on the **strength of the bonds** between the enzyme and the inhibitor.

1) If they're **strong, covalent bonds**, the inhibitor can't be removed easily and the inhibition is **irreversible**.

2) If they're **weaker hydrogen bonds** or weak **ionic bonds**, the inhibitor can be removed and the inhibition is **reversible**.

Factors Affecting Enzyme Activity

Some *Metabolic Poisons* are *Enzyme Inhibitors*

Metabolic **poisons interfere** with **metabolic reactions** (the reactions that occur in cells), causing **damage**, **illness** or **death** — they're often **enzyme inhibitors**.
In the **exam** you might be asked to **describe the action** of one **named poison**, for example:

1) **Cyanide** is an **irreversible** inhibitor of **cytochrome c oxidase**, an enzyme that catalyses **respiration** reactions. Cells that can't respire **die**.

2) **Malonate** inhibits **succinate dehydrogenase** (which also catalyses respiration reactions).

3) **Arsenic** inhibits the action of **pyruvate dehydrogenase**, yet another enzyme that catalyses **respiration** reactions.

Gillian didn't think Hugo would find it quite so funny when he realised she'd spiked his food with an irreversible enzyme inhibitor. Mwah ha ha ha.

Some *Drugs* Work by *Inhibiting Enzymes*

Some **medicinal drugs** are **enzyme inhibitors**, for example:

1) Some **antiviral** drugs (drugs that stop **viruses** like **HIV**) — e.g. **reverse transcriptase inhibitors** inhibit the enzyme **reverse transcriptase**, which catalyses the **replication** of **viral DNA**. This **prevents** the virus from **replicating**.

2) Some **antibiotics** — e.g. **penicillin** inhibits the enzyme **transpeptidase**, which **catalyses** the **formation** of **proteins** in bacterial cell walls. This **weakens the cell wall** and prevents the bacterium from regulating its osmotic pressure. As a result the cell **bursts** and the bacterium is **killed**.

Practice Questions

Q1 What are cofactors and coenzymes?

Q2 What's the difference between competitive and non-competitive enzyme inhibitors?

Q3 Name one metabolic poison and describe how it works.

Q4 Describe one medicinal use of enzyme inhibitors.

Exam Questions

Q1 During an experiment hexokinase (an enzyme that catalyses reactions important in respiration) was found to work only in the presence of magnesium ions and to work slower when aluminium ions were also present.

a) Suggest a possible reason why hexokinase only works when magnesium ions are present. [2 marks]

b) Suggest a possible reason why hexokinase works slower when aluminium ions are present. [2 marks]

c) Explain why aluminium ions are a metabolic poison. [1 mark]

Q2 HIV uses protease enzymes to catalyse the breakdown of proteins. It uses the products of the reaction to replicate new viruses. Ritonavir is a drug used to treat HIV. Its molecules have a similar shape to the protein molecules which are the substrate for HIV protease. Suggest how Ritonavir will affect HIV. Explain your answer. [5 marks]

Activity — mine is usually inhibited by pizza and a movie...

Crikey, it's like a rubbish soap or something — one minute the enzymes are trying to kill us, the next they're bringing us back to life, and all the while there are some things trying to stop them, and others trying to help them — if you can follow the ins, outs, ups and downs of some crazy soap then you can follow this. Everybody needs good en-zymes...

Balanced Diet

To maintain good health you need a balanced diet containing the right amount of each essential nutrient.
If you eat too much of something it can badly affect your health... and your waistline.

A **Balanced Diet** Supplies All the **Essential Nutrients**

A balanced diet gives you all the **nutrients** you need, plus **fibre** and **water**. There are **five** important nutrients — **carbohydrates**, **proteins**, **fats**, **vitamins** and **mineral salts**. Each nutrient has different functions in the body:

NUTRIENTS	FUNCTIONS
Carbohydrates	Provide energy.
Fats (lipids)	Act as an energy store, provide insulation, make up cell membranes, physically protect organs.
Proteins	Needed for growth, the repair of tissues and to make enzymes.
Vitamins	Different vitamins have different functions, e.g. vitamin D is needed for calcium absorption, vitamin K is needed for blood clotting.
Mineral salts	Different mineral salts have different functions, e.g. iron is needed to make haemoglobin in the blood, calcium is needed for bone formation.

Fibre	Aids movement of food through gut.
Water	It is used in chemical reactions. We need a constant supply to replace water lost through urinating, breathing and sweating.

Mmm... paper plates, delicious and nutritious...

Not Getting the **Right Amount** of **Each Nutrient** Causes **Malnutrition**

Basically, **malnutrition** is caused by having **too little** or **too much** of some nutrients in your diet. There are three causes:

1) Not having **enough food** — you get **too little** of **every nutrient**.
2) Having an **unbalanced diet**:
   •   Getting **too little** of a nutrient can lead to all kinds of **deficiency illnesses**, e.g. getting too little **iron** in your diet causes **anaemia**.
   •   Getting **too many** carbohydrates or fats can lead to **obesity**.
3) Not being able to **absorb the nutrients** from digestion into your **bloodstream** properly. E.g. coeliac disease reduces absorption of nutrients from the small intestine. This also causes **deficiency illnesses**.

Over-Nutrition and **Lack of Exercise** can Lead to **Obesity**

Obesity is a bigger problem in developed countries.

Obesity is a common **dietary condition** caused by eating **too much food**.

Hear ye, hear ye! I want more food.

1) **Obesity** is defined as being **20%** (or more) **over the recommended body weight**.
2) **Too much sugary** or **fatty food** and **too little exercise** are the main causes of obesity.
3) People can also be obese due to an **underactive thyroid gland**, but this problem isn't common.
4) Obesity can increase the risk of **diabetes**, **arthritis**, **high blood pressure**, **coronary heart disease** (CHD) and even some forms of **cancer**.

Balanced Diet

An *Unhealthy Diet* Can Increase the Risk of *Coronary Heart Disease*

Coronary Heart Disease (CHD) is the result of **reduced** blood flow to the heart. It can lead to **chest pain** (angina) and **heart attacks**. It's caused by **atherosclerosis** — the narrowing and hardening of the **coronary arteries** (the blood vessels that supply the heart).

1) A diet **high** in **saturated fat** raises **blood cholesterol** level (see below). This increases the build up of **fatty deposits** in the **arteries** (called atheromas), which **causes atherosclerosis**.

2) A diet **high in salt** can cause **high blood pressure**. This can **damage artery walls**, which **causes atherosclerosis**.

See p. 86 for more on atherosclerosis and CHD.

The Body *Regulates Blood Cholesterol Level* using *HDLs* and *LDLs*

1) **Cholesterol** is a **lipid** made in the body.

2) Some is **needed** for the body to **function normally**.

3) Cholesterol needs to be attached to a **protein** to be moved around, so the body forms **lipoproteins** — substances composed of both **protein** and **lipid**. There are **two types** of lipoprotein:

High density lipoproteins (HDLs) are **mainly protein**. They transport **cholesterol** from **body tissues** to the **liver** where it's **recycled** or **excreted**. Their function is to **reduce blood cholesterol** when the level is **too high**.

Low density lipoproteins (LDLs) are **mainly lipid**. They transport cholesterol from the **liver** to the **blood**, where it circulates until needed by cells. Their function is to **increase blood cholesterol** when the level is **too low**.

4) A diet **high** in **saturated fat raises LDL** level — so more cholesterol is transported **to the blood**, increasing total blood cholesterol and **increasing** the risk of CHD.

5) A diet **high** in **polyunsaturated fat raises HDL** level — so more cholesterol is transported **from the blood** to the liver, decreasing total blood cholesterol and **decreasing** the risk of CHD.

John decided to live on the edge and ordered a fry-up.

Practice Questions

Q1 Briefly describe what is meant by a balanced diet.

Q2 Give three causes of malnutrition.

Q3 Briefly describe how a diet high in salt can increase the risk of CHD.

Q4 Describe the differences between high density lipoproteins and low density lipoproteins.

Exam Questions

Q1 Explain how a diet high in saturated fat can increase the risk of coronary heart disease. [4 marks]

Q2 A patient at risk from CHD had the level of high density lipoproteins (HDLs) in his blood monitored for six months. Over this period the level of HDLs increased from 60 mg/dl to 100 mg/dl.

a) Suggest how the patient's total blood cholesterol level changed over this period. Explain your answer. [2 marks]

b) Suggest how the patient might have changed his diet to try to increase his HDL level. [1 mark]

Healthy food tastes just as good as stuff that's bad for you — yeah right...

I hate cauliflower cheese, it looks like melted brains — but a balanced diet means eating a bit of everything and not too much of anything. So when you've finished feeding your cauliflower cheese to the dog, be sure to cover the page and write out the bit about HDLs and LDLs plenty of times — it's easy to confuse them. In fact, remind me which is which...

Food Production

The ever increasing need for food has been partly met by increasing the productivity of the plants and animals we eat. There are short-term ways to do this (like using pesticides), and long-term ways to do this (like selective breeding).

Humans *Ultimately* Depend *on* Plants *for Food*

1) Humans **rely on plants** for **food** because plants are at the **start of all food chains**.

2) Plants use the **energy from sunlight** to convert **carbon dioxide** and **water** into **complex organic compounds** (such as carbohydrates).

3) **Humans**, and other **animals**, eat, digest and absorb the compounds, which they use for energy and to grow.

4) We grow plants for **direct consumption** and to **feed animals**, which we then eat.

5) Many modern farming methods aim to **maximise productivity** by **increasing** plant and animal **growth**.

Turnip
eaten by...
Steve
Steve wasn't happy with his turnip.

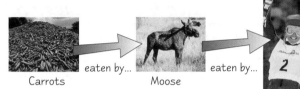

Carrots
eaten by...
Moose
eaten by...
Helga
Helga's moose mousse went down a treat.

Fertilisers *and* Pesticides Increase Food Production

Fertilisers

1) Fertilisers are **chemicals** that **increase crop yields** by providing **minerals** (such as nitrate, phosphate and potassium) that plants need to grow.

2) Minerals in the soil are **used up** during crop growth. Fertilisers **replace** these minerals, so that a **lack** of minerals doesn't **limit** growth of the next crop.

3) Fertilisers can be **natural** — made by natural processes (e.g. compost and manure), or **artificial** — made by humans.

Pesticides

1) Pesticides are **chemicals** that **increase crop yields** by **killing pests** that feed on the crops. This means **fewer plants** are **damaged** or **destroyed**.

2) Pests include microorganisms, insects or mammals (e.g. rats).

3) Pesticides may be **specific** and kill only **one** pest species, or **broad**, and kill a **range** of different species — this could mean that some **non-pest species** are also harmed.

Animals *Can be Given* Antibiotics *to Increase Food Production*

1) Animals farmed for food are sometimes given **antibiotics** — chemicals that **kill** or **inhibit** the growth of **bacteria**.

2) Antibiotics help to treat or prevent **diseases** caused by bacteria.

3) Animals normally **use energy** fighting diseases, which reduces the amount of energy available for **growth**. Giving them antibiotics means animals can use **more energy** to grow, **increasing food production**.

4) Antibiotics also help to **promote** the growth of animals.

5) This is thought to be because the antibiotics **influence bacteria** in the animals' gut, allowing the animals to **digest** food **more efficiently**.

6) This can increase both the **growth rate** of the animal and its **size** when mature.

Food Production

Selective Breeding *Increases* Crop Yields...

1) Selective breeding involves **selecting** plants with **good characteristics** (e.g. high yield, disease resistance or pest resistance) to **reproduce** together in order to **increase productivity**.

2) Here's an example of how it's done:

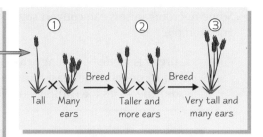

Tall · Many ears → Breed → Taller and more ears → Breed → Very tall and many ears

1) Select plants with **good characteristics** that will increase **crop yield**, e.g. a **tall** corn plant and a corn plant that produces **multiple ears**. Breed them **together**.

2) Select the **offspring** with the best characteristics, e.g. tallest with the most ears, and breed them **together**.

3) **Continue** this over **several generations** until a high-yielding plant is produced, e.g. **very tall** with **multiple ears** of corn.

3) Selective breeding is carried out in the same way to produce plants that are **resistant to disease or pests**.

1) Plants showing a high level of **resistance** are **bred together**.

2) The offspring that show **most resistance** are then bred together.

3) This continues over **several generations** to produce a crop that is disease or pest resistant.

...and the **Productivity** of Animals

Selective breeding can also be used to **increase** the **productivity of animals**. Useful characteristics such as **fast growth rate** and **high meat**, **milk** or **egg yields** can be developed. For example:

1) Select animals with **good characteristics** that will increase meat yield, e.g. the **largest** cows and bulls. Breed them **together**.

2) Select the **offspring** with the best characteristics, e.g. largest, and breed them **together**.

3) **Continue** this over **several generations** until cows with very high meat yields are produced, e.g. **very large cows**.

Daisy was a big cow, just like her mum — though she hadn't seen her around for a while...

Practice Questions

Q1 What type of organism is the basis of all food chains?

Q2 Briefly explain how fertilisers can increase crop yields.

Q3 Briefly explain how using antibiotics increases meat productivity.

Exam Question

Q1 Wheat is an important food crop that has been grown by farmers for over 5000 years.
Modern wheat plants have much larger grains than the wheat plants that were grown 5000 years ago.

a) Explain how selective breeding has led to wheat plants with larger grains than earlier wheat plants. [3 marks]

b) The Hessian fly is a pest of wheat crops. Describe how Hessian fly infestation would affect the wheat crop yield and suggest both a short-term and a long-term solution to the infestation. [3 marks]

Better food productivity — I'm over the moooooon...

Back in the olden days the steaks weren't as fat or the potatoes so appetising... the grass was less green too. After all this talk of food you'll need a snack — go get one and have a break. I'm having one, so you better too. Aaah, tea...

Microorganisms and Food

The waste products of some microorganisms can be harmful and contaminate food. Other microorganisms can be useful for food production though — cheese tastes delicious until you remember it's really mouldy milk.

Microorganisms can be used to *Make Food*

Microorganisms such as **bacteria**, **yeast** and other **fungi** are used in the production of many foods and drinks. Some microorganisms can **convert sugar** into other substances that humans can then use for **food production**. For example:

1) **Bread** is made by mixing yeast (a fungus), **sugar**, **flour** and **water** into a dough. The yeast turn the sugar into **ethanol** and **carbon dioxide** — it's the carbon dioxide that makes the bread **rise**.

2) **Wine** is made by adding **yeast** to **grape juice**. The yeast turn the sugar in the grape juice into **ethanol** (alcohol) and **carbon dioxide**.

3) **Cheese** is made by adding **bacteria** to milk. The bacteria turn the sugar in the milk into **lactic acid**, which causes the milk to **curdle**. An enzyme is then used to turn the curdled milk into **curds** and **whey**. The curds are separated off and left to **ripen** into **cheese**. Nice.

4) **Yoghurt** is also made by adding bacteria to milk. The bacteria turn the sugar in the milk into lactic acid, causing the milk to **clot** and **thicken** into yoghurt.

Using *Microorganisms* to *Make Food* has *Advantages*...

1) Populations of microorganisms **grow rapidly** under the right **conditions**, so food can be produced **quickly**.

2) Microorganisms can **grow** on a **range** of **inexpensive** materials.

3) Their environment can be **artificially controlled** — so you can potentially **grow food anywhere** and at **any time of the year**.

4) Conditions for growth are **easy to create**.

5) Some of the food made using microorganisms often **lasts longer** in **storage** than the raw product they're made from, e.g. **cheese** can be stored for longer than **milk**.

...and *Disadvantages*

1) There's a **high risk** of **food contamination**. The conditions created to grow the **desirable** microorganisms are also favourable to **harmful** microorganisms. They could cause the foods produced to **spoil** (go off), or if eaten, cause illnesses such as **food poisoning**.

2) The conditions required to grow microorganisms can be simple to create, but **small changes** in temperature or pH can **easily kill** the microorganisms.

Being served microorganisms for tea pushed Geoff over the edge.

Microorganisms and Food

Food Spoilage by Microorganisms can be Prevented

Food spoilage can be caused by the **growth** of **unwanted microorganisms** — as the organisms grow they break down the food, **contaminating** it with **waste products**. **Preventing** food spoilage involves either **killing** the microorganisms or **depriving** the microorganisms of the conditions they need to grow — this either **slows down** or **stops** their growth.

1) Salting prevents microorganisms taking in water...

Salting is simply **adding salt** to foods. Salt **inhibits the growth** of microorganisms by interfering with their ability to **absorb water** (which they need to survive). Some **meats** are preserved by salting, and **tinned foods** are often preserved in **brine** (a mixture of salt and water).

2) ...adding sugar can have the same effect.

Adding **sugar** also **inhibits the growth** of microorganisms by interfering with their ability to **absorb water**. For example, the high sugar content of **fruit jams** reduces the growth of microorganisms, giving the jam a **long shelf life**.

3) Freezing slows the growth of microorganisms.

Freezers keep foods below –18 °C. This **slows down reactions** taking place in microorganisms and **freezes the water** in the food, so the microorganisms **can't** use it. Freezing can preserve foods for **many months**.

4) Pickling in acidic vinegar inhibits the growth of microorganisms.

Vinegar has a **low pH**, which reduces **enzyme activity** (see p. 68) in microorganisms. This means they can't function properly, **inhibiting their growth**. Vinegar is used to **pickle** foods like onions.

5) Heat treatment kills microorganisms...

Heat treatment involves heating food to a **high temperature**, which **kills** any microorganisms present. **Pasteurisation** is one form of heat treatment — it involves raising **liquids** such as **milk** to a high temperature.

6) ...and so does irradiation.

Irradiation involves exposing foods to **radiation**, e.g. **X-rays** or **gamma rays**. This treatment **kills** any microorganisms present and can **extend shelf life** considerably.

Practice Questions

Q1 Name three foods made using microorganisms.

Q2 Describe two disadvantages of using microorganisms in food production.

Q3 Describe how pickling preserves food.

Exam Question

Q1 Mycoprotein is a protein-rich food produced from an edible fungus. The fungus is grown in an environment where conditions are carefully controlled. It's then heat-treated before being processed into the final product.

a) Explain why the mycoprotein is heat-treated. [2 marks]

b) Suggest three advantages of producing protein-rich foods from fungi compared to producing protein-rich foods from cows. [3 marks]

Hmm — I believe I'll have the irradiated beef with the pickled sprouts...

Ye scurvy dogs! You see, pirates didn't just eat salted pork because they liked the taste — they knew a thing or two about food spoilage. Pity they couldn't say the same about the whole fresh fruit/scurvy/nice teeth thing. Learn the six ways of preventing food spoilage and you'll find your way to a great chest of treasure. Well, quite a few marks anyway...

Infectious Disease

Health can be affected by loads of things, especially infection with microorganisms...

Disease can be Caused by Different Things

1) In the exam you could be asked to **discuss** what **health** and **disease** mean. So here goes...
   - **Health** is a **state** of **physical**, **mental** and **social well-being**, which includes the **absence** of **disease** and **infirmity** (weakness of body or mind).
   - **Disease** is a **condition** that **impairs** the **normal functioning** of an **organism**.

2) A disease can be caused by **infection** with **pathogens** or **parasites**. You need to be able to discuss what the terms pathogen and parasite mean:
   - A **pathogen** is an organism that can cause **disease**. **Bacteria**, **fungi** and **viruses** are all pathogens.
   - A **parasite** is an organism that **lives on** or **in** another organism (the host) and causes **damage** to that organism. **Tapeworms**, **roundworms** and **fleas** are all examples of parasites. Some parasites cause disease, so they're also pathogens.

3) Diseases can also be **caused** by **genetic defects**, **nutritional deficiencies** and **environmental factors** (e.g. toxic chemicals). **Infectious diseases** are diseases that can be **passed between individuals**, e.g. malaria, HIV and TB.

Malaria is Caused by the Parasite Plasmodium

1) *Plasmodium* is a **eukaryotic**, **single-celled parasite**.
2) It's **transmitted** by **mosquitoes** — **insects** that **feed** on the **blood** of **animals**, including **humans**.
3) The mosquitoes are **vectors** — they **don't** cause the disease themselves, but they **spread** the infection by **transferring** the parasite from one host to another.
4) Mosquitoes **transfer** the *Plasmodium* parasite into an animal's blood when they **feed** on them.
5) *Plasmodium* infects the **liver** and **red blood cells**, and **disrupts** the **blood supply** to vital organs.

AIDS is Caused by the HIV Virus

1) The **human immunodeficiency virus** (**HIV**) infects human white blood cells.
2) HIV (and all other viruses) can only **reproduce inside** the **cells** of the organism it has infected because it doesn't have the equipment (such as enzymes and ribosomes) to replicate on its own.
3) After the virus has reproduced, it **kills** the **white blood cells** as it **leaves**.
4) HIV infection leads to **acquired immune deficiency syndrome** (**AIDS**).
5) AIDS is a condition where the **immune system deteriorates** and eventually **fails** due to the loss of white blood cells. It makes the sufferer more **vulnerable** to **other infections**, like pneumonia.
6) HIV is **transmitted** in **three** main ways:

   - Via unprotected **sexual intercourse**.
   - Through **infected bodily fluids** (like blood), e.g. **sharing needles**, **blood transfusions**.
   - From **mother** to **fetus** (through the placenta, breast milk or during childbirth).

Tuberculosis (TB) is Caused by a Bacterium

1) **Tuberculosis** (TB) is a **lung disease caused** by the **bacterium** *Mycobacterium tuberculosis*.
2) TB spreads by '**droplet infection**' — when an infected person **coughs** or **sneezes**, **tiny droplets** of **saliva** and **mucus** containing the bacteria are released from their mouth and nose. These droplets are then **breathed** in by other people.
3) Many people with tuberculosis are infected but **don't show** any symptoms. But if they become **weakened**, e.g. by another disease or malnutrition, then the infection can become **active**. They'll show the symptoms and be able to pass on the infection.

Infectious Disease

Malaria, AIDS/HIV and TB Have a Global Impact

1) **Malaria**, **HIV** and **TB** are most **common** in **sub-Saharan Africa** and other **developing countries**. This is because:

- There's **limited access** to good **healthcare** — **drugs** are **not** always **available**, people are **less likely** to be **diagnosed** and **treated**, **blood donations** aren't always **screened** for infectious diseases and **surgical equipment** isn't always **sterile**.
- There's **limited health education** to inform people how to **avoid infectious diseases** — e.g. fewer people know about the **transmission** of **HIV** and that it can be **prevented** by **safe-sex** practices, e.g. using condoms.
- There's **limited equipment** to **reduce** the **spread** of infections — e.g. fewer people have **mosquito nets** to reduce the chance of infection with **malaria**.
- There are **overcrowded** conditions — this **increases** the **risk** of **TB infection** by **droplet transmission** (see previous page).

2) The **prevalence** of malaria, HIV and TB in developing countries, like sub-Saharan Africa, **slows** down **social** and **economic development** because these diseases **increase death rates**, **reduce productivity** (fewer people are able to work) and result in **high healthcare costs**.

3) **Studying** the **global distribution** of these diseases is **important** for many reasons:

- The information can be used to find out **where** people are most **at risk**.
- Any data collected can be used to **predict** where **epidemics** are most likely to occur.
- It's important for **research** (e.g. into how it's spread).
- It allows organisations to provide **aid** where it's **needed most**.

Practice Questions

Q1 Explain what is meant by the term health.

Q2 What causes malaria?

Q3 Describe how HIV can be transmitted between individuals.

Exam Questions

Q1 Africa has the highest number of deaths from tuberculosis and the USA has the lowest number of deaths.

a) State what causes tuberculosis and describe how it is transmitted between individuals. [4 marks]

b) Suggest three reasons why more deaths from tuberculosis occur in Africa than in the USA. [3 marks]

c) Suggest two reasons why it is important that other countries study the distribution of tuberculosis. [2 marks]

Q2 AIDS has killed more than 25 million people since it was first recognised in 1981.

a) Name the pathogen that causes AIDS. [1 mark]

b) Describe four ways that the spread of this pathogen can be reduced. [4 marks]

My computer has a virus — I knew I shouldn't have sneezed on it...

Malaria, AIDS and TB aren't the nicest things to learn about, but unfortunately they could pop up in the exam. Even though these diseases aren't that common in the UK (because we have free access to healthcare, good health education, low poverty, good nutrition etc.) they cause many problems in other countries across the world.

The Immune System

Well, all that stuff about disease is making me feel a bit on edge. But your body has some state-of-the-art defences to protect you against pathogens and parasites. First up, the skin and mucus membranes...

The Skin and Mucus Membranes are the Body's Primary Defences...

Your body has a number of **primary defences** that help **prevent pathogens** and **parasites** from **entering** it. These include the **skin** and **mucus membranes**:

SKIN

This acts as a **physical barrier**, **blocking pathogens** from **entering** the body. It also acts as a **chemical barrier** by producing **chemicals** that are **antimicrobial** and can **lower pH**, **inhibiting** the **growth** of pathogens.

MUCOUS MEMBRANES

They **protect body openings** that are **exposed** to the **environment** (such as the mouth, nostrils, ears, genitals and anus). Some membranes **secrete mucus** — a sticky substance that **traps pathogens** and contains **antimicrobial enzymes**.

...but if a Pathogen Gets Past Those the Immune System Responds

If a pathogen or parasite gets **past** the **primary defences** and **enters** the body, the **immune system** will respond.

An **immune response** is the body's **reaction** to a **foreign antigen**.

1) **Antigens** are **molecules** (usually proteins or polysaccharides) found on the **surface** of **cells**.

2) When a pathogen (like a bacterium) **invades** the body, the antigens on its cell surface are **identified as foreign**, which **activates** cells in the immune system.

There are Four Main Stages Involved in the Immune Response

(1) Phagocytes Engulf Pathogens

A **phagocyte** (e.g. a macrophage) is a type of **white blood cell** that carries out **phagocytosis** (engulfment of pathogens). They're found in the **blood** and in **tissues** and are the **first** cells to **respond** to a pathogen inside the body. Here's how they work:

1) A phagocyte **recognises** the **antigens** on a pathogen.

2) The cytoplasm of the phagocyte moves round the pathogen, **engulfing** it.

3) The pathogen is now contained in a **phagocytic vacuole** (a bubble) in the cytoplasm of the phagocyte.

4) A **lysosome** (an organelle that contains **digestive enzymes**) **fuses** with the phagocytic vacuole. The enzymes **break down** the pathogen.

5) The phagocyte then **presents** the pathogen's antigens. It sticks the antigens on its **surface** to **activate** other immune system cells.

The Immune System

2) Phagocytes **Activate T lymphocytes**

1) A **T lymphocyte** is another type of **white blood cell**.

2) Their surface is covered with **receptors**.

3) The receptors **bind to antigens** presented by the phagocytes.

4) Each T lymphocyte has a **different receptor** on its surface.

5) When the receptor on the surface of a T lymphocyte meets a **complementary antigen**, it binds to it — so each T lymphocyte will bind to a **different antigen**. This process **activates** the T lymphocyte and is known as **clonal selection**.

6) The activated T lymphocyte then undergoes **clonal expansion** — it **divides** to produce clones, which then **differentiate** into **different types** of T lymphocytes that carry out **different functions**:

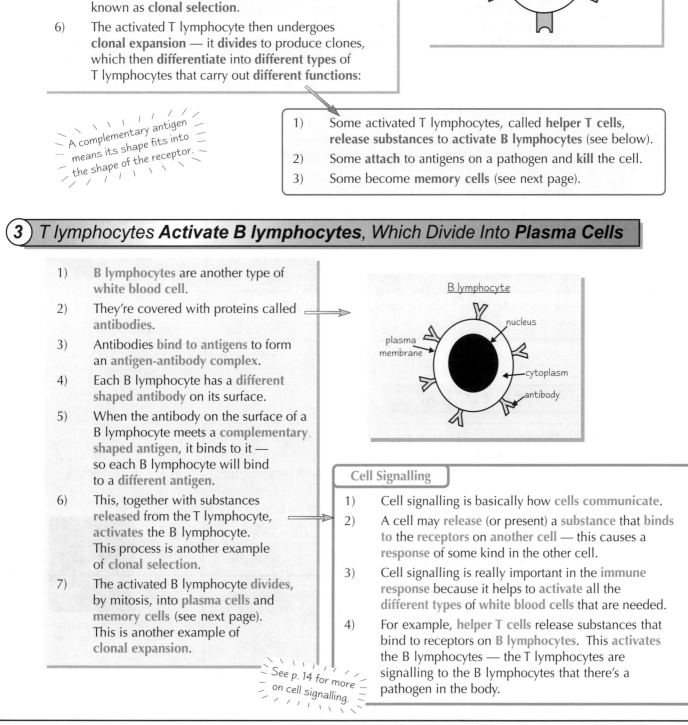

T lymphocyte

nucleus

plasma membrane

cytoplasm

receptor

A complementary antigen means its shape fits into the shape of the receptor.

1) Some activated T lymphocytes, called **helper T cells**, **release substances** to **activate B lymphocytes** (see below).

2) Some **attach** to antigens on a pathogen and **kill** the cell.

3) Some become **memory cells** (see next page).

3) T lymphocytes **Activate B lymphocytes**, Which Divide Into **Plasma Cells**

1) **B lymphocytes** are another type of **white blood cell**.

2) They're covered with proteins called **antibodies**.

3) Antibodies **bind to antigens** to form an **antigen-antibody complex**.

4) Each B lymphocyte has a **different shaped antibody** on its surface.

5) When the antibody on the surface of a B lymphocyte meets a **complementary shaped antigen**, it binds to it — so each B lymphocyte will bind to a **different antigen**.

6) This, together with substances **released** from the T lymphocyte, **activates** the B lymphocyte. This process is another example of **clonal selection**.

7) The activated B lymphocyte **divides**, by mitosis, into **plasma cells** and **memory cells** (see next page). This is another example of **clonal expansion**.

B lymphocyte

nucleus

plasma membrane

cytoplasm

antibody

Cell Signalling

1) Cell signalling is basically how **cells communicate**.

2) A cell may **release** (or present) a **substance** that **binds to the receptors** on **another cell** — this causes a **response** of some kind in the other cell.

3) Cell signalling is really important in the **immune response** because it helps to **activate** all the **different types** of **white blood cells** that are needed.

4) For example, **helper T cells** release substances that bind to receptors on **B lymphocytes**. This **activates** the B lymphocytes — the T lymphocytes are signalling to the B lymphocytes that there's a pathogen in the body.

See p. 14 for more on cell signalling.

The Immune System

4) Plasma Cells Make More Antibodies to a Specific Antigen

1) Plasma cells are **clones** of the B lymphocyte (they're **identical** to the B lymphocyte).

2) They secrete **loads** of the **antibody**, specific to the antigen, into the blood.

3) These antibodies will bind to the antigens on the surface of the pathogen to form **lots** of **antigen-antibody complexes**.

4) You need to **learn** the **structure** of antibodies:

An Antigen-Antibody Complex

antigen
variable regions (orange)
light chain
hinge protein
disulfide bridge
heavy chain
constant regions (blue)

- The **variable regions** of the antibody form the **antigen binding sites**. The **shape** of the variable region is **complementary** to a particular antigen. The variable regions **differ** between antibodies.
- The **hinge region** allows **flexibility** when the antibody binds to the antigen.
- The **constant regions** allow binding to **receptors** on **immune system cells**, e.g. phagocytes. The constant region is the **same in all** antibodies.
- **Disulfide bridges** (a type of bond) hold the polypeptide chains together.

5) Antibodies **help** to **clear** an **infection** by:

1) <u>Agglutinating pathogens</u> — each antibody has **two binding sites**, so an antibody can **bind** to **two pathogens** at the **same time** — the pathogens become **clumped together**. Phagocytes then bind to the antibodies and phagocytose a lot of pathogens **all at once**.

2) <u>Neutralising toxins</u> — antibodies can **bind** to the **toxins** produced by pathogens. This **prevents** the toxins from **affecting human cells**, so the toxins are **neutralised** (inactivated). The toxin-antibody complexes are also phagocytosed.

3) <u>Preventing the pathogen binding to human cells</u> — when antibodies bind to the antigens on pathogens, they may **block** the cell surface **receptors** that the pathogens need to **bind to the host cells**. This means the pathogen **can't attach to** or **infect** the host cells.

Agglutination

antibody

pathogen
antigen

The Primary Response is Slow...

1) When a **pathogen** enters the body for the **first time** the **antigens** on its surface **activate** the **immune system**. This is called the **primary response**.

2) The primary response is **slow** because there **aren't many B lymphocytes** that can make the antibody needed to bind to it.

3) Eventually the body will produce **enough** of the right antibody to overcome the infection. Meanwhile the infected person will show **symptoms** of the disease.

4) After being exposed to an antigen, both T and B lymphocytes produce **memory cells**. These memory cells **remain in the body** for a **long** time. Memory T lymphocytes remember the **specific antigen** and will recognise it a second time round. Memory B lymphocytes record the specific **antibodies** needed to bind to the antigen.

5) The person is now **immune** — their immune system has the **ability** to respond **quickly** to a second infection.

Don't get the primary response mixed up with primary defences (see p. 80).

Neil's primary response — to his parents.

The Immune System

...the Secondary Response is Faster

1) If the **same pathogen** enters the body again, the immune system will produce a **quicker, stronger** immune response — the **secondary response**.

2) **Memory B lymphocytes** divide into **plasma cells** that produce the right antibody to the antigen. **Memory T lymphocytes** divide into the **correct type** of **T lymphocytes** to kill the cell carrying the antigen.

3) The secondary response often gets rid of the pathogen **before** you begin to show any **symptoms**.

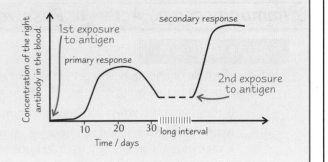

In the exam you might be asked to **compare** and **contrast** the primary and secondary immune response — basically say how they're **similar** and say how they're **different**. These are summarised in the table below:

	Primary response	Secondary response
Pathogen	Enters for 1st time	Enters for 2nd time
Speed of response	Slow	Fast
Cells activated	B and T lymphocytes	Memory cells
Symptoms	Yes	No

Practice Questions

Q1 Name two primary defences against pathogens and parasites.

Q2 Define the term immune response.

Q3 What are antigens?

Q4 What structures are found on the surface of T lymphocytes?

Q5 Draw and label the structure of a B lymphocyte.

Q6 Draw and label the structure of an antibody.

Q7 Give two differences between the primary and secondary response.

These questions cover pages 80-83.

Exam Questions

Q1 Describe how a phagocyte responds to an invading pathogen. [6 marks]

Q2 Describe the function of antibodies. [3 marks]

Q3 Emily had chickenpox as a child. She was exposed to the virus that causes it as a teenager but did not experience any symptoms. Explain why. [10 marks]

The student-revision complex — only present the night before an exam...

Memory cells are still B and T lymphocytes, but they're the ones that stick around for a long time. So if a pathogen is stupid enough to invade the body again, these cells can immediately divide into more of themselves, and release antibodies specifically against the pathogen or bind to the pathogen and destroy it. Ha ha (evil laugh).

Immunity and Vaccinations

The primary response gives you immunity against a disease, but only after you've gotten ill. If only there was a way to stimulate memory cell production without getting the disease... Well, there is — vaccination.

Immunity can be *Active* or *Passive*

ACTIVE IMMUNITY

This is the type of immunity you get when **your immune system makes its own antibodies** after being **stimulated** by an **antigen**. There are **two** different types of active immunity:

1) **Natural** — this is when you become immune after **catching a disease**.

2) **Artificial** — this is when you become immune after you've been given a **vaccination** containing a harmless dose of antigen (see below).

PASSIVE IMMUNITY

This is the type of immunity you get from being **given antibodies made by a different organism** — your immune system **doesn't** produce any antibodies of its own. Again, there are **two** types:

1) **Natural** — this is when a **baby** becomes immune due to the antibodies it receives from its **mother**, through the **placenta** and in **breast milk**.

2) **Artificial** — this is when you become immune after being **injected** with **antibodies** from **someone else**. E.g. If you contract tetanus you can be injected with antibodies against the tetanus toxin, collected from blood donations.

In the exam you might be asked to **compare** and **contrast** these types of immunity:

Active immunity	Passive immunity
Exposure to antigen	No exposure to antigen
It takes a while for protection to develop	Protection is immediate
Protection is long-term	Protection is short-term
Memory cells are produced	Memory cells aren't produced

Vaccines Help to *Control Disease*

1) While your B lymphocytes are busy **dividing** to build up their numbers to deal with a pathogen (i.e. the **primary response** — see p. 82), you **suffer** from the disease. **Vaccination** can help avoid this.

2) Vaccines **contain antigens** that cause your body to **produce memory cells** against a particular pathogen, **without** the pathogen **causing disease**. This means you become **immune** without getting any **symptoms**... genius.

3) If most people in a **community** are **vaccinated**, the disease becomes extremely **rare**. This means that even people who haven't been vaccinated are **unlikely** to get the disease, because there's no one to catch it from. This is called **herd immunity**.

4) Vaccines always contain antigens — these may be **free** or attached to a **dead** or **attenuated** (weakened) **pathogen**.

5) Vaccines may be **injected** or taken **orally**. The **disadvantages** of taking a vaccine orally are that it could be **broken down** by **enzymes** in the gut or the **molecules** of the vaccine may be **too large** to be **absorbed** into the blood.

6) Sometimes **booster** vaccines are given later on (e.g. after several years) to **make sure** that memory cells are produced.

Paul couldn't understand why his herd immunity wasn't working...

Immunity and Vaccinations

New Influenza Vaccines Have to be Developed Every Year

1) The **influenza virus** causes **influenza** (flu).

2) **Proteins (neuraminidase** and **haemagglutinin)** on the **surface** of the influenza virus act as **antigens**, **triggering** the immune system.

3) These antigens can **change regularly**, forming **new strains** of the virus.

4) **Memory cells** produced from **vaccination** with **one strain** of flu will **not recognise** other strains with **different antigens**.

5) Every year there are **different strains** of the influenza virus **circulating** in the **population**, so a **different vaccine** has to be made.

6) **Laboratories** collect **samples** of these different strains, and organisations, such as the **WHO** (World Health Organisation) and **CDC** (Centre for Disease Control), **test** the **effectiveness** of different influenza **vaccines** against them.

7) **New vaccines** are **developed** and one is chosen **every year** that is the **most effective** against the **recently** circulating influenza viruses.

8) Governments and health authorities then implement a **programme** of **vaccination** using this most **suitable** vaccine. This is a good example of how society uses science to inform **decision making**.

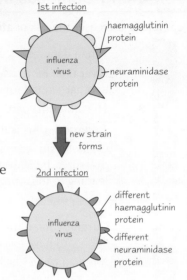

Possible Sources of Medicines Need to be Protected

1) Many **medicinal drugs** are manufactured **using natural compounds** found in **plants, animals** or **microorganisms**. E.g. **penicillin** is obtained from a **fungus**, some **cancer drugs** are made using **soil bacteria**, and **daffodils** are now grown to produce a drug used to treat **Alzheimer's disease**.

2) Only a **small proportion** of organisms have been **investigated** so far, so it's possible that plants or microorganisms **exist** that contain compounds that could be used to treat **currently incurable** diseases, such as AIDS.

3) Possible **sources of drugs** need to be **protected** by **maintaining** the **biodiversity** (the variety of different species) on Earth. If we **don't** protect them, some species could **die** out before we get a **chance** to study them.

4) Even organisms that have **already** been studied could still prove to be **useful** sources of medicines as **new techniques** are developed for identifying, purifying and testing compounds.

Practice Questions

Q1 What is the difference between active and passive immunity?
Q2 Explain the difference between natural passive immunity and artificial passive immunity.
Q3 Give two advantages of vaccination.
Q4 Why is protecting biodiversity important for the development of new medicines?

Exam Question

Q1 Influenza is caused by a virus that constantly changes its antigens.

   a) Explain why a new influenza vaccine is made every year. [3 marks]

   b) Describe how new influenza vaccines are chosen every year. [3 marks]

An injection of dead bugs — roll on my next vaccine...

The influenza virus is so clever that it would almost make you think it had a mind of its own. I mean, as soon as we catch up with it and develop a vaccine, off it goes and changes its surface antigens again. Influenza virus: one, humans: nil. This is one of the ways viruses have evolved to avoid your immune system. Well, clever them.

Smoking and Disease

Don't worry I won't lecture you about smoking, but you do need to know how it affects a person's health for the exam...

Smoking Damages the Cardiovascular System...

Smoking increases the risk of **atherosclerosis**, **coronary heart disease** (CHD) and **stroke**:

Atherosclerosis

1) When **damage** occurs to the lining of an **artery**, **white blood cells** move into the area.
2) Over time **more** white blood cells, **lipids** and **connective tissue** build up and harden to form a **fibrous plaque** at the site of damage — an **atheroma**.
3) The atheroma partially **blocks** the **lumen** of the artery and **restricts blood flow**.
4) **Atherosclerosis** is the **hardening** of **arteries** due to the formation of **atheromas**.
5) Cigarette smoke contains **nicotine**, which causes an **increase** in **blood pressure**. Increased blood pressure can cause **damage** to the arteries, leading to the formation of more **atheromas**.

normal artery
lumen (space in centre)
atheroma
lumen shrinks, so it's more difficult for blood to pass through

Coronary Heart Disease (CHD)

1) **Coronary heart disease** is when the **coronary arteries** (arteries that supply blood to the heart) have lots of **atheromas** in them. This **restricts blood flow** to the **heart**.
2) A reduction in blood flow **reduces** the amount of **oxygen** an area of the heart gets. This can cause **pain** (angina) or a **heart attack**.
3) Smoking **increases** the **risk** of CHD because **carbon monoxide** irreversibly combines with **haemoglobin**, **reducing** the amount of **oxygen** transported in the blood, which reduces the amount of oxygen available to tissues, including the **heart**.
4) Also, **nicotine** in cigarette smoke makes **platelets** (cells involved in blood clotting) **sticky**, increasing the chance of **blood clots forming**. If clotting happens in the **coronary arteries** it could cause a **heart attack**.
5) The presence of **atheromas** also increases the risk of **blood clots forming** (and smoking increases atheroma formation — see above).

CHD is a type of cardiovascular disease.

Stroke

1) A **stroke** is a **rapid loss** of **brain function** due to a **disruption** in the **blood supply** to the **brain**.
2) This can be caused by a **blood clot** in an **artery** leading to the brain, which **reduces** the amount of blood, and therefore **oxygen**, that can reach the brain.
3) Nicotine **increases** the risk of stroke because it increases the risk of **clots forming** (see above).
4) Carbon monoxide also **increases** the **risk** of stroke because it **reduces** the amount of oxygen available to the brain by combining with haemoglobin (see above).

...and the Gas Exchange System

Lung Cancer

1) Cigarette smoke contains many **carcinogens** (chemicals that can cause a cell to become cancerous).
2) These carcinogens may cause mutations in the **DNA** of **lung cells**, which could lead to **uncontrolled cell growth** and the **formation** of a **malignant** (cancerous) **tumour**.
3) Malignant tumours **grow uncontrollably**, **blocking air flow** to areas of the lung.
4) This **decreases gas exchange** and leads to a **shortness of breath** because the body is struggling to take in **enough oxygen**.
5) The tumour uses **lots of nutrients** and **energy** to grow, which causes **weight loss**.

Chronic Bronchitis

1) Chronic bronchitis is **inflammation** of the lungs.
2) The upper respiratory tract is lined with **goblet cells** that produce **mucus** to **trap microorganisms**. The tract is also lined with **cilia** that 'beat' to move the mucus towards the **throat** so it can be **removed**.
3) Cigarette smoke **damages** the **cilia** and causes the goblet cells to produce **more mucus**.
4) The mucus **accumulates** in the lungs, which causes **increased coughing** to try and remove the mucus.
5) **Microorganisms multiply** in the mucus and cause **lung infections** that lead to **inflammation**, which **decreases gas exchange**.
6) Chronic bronchitis is a type of **chronic obstructive pulmonary disease** (COPD). COPD is a group of diseases that involve permanent airflow reduction.

Smoking and Disease

Emphysema

Emphysema is also a type of COPD.

1) Emphysema is a lung disease caused by **smoking** or long-term exposure to **air pollution** — foreign particles in the smoke (or air) become **trapped** in the alveoli.

2) This causes **inflammation**, which encourages **phagocytes** to the area. The phagocytes produce an **enzyme** that breaks down **elastin** (an elastic protein found in the **walls** of the **alveoli**).

3) The alveolar walls are **destroyed** and the **elasticity** of the lungs is **lost**.

4) This **reduces** the **surface area** of the alveoli, so the **rate** of **gaseous exchange decreases**.

5) Symptoms of emphysema include **shortness of breath** and **wheezing**. People with emphysema have an **increased breathing rate** as they try to increase the amount of air (containing oxygen) reaching their lungs.

You Might Have to *Evaluate Evidence Linking Smoking* to *Disease* or *Death*

Here's an **example** of the kind of thing you might get:

The graph shows the results of a study involving **34 439 male British doctors**. **Questionnaires** were used to find out the smoking habits of the doctors. The number of **deaths** among the participants from ischaemic heart disease (coronary heart disease) was counted, and **adjustments** were made to account for **differences in age**.

1) The graph shows that the **number** of deaths from ischaemic heart disease **increased** as the number of cigarettes smoked per day **increased**. **Fewer former smokers** and **non-smokers** died of ischaemic heart disease than smokers.

2) So you can conclude that there's a **positive correlation** between the number of cigarettes smoked per day by **male doctors** and the **mortality rate** from ischaemic heart disease. You **can't** say that smoking more **causes** an increased risk of dying from ischaemic heart disease though. There could be **other factors** causing the pattern, e.g. heavier smokers may **drink more alcohol** and it could be the alcohol (not smoking) that increases the risk of heart disease.

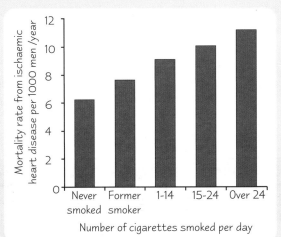

3) You might have to evaluate the study — you basically need to think about how the study **method could affect the results**. For example:

- A **large sample size** was used — 34 439. The **bigger** the sample size the **more reliable** the results.
- People (even doctors) can tell **porkies** on **questionnaires**, reducing the **reliability** of results.
- The study **only** used doctors — this could have swayed the results. Doctor's might be more likely to **avoid** the other risk factors associated with cardiovascular disease (e.g. alcohol, poor diet) and so this might **bias** the data.
- All the participants have the same job but they **weren't matched** otherwise, e.g. they might not be the same weight, or they might do different amounts of exercise a week, etc. This could have affected the results. Just like in an experiment you need to **control** as many **variables** as possible.

Practice Question

Q1 Explain how nicotine increases the risk of atheromas forming.

Exam Question

Q1 Smoking can damage the mammalian gas exchange system, causing emphysema and lung cancer. Explain how smoking can lead to each of these diseases and explain the symptoms they produce. [12 marks]

Smoky bacon — so it's okay for pigs to smoke then?

Whatever your views on smoking, you need to be objective when looking at study data. For the exam you need to make sure you can explain how smoking affects the lungs and how nicotine and carbon monoxide muck up the heart.

Studying Biodiversity

Bet you've noticed how there are loads of different living things in the world — well that's biodiversity in a nutshell.

Biodiversity is the Variety of Organisms

Before you can sink your teeth into the real meat of biodiversity, there are a few definitions you need to know:

1) **Biodiversity** — the **variety** of **living organisms** in an **area**.

2) **Species** — a group of **similar organisms** able to **reproduce** to give **fertile offspring**.

3) **Habitat** — the **area inhabited** by a species. It includes the **physical** factors, like the soil and temperature range, and the **living** (biotic) factors, like availability of food or the presence of predators.

Pete wasn't sure that the company's new increased biodiversity policy would be good for productivity.

Areas with a **high** biodiversity are those with lots of **different species**.

Biodiversity Can be Considered at Different Levels

1) **Habitat diversity** — the number of **different habitats** in an **area**. For example, a coastal area could contain many different habitats — beaches, sand dunes, mudflats, salt marshes etc.

2) **Species diversity** — the number of **different species** and the **abundance** of each species in an **area**. For example, a woodland could contain many different species of plants, insects, birds and mammals.

3) **Genetic diversity** — the variation of **alleles** within a species (or a population of a species). For example, human blood type is determined by a gene with four different alleles.

Alleles are different versions of genes.

Sampling Can be Used to Measure Biodiversity

In most cases it'd be **too time-consuming** to count every individual organism in a habitat. Instead, a **sample** of the population is taken. **Estimates** about the whole habitat are based on the sample. Here's what sampling involves:

1) **Choose** an **area** to **sample** — a small area within the habitat being studied.

2) **Count** the number of individuals of **each species**. How you do this depends on **what** you're counting, for example:

   - For plants you'd use a **quadrat** (a frame which you place on the ground).
   - For flying insects you'd use a **sweepnet** (a net on a pole).
   - For ground insects you'd use a **pitfall trap** (a small pit that insects can't get out of).
   - For aquatic animals you'd use a **net**.

3) **Repeat** the process — take as many samples as possible. This gives a better indication of the **whole habitat**.

4) Use the results to **estimate** the total number of individuals or the total number of different species in the habitat being studied.

5) When sampling **different habitats** and comparing them, always use the **same sampling technique**.

Even when randomly selecting samples, you still need to do as many repeats as possible.

The Sample Has to be Random

To avoid **bias** in your results, the sample should be random. For example:

If you were looking at plant species in a field you could pick random sample sites by dividing the field into a **grid** and using a **random number generator** to select coordinates.

Studying Biodiversity

Species Richness and Species Evenness Affect Biodiversity

The **greater** the **species richness** and **species evenness** in an area, the **higher** the biodiversity.

1) **Species richness** is the number of **different species** in an area. The **higher** the number of species, the **greater** the species richness. It's measured by taking random samples of a habitat (see previous page) and counting the number of different species.

2) **Species evenness** is a measure of the **relative abundance** of **each species** in an area. The **more similar** the **population size** of each species, the **greater** the species evenness. It's measured by taking random samples of a habitat, and counting the **number of individuals** of each different species.

Example Habitat X and habitat Y both contain **two different species** and **30 individual organisms**.

	Habitat X	Habitat Y
species 1	28	15
species 2	2	15
total	30	30

- **Species richness** in the two habitats is the **same** — 2.
- In **habitat Y** the individual organisms are **more evenly distributed** between the different species — it has **greater species evenness**.

Diversity is Measured using Simpson's Index of Diversity

1) Species present in a habitat in very **small** numbers shouldn't be treated the same as those with **bigger** populations.

2) **Simpson's Index of Diversity** takes into account both **species richness** and **species evenness**.

3) Simpson's Index of Diversity (**D**) can be calculated using this formula.

4) Simpson's Index of Diversity is always a value **between 0 and 1**. The **closer to 1** the index is, the **more diverse** the habitat. The greater the species richness and evenness, the higher the number.

$$D = 1 - \left(\sum \left(\frac{n}{N} \right)^2 \right)$$

n = **Total number** of individuals of **one** species
N = **Total number** of organisms of **all** species
Σ = '**Sum of**' (i.e. added together)

Here's a simple example of the index of diversity in a field:

There are 3 different species of flower in this field — a red species, a white and a blue. There are 11 organisms altogether, so N = 11. There are 3 of the red species, 5 of the white and 3 of the blue. So the index of diversity for this field is:

$$D = 1 - \left(\left(\frac{3}{11} \right)^2 + \left(\frac{5}{11} \right)^2 + \left(\frac{3}{11} \right)^2 \right) = 1 - 0.36 = 0.64$$

You need to work out the (n/N)² bit for each different species then add them all together.

The field has an index of diversity of 0.64, which is fairly high.

Practice Questions

Q1 What is meant by habitat diversity, species diversity and genetic diversity?

Q2 Why is it important that samples of a habitat are taken at random?

Exam Question

Q1 A group of students is investigating the diversity of millipedes (small ground insects) in a habitat. They want to find out the species richness and species evenness in the area.

a) Describe what is meant by species richness and species evenness. [2 marks]

b) Describe how the students could measure species evenness in the habitat. [4 marks]

Species richness — goldfish and money spiders top the list...

OK, so this isn't exactly the easiest of things to get your head around — I thought ecology was meant to be straightforward. Make sure you know the definitions of species richness and species evenness and can describe how you'd measure them. As for Simpson's Index of Diversity — well, sometimes I wish I was still a fresh-faced sixth-former, but this sure ain't one of them.

Global Biodiversity

One of the problems with this biodiversity lark is that it's really difficult to measure on a global scale — even top scientists can't seem to agree. One thing they do agree on is that climate change is affecting biodiversity...

Current **Estimates** of **Global Biodiversity Vary**

Global biodiversity is the **total number** of species on Earth. This includes:

1) **Named species** — scientists have named between 1.5 and 1.75 million species. This figure isn't exact because there's no central database of all species and some scientists have **different opinions** about the classification of certain species.

2) **Unnamed species** — scientists agree that a large proportion of the species on Earth **have not been named** — many species are **undiscovered**, or are known but haven't yet been named.

This strange-looking two-headed dog is among those not yet named.

Scientists **estimate** that the **total number** of species on Earth ranges from about 5 million to 100 million. Some of the most recent estimates are around 14 million. There are lots of reasons why scientists have such different ideas:

1) **Different scientists** have used **different techniques** to make their estimates.

2) Relatively **little is known** about some **groups** of organisms (e.g. bacteria and insects) — there could be **many more** than we think.

3) Biodiversity varies in **different parts** of the world — the greatest diversity is near the **equator** and it **decreases** towards the **poles**. Tropical rainforests are **largely unexplored** — this might mean current estimates of global biodiversity are **too low**.

Scientific uncertainty makes biodiversity hard to measure.

Estimates of global biodiversity **change** as scientists find out new things — this is an example of the **tentative nature** of scientific knowledge.

Climate Change Affects Biodiversity...

1) **Climate change** is the **variation** in the Earth's climate, e.g. things like changes in **temperature** and **rainfall patterns**.

2) It occurs **naturally**, but the **scientific consensus** is that the climate change we're **experiencing at the moment** is **caused** by **humans** increasing emissions of **greenhouse gases** (such as **carbon dioxide**).

3) Greenhouse gases cause **global warming** (**increasing global average temperature**), which causes **other types** of climate change, e.g. changing rainfall patterns.

4) Climate change will affect **different areas** of the world in **different ways** — some places will get **warmer**, some **colder**, some **wetter** and others **drier**. All of these are likely to **affect global biodiversity**:

- Most species need a particular **climate** to survive.
- A change in climate may mean that an area that was previously **inhabitable** becomes **uninhabitable** (and **vice versa**).
- This may cause an **increase** or **decrease** in the **range** of some species (the area in which they live). This could increase or decrease biodiversity.
- Some species may be forced to **migrate** to a more suitable area, causing a change in **species distribution**. Migrations usually **decrease** biodiversity in the areas the species migrate from, and **increase** biodiversity in the areas they migrate to.
- If there isn't a suitable habitat to migrate to, the species is a plant and **can't migrate**, or if the change is **too fast**, the species may become **extinct**. This will **decrease** biodiversity.

Range change example

The southern **range** limit of the **Sooty Copper Butterfly** has **moved** 60 miles north in recent decades.

Extinction example

Corals die if water temperature **changes** by just one or two degrees. In 1998 a coral reef near Panama was badly damaged because the water **temperature** had **increased** — at least one species of coral became **extinct** as a result.

Global Biodiversity

...the *Spread* of *Disease*...

Changing climate may also contribute to the **spread of disease**, for example:

1) The **ranges** of some **insects** that **carry disease** might become **greater**. E.g. as areas become **warmer** and **wetter** insects like mosquitoes, which can carry **malaria**, will spread into areas that were **previously uninhabitable**, **bringing the disease** with them. This change in distribution could lead to an increase in biodiversity, though the **spread of diseases** could **reduce biodiversity** — with some species suffering population decline, or even extinction.

2) Warmer and wetter conditions may also encourage the spread of **fungal diseases**. This could also lead to an increase or decrease in biodiversity.

...and *Agricultural Patterns*

Changes in **temperature**, **rainfall**, the **timing of the seasons**, and the **frequency of flood** and **drought** will affect **patterns of agriculture**. This may also affect biodiversity:

1) Land that was **previously unsuitable** becomes **available** for agriculture — areas of that were previously too hot or too dry to support much biodiversity can be farmed, **increasing** the biodiversity in an area.

2) **Different crops** need **different conditions** so, as the climate in an area changes, so will the **crops grown**. This could **disrupt food chains** — some **existing species** will be left **without** a source of food, and new food sources will be provided for **other species**. This could **increase** or **decrease** biodiversity in an area.

3) **Extreme weather events** and **unexpected conditions**, such as a **flood** or a **drought** or a change in the **timing of the seasons**, might result in **crop failure**. This could **disrupt food chains** and **decrease biodiversity**.

Practice Questions

Q1 Suggest two reasons why estimates of global biodiversity vary so widely.

Q2 Explain how changing patterns of agriculture might affect biodiversity.

Exam Question

Q1 The Living Planet Index measures trends in the Earth's biodiversity. It is calculated using population data from over 1000 species. The graph below shows how the Living Planet Index changed between 1970 and 2000.

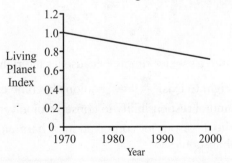

a) Suggest why the Living Planet Index does not use population data from all the species on Earth. [1 mark]

b) Describe the pattern shown on the graph. [1 mark]

c) Describe how climate change during the last 30 years could have decreased global biodiversity. [5 marks]

Mosquitoes — coming soon to a climate near you...

All of this makes the future look a bit bleak — plagues of mosquitoes in places they never used to be, half the country underwater and loads of different species dying out — I bet you thought this section was going to be all about fluffy animals. Now you know why biodiversity's at risk, it's time to take a look at why it's so important and worth saving...

Importance of Biodiversity

You're probably wondering what all this fuss about biodiversity is for. Well, biodiversity provides us with the means to make nice clothes and good food, so it's a pretty good idea not to reduce it.

Maintaining Biodiversity is Important for Economic Reasons...

Many species of animals and plants are important to the **global economy**. Products derived from plant and animal species are traded on a local and global scale. They include things like...

1) **Food** and **drink** — plants and animals are the source of almost all **food** and some **drinks**.
2) **Clothing** — a lot of **fibres** and **fabrics** are made from plants and animals (e.g. cotton from plants and leather from animals).
3) **Drugs** — many are made from compounds from plants (e.g. the painkiller **morphine** is made from **poppies**).
4) **Fuels** — we use a number of organisms to produce **renewable** fuels, including ethanol and biogas. Fossil fuels are **non-renewable** (they'll run out), so other sources are of **major economic importance**.
5) **Other industrial materials** — a huge variety of other materials are produced from plant and animal species, including **wood**, **paper**, **dyes**, **adhesives**, **oils**, **rubber** and chemicals such as **pesticides**.

It's important to conserve all the organisms we currently use to make products, as well as those we **don't currently use** — they may provide us with **new products** in the **future**, e.g. new drugs for diseases we can't yet cure.

...Ecological Reasons...

The ecological reasons for maintaining biodiversity are all down to the **complex relationships** between **organisms** and their **environments**. The loss of **just one species** can have pretty **drastic effects**, for example:

1) **Disruption** of **food chains**, e.g. some species of bear feed on salmon, which feed on herring. If the number of herring decline it can affect **both** the salmon and the bear populations.
2) **Disruption** of **nutrient cycles**, e.g. decomposers like worms improve the **quality of soil** by recycling nutrients. If worm numbers decline, soil quality will be affected. This will affect the **growth** of plants and the **amount of food** available to animals.
3) **Loss of habitats**, e.g. hedgerows are **wildlife corridors** — they enable organisms to move between different habitats **safely**. If they're removed species can become **isolated** and availability of **food** and **nesting sites** for many species will be **reduced**.
4) **Habitat destruction** can also affect **climate**, e.g. CO_2 is stored in trees and bogs — the destruction of forests and peat bogs is contributing to **climate change** (see p. 90).

All these ecological reasons also have knock-on economic effects.

...Ethical Reasons...

Some people believe that we should conserve species simply because it's the **right thing to do**.

1) Many believe organisms have a **right to exist** — they shouldn't become **extinct** as a result of our activities.
2) Some people believe we have a **moral responsibility** to conserve biodiversity for **future** human generations.
3) There are also **religious** and **spiritual** reasons for conservation — **harmony** with the **natural world** is important to many beliefs and philosophies.

...and Aesthetic Reasons

Others believe we should conserve biodiversity because it brings **joy** to millions of people.

1) Areas **rich** in biodiversity provide a pleasant, **attractive environment** that people can enjoy.
2) The more biodiversity in an area the more **visitors** the area is likely to **attract** — this also has economic advantages.

Importance of Biodiversity

Maintaining Biodiversity is Important to Agriculture

In addition to all those economic, ecological, ethical and aesthetic reasons you now know all about, maintaining the biodiversity of wild plants and animals has some **benefits** for **agriculture**.

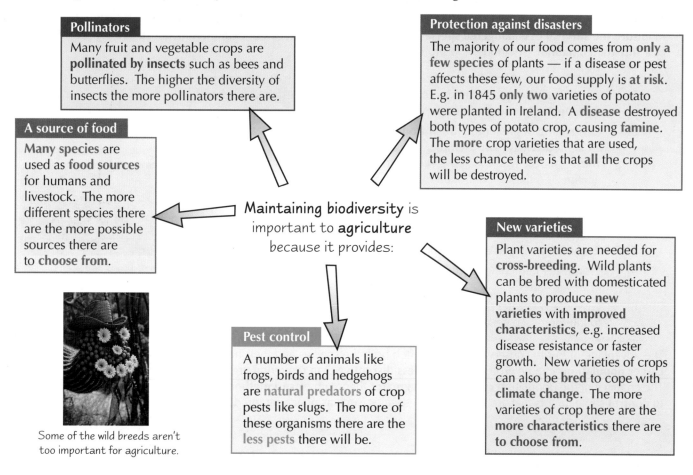

Pollinators

Many fruit and vegetable crops are **pollinated by insects** such as bees and butterflies. The higher the diversity of insects the more pollinators there are.

Protection against disasters

The majority of our food comes from **only a few species** of plants — if a disease or pest affects these few, our food supply is **at risk**. E.g. in 1845 **only two** varieties of potato were planted in Ireland. A **disease** destroyed both types of potato crop, causing **famine**. The **more** crop varieties that are used, the less chance there is that **all** the crops will be destroyed.

A source of food

Many species are used as **food sources** for humans and livestock. The more different species there are the more possible sources there are to **choose from**.

Maintaining biodiversity is important to **agriculture** because it provides:

New varieties

Plant varieties are needed for **cross-breeding**. Wild plants can be bred with domesticated plants to produce **new varieties** with **improved characteristics**, e.g. increased disease resistance or faster growth. New varieties of crops can also be **bred** to cope with **climate change**. The more varieties of crop there are the **more characteristics** there are **to choose from**.

Pest control

A number of animals like frogs, birds and hedgehogs are **natural predators** of crop pests like slugs. The more of these organisms there are the **less pests** there will be.

Some of the wild breeds aren't too important for agriculture.

Practice Questions

Q1   Suggest why maintaining biodiversity of plants is important to the drugs industry.

Q2   Give an economic reason for the conservation of biodiversity.

Q3   Give an ethical reason for the conservation of biodiversity.

Q4   Give an aesthetic reason for the conservation of biodiversity.

Q5   Suggest two characteristics that could be improved by cross-breeding domesticated plants with wild varieties.

Exam Questions

Q1   Explain why decreasing biodiversity could have adverse ecological implications.   [4 marks]

Q2   Briefly explain why maintaining biodiversity is important to the agricultural industry.   [5 marks]

Hippy or not — better start hugging those trees...

So, it turns out biodiversity is pretty important. Without it, not only would your life lack its little luxuries, like toilet paper with aloe vera, and fancy designer clothes, just surviving would be tricky — there'd be nothing to eat and fewer drugs to treat you when you're ill. Make sure you learn all the reasons for maintaining biodiversity — they might just crop up in the exam.

Conservation and Biodiversity

I'm sure no animals like being snatched from the African plains and taken to live in a safari park in Kidderminster, but sometimes they just don't know what's best for them...

In Situ Conservation Keeps Species in Their Natural Habitat

In situ conservation means **on site** — it involves protecting species in their **natural habitat**. Conservation is important to **ensure the survival** of **endangered species** — species which are at risk of **extinction** because of a **low** population, or a **threatened habitat**. Methods of *in situ* conservation include:

1) Establishing **protected areas** such as **national parks** and **nature reserves** — habitats and species are protected in these areas by **restricting urban development**, **industrial development** and **farming**.

2) **Controlling** or **preventing the introduction** of species that **threaten** local biodiversity. For example, grey squirrels are not native to Britain. They **compete** with the native red squirrel and have caused a population **decline**. So they're controlled in some areas.

3) **Protecting habitats** — e.g. controlling water levels to conserve wetlands and coppicing (trimming trees) to conserve woodlands. This allows organisms to **continue living** in their **natural habitat**.

4) **Restoring damaged areas** — such as a coastline polluted by an oil spill.

5) **Promoting** particular species — this could be by protecting **food sources** or **nesting sites**.

6) Giving **legal protection** to **endangered species**, e.g. making it illegal to kill them (see next page).

Jim reckoned he'd seen the last of those red squirrels — but he hadn't counted on their friends turning up.

The advantage of *in situ* conservation is that often both the **species** and their **habitat** are conserved. **Larger populations** can be protected and it's **less disruptive** than removing organisms from their habitats. The chances of the population **recovering** are **greater** than with *ex situ* methods (see below). But, it can be **difficult to control** some factors that are **threatening** a species (such as poaching, predators or climate change).

Ex Situ Conservation Removes Species from Their Natural Habitat

Ex situ conservation means **off site** — it involves protecting a species by **removing** part of the population from a **threatened habitat** and placing it in a **new location**. *Ex situ* conservation is often a **last resort**. Methods of *ex situ* conservation include:

1) **Relocating** an organism to a **safer area**, e.g. five white rhinos were recently relocated from the Congo to Kenya because they were in danger from **poachers** who kill them for their ivory.

2) **Breeding** organisms in **captivity** then **reintroducing** them to the wild when they are **strong enough**, e.g. sea eagles have been reintroduced to Britain through a captive breeding programme. Breeding is carried out in **animal sanctuaries** and **zoos**.

3) **Botanic gardens** are controlled environments used to grow a variety of **rare** plants for the purposes of **conservation**, **research**, **display** and **education**. **Endangered** plant species as well as species that are **extinct in the wild** can be grown and **reintroduced** into suitable habitats.

4) **Seed banks** — seeds can be frozen and stored in seed banks for over a century without losing their **fertility**. Seed banks provide a useful source of seeds if **natural reserves** are **destroyed**, for example by **disease** or other **natural disasters**.

The advantages of *ex situ* conservation are that it can be used to protect individual animals in a **controlled environment** — things like predation and hunting can be managed more easily. It can also be used to **reintroduce** species that have **left an area**. But, there are disadvantages — usually only a **small number** of individuals can be cared for. It can be **difficult** and **expensive** to create and **sustain** the **right environment**. *Ex situ* conservation is usually **less successful** than *in situ* methods — many species can't **breed successfully** in captivity, or don't **adapt** to their new environment when moved to a new location.

Conservation and Biodiversity

International Cooperation is *Important* in *Species Conservation*

Information about **threats** to biodiversity needs to be **shared** and countries need to decide on **conservation methods** and **implement them together**. Here are a couple of examples of successful international cooperation:

Rio Convention on Biodiversity

1) It aims to **develop international strategies** on the conservation of biodiversity and how to use animal and plant resources in a **sustainable** way.
2) The convention made it part of **international law** that conserving biodiversity is **everyone's responsibility**.
3) It also provides **guidance** to governments on how to conserve biodiversity.

CITES Agreement

1) CITES (**Convention** on **International Trade** in **Endangered Species**) is an agreement designed to increase **international cooperation** in **regulating trade** in wild animal and plant specimens.
2) The member countries all agreed to make it **illegal** to **kill** endangered species.
3) The agreement helps to **conserve** species by **limiting** trade through **licensing**, and by making it **illegal** to trade in products made from endangered animals (such as rhino ivory and leopard skins).
4) It's also designed to **raise awareness** of threats to biodiversity through **education**.

International cooperation is really **important** — it'd be pointless making hunting endangered species illegal in one country if poachers could just go and hunt them in another country.

Environmental Impact Assessments are Used to Inform *Planning Decisions*

An **Environmental Impact Assessment** (**EIA**) is an assessment of the **impact** a development project (such as building a new shopping centre or power station) might have on the environment. It involves:

1) **Estimating** biodiversity on the project site and **evaluating** how the development might **affect** biodiversity.
2) **Identifying** ways that biodiversity could be **conserved**.
3) Identifying threatened or **endangered species** on the project site and the **laws** relating to their conservation.
4) Deciding on **planning stipulations** — measures that will have to be implemented if the project proceeds, e.g. **relocating** or **protecting** endangered species.

Local authorities are often under pressure from **conservationists** who argue that developments **damage** the environment and **disturb** wildlife — they feel that habitats should be **left alone**.

Environmental impact assessments ensure that **decision makers** consider the **environmental impact** of development projects — they're used by local authorities to decide **if** and **how** projects will proceed.

Practice Questions

Q1 Describe how botanic gardens and seed banks help in the conservation of biodiversity.

Q2 What is CITES and how does it help to conserve endangered species?

Q3 Explain what environmental impact assessments are and describe how they are used.

Exam Question

Q1 The hawksbill turtle is an endangered species of sea turtle threatened by hunting and loss of nesting sites. They have slow reproductive, growth and development rates and their numbers are in rapid decline.

a) Suggest how the hawksbill turtle could be conserved by *in situ* and *ex situ* conservation methods. [5 marks]

b) Describe the disadvantages of using *ex situ* conservation methods. [4 marks]

c) Suggest why international cooperation is important to the conservation of the hawksbill turtle. [1 mark]

The path of true conservation ne'er did run smooth...

I'm sure the animals being forcibly removed from their homes are just as bemused as you are right now but I'm afraid it's another case of having to learn the facts. Plain and simple. Don't be put off by things like 'in' or 'ex' situ — that's just a way of saying 'on' or 'off' site that makes people feel clever when they say them. In fact, I'm feeling rather clever right now.

Classification Basics

For hundreds of years people have been putting organisms into groups to make it easier to recognise and name them. For example, my brother is a member of the species Idioto bigearian (Latin for idiots with big ears).

Classification *is All About* Grouping Together Similar Organisms

Classification is the act of **arranging organisms** into **groups** based on their **similarities** and **differences**. This makes it **easier** for scientists to **identify** them and to **study** them. **Taxonomy** is the **study** of classification. There are a few different classification systems in use, but they all involve placing organisms into groups in a **taxonomic hierarchy**:

1)   There are **eight levels** of groups (called taxonomic groups) used in classification.

2)   **Similar organisms** are first sorted into one of **three** very **large groups** called **domains**, e.g. animals, plants and fungi are in the Eukarya domain.

3)   **Similar organisms** are then sorted into **slightly smaller groups** called **kingdoms**, e.g. all animals are in the animal kingdom.

4)   **Similar** organisms from that kingdom are then grouped into a **phylum**. **Similar** organisms from each phylum are then grouped into a **class**, and **so on** down the eight levels of the taxonomic hierarchy.

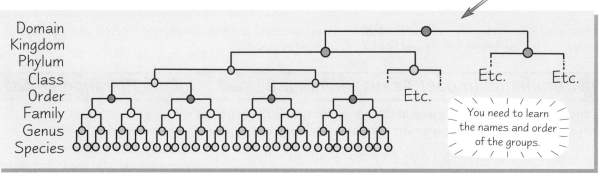

You need to learn the names and order of the groups.

5)   As you move **down** the hierarchy, there are **more groups** at each level but **fewer organisms** in each group.

6)   The hierarchy **ends** with **species** — the groups that contain only **one type** of organism (e.g. humans, dog, *E. coli* and about 50 million other living species).

Organisms *Can be Placed into One of* Five Kingdoms

You need to **know** these five kingdoms and the **general characteristics** of the organisms in each of them:

KINGDOM	EXAMPLES	FEATURES
Prokaryotae (Monera)	bacteria	prokaryotic, unicellular (single-celled), no nucleus, less than 5 μm
Protoctista	algae, protozoa	eukaryotic cells, usually live in water, single-celled or simple multicellular organisms
Fungi	moulds, yeasts, mushrooms	eukaryotic, chitin cell wall, saprotrophic (absorb substances from dead or decaying organisms)
Plantae	mosses, ferns, flowering plants	eukaryotic, multicellular, cell walls made of cellulose, can photosynthesise, contain chlorophyll, autotrophic (produce their own food)
Animalia	nematodes (roundworms), molluscs, insects, fish, reptiles, birds, mammals	eukaryotic, multicellular, no cell walls, heterotrophic (consume plants and animals)

Classification Basics

The **Binomial Naming System** is Used in **Classification**

1) The **nomenclature** (**naming system**) used for classification is called the **binomial system** — all organisms are given **one** internationally accepted scientific **name** in **Latin** that has **two parts**.

2) The **first part** of the name is the **genus** name and has a capital letter. The **second part** is the **species** name and begins with a lower case letter. E.g. using the binomial system humans are *Homo sapiens*. Names are always written in *italics* (or they're <u>underlined</u> if they're **handwritten**).

3) The binomial system helps to avoid the **confusion** of using **common names**. E.g. over 100 different plant species are called **raspberries** and one species of buttercup has over 90 different common names.

Phylogeny Tells Us About the **Evolutionary History** of Organisms

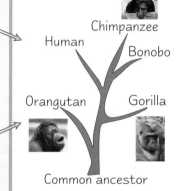

1) **Phylogeny** is the study of the **evolutionary history** of groups of **organisms**.

2) All organisms have **evolved** from shared common ancestors (**relatives**). E.g. members of the Hominidae family (great apes and humans) evolved from a common ancestor. First orangutans **diverged** (evolved to become a **different species**) from this common ancestor. Next gorillas diverged, then humans, closely followed by bonobos and chimpanzees.

3) Phylogeny tells us **who's related** to whom and how **closely related** they are.

4) Closely related species **diverged** away from each other **most recently**. E.g. the phylogenetic tree opposite shows the **Hominidae tree**. Humans and **chimpanzees** are **closely** related, as they diverged very **recently**. You can see this because their branches are **close** together. Humans and orangutans are more **distantly** related, as they diverged longer ago, so their branches are **further** apart.

Classification systems now take into account **phylogeny** when arranging organisms into **groups**.

Practice Questions

Q1 List the taxonomic hierarchy in order, starting with the largest groups.

Q2 List two features of the kingdom Fungi.

Q3 List two features of the kingdom Animalia.

Exam Questions

Q1 Define the following terms:
   a) classification   [1 mark]
   b) taxonomy   [1 mark]
   c) phylogeny   [1 mark]

Q2 Describe the binomial system of naming organisms.   [3 marks]

Snozcumber kingdom features — long, thin, green, filled with snot...

Make sure that you really understand all the basics on these pages before delving any deeper into this section. Remembering the order of the groups in the taxonomic hierarchy is about as easy as licking your elbow... try making up a mnemonic to help (like 'Dopey King Prawns Can't Order Fried Green Sausages' for Domain, Kingdom, Phylum, Class, Order, Family, etc.).

Evolution of Classification Systems

Classification systems and the groups organisms are placed in aren't set in stone. New technology and new evidence can lead to changes in these systems and the reclassification of organisms.

Classification Systems are now Based on a Range of Evidence

1) Early classification systems **only** used **observable features** (things you can see) to place organisms into groups, e.g. whether they lay eggs, can fly or can cook a mean chilli...

2) But this method has **problems**. Scientists don't always agree on the **relative importance** of different features and groups based **solely** on **physical features** may not show how **related** organisms are.

> For example, **sharks** and **whales look** quite similar and they both **live** in the **sea**. But they're **not** actually closely related.

3) Classification systems are **now** based on observable features **along** with **other evidence**.

4) The **more similar** organisms are, the **more related** they are. We now use a wide range of evidence to see **how similar**, and therefore how related, organisms are. For example:

> 1) **Molecular evidence** — the similarities in **proteins** and **DNA**. **More closely related** organisms will have **more similar** molecules. You can **compare** things like how **DNA** is **stored**, the **sequence** of DNA **bases** (see page 62) and the **sequence** of **amino acids** in **proteins** from different organisms. E.g. the **base sequence** for human and chimpanzee **DNA** is about 94% the **same**.
>
> 2) **Embryological evidence** — the similarities in the **early stages** of an organism's **development**.
>
> 3) **Anatomical evidence** — the similarities in **structure** and **function** of different body parts.
>
> 4) **Behavioural evidence** — the similarities in **behaviour** and **social organisation** of organisms.

5) **New technologies** (e.g. new **DNA** techniques, better **microscopes**) can result in **new discoveries** being made.

6) Scientists can share their new discoveries in **meetings** and **scientific journals** (see p. 1). How organisms are **classified** is **continually revised** to take account of any **new findings** that scientists **discover**.

> For example, skunks **were** classified in the family **Mustelidae** until **molecular evidence** revealed their **DNA sequence** was significantly different to other members of that family. So they were reclassified into the family **Mephitidae**.

Five Kingdoms Vs Three Domains

The **three domain classification system** shown on page 96 is relatively new, and was suggested because of **new evidence**:

1) In the older **system** the **largest groups** were the **five kingdoms** — all organisms were placed into **one** of these groups.

2) In 1990, the three domain system was proposed. This new system has three domains — **large superkingdoms** that are **above** the kingdoms in the **taxonomic hierarchy** (see p. 96).

3) In the **three domain system**, organisms with cells that **contain a nucleus** are placed in the domain **Eukarya** (this includes four of the five kingdoms). Organisms that were in the kingdom **Prokaryotae** (which contains unicellular organisms **without a nucleus**) are separated into two domains — the **Archaea** and **Bacteria**.

4) The **lower** hierarchy stays the **same** — Kingdom, Phylum, Class, Order, Family, Genus, Species.

5) The three domain system was proposed because of **new evidence**, mainly molecular. E.g. the **Prokaryotae** were **reclassified** into **two domains** because new evidence showed **large differences** between the Archaea and Bacteria. The new evidence included:

> • **Molecular evidence** — The enzyme RNA polymerase (needed to make RNA) is different in Bacteria and Archaea. Archaea, but not Bacteria, have similar histones (proteins that bind to DNA) to Eukarya.
>
> • **Cell membrane evidence** — The bonds of the lipids (see p. 58) in the cell membranes of Bacteria and Archaea are different. The development and composition of flagellae (see p. 7) are also different.

6) Most scientists now **agree** that Archaea and Bacteria **evolved separately** and that Archaea are **more closely related** to Eukarya than Bacteria. The three-domain system reflects how **different** the Archaea and Bacteria are.

Dichotomous Keys

Dichotomous Keys can be used to Identify Organisms

1) **Dichotomous keys** provide a way to **identify organisms** based on **observable features** (e.g. colour, type of leaves).

2) They consist of a **series of questions**, each with **only two** possible answers.
Each **answer** leads to the **name** of the organism or **another question**, and so on, until the organism is **identified**.

3) In the **exam** you could be asked to **use** a dichotomous key to **identify** some organisms.
For example, the dichotomous key below can be used to identify **seaweeds**:

1.	Is it bright, grassy green?	Yes	Sea lettuce
		No	Go to 2.
2.	Is it reddish brown?	Yes	Irish moss
		No	Go to 3.
3.	Does it have a large, root-like structure?	Yes	Kelp
		No	Go to 4.
4.	Does it have air bladders (pockets of air) in the leaves?	Yes	Bladder wrack
		No	Go to 5.
5.	Is the leaf edge saw-toothed?	Yes	Saw wrack
		No	Go to 6.
6.	Is the leaf rolled in at the edges?	Yes	Channelled wrack
		No	Spiral wrack

Bright, grassy green?
Yes. Sea lettuce?
Not so sure.

Using the **key** to identify this seaweed, the answer to question 1 is **yes** (it's **bright, grassy green**) — so it's **sea lettuce**.

For this seaweed, the answers to questions 1, 2 and 3 are **no**. The answer to question 4 is **yes** (it has **air bladders**) — so it's **bladder wrack**.

Answer 1 is **no**, but answer 2 is yes (it's **reddish brown**) — so it's **Irish moss**.

Answers 1, 2, 3 and 4 are **no**, but 5 is **yes** (it's got **saw-toothed edges**) — so it's **saw wrack**.

Practice Questions

Q1 What evidence were the first classification systems solely based on?

Q2 What is meant by a domain?

Q3 What is a dichotomous key?

A B C

1.	Is it covered with hair-like filaments?	Yes	*Trichodesmium*
		No	Go to 2.
2.	Is it unicellular and oval shaped?	Yes	*Synechococcus*
		No	Go to 2.
3.	Is it unicellular and rod shaped?	Yes	*Lyngbya*
		No	Go to 3.
4.	Is it spiral shaped?	Yes	*Spirulina*
		No	Go to 2.
5.	Is it a long chain of spherical cells?	Yes	*Anabaena*
		No	*Dermocarpa*

Exam Question

Q1 The key above can be used to identify different types of Cyanobacteria (bacteria that can photosynthesise).

a) Use the key to identify the Cyanobacteria labelled A, B and C above. [3 marks]

b) The three domain system of classification places Cyanobacteria in the domain Bacteria.
Describe three differences between organisms in the Bacteria and Archaea domains. [3 marks]

Why did the starfish blush? — because the seaweed... (classic)

*So there you have it — these four little pages are all you need to learn about classification and identifying organisms.
You'll be a bona fide taxonomist before you know it. Taxonomists are great fun — with their crazy little classification systems.*

Variation

Ever wondered why no two people are exactly alike? No, well nor have I actually, but it's time to start thinking about it.
This variation is partly genetic and partly due to differences in the environment.

Variation *Exists Between* All Individuals

Variation is the **differences** that exist between **individuals**. Every individual organism is
unique — even **clones** (such as identical twins) show some **variation**. It can occur:

Here's how I remember
which is which — Int-**er**
means diff-**er**-ent species.

1) <u>Within species</u> — Variation within a species is called **intraspecific** variation. For example,
individual European robins weigh **between** 16 g and 22 g and show some variation in
many other characteristics including length, wingspan, colour and beak size.

2) <u>Between species</u> — The variation between **different species** is called **interspecific** variation.
For example, the **lightest** species of bird is the bee hummingbird, which weighs around
1.6 g on average. The **heaviest** species of bird is the ostrich, which can weigh up to
160 kg (100 000 times as much).

No matter what
anyone said,
Malcolm knew size
was important.

Variation *can be* Continuous...

Continuous variation is when the **individuals** in a population vary **within a range** — there are **no distinct categories**,
e.g. **humans** can be **any height** within a range (139 cm, 175 cm, 185.9 cm, etc.), **not just** tall or short.
Here are some more examples:

The categories
are <u>not</u> distinct

Animals

1) **Milk yield** — e.g. cows can produce any volume of milk within a range.
2) **Mass** — e.g. humans can be any mass within a range.

Plants

1) **Number of leaves** — e.g. a tree can have any number of leaves within a range.
2) **Mass** — e.g. the mass of the seeds from a flower head varies within a range.

Microorganisms

1) **Width** — e.g. the width of *E. coli* bacteria varies within a range.
2) **Length** — e.g. the length of the flagellum (see p. 7) can vary within a range.

...or Discontinuous

Discontinuous variation is when there are two or more **distinct categories** — each individual
falls into **only one** of these categories, there are **no intermediates**. Here are some examples:

Four distinct
blood groups

Animals

1) **Sex** — e.g. humans can be either male or female.
2) **Blood group** — e.g. humans can be group A, B, AB or O.

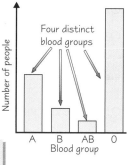

Plants

1) **Colour** — e.g. courgettes are either yellow, dark green or light green.
2) **Seed shape** — e.g. some pea plants have smooth seeds and some have wrinkled seeds.

Microorganisms

1) **Antibiotic resistance** — e.g. bacteria are either resistant or not.
2) **Pigment production** — e.g. some types of bacteria can produce a coloured pigment, some can't.

Variation

Variation can be Caused by Genes, the Environment, or Both

Variation can be caused by **genetic factors**, **environmental factors** or a combination of **both**:

1 Genetic factors

1) **Different species** have **different genes**.
2) Individuals of the **same species** have the **same genes**, but **different versions** of them (called **alleles**).
3) The genes and alleles an organism has make up its **genotype**.
4) The differences in **genotype** result in **variation** in **phenotype** — the **characteristics** displayed by an organism.
5) Examples of variation caused **only** by genetic factors include **blood group** in humans (O, A, B or AB) and **antibiotic resistance** in bacteria.
6) You **inherit** your genes from your parents. This means variation caused by genetic factors is **inherited**.

2 Environmental factors

1) Variation can also be caused by **differences in the environment**, e.g. climate, food, lifestyle.
2) Characteristics controlled by environmental factors can **change** over an organism's life.
3) Examples of variation caused **only** by environmental factors include **accents** and whether people have **pierced ears**.

3 Both

Genetic factors determine the characteristics an organism's **born with**, but **environmental factors** can **influence** how some characteristics **develop**. For example:

1) **Height** — **genes** determine how tall an organism **can grow** (e.g. tall parents tend to have tall children). But **diet or nutrient availability** affect how tall an organism **actually grows**.
2) **Flagellum** — **genes** determine if a microorganism **can grow** a flagellum, but some will only **start to grow** them in **certain environments**, e.g. if metal ions are present.

Practice Questions

Q1 What is variation?

Q2 Describe what is meant by continuous variation and give one example.

Q3 Describe what is meant by discontinuous variation and give one example.

Q4 Briefly describe what is meant by variation caused by environmental factors.

Exam Question

Q1 The graph shows the results of an investigation into the effects of temperature on the length of time it took for ladybird larvae to emerge as adults. Two species of ladybird were investigated, species A and species B.

a) Describe the results of the study. [3 marks]

b) Explain what causes the variation between the species and within each species. [4 marks]

Environmental Factor — the search is on for the most talented environment...

It's amazing to think how many factors and genes influence the way we look and behave. It's the reason why every single organism is unique. My parents have often said they're glad they'll never have another child as 'unique' as me.

Adaptations

All the variation between and within species means that some organisms are better adapted to their environment than others...

Adaptations make Organisms Well Suited to Their Environment

1) Being **adapted** to an environment means an organism has features that **increase** its **chances of survival** and **reproduction**, and also the chances of its **offspring reproducing successfully**.

2) These features are called **adaptations** and can be behavioural, physiological and anatomical (see below).

3) Adaptations develop because of **evolution** by **natural selection** (see the next page).

4) In each generation, the **best-adapted individuals** are more likely to survive and reproduce — passing their adaptations on to their **offspring**. Individuals that are less well adapted are more likely to **die before reproducing**.

Adaptations can be Behavioural, Physiological and Anatomical

Behavioural adaptations

Ways an organism **acts** that increase its chance of survival. For example:

- **Possums** sometimes '**play dead**' — if they're being threatened by a **predator** they play dead to **escape attack**. This **increases** their chance of **survival**.

- **Scorpions dance** before **mating** — this makes sure they attract a mate of the **same species**, increasing the likelihood of **successful mating**.

Sid and Nancy were well adapted to hiding in candyfloss shops.

Physiological adaptations

Processes inside an organism's body that increase its chance of survival. For example:

- **Brown bears hibernate** — they **lower their metabolism** (all the chemical reactions taking place in their body) over **winter**. This **conserves energy**, so they don't need to look for **food** in the months when it's scarce — **increasing** their chance of **survival**.

- **Some bacteria** produce **antibiotics** — these **kill** other species of bacteria in the area. This means there's **less competition**, so they're **more likely** to **survive**.

Anatomical (structural) adaptations

Structural features of an organism's body that increase its chance of survival. For example:

- **Otters** have a **streamlined shape** — making it easier to **glide** through the **water**. This makes it easier for them to **catch prey** and **escape predators**, increasing their chance of **survival**.

- **Whales** have a **thick layer** of **blubber** (fat) — this helps to keep them **warm** in the cold sea. This increases their chance of survival in places where their **food** is found.

Practice Questions

Q1 What is meant by the term adaptation?

Q2 Describe the differences between behavioural, physiological and anatomical adaptations.

Exam Question

Q1 Hedgehogs are commonly found in gardens across the UK. They are brown with long, spiky fur, small ears and claws. They hibernate over winter and can roll into a ball when alarmed.

Give one behavioural, one physiological and two anatomical adaptations of hedgehogs, and suggest how each helps them to survive. [8 marks]

I'm perfectly adapted — for staying in bed...

Adaptations are features that make an organism more likely to survive and reproduce. Repetitive? Yes, but that's why it's so easy to learn. Adaptations develop because of evolution by natural selection, which is on the next page. Lucky you.

The Theory of Evolution

Evolution is the slow and continual change of organisms from one generation to the next. It explains how advantageous adaptations become common within a population of organisms...

Darwin Published his Theory of Evolution by Natural Selection in 1859

Scientists use **theories** to attempt to **explain** their **observations** — Charles Darwin was no exception. Darwin made **four** key observations about the world around him.

<u>Observations:</u>

1) Organisms produce **more offspring** than **survive**.

2) There's **variation** in the characteristics of members of the **same species**.

3) Some of these characteristics can be **passed on** from one generation to the next.

4) Individuals that are **best adapted** to their environment are more likely to **survive**.

Natural selection is one process by which evolution occurs.

Darwin wrote his theory of **evolution by natural selection** to **explain** his observations:

<u>Theory:</u>

1) Individuals within a population **show variation** in their **phenotypes** (their characteristics).

2) **Predation, disease** and **competition** create a **struggle for survival**.

3) Individuals with **better adaptations** (characteristics that give a selective advantage, e.g. being able to run away from predators faster) are **more likely to survive**, **reproduce** and **pass on** their advantageous adaptations to their **offspring**.

4) Over time, the **number** of individuals with the advantageous adaptations **increases**.

5) Over generations this leads to **evolution** as the favourable adaptations become **more common** in the population.

At first, there was some **opposition** to Darwin's theory as it conflicted with some **religious beliefs**. Over time the theory has become **increasingly accepted** as more **evidence** has been found to support it and no evidence has been shown to disprove it. Evidence increases scientists' **confidence** in a theory — the more evidence there is, the more chance of something becoming an **accepted scientific explanation** (see pages 1-2).

Evolution can Lead to Speciation

Speciation is the **formation of a new species**:

1) A **species** is defined as a group of **similar organisms** that can **reproduce** to produce **fertile offspring**.

2) Species can exist as **one** or **more populations**, e.g. there are populations of the American black bear in parts of the USA and in parts of Canada.

3) Speciation happens when **populations** of the **same species** evolve to become so different that they can't breed with one another to produce **fertile** offspring.

Here's an example to show you **how** evolution can lead to speciation:

Darwin's finches

Darwin observed 14 species of finch on the **Galapagos Islands** — a group of islands in the Pacific Ocean. Each species of finch was unique to a single island. Although the finches were similar, the size and shape of their **beaks** differed — they were adapted to the **food sources** found on their specific island. Darwin theorised that:

1) All the species of finch had a **common ancestor**.

2) Different populations became **isolated** on different islands.

3) Each population **evolved adaptations** to their environment.

4) The populations evolved to become so different that they could no longer **breed** to produce **fertile offspring**.

5) They had evolved into **separate species**.

The Theory of Evolution

Because there's so much evidence to support the theory of evolution it's pretty much considered scientific fact now...

*There's **Plenty of Evidence** to **Support Evolution***

Fossil Record Evidence

Fossils are the **remains** of organisms **preserved in rocks**.
By arranging fossils in chronological (date) order, **gradual changes** in organisms can be observed that provide **evidence** of evolution.

Example — The fossil record of the **horse** shows a **gradual change** in characteristics, including increasing **size** and **hoof** development.

DNA Evidence

1) The theory of evolution suggests that all organisms have **evolved** from shared **common ancestors**.
2) Closely related species **diverged** (evolved to become different species) **more recently**.
3) Evolution is caused by **gradual changes** in the **base sequence** of organisms' **DNA**.
4) So, organisms that diverged away from each other more recently, should have **more similar DNA**, as **less time** has passed for changes in the DNA sequence to occur. This is exactly what scientists have found.

See p. 62 for more on DNA.

Example — Humans, chimps and mice all evolved from a common ancestor. Humans and mice diverged a **long time ago**, but humans and chimps diverged **quite recently**. The **DNA base sequence** of humans and chimps is 94% the same, but human and mouse DNA is only 85% the same.

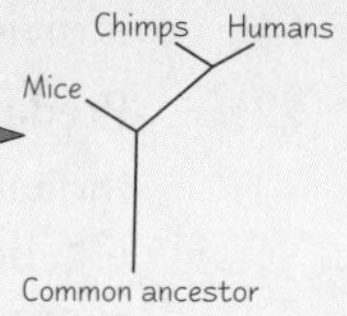

Molecular Evidence

In addition to DNA, the similarities in **other molecules** provide evidence.
Scientists compare the **sequence** of **amino acids** in **proteins** (see p. 64), and compare **antibodies**.
Organisms that diverged away from each other **more recently** have **more similar molecules**, as **less time** has passed for changes in proteins and other molecules to occur.

Populations** of **Bacteria** can **Evolve Resistance** to **Antibiotics

Antibiotics are drugs that **kill or inhibit the growth** of bacteria. Scientists have observed the evolution of **antibiotic resistance** in many species of bacteria. For example, MRSA (methicillin-resistant *Staphylococcus aureus*) is a **strain** (type) of bacteria that's resistant to the antibiotic methicillin.

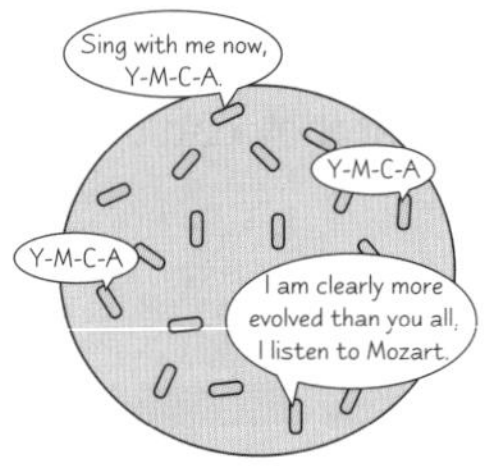

The **evolution** of antibiotic resistance can be explained by **natural selection**:

1) There is **variation** in a population of bacteria. **Genetic mutations** make some bacteria naturally **resistant** to an antibiotic.
2) If the population of bacteria is exposed to that antibiotic, only the individuals with resistance will **survive** to **reproduce**.
3) The **alleles** which cause the antibiotic resistance will be **passed on** to the next generation, and so the population will evolve to become resistant to the drug.

*The Evolution of **Antibiotic Resistance** has **Implications** for **Humans***

1) **Infections** caused by antibiotic-resistant bacteria (such as MRSA) are **harder to treat** — some species of bacteria are resistant to **a lot of different antibiotics**. It takes doctors a while to figure out which antibiotics will get rid of the infection, and in that time the **patient** could become **very ill** or **die**.
2) There could come a point where a bacterium has developed resistance to **all known antibiotics**. To prevent this **new antibiotics** need to be **developed**. This takes **time** and costs a lot of **money**.

Different strains of one species of bacteria can be resistant to different antibiotics — one antibiotic won't always kill all of them.

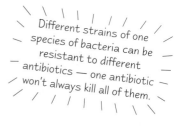

The Theory of Evolution

Populations of Insects can Evolve Resistance to Pesticides

Pesticides are chemicals that **kill pests** (e.g. insects that damage crops). Scientists have observed the evolution of **pesticide resistance** in many species of insect. For example, some populations of **mosquito** have **evolved resistance** to the pesticide **DDT**. Some populations of **pollen beetles** (which damage the crop oilseed rape) are resistant to **pyrethroid** pesticides.

Janet was resistant to DDT but not to Malcolm's smooth talking.

The evolution of **pesticide resistance** can be explained by **natural selection**:

1) There is **variation** in a population of insects. **Genetic mutations** make some insects naturally **resistant** to a pesticide.

2) If the population of insects is exposed to that pesticide, only the individuals with resistance will **survive** to **reproduce**.

3) The **alleles** which cause the pesticide resistance will be **passed on** to the next generation, and so the population will evolve to become more resistant to the chemical.

The Evolution of Pesticide Resistance has Implications for Humans

The implications for humans are pretty similar to those for antibiotic resistance:

1) **Crop infestations** with **pesticide-resistant** insects are **harder** to **control** — some insects are resistant to **lots of different pesticides**. It takes farmers a while to figure out which pesticide will kill the insect and in that time **all** the crop could be **destroyed**. If the insects are resistant to specific pesticides (ones that only kill that insect), farmers might have to use **broader pesticides** (those that kill a range of insects), which could kill beneficial insects.

2) If **disease-carrying** insects (e.g. mosquitoes) become pesticide-resistant, the **spread of disease** could **increase**.

3) A population of insects could **evolve resistance** to **all** pesticides in use. To prevent this **new pesticides** need to be **produced**. This takes **time** and costs **money**.

Practice Questions

Q1 What four key observations did Darwin make?

Q2 Define speciation.

Q3 Briefly describe how fossil evidence supports the theory of evolution.

These questions cover pages 103-105.

Exam Questions

Q1 Outline Darwin's theory of evolution by natural selection. [4 marks]

Q2 The diamondback moth is a pest of many crops. In 1953 it became resistant to the pesticide DDT and by 1981 it had become resistant to 36 other pesticides.

   a) Explain how the diamondback moth populations could have developed DDT resistance. [4 marks]

   b) Describe two possible implications of the diamondback moth developing resistance to pesticides. [2 marks]

The fossil record — it rocks...

Evolution by natural selection isn't that bad really... just remember that any adaptation that increases the chances of an organism surviving (e.g. by avoiding being killed by antibiotics) or getting laid (no explanation required) will increase in the population due to the process of natural selection. Now I know why mullets have disappeared... so unattractive...

How to Interpret Data

Science is all about getting good evidence to test your theories... so scientists need to be able to spot a badly designed experiment a mile off, and be able to interpret the results of an experiment properly.
Being the cheeky little monkeys they are, your exam board will want to make sure you can do it too.
Here's a quick reference section to show you how to go about interpreting data-style questions.

You Might get **Data** to **Interpret** in the **Exam**

Here's an example of the kind of data you might get:

Experiment A

Experiment A examined the effect of temperature on the rate of an enzyme-controlled reaction. The rate of reaction for enzyme X was measured at six different temperatures (from 10 to 60 °C). All other variables were kept constant.

A negative control containing all solutions except the enzyme was included. The rate of reaction for the negative control was zero at each temperature used. The results are shown in the graph on the right.

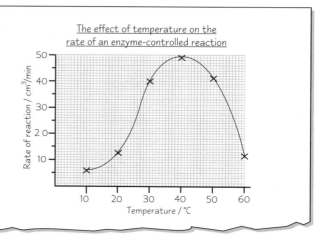

You Need to be Able to **Read Graphs**

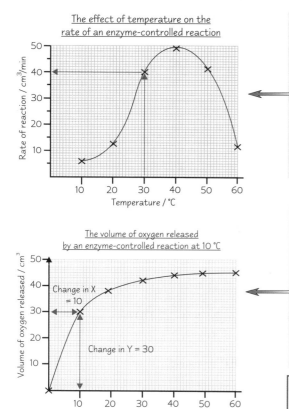

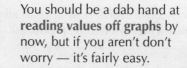

Susie was worried by all the talk of gir-raffe paper.

1) You should be a dab hand at **reading values off graphs** by now, but if you aren't don't worry — it's fairly easy.

2) For example, if you want to know what the rate of reaction was at **30 °C** you find 30 on the x-axis and **go up** until you hit the line — then go **across** to the y-axis and **read off the value** (40 cm³/min).

3) Don't forget to put the **units** on your answer.

A little trickier is calculating the **gradient** of the graph:

$$\text{Gradient} = \frac{\text{Change in Y}}{\text{Change in X}} \qquad \text{Units} = \frac{Y}{X}$$

The x-axis is horizontal, the y-axis is vertical.

For example, if you want to know the **rate of a reaction** over the first 10 seconds:

$$\text{Gradient} = \text{rate of reaction} = \frac{30}{10} = 3 \qquad \text{Units} = \frac{cm^3}{s} = cm^3/s$$

The **answer** is 3 cm³/s.

If you **aren't** told what to use (e.g. over the first 10 seconds) then use the **largest area** you can from the **straightest** part of the graph.

Reading graphs... I didn't realise they were so intelligent...

This is pretty bog-standard stuff but it's really important that you get it right — graph questions are easy marks in the exam... It can be quite easy to forget to do the simple things, like including units — make sure you don't miss them out.

How to Evaluate and Describe Experiments

Experiments *Have to be* Designed Carefully

Any experiment has to be carried out properly to get a **reliable result**.
Here are some of the things that should be done:

1) <u>Only one variable should change</u> — Variables are **quantities** that have the **potential to change**, e.g. temperature. You should only ever **change one variable** in an experiment. Then you can be sure that changing that variable is the **reason** for **any effects** you see. You need to **measure** something to see if the variable is having an **effect** (e.g. volume).

   - The variable that you **change** is called the **independent variable**.
   - The variable that you **measure** is called the **dependent variable**.

2) <u>All the other variables should be controlled</u> — When you're investigating a variable you need to keep **everything else** that could affect it **constant**. This means you can be sure that **only** your independent variable is causing any effects seen.

3) <u>Experiments should be repeated</u> — Reliable results are **reproducible**. A good experiment includes **repeated** measurements, so you can see if the results are reproducible.

4) <u>Negative controls should be used</u> — Negative controls are used to check that **nothing else** included in the experiment is **affecting** the thing you're measuring (the dependent variable).

The same principles apply to **studies** — the **more people** included the better (this is a bit like having loads of repeats), as many **variables** should be **controlled** as possible, and a **control group** should be used if appropriate.

A reliable result is a result that can be <u>consistently reproduced</u> in independent experiments. If the results are reproducible they're more likely to be <u>true</u>.

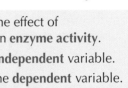
Harold's experiment wasn't very well designed, but it sure did look good.

> **EXAMPLE** | Investigating the effect of **temperature** on **enzyme activity**.
>
> 1) Temperature is the **independent** variable.
> 2) Enzyme activity is the **dependent** variable.
> 3) pH, volume, substrate concentration and enzyme concentration should all **stay the same**.
> 4) The experiment should be **repeated** at least **three times** at each temperature used.
> 5) A **negative control**, containing everything used **except the enzyme**, should be measured at each temperature used. No enzyme activity should be seen with these controls.

You Need to Be Able to Describe *a Good Experiment*

You could be asked to describe an experiment in the exam. You need to:

1) **Plan what you're going to write** before you start — roughly jot down the **sequence** of the experiment.

2) Describe the **sequence** of the experiment — what you do first, then second, then third etc. Use the **proper names** for the **equipment** and **reagents**, e.g. spectrophotometer, Benedict's reagent, etc. Don't forget to mention any **calculation steps**, e.g. finding averages. Be **specific** about what you would do.

3) If it's a **test** (e.g. a test for sugar), describe what **results** you'd expect — e.g. what **colour change** you'd expect.

Patrick had spent ages on his plan. He wasn't convinced the examiners would like it though...

Catalase catalyses the breakdown of hydrogen peroxide into water and oxygen.

> **EXAMPLE** | Investigating the effect of **temperature** on **catalase activity**.
>
> 1) Set up test tubes containing the **same concentration** of hydrogen peroxide.
> 2) Set up the apparatus to measure the **volume** of oxygen produced from each test tube.
> 3) Put each test tube in a **water bath** set to a different temperature (e.g. 10 °C, 20 °C, 30 °C and 40 °C).
> 4) Add the **same volume** of catalase to each test tube and **record** how much oxygen is produced in the **first minute** (60 s) of the reaction.
> 5) A **negative control** reaction, not containing catalase, should be carried out at each temperature.
> 6) **Repeat** the experiment at each temperature three times, and use the results to find an average volume.
> 7) **Calculate the average** rate of reaction at each temperature by dividing the volume produced by the time taken (cm^3/second).

Controls — I think I prefer the remote kind...

This page should give you a fair idea of the points to think about when describing an experiment. Just remember to take your time and make sure you've included all the main points — constants, specifics, measurements, repeats and controls.

A2-Level

Biology

Exam Board: OCR

Communication and Homeostasis Basics

Ah, there's nothing like a nice long section to start you off on the second half of the book — welcome to A2 Biology.

Responding to their Environment Helps Organisms Survive

1) **Animals increase** their **chances** of **survival** by **responding** to **changes** in their **external environment**, e.g. by **avoiding harmful environments** such as places that are too hot or too cold.

2) They also **respond** to **changes** in their **internal environment** to make sure that the **conditions** are always **optimal** for their **metabolism** (all the chemical reactions that go on inside them).

3) **Plants** also **increase** their **chances** of **survival** by **responding** to **changes** in their **environment** (see p. 204).

4) Any **change** in the internal or external **environment** is called a **stimulus**.

Receptors Detect Stimuli and Effectors Produce a Response

1) **Receptors detect stimuli**.

2) Receptors are **specific** — they only **detect one particular stimulus**, e.g. light, pressure or glucose concentration.

3) There are **many different types** of receptor that each detect a **different type of stimulus**.

4) Some receptors are **cells**, e.g. photoreceptors are receptor cells that connect to the nervous system. Some receptors are **proteins** on **cell surface membranes**, e.g. glucose receptors are proteins found in the cell membranes of some pancreatic cells.

5) **Effectors** are cells that bring about a **response** to a **stimulus**, to produce an **effect**. Effectors include **muscle cells** and cells found in **glands**, e.g. the **pancreas**.

Receptors Communicate with Effectors Via Hormones and Nerves

1) Receptors **communicate** with effectors via the **nervous system** (see p. 112) or the **hormonal system** (see p. 118), or sometimes using **both**.

2) **Nervous** and **hormonal communication** are both **examples** of **cell signalling** (ways cells communicate with each other).

Homeostasis is the Maintenance of a Constant Internal Environment

1) **Changes** in your **external environment** can affect your **internal environment** — the blood and tissue fluid that surrounds your cells.

2) **Homeostasis** involves **control systems** that keep your **internal environment** roughly **constant** (within **certain limits**).

3) **Keeping** your internal environment **constant** is vital for cells to **function normally** and to **stop** them being **damaged**.

4) It's particularly important to **maintain** the right **core body temperature**. This is because temperature affects **enzyme activity**, and enzymes **control** the **rate** of **metabolic reactions**:

   - If **body temperature is too high** (e.g. 40 °C) **enzymes** may become **denatured**. The enzyme's molecules **vibrate too much**, which **breaks** the **hydrogen bonds** that hold them in their **3D shape**. The **shape** of the enzyme's **active site** is **changed** and it **no longer works** as a **catalyst**. This means **metabolic reactions** are **less efficient**.

   - If body temperature is **too low enzyme activity** is **reduced**, **slowing** the rate of **metabolic reactions**.

   - The **highest rate** of enzyme activity happens at their **optimum temperature** (about **37 °C** in humans).

5) It's also important to **maintain** the right **concentration** of **glucose** in the **blood**, so there's always enough available for respiration.

There's more about control of body temperature on p. 120 and control of blood glucose on p. 122.

Communication and Homeostasis Basics

Homeostatic Systems Detect a Change and Respond by Negative Feedback

1) Homeostatic systems involve **receptors**, a **communication system** and **effectors** (see the previous page).

2) Receptors detect when a level is **too high** or **too low**, and the information's communicated via the **nervous** system or the **hormonal** system to **effectors**.

3) The effectors respond to **counteract** the change — bringing the level **back** to **normal**.

4) The mechanism that **restores** the level to **normal** is called a **negative feedback** mechanism.

5) Negative feedback **keeps** things around the **normal** level, e.g. body temperature is usually kept **within 0.5 °C** above or below **37 °C**.

6) Negative feedback only works within **certain limits** though — if the change is **too big** then the **effectors** may **not** be able to **counteract** it, e.g. a huge drop in body temperature caused by prolonged exposure to cold weather may be too large to counteract.

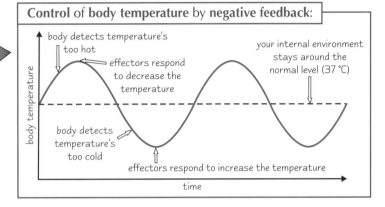

Control of **body temperature** by **negative feedback:**

body detects temperature's too hot

effectors respond to decrease the temperature

your internal environment stays around the normal level (37 °C)

body detects temperature's too cold

effectors respond to increase the temperature

time

Positive Feedback Mechanisms Amplify a Change from the Normal Level

1) Some changes trigger a **positive feedback** mechanism, which **amplifies** the change.

2) The effectors respond to **further increase** the level **away** from the **normal** level.

3) Positive feedback is useful to **rapidly activate** something, e.g. a **blood clot** after an injury:

- **Platelets** become **activated** and release a **chemical** — this triggers **more platelets** to be activated, and so on.
- Platelets **very quickly** form a **blood clot** at the injury site.
- The process **ends** with **negative feedback**, when the body detects the **blood clot** has been **formed**.

4) Positive feedback **isn't** involved in **homeostasis** because it **doesn't** keep your internal environment **constant**.

Practice Questions

Q1 Why do organisms respond to changes in their environment?

Q2 What is a stimulus?

Q3 Give two types of effector.

Q4 What is cell signalling?

Q5 What is a negative feedback mechanism?

Q6 What type of mechanism amplifies a change from the normal level?

Exam Question

Q1 a) Define homeostasis. [1 mark]

b) Describe the role of receptors, communication systems and effectors in homeostasis. [3 marks]

Responding to questions in an exam helps you to pass...

Animals respond to changes in their internal and external environment. They respond to internal changes so that they can keep conditions just right for all their bodily reactions. Maintaining this constant environment is called homeostasis — basically you just need to remember that if one thing goes up the body responds to bring it down, and vice versa.

The Nervous System and Neurones

The nervous system helps organisms to respond to the environment, so you need to know a bit more about it...

The **Nervous System** Sends Information as **Nerve Impulses**

1) The **nervous system** is made up of a **complex network** of cells called **neurones**.
There are **three main types** of neurone:

- **Sensory neurones** transmit nerve impulses from **receptors** to the **central nervous system** (CNS) — the **brain** and **spinal cord**.
- **Motor neurones** transmit nerve impulses from the **CNS** to **effectors**.
- **Relay neurones** transmit nerve impulses **between** sensory neurones and motor neurones.

2) A stimulus is detected by **receptor cells** and a **nerve impulse** is sent along a **sensory neurone**.

3) When a **nerve impulse** reaches the end of a neurone chemicals called **neurotransmitters** take the information across to the **next neurone**, which then sends a **nerve impulse** (see p. 116).

4) The **CNS processes** the information, **decides what to do** about it and sends impulses along **motor neurones** to an **effector**.

> Nerve impulses are electrical impulses. They're also called action potentials.

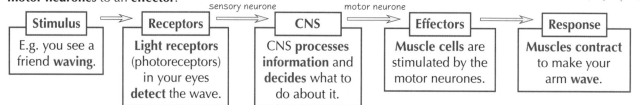

Stimulus		Receptors		CNS		Effectors		Response
E.g. you see a friend **waving**.		**Light receptors** (photoreceptors) in your eyes **detect** the wave.		CNS **processes information** and **decides** what to do about it.		**Muscle cells** are stimulated by the motor neurones.		**Muscles contract** to make your arm **wave**.

sensory neurone *motor neurone*

Sensory Receptors Convert Stimulus Energy into Nerve Impulses

1) **Different stimuli** have **different forms** of **energy**, e.g. light energy or chemical energy.

2) But your **nervous system** only sends information in the form of **nerve impulses** (electrical impulses).

3) **Sensory receptors convert** the energy of a **stimulus** into **electrical energy**.

4) So, sensory receptors act as **transducers** — something that **converts** one form of energy into another.

5) Here's a bit more about how receptor cells that communicate information via the **nervous system** work:

- When a nervous system receptor is in its **resting state** (not being stimulated), there's a **difference in charge** between the **inside** and the **outside** of the cell — this is generated by ion pumps and ion channels. This means there's a **voltage** across the membrane. Voltage is also known as **potential difference**.

- The **potential difference** when a cell is at **rest** is called its **resting potential**. When a stimulus is detected, the cell membrane is **excited** and becomes **more permeable**, allowing **more ions** to move **in** and **out** of the cell — **altering** the potential difference. The **change** in **potential difference** due to a stimulus is called the **generator potential**.

- A **bigger stimulus** excites the membrane more, causing a **bigger movement** of ions and a **bigger change** in potential difference — so a **bigger generator potential** is produced.

- If the **generator potential** is **big enough** it'll trigger an **action potential** (nerve impulse) along a neurone. An action potential is only triggered if the generator potential reaches a certain level called the **threshold** level.

- If the stimulus is **too weak** the generator potential **won't reach** the **threshold**, so there's **no action potential**.

You Need to **Learn** the **Structure** of **Sensory Neurones**...

1) All neurones have a **cell body** with a **nucleus** (plus **cytoplasm** and all the other **organelles** you usually get in a cell).

2) The cell body has **extensions** that **connect** to **other neurones** — **dendrites** carry nerve impulses **towards** the **cell body**, and **axons** carry nerve impulses **away** from the **cell body**.

3) Sensory neurones have **one long dendrite** that carries nerve impulses from **receptor cells** to the **cell body**, and **one short axon** that carries nerve impulses from the **cell body** to the **CNS**.

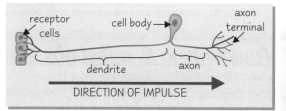

receptor cells — cell body — axon / axon terminal

dendrite — axon

DIRECTION OF IMPULSE

The Nervous System and Neurones

...and *Motor Neurones*

Motor neurones have **many short dendrites** that carry nerve impulses from the **central nervous system (CNS)** to the **cell body**, and **one long axon** that carries nerve impulses from the **cell body** to **effector cells**.

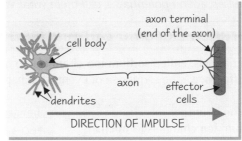

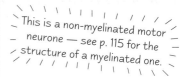
This is a non-myelinated motor neurone — see p. 115 for the structure of a myelinated one.

Neurone *Cell Membranes* are *Polarised* at *Rest*

1) In a neurone's **resting state** (when it's not being stimulated), the **outside** of the membrane is **positively charged** compared to the **inside**. This is because there are **more positive ions outside** the cell than inside.

2) So the membrane is **polarised** — there's a **difference in charge**.

3) The voltage across the membrane when it's at rest is called the **resting potential** — it's about **–70 mV**.

4) The resting potential is created and maintained by **sodium-potassium pumps** and **potassium ion channels** in a neurone's membrane:

Sodium-potassium pump		**Potassium ion channel**
These pumps use **active transport** to move **three sodium ions (Na$^+$) out** of the neurone for every **two potassium ions (K$^+$) moved in.** ATP is needed to do this.	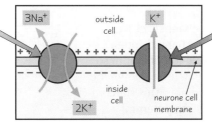	These channels allow **facilitated diffusion** of **potassium ions (K$^+$) out** of the neurone, down their **concentration gradient**.

- The sodium-potassium pumps move **sodium ions out** of the neurone, but the membrane **isn't permeable** to **sodium ions**, so they **can't diffuse back in**. This creates a **sodium ion electrochemical gradient** (a **concentration gradient** of **ions**) because there are **more** positive sodium ions **outside** the cell than inside.

- The sodium-potassium pumps also move **potassium ions in** to the neurone, but the membrane **is permeable** to **potassium ions** so they **diffuse back out** through potassium ion channels.

- This makes the **outside** of the cell **positively charged** compared to the inside.

Practice Questions

Q1 What is the function of a motor neurone?

Q2 What do sensory receptors convert energy into?

Q3 Name the pumps and channels that maintain a neurone's resting potential.

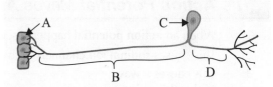

Exam Question

Q1 Bright light causes circular iris muscles in an animal's eyes to contract, which constricts the pupils and protects the eyes. Describe and explain the roles of receptors and effectors for this response. [5 marks]

Q2 The diagram above is of a sensory neurone. Name parts A to D. [4 marks]

Vacancy — talented gag writer required for boring biology topics...

Actually, it's not that boring, it's just all the stuff about sensory receptors and resting potentials can be a bit tricky to get your head around. Just take your time and try scribbling it all down a few times till it starts to make some kind of sense. Then you can finish off by drawing loads of sensory and motor neurones, until you can label them in your sleep.

Action Potentials

Electrical impulses, nerve impulses, action potentials... call them what you will, you need to know how they work.

Neurone **Cell Membranes** Become **Depolarised** when they're **Stimulated**

A **stimulus** triggers other ion channels, called **sodium ion channels**, to **open**. If the stimulus is big enough, it'll trigger a **rapid change** in **potential difference**. The sequence of events that happen are known as an **action potential**:

① **Stimulus** — this **excites** the neurone cell membrane, causing **sodium ion channels** to **open**. The membrane becomes **more permeable** to sodium, so **sodium ions diffuse into** the neurone down the sodium ion electrochemical gradient. This makes the **inside** of the neurone **less negative**.

② **Depolarisation** — if the potential difference reaches the **threshold** (around **−55 mV**), **voltage-gated sodium ion channels open**. More sodium ions diffuse into the neurone.

> *Voltage-gated ion channels open at a certain voltage.*

③ **Repolarisation** — at a potential difference of around **+30 mV** the **sodium ion channels close** and **voltage-gated potassium ion channels open**. The membrane is **more permeable** to potassium so **potassium ions diffuse out** of the neurone down the potassium ion concentration gradient. This starts to get the membrane **back** to its **resting potential**.

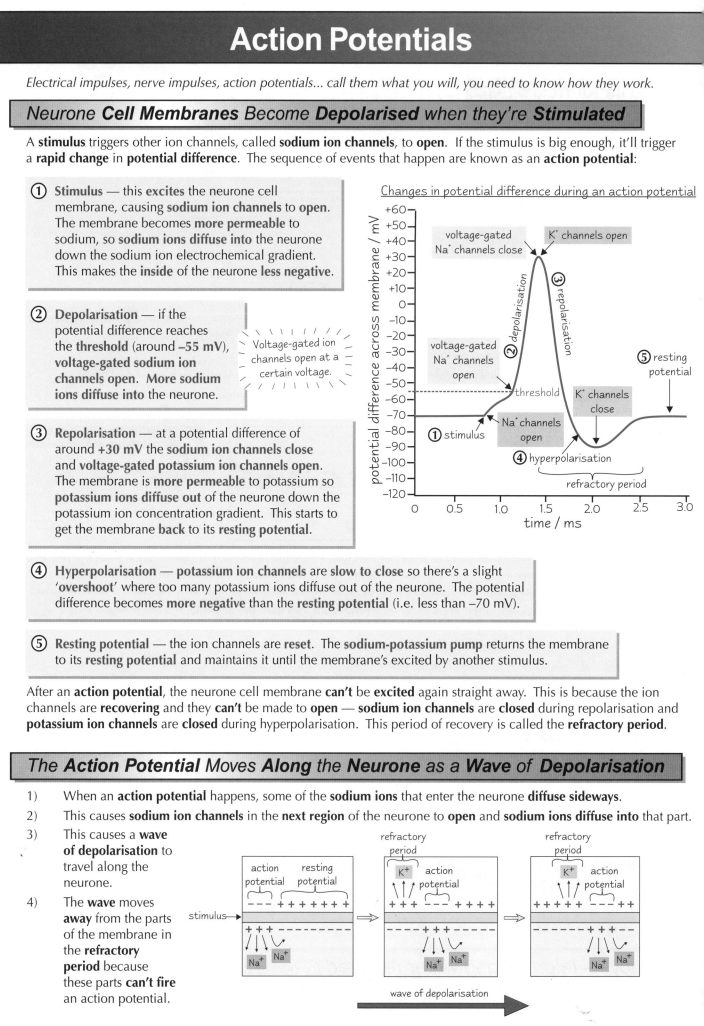

Changes in potential difference during an action potential

④ **Hyperpolarisation** — **potassium ion channels** are **slow to close** so there's a slight 'overshoot' where too many potassium ions diffuse out of the neurone. The potential difference becomes **more negative** than the **resting potential** (i.e. less than −70 mV).

⑤ **Resting potential** — the ion channels are **reset**. The **sodium-potassium pump** returns the membrane to its **resting potential** and maintains it until the membrane's excited by another stimulus.

After an **action potential**, the neurone cell membrane **can't** be **excited** again straight away. This is because the ion channels are **recovering** and they **can't** be made to **open** — sodium ion channels are **closed** during repolarisation and **potassium ion channels** are **closed** during hyperpolarisation. This period of recovery is called the **refractory period**.

The **Action Potential** Moves **Along** the **Neurone** as a **Wave** of **Depolarisation**

1) When an **action potential** happens, some of the **sodium ions** that enter the neurone **diffuse sideways**.

2) This causes **sodium ion channels** in the **next region** of the neurone to **open** and **sodium ions diffuse into** that part.

3) This causes a **wave of depolarisation** to travel along the neurone.

4) The **wave** moves **away** from the parts of the membrane in the **refractory period** because these parts **can't fire** an action potential.

wave of depolarisation

Action Potentials

A *Bigger Stimulus* Causes *More Frequent Impulses*

1) Once the threshold is reached, an action potential will **always fire** with the **same change in voltage**, no matter how big the stimulus is.

2) If **threshold isn't reached**, an action potential **won't fire**.

3) A **bigger stimulus** won't cause a bigger action potential, but it will cause them to fire **more frequently**.

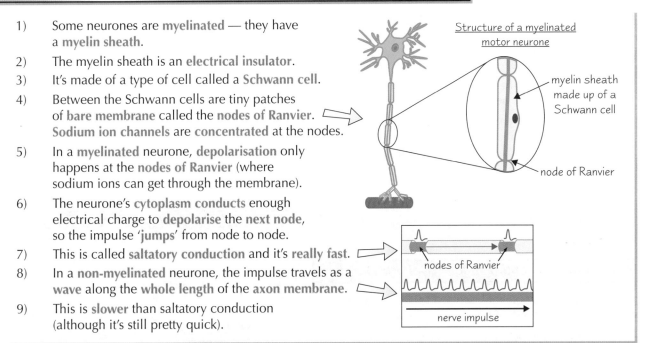

Action Potentials Go Faster in *Myelinated Neurones*

1) Some neurones are **myelinated** — they have a **myelin sheath**.

2) The myelin sheath is an **electrical insulator**.

3) It's made of a type of cell called a **Schwann cell**.

4) Between the Schwann cells are tiny patches of **bare membrane** called the **nodes of Ranvier**. **Sodium ion channels** are **concentrated** at the nodes.

5) In a **myelinated** neurone, **depolarisation** only happens at the **nodes of Ranvier** (where sodium ions can get through the membrane).

6) The neurone's **cytoplasm conducts** enough electrical charge to **depolarise** the **next node**, so the impulse 'jumps' from node to node.

7) This is called **saltatory conduction** and it's **really fast**.

8) In a **non-myelinated** neurone, the impulse travels as a **wave** along the **whole length** of the **axon membrane**.

9) This is **slower** than saltatory conduction (although it's still pretty quick).

Practice Questions

Q1 Briefly describe how an action potential moves along a neurone.

Q2 What are nodes of Ranvier?

Exam Questions

Q1 The graph shows an action potential across an axon membrane following the application of a stimulus.

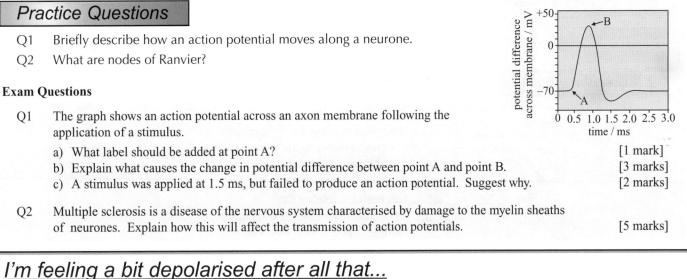

a) What label should be added at point A? [1 mark]
b) Explain what causes the change in potential difference between point A and point B. [3 marks]
c) A stimulus was applied at 1.5 ms, but failed to produce an action potential. Suggest why. [2 marks]

Q2 Multiple sclerosis is a disease of the nervous system characterised by damage to the myelin sheaths of neurones. Explain how this will affect the transmission of action potentials. [5 marks]

I'm feeling a bit depolarised after all that...

Action potentials are potentially confusing. The way I remember them is that polarisation is a difference in charge across a cell's membrane — during depolarisation that difference becomes smaller and during repolarisation it gets bigger again.

Synapses

When an action potential arrives at the end of a neurone the information has to be passed on to the next cell — this could be another neurone, a muscle cell or a gland cell.

A **Synapse** is a **Junction** Between a **Neurone** and the **Next Cell**

1) A **synapse** is the junction between a **neurone** and another **neurone**, or between a **neurone** and an **effector cell**, e.g. a muscle or gland cell.

2) The **tiny gap** between the cells at a synapse is called the **synaptic cleft**.

3) The **presynaptic neurone** (the one before the synapse) has a **swelling** called a **synaptic knob**. This contains **synaptic vesicles** filled with **chemicals** called **neurotransmitters**.

4) When an **action potential** reaches the end of a neurone it causes **neurotransmitters** to be **released** into the synaptic cleft. They **diffuse across** to the **postsynaptic membrane** (the one after the synapse) and **bind** to **specific receptors**.

5) When neurotransmitters bind to receptors they might **trigger** an **action potential** (in a neurone), cause **muscle contraction** (in a muscle cell), or cause a **hormone** to be **secreted** (from a gland cell).

6) Neurotransmitters are **removed** from the **cleft** so the **response** doesn't keep happening, e.g. they're taken back into the **presynaptic neurone** or they're **broken down** by **enzymes** (and the products are taken into the neurone).

7) There are many **different** neurotransmitters, e.g. **acetylcholine (ACh)** and **noradrenaline**. Synapses that use acetylcholine are called **cholinergic synapses**. Their structure is exactly the **same** as in the diagram above. They bind to receptors called **cholinergic receptors**, and they're broken down by an enzyme called **acetylcholinesterase (AChE)**.

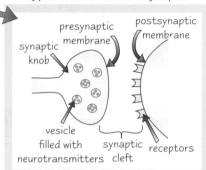

Typical structure of a synapse

presynaptic membrane
postsynaptic membrane
synaptic knob
vesicle filled with neurotransmitters
synaptic cleft
receptors

Here's How **Neurotransmitters Transmit Nerve Impulses Between Neurones**

1 An **Action Potential** Triggers **Calcium Influx**

1) An action potential (see p. 114) arrives at the **synaptic knob** of the **presynaptic neurone**.

2) The action potential stimulates **voltage-gated calcium ion channels** in the **presynaptic neurone** to **open**.

3) **Calcium ions diffuse into** the synaptic knob. (They're pumped out afterwards by active transport.)

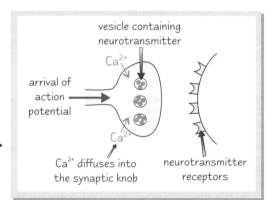

vesicle containing neurotransmitter
Ca^{2+}
arrival of action potential
Ca^{2+}
Ca^{2+} diffuses into the synaptic knob
neurotransmitter receptors

2 **Calcium Influx** Causes **Neurotransmitter Release**

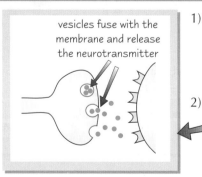

vesicles fuse with the membrane and release the neurotransmitter

1) The influx of **calcium ions** into the synaptic knob causes the **synaptic vesicles** to **move** to the **presynaptic membrane**. They then **fuse** with the presynaptic membrane.

2) The **vesicles release** the neurotransmitter into the **synaptic cleft** — this is called **exocytosis**.

Synapses

③ The *Neurotransmitter* *Triggers* an *Action Potential* in the *Postsynaptic Neurone*

1) The neurotransmitter **diffuses** across the **synaptic cleft** and **binds** to specific **receptors** on the **postsynaptic membrane**.

2) This causes **sodium ion channels** in the **postsynaptic neurone** to **open**.

3) The **influx** of **sodium ions** into the postsynaptic membrane causes **depolarisation**. An **action potential** on the **postsynaptic membrane** is generated if the **threshold** is reached.

4) The **neurotransmitter** is **removed** from the **synaptic cleft** so the **response** doesn't keep happening.

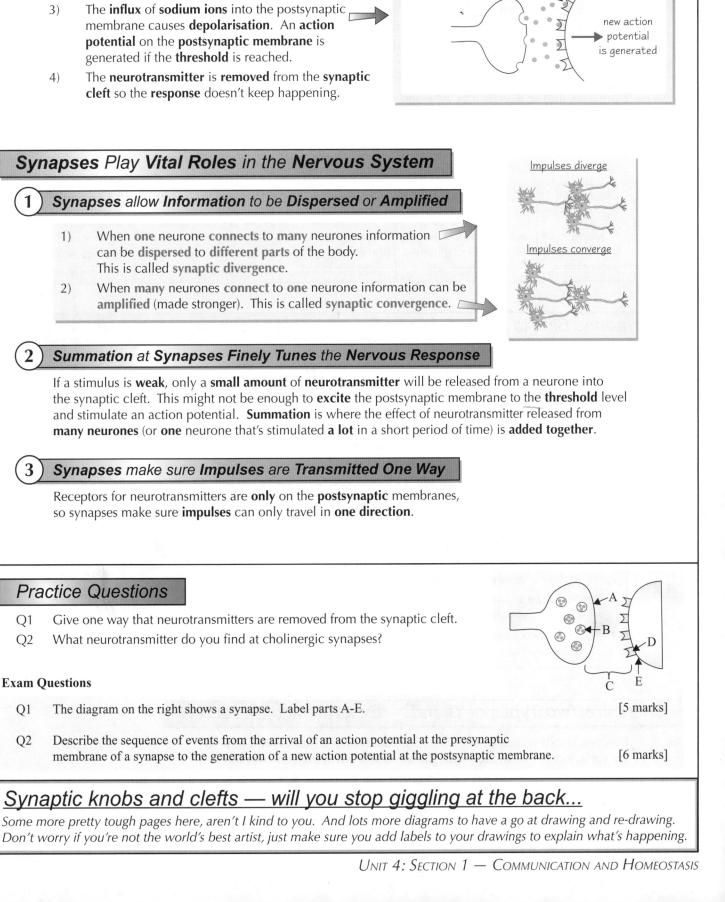

neurotransmitter diffuses across and binds to receptors

new action potential is generated

Synapses Play **Vital Roles** in the **Nervous System**

① *Synapses* allow *Information* to be *Dispersed* or *Amplified*

1) When **one** neurone **connects** to **many** neurones information can be **dispersed** to **different parts** of the body. This is called **synaptic divergence**.

2) When **many** neurones **connect** to **one** neurone information can be **amplified** (made stronger). This is called **synaptic convergence**.

Impulses diverge

Impulses converge

② *Summation* at *Synapses Finely Tunes* the *Nervous Response*

If a stimulus is **weak**, only a **small amount** of **neurotransmitter** will be released from a neurone into the synaptic cleft. This might not be enough to **excite** the postsynaptic membrane to the **threshold** level and stimulate an action potential. **Summation** is where the effect of neurotransmitter released from **many neurones** (or **one** neurone that's stimulated **a lot** in a short period of time) is **added together**.

③ *Synapses* make sure *Impulses* are *Transmitted One Way*

Receptors for neurotransmitters are **only** on the **postsynaptic** membranes, so synapses make sure **impulses** can only travel in **one direction**.

Practice Questions

Q1 Give one way that neurotransmitters are removed from the synaptic cleft.

Q2 What neurotransmitter do you find at cholinergic synapses?

Exam Questions

Q1 The diagram on the right shows a synapse. Label parts A-E. [5 marks]

Q2 Describe the sequence of events from the arrival of an action potential at the presynaptic membrane of a synapse to the generation of a new action potential at the postsynaptic membrane. [6 marks]

Synaptic knobs and clefts — will you stop giggling at the back...

Some more pretty tough pages here, aren't I kind to you. And lots more diagrams to have a go at drawing and re-drawing. Don't worry if you're not the world's best artist, just make sure you add labels to your drawings to explain what's happening.

The Hormonal System and Glands

Now you've seen how the nervous system helps us respond to our environment, it's on to the hormonal system...

The **Hormonal System** Sends Information as **Chemical Signals**

1) The **hormonal system** is made up of **glands** (called **endocrine glands**) and **hormones**:
   - **Endocrine glands** are groups of cells that are specialised to **secrete hormones**. E.g. the **pancreas** secretes **insulin**.
   - **Hormones** are '**chemical messengers**'. Many hormones are **proteins** or **peptides**, e.g. **insulin**. Some hormones are **steroids**, e.g. **progesterone**.

   The hormonal system is also called the endocrine system.

2) **Hormones** are **secreted** when an **endocrine gland** is **stimulated**:
   - Glands can be **stimulated** by a **change** in **concentration** of a specific **substance** (sometimes **another hormone**).
   - They can also be **stimulated** by **electrical impulses**.

3) Hormones **diffuse directly into** the **blood**, then they're **taken** around the body by the **circulatory system**.

4) They **diffuse out** of the blood **all over** the **body** but each hormone will only **bind to specific receptors** for that hormone, found on the membranes of some cells, called **target cells**. Tissue that contains target cells is called **target tissue**.

5) The hormones trigger a **response** in the **target cells** (the **effectors**).

Stimulus	→	Receptors	→	Hormone	→	Effectors	→	Response
E.g. **low blood glucose** concentration.		**Receptors** on **pancreas** cells detect the low blood glucose concentration.		The pancreas **releases** the hormone **glucagon** into the blood.		**Target cells** in the **liver** detect glucagon and convert glycogen into glucose.		**Glucose** is released into the blood, so **glucose** concentration **increases**.

Hormones Bind to **Receptors** and Cause a **Response** via **Second Messengers**

1) A **hormone** is called a **first messenger** because it carries the chemical message the **first part** of the way, from the **endocrine gland** to the **receptor** on the **target cells**.

2) When a hormone **binds** to its receptor it **activates** an **enzyme** in the **cell membrane**.

3) The enzyme catalyses the **production** of a **molecule** inside the cell called a **signalling molecule** — this molecule **signals** to **other parts** of the cell to **change** how the cell **works**.

4) The **signalling molecule** is called a **second messenger** because it carries the chemical message the **second part** of the way, from the **receptor** to **other parts** of the **cell**.

5) Second messengers **activate** a **cascade** (a chain of reactions) **inside** the cell. Here's an **example** you need to **learn**:

- The hormone **adrenaline** is a **first messenger**.
- It binds to **specific receptors** in the **cell membranes** of many cells, e.g. liver cells.
- When adrenaline binds it **activates** an **enzyme** in the membrane called **adenylate cyclase**.
- **Activated adenylate cyclase** catalyses the production of a **second messenger** called **cyclic AMP** (**cAMP**).
- cAMP **activates** a **cascade**, e.g. a cascade of enzyme reactions make **more glucose available** to the cell.

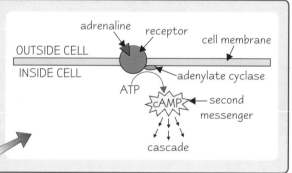

There are **Two Types** of Gland — **Exocrine** and **Endocrine**

1) Exocrine glands secrete chemicals through **ducts** (tubes) into **cavities** or onto the **surface** of the body, e.g. **sweat glands** secrete **sweat** onto the **skin surface**.

2) They usually secrete **enzymes**, e.g. **digestive glands** secrete **digestive enzymes** into the **gut**.

3) **Endocrine** glands secrete **hormones directly** into the **blood**.

4) **Some organs** have exocrine tissue **and** endocrine tissue, so act as both types of gland.

The Hormonal System and Glands

The Pancreas is an Exocrine and an Endocrine Gland

The pancreas is a gland that's found **below** the **stomach**.
You need to know about its exocrine function and its endocrine function:

Exocrine function of the pancreas

1) **Most** of the pancreas is exocrine tissue.
2) The exocrine cells are called **acinar cells**.
3) They're found in **clusters** around the **pancreatic duct** — a duct that goes to the **duodenum** (part of the small intestine).
4) The acinar cells **secrete digestive enzymes** into the **pancreatic duct**.
5) The enzymes **digest food** in the **duodenum**, e.g. **amylase** breaks down **starch** to **glucose**.

Endocrine function of the pancreas

1) The areas of **endocrine** tissue are called the **islets of Langerhans**.
2) They're found in clusters around **blood capillaries**.
3) The islets of Langerhans **secrete hormones** directly into the **blood**.
4) They're made up of **two types** of cell:
   - **Alpha (α) cells** secrete a **hormone** called **glucagon**.
   - **Beta (β) cells** secrete a **hormone** called **insulin**.
5) **Glucagon** and **insulin** help to **control blood glucose concentration** (see p. 122).

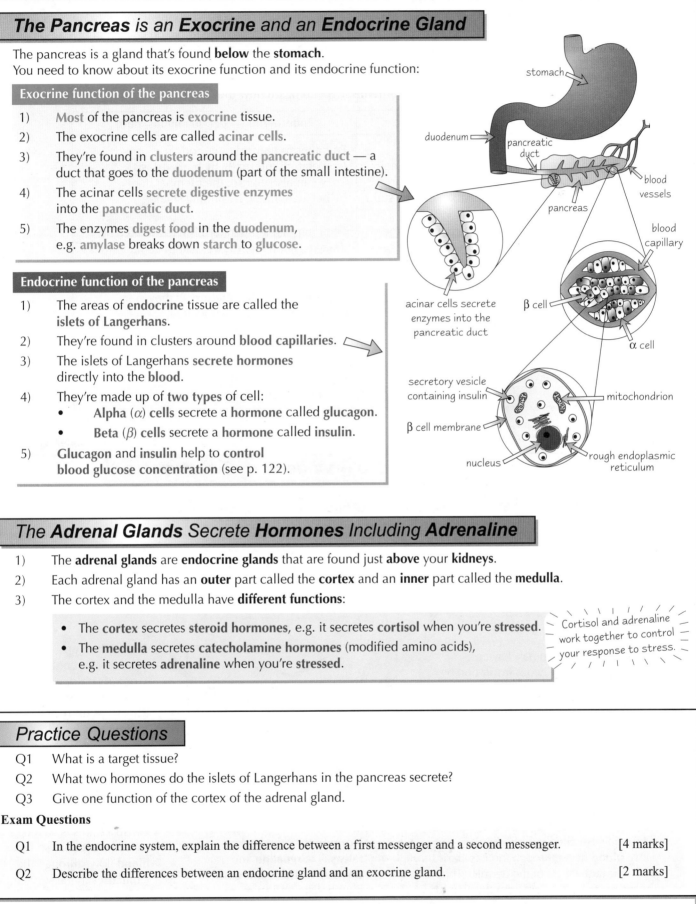

acinar cells secrete enzymes into the pancreatic duct

β cell — α cell — secretory vesicle containing insulin — mitochondrion — β cell membrane — nucleus — rough endoplasmic reticulum

The Adrenal Glands Secrete Hormones Including Adrenaline

1) The **adrenal glands** are **endocrine glands** that are found just **above** your **kidneys**.
2) Each adrenal gland has an **outer** part called the **cortex** and an **inner** part called the **medulla**.
3) The cortex and the medulla have **different functions**:

- The **cortex** secretes **steroid hormones**, e.g. it secretes **cortisol** when you're **stressed**.
- The **medulla** secretes **catecholamine hormones** (modified amino acids), e.g. it secretes **adrenaline** when you're **stressed**.

Cortisol and adrenaline work together to control your response to stress.

Practice Questions

Q1 What is a target tissue?
Q2 What two hormones do the islets of Langerhans in the pancreas secrete?
Q3 Give one function of the cortex of the adrenal gland.

Exam Questions

Q1 In the endocrine system, explain the difference between a first messenger and a second messenger. [4 marks]
Q2 Describe the differences between an endocrine gland and an exocrine gland. [2 marks]

Islets of Langerhans — sounds like an exotic beach to me...

All this talk of the "islets of Langerhans" and I can think of nothing else but sun, sea and sand... but it's secretions, second messengers and cyclic AMP for you, until your exams are over and you can start planning any holidays.

Homeostasis — Control of Body Temperature

Homeostasis is responsible for controlling body temperature in mammals like you — stopping you freezing or becoming a hot sweaty mess. Other organisms control their body temperature differently. Read on, oh chosen one, read on...

Temperature *is* Controlled Differently *in* Ectotherms *and* Endotherms

Animals are classed as either **ectotherms** or **endotherms**, depending on how they **control** their body temperature:

Ectotherms — e.g. reptiles, fish	Endotherms — e.g. mammals, birds
Ectotherms **can't control** their body temperature **internally** — they **control** their temperature by **changing** their **behaviour** (e.g. reptiles gain heat by basking in the sun).	Endotherms **control** their body temperature **internally** by **homeostasis**. They can also control their temperature by **behaviour** (e.g. by finding shade).
Their **internal** temperature **depends** on the **external temperature** (their surroundings).	Their internal temperature is **less affected** by the **external temperature** (within certain limits).
Their **activity** level **depends** on the external temperature — they're **more** active at **higher** temperatures and **less** active at **lower** temperatures.	Their **activity** level is largely **independent** of the **external temperature** — they can be active at any temperature (within certain limits).
They have a **variable metabolic rate** and they **generate** very **little heat** themselves.	They have a constantly **high metabolic rate** and they **generate** a **lot of heat** from metabolic reactions.

Mammals *have* Many Mechanisms *to* Change Body Temperature

Mechanisms to REDUCE body temperature:

Sweating — **more sweat** is secreted from **sweat glands** when the body's too hot. The water in sweat **evaporates** from the surface of the skin and **takes heat** from the body. The **skin is cooled**.

Hairs lie flat — mammals have a layer of **hair** that provides **insulation** by **trapping air** (air is a poor conductor of heat). When it's hot, **erector pili muscles relax** so the hairs lie flat. **Less air** is trapped, so the skin is **less insulated** and **heat** can be **lost** more easily.

Vasodilation — when it's hot, **arterioles** near the surface of the skin **dilate** (this is called **vasodilation**). **More blood** flows through the **capillaries** in the surface layers of the dermis. This means **more heat** is **lost** from the skin by **radiation** and the **temperature** is **lowered**.

Mechanisms to INCREASE body temperature:

Shivering — when it's cold, **muscles contract** in **spasms**. This makes the body **shiver** and **more heat** is **produced** from **increased respiration**.

Hormones — the body releases **adrenaline** and **thyroxine**. These **increase metabolism** and so **more heat is produced**.

Much less sweat — **less sweat** is secreted from sweat glands when it's cold, **reducing** the amount of **heat loss**.

Hairs stand up — **erector pili muscles contract** when it's cold, which makes the **hairs stand up**. This **traps more air** and so **prevents heat loss**.

Vasoconstriction — when it's cold, **arterioles** near the surface of the skin **constrict** (this is called **vasoconstriction**) so **less blood** flows through the **capillaries** in the surface layers of the dermis. This **reduces heat loss**.

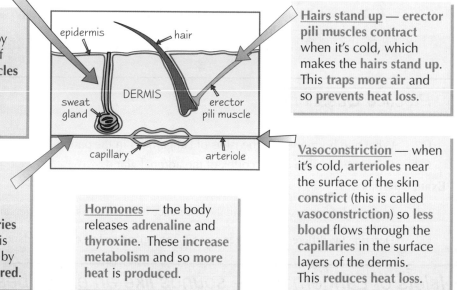

epidermis · hair · DERMIS · sweat gland · erector pili muscle · capillary · arteriole

Homeostasis — Control of Body Temperature

The **Hypothalamus Controls** Body Temperature in **Mammals**

1) **Body temperature** in mammals is **maintained** at a **constant level** by a part of the **brain** called the **hypothalamus**.

2) The hypothalamus **receives information** about **temperature** from **thermoreceptors** (temperature receptors):

 • Thermoreceptors in the **hypothalamus** detect **internal temperature** (the temperature of the blood).

 • Thermoreceptors in the **skin** (called **peripheral temperature receptors**) detect **external temperature** (the temperature of the skin).

3) Thermoreceptors send **impulses** along **sensory neurones** to the **hypothalamus**, which sends **impulses** along **motor neurones** to **effectors** (e.g. **skeletal muscles**, or **sweat glands** and **erector pili muscles** in the **skin**).

4) The effectors respond to **restore** the body temperature **back to normal**. Here's how it all works:

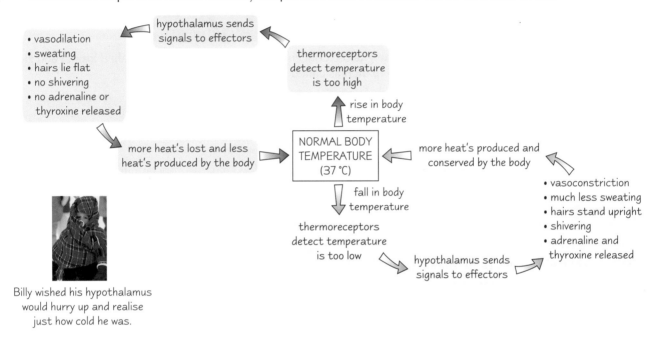

Billy wished his hypothalamus would hurry up and realise just how cold he was.

Practice Questions

Q1 Give four differences between ectotherms and endotherms.

Q2 Which type of animal has more control over their body temperature, ectotherms or endotherms?

Q3 How does sweating reduce body temperature?

Q4 How does vasodilation help the body to lose heat?

Q5 Which part of the brain is responsible for maintaining a constant body temperature in mammals?

Exam Questions

Q1 Snakes are usually found in warm climates. Suggest why they are not usually found in cold climates. Explain your answer. [4 marks]

Q2 Mammals that live in cold climates have thick fur and layers of fat beneath their skin to keep them warm. Describe and explain two other ways they maintain a constant body temperature in cold conditions. [4 marks]

Q3 Describe and explain how the body detects a high external temperature. [2 marks]

Sweat, hormones and erector muscles — ooooh errrrrrr...

The mechanisms that change body temperature are pretty good and can cope with some extreme temperatures, but I reckon I could think up some slightly less embarrassing ways of doing it, instead of getting all red-faced and stinky. Mind you, it seems like ectotherms have got it sussed with their whole sunbathing thing — now that's definitely the life...

Homeostasis — Control of Blood Glucose

These pages are all about how homeostasis helps you to not go totally hyper when you stuff your face with sweets.

Eating and Exercise Change the Concentration of Glucose in your Blood

1) **All cells** need a constant **energy supply** to work — so **blood glucose concentration** must be carefully **controlled**.

2) The **concentration** of **glucose** in the blood is **normally** around **90 mg per 100 cm³** of blood.
It's **monitored** by cells in the **pancreas**.

3) Blood glucose concentration **rises** after **eating food** containing **carbohydrate**.

4) Blood glucose concentration **falls** after **exercise**, as **more glucose** is used in **respiration** to **release energy**.

Insulin and Glucagon Control Blood Glucose Concentration

The hormonal system (see p. 118) **controls** blood glucose concentration using **two hormones** called **insulin** and **glucagon**.
They're both **secreted** by clusters of cells in the **pancreas** called the **islets of Langerhans**:

> **Beta (β) cells** secrete **insulin** into the blood.

> **Alpha (α) cells** secrete **glucagon** into the blood.

Insulin and glucagon act on **effectors**, which respond to **restore** the blood glucose concentration to the **normal level**:

Insulin lowers blood glucose concentration when it's too high

1) Insulin binds to **specific receptors** on the cell membranes of **liver cells** and **muscle cells**.

2) It **increases** the **permeability** of cell membranes to glucose, so the cells **take up more glucose**.

3) Insulin also **activates enzymes** that convert **glucose** into **glycogen**.

4) Cells are able to **store glycogen** in their cytoplasm, as an **energy source**.

5) The process of **forming glycogen** from glucose is called **glycogenesis**.

Liver cells are also called hepatocytes.

```
        activated
        by insulin
            │
            ▼
      glycogenesis
GLUCOSE ──────────→ GLYCOGEN
```

'Genesis' means 'making' — so glycogenesis means making glycogen.

6) Insulin also **increases** the **rate** of **respiration** of glucose, especially in muscle cells.

Glucagon raises blood glucose concentration when it's too low

1) Glucagon binds to **specific receptors** on the cell membranes of **liver cells**.

2) Glucagon **activates enzymes** that **break down glycogen** into **glucose**.

3) The process of **breaking down glycogen** is called **glycogenolysis**.

4) Glucagon also promotes the formation of glucose from **fatty acids** and **amino acids**.

5) The process of **forming glucose** from **non-carbohydrates** is called **gluconeogenesis**.

'Lysis' means 'splitting' — so glycogenolysis means splitting glycogen.

```
FATTY ACIDS                          glycogenesis
AMINO ACIDS ──────────→ GLUCOSE ⇄──────────── GLYCOGEN
          gluconeogenesis        glycogenolysis
                    ↖        ↗
                     activated
                     by glucagon
```

Melvin had finally mastered the ancient "chair-lysis" move.

6) Glucagon **decreases** the **rate** of **respiration** of glucose in cells.

Homeostasis — Control of Blood Glucose

Negative Feedback Mechanisms Keep Blood Glucose Concentration Normal

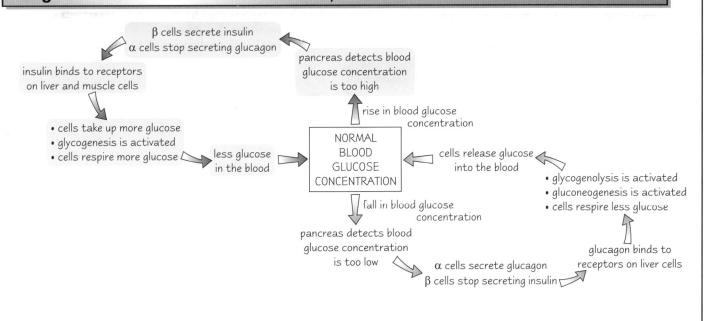

Beta (β) Cells Secrete Insulin when they're Depolarised

β cells **contain insulin** stored in **vesicles**. β cells **secrete insulin** when they **detect high blood glucose concentration**. Here's how it happens:

1) When blood glucose concentration is **high**, **more glucose enters** the β cells by **facilitated diffusion**.

2) **More glucose** in a β cell causes the rate of **respiration** to **increase**, making **more ATP**.

3) The **rise** in **ATP** triggers the **potassium ion channels** in the β cell plasma membrane to **close**.

4) This means **potassium ions** (K⁺) **can't** get through the membrane — so they **build up inside** the cell.

5) This makes the **inside** of the β cell **less negative** because there are **more positively-charged** potassium ions **inside** the cell — so the plasma membrane of the β cell is **depolarised**.

6) Depolarisation triggers **calcium ion channels** in the membrane to **open**, so **calcium ions diffuse into** the β cell.

7) This causes the **vesicles** to **fuse** with the **β cell plasma membrane**, releasing insulin (this is called **exocytosis**).

Practice Questions

Q1   Why does your blood glucose concentration fall after exercise?

Q2   What's the process of breaking down glycogen into glucose called?

Q3   Give two effects of glucagon on liver cells.

Exam Questions

Q1   Describe and explain how hormones return blood glucose concentration to normal after a meal.   [5 marks]

Q2   Suggest the effect on a β cell of respiration being inhibited.   [2 marks]

My α cells detect low glucose — urgent tea and biscuit break needed...

Aaaaargh there are so many stupidly complex names to learn and they all look and sound exactly the same to me.
You can't even get away with sneakily misspelling them all in your exam — like writing 'glycusogen' or 'glucogenesisolysis'.
Nope, examiners have been around for centuries, so I'm afraid old tricks like that just won't work on them. Grrrrrrr.

Diabetes and Control of Heart Rate

Phew, finally the last two pages in the section. Just a couple of loose ends to tidy up and you're home free.

Diabetes Occurs when Blood Glucose Concentration is Not Controlled

Diabetes mellitus is a condition where **blood glucose** concentration **can't** be **controlled** properly. There are **two types**:

Type I diabetes (also called insulin-dependent diabetes)

1) In Type I diabetes, the β cells in the islets of Langerhans **don't produce** any **insulin**.

2) After **eating**, the blood glucose level **rises** and **stays high** — this is a condition called **hyperglycaemia**, which can result in **death** if left untreated.
The kidneys **can't reabsorb** all this glucose, so some of it's **excreted** in the urine.

3) Type 1 diabetes usually develops in children or young adults.

Type II diabetes (also called non-insulin-dependent diabetes)

1) **Type II** diabetes is usually acquired **later** in **life** than Type I, and it's often linked with **obesity**.

2) It occurs when the β cells **don't produce enough insulin** or when the body's **cells don't respond** properly to **insulin**. Cells don't respond properly because the insulin **receptors** on their membranes **don't work** properly, so the cells **don't** take up enough glucose. This means the **blood glucose concentration** is **higher** than normal.

Insulin can be Produced by Genetically Modified Bacteria

1) Insulin **used** to be **extracted** from **animal pancreases** (e.g. **pigs** and **cattle**), to treat people with **Type I** diabetes.

2) But **nowadays**, **human insulin** can be made by **genetically modified (GM) bacteria** (see p. 186).

3) Using **GM bacteria** to produce insulin is **much better** for many reasons, for example:

- **Producing** insulin using GM bacteria is **cheaper** than extracting it from animal pancreases.
- **Larger quantities** of insulin can be produced using GM bacteria.
- GM bacteria make **human insulin**. This is **more effective** than using **pig** or **cattle insulin** (which is slightly different to human insulin) and it's **less likely** to trigger an **allergic response** or be **rejected** by the **immune system**.
- Some people **prefer** insulin from **GM bacteria** for **ethical** or **religious** reasons. E.g. some **vegetarians** may **object** to the **use** of **animals**, and some **religious people object** to using insulin from **pigs**.

Stem Cells Could be Used to Cure Diabetes

1) Stem cells are **unspecialised cells** — they have the **ability** to **develop** into **any type** of cell.

2) Using stem cells could **potentially cure** diabetes — here's how:

- **Stem cells** could be **grown** into β **cells**.
- The β cells would then be **implanted** into the **pancreas** of a person with **Type I diabetes**.
- This means the person would be able to **make insulin** as **normal**.
- This treatment is **still being developed**. But if it's effective, it'll **cure** people with Type I diabetes — they **won't** have to have **regular injections** of **insulin**.

Look back at p. 24 if you need to remind yourself about stem cells.

Diabetes and Control of Heart Rate

The Control of Heart Rate Involves Both the Nervous and Hormonal Systems

The **nervous system** helps to control heart rate in these ways:

1) The **sinoatrial node (SAN)** generates **electrical impulses** that cause the **cardiac muscles** to **contract**.

2) The **rate** at which the SAN fires (i.e. heart rate) is **unconsciously controlled** by a part of the **brain** called the **medulla**.

3) Animals need to **alter** their **heart rate** to **respond** to **internal stimuli**, e.g. to prevent fainting due to low blood pressure or to make sure the heart rate is high enough to supply the body with enough oxygen.

4) **Stimuli** are **detected** by **pressure receptors** and **chemical receptors**:

- There are **pressure receptors** called **baroreceptors** in the **aorta** and the **vena cava**. They're stimulated by **high** and **low blood pressure**.

- There are **chemical receptors** called **chemoreceptors** in the **aorta**, the **carotid artery** (a major artery in the neck) and in the **medulla**. They **monitor** the **oxygen** level in the **blood** and also **carbon dioxide** and **pH** (which are indicators of O_2 level).

5) Electrical impulses from receptors are sent **to the medulla** along **sensory** neurones. The medulla processes the information and sends impulses to the SAN along **motor** neurones. Here's how it all works:

STIMULUS	RECEPTOR	NEURONE	EFFECTOR	RESPONSE
High blood pressure.	Baroreceptors detect high blood pressure.	Impulses are sent to the medulla, which sends impulses along the vagus nerve. This secretes acetylcholine, which binds to receptors on the SAN.	Cardiac muscles	Heart rate slows down to reduce blood pressure back to normal.
Low blood pressure.	Baroreceptors detect low blood pressure.	Impulses are sent to the medulla, which sends impulses along the accelerator nerve. This secretes noradrenaline, which binds to receptors on the SAN.	Cardiac muscles	Heart rate speeds up to increase blood pressure back to normal.
High blood O_2, low CO_2 or high pH levels.	Chemoreceptors detect chemical changes in the blood.	Impulses are sent to the medulla, which sends impulses along the vagus nerve. This secretes acetylcholine, which binds to receptors on the SAN.	Cardiac muscles	Heart rate decreases to return O_2, CO_2 and pH levels back to normal.
Low blood O_2, high CO_2 or low pH levels.	Chemoreceptors detect chemical changes in the blood.	Impulses are sent to the medulla, which sends impulses along the accelerator nerve. This secretes noradrenaline, which binds to receptors on the SAN.	Cardiac muscles	Heart rate increases to return O_2, CO_2 and pH levels back to normal.

The **hormonal system** helps to control heart rate in these ways:

1) When an organism is **threatened** (e.g. by a predator) the **adrenal glands** release **adrenaline**.

2) Adrenaline **binds** to **specific receptors** in the **heart**. This causes the cardiac muscle to **contract more frequently** and with **more force**, so **heart rate increases** and the heart **pumps more blood**.

Practice Questions

Q1 What is diabetes?

Q2 Briefly describe how stem cells could be used to cure diabetes.

Exam Questions

Q1 Explain why someone with diabetes can produce insulin but can't control their blood glucose concentration. [3 marks]

Q2 Give two advantages of using insulin produced by genetically modified (GM) bacteria over using insulin extracted from animal pancreases. [2 marks]

Q3 a) Explain how high blood pressure in the aorta causes the heart rate to slow down. [5 marks]
     b) What would be the effect of severing the nerves from the medulla to the sinoatrial node (SAN)? [2 marks]

My heart rate seems to be controlled by the boy next door...

So, the hormonal system can work with the nervous system to control processes such as heart rate. However, sometimes the hormonal system goes wrong and causes problems, like diabetes. Luckily advances in medical technology (e.g. synthetic insulin and stem cells) have helped to treat these problems. Congratulations, you've made it to the end of the first A2 section.

The Liver and Excretion

Liver — not just what your grandparents eat with onions. The liver has loads of functions, but the one you need to know about is its job in excretion. It's great at breaking things down like excess amino acids and other harmful substances.

Excretion is the Removal of Waste Products from the Body

All the **chemical reactions** that happen in your cells make up your **metabolism**. Metabolism produces **waste products** — substances that **aren't needed** by the cells, such as **carbon dioxide** and **nitrogenous** (nitrogen-containing) **waste**. Many of these products are **toxic**, so if they were allowed to **build up** in the body they would cause **damage**. This is where **excretion** comes in. Excretion is the **removal** of the **waste products of metabolism** from the body.

> For example, carbon dioxide is a waste product of respiration. **Too much** in the blood is toxic, so it's removed from the body by the lungs (e.g. in mammals) or gills (e.g. in fish). The lungs and gills act as **excretory organs**.

The Liver is Involved in Excretion

One of the functions of the **liver** is to **break down** metabolic waste products and other substances that can be **harmful**, like **drugs** and **alcohol**. They're broken down into **less harmful** products that can then be **excreted**.

You need to learn all the different **veins**, **arteries** and **ducts** connected to the liver:

1) The **hepatic artery** supplies the liver with **oxygenated blood** from the heart, so the liver has a good supply of **oxygen** for **respiration**, providing plenty of **energy**.

2) The **hepatic vein** takes **deoxygenated blood** away from the liver.

3) The **hepatic portal vein** brings blood from the **duodenum** and **ileum** (parts of the small intestine), so it's rich in the products of **digestion**. This means any ingested harmful substances are **filtered out** and **broken down straight away**.

4) The **bile duct** takes **bile** (a substance produced by the liver to **emulsify fats**) to the **gall bladder** to be **stored**.

You need to learn about the **structure** of the liver too:

1) The liver is made up of **liver lobules** — cylindrical structures made of **cells** called **hepatocytes** that are arranged in rows **radiating** out from the centre.

2) Each lobule has a **central vein** in the middle that connects to the **hepatic vein**. **Many branches** of the **hepatic artery**, **hepatic portal vein** and **bile duct** are also found connected to each lobule (only one of each is shown in the picture).

3) The **hepatic artery** and the **hepatic portal vein** are connected to the **central vein** by **capillaries** called **sinusoids**.

4) Blood runs **through** the sinusoids, past the hepatocytes that **remove harmful substances** and **oxygen** from the blood.

5) The harmful substances are **broken down** by the hepatocytes into **less harmful** substances that then **re-enter** the blood.

6) The blood runs to the **central vein**, and the central veins from all the lobules **connect** up to form the **hepatic vein**.

7) Cells called **Kupffer cells** are also attached to the walls of the sinusoids. They **remove bacteria** and **break down** old **red blood cells**.

8) The **bile duct** is connected to the **central vein** by tubes called **canaliculi**.

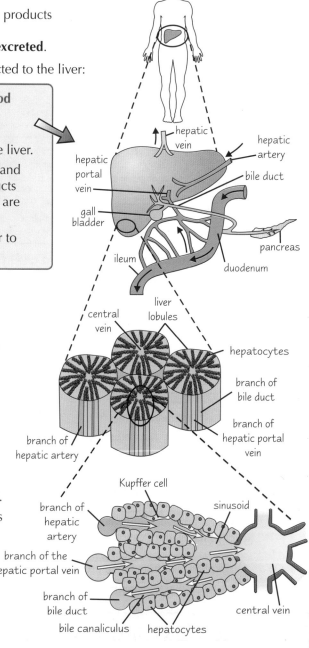

The Liver and Excretion

Excess Amino Acids are Broken Down by the Liver

One of the liver's most important roles is getting rid of **excess amino acids** produced by eating and **digesting protein**.
Amino acids contain **nitrogen** in their **amino groups**. **Nitrogenous substances can't** usually be **stored** by the body.
This means **excess** amino acids can be **damaging** to the body, so they must be **used** by the body (e.g. to make
proteins) or be **broken down and excreted**. Here's how excess amino acids are **broken down** in the **liver**:

1) First, the nitrogen-containing amino groups are removed from any
   excess amino acids, forming ammonia and organic acids — this process
   is called deamination.

2) The organic acids can be respired to give ATP or converted to carbohydrate
   and stored as glycogen.

3) Ammonia is too toxic for mammals to excrete directly, so it's combined with
   CO_2 in the ornithine cycle to create urea.

4) The urea is released from the liver into the blood. The kidneys then filter the blood
   and remove the urea as urine (see p. 128-129), which is excreted from the body.

Josie felt that warm feeling
that meant a little bit of
urea had just slipped out.

The Liver Removes Other Harmful Substances from the Blood

The **liver** also breaks down other harmful substances, like **alcohol**, **drugs** and **unwanted hormones**.
They're broken down into **less harmful compounds** that can then be **excreted** from the body
— this process is called **detoxification**. Some of the harmful products broken down by the liver include:

1) Alcohol (ethanol) — a toxic substance that can damage cells. It's broken down by the liver
   into ethanal, which is then broken down into a less harmful substance called acetic acid.
   Excess alcohol over a long period can lead to cirrhosis of the liver — this is when the cells
   of the liver die and scar tissue blocks blood flow.

2) Paracetamol — a common painkiller that's broken down by the liver.
   Excess paracetamol in the blood can lead to liver and kidney failure.

3) Insulin — a hormone that controls blood glucose concentration (see page 122). Insulin is
   also broken down by the liver as excess insulin can cause problems with blood sugar levels.

Practice Questions

Q1 Define excretion.
Q2 Why is excretion needed?
Q3 Which blood vessel brings oxygenated blood to the liver?
Q4 Name the blood vessel that brings blood to the liver from the small intestine.
Q5 What are liver lobules?

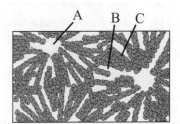

Exam Questions

Q1 Name the parts of the liver shown in the diagram on the right. [3 marks]

Q2 Explain why the concentration of urea in urine might increase after eating a meal that's rich in protein. [6 marks]

Lots of important functions — can't liver without it...

*Poor little amino acids, doing no harm then suddenly they're broken down and excreted. As upsetting as it is, however,
you need to learn how they're broken down in the liver. It's a heart-wrenching tale of separation — the amino group
and the organic acid are torn from each other's life. Right, enough of that nonsense. Learn it and learn it good.*

The Kidneys and Excretion

So you've learnt about how the liver does a pretty good job at breaking down stuff for excretion.
Now you get to learn that the kidneys like to play a part in this excretion malarkey too...

The **Kidneys** are **Organs** of **Excretion**

One of the main **functions** of the **kidneys** is to **excrete waste products**, e.g. **urea** produced by
the **liver**. They also **regulate** the body's **water content** (see p. 130-131). Here's an overview
of how they excrete waste products (you need to **learn** the **structure** of the kidneys too):

1) Blood **enters** the kidney through the **renal artery** and then
passes through **capillaries** in the **cortex** of the kidneys.

2) As the blood passes through the capillaries, **substances**
are **filtered out of the blood** and into **long tubules** that surround
the capillaries. This process is called **ultrafiltration** (see below).

3) **Useful substances** (e.g. glucose) are **reabsorbed** back into
the blood from the tubules in the **medulla** — this is called
selective reabsorption (see next page).

4) The remaining **unwanted substances** (e.g. urea) pass along
the tubules, then along the **ureter** to the **bladder**,
where they're **expelled** as **urine**.

5) The filtered blood passes out of the kidneys through the **renal vein**.

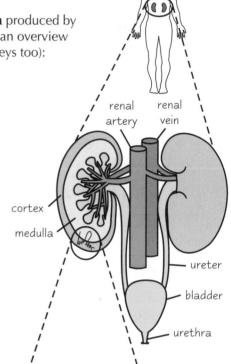

Blood is **Filtered** at the **Start** of the **Nephrons**

The **long tubules** along with the bundle of **capillaries**
where the blood is **filtered** are called **nephrons**
— there are **thousands** of nephrons in each kidney.

1) Blood from the **renal artery** enters smaller
arterioles in the **cortex**.

2) Each arteriole splits into a structure called a **glomerulus**
— a **bundle** of **capillaries** looped inside a hollow ball
called a **renal capsule** (or **Bowman's capsule**).

3) This is where **ultrafiltration** takes place.

4) The **arteriole** that takes blood **into** each glomerulus
is called the **afferent** arteriole, and the arteriole
that takes the filtered blood **away** from the
glomerulus is called the **efferent** arteriole.

5) The **efferent** arteriole is **smaller** in **diameter** than the afferent
arteriole, so the blood in the glomerulus is under **high pressure**.

6) The high pressure **forces liquid** and **small molecules**
in the blood **out** of the **capillary** and **into** the **renal capsule**.

7) The liquid and small molecules pass through **three** layers
to get into the renal capsule and **enter** the nephron **tubules**
— the **capillary wall**, a membrane (called the **basement
membrane**) and the **epithelium** of the renal capsule.
Larger molecules like **proteins** and **blood cells**
can't pass through and **stay** in the blood.

8) The liquid and small molecules, now called **filtrate**,
pass along the rest of the nephron and **useful substances**
are **reabsorbed** along the way — see next page.

9) Finally, the filtrate flows through the **collecting duct**
and passes out of the kidney along the **ureter**.

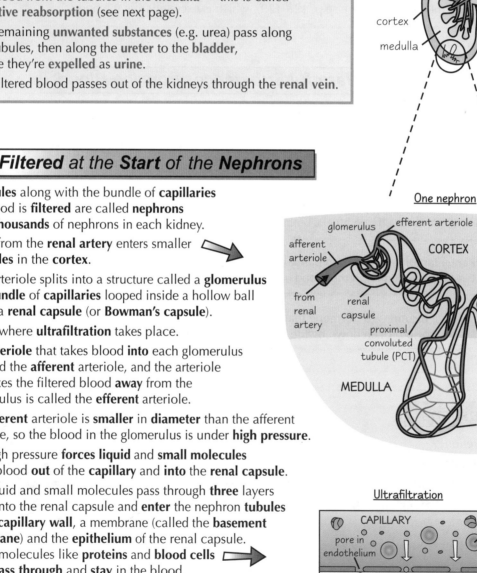

One nephron

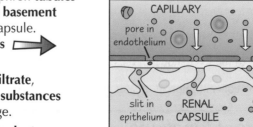

Ultrafiltration

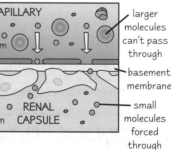

The Kidneys and Excretion

Useful Substances are Reabsorbed Along the Nephron Tubules

1) **Selective reabsorption** takes place as the filtrate flows along the **proximal convoluted tubule** (**PCT**), through the **loop of Henle**, and along the **distal convoluted tubule** (**DCT**).

2) **Useful substances** leave the tubules of the nephrons and **enter** the capillary network that's **wrapped** around them (see diagram on previous page).

3) The **epithelium** of the wall of the PCT has **microvilli** to provide a **large surface area** for the **reabsorption** of useful materials from the **filtrate** (in the tubules) into the **blood** (in the capillaries).

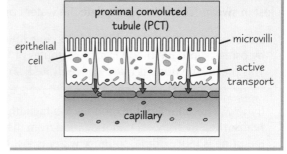

4) Useful solutes like **glucose**, **amino acids**, **vitamins** and some **salts** are reabsorbed along the PCT by **active transport** and **facilitated diffusion**.

5) Some **urea** is also reabsorbed by **diffusion**.

6) **Water** enters the blood by **osmosis** because the **water potential** of the blood is **lower** than that of the filtrate. Water is reabsorbed from the **loop of Henle**, **DCT** and the **collecting duct** (see next page).

Water potential basically describes the tendency of water to move from one area to another. Water will move from an area of higher water potential to an area of lower water potential — it moves down the water potential gradient.

7) The filtrate that remains is **urine**, which passes along the **ureter** to the **bladder**.

Urine is usually **made up of**:
- **Water** and **dissolved salts**.
- **Urea**.
- Other substances such as **hormones** and **excess vitamins**.

The volume of water in urine varies depending on how much you've drunk (see p. 130). The amount of urea also varies depending on how much protein you've eaten (see p. 127).

Urine **doesn't** usually contain:
- **Proteins** and **blood cells** — they're **too big** to be **filtered out** of the blood.
- **Glucose, amino acids** and **vitamins** — they're **actively reabsorbed** back into the blood (see above).

Ali was going to selectively absorb all the green jelly beans.

Practice Questions

Q1 Which blood vessel supplies the kidney with blood?

Q2 What are the bundles of capillaries found in the cortex of the kidneys called?

Q3 What is selective reabsorption?

Q4 Why aren't proteins normally found in urine?

Exam Question

Q1
  a) Name the structures labelled A-D shown in the diagram. [4 marks]
  b) In which structure (B-D) does ultrafiltration take place? [1 mark]
  c) Describe and explain the process of ultrafiltration. [5 marks]

Mmm — it's steak and excretion organ pie for dinner...

Excretion is a pretty horrible sounding word I know, but it's gotta be done. Speaking of horrible, I've never been able to eat kidney ever since I learnt all about this urine production business. Shame really because I used to love it sooooo much — I'd have kidneys on toast for breakfast, kidney sandwiches for lunch, kidney soup for tea, and kidney ice cream for pudding.

Controlling Water Content

More lovely kidney to gobble up on these pages — this time it's their role in controlling the water content of the blood. Busy things, these kidneys.

The **Kidneys** Regulate the **Water Content** of the **Blood**

Water is **essential** to keep the body **functioning**, so the **amount** of water in the **blood** needs to be kept **constant**. Mammals excrete **urea** (and other waste products) in **solution**, which means **water** is **lost** during excretion. Water is also lost in **sweat**. The kidneys **regulate** the water content of the blood (and urine), so the body has just the **right amount**:

If the water content of the blood is too **low** (the body is **dehydrated**), **more** water is **reabsorbed** by osmosis **into** the blood from the tubules of the nephrons (see p. 128-129 for more). This means the urine is **more concentrated**, so **less** water is **lost** during excretion.

If the water content of the blood is too **high** (the body is too **hydrated**), **less** water is **reabsorbed** by osmosis **into** the blood from the tubules of the nephrons. This means the urine is **more dilute**, so **more** water is **lost** during excretion (see next page).

Brad liked his urine to be dilute.

Regulation of the water content of the blood takes place in the **middle** and **last parts** of the nephron — the **loop of Henle**, the **distal convoluted tubule** (DCT) and the **collecting duct** (see below). The **volume** of water reabsorbed is controlled by **hormones** (see next page).

The **Loop of Henle** has a **Countercurrent Multiplier Mechanism**

The **loop of Henle** is made up of two 'limbs' — the **descending** limb and the **ascending** limb. They help set up a mechanism called the **countercurrent multiplier mechanism**. It's this mechanism that helps to **reabsorb water** back into the blood. Here's how it **works**:

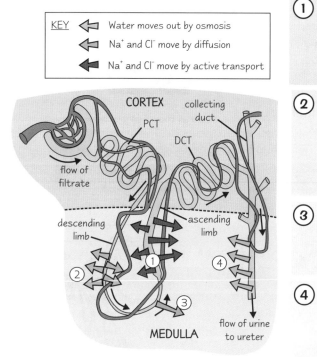

KEY
- ⇐ Water moves out by osmosis
- ⇐ Na⁺ and Cl⁻ move by diffusion
- ⇐ Na⁺ and Cl⁻ move by active transport

CORTEX — collecting duct — PCT — DCT — flow of filtrate — descending limb — ascending limb — MEDULLA — flow of urine to ureter

(1) Near the **top of the ascending** limb, Na^+ and Cl^- ions are **actively pumped out** into the **medulla**. The ascending limb is **impermeable** to **water**, so the water **stays inside** the tubule. This creates a **low water potential** in the **medulla**, because there's a **high concentration** of ions.

(2) Because there's a **lower** water potential in the **medulla** than in the descending limb, **water** moves **out** of the **descending limb** into the **medulla** by **osmosis**. This makes the **filtrate more concentrated** (the ions can't diffuse out — the descending limb isn't permeable to them). The water in the medulla is **reabsorbed** into the **blood** through the **capillary network**.

(3) Near the **bottom of the ascending** limb Na^+ and Cl^- ions **diffuse out** into the **medulla**, further **lowering** the **water potential** in the medulla. (The ascending limb is **impermeable** to **water**, so it **stays in the tubule**.)

(4) The first three stages massively **increase** the **ion concentration** in the **medulla**, which **lowers** the **water potential**. This causes **water** to **move out** of the **collecting duct** by **osmosis**. As before, the water in the medulla is **reabsorbed** into the **blood** through the **capillary network**.

The **volume** of water **reabsorbed** from the collecting duct into the capillaries is **controlled** by **changing the permeability** of the **collecting duct** (see next page).

Different animals have **different length loops of Henle**. The **longer** an animal's loop of Henle, the **more water they can reabsorb** from the filtrate. When there's a longer ascending limb, **more ions** are **actively pumped out** into the medulla, which creates a **really low water potential** in the medulla. This means **more water** moves **out** of the nephron and collecting duct **into** the **capillaries**, giving very **concentrated urine**. Animals that live in areas where there's **little water** usually have **long loops** to **save** as much **water** as possible.

Controlling Water Content

Water Reabsorption is Controlled by Hormones

1) The water content, and so water potential, of the blood is **monitored** by cells called **osmoreceptors** in a part of the **brain** called the **hypothalamus**.

2) When the osmoreceptors are **stimulated** by **low** water content in the blood, the hypothalamus sends **nerve impulses** to the **posterior pituitary gland** to release a **hormone** called **antidiuretic hormone** (ADH) into the blood.

3) ADH makes the walls of the DCT and collecting duct **more permeable** to **water**.

4) This means **more water** is **reabsorbed** from these tubules **into** the medulla and into the blood by osmosis. A **small** amount of **concentrated urine** is produced, which means **less water** is **lost** from the body.

It's called antidiuretic hormone because diuresis is when lots of dilute urine is produced, so anti means a small amount of concentrated urine is produced.

Here's how ADH changes the **water content** of the **blood** when it's too **low** or too **high**:

1 Blood ADH Level Rises When You're Dehydrated

Dehydration is what happens when you **lose water**, e.g. by sweating during exercise, so the **water content** of the blood needs to be **increased**:

1) The **water content** of the blood **drops**, so its **water potential drops**.

2) This is detected by **osmoreceptors** in the **hypothalamus**.

3) The **posterior pituitary gland** is stimulated to release **more ADH** into the blood.

4) **More ADH** means that the DCT and collecting duct are **more permeable**, so **more water** is **reabsorbed** into the blood by osmosis.

5) A **small amount** of **highly concentrated** urine is produced and **less water** is **lost**.

Dehydrated? Me? As if...

2 Blood ADH Level Falls When You're Hydrated

If you're **hydrated**, you've taken in **lots of water**, so the **water content** of the blood needs to be **reduced**:

1) The **water content** of the blood **rises**, so its **water potential rises**.

2) This is detected by the **osmoreceptors** in the **hypothalamus**.

3) The **posterior pituitary gland** releases **less ADH** into the blood.

4) **Less ADH** means that the DCT and collecting duct are **less permeable**, so **less water** is **reabsorbed** into the blood by osmosis.

5) A **large amount** of **dilute** urine is produced and **more water** is **lost**.

Practice Questions

Q1 In which parts of the nephron does water reabsorption take place?

Q2 Describe what happens along the descending limb of the loop of Henle.

Q3 Which cells monitor the water content of the blood?

Q4 Which gland releases ADH?

Exam Questions

Q1 Describe and explain how water is reabsorbed into the capillaries from the nephron. [6 marks]

Q2 The level of ADH in the blood rises during strenuous exercise. Explain the cause of the increase and the effect it has on kidney function. [6 marks]

If you don't understand what ADH does, ur-ine trouble...

Seriously though, there are two main things to learn from these pages — how water is reabsorbed from the tubules in the kidney, and how the water content of the blood is regulated by osmoreceptors, the hypothalamus and the posterior pituitary gland. Keep writing it down until you've got it sorted in your head, and you'll be just fine. Now I need a wee.

Kidney Failure and Detecting Hormones

Everything's fine while the kidneys are working well, but when they get damaged things don't run quite so smoothly.

Kidney Failure is When the Kidneys Stop Working Properly

Kidney failure is also called renal failure.

Kidney failure is when the kidneys **can't** carry out their **normal functions** because they **can't work properly**. Kidney failure can be **caused** by many things including:

1) **Kidney infections** — these can cause **inflammation** (swelling) of the kidneys, which can **damage** the cells. This **interferes** with **filtering** in the renal capsules, or with **reabsorption** in the other parts of the nephrons.

2) **High blood pressure** — this can damage the **glomeruli**. The blood in the glomeruli is already under **high pressure** but the **capillaries** can be **damaged** if the blood pressure gets **too high**. This means **larger** molecules like **proteins** can get through the capillary walls and into the **urine**.

Kidney failure causes **lots of problems**, for example:

1) **Waste products** that the kidneys would normally **remove** (e.g. **urea**) begin to **build up** in the blood. **Too much** urea in the blood causes **weight loss** and **vomiting**.

2) **Fluid** starts to **accumulate** in the tissues because the kidneys **can't remove excess water** from the blood. This causes **parts of the body** to **swell**, e.g. the person's legs, face and abdomen can swell up.

3) The balance of **ions** in the body becomes, well, unbalanced. The blood may become **too acidic**, and an imbalance of calcium and phosphate can lead to **brittle bones**. **Salt build-up** may cause more **water retention**.

4) **Long-term** kidney failure causes **anaemia** — a **lack** of **haemoglobin** in the blood.

If the problems caused by kidney failure **can't be controlled**, it can eventually lead to **death**.

Renal Dialysis and Kidney Transplants can be used to Treat Kidney Failure

When the kidneys can no longer **function** (i.e. they've **totally failed**), a person is unable to **survive** without **treatment**. There are **two** main treatment options:

Renal dialysis

1) **Renal dialysis** is where a machine is used to filter a patient's blood.
- The patient's blood is passed through a **dialysis machine** — the **blood** flows on one side of a **partially permeable membrane** and **dialysis fluid** flows on the other side.
- **Waste products** and **excess water** and **ions** diffuse across the membrane into the dialysis fluid, **removing** them from the blood.
- **Blood cells** and **larger** molecules like **proteins** are **prevented** from **leaving** the blood.
2) Patients can feel increasingly **unwell** between dialysis sessions because **waste products** and **fluid** starts to build up in their **blood**.
3) Each dialysis session takes **three to five hours**, and patients need **two or three sessions a week**, usually in **hospital**. This is **quite expensive** and is pretty **inconvenient** for the patient.
4) But dialysis can keep a person **alive** until a **transplant** is available (see below), and it's a lot **less risky** than having the **major surgery** involved in a transplant.

Kidney transplant

1) A **kidney transplant** is where a **new kidney** is implanted into a patient's body to **replace** a damaged kidney.
2) The new kidney has to be from a person with the **same blood** and **tissue type**. They're often donated from a **living relative**, as people can survive with **only one** kidney. They can also come from **other people** who've recently **died** — organ donors.
3) Transplants have a lot of **advantages** over dialysis:
- It's **cheaper** to give a person a transplant than keep them on dialysis for a **long time**.
- It's **more convenient** for a person than regular dialysis sessions.
- Patients don't have the problem of feeling **unwell** between dialysis sessions.
4) But there are also **disadvantages** to having a kidney transplant:
- The patient will have to undergo a **major operation**, which is **risky**.
- The **immune system** may **reject** the transplant, so the patient has to take **drugs** to **suppress it**.

Kidney Failure and Detecting Hormones

Urine is used to Test for Pregnancy and Steroid Use

Urine is made by **filtering** the **blood**, so you can have a look at what's in a person's blood by **testing** their **urine**. For example, you can test if a woman is **pregnant** by looking for a **hormone** that only pregnant women produce, and you can test **athletes** for the presence of **banned drugs** like **steroids**:

TESTING FOR PREGNANCY

Pregnancy tests detect the hormone **human chorionic gonadotropin (hCG)** that's only found in the **urine** of **pregnant women**:

1) A **stick** is used with an **application area** that contains **antibodies for hCG** bound to a **coloured bead** (**blue**).

2) When urine is applied to the application area any hCG will **bind** to the antibody on the beads.

3) The urine **moves** up to the **test strip**, **carrying** the **beads** with it.

4) The test strip has **antibodies to hCG** stuck in place (**immobilised**).

5) If there **is hCG present** the test strip turns **blue** because the **immobilised** antibody binds to any **hCG** attached to the **blue** beads, concentrating the **blue beads** in that area. If **no hCG** is present, the beads will **pass through** the test area **without** binding to anything, and so it **won't** go blue.

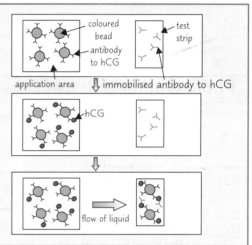

TESTING FOR STEROIDS

1) **Anabolic steroids** are **drugs** that **build up muscle tissue**.

2) **Testosterone** is an anabolic steroid, and there are other common ones such as **Nandrolone**.

3) Some **athletes** are **banned** from taking anabolic steroids. This is to try to stop the misuse of steroids that can have **dangerous side-effects**, such as **liver damage**. Also, it's considered **unfair** for some athletes to use steroids.

4) Steroids are **removed from the blood** in the **urine**, so athletes regularly have their **urine tested** for steroids.

5) Urine is tested for steroids (or the **products** made when they're **broken down**) by a technique called **gas chromatography**.

6) The urine sample is **vaporised** (turned into a **gas**) and passed through a column containing a **liquid**. **Different substances** move through the column at **different speeds**. The length of time taken for substances in the **sample** to pass through the column is **compared** to the time taken for a **steroid** to pass through the column. If the time taken is the **same** then the sample **contains the steroid**.

Practice Questions

Q1 Give one effect of kidney failure on the body.

Q2 What is renal dialysis?

Q3 What substance does a pregnancy test detect in a urine sample?

Exam Questions

Q1 Discuss the advantages and disadvantages of kidney transplants. [5 marks]

Q2 Describe and explain how urine can be used to detect steroid use. [5 marks]

Kidney failure, kidney infections, kidney transplants, kidney beans...

So you can either treat kidney failure with a kidney transplant or you can use kidney dialysis to filter the blood a few times a week. Both treatments come with their advantages and disadvantages, so make sure you can sum them both up. Here's a tip — you can usually use the disadvantages of one treatment to come up with the advantages of the other.

Photosynthesis, Respiration and ATP

OK, this isn't the easiest topic in the world, but 'cos I'm feeling nice today we'll take it slowly, one bit at a time...

Biological Processes Need Energy

Plant and animal cells **need energy** for biological processes to occur:

- **Plants** need energy for things like **photosynthesis**, **active transport** (e.g. to take in minerals via their roots), **DNA replication**, **cell division** and **protein synthesis**.
- **Animals** need energy for things like **muscle contraction**, maintenance of **body temperature**, **active transport**, DNA replication, cell division and protein synthesis.

Without energy, these biological processes would stop and the plant or animal would die.

Photosynthesis Stores Energy in Glucose

1) **Plants** are **autotrophs** — they can **make** their **own food** (**glucose**). They do this using **photosynthesis**.
2) **Photosynthesis** is the process where **energy** from **light** is used to **make glucose** from H_2O and CO_2 (the light energy is **converted** to **chemical energy** in the form of glucose).
3) Photosynthesis occurs in a **series** of **reactions**, but the overall equation is:

$$6CO_2 + 6H_2O + \text{Energy} \longrightarrow C_6H_{12}O_6 \text{ (glucose)} + 6O_2$$

4) So, energy is **stored** in the **glucose** until the plants **release** it by **respiration**.
5) **Animals** are **heterotrophs** — they **can't make** their **own food**. So, they obtain glucose by **eating plants** (or **other animals**), then respire the glucose to release energy.

Respiration in plants and animals needs glucose from photosynthesis to occur.

Cells Release Energy from Glucose by Respiration

1) **Plant** and **animal** cells **release energy** from **glucose** — this process is called **respiration**.
2) This energy is used to power all the **biological processes** in a cell.
3) There are two types of respiration:
   - **Aerobic respiration** — respiration **using oxygen**.
   - **Anaerobic respiration** — respiration **without oxygen**.
4) Aerobic respiration produces **carbon dioxide** and **water**, and releases **energy**. The overall equation is:

$$C_6H_{12}O_6 \text{ (glucose)} + 6O_2 \longrightarrow 6CO_2 + 6H_2O + \text{Energy}$$

ATP is the Immediate Source of Energy in a Cell

1) A cell **can't** get its energy **directly** from glucose.
2) So, in respiration, the **energy released** from glucose is used to **make ATP** (adenosine triphosphate). ATP is made from the nucleotide base **adenine**, combined with a **ribose sugar** and **three phosphate groups**.
3) It **carries energy** around the cell to where it's **needed**.
4) **ATP is synthesised** from **ADP** and **inorganic phosphate** (P_i) using energy from an **energy-releasing** reaction, e.g. the **breakdown** of glucose in **respiration**. The energy is stored as **chemical energy** in the **phosphate bond**. The enzyme **ATP synthase** catalyses this reaction.

5) ATP **diffuses** to the part of the cell that **needs** energy.
6) Here, it's **broken down** back into **ADP** and **inorganic phosphate** (P_i). Chemical **energy** is **released** from the phosphate bond and used by the cell. **ATPase** catalyses this reaction.
7) The ADP and inorganic phosphate are **recycled** and the process starts again.

Inorganic phosphate (P_i) is just the fancy name for a single phosphate.

Photosynthesis, Respiration and ATP

ATP has Specific Properties that Make it a Good Energy Source

1) ATP stores or releases only a **small**, **manageable amount** of energy at a time, so **no** energy is **wasted**.

2) It's a **small**, **soluble** molecule so it can be **easily transported** around the cell.

3) It's **easily broken down**, so energy can be **easily released**.

4) It can **transfer energy** to another molecule by transferring one of its **phosphate groups**.

5) ATP **can't pass out** of the **cell**, so the cell **always** has an immediate supply of energy.

Karen needed a lot of energy just to keep her headdress on...

You Need to Know Some Basics Before You Start

There are some pretty confusing technical terms in this section that you need to get your head around:

- **Metabolic pathway** — a **series** of **small reactions** controlled by **enzymes**, e.g. **respiration** and **photosynthesis**.

- **Phosphorylation** — **adding phosphate** to a molecule, e.g. **ADP** is phosphorylated to **ATP** (see previous page).

- **Photophosphorylation** — **adding phosphate** to a molecule using **light**.

- **Photolysis** — the **splitting** (lysis) of a molecule using **light** (photo) energy.

- **Hydrolysis** — the **splitting** (lysis) of a molecule using **water** (hydro).

- **Decarboxylation** — the **removal** of **carbon dioxide** from a molecule.

- **Dehydrogenation** — the **removal** of **hydrogen** from a molecule.

- **Redox reactions** — reactions that involve **oxidation** and **reduction**.

> **Remember redox reactions:**
>
> 1) If something is **reduced** it has **gained electrons** (e⁻), and may have **gained hydrogen** or lost oxygen.
>
> 2) If something is **oxidised** it has **lost electrons**, and may have **lost hydrogen** or gained oxygen.
>
> 3) Oxidation of one molecule **always** involves reduction of another molecule.

One way to remember electron and hydrogen movement is OILRIG. Oxidation Is Loss, Reduction Is Gain.

Photosynthesis and Respiration Involve Coenzymes

1) A **coenzyme** is a molecule that **aids** the **function** of an **enzyme**.

2) They work by **transferring** a **chemical group** from one molecule to another.

3) A coenzyme used in **photosynthesis** is **NADP**. NADP transfers **hydrogen** from one molecule to another — this means it can **reduce** (give hydrogen to) or **oxidise** (take hydrogen from) a molecule.

4) Examples of coenzymes used in **respiration** are: **NAD**, **coenzyme A** and **FAD**.

   - NAD and FAD transfer **hydrogen** from one molecule to another — this means they can **reduce** (give hydrogen to) or **oxidise** (take hydrogen from) a molecule.

   - **Coenzyme A** transfers **acetate** between molecules (see pages 145-146).

When hydrogen is transferred between molecules, electrons are transferred too.

Practice Questions

Q1 Write down three biological processes in animals that need energy.

Q2 What is photosynthesis?

Q3 What is the overall equation for aerobic respiration?

Q4 How many phosphate groups does ATP have?

Q5 Give the name of a coenzyme involved in photosynthesis.

Exam Question

Q1 ATP is the immediate source of energy inside a cell.
Describe how the synthesis and breakdown of ATP meets the energy needs of a cell. [6 marks]

Oh dear, I've used up all my ATP on these two pages...

Well, I won't beat about the bush, this stuff is pretty tricky... nearly as hard as a cross between Mr T, Hulk Hogan and Arnie. But, with a little patience and perseverance (and plenty of [chocolate] [coffee] [marshmallows] — delete as you wish), you'll get there. Once you've got these pages straight in your head, the next ones will be easier to understand.

Photosynthesis

Right, pen at the ready. Check. Brain switched on. Check. Cuppa piping hot. Check. Sweets on standby. Check. Okay, I think you're all sorted to start photosynthesis. Finally, take a deep breath and here we go...

Photosynthesis Takes Place in the Chloroplasts of Plant Cells

1) **Chloroplasts** are **small, flattened organelles** found in **plant cells**.

2) They have a **double membrane** called the **chloroplast envelope**.

3) **Thylakoids** (fluid-filled sacs) are **stacked up** in the chloroplast into structures called **grana** (singular = **granum**). The grana are **linked** together by bits of thylakoid membrane called **lamellae** (singular = **lamella**).

4) Chloroplasts contain **photosynthetic pigments** (e.g. **chlorophyll a**, **chlorophyll b** and **carotene**). These are **coloured substances** that **absorb** the **light energy** needed for photosynthesis. The pigments are found in the **thylakoid membranes** — they're attached to **proteins**. The protein and pigment is called a **photosystem**.

5) A photosystem contains **two types** of photosynthetic pigments — **primary** pigments and **accessory** pigments. Primary pigments are **reaction centres** where **electrons** are **excited** during the light-dependent reaction (see next page). Accessory pigments **surround** the primary pigments and **transfer light energy** to them.

6) There are **two photosystems** used by plants to capture light energy. **Photosystem I** (or PSI) absorbs light best at a wavelength of **700 nm** and **photosystem II** (PSII) absorbs light best at **680 nm**.

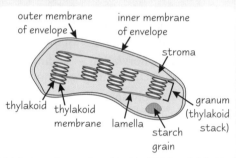

outer membrane of envelope
inner membrane of envelope
stroma
granum (thylakoid stack)
thylakoid
thylakoid membrane
lamella
starch grain

7) Contained within the inner membrane of the chloroplast and **surrounding** the thylakoids is a gel-like substance called the **stroma**. It contains **enzymes**, **sugars** and **organic acids**.

8) Carbohydrates produced by photosynthesis and not used straight away are stored as **starch grains** in the **stroma**.

Photosynthesis can be Split into Two Stages

There are actually **two stages** that make up **photosynthesis**:

See p. 138 for loads more information on the Calvin cycle.

1 The Light-Dependent Reaction

1) As the name suggests, this reaction **needs light energy**.

2) It takes place in the **thylakoid membranes** of the chloroplasts.

3) Here, light energy is absorbed by **photosynthetic pigments** in the **photosystems** and converted to **chemical energy**.

4) The light energy is used to add a phosphate group to ADP to form **ATP**, and to reduce NADP to form **reduced NADP**. **ATP transfers energy** and reduced **NADP transfers hydrogen** to the light-independent reaction.

5) During the process H_2O is **oxidised** to O_2.

2 The Light-Independent Reaction

1) This is also called the **Calvin cycle** and as the name suggests it **doesn't use light energy** directly. (But it does **rely** on the **products** of the light-dependent reaction.)

2) It takes place in the **stroma** of the chloroplasts.

3) Here, the **ATP** and **reduced NADP** from the light-dependent reaction supply the **energy** and **hydrogen** to make **glucose** from CO_2.

In the Light-Dependent Reaction ATP is Made by Photophosphorylation

In the light-dependent reaction, the **light energy** absorbed by the photosystems is used for **three** things:

1) Making **ATP** from **ADP** and **inorganic phosphate**. This reaction is called **photophosphorylation** (see p. 135).

2) Making **reduced NADP** from **NADP**.

3) Splitting **water** into **protons** (H^+ ions), **electrons** and **oxygen**. This is called **photolysis** (see p. 135).

The light-dependent reaction actually includes **two types** of **photophosphorylation** — **non-cyclic** and **cyclic**. Each of these processes has **different products**.

Photosynthesis

Non-cyclic Photophosphorylation Produces ATP, Reduced NADP and O₂

To understand the process you need to know that the photosystems (in the thylakoid membranes) are **linked** by **electron carriers**. Electron carriers are **proteins** that **transfer electrons**. The photosystems and electron carriers form an **electron transport chain** — a **chain** of **proteins** through which **excited electrons flow**. All the processes in the diagrams are happening together — I've just split them up to make it easier to understand.

1 **Light energy excites electrons in chlorophyll**

- **Light energy** is absorbed by **PSII**.
- The light energy **excites electrons** in **chlorophyll**.
- The electrons move to a **higher energy level** (i.e. they have more energy).
- These high-energy electrons **move** along the **electron transport chain** to **PSI**.

2 **Photolysis of water produces protons (H⁺ ions), electrons and O₂**

- As the excited electrons **from chlorophyll leave PSII** to **move along** the electron transport chain, they must be **replaced**.
- **Light** energy splits **water** into **protons** (H⁺ ions), **electrons** and **oxygen**. (So the O₂ in photosynthesis comes from water.)
- The reaction is: $H_2O \longrightarrow 2H^+ + \frac{1}{2}O_2$

Not all of the electron carriers are shown in these diagrams.

3 **Energy from the excited electrons makes ATP...**

- The excited electrons **lose energy** as they **move along** the **electron transport chain**.
- This energy is used to **transport protons into** the **thylakoid** so that the thylakoid has a **higher concentration** of protons than the stroma. This forms a **proton gradient** across the membrane.
- Protons move **down** their concentration gradient, into the stroma, **via** an enzyme called **ATP synthase**. The energy from this movement combines **ADP** and **inorganic phosphate** (P_i) to form **ATP**.

Chemiosmosis is the name of the process where the movement of H⁺ ions across a membrane generates ATP. This process also occurs in respiration (see p. 147).

4 **...and generates reduced NADP.**

- Light energy is **absorbed** by PSI, which excites the electrons again to an **even higher** energy level.
- Finally, the electrons are **transferred** to **NADP**, along with a **proton** (H⁺ ion) from the **stroma**, to form **reduced NADP**.

Remember a 'proton' is just another word for a hydrogen ion (H⁺).

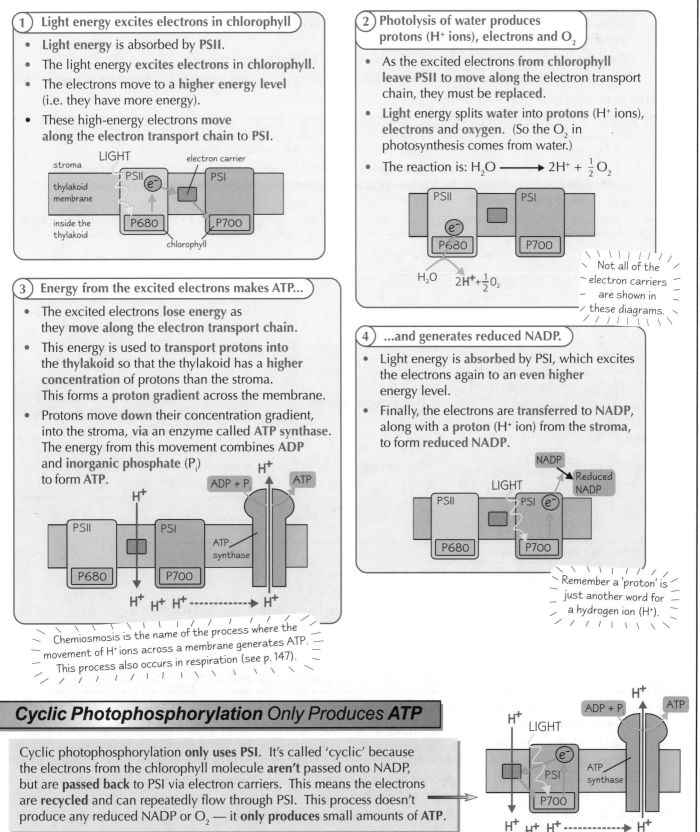

Cyclic Photophosphorylation Only Produces ATP

Cyclic photophosphorylation **only uses PSI**. It's called 'cyclic' because the electrons from the chlorophyll molecule **aren't** passed onto NADP, but are **passed back** to PSI via electron carriers. This means the electrons are **recycled** and can repeatedly flow through PSI. This process doesn't produce any reduced NADP or O₂ — it **only produces** small amounts of **ATP**.

Photosynthesis

Don't worry, you're over the worst of photosynthesis now. Instead of electrons flying around, there's a nice cycle of reactions to learn. What more could you want from life? Money, fast cars and nice clothes have nothing on this...

The **Light-Independent** Reaction is also called the **Calvin Cycle**

1) The Calvin cycle takes place in the **stroma** of the chloroplasts.

2) It makes a molecule called **triose phosphate** from **CO_2** and **ribulose bisphosphate** (a 5-carbon compound). Triose phosphate can be used to make **glucose** and other **useful organic substances** (see below).

3) There are a few steps in the cycle, and it needs **ATP** and **H^+ ions** to keep it going.

4) The reactions are linked in a **cycle**, which means the starting compound, **ribulose bisphosphate**, is **regenerated**.

The Calvin cycle is also called carbon fixation, because carbon from CO_2 is 'fixed' into an organic molecule.

Here's what happens at each stage in the cycle:

1 **Carbon dioxide is combined with ribulose bisphosphate to form two molecules of glycerate 3-phosphate**

- **CO_2** enters the leaf through the **stomata** and diffuses into the **stroma** of the chloroplast.

- Here, it's combined with **ribulose bisphosphate (RuBP)**, a **5-carbon** compound. This gives an **unstable 6-carbon** compound, which quickly breaks down into **two** molecules of a **3-carbon** compound called **glycerate 3-phosphate (GP)**.

- **Ribulose bisphosphate carboxylase (rubisco)** catalyses the reaction between **CO_2** and **ribulose bisphosphate**.

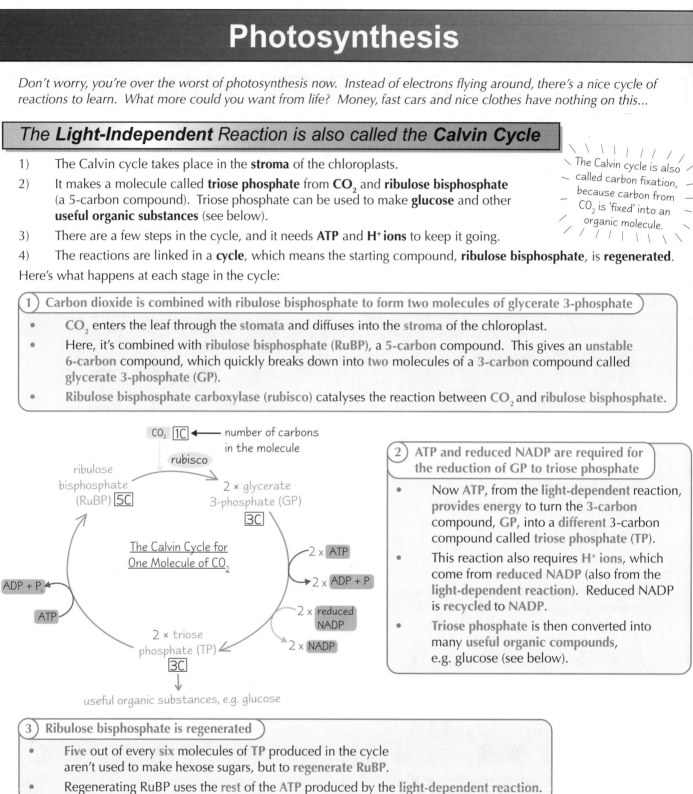

2 **ATP and reduced NADP are required for the reduction of GP to triose phosphate**

- Now **ATP**, from the **light-dependent** reaction, **provides energy** to turn the **3-carbon** compound, **GP**, into a **different** 3-carbon compound called **triose phosphate (TP)**.

- This reaction also requires **H^+ ions**, which come from **reduced NADP** (also from the **light-dependent reaction**). Reduced NADP is **recycled** to NADP.

- **Triose phosphate** is then converted into many **useful organic compounds**, e.g. glucose (see below).

3 **Ribulose bisphosphate is regenerated**

- **Five** out of every **six** molecules of **TP** produced in the cycle aren't used to make hexose sugars, but to **regenerate RuBP**.

- Regenerating RuBP uses the **rest** of the **ATP** produced by the **light-dependent reaction**.

TP and **GP** are **Converted** into **Useful Organic Substances** like **Glucose**

The Calvin cycle is the starting point for making **all** the organic substances a plant needs. **Triose phosphate** (TP) and **glycerate 3-phosphate** (GP) molecules are used to make **carbohydrates**, **lipids** and **amino acids**:

- **Carbohydrates** — hexose sugars (e.g. glucose) are made by joining **two triose phosphate molecules** together and **larger** carbohydrates (e.g. sucrose, starch, cellulose) are made by joining **hexose sugars** together in **different ways**.

- **Lipids** — these are made using **glycerol**, which is synthesised from **triose phosphate**, and **fatty acids**, which are synthesised from **glycerate 3-phosphate**.

- **Amino acids** — some amino acids are made from **glycerate 3-phosphate**.

Photosynthesis

The **Calvin Cycle** Needs to Turn **Six Times** to Make **One Hexose Sugar**

1) **Three turns** of the cycle produces **six** molecules of **triose phosphate** (TP), because two molecules of TP are made for every one CO_2 molecule used.
2) **Five** out of **six** of these TP molecules are used to **regenerate ribulose bisphosphate** (RuBP).
3) This means that for **three turns** of the cycle only **one TP** is produced that's used to make a **hexose sugar**.
4) A hexose sugar has **six carbons** though, so **two TP** molecules are needed to form one hexose sugar.
5) This means the cycle must turn **six times** to produce **two molecules** of **TP** that can be used to make **one hexose sugar**.
6) Six turns of the cycle need **18 ATP** and **12 reduced NADP** from the light-dependent reaction.

The **Structure** of a **Chloroplast** is **Adapted** for **Photosynthesis**

1) The **chloroplast envelope** keeps the **reactants** for photosynthesis **close** to their **reaction sites**.
2) The **thylakoids** have a **large surface area** to allow as much **light energy** to be **absorbed** as possible.
3) **Lots** of **ATP synthase** molecules are present in the thylakoid membranes to **produce ATP** in the light-dependent reaction.
4) The **stroma** contains all the **enzymes**, **sugars** and **organic acids** for the light-independent reaction to take place.

Practice Questions

Q1 Name two photosynthetic pigments in the chloroplasts of plants.
Q2 At what wavelength does photosystem I absorb light best?
Q3 What three substances does non-cyclic photophosphorylation produce?
Q4 Which photosystem is involved in cyclic photophosphorylation?
Q5 Where in the chloroplasts does the light-independent reaction occur?
Q6 Name two organic substances made from triose phosphate.
Q7 How many CO_2 molecules need to enter the Calvin cycle to make one hexose sugar?
Q8 Describe two ways in which a chloroplast is adapted for photosynthesis.

These questions cover pages 136-139.

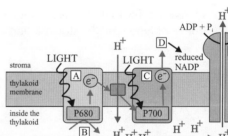

Exam Questions

Q1 The diagram above shows the light-dependent reaction of photosynthesis.
a) Where precisely in a plant does the light-dependent reaction of photosynthesis occur? [1 mark]
b) What is A? [1 mark]
c) Describe process B and explain its purpose. [4 marks]
d) What is reactant D? [1 mark]

Q2 Rubisco is an enzyme that catalyses the first reaction of the Calvin cycle. CA1P is an inhibitor of rubisco.
a) Describe how triose phosphate is produced in the Calvin cycle. [6 marks]
b) Briefly explain how ribulose bisphosphate (RuBP) is regenerated in the Calvin cycle. [2 marks]
c) Explain the effect that CA1P would have on glucose production. [3 marks]

Calvin cycles — bikes made by people that normally make pants...

Next thing we know there'll be male models swanning about in their pants riding highly fashionable bikes. Sounds awful I know, but let's face it, anything would look better than cycling shorts. Anyway, it would be a good idea to go over these pages a couple of times — you might not feel as if you can fit any more information in your head, but you can, I promise.

Limiting Factors in Photosynthesis

Now you know what photosynthesis is it's time to find out what conditions make it speedy and what slows it down. I'd start by making sure you have the best conditions for revision — oodles of biscuits and your thinking cap on.

There are **Optimum Conditions** for Photosynthesis

The **ideal conditions** for photosynthesis vary from one plant species to another, but the conditions below would be ideal for **most** plant species in temperate climates like the UK.

1. **High light intensity** of a certain **wavelength**

- Light is needed to provide the **energy** for the **light-dependent reaction** — the **higher** the **intensity** of the light, the **more energy** it provides.

- Only certain **wavelengths** of light are used for photosynthesis. The photosynthetic pigments chlorophyll a, chlorophyll b and carotene only **absorb** the **red** and **blue** light in sunlight. (**Green** light is **reflected**, which is why plants look green.)

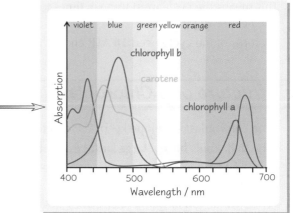

2. **Temperature** around 25 °C

- Photosynthesis involves **enzymes** (e.g. ATP synthase, rubisco). If the temperature falls **below 10 °C** the enzymes become **inactive**, but if the temperature is **more than 45 °C** they may start to **denature**.

- Also, at **high** temperatures **stomata close** to avoid losing too much water. This causes photosynthesis to slow down because **less CO_2** enters the leaf when the stomata are closed.

3. **Carbon dioxide at 0.4%**

- Carbon dioxide makes up **0.04%** of the gases in the atmosphere.
- Increasing this to **0.4%** gives a **higher rate** of photosynthesis, but any higher and the stomata start to **close**.

> Plants also need a constant supply of water — too little and photosynthesis has to stop but too much and the soil becomes waterlogged (reducing the uptake of magnesium for chlorophyll a).

Light, Temperature and CO_2 can all Limit Photosynthesis

1) **All three** of these things need to be at the **right level** to allow a plant to photosynthesise as quickly as possible.

2) If any **one** of these factors is **too low** or **too high**, it will **limit photosynthesis** (slow it down). Even if the other two factors are at the perfect level, it won't make **any difference** to the speed of photosynthesis as long as that factor is at the wrong level.

3) On a warm, sunny, windless day, it's usually **CO_2** that's the limiting factor, and at night it's the **light intensity**.

4) However, **any** of these factors could become the limiting factor, depending on the **environmental conditions**.

All that Murray and Fraser knew was that limiting photosynthesis was a tasty business...

Limiting Factors in Photosynthesis

You Might Have to **Interpret Graphs** About **Limiting Factors**

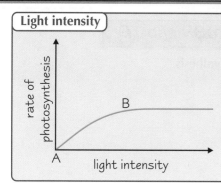

Between points A and B, the rate of photosynthesis is limited by the **light intensity**. So as the light intensity **increases**, so can the rate of photosynthesis. Point B is the **saturation point** — increasing light intensity after this point makes no difference, because **something else** has become the limiting factor. The graph now **levels off**.

The saturation point is where a factor is no longer limiting the reaction — something else has become the limiting factor.

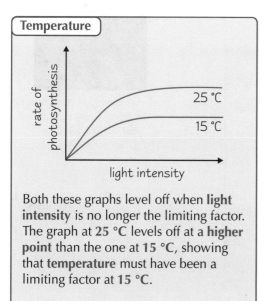

Both these graphs level off when **light intensity** is no longer the limiting factor. The graph at **25 °C** levels off at a **higher point** than the one at **15 °C**, showing that **temperature** must have been a limiting factor at **15 °C**.

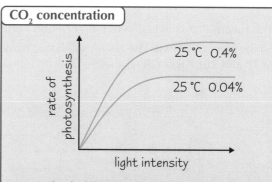

Again, both these graphs level off when **light intensity** is no longer the limiting factor. The graph at **0.4% CO_2** levels off at a **higher point** than the one at **0.04%**, so CO_2 **concentration** must have been a limiting factor at **0.04% CO_2**. The limiting factor here **isn't temperature** because it's the **same** for both graphs (25 °C).

Practice Questions

Q1   Why is a high light intensity an optimum condition for photosynthesis?

Q2   What is the optimum concentration of carbon dioxide for photosynthesis?

Q3   What is the limiting factor for photosynthesis on a warm, sunny day?

Q4   What is the limiting factor for photosynthesis at night?

Exam Question

Q1   An experiment was carried out to investigate how temperature affects photosynthesis.
The rate of photosynthesis was measured at 10 °C, 25 °C and 45 °C.
At which temperature would the rate of photosynthesis have been greatest? Explain your answer.   [4 marks]

I'm a whizz at the factors that limit revision...

... watching Hollyoaks, making tea, watching EastEnders, walking the dog... not to mention staring into space (one of my favourites). These pages aren't that bad though. You just need to learn how light, CO_2 and temperature affect the rate of photosynthesis. Try shutting the book and writing down what you know — you'll be amazed at what you remember.

Limiting Factors in Photosynthesis

Well, I hope you didn't think we'd finished covering limiting factors.... ohhhhhh no, I could write a whole book on them. But just for you I've added an experiment to spice things up a bit. Woo hoo.

Light, Temperature and CO$_2$ Affect the Levels of GP, RuBP and TP

Light intensity, temperature and CO$_2$ concentration all affect the rate of photosynthesis, which means they affect the levels of GP, RuBP and TP in the Calvin cycle.

1. Light intensity

- In **low light intensities**, the products of the light-dependent stage (**reduced NADP** and **ATP**) will be in **short supply**.

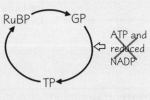

- This means that **conversion of GP** to TP and RuBP is **slow**.
- So the level of **GP** will **rise** (as it's still being made) and levels of **TP** and **RuBP** will **fall** (as they're used up to make GP).

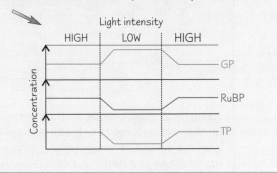

Derek knew that a low light intensity would increase the level of romance.

2. Temperature

- All the reactions in the Calvin cycle are catalysed by **enzymes** (e.g. rubisco).
- At **low temperatures**, all of the reactions will be **slower** as the enzymes work more **slowly**.

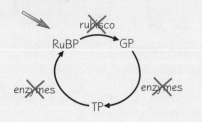

- This means the levels of **RuBP**, **GP** and **TP** will **fall**.
- GP, TP and RuBP are affected in the same way at **very high temperatures**, because the **enzymes** will start to **denature**.

3. Carbon dioxide concentration

- At **low CO$_2$ concentrations**, **conversion of RuBP to GP** is also **slow** (as there's less CO$_2$ to combine with RuBP to make GP).

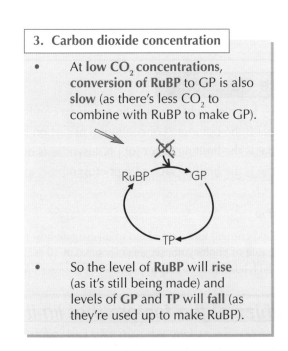

- So the level of **RuBP** will **rise** (as it's still being made) and levels of **GP** and **TP** will **fall** (as they're used up to make RuBP).

Limiting Factors in Photosynthesis

Limiting Factors can be Investigated using Pondweed

1) **Canadian pondweed** (*Elodea*) can be used to measure the effect of light intensity, temperature and CO_2 concentration on the **rate of photosynthesis**.

> Remember photosynthesis produces glucose and oxygen (see page 134).

2) The rate at which **oxygen** is **produced** by the pondweed can be easily **measured** and this **corresponds** to the rate of photosynthesis.

3) For example, the **apparatus** below is used to **measure** the **effect** of **light intensity** on photosynthesis.

- A **test tube** containing the **pondweed** and **water** is connected to a **capillary tube** full of water.
- The tube of water is connected to a **syringe**.
- A **source of white light** is placed at a **specific distance** from the pondweed.
- The pondweed is left to photosynthesise for a **set amount of time**. As it photosynthesises, the **oxygen released** will **collect** in the **capillary tube**.
- At the end of the experiment, the syringe is used to **draw** the gas **bubble** in the tube **up** alongside a **ruler** and the **length** of the gas bubble (volume of O_2) is **measured**.
- Any **variables** that could affect the results should be **controlled**, e.g. temperature, the time the weed is left to photosynthesise.
- The experiment is **repeated** and the **average** length of gas bubble is calculated, to make the results **more reliable**.
- The whole experiment is then **repeated** with the **light source** placed at **different distances** from the pondweed.

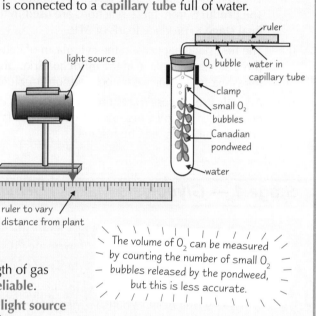

light source

ruler

O_2 bubble   water in capillary tube

clamp

small O_2 bubbles

Canadian pondweed

water

ruler to vary distance from plant

> The volume of O_2 can be measured by counting the number of small O_2 bubbles released by the pondweed, but this is less accurate.

4) The apparatus above can be adapted to **measure** the **effect** of **temperature** on photosynthesis — the test tube of pondweed is put in a **beaker of water** at a **set temperature** (then the experiment's repeated with different temperatures of water).

Practice Questions

Q1   How does a low CO_2 concentration in the air affect the level of TP in a plant?

Q2   In an experiment on the rate of photosynthesis, how can light intensity be varied?

Q3   In the experiment above, give two variables that must be controlled.

Exam Questions

Q1   A scientist was investigating the effect of different conditions on the levels of GP, TP and RuBP in a plant. Predict the results of his experiment under the following conditions. Explain your answers.
a) Low light intensity, optimum temperature and optimum CO_2 concentration.   [3 marks]
b) Low temperature, optimum light intensity and optimum CO_2 concentration.   [3 marks]

Q2   Briefly describe the apparatus and method you would use to investigate how temperature affects photosynthesis in Canadian pondweed.   [6 marks]

Aah, Canadian pondweed — a biology student's best friend...

Well... sometimes — usually you end up staring endlessly at it while it produces lots of tiny bubbles. Thrilling. If you have to describe an experiment in the exam make sure you include details about the apparatus, the method and the variables you'd keep constant to make your results more reliable. Examiners love reliability (but then they're a bit weird — I love cake).

Aerobic Respiration

From the last gazillion pages you know that plants make their own glucose. Unfortunately, that means now you need to learn how plant and animal cells release energy from glucose. It's not the easiest thing in the world to understand, but it'll make sense once you've gone through it a couple of times.

There are **Four Stages** in **Aerobic Respiration**

1) The four stages in aerobic respiration are **glycolysis**, the **link reaction**, the **Krebs cycle** and **oxidative phosphorylation**.

2) The **first three** stages are a **series of reactions**. The **products** from these reactions are **used** in the **final stage** to produce loads of ATP.

3) The **first** stage happens in the **cytoplasm** of cells and the **other three** stages take place in the **mitochondria**. You might want to refresh your memory of mitochondrion structure before you start.

4) All cells use **glucose** to **respire**, but organisms can also **break down** other **complex organic molecules** (e.g. fatty acids, amino acids), which can then be respired.

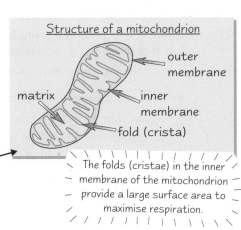

Structure of a mitochondrion

outer membrane
matrix
inner membrane
fold (crista)

The folds (cristae) in the inner membrane of the mitochondrion provide a large surface area to maximise respiration.

Stage 1 — **Glycolysis** Makes **Pyruvate** from **Glucose**

1) Glycolysis involves splitting **one molecule** of glucose (with 6 carbons — 6C) into **two** smaller molecules of **pyruvate** (3C).

2) The process happens in the **cytoplasm** of cells.

3) Glycolysis is the **first stage** of both aerobic and anaerobic respiration and **doesn't need oxygen** to take place — so it's an **anaerobic** process.

Respiration Map

You are here

Glycolysis

Link Reaction

Krebs Cycle

Oxidative Phosphorylation

There are **Two Stages** in Glycolysis — **Phosphorylation** and **Oxidation**

First, **ATP** is **used** to **phosphorylate glucose** to triose phosphate. Then **triose phosphate** is oxidised, releasing ATP. Overall there's a **net gain** of **2 ATP**.

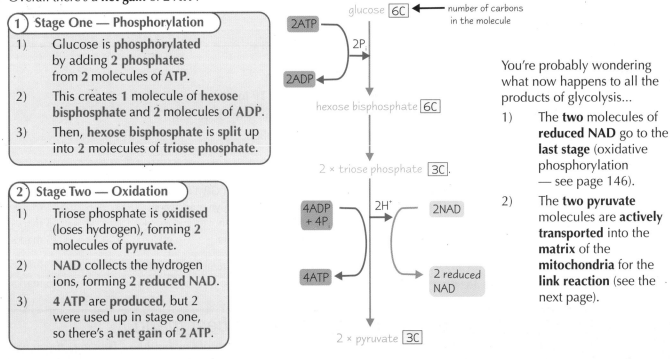

1 Stage One — Phosphorylation

1) Glucose is **phosphorylated** by adding **2 phosphates** from **2 molecules** of ATP.

2) This creates **1 molecule** of **hexose bisphosphate** and **2 molecules** of ADP.

3) Then, **hexose bisphosphate** is **split up** into **2 molecules** of **triose phosphate**.

2 Stage Two — Oxidation

1) Triose phosphate is **oxidised** (loses hydrogen), forming **2 molecules** of **pyruvate**.

2) **NAD** collects the hydrogen ions, forming **2 reduced NAD**.

3) **4 ATP are produced**, but 2 were used up in stage one, so there's a **net gain** of **2 ATP**.

glucose 6C ← number of carbons in the molecule

2ATP
2P$_i$
2ADP

hexose bisphosphate 6C

2 × triose phosphate 3C

4ADP + 4P$_i$
2H$^+$
2NAD
4ATP
2 reduced NAD

2 × pyruvate 3C

You're probably wondering what now happens to all the products of glycolysis...

1) The **two** molecules of **reduced NAD** go to the **last stage** (oxidative phosphorylation — see page 146).

2) The **two pyruvate** molecules are **actively transported** into the **matrix** of the **mitochondria** for the **link reaction** (see the next page).

Aerobic Respiration

Stage 2 — the Link Reaction converts Pyruvate to Acetyl Coenzyme A

The **link reaction** takes place in the **mitochondrial matrix**:

1) **Pyruvate is decarboxylated — one carbon atom is removed** from pyruvate in the form of **CO_2**.

2) **NAD is reduced** — it collects **hydrogen** from pyruvate, changing **pyruvate** into **acetate**.

3) **Acetate** is combined with **coenzyme A (CoA)** to form **acetyl coenzyme A (acetyl CoA)**.

4) **No ATP** is produced in this reaction.

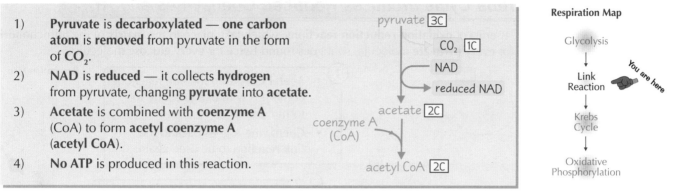

Respiration Map

Glycolysis
↓
Link Reaction → You are here
↓
Krebs Cycle
↓
Oxidative Phosphorylation

The Link Reaction occurs Twice for every Glucose Molecule

Two pyruvate molecules are made for **every glucose molecule** that enters glycolysis. This means the **link reaction** and the third stage (the **Krebs cycle**) happen **twice** for every glucose molecule. So for each glucose molecule:

- Two molecules of **acetyl coenzyme A** go into the Krebs cycle (see page 146).
- Two CO_2 **molecules** are released as a waste product of respiration.
- Two molecules of **reduced NAD** are formed and go to the last stage (oxidative phosphorylation, see page 146).

Mitochondria are Adapted for Respiration

Mitochondria are **adapted** to their **function** in the following ways:

1) The **inner membrane** is **folded** into **cristae**, which **increases** the membrane's **surface area** to **maximise respiration**.

2) There are **lots of ATP synthase** molecules in the **inner membrane** to produce **lots of ATP** in the **final stage** of respiration.

3) The **matrix** contains all the **reactants** and **enzymes** needed for the **Krebs cycle** to take place.

Practice Questions

Q1 Where in the cell does glycolysis occur?

Q2 Is glycolysis an anaerobic or aerobic process?

Q3 How many ATP molecules are used up in glycolysis?

Q4 What is the product of the link reaction?

Exam Questions

Q1 Describe how a 6-carbon molecule of glucose is converted to pyruvate. [6 marks]

Q2 The link reaction of respiration occurs in the mitochondrial matrix.
b) Describe what happens in the link reaction. [3 marks]
a) Explain two ways in which a mitochondrion is adapted to its function. [2 marks]

No ATP was harmed during this reaction...

Ahhhh... too many reactions. I'm sure your head hurts now, 'cause mine certainly does. Just think of revision as like doing exercise — it can be a pain while you're doing it (and maybe afterwards too), but it's worth it for the well-toned brain you'll have. Just keep going over and over it, until you get the first two stages of respiration straight in your head. Then relax.

Aerobic Respiration

As you've seen, glycolysis produces a net gain of two ATP. Pah, we can do better than that.
The Krebs cycle and oxidative phosphorylation are where it all happens — ATP galore.

Stage 3 — the **Krebs Cycle** Produces **Reduced Coenzymes** and **ATP**

The Krebs cycle involves a series of **oxidation-reduction reactions**, which take place in the **matrix** of the **mitochondria**. The cycle happens **once** for **every pyruvate** molecule, so it goes round **twice** for **every glucose** molecule.

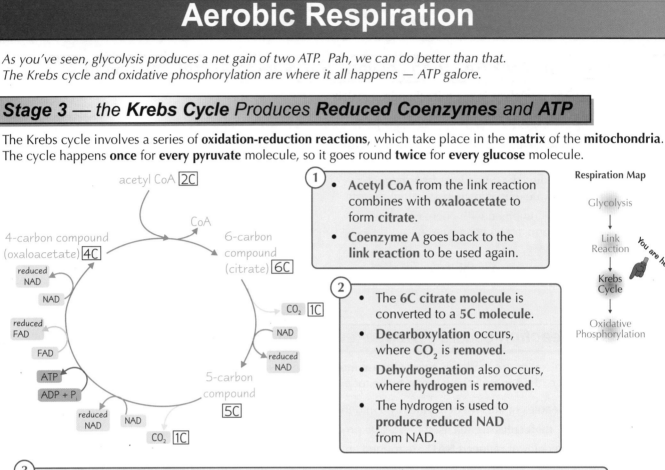

1
- **Acetyl CoA** from the link reaction combines with **oxaloacetate** to form **citrate**.
- **Coenzyme A** goes back to the **link reaction** to be used again.

2
- The **6C citrate molecule** is converted to a **5C molecule**.
- **Decarboxylation** occurs, where CO_2 is **removed**.
- **Dehydrogenation** also occurs, where **hydrogen** is **removed**.
- The hydrogen is used to **produce reduced NAD** from NAD.

Respiration Map

Glycolysis

Link Reaction — *You are here*

Krebs Cycle

Oxidative Phosphorylation

3
- The **5C molecule** is then converted to a **4C molecule**. (There are some intermediate compounds formed during this conversion, but you don't need to know about them.)
- **Decarboxylation** and **dehydrogenation** occur, producing **one** molecule of **reduced FAD** and **two** of **reduced NAD**.
- **ATP** is **produced** by the **direct transfer** of a **phosphate** group from an **intermediate** compound to **ADP**. When a phosphate group is directly transferred from one molecule to another it's called **substrate-level phosphorylation**. **Citrate** has now been **converted** into **oxaloacetate**.

Some **Products** of the **Krebs Cycle** are Used in **Oxidative Phosphorylation**

Some products are **reused**, some are **released** and others are used for the **next stage** of respiration:

Product from one Krebs cycle	Where it goes
1 coenzyme A	Reused in the next link reaction
Oxaloacetate	Regenerated for use in the next Krebs cycle
2 CO_2	Released as a waste product
1 ATP	Used for energy
3 reduced NAD	To oxidative phosphorylation
1 reduced FAD	To oxidative phosphorylation

Mr Krebs

Talking about oxidative phosphorylation was always a big hit with the ladies...

Stage 4 — **Oxidative Phosphorylation** Produces *Lots* of **ATP**

1) Oxidative phosphorylation is the process where the **energy** carried by **electrons**, from **reduced coenzymes** (reduced NAD and reduced FAD), is used to **make ATP**. (The whole point of the previous stages is to make reduced NAD and reduced FAD for the final stage.)

2) Oxidative phosphorylation involves two processes — the **electron transport chain** and **chemiosmosis** (see the next page).

Respiration Map

Glycolysis

Link Reaction

Krebs Cycle

Oxidative Phosphorylation — *You are here*

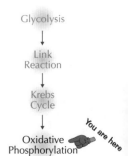

Aerobic Respiration

Protons are Pumped Across the Inner Mitochondrial Membrane

So now on to how **oxidative phosphorylation** actually **works**:

1) **Hydrogen atoms** are released from **reduced NAD** and **reduced FAD** as they're oxidised to NAD and FAD. The H atoms **split** into **protons (H⁺)** and **electrons (e⁻)**.

2) The **electrons** move along the **electron transport chain** (made up of three **electron carriers**), **losing energy** at each carrier.

3) This energy is used by the electron carriers to **pump protons** from the **mitochondrial matrix into** the **intermembrane space** (the space **between** the inner and outer **mitochondrial membranes**).

4) The **concentration** of **protons** is now **higher** in the **intermembrane space** than in the mitochondrial matrix — this forms an **electrochemical gradient** (a **concentration gradient** of **ions**).

5) Protons **move down** the **electrochemical gradient**, back into the mitochondrial matrix, via **ATP synthase**. This **movement** drives the synthesis of **ATP** from **ADP** and **inorganic phosphate** (P_i).

6) The movement of H⁺ ions across a membrane, which generates ATP, is called **chemiosmosis**.

7) In the mitochondrial matrix, at the end of the transport chain, the **protons**, **electrons** and **O₂** (from the blood) combine to form **water**. Oxygen is said to be the final **electron acceptor**.

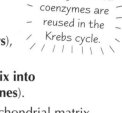

The regenerated coenzymes are reused in the Krebs cycle.

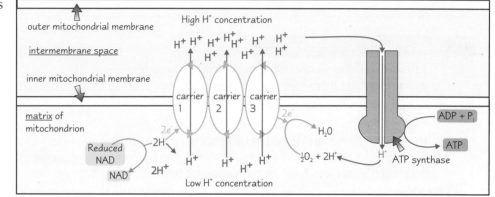

32 ATP Can be Made from One Glucose Molecule

As you know, **oxidative phosphorylation makes ATP** using energy from the reduced coenzymes — **2.5 ATP** are made from each **reduced NAD** and **1.5 ATP** are made from each **reduced FAD**. The table on the right shows **how much** ATP a cell can make from **one molecule** of **glucose** in **aerobic respiration**. (Remember, one molecule of glucose produces 2 pyruvate, so the link reaction and Krebs cycle happen twice.)

Stage of respiration	Molecules produced	Number of ATP molecules
Glycolysis	2 ATP	2
Glycolysis	2 reduced NAD	2 × 2.5 = 5
Link Reaction (×2)	2 reduced NAD	2 × 2.5 = 5
Krebs cycle (×2)	2 ATP	2
Krebs cycle (×2)	6 reduced NAD	6 × 2.5 = 15
Krebs cycle (×2)	2 reduced FAD	2 × 1.5 = 3
		Total ATP = 32

The number of ATP produced per reduced NAD or reduced FAD was thought to be 3 and 2, but new research has shown that the figures are nearer 2.5 and 1.5.

Practice Questions

Q1   Where in the cell does the Krebs cycle occur?

Q2   How many times does decarboxylation happen during one turn of the Krebs cycle?

Q3   What do the electrons lose as they move along the electron transport chain in oxidative phosphorylation?

Exam Question

Q1   Carbon monoxide inhibits the final electron carrier in the electron transport chain.
   a) Explain how this affects ATP production via the electron transport chain. [2 marks]
   b) Explain how this affects ATP production via the Krebs cycle. [2 marks]

The electron transport chain isn't just a FAD with the examiners...

Oh my gosh, I didn't think it could get any worse... You may be wondering how to learn these pages of crazy chemistry, but basically you have to put in the time and go over and over it. Don't worry though, it WILL pay off, and before you know it you'll be set for the exam. And once you know this section you'll be able to do anything, e.g. world domination...

Respiration Experiments

Congratulations — you've done all the main reactiony bits of respiration, so now it's time for some exciting experiments. When I say 'exciting', I'm using the word loosely. But I've got to say something positive to keep the morale up.

Scientific Experiments Provide Evidence for Chemiosmosis

Before the 1960s, scientists **didn't** understand the **connection** between the **electron transport chain** and **ATP synthesis** in respiration. One idea was that **energy lost** from **electrons moving** down the **electron transport chain** creates a **proton gradient** (a concentration gradient of H^+ ions), which is then used to **synthesise ATP** — this is called the **chemiosmotic theory**. Nowadays, there's quite a lot of **experimental evidence** supporting this theory:

Experiment One — Low pH

1) The **pH** of the **intermembrane space** in mitochondria was found to be **lower** than the pH of the **matrix**.

2) A **lower pH** means the intermembrane space is **more acidic** — it has a **higher concentration** of H^+ ions.

3) This observation shows that a **proton gradient exists** between the intermembrane space and the matrix of mitochondria.

The chemiosmotic theory is the most widely accepted theory for linking the electron transport chain to ATP synthesis.

Experiment Two — Artificial Vesicles

1) **Artificial vesicles** were created from **phospholipid bilayers** to **represent** the **inner mitochondrial membrane**.

2) **Proton pumps** from bacteria and **ATP synthase** were added to the vesicle membranes.

3) The **proton pumps** are **activated** by **light**, so when light was shone onto these vesicles they started to **pump protons**. The **pH inside** the vesicles **decreased** — protons were being **pumped into** the vesicle from outside.

4) When **ADP** and P_i were **added** to the solution **outside** the vesicles, **ATP** was **synthesised**.

5) This artificial system shows that a **proton gradient** can be **used** to **synthesise ATP** (but doesn't show that this happens in mitochondria).

Experiment Three — Mitochondria

1) Mitochondria were put into a **slightly alkaline solution** (pH8).

2) They were left until the **whole** of each mitochondrion (matrix and intermembrane space) **became pH8**.

3) When these mitochondria were given **ADP** and P_i **no ATP** was produced.

4) Then the mitochondria were **transferred** to a **more acidic solution** of pH4 (i.e. one with a **higher concentration** of **protons**).

5) The **outer membrane** of the mitochondrion is **permeable** to **protons** — the protons **moved into** the **intermembrane space**, creating a **proton gradient** across the **inner mitochondrial membrane**.

6) In the presence of **ADP** and P_i, **ATP was produced**.

7) This experiment shows that a **proton gradient** can be **used** by mitochondria to **make ATP**.

Experiment Four — Uncouplers

1) **Uncouplers** are substances that **destroy** the **proton gradient** across the **inner mitochondrial membrane**.

2) An **uncoupler** was added to mitochondria, along with **reduced NAD**, and **ADP** and P_i.

3) **No ATP** was made.

4) This experiment shows that a **proton gradient** is required to **synthesise ATP** in **mitochondria**.

Respiration Experiments

The Rate of Respiration can be Measured using a Respirometer

1) The volume of **oxygen taken up** or the volume of **carbon dioxide produced indicates** the **rate** of **respiration**.

2) A **respirometer** measures the rate of **oxygen** being **taken up** — the **more** oxygen taken up, the **faster** the rate of respiration.

3) Here's how you can use a **respirometer** to **measure** the volume of **oxygen taken up** by some **woodlice**:

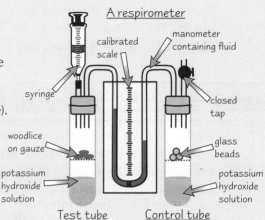

A respirometer

- The apparatus is set up as shown on the right.
- **Each tube** contains **potassium hydroxide** solution (or soda lime), which **absorbs carbon dioxide**.
- The **control tube** is set up in exactly the **same way** as the test tube, but **without** the **woodlice**, to make sure the **results** are **only** due to the woodlice **respiring** (e.g. it contains beads that have the same mass as the woodlice).
- The **syringe** is used to set the **fluid** in the **manometer** to a **known level**.
- The apparatus is **left** for a **set** period of **time** (e.g. 20 minutes).
- During that time there'll be a **decrease** in the **volume** of the **air** in the test tube, due to **oxygen consumption** by the **woodlice** (all the CO_2 produced is absorbed by the potassium hydroxide).
- The decrease in the volume of the air will **reduce the pressure** in the tube and cause the **coloured liquid** in the manometer to **move towards** the test tube.
- The **distance moved** by the **liquid** in a **given time** is **measured**. This value can then be used to **calculate** the **volume of oxygen** taken in by the woodlice **per minute**.
- Any **variables** that could **affect** the results are **controlled**, e.g. temperature, volume of potassium hydroxide solution in each test tube.

4) To produce more **reliable** results the experiment is **repeated** and a **mean volume** of O_2 is calculated.

Practice Questions

Q1 What is the chemiosmotic theory?

Q2 What does a respirometer measure?

Exam Questions

Q1 In the first stage of an experiment, mitochondria were put in a solution at pH 9.1 and left until each mitochondrion had a pH of 9.1 throughout its compartments. In the presence of ADP and P_i, no ATP was produced. During the second stage of the experiment, the same mitochondria were placed in a solution at pH 3.7. In the presence of ADP and P_i, ATP was produced.
- a) Why was no ATP produced during the first part of the experiment? [1 mark]
- b) What would the pH of the intermembrane space have been during the second stage of the experiment? [1 mark]
- c) Do these results support the chemiosmotic theory? Explain your answer. [1 mark]

Q2 A respirometer is set up as shown in the diagram on this page.
- a) Explain the purpose of the control tube. [1 mark]
- b) Explain what would happen if there was no potassium hydroxide in the tubes. [2 marks]
- c) What other substance could be measured to find out the rate of respiration? [1 mark]

My results are dodgy — I'm sure the woodlice are holding their breath...

Okay, that wasn't very funny, but this page doesn't really give me any inspiration. You probably feel the same way. It's just one of those pages that you have to plough through. You could try drawing a few pretty diagrams to get the experiments in your head. And after you've got it sorted do something exciting, like trying to stick your toe in your ear...

Aerobic and Anaerobic Respiration

We're on the home stretch now ladies and gents — these are the last two pages in the section.

There are **Two Types** of **Anaerobic Respiration**

1) **Anaerobic** respiration **doesn't use oxygen**.

2) It **doesn't** involve the **link reaction**, the **Krebs cycle** or **oxidative phosphorylation**.

3) There are **two types** of anaerobic respiration — **alcoholic fermentation** and **lactate fermentation**.

4) These two processes are **similar**, because they both take place in the **cytoplasm**, they both produce **two ATP** per molecule of glucose and they both **start** with **glycolysis** (which produces **pyruvate**).

5) They **differ** in **which organisms** they occur in and what happens to the **pyruvate** (see below).

Lactate Fermentation Occurs in **Mammals** and Produces **Lactate**

1) **Reduced NAD** (from glycolysis) transfers **hydrogen** to **pyruvate** to form **lactate** and **NAD**.

2) **NAD** can then be reused in **glycolysis**.

reduced NAD → NAD

pyruvate → lactate (lactic acid)

Some bacteria carry out lactate fermentation.

The production of lactate **regenerates NAD**. This means **glycolysis** can **continue** even when there **isn't** much oxygen around, so a **small amount of ATP** can still be **produced** to keep some biological process going... clever.

Alcoholic Fermentation Occurs in **Yeast Cells** and Produces **Ethanol**

1) **CO$_2$** is **removed** from **pyruvate** to form **ethanal**.

2) **Reduced NAD** (from glycolysis) transfers **hydrogen** to **ethanal** to form **ethanol** and **NAD**.

3) **NAD** can then be reused in **glycolysis**.

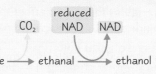

CO$_2$ reduced NAD → NAD

pyruvate → ethanal → ethanol

Alcoholic fermentation also occurs in plants.

The production of ethanol also **regenerates NAD** so **glycolysis** can **continue** when there isn't much oxygen around.

Aerobic Respiration **Doesn't Release** as **Much Energy** as **Possible**...

In theory, **aerobic respiration** can make **32 ATP** per **glucose molecule** (see page 147). But in reality the **actual yield** is **lower** because:

1) Some of the **reduced NAD** formed during the **first three stages** of aerobic respiration is used in **other reduction reactions** in the cell instead of in **oxidative phosphorylation**.

2) **Some ATP** is **used up** by **actively transporting** substances **into the mitochondria** during respiration, e.g. **pyruvate** (formed at the end of glycolysis), **ADP** and **phosphate** (both needed for making ATP).

3) The **inner mitochondrial membrane is leaky** — some **protons** may **leak** into the **matrix** without passing through **ATP synthase** and **without making ATP**.

...but it Still **Releases More Energy** than **Anaerobic** Respiration

1) The **ATP yield** from **anaerobic** respiration is **always lower** than from **aerobic** respiration.

2) This is because **anaerobic respiration** only includes **one energy-releasing stage** (glycolysis), which only produces **2 ATP** per glucose molecule.

3) The energy-releasing reactions of the **Krebs cycle** and **oxidative phosphorylation** need **oxygen**, so they **can't** occur during anaerobic respiration.

Aerobic and Anaerobic Respiration

Cells Can Respire Different Substrates

1) Cells **respire glucose**, but they also respire **other carbohydrates**, **lipids** and **proteins**.

2) Any **biological molecule** that can be **broken down** in **respiration** to **release energy** is called a **respiratory substrate**.

3) When an organism respires a specific **respiratory substrate**, the **respiratory quotient** (RQ) can be **worked out**.

4) The **respiratory quotient** is the volume of **carbon dioxide** produced when that **substrate is respired**, **divided** by the volume of **oxygen consumed**, in a set period of **time**.

Proteins and lipids enter respiration at the Krebs cycle.

$$RQ = \frac{\text{Volume of } CO_2 \text{ released}}{\text{Volume of } O_2 \text{ consumed}}$$

5) For example, you can work out the **RQ** for cells that **only respire glucose**:
   - The basic equation for aerobic respiration using glucose is: $C_6H_{12}O_6 + 6O_2 \rightarrow 6CO_2 + 6H_2O + \text{energy}$
   - The RQ of glucose = molecules of CO_2 **released** ÷ molecules of O_2 **consumed**
   $$= 6 \div 6 = 1.$$

6) Respiratory quotients have been worked out for the respiration of **other respiratory substrates**. **Lipids** and **proteins** have an RQ value **lower than one** because **more oxygen** is needed to oxidise fats and lipids than to oxidise carbohydrates.

Respiratory Substrate	RQ
Lipids (triglycerides)	0.7
Proteins or amino acids	0.9
Carbohydrates	1

The Respiratory Quotient tells you what Substrate is being Respired

1) The **respiratory quotient** for an organism is **useful** because it tells you **what kind** of **respiratory substrate** an organism is respiring and what **type** of **respiration** it's using (aerobic or anaerobic).

2) For example, under **normal conditions** the usual **RQ** for humans is between **0.7** and **1.0**. An RQ in this range shows that some **fats** (lipids) are being used for respiration, as well as **carbohydrates** like glucose. Protein **isn't** normally used by the body for respiration unless there's **nothing else**.

3) **High RQs** (greater than 1) mean that an organism is **short of oxygen**, and is having to respire **anaerobically** as well as aerobically.

4) **Plants** sometimes have a **low RQ**. This is because the CO_2 released in respiration is **used** for **photosynthesis** (so it's not measured).

Practice Questions

Q1 What molecule is made when CO_2 is removed from pyruvate during alcoholic fermentation?
Q2 Does anaerobic respiration release more or less energy per glucose molecule than aerobic respiration?
Q3 What is a respiratory substrate?

Exam Questions

Q1 A culture of mammalian cells was incubated with glucose, pyruvate and antimycin C. Antimycin C inhibits an electron carrier in the electron transport chain of aerobic respiration. Explain why these cells can still produce lactate. [1 mark]

Q2 This equation shows the aerobic respiration of a fat called triolein: $C_{57}H_{104}O_6 + 80O_2 \rightarrow 52H_2O + 57CO_2$ Calculate the respiratory quotient for this reaction. Show your working. [2 marks]

My little sis has an RQ of 157 — she's really clever...

I know, I'm really pushing the boundary between humour and non-humour here. But, at least we've come to the end of the section — and what a section it was. You might think it's unfair finishing it off with nasty calculations, but if you understand how to work out the RQ you'll be one step closer to being sorted for the exam.

DNA, RNA and Protein Synthesis

You learnt how DNA and its mysterious cousin RNA are used to produce proteins at AS, but irritatingly you need to know it at A2 as well (with a few extra bits thrown in — unlucky).

DNA is Made of **Nucleotides** that Have a **Sugar**, a **Phosphate** and a **Base**

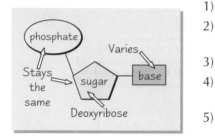

1) DNA is a **polynucleotide** — it's made up of lots of **nucleotides** joined together.
2) Each nucleotide is made from a **pentose sugar** (with 5 carbon atoms), a **phosphate** group and a **nitrogenous base**.
3) The **sugar** in DNA nucleotides is a **deoxyribose** sugar.
4) Each nucleotide has the **same sugar and phosphate**. The **base** on each nucleotide can **vary** though.
5) There are **four** possible bases — adenine (**A**), thymine (**T**), cytosine (**C**) and guanine (**G**).

You learnt a lot of this at AS but you need to know it for A2 as well.

Two Polynucleotide Strands **Join Together** to Form a **Double-Helix**

1) DNA nucleotides join together to form **polynucleotide strands**.
2) The nucleotides join up between the **phosphate** group of one nucleotide and the **sugar** of another, creating a **sugar-phosphate backbone**.
3) **Two** DNA polynucleotide strands join together by **hydrogen bonding** between the bases.
4) Each base can only join with one particular partner — this is called **complementary base pairing**.
5) **Adenine** always pairs with **thymine** (**A - T**) and **guanine** always pairs with **cytosine** (**G - C**). →
6) The two strands **wind up** to form the **DNA double-helix**.

When two strands have bases that pair up the strands are said to be complementary to each other:

```
A T C G G
| | | | |
T A G C C
```

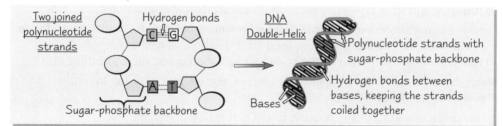

DNA Contains **Genes** Which are **Instructions** for **Proteins**

Polypeptide is just another word for a protein.

1) Genes are **sections of DNA**. They're found on **chromosomes**.
2) Genes **code** for **proteins** (polypeptides), including **enzymes** — they contain the **instructions** to make them.
3) Proteins are made from **amino acids**. Different proteins have a **different number** and **order** of amino acids.
4) It's the **order** of **bases** in a gene that determines the **order of amino acids** in a particular **protein**.
5) Each amino acid is coded for by a sequence of **three bases** (called a **triplet** or a **codon**) in a gene.
6) **Different sequences** of bases code for different amino acids — this is the **genetic code**.

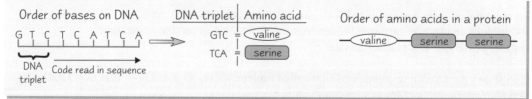

7) Some amino acids are coded for by **more than one** triplet, e.g. CGA, CGG, CGT and CGC all code for arginine.
8) Other triplets are used to tell the cell when to **start** and **stop** production of the protein — these are called **start** and **stop codons**. They're found at the **beginning** and **end** of the gene. E.g. TAG is a stop codon.

Stop codons are also called stop signals.

DNA, RNA and Protein Synthesis

DNA is Copied into RNA for Protein Synthesis

1) DNA molecules are found in the **nucleus** of the cell, but the organelles for protein synthesis (**ribosomes**) are found in the **cytoplasm**.

2) DNA is too large to move out of the nucleus, so a section is **copied** into **RNA**. This process is called **transcription** (see next page).

3) RNA is a **single** polynucleotide strand — it contains the sugar **ribose**, and **uracil (U)** replaces thymine as a base. Uracil **always pairs** with **adenine** during protein synthesis.

4) The RNA **leaves** the nucleus and joins with a **ribosome** in the cytoplasm, where it can be used to synthesise a **protein**. This process is called **translation** (see page 155).

5) There are actually two types of RNA you need to know about:

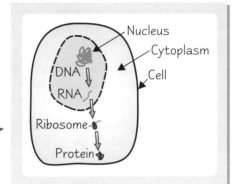

Messenger RNA (mRNA)
- Made in the **nucleus**.
- **Three adjacent bases** are called a **codon**.
- It **carries the genetic code** from the DNA in the **nucleus** to the **cytoplasm**, where it's used to make a **protein** during **translation**.

Codons and anticodons are sometimes referred to as triplets.

Transfer RNA (tRNA)
- Found in the **cytoplasm**.
- It has an **amino acid binding site** at one end and a **sequence** of **three bases** at the other end called an **anticodon**.
- It **carries the amino acids** that are used to make **proteins** to the **ribosomes** during **translation**.

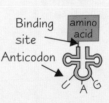

Practice Questions

Q1 Name the four possible bases in DNA.
Q2 Which DNA bases pair together in complementary base pairing?
Q3 What determines the order of amino acids in a protein?
Q4 Name the bases found in RNA.
Q5 What are three adjacent bases in mRNA called?
Q6 Where in the cell is mRNA made?

Amino Acid	DNA sequence
Serine	AGA
Leucine	GAT
Tyrosine	ATA
Valine	CAC
Alanine	CGT
Arginine	GCG

Exam Questions

Q1 Describe the role of mRNA and the role of tRNA. [2 marks]

Q2 A piece of DNA has the following nucleotide sequence: AGAAGAATACACCGT
    a) How many amino acids does this sequence code for? [1 mark]
    b) Using the table above, write down the amino acid sequence it codes for. [2 marks]

Genes, genes are good for your heart, the more you eat, the more you...

Hurrah — finally some pages with something familiar on. But just because you learnt some of it at AS doesn't mean you can skip them. You really need to get your head around how DNA and RNA work together to produce proteins or the next two pages are going to be a teeeny weeny bit tricky. Don't say I didn't warn you. Turn over too quickly at your own peril...

Transcription and Translation

Time to find out how RNA works its magic to make proteins. It gets a bit complicated but bear with it.

First Stage of Protein Synthesis — Transcription

During transcription an **mRNA copy** of a gene (a section of DNA) is made in the **nucleus**:

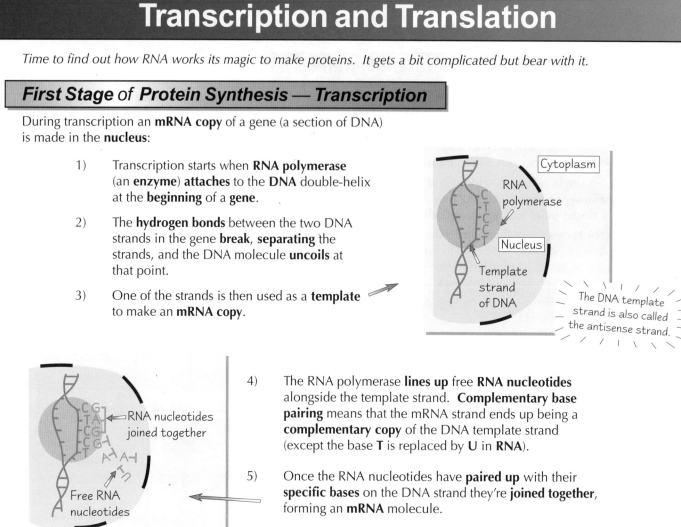

1) Transcription starts when **RNA polymerase** (an **enzyme**) **attaches** to the **DNA** double-helix at the **beginning** of a **gene**.

2) The **hydrogen bonds** between the two DNA strands in the gene **break**, **separating** the strands, and the DNA molecule **uncoils** at that point.

3) One of the strands is then used as a **template** to make an **mRNA copy**.

The DNA template strand is also called the antisense strand.

4) The RNA polymerase **lines up** free **RNA nucleotides** alongside the template strand. **Complementary base pairing** means that the mRNA strand ends up being a **complementary copy** of the DNA template strand (except the base **T** is replaced by **U** in **RNA**).

5) Once the RNA nucleotides have **paired up** with their **specific bases** on the DNA strand they're **joined together**, forming an **mRNA** molecule.

6) The RNA polymerase moves **along** the DNA, separating the strands and **assembling** the mRNA strand.

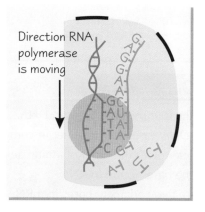

7) The **hydrogen bonds** between the uncoiled strands of DNA **re-form** once the RNA polymerase has passed by and the strands **coil back into a double-helix**.

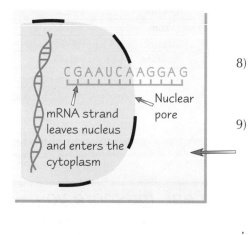

8) When RNA polymerase reaches a **stop codon**, it stops making mRNA and **detaches** from the DNA.

9) The **mRNA** moves **out** of the **nucleus** through a **nuclear pore** and attaches to a **ribosome** in the cytoplasm, where the next stage of protein synthesis takes place (see next page).

Transcription and Translation

Second Stage of Protein Synthesis — Translation

Translation occurs at the **ribosomes** in the **cytoplasm**. During **translation**, **amino acids** are **joined together** to make a **polypeptide chain** (protein), following the sequence of **codons** carried by the mRNA.

1) The **mRNA attaches** itself to a **ribosome** and **transfer RNA** (**tRNA**) molecules **carry amino acids** to the ribosome.

2) A tRNA molecule, with an **anticodon** that's **complementary** to the **first codon** on the mRNA, attaches itself to the mRNA by **complementary base pairing**.

3) A second tRNA molecule attaches itself to the **next codon** on the mRNA in the **same way**.

4) The two amino acids attached to the tRNA molecules are **joined** by a **peptide bond**. The first tRNA molecule **moves away**, leaving its amino acid behind.

5) A third tRNA molecule binds to the **next codon** on the mRNA. Its amino acid **binds** to the first two and the second tRNA molecule **moves away**.

6) This process continues, producing a chain of linked amino acids (a **polypeptide chain**), until there's a **stop codon** on the mRNA molecule.

7) The polypeptide chain (**protein**) **moves away** from the ribosome and translation is complete.

anticodon on tRNA U A C / codon on mRNA A U G

Protein synthesis is also called polypeptide synthesis as it makes a polypeptide (protein)

Practice Questions

Q1 What are the two stages of protein synthesis called?
Q2 Where does the first stage of protein synthesis take place?
Q3 When does RNA polymerase stop making mRNA?
Q4 Where does the second stage of protein synthesis take place?

Exam Questions

Q1 A drug that inhibits cell growth is found to be able to bind to DNA, preventing RNA polymerase from binding. Explain how this drug will affect protein synthesis. [2 marks]

Q2 A polypeptide chain (protein) from a eukaryotic cell is 10 amino acids long.
a) Predict how long the mRNA for this protein would be in nucleotides (without the start and stop codons). Explain your answer. [2 marks]
b) Describe how the mRNA is translated into the polypeptide chain. [6 marks]

The only translation I'm interested in is a translation of this page into English...

So you start off with DNA, lots of cleverness happens and bingo... you've got a protein. Only problem is you need to know the cleverness bit in quite a lot of detail. So scribble it down, recite it to yourself, explain it to your best mate or do whatever else helps you remember the joys of protein synthesis. And then think how clever you must be to know it all.

Control of Protein Synthesis and Body Plans

Proteins aren't just made willy-nilly — there's some control over when they're synthesised...

Genes can be Switched On or Off

1) **Protein synthesis** can be **controlled** at the **genetic level** by **altering** the rate of **transcription** of genes. E.g. **increased** transcription produces **more mRNA**, which can be used to make **more protein**.

> Transcription is covered on page 154.

2) Genetic control of protein production in **prokaryotes** (e.g. bacteria) often involves **operons**.

3) An operon is a **section** of **DNA** that contains **structural genes**, **control elements** and sometimes a **regulatory gene**:

- The structural genes code for **useful proteins**, such as **enzymes** — they're all **transcribed together**.

- The control elements include a **promoter** (a DNA sequence located **before** the structural genes that **RNA polymerase** binds to) and an **operator** (a DNA sequence that proteins called **transcription factors** bind to).

- The regulatory gene codes for a **transcription factor** — a protein that **binds** to **DNA** and **switches** genes **on** or **off** by **increasing** or **decreasing** the **rate** of **transcription**. Factors that **increase** the rate are called **activators** and those that **decrease** the rate are called **repressors**.

The only control Brad had over his jeans was some braces.

4) The **shape** of a transcription factor determines whether it **can bind to DNA** or **not**, and can be **altered** by the binding of some molecules, e.g. hormones and sugars.

5) This means the **amount** of some **molecules** in an environment or a cell can **control** the **synthesis** of some **proteins** by affecting **transcription factor binding**. You need to learn this example:

EXAMPLE: The *lac* operon in *E. coli*

1) *E. coli* is a bacterium that **respires glucose**, but it can use **lactose** if glucose isn't available.

2) The genes that produce the **enzymes** needed to **respire lactose** are found on an operon called the **lac operon**.

3) The lac operon has **three structural genes** — **lacZ**, **lacY** and **lacA**, which produce proteins that help the bacteria digest lactose (including **β-galactosidase** and **lactose permease**).

4) Here's how it works:

Lactose NOT present

The **regulatory** gene (lacI) produces the **lac repressor**, which **binds** to the **operator** site when there's **no lactose** present and **blocks transcription**.

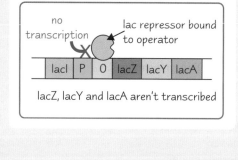

lacZ, lacY and lacA aren't transcribed

Lactose present

When **lactose is present**, it **binds** to the **repressor**, **changing** the repressor's **shape** so that it can **no longer bind** to the operator site.

RNA polymerase can now begin **transcription** of the structural genes.

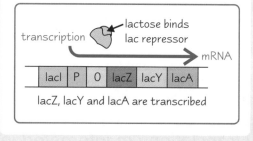

lacZ, lacY and lacA are transcribed

Control of Protein Synthesis and Body Plans

Some Genes Control the Development of Body Plans

1) A **body plan** is the **general structure** of an organism, e.g. the *Drosophila* fruit fly has various **body parts** (head, abdomen, etc.) that are **arranged** in a **particular way** — this is its body plan.

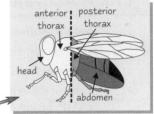

2) **Proteins control** the **development** of a body plan — they help set up the basic body plan so that everything is in the right place, e.g. legs grow where legs should grow.

3) The proteins that control body plan development are **coded for** by genes called **homeotic genes**. E.g. two homeotic gene clusters control the development of the *Drosophila* body plan — one controls the development of the head and anterior thorax and the other controls the development of the posterior thorax and abdomen.

4) **Similar homeotic genes** are found in **animals**, **plants** and **fungi**, which means that body plan development is controlled in a similar way in flies, mice, humans, etc. Here's how homeotic genes control development:

   - Homeotic genes have **regions** called **homeobox sequences** that code for a part of the protein called the **homeodomain**.

   - The homeodomain **binds** to specific **sites** on **DNA**, enabling the protein to work as a **transcription factor** (see previous page).

   - The proteins bind to DNA at the **start** of **developmental genes**, **activating** or **repressing transcription** and so altering the production of proteins involved in the development of the body plan.

Programmed Cell Death is Involved in the Development of Body Plans

1) Some cells **die** and **break down** as a **normal** part of **development**.

2) This is a **highly controlled process** called apoptosis, or **programmed cell death**.

3) Once **apoptosis** has been **triggered** the **cell** is **broken down** in a series of steps:
   - The cell produces **enzymes** that **break down** important cell components such as **proteins** in the cytoplasm and **DNA** in the nucleus.
   - As the cell's contents are broken down it begins to **shrink** and **breaks up** into **fragments**.
   - The **cell fragments** are **engulfed** by **phagocytes** and **digested**.

4) Apoptosis is involved in the development of **body plans** — mitosis and **differentiation create** the bulk of the **body parts** and then apoptosis **refines** the parts by **removing** the **unwanted structures**. For example:

   - When hands and feet first develop the digits (fingers and toes) are connected. They're only separated when cells in the connecting tissue undergo apoptosis.

   - As tadpoles develop into frogs their tail cells are removed by apoptosis.

   - An excess of nerve cells are produced during the development of the nervous system. Nerve cells that aren't needed undergo apoptosis.

5) All cells contain **genes** that code for proteins that **promote** or **inhibit apoptosis**.

6) During development, genes that **control** apoptosis are **switched on** and off in **appropriate** cells, so that **some die** and the **correct body plan develops**.

Practice Questions

Q1 What does a transcription factor do?

Q2 What is a body plan?

Q3 Give one example of how apoptosis is used during the development of a body plan.

Exam Question

Q1 Explain how the presence of lactose causes *E. coli* to produce ß-galactosidase and lactose permease. [4 marks]

Too much revision can activate programmed cell death in your brain....

OK, maybe that's not completely true. There are a lot of 'interesting' words to remember on these two pages — I bet you're glad you decided to study biology. Some of these concepts are quite hard to get your head round but keep going over it until it all makes sense — it'll click eventually. Then you can dazzle your friends with your knowledge of gene control...

Protein Activation and Gene Mutation

Some proteins need activating before they'll work — cyclic AMP gives them a molecular kick up their amino acid backside. Proteins can also be affected by mutations in DNA... sounds like it's a hard life being a protein...

cAMP Activates Some Proteins by Altering Their Shape

1) **Protein synthesis** can be controlled at the **genetic level** by **molecules** (see page 156).

2) Some proteins produced by protein synthesis **aren't active** though — they have to be **activated** to work.

3) **Protein activation** is also controlled by **molecules**, e.g. **hormones** and **sugars**.

4) Some of these molecules work by **binding** to **cell membranes** and **triggering** the production of cyclic **AMP** (**cAMP**) **inside** the **cell**.

5) cAMP then **activates proteins** inside the cell by **altering** their **three-dimensional** (3D) **structure**.

6) For example, altering the 3D structure can **change** the **active site** of an enzyme, making it become **more** or **less active**.

7) For example, cAMP activates **protein kinase A** (**PKA**):

> 1) **PKA** is an **enzyme** made of four subunits.
>
> 2) When cAMP **isn't bound**, the four units are bound together and are **inactive**.
>
> 3) When cAMP **binds**, it causes a **change** in the enzyme's **3D structure**, releasing the active subunits — PKA is now **active**.

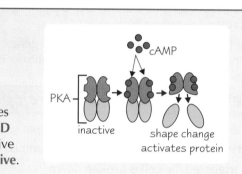

cAMP is a secondary messenger — it relays the message from the control molecule, e.g. the hormone, to the inside of the cell (see page 118).

Mutations are Changes to the Base Sequence of DNA

1) Any change to the **base (nucleotide) sequence** of DNA is called a **mutation**.

2) The **types** of mutations that can occur include:

- **Substitution** — one base is swapped for another, e.g. ATGCCT becomes ATTCCT
- **Deletion** — one base is removed, e.g. ATGCCT becomes ATCCT
- **Insertion** — one base is added, e.g. ATGCCT becomes ATGACCT
- **Duplication** — one or more bases are repeated, e.g. ATGCCT becomes ATGCCCCT
- **Inversion** — a sequence of bases is reversed, e.g. ATGCCT becomes ACCGTT

3) The **order** of **DNA bases** in a gene determines the **order of amino acids** in a particular **protein**. If a mutation occurs in a gene, the **primary structure** (amino acid chain) of the protein it codes for could be **altered**:

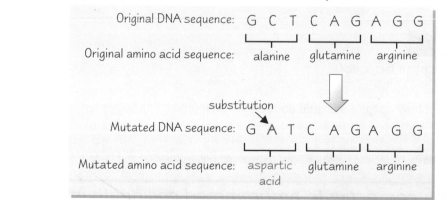

4) This may **change** the final **3D shape** of the protein so it **doesn't work properly**, e.g. **active sites** in enzymes may not form properly, meaning that **substrates can't bind** to them.

Protein Activation and Gene Mutation

Mutations can be Neutral, Beneficial or Harmful

1) Some mutations can have a **neutral effect** on a protein's **function**. They may have a neutral effect because:

   - The mutation changes a base in a triplet, but the amino acid that the triplet codes for **doesn't change**. This happens because **some amino acids** are coded for by **more than one triplet**. E.g. both **TAT** and **TAC** code for **tyrosine**, so if TAT is changed to TAC the amino acid won't change.

   - The mutation produces a triplet that codes for a **different amino acid**, but the amino acid is **chemically similar** to the original so it functions like the original amino acid. E.g. **arginine (AGG)** and **lysine (AAG)** are coded for by similar triplets — a **substitution** mutation can **swap** the amino acids. But this mutation would have a **neutral effect** on a **protein** as the amino acids are **chemically similar**.

   - The mutated triplet codes for an amino acid **not involved** with the protein's **function**, e.g. one that's located **far away** from an enzyme's **active site**, so the protein **works** as it **normally** does.

2) A **neutral effect** on protein function **won't** affect an **organism** overall.

3) However, some mutations **do** affect a protein's **function** — they can make a protein **more** or **less active**, e.g. by **changing** the **shape** of an enzyme's **active site**.

4) If protein function **is affected** it can have a **beneficial** or **harmful** effect on the **whole organism**:

Mutations with beneficial effects	Mutations with harmful effects
• These have an **advantageous effect** on an organism, i.e. they **increase** its chance of **survival**. • E.g. some bacterial **enzymes break down** certain **antibiotics**. **Mutations** in the genes that code for these enzymes could make them work on a **wider range** of antibiotics. This is **beneficial** to the **bacteria** because antibiotic resistance can help them to survive.	• These have a **disadvantageous effect** on an organism, i.e. they **decrease** its chance of **survival**. • E.g. **cystic fibrosis** (CF) can be caused by a **deletion** of three bases in the gene that codes for the **CFTR** (cystic fibrosis transmembrane conductance regulator) **protein**. The mutated CFTR protein **folds incorrectly**, so it's **broken down**. This leads to **excess mucus production**, which affects the **lungs** of CF sufferers.

Mutations that are beneficial to the organism are passed on to future generations by the process of natural selection (see p. 170).

Practice Questions

Q1 How does cAMP activate a protein?

Q2 Give two reasons why a mutation may have a neutral effect on a protein's function.

Amino acid	DNA triplet
Methionine	ATG
Tyrosine	TAT or TAC
Serine	TCA or TCC
Glycine	GGC or GGT
Cysteine	TGT or TGC

Exam Questions

Q1 a) Define the term mutation. [1 mark]
    b) Describe two types of mutation that occur in DNA. [2 marks]

Q2 A gene begins with the following DNA sequence: ATGTATTCAGGCTGT
    A mutation occurred where the ninth base was substituted by cytosine (C).
    a) Write down the mutated DNA sequence. [1 mark]
    b) Using the table, explain the effect that the mutation would have on the protein. [3 marks]

Mutations in adolescent turtles can enhance their ninja skills...

The important thing to remember about cAMP is that it alters the 3D structure of proteins — you can't just say that it activates proteins, you need to say how it does it as well. Don't forget that mutations can be harmless and that some can improve the way a protein functions — it's easy to associate 'mutation' with 'bad', but don't fall into that trap.

Meiosis

To kick-start this section we have a well-known A2-Biology crowd-pleaser... meiosis. If you thought mitosis was exciting at AS then you ain't seen nothing yet.

DNA from **One Generation** is **Passed** to the Next by **Gametes**

1) **Gametes** are the **sperm** cells in males and **egg** cells in females. They join together at **fertilisation** to form a **zygote**, which divides and develops into a **new organism**.

2) Normal **body cells** have the **diploid number** (**2n**) of chromosomes — meaning each cell contains **two** of each chromosome, one from the mum and one from the dad.

3) **Gametes** have the **haploid** (**n**) number — there's only one copy of each chromosome.

4) At **fertilisation**, a **haploid sperm** fuses with a **haploid egg**, making a cell with the **normal diploid number** of chromosomes (2n).

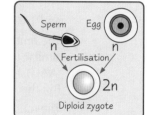

Gametes are Formed by **Meiosis**

Meiosis is a type of **cell division** that happens in the reproductive organs to **produce gametes**. Cells that divide by meiosis are **diploid** to start with, but the cells that are formed from meiosis are **haploid** — the chromosome number halves. Cells formed by meiosis are all **genetically different** because each new cell ends up with a **different combination** of chromosomes.

Gametes Divide Twice in **Meiosis**

Before meiosis, **interphase** happens — the cell's DNA unravels and **replicates** so there are **two** copies of each chromosome in each cell. Each copy of the chromosome is called a **chromatid** and a pair are called **sister chromatids** — they're joined in the middle by a **centromere**. After interphase, the cells enter meiosis where they **divide twice** — the first division is called **meiosis I** and the second is called **meiosis II**. There are **four similar stages** to each division called **prophase**, **metaphase**, **anaphase** and **telophase**:

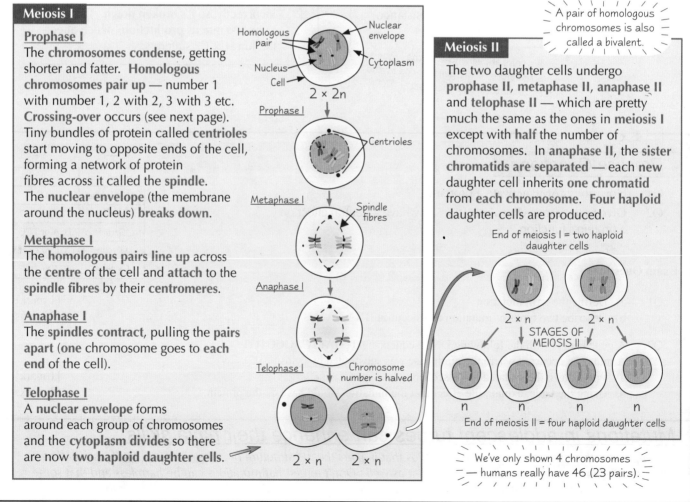

Meiosis I

Prophase I
The **chromosomes condense**, getting shorter and fatter. **Homologous chromosomes pair up** — number 1 with number 1, 2 with 2, 3 with 3 etc. **Crossing-over** occurs (see next page). Tiny bundles of protein called **centrioles** start moving to opposite ends of the cell, forming a network of protein fibres across it called the **spindle**. The **nuclear envelope** (the membrane around the nucleus) **breaks down**.

Metaphase I
The **homologous pairs line up** across the **centre of the cell** and **attach to the spindle fibres** by their **centromeres**.

Anaphase I
The **spindles contract**, pulling the **pairs apart** (**one chromosome goes to each end of the cell**).

Telophase I
A **nuclear envelope** forms around each group of chromosomes and the **cytoplasm divides** so there are now **two haploid daughter cells**.

Meiosis II

The two daughter cells undergo **prophase II, metaphase II, anaphase II and telophase II** — which are pretty much the same as the ones in **meiosis I** except with **half** the number of chromosomes. In **anaphase II**, the **sister chromatids are separated** — each **new** daughter cell inherits **one chromatid** from **each chromosome**. **Four haploid daughter cells** are produced.

Meiosis

Meiosis *Produces Cells that are* Genetically Different

Genetic variation is the **differences** that exist between **individuals' genetic material**. The reason meiosis is important is that it **creates** genetic variation — it makes gametes that are all genetically different. It does this in three ways:

(1) Crossing-over of chromatids

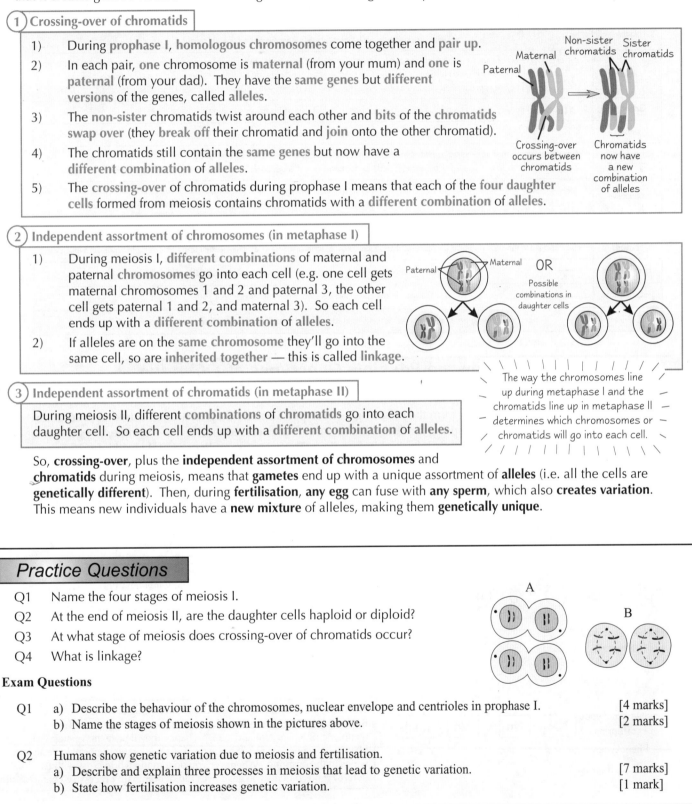

1) During **prophase I**, **homologous chromosomes** come together and **pair up**.

2) In each pair, **one** chromosome is **maternal** (from your mum) and **one** is **paternal** (from your dad). They have the **same genes** but **different versions** of the genes, called **alleles**.

3) The **non-sister** chromatids twist around each other and **bits** of the **chromatids** **swap over** (they **break off** their chromatid and **join** onto the other chromatid).

4) The chromatids still contain the **same genes** but now have a **different combination** of **alleles**.

5) The **crossing-over** of chromatids during prophase I means that each of the **four daughter cells** formed from meiosis contains chromatids with a **different combination** of **alleles**.

(2) Independent assortment of chromosomes (in metaphase I)

1) During meiosis I, **different combinations** of maternal and paternal **chromosomes** go into each cell (e.g. one cell gets maternal chromosomes 1 and 2 and paternal 3, the other cell gets paternal 1 and 2, and maternal 3). So each cell ends up with a **different combination** of **alleles**.

2) If alleles are on the **same chromosome** they'll go into the same cell, so are **inherited together** — this is called **linkage**.

(3) Independent assortment of chromatids (in metaphase II)

During meiosis II, different **combinations** of **chromatids** go into each daughter cell. So each cell ends up with a **different combination** of **alleles**.

> The way the chromosomes line up during metaphase I and the chromatids line up in metaphase II determines which chromosomes or chromatids will go into each cell.

So, **crossing-over**, plus the **independent assortment of chromosomes** and **chromatids** during meiosis, means that **gametes** end up with a unique assortment of **alleles** (i.e. all the cells are **genetically different**). Then, during **fertilisation**, **any egg** can fuse with **any sperm**, which also **creates variation**. This means new individuals have a **new mixture** of alleles, making them **genetically unique**.

Practice Questions

Q1 Name the four stages of meiosis I.

Q2 At the end of meiosis II, are the daughter cells haploid or diploid?

Q3 At what stage of meiosis does crossing-over of chromatids occur?

Q4 What is linkage?

Exam Questions

Q1 a) Describe the behaviour of the chromosomes, nuclear envelope and centrioles in prophase I. [4 marks]
   b) Name the stages of meiosis shown in the pictures above. [2 marks]

Q2 Humans show genetic variation due to meiosis and fertilisation.
   a) Describe and explain three processes in meiosis that lead to genetic variation. [7 marks]
   b) State how fertilisation increases genetic variation. [1 mark]

Physics — that's what I call crossing-over to the dark side...

You're probably sat there thinking about the good old days of AS, where meiosis didn't seem that hard... But, as your teachers will say, this is sooooo much more interesting. And I'm afraid that even if you don't agree with that, you still have to get your head around this lot. Go over it again and again until you start dreaming about chromosomes...

Inheritance

If you know the alleles two organisms have you can work out the alleles their offspring might have if they get jiggy with it.

You **Need to Know** These **Genetic Terms**

TERM	DESCRIPTION
Gene	A sequence of bases on a DNA molecule that codes for a protein (polypeptide), which results in a characteristic, e.g. the gene for eye colour.
Allele	A different version of a gene. Most plants and animals, including humans, have two alleles of each gene, one from each parent. The order of bases in each allele is slightly different — they code for different versions of the same characteristic. They're represented using letters, e.g. the allele for brown eyes (B) and the allele for blue eyes (b).
Genotype	The alleles an organism has, e.g. BB, Bb or bb for eye colour.
Phenotype	The characteristics the alleles produce, e.g. brown eyes.
Dominant	An allele whose characteristic appears in the phenotype even when there's only one copy. Dominant alleles are shown by a capital letter. E.g. the allele for brown eyes (B) is dominant — if a person's genotype is Bb or BB, they'll have brown eyes.
Recessive	An allele whose characteristic only appears in the phenotype if two copies are present. Recessive alleles are shown by a lower case letter. E.g. the allele for blue eyes (b) is recessive — if a person's genotype is bb, they'll have blue eyes.
Codominant	Alleles that are both expressed in the phenotype — neither one is recessive, e.g. the alleles for haemoglobin.
Locus	The fixed position of a gene on a chromosome. Alleles of a gene are found at the same locus on each chromosome in a pair.
Homozygote	An organism that carries two copies of the same allele, e.g. BB or bb.
Heterozygote	An organism that carries two different alleles, e.g. Bb.
Carrier	A person carrying an allele which is not expressed in the phenotype but that can be passed on to offspring.

'Codes for' means 'contains the instructions for'.

Genetic Diagrams Show the **Possible Genotypes** of **Offspring**

Individuals have **two alleles** for **each gene**. **Gametes** contain only **one allele** for each gene. When two gametes fuse together, the alleles they contain form the **offspring's genotype**. **Genetic diagrams** can be used to **predict** the **genotypes** and **phenotypes** of the offspring produced if two parents are **crossed** (bred). For example, the genetic diagram below shows how **wing length** is inherited in fruit flies. This is an example of **monohybrid inheritance** — the inheritance of a **single characteristic** (gene) controlled by **different alleles**.

N — normal wings allele
n — vestigial (little) wings allele

Parents' genotypes   NN   **x**   nn

Gametes' alleles   (N) (N)   (n) (n)

Possible genotypes of F₁ offspring   Nn   Nn **x** Nn   Nn

Gametes' alleles   (N) (n) (N) (n)

Possible genotypes of F₂ offspring   NN   Nn   Nn   nn
Phenotypes   Normal   Normal   Normal   Vestigial
Ratio in F₂ offspring   3 : 1

The allele for **normal wings** is **dominant**, so it's shown by a **capital** letter N. Any flies that have even one N allele will have normal wings.

One parent is **homozygous** with **normal wings** (NN) and one is **homozygous** with **vestigial wings** (nn).

The normal winged parent **only** produces gametes with the allele for **normal wings** (N). The vestigial winged parent **only** produces gametes with the allele for **vestigial wings** (n).

The first set of offspring is called the F₁ generation.

All F₁ offspring are **heterozygous** (Nn), as one allele is inherited from **each** parent.

The second set of offspring is called the F₂ generation.

The gametes produced by the F₁ offspring may contain the allele for **either normal** (N) or **vestigial wings** (n).

The F₂ offspring could have **either** normal or vestigial wings. But there's a **75%** chance they'll have the **normal wings** phenotype (genotype of NN or Nn) and a **25%** chance they'll have the **vestigial wings** phenotype (genotype nn). So you'd expect a **3:1** ratio of normal : vestigial wings in the offspring. **Whenever** you do a monohybrid cross with **two heterozygous** parents you get a **3:1** ratio of **dominant : recessive** characteristic.

A **Punnett square** is just another way of showing a **genetic diagram**:

First work out the alleles the **gametes** would have. → Parents' genotypes   NN   nn
Gametes' alleles   (N)(N) (n)(n)

Then **cross** the **parents' gametes** to show the possible genotypes of the F₁ generation — all heterozygous, Nn. →

F₁	(n)	(n)
(N)	Nn	Nn
(N)	Nn	Nn

Inheritance

Some Genes Have Codominant Alleles

Occasionally, alleles show **codominance** — **both alleles** are expressed in the **phenotype**, **neither one** is recessive. One example in humans is the allele for **sickle-cell anaemia**:

1) People who are **homozygous** for **normal haemoglobin** ($H^N H^N$) don't have the disease.

2) People who are **homozygous** for **sickle haemoglobin** ($H^S H^S$) have **sickle-cell anaemia** — all their **blood cells** are **sickle-shaped** (crescent-shaped).

3) People who are **heterozygous** ($H^N H^S$) have an **in-between** phenotype, called the **sickle-cell trait** — they have **some** normal haemoglobin and some sickle haemoglobin. The two alleles are **codominant** because they're **both** expressed in the **phenotype**.

4) The **genetic diagram** shows the possible offspring from **crossing** two parents with **sickle-cell trait** (**heterozygous**).

You need to be able to work out genetic diagrams for codominant alleles and sex-linked characteristics.

Some Characteristics are Sex-linked

1) The genetic information for **gender** (**sex**) is carried on two **sex chromosomes**.

2) In mammals, **females** have **two X** chromosomes (XX) and **males** have **one X** and **one Y** chromosome (XY).

3) A **characteristic** is said to be **sex-linked** when the allele that codes for it is located on a **sex chromosome**.

4) The **Y chromosome** is **smaller** than the X chromosome and carries **fewer genes**. So most genes on the sex chromosomes are **only carried** on the X chromosome (called **X-linked** genes).

5) As **males** only have **one X chromosome** they often only have **one allele** for sex-linked genes. So because they **only** have one copy they **express** the **characteristic** of this allele even if it's **recessive**. This makes males **more likely** than females to show **recessive phenotypes** for genes that are sex-linked.

6) Genetic disorders caused by **faulty alleles** on sex chromosomes include **colour blindness** and **haemophilia**. The faulty alleles for both of these disorders are carried on the X chromosome — they're called **X-linked disorders**.

> **Example** Colour blindness is a **sex-linked disorder** caused by a faulty allele carried on the **X chromosome**. As it's sex-linked **both** the chromosome and the allele are **represented** in the genetic diagram, e.g. X^n, where **X** represents the **X chromosome** and n the **faulty allele** for **colour vision**. The Y chromosome doesn't have an allele for colour vision so is **just represented** by **Y**. Females would need **two copies** of the **recessive allele** to be colour blind, while males only need **one copy**. This means colour blindness is **much rarer** in **women** than **men**.
>
> N — normal colour vision allele
> n — faulty colour vision allele

Practice Questions

Q1 What is meant by the terms genotype, phenotype, dominant allele and recessive allele?

Q2 What is a codominant allele?

Exam Question

Q1 Haemophilia A is a sex-linked genetic disorder caused by a recessive allele carried on the X chromosome (X^h).
a) Draw a genetic diagram for a female carrier and a male sufferer to predict their offspring's genotype. [3 marks]
b) Explain why haemophilia is more common in males than females. [3 marks]

If there's a dominant revision allele I'm definitely homozygous recessive...

OK, so there are a lot of fancy words on these pages and yes, you do need to know them all. Sorry about that. But don't despair — once you've learnt what the words mean and know how genetic diagrams work it'll all just fall into place.

Phenotypic Ratios and Epistasis

Right, this stuff is fairly hard, so if you don't get it first time don't panic.
Make sure you're happy with the genetic diagrams on the previous pages before you get stuck into these two.

Genetic Diagrams can Show how More Than One Characteristic is Inherited

You can use genetic diagrams to work out the chances of offspring inheriting certain **combinations** of characteristics. For example, you can look at how **two different genes** are inherited — **dihybrid inheritance**. The diagram below is a dihybrid cross showing how wing size **and** colour are inherited in **fruit flies**.

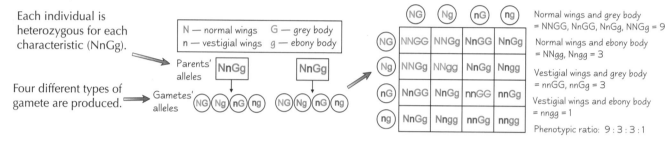

Each individual is heterozygous for each characteristic (NnGg).

Four different types of gamete are produced.

N — normal wings   G — grey body
n — vestigial wings   g — ebony body

Parents' alleles: NnGg   NnGg

Gametes' alleles: NG Ng nG ng   NG Ng nG ng

	NG	Ng	nG	ng
NG	NNGG	NNGg	NnGG	NnGg
Ng	NNGg	NNgg	NnGg	Nngg
nG	NnGG	NnGg	nnGG	nnGg
ng	NnGg	Nngg	nnGg	nngg

Normal wings and grey body
= NNGG, NnGG, NnGg, NNGg = 9

Normal wings and ebony body
= NNgg, Nngg = 3

Vestigial wings and grey body
= nnGG, nnGg = 3

Vestigial wings and ebony body
= nngg = 1

Phenotypic ratio: 9 : 3 : 3 : 1

Phenotypic Ratios can be Predicted

The **phenotypic ratio** is the **ratio of different phenotypes** in offspring. Genetic diagrams allow you to **predict** the phenotypic ratios in F_1 and F_2 offspring. You need to **remember** the ratios for the following crosses:

Type of cross	Parents	Phenotypic ratio in F_1	Phenotypic ratio in F_2
Monohybrid	Homozygous dominant × homozygous recessive (e.g. NN × nn)	All heterozygous offspring (e.g. Nn)	3 : 1 dominant : recessive
Dihybrid	Homozygous dominant × homozygous recessive (e.g. NNGG × nngg)	All heterozygous offspring (e.g. NnGg)	9 : 3 : 3 : 1 dominant both : dominant 1st recessive 2nd : recessive 1st dominant 2nd : recessive both
Codominant	Homozygous for one allele × homozygous for the other allele (e.g. H^NH^N x H^SH^S)	All heterozygous offspring (e.g. H^NH^S)	1 : 2 : 1 homozygous for one allele : heterozygous : homozygous for the other allele

Sometimes you **won't** get the **expected** (predicted) phenotypic ratio — it'll be quite different. This can be because of **epistasis** (coming up next) or **linkage** (see page 161).

An Epistatic Gene Masks the Expression of Another Gene

1) **Many different genes** can control the **same** characteristic — they **interact** to form the phenotype.

2) This can be because the **allele** of one gene **masks** (blocks) **the expression** of the alleles of other genes — this is called **epistasis**.

Example 1 In humans a **widow's peak** (see picture) is controlled by one gene and **baldness** by others. If you have the **alleles** that code for baldness, it **doesn't matter** whether you have the allele for a widow's peak or not, as you have **no hair**. The baldness genes are **epistatic** to the widow's peak gene, as the baldness genes **mask** the expression of the widow's peak gene.

I'm still dashing, even with my widow's peak.

Example 2 **Flower pigment** in a plant is controlled by two genes. **Gene 1** codes for a **yellow pigment** (Y is the dominant yellow allele) and **gene 2** codes for an enzyme that **turns** the yellow pigment **orange** (R is the dominant orange allele). If you **don't have the Y** allele it **won't matter** if you have the R allele or not as the flower **will be colourless**. Gene 1 is **epistatic** to gene 2 as it can **mask** the expression of gene 2.

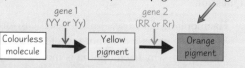

gene 1 (YY or Yy)   gene 2 (RR or Rr)

Colourless molecule → Yellow pigment → Orange pigment

3) **Crosses** involving epistatic genes **don't result** in the **expected phenotypic ratios** given above, e.g. if you cross **two heterozygous orange** flowered plants (YyRr) from the above example you wouldn't get the expected **9 : 3 : 3 : 1** phenotypic ratio for a **normal dihybrid cross** (see next page).

Phenotypic Ratios and Epistasis

You can **Predict** the **Phenotypic Ratios** for Some **Epistatic Genes**

Just as you can **predict** the phenotypic ratios for **normal dihybrid crosses** (see previous page), you can predict the phenotypic ratios for dihybrid crosses involving some **epistatic genes** too:

A dihybrid cross involving a recessive epistatic allele — 9 : 3 : 4

Having **two copies** of the **recessive** epistatic allele **masks** (**blocks**) the expression of the **other gene**. If you cross a **homozygous recessive** parent with a **homozygous dominant** parent you will get a **9 : 3 : 4** phenotypic ratio of **dominant both : dominant epistatic recessive other : recessive epistatic** in the **F₂ generation**.

E.g. the **flower example** from the **previous page** is an example of a **recessive epistatic allele**. If a plant is **homozygous recessive** for the **epistatic gene** (**yy**) then it will be **colourless**, **masking** the expression of the orange gene. So if you cross homozygous parents, you should get a **9 : 3 : 4** ratio of **orange : yellow : white** in the **F₂ generation**. You can check the **phenotypic ratio** is right **using a genetic diagram**:

F₁ cross
YYRR × yyrr = all YyRr | YyRr |

F₂ cross

	YR	Yr	yR	yr
YR	YYRR	YYRr	YyRR	YyRr
Yr	YYRr	YYrr	YyRr	Yyrr
yR	YyRR	YyRr	yyRR	yyRr
yr	YyRr	Yyrr	yyRr	yyrr

YyRr

Orange
= YYRR, YYRr, YyRR, YyRr = 9
Yellow
= Yyrr, YYrr = 3
White = yyRR, yyRr, yyrr = 4
Phenotypic ratio:
9 : 3 : 4

A dihybrid cross involving a dominant epistatic allele — 12 : 3 : 1

Having **at least one** copy of the **dominant epistatic** allele **masks** (**blocks**) the expression of the other gene. Crossing a **homozygous recessive** parent with a **homozygous dominant** parent will produce a **12 : 3 : 1** phenotypic ratio of **dominant epistatic : recessive epistatic dominant other : recessive both** in the F₂ generation.

E.g. **squash colour** is controlled by two genes — the **colour epistatic gene** (**W/w**) and the **yellow gene** (**Y/y**). The **no-colour, white** allele (**W**) is **dominant** over the **coloured** allele (**w**), so **WW** or **Ww** will be **white** and **ww** will be **coloured**. The yellow gene has the **dominant yellow** allele (**Y**) and the **recessive green** allele (**y**). So if the plant has **at least one W**, then the squash **will be white**, **masking** the expression of the yellow gene. So if you cross **wwyy** with **WWYY**, you'll get a **12 : 3 : 1** ratio of **white : yellow : green** in the F₂ generation. Here's a **genetic diagram** to prove it:

F₁ cross
WWYY × wwyy = all WwYy | WwYy |

F₂ cross

	WY	Wy	wY	wy
WY	WWYY	WWYy	WwYY	WwYy
Wy	WWYy	WWyy	WwYy	Wwyy
wY	WwYY	WwYy	wwYY	wwYy
wy	WwYy	Wwyy	wwYy	wwyy

WwYy

White = WWYY, WWYy, WWyy, WwYY, WwYy, Wwyy = 12
Yellow = wwYY, wwYy = 3
Green = wwyy = 1
Phenotypic ratio: 12 : 3 : 1

Practice Questions

Q1 What phenotypic ratio would be produced in the F₁ generation and the F₂ generation by the cross aabb × AABB (assuming no epistasis)?

Q2 Describe epistasis.

Exam Questions

Homozygous curly hair (hhss) crossed with a homozygous bald (HHSS)

Phenotypes of the F₂ offspring produced		
Bald	Straight hair	Curly hair
36	9	3

Q1 Colour (R red, r pink) and lines (G green, g white) are controlled by two genes in the Snozcumber plant. Draw a genetic diagram of the cross: homozygous for red and white lines × homozygous for pink and green lines.   [3 marks]

Q2 Coat colour in mice is controlled by two genes. Gene 1 controls whether fur is coloured (C) or albino (c). Gene 2 controls whether the colour is grey (G) or black (g). Gene 1 is epistatic over gene 2. Describe and explain the phenotypic ratio produced in the F₂ generation from a CCGG × ccgg cross.   [4 marks]

Q3 Hair type in Dillybopper beetles is controlled by two genes: hair (H bald, h hair) and type (S straight, s curly). The F₂ offspring of a cross are shown in the table. Explain the phenotypic ratio shown by the cross.   [3 marks]

Biology students — 9 : 1 phenotypic ratio normal : geek...

I don't know about you but I think I need a lie-down after these pages. Epistasis is a bit of a tricky topic, but you just need to understand what it is and learn the phenotypic ratios for the different types of epistasis — dominant and recessive.

The Chi-Squared Test

Just when you thought it was safe to turn the page... I stick in some maths. Surprise!

The **Chi-Squared Test** Can Be Used to **Check** the **Results** of **Genetic Crosses**

1) The **chi-squared** (χ^2) **test** is a **statistical test** that's used to see if the **results** of an experiment **support** a **theory**.

2) First, the theory is used to **predict** a **result** — this is called the **expected result**.
Then, the experiment is carried out and the **actual result** is recorded — this is called the **observed result**.

3) To see if the results support the theory you have to make a **hypothesis** called the **null hypothesis**.

4) The null hypothesis is always that there's **no significant difference** between the observed and expected results (your experimental result will usually be a bit different from what you expect, but you need to know if the difference is just **due to chance**, or because your **theory is wrong**).

5) The χ^2 **test** is then carried out and the **outcome** either **supports** or **rejects** the **null hypothesis**.

6) You can use the χ^2 test in **genetics** to test theories about the **inheritance** of **characteristics**. For example:

> **Theory**: **Wing length** in fruit flies is controlled by a **single gene** with **two alleles** (**monohybrid inheritance**). The **dominant** allele (N) gives **normal** wings, and the **recessive** allele (n) gives **vestigial** wings.
>
> **Expected results**: With monohybrid inheritance, if you cross a **homozygous dominant** parent with a **homozygous recessive** parent, you'd expect a **3 : 1 phenotypic ratio** of **normal : vestigial** wings in the F_2 generation (see p. 162).
>
> **Observed results**: The **experiment** (of crossing a homozygous dominant parent with a homozygous recessive parent) is **carried out** on fruit flies and the **number of offspring** with normal and vestigial wings is **counted**.
>
> **Null hypothesis**: There's **no significant difference** between the observed and expected results.
>
> (If the χ^2 test shows the observed and expected results are **not significantly different** the null hypothesis is **accepted** — the data supports the **theory** that wing length is controlled by **monohybrid inheritance**.)

First, **Work** out the **Chi-Squared Value...**

The best way to understand the χ^2 test is to work through an example — here's one for testing the **wing length** of **fruit flies** as explained above.

Chi-squared χ^2 is calculated using this formula: $\implies$ $$\chi^2 = \sum \frac{(O-E)^2}{E}$$
where **O** = **observed** result and **E** = **expected** result.

You don't need to learn the formula for chi-squared — it'll be given to you in the exam.

The easiest way to calculate χ^2 is to work it out in **stages** using a table:

(1) First, the **number of offspring** (out of a total of 160) **expected** for each phenotype is worked out. E for normal wings: 160 (total) ÷ 4 (ratio total) × 3 (predicted ratio for normal wings) = 120. E for vestigial wings: 160 ÷ 4 × 1 = 40.

Phenotype	Ratio	Expected Result (E)	Observed Result (O)
Normal wings	3	120	
Vestigial wings	1	40	

(2) Then the **actual number** of offspring **observed** with each phenotype (out of the 160 offspring) is **recorded**, e.g. 111 with normal wings.

Phenotype	Ratio	Expected Result (E)	Observed Result (O)
Normal wings	3	120	111
Vestigial wings	1	40	49

(3) The results are used to work out χ^2, taking it **one step at a time**:

(a) First calculate **O – E** (subtract the **expected result** from the **observed result**) for each phenotype. E.g. for normal wings: 111 – 120 = –9.

(b) Then the resulting numbers are **squared**, e.g. $9^2 = 81$

Phenotype	Ratio	Expected Result (E)	Observed Result (O)	O – E	$(O - E)^2$	$\frac{(O-E)^2}{E}$
Normal wings	3	120	111	–9	81	0.675
Vestigial wings	1	40	49	9	81	2.025

$$\sum \frac{(O-E)^2}{E} = \boxed{2.7}$$

(c) These figures are divided by the **expected results**, e.g. 81 ÷ 120 = 0.675.

(d) Finally, the numbers are **added** together to get χ^2, e.g. 0.675 + 2.025 = **2.7**.

Remember, you need to work it out for each phenotype first, then add all the numbers together.

The Chi-Squared Test

...Then **Compare** it to the **Critical Value**

1) To find out if there **is** no significant difference between your observed and expected results you need to **compare** your χ^2 **value** to a **critical value**.

2) The critical value is the value of χ^2 that corresponds to a 0.05 (**5%**) level of **probability** that the **difference** between the observed and expected results is **due to chance**.

3) If your χ^2 value is **smaller** than the critical value then there **is no significant difference** between the observed and expected results — the **null hypothesis** is **accepted**. E.g. for the example on the previous page the χ^2 value is **2.7**, which is **smaller** than the critical value of **3.84** — there's **no significant difference** between the observed and expected results. This means the **theory** that wing length in fruit flies is controlled by **monohybrid inheritance** is **supported**.

4) If your χ^2 value is **larger** than the critical value then there **is a significant difference** between the observed and expected results (something **other than chance** is causing the difference) — the **null hypothesis** is **rejected**.

5) In the exam you might be **given** the **critical value** or asked to **work it out** from a **table**:

Using a χ^2 table:

If you're not given the critical value, you may have to find it yourself from a χ^2 **table** — this shows a range of **probabilities** that correspond to different **critical values** for different **degrees of freedom** (explained below). Biologists normally use a **probability** level of **0.05** (5%), so you only need to look in that column.

- First, the **degrees of freedom** for the experiment are worked out — this is the **number of classes** (number of phenotypes) **minus one**. E.g. 2 – 1 = 1.
- Next, the **critical value** corresponding to a **probability** of **0.05** at **one degree of freedom** is found in the table — here it's **3.84**.
- Then just **compare** your χ^2 value of **2.7** to this critical value, as explained above.

degrees of freedom	no. of classes	Critical values					
1	2	0.46	1.64	2.71	3.84	6.64	10.83
2	3	1.39	3.22	4.61	5.99	9.21	13.82
3	4	2.37	4.64	6.25	7.82	11.34	16.27
4	5	3.36	5.99	7.78	9.49	13.28	18.47
probability that result is due to chance only		0.50 (50%)	0.20 (20%)	0.10 (10%)	0.05 (5%)	0.01 (1%)	0.001 (0.1%)

Practice Questions

Q1 What is a χ^2 test used for?

Q2 What can the results of the χ^2 test tell you?

Q3 How do you tell if the difference between your observed and expected results is due to chance?

Exam Question

Q1 A scientist is investigating petal colour in a flower. It's thought to be controlled by two separate genes (dihybrid inheritance), the colour gene — B = blue, b = purple, and the spots gene — W = white, w = yellow. A cross involving a homozygous dominant parent and a homozygous recessive parent should give a 9 : 3 : 3 : 1 ratio in the F_2 generation. The scientist observes the number of offspring showing each of four phenotypes in 240 F_2 offspring. Her results are shown in the table.

Her null hypothesis is that there is no significant difference between the observed and expected ratios.

a) Complete the table to calculate χ^2 for this experiment. [4 marks]

b) The critical value for this experiment is 7.82. Explain whether the χ^2 value supports or rejects the null hypothesis. [2 marks]

Phenotype	Ratio	Expected Result (E)	Observed Result (O)	O – E	O – E^2	$\frac{(O-E^2)}{E}$
Blue with white spots	9	135	131			
Purple with white spots	3	45	52			
Blue with yellow spots	3	45	48			
Purple with yellow spots	1	15	9			
					$\sum \frac{(O-E)^2}{E} =$	

The expected result of revising these pages — boredom...

...the observed result — boredom (except for the maths geeks among you). Don't worry if you're not brilliant at maths though, you don't have to be to do the chi-squared test — just make sure you know the steps above off by heart. You could even practise going through the example on these pages without looking at the book... go on, you know you want to.

Unit 5: Section 2 — Inheritance

Variation

Some people are tall, others are short. Some people wear glasses, others don't. Some people like peanut butter sandwiches, others... well, you get the picture. Basically variety is the spice of life and here's why we're all different.

Variation Exists Between All Individuals

1) **Variation** is the **differences** that exist between **individuals**. Every individual organism is **unique** — even **clones** (such as identical twins) show **some variation**.

2) Variation can occur **within species**, e.g. **individual** European robins weigh **between** 16 g and 22 g and show some variation in many other characteristics including length, wingspan, colour and beak size.

3) It can also occur **between species**, e.g. the **lightest** species of bird is the bee hummingbird, which weighs around 1.6 g on average and the **heaviest** species of bird is the ostrich, which can weigh up to 160 kg (100 000 times as much).

Variation — a concept lost on the army.

Variation can be Continuous...

1) **Continuous variation** is when the **individuals** in a population vary **within a range** — there are **no distinct categories**, e.g. **humans** can be **any height** within a range (139 cm, 175 cm, 185.9 cm, etc.), not just tall or short. ⟹

2) Some more examples of continuous variation include:

- **Finger length** — e.g. a human finger can be any length within a range.
- **Plant mass** — e.g. the mass of the seeds from a flower head varies within a range.

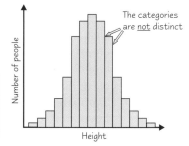

The categories are not distinct

...or Discontinuous

1) **Discontinuous variation** is when there are two or more **distinct categories** — each individual falls into **only one** of these categories, there are **no intermediates**.

2) Here are some examples of discontinuous variation:

- **Sex** — e.g. animals can be either male or female.
- **Blood group** — e.g. humans can be group A, B, AB or O. ⟹

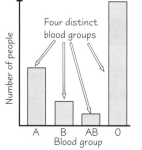

Four distinct blood groups

Variation can be Influenced by Your Genes...

1) **Different species** have **different genes**.

2) Individuals of the **same species** have the **same genes**, but **different versions** of them (called **alleles**).

3) The genes and alleles an organism has make up its **genotype**.

4) The **differences** in genotype result in **variation** in phenotype — the **characteristics** displayed by an organism. (Variation in phenotype is also referred to as **phenotypic variation**.)

> **EXAMPLE**   Human blood group — there are **three** different **blood group alleles**, which result in **four different blood groups**.

5) **Inherited** characteristics that show **continuous** variation are usually **influenced** by **many genes** — these characteristics are said to be **polygenic**. For example, **human skin colour** is polygenic — it comes in **loads** of **different shades** of colour.

6) **Inherited** characteristics that show **discontinuous** variation are usually influenced by only **one gene** (or a **small number** of genes), e.g. **violet flower colour** (either coloured or white) is controlled by only one gene. Characteristics controlled by **only one gene** are said to be **monogenic**.

Variation

...the **Environment**...

Variation can also be caused by **differences in the environment**, e.g. climate, food, lifestyle.
Characteristics controlled by environmental factors can **change** over an organism's life.

EXAMPLES

1) **Accent** — this is determined by **environmental factors only**, including **where you live** now, where you **grew up** and the accents of **people around you**.

2) **Pierced ears** — this is also **only** determined by **environmental factors**, e.g. **fashion**, **peer pressure**.

...or **Both**

Genetic factors determine genotype and the characteristics an organism's **born with**, but **environmental factors** can **influence** how some characteristics **develop**. Most phenotypic variation is caused by the **combination** of **genotype** and **environmental factors**. Phenotypic variation influenced by both usually shows **continuous variation**.

EXAMPLES

1) **Height of pea plants** — pea plants come in **tall** and **dwarf** forms (**discontinuous** variation), which is determined by **genotype**. However, the **exact height** of the tall and dwarf plants **varies** (**continuous** variation) because of **environmental factors** (e.g. **light intensity** and **water availability** ⟹ affect how tall a plant grows).

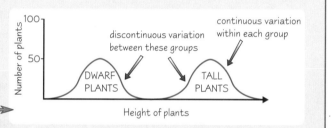

2) **Human body mass** — this is **partly genetic** (large parents often have large children), but it's also **strongly influenced** by **environmental factors**, like **diet** and **exercise**. Body mass **varies** within a **range**, so it's **continuous** variation.

Practice Questions

Q1   What is variation?

Q2   Describe what is meant by discontinuous variation and give one example.

Q3   Briefly describe what is meant by variation caused by genotype.

Puppy	Mass / kg	Colour	Puppy	Mass / kg	Colour	Puppy	Mass / kg	Colour
1	10.04	yellow	6	10.39	yellow	11	9.25	black
2	10.23	chocolate	7	10.55	chocolate	12	11.06	black
3	15.65	black	8	15.87	chocolate	13	12.45	yellow
4	18.99	black	9	16.99	black	14	14.99	yellow
5	9.45	black	10	10.47	yellow	15	10.93	chocolate

Exam Questions

Q1   The mass and coat colour of 15 Labrador puppies is shown in the table.
a) What type of variation (continuous or discontinuous) is shown by the coat colour of the puppies?   [1 mark]
b) Calculate the range of puppy mass.   [1 mark]
c) Which of the characteristics described in the table is most likely to be influenced by both genotype and the environment? Explain your answer.   [2 marks]

Q2   Give an example of a human characteristic influenced by both genotype and the environment. Explain your answer.   [2 marks]

Revision boredom shows discontinuous variation — always bored with it...

Hopefully you remember a lot of the info on these pages from AS, but I'm afraid you still need to know it off by heart for your A2 exam. Test yourself on examples of continuous and discontinuous variation — you never know when a sneaky question could pop up on them. Then, rest your brain so it's well and truly ready for a bit of evolution...

Evolution by Natural Selection and Genetic Drift

Variation between individuals of a species means that some organisms are better adapted to their environment than others — so they're more likely to survive and reproduce. Which leads us nicely on to evolution by natural selection...

Evolution *is a* Change *in* Allele Frequency

1) The complete range of **alleles** present in a **population** is called the **gene pool**.
2) **New alleles** are usually generated by **mutations** in **genes**.
3) How **often** an **allele occurs** in a population is called the **allele frequency**. It's usually given as a **percentage** of the total population, e.g. 35%, or a **number**, e.g. 0.35.
4) The **frequency** of an **allele** in a population **changes** over time — this is **evolution**.

A population is a group of organisms of the same species living in a particular area.

Evolution *Occurs by* Natural Selection

Variation is generated by meiosis and mutations.

1) **Individuals** within a population **vary** because they have **different alleles**.
2) **Predation, disease** and **competition** (**selection pressures**) create a **struggle for survival**.
3) Because individuals vary, some are **better adapted** to the selection pressures than others.
4) Individuals that have an allele that **increases** their **chance of survival** (a **beneficial** allele) are **more likely** to **survive, reproduce** and **pass on** the beneficial allele, than individuals with different alleles.
5) This means that a **greater proportion** of the next generation **inherit** the **beneficial allele**.
6) They, in turn, are **more likely** to **survive, reproduce** and **pass on** their genes.
7) So the **frequency** of the beneficial allele **increases** from generation to generation.
8) This process is called **natural selection**.

A selection pressure is anything that affects an organism's chance of survival and reproduction.

The Environment *Affects* Which Characteristics Become More Common

Whether the **environment** is **changing** or **stable** affects **which characteristics are selected for** by natural selection:

When the **environment isn't changing** much, individuals with alleles for characteristics towards the **middle** of the range are more likely to **survive** and **reproduce**. This is called **stabilising selection** and it **reduces the range** of possible **phenotypes**.

EXAMPLE In any **mammal population** there's a **range** of **fur length**. In a **stable climate**, having fur at the **extremes** of this range **reduces** the **chances** of **surviving** as it's harder to maintain the **right body temperature**. Animals with alleles for **average fur length** are the **most** likely to **survive, reproduce** and **pass on** their alleles. So these alleles **increase** in **frequency**. The **proportion** of the **population** with **average fur length increases** and the **range** of fur lengths **decreases**.

When there's a **change** in the environment, individuals with alleles for characteristics of an **extreme type** are more likely to **survive** and **reproduce**. This is called **directional selection**.

EXAMPLE If the environment becomes **very cold**, individual mammals with **alleles** for **long fur length** will find it **easier** to **maintain** the **right body temperature** than animals with short fur length. So they're **more likely** to **survive, reproduce** and **pass on** their alleles. Over time the **frequency** of alleles for **long fur length increases**.

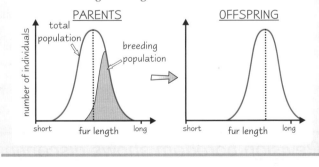

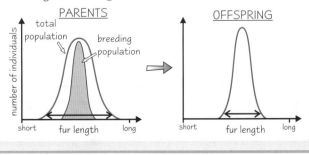

Evolution by Natural Selection and Genetic Drift

Evolution Also Occurs via Genetic Drift

1) **Natural selection** is just **one** process by which **evolution** occurs.

2) Evolution **also** occurs due to **genetic drift** — instead of **environmental factors** affecting which individuals **survive**, **breed** and pass on their alleles, **chance** dictates **which alleles** are **passed on**. Here's how it works:

> • Individuals within a population show variation in their genotypes (e.g. A and B). → genotype A (4) / genotype B (4)
> • By chance, the allele for one genotype (B) is passed on to the offspring more often than others.
> • So the number of individuals with the allele increases. → genotype A (3) / genotype B (5)
> • If by chance the same allele is passed on more often again and again, it can lead to evolution as the allele becomes more common in the population. → genotype A (1) / genotype B (7)

3) Natural selection and genetic drift work **alongside each other** to drive evolution, but one process can drive evolution **more** than the other depending on the **population size**.

4) **Evolution by genetic drift** usually has a **greater effect** in **smaller populations** where **chance** has a **greater influence**. In larger populations any chance factors tend to **even out** across the whole population.

5) The evolution of **human blood groups** is a good example of **genetic drift**:

> Different **Native American tribes** show different **blood group frequencies**. For example, **Blackfoot Indians** are mainly **group A**, but **Navajos** are mainly **group O**. Blood group doesn't affect **survival** or **reproduction**, so the differences **aren't** due to evolution by natural selection. In the past, human populations were much **smaller** and were often found in **isolated groups**. The blood group differences were due to evolution by genetic drift — by **chance** the allele for **blood group O** was **passed on more often** in the **Navajo tribe**, so over time this **allele** and blood group became **more common**.

6) Evolution by genetic drift also has a greater effect if there's a **genetic bottleneck** — e.g. when a large population **suddenly becomes smaller** because of a **natural disaster**. For example:

> The **mice** in a **large population** are either **black or grey**. The coat colour **doesn't** affect their **survival** or **reproduction**. A **large flood** hits the population and the **only survivors** are **grey** mice and **one black mouse**. **Grey** becomes the **most common colour** due to **genetic drift**.

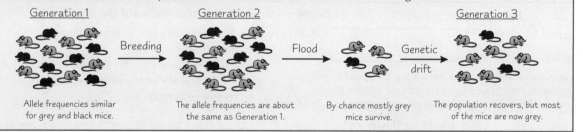

Generation 1 → Breeding → Generation 2 → Flood → Genetic drift → Generation 3

Allele frequencies similar for grey and black mice.   The allele frequencies are about the same as Generation 1.   By chance mostly grey mice survive.   The population recovers, but most of the mice are now grey.

Practice Questions

Q1 What is evolution?

Q2 What is allele frequency?

Q3 What is genetic drift?

Exam Question

Q1 Before the 1800s, there were more pale-coloured peppered moths than dark peppered moths in Manchester. The pale moths were camouflaged on the trees they lived on. During the 1800s, air pollution in Manchester rose and blackened many of the trees. By the end of the 1800s, dark moths had become more common. Explain how natural selection gave rise to the increase in dark moths.

[5 marks]

I've evolved to revise for hours and still not remember things...

The trickiest thing here is tying all the information together in your head. Basically, natural selection and genetic drift drive evolution. And the characteristics selected for in natural selection are determined by what the environment's like.

Hardy-Weinberg Principle and Artificial Selection

*Now you know what allele frequency is you need to be able to calculate it. So switch your maths brain on now.
Then you can take a breather on the right-hand page and learn all about artificial selection.*

The **Hardy-Weinberg Principle** Predicts That **Allele Frequencies Won't Change**

1) The **Hardy-Weinberg principle** predicts that the **frequencies** of **alleles** in a population **won't change** from **one generation** to the **next**.

2) But this prediction is **only true** under **certain conditions** — it has to be a **large population** where there's **no immigration**, **emigration**, **mutations** or **natural selection**. There also needs to be **random mating** — all possible genotypes can breed with all others.

3) The **Hardy-Weinberg equations** (see below) are based on this principle. They can be used to **estimate the frequency** of particular **alleles** and **genotypes** within populations.

4) If the allele frequencies **do change** between generations in a large population then immigration, emigration, natural selection or mutations have happened.

The **Hardy-Weinberg Equations** Can be Used to **Predict Allele Frequency**...

1) You can **figure out** the frequency of one allele if you **know the frequency of the other**, using this equation:

$$p + q = 1$$

Where: p = the **frequency** of the **dominant** allele
q = the **frequency** of the **recessive** allele

The **total frequency** of **all possible alleles** for a characteristic in a certain population is 1.0. So the frequencies of the **individual alleles** (the dominant one and the recessive one) must **add up to 1.0**.

2) E.g. a species of plant has either **red** or **white** flowers. Allele **R** (red) is **dominant** and allele **r** (white) is **recessive**. If the frequency of **R** is **0.4**, then the frequency of **r** is 1 − 0.4 = **0.6**.

*Make sure you **learn** both equations.*

...**Genotype Frequency**...

1) You can **figure out** the frequency of one genotype if you **know the frequencies of the others**, using this equation:

$$p^2 + 2pq + q^2 = 1$$

Where p^2 = the **frequency** of the **homozygous dominant genotype**
$2pq$ = the **frequency** of the **heterozygous genotype**
q^2 = the **frequency** of the **homozygous recessive genotype**

The **total frequency** of **all possible genotypes** for one characteristic in a certain population is 1.0. So the frequencies of the **individual genotypes** must **add up to 1.0**.

2) E.g. if there are **two alleles** for **flower colour** (R and r), there are **three possible genotypes** — RR, Rr and rr. If the frequency of genotype RR (p^2) is **0.34** and the frequency of genotype Rr ($2pq$) is **0.27**, the frequency of genotype rr (q^2) must be 1 − 0.34 − 0.27 = **0.39**.

...and the **Percentage** of a **Population** that has a **Certain Genotype**

The **frequency** of **cystic fibrosis** (genotype ff) in the UK is currently approximately **1 birth in 2000**. From this information you can estimate the **proportion** of people in the UK that are cystic fibrosis **carriers** (Ff). To do this you need to find the **frequency** of **heterozygous genotype Ff**, i.e. **2pq**, using **both equations**:

EXAMPLE

First calculate q:
- Frequency of cystic fibrosis (homozygous recessive, ff) is 1 in 2000
- ff = q^2 = 1 ÷ 2000 = 0.0005
- So, $q = \sqrt{0.0005} = 0.022$

Next calculate p:
- using $p + q = 1$, $p = 1 - q$
- $p = 1 - 0.022$
- $p = 0.978$

Then calculate 2pq:
- $2pq = 2 \times 0.978 \times 0.022$
- $2pq = 0.043$

The **frequency** of **genotype Ff** is **0.043**, so the **percentage** of the UK population that are **carriers** is **4.3%**.

Hardy-Weinberg Principle and Artificial Selection

Artificial Selection *Involves* Breeding *Individuals with* Desirable Traits

Artificial selection is when **humans select individuals** in a population to **breed together** to get **desirable traits**. There are two examples you need to **learn**:

Artificial selection is also called selective breeding, which you might remember from AS (see p. 75).

Modern Dairy Cattle

Modern **dairy cows** produce **many litres of milk** a day as a result of **artificial selection**:

1) Farmers **select a female** with a **very high milk yield** and a **male** whose **mother** had a very high milk yield and **breed** these two **together**.

2) Then they **select** the **offspring** with the **highest milk yields** and **breed** them **together**.

3) This is continued over **several generations** until a **very high milk-yielding cow** is produced.

Bread Wheat

Bread wheat (*Triticum aestivum*) is the plant from which **flour** is produced for **bread-making**. It produces a **high yield** of wheat because of **artificial selection** by **humans**:

1) Wheat plants with a **high wheat yield** (e.g. large ears) are **bred together**.

2) The **offspring** with the **highest yields** are then **bred together**.

3) This is continued over **several generations** to produce a plant that has a **very high yield**.

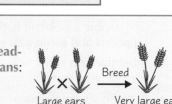

Large ears × — Breed → Very large ears

You Need to be Able to Compare Natural Selection *and* Artificial Selection

You need to be able to describe the **similarities** and **differences** between **natural** and **artificial selection**:

Similarities:
- Both change the **allele frequencies** in the next generation — the **alleles** that **code** for the **beneficial/desirable characteristic** will become **more common** in the next generation.
- Both may make use of **random mutations** when they occur — if a random mutation produces an **allele** that gives a **beneficial/desirable phenotype**, it will be **selected for** in the next generation.

Differences:
- In natural selection, the organisms that reproduce are **selected by the environment** but in artificial selection this is **carried out by humans**.
- Artificial selection aims for a **predetermined result**, e.g. a farmer aims for a higher yield of milk, but in natural selection the **result is unpredictable**.
- Natural selection makes the species **better adapted** to the **environment**, but artificial selection makes the species **more useful** for **humans**.

Practice Questions

Q1 Which term represents the frequency of the dominant allele in the Hardy-Weinberg equations?

Q2 Describe two similarities between natural and artificial selection.

Exam Questions

Q1 A species of dog has either a black or brown coat. Allele B (black) is dominant and allele b (brown) is recessive. If the frequency of the b allele is 0.23, what is the frequency of the B allele? [1 mark]

Q2 Modern beef cattle (raised for meat production) produce a very high meat yield. Explain how artificial selection by farmers could have led to this. [3 marks]

This stuff's surely not that bad — Hardly worth Weining about...

Not many of you will be thrilled with the maths content on the left-hand page, but don't worry 'cause you just need to know the equations off by heart and what the terms in them mean. Then in the exam you'll be able to put the numbers in the correct places in the equation and, hey presto, you'll have your answer. Oh, and don't forget to take a calculator...

Speciation

Evolution leads to the development of lots of different species. Unfortunately for some species, the biologists had run out of good names, e.g. Colon rectum *(a type of beetle) and* Aha ha *(an Australian wasp). Oh dear.*

Speciation *is the Development of a* New Species

1) A **species** is defined as a group of **similar organisms** that can **reproduce** to give **fertile offspring**.

2) **Speciation** is the development of a **new species**.

3) It occurs when **populations** of the **same species** become **reproductively isolated** — changes in allele frequencies cause changes in phenotype that mean they can **no longer breed** together to produce **fertile offspring**.

Geographical Isolation *and* Natural Selection *Lead to* Speciation

1) Geographical isolation happens when a **physical barrier divides** a population of a species — **floods**, **volcanic eruptions** and **earthquakes** can all cause barriers that isolate some individuals from the main population.

2) **Conditions** on either side of the barrier will be slightly **different**. For example, there might be a **different climate** on each side.

Geographical isolation is also known as ecological isolation.

3) Because the environment is different on each side, **different characteristics** will become **more common** due to **natural selection** (because there are **different selection pressures**):

- Because different **characteristics** will be **advantageous** on each side, the **allele frequencies** will change in each population, e.g. if one allele is more advantageous on one side of the barrier, the frequency of that allele on that side will **increase**.

- **Mutations** will take place **independently** in each population, also changing the **allele frequencies**.

- The changes in allele frequencies will lead to changes in **phenotype frequencies**, e.g. the advantageous characteristics (**phenotypes**) will become more common on that side.

4) Eventually, individuals from different populations will have changed so much that they won't be able to breed with one another to produce **fertile** offspring — they'll have become **reproductively isolated**.

5) The two groups will have become separate **species**.

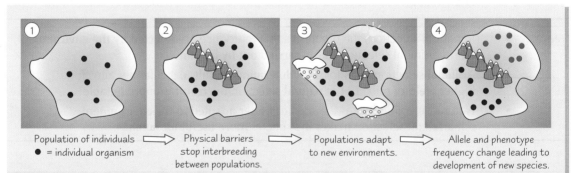

| ① Population of individuals ● = individual organism | ⇒ | ② Physical barriers stop interbreeding between populations. | ⇒ | ③ Populations adapt to new environments. | ⇒ | ④ Allele and phenotype frequency change leading to development of new species. |

Reproductive Isolation *Occurs in Many Ways*

Reproductive isolation occurs because the **changes** in the alleles and phenotypes of the two populations **prevent** them from **successfully breeding together**. These changes include:

1) **Seasonal changes** — individuals from the same population develop different flowering or mating seasons, or become sexually active at different times of the year.

2) **Mechanical changes** — changes in genitalia prevent successful mating.

3) **Behavioural changes** — a group of individuals develop courtship rituals that aren't attractive to the main population.

Janice's courtship ritual was still successful in attracting mates.

A population **doesn't** have to become **geographically isolated** to become **reproductively isolated**. Random mutations could occur **within a population**, resulting in the changes mentioned above, **preventing** members of that population breeding with other members of the species.

Speciation

There are Different Ways to Classify Species

1) The traditional definition of a species is a group of **similar organisms** that can **reproduce** to give **fertile offspring**. This way of defining a species is called the **biological species concept**.

2) Scientists can have problems when using this definition, e.g. problems deciding **which species** an organism belongs to or if it's a new, **distinct species**.

3) This is because you can't always see their **reproductive behaviour** — you can't always tell if different organisms can reproduce to give **fertile offspring**. For example:

> 1) They might be **extinct**, so you **can't** study their reproductive behaviour.
>
> 2) They might **reproduce asexually** — they never **reproduce together** even if they belong to the same species, e.g. bacteria.
>
> 3) There might be **practical** and **ethical issues** involved — you can't see if some organisms reproduce successfully in the wild (due to geography) and you can't study them in a lab (because it's unethical, e.g. humans and chimps are classed as separate species but has anyone ever tried mating them...).

4) Because of these problems, scientists sometimes use the **phylogenetic species concept** to classify organisms.

5) Phylogenetics is the **study** of the **evolutionary history** of groups of organisms (you might remember it from AS — take a look back at p. 97).

6) All organisms have **evolved** from shared common ancestors (**relatives**). The **more closely related** two species are, the **more recently** their last common ancestor will be.

7) Phylogenetics tells us **what's related** to what and how **closely related** they are.

The phylogenetic concept is also called the cladistic or evolutionary species concept.

8) Scientists can use phylogenetics to decide **which species** an organism belongs to or if it's a **new species** — if it's **closely related** to members of another species then it's probably the **same species**, but if it's **quite different** to any known species it's probably a **new species**.

9) There are also **problems** with classifying organisms using this concept, e.g. there's no cut-off to say how different two organisms have to be to be different species. For example, **chimpanzees** and **humans** are **different species** but about **94%** of our DNA is exactly the **same**.

Practice Questions

Q1 What is speciation?

Q2 What two concepts can be used to classify a species?

Exam Question

Q1 The diagram shows an experiment conducted with fruit flies. One population was split in two and each population was fed a different food. After many generations the two populations were placed together and it was observed that they were unable to breed together.

Group fed starch-based food

Many generations pass

Single species of fruit fly

Group fed maltose-based food

a) What evidence shows that speciation occurred? [1 mark]

b) Explain why the experiment resulted in speciation. [3 marks]

c) Suggest two possible reasons why members of the two populations were not able to breed together. [2 marks]

d) During the experiment, populations of fruit flies were artificially isolated. Suggest one way that populations of organisms could become isolated naturally. [1 mark]

Chess club members — self-enforced reproductive isolation...

These gags get better and better... Anyway, it's a bit of a toughie getting your head round the different mechanisms that can produce a new species. It doesn't help that reproductive isolation can happen on its own OR as a result of geographical isolation. Also, when reproductive isolation is caused by seasonal changes it's sometimes called seasonal isolation.

Cloning

Please don't try doing this at home — you'll only confuse people if there are 27 copies of you in the house...

Cloning makes Cells or Organisms Genetically Identical to Another Organism

Cloning is the process of producing **genetically identical cells** or **organisms** from the cells of an **existing organism**. Cloning can occur **naturally** in some **plants** and **animals**, but it can also be carried out **artificially**. You need to know about the **two types** of **artificial cloning** used for **animals**:

Reproductive cloning

1) **Reproductive cloning** is used to make a **complete organism** that's **genetically identical** to **another organism**.

2) Scientists use cloned animals for **research purposes**, e.g. they can **test new drugs** on cloned animals. They're all genetically identical, so the **variables** that come from **genetic differences** (e.g. the likelihood of developing cancer) are **removed**. This means the **results** are more **reliable**.

3) Reproductive cloning can be used to **save endangered animals** from **extinction** by cloning new individuals.

4) It can also be used by **farmers** to **increase** the **number** of animals with **desirable characteristics** to **breed from**, e.g. a prize-winning cow with high milk production could be cloned.

5) Loads of different animals have been cloned, e.g. **sheep**, **cattle**, **pigs** and **horses**.

Non-reproductive cloning

1) **Non-reproductive cloning** is used to make **embryonic stem cells** that are **genetically identical** to **another organism**. It's also called **therapeutic cloning**.

2) Embryonic stem cells are harvested from young **embryos**.

3) They have the **potential** to become **any cell type** in an organism, so scientists think they could be used to **replace damaged tissues** in a **range** of **diseases**, e.g. heart disease, spinal cord injuries, degenerative brain disorders like Parkinson's disease.

4) If replacement tissue is made from cloned embryonic stem cells that are **genetically identical** to the **patient's own cells** then the tissue **won't be rejected** by their immune system.

Take a look back at the stuff you learnt about stem cells at AS-level on p. 24.

Animals are Artificially Cloned by Nuclear Transfer

Reproductive and **non-reproductive** cloning are **both carried out** using a technique called **nuclear transfer**. Here's how it's done with **sheep** (but the **principles** are the **same** for **any animal**):

1) A **body cell** is taken from sheep A. The **nucleus** is **extracted** and **kept**.

2) An **egg cell** is taken from sheep B. Its nucleus is **removed** to form an **enucleated egg cell**.

3) The nucleus from sheep A is **inserted** into the enucleated egg cell — the egg cell from **sheep B** now contains the **genetic information** from **sheep A**.

4) The egg cell is **stimulated** to **divide** and an **embryo** is formed.

5) In **reproductive cloning** the embryo is **implanted** into a **surrogate mother**. A **lamb** is produced that's a **genetically identical** copy of **sheep A**.

6) In **non-reproductive cloning** stem cells are **harvested** from the embryo. The stem cells are **genetically identical** to the cells in **sheep A**.

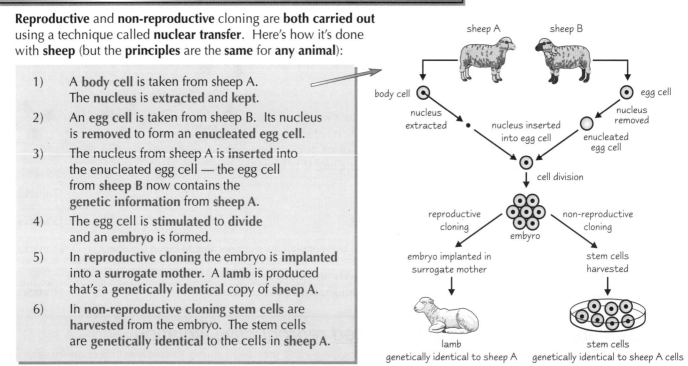

sheep A   sheep B

body cell — nucleus extracted

egg cell — nucleus removed

nucleus inserted into egg cell

enucleated egg cell

cell division

reproductive cloning — embryo implanted in surrogate mother — lamb genetically identical to sheep A

embryo

non-reproductive cloning — stem cells harvested — stem cells genetically identical to sheep A cells

Cloning

Cloning Animals has Advantages and Disadvantages

Advantages

- **Desirable genetic characteristics** (e.g. high milk production in cows) are **always passed on** to clones — this **doesn't always** happen with **sexual reproduction**.
- **Infertile animals** can be **reproduced**.
- **Animals** can be **cloned** at **any time** — farmers wouldn't have to wait until a breeding season to produce new animals.

Disadvantages

- **Undesirable genetic characteristics** (e.g. a weak immune system) are **always passed on** to clones.
- Reproductive cloning is very **difficult, time-consuming** and **expensive** — **Dolly the sheep** was created after 277 nuclear transfer **attempts**.
- Some evidence suggests that clones **may not live as long** as natural offspring.

There are Ethical Issues to do with Human Cloning

1) The use of **human embryos** as a source of stem cells is **controversial**. The embryos are usually **destroyed** after the embryonic stem cells have been harvested — some people believe that doing this is **destroying a human life**.

2) Some people think a **cloned human** would have a **lower quality of life**, e.g. they might suffer **social exclusion** or have difficulty developing their own **personal identity**.

3) Some people think that cloning humans would be **wrong** because it **undermines** natural **sexual reproduction**, and traditional **family structures**.

Reproductive cloning of humans is currently illegal in the UK.

Plants can be Artificially Cloned using Tissue Culture

1) **Plants** can be **cloned** from existing plants using a technique called **tissue culture**. Here's how it's done:

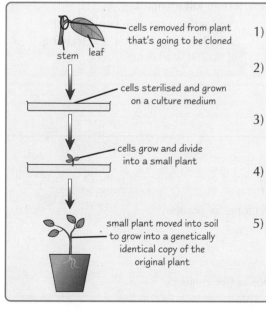

cells removed from plant that's going to be cloned

stem   leaf

cells sterilised and grown on a culture medium

cells grow and divide into a small plant

small plant moved into soil to grow into a genetically identical copy of the original plant

1) **Cells** are taken from the original plant that's going to be cloned.

2) Cells from the **stem** and **root tips** are used because they're **stem cells** — like in humans, plant stem cells can develop into **any type of cell**.

3) The cells are **sterilised** to kill any **microorganisms** — bacteria and fungi **compete** for nutrients with the **plant cells**, which **decreases** their **growth rate**.

4) The cells are placed on a **culture medium** containing plant **nutrients** (like **glucose** for **respiration**) and **growth factors** (such as **auxins**).

5) When the cells have **divided** and **grown** into a **small plant** they're taken out of the medium and **planted in soil** — they'll develop into plants that are **genetically identical** to the **original plant**.

2) Tissue culture is used to clone plants that **don't readily reproduce** or are **endangered** or **rare**, e.g. British orchids.

3) It's also used to grow **whole plants** from **genetically engineered plant cells**.

4) **Micropropagation** is when tissue culture is used to produce **lots** of cloned plants **very quickly**. **Cells** are taken from developing cloned plants and **subcultured** (grown on another fresh culture medium) — **repeating** this process creates **large numbers** of clones.

Cloning

Some Plants can Produce Natural Clones by Vegetative Propagation

Vegetative propagation is the natural production of plant clones from **non-reproductive tissues**, e.g. roots, leaves and stems. Plants grow **structures** on roots, leaves or stems that can **grow** into an identical **new plant**. You need to know how **elm trees** produce clones from structures called **suckers**:

1) A sucker is a **shoot** that grows from the **shallow roots** of an elm tree.

2) Suckers grow from **sucker buds** (undeveloped shoots) that are scattered around the tree's **root system**. The buds are **normally dormant**.

3) During times of **stress** (e.g. drought, damage or disease) or when a tree is **dying**, the **buds** are **activated** and suckers begin to form.

4) Suckers can pop up many metres **away** from the parent tree, which can help to **avoid** the **stress** that triggered their growth.

5) They eventually form completely **separate trees** — **clones** of the tree that the suckers grew from.

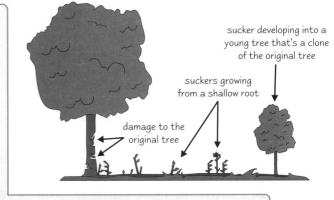

sucker developing into a young tree that's a clone of the original tree

suckers growing from a shallow root

damage to the original tree

Plant Cloning in Agriculture has Advantages and Disadvantages

Advantages

- **Desirable genetic characteristics** (e.g. high fruit production) are **always passed on** to clones. This **doesn't always** happen when plants **reproduce sexually**.

- Plants can be reproduced in **any season** because tissue culture (see previous page) is carried out **indoors**.

- **Sterile plants** can be **reproduced**.

- Plants that take a **long time** to produce **seeds** can be **reproduced quickly**.

Disadvantages

- **Undesirable genetic characteristics** (e.g. producing fruit with lots of seeds) are **always passed on** to clones.

- **Cloned plant populations** have **no genetic variability**, so a **single disease** could **kill** them all.

- **Production costs** are **very high** due to **high energy use** and the **training** of skilled workers.

Practice Questions

Q1 What type of cells are made by non-reproductive cloning?

Q2 Name the technique that can be used to produce artificial clones of plants.

Q3 Give one disadvantage of plant cloning in agriculture.

These questions cover pages 176-178.

Exam Question

Q1 Scientists in the UK are using stem cells produced by non-reproductive cloning to research treatments for diseases like Parkinson's disease.

   a) How does reproductive cloning differ from non-reproductive cloning?   [2 marks]

   b) Briefly describe the technique they might use to carry out non-reproductive cloning.   [6 marks]

I ain't makin' no cloned elm tree, sucker...

Although it would be nice to have lots of clones doing your revision, exams and PE lessons, it's not going to happen. Sadly there's only one of you, and you need to learn about the different types of cloning, how they're done and their advantages and disadvantages. There are ethical issues with human cloning too — it's not everyone's cup of tea...

Biotechnology

The global biotechnology industry is humongous, but fortunately you've only got to learn three pages about it...

Biotechnology is the Use of Living Organisms in Industry

1) **Biotechnology** is the **industrial use** of **living organisms** to produce **food**, **drugs** and **other products**, e.g. yeast is used to make wine.

2) The living organisms used are mostly **microorganisms** (bacteria and fungi). Here are a few reasons why:

> - Their **ideal growth conditions** can be **easily** created.
> - They grow **rapidly** under the right conditions, so **products** can be made **quickly**.
> - They can grow on a **range** of **inexpensive** materials.
> - They can be grown at **any time** of the year.

3) Biotechnology also **uses parts** of **living organisms** (such as **enzymes**) to make products, e.g. rennet (a mix of enzymes) is extracted from calf stomachs and used to make cheese.

4) Enzymes used in industry can be **contained within the cells** of organisms — these are called **intracellular enzymes**.

5) Enzymes are also used that **aren't contained within cells** — these are called **isolated enzymes**. **Some** are **secreted naturally** by microorganisms (called **extracellular enzymes**), but others have to be **extracted**.

6) **Naturally secreted** enzymes are **cheaper** to use because it can be **expensive** to **extract** enzymes from cells.

Hooray, the rennet extractor's here.

Isolated Enzymes can be Immobilised

1) **Isolated enzymes** used in industry can become **mixed in** with the **products** of a reaction.

2) The **products** then need to be **separated** from this mixture, which can be **complicated** and **costly**.

3) This is **avoided** in large-scale production by using **immobilised enzymes** — enzymes that are **attached** to an **insoluble material** so they **can't** become mixed with the products.

4) There are **three main ways** that enzymes are **immobilised**:

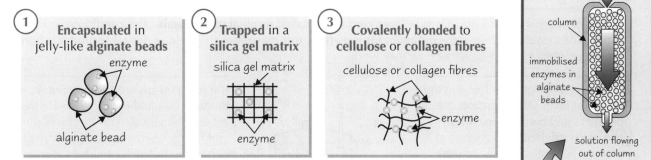

5) In industry, the **substrate solution** for a reaction is run through a **column** of **immobilised enzymes**.

6) The **active sites** of the enzymes are still **available** to **catalyse** the reaction but the solution flowing **out of** the column will **only** contain the **desired product**.

7) Here are some of the **advantages** of using **immobilised enzymes** in industry:

> - Columns of immobilised enzymes can be **washed** and **reused** — this **reduces** the **cost** of running a reaction on an **industrial scale** because you don't have to **keep buying** new enzymes.
> - The product **isn't mixed** with the enzymes — **no money** or **time** is **spent** separating them out.
> - Immobilised enzymes are **more stable** than free enzymes — they're less likely to **denature** (become inactive) in **high temperatures** or **extremes** of **pH**.

Biotechnology

Closed Cultures of Microorganisms follow a Standard Growth Curve

1) A **culture** is a **population** of one type of microorganism that's been grown under **controlled conditions**.

2) A **closed culture** is when growth takes place in a vessel that's **isolated** from the **external environment** — extra nutrients **aren't added** and waste products **aren't removed** from the vessel **during growth**.

3) In a closed culture a population of microorganisms follows a **standard growth curve**:

> ① **Lag phase** — the population size **increases slowly** because the **microorganisms** have to make enzymes and other molecules before they can reproduce. This means the **reproduction rate** is **low**.
>
> ② **Exponential phase** — the population size **increases quickly** because the culture **conditions** are at their **most favourable** for **reproduction** (**lots of food** and **little competition**). The number of microorganisms **doubles** at **regular intervals**.
>
> ③ **Stationary phase** — the population size **stays level** because the **death rate** of the microorganisms **equals** their **reproductive rate**. Microorganisms **die** because there's **not enough food** and poisonous **waste products build up**.
>
> ④ **Decline phase** — the population size **falls** because the **death rate** is **greater** than the **reproductive rate**. This is because food is very **scarce** and waste products are at **toxic levels**.

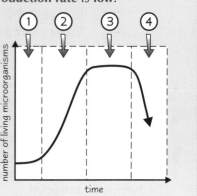

4) When growing conditions are **favourable** (e.g. during the **exponential phase**) microorganisms produce **primary metabolites** — **small molecules** that are **essential** for the **growth** of the microorganisms.

5) When growing conditions are **less favourable** (e.g. during the **stationary phase**) some microorganisms produce **secondary metabolites** — molecules that **aren't essential** for **growth** but are **useful** in **other ways**.

6) **Secondary metabolites** help microorganisms **survive**, e.g. the **antibiotic penicillin** is a secondary metabolite made by *Penicillium* (a fungus). It **kills bacteria** that **inhibit** its **growth**.

7) Some secondary metabolites are **desirable** to **biotechnology industries**, e.g. *Penicillium* is **cultured** on an **industrial scale** to produce lots of penicillin — it's used to treat **bacterial infections** in humans and animals.

Microorganisms are Grown in Fermentation Vessels

Cultures of microorganisms are grown in **large containers** called **fermentation vessels**. The **conditions** inside the fermentation vessels are kept at the **optimum for growth** — this **maximises** the **yield** of **desirable products** from the microorganisms. Here's a bit about how they work:

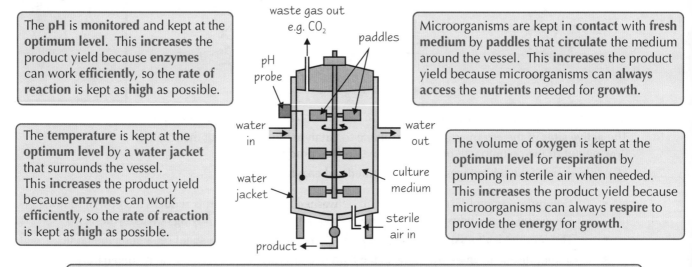

The **pH** is **monitored** and kept at the **optimum level**. This **increases** the product yield because **enzymes** can work **efficiently**, so the **rate of reaction** is kept as **high** as possible.

Microorganisms are kept in **contact** with **fresh medium** by **paddles** that **circulate** the medium around the vessel. This **increases** the product yield because microorganisms can **always access** the **nutrients** needed for **growth**.

The **temperature** is kept at the **optimum level** by a **water jacket** that surrounds the vessel. This **increases** the product yield because **enzymes** can work **efficiently**, so the **rate of reaction** is kept as **high** as possible.

The volume of **oxygen** is kept at the **optimum level** for **respiration** by pumping in sterile air when needed. This **increases** the product yield because microorganisms can always **respire** to provide the **energy** for **growth**.

Vessels are **sterilised** between uses with **superheated steam** to kill any **unwanted organisms**. This **increases** the product yield because the microorganisms **aren't competing** with other organisms.

Biotechnology

There are Two Main Culture Methods — Batch and Continuous

1) **Batch culture** is where microorganisms are grown in **individual batches** in a fermentation vessel — when one culture **ends** it's **removed** and then a **different batch** of microorganisms is grown in the vessel.

2) **Continuous culture** is where microorganisms are **continually grown** in a fermentation vessel **without stopping**.

3) Here are some of the **differences** between batch culture and continuous culture:

Batch Culture	Continuous Culture
A fixed volume of growth medium (nutrients) is added to the fermentation vessel at the start of the culture and no more is added. The culture is a closed system.	Growth medium flows through the vessel at a steady rate so there's a constant supply of fresh nutrients. The culture is an open system.
Each culture goes through the lag, exponential and stationary growth phases.	The culture goes through the lag phase but is then kept at the exponential growth phase.
The product is harvested once, during the stationary phase.	The product is continuously taken out of the fermentation vessel at a steady rate.
The product yield is relatively low — stopping the reaction and sterilising the vessel between fermentations means there's a period when no product is being harvested.	The product yield is relatively high — microorganisms are constantly growing at an exponential rate.
If contamination occurs it only affects one batch. It's not very expensive to discard the contaminated batch and start a new one.	If the culture is contaminated the whole lot has to be discarded — this is very expensive when the cultures are done on an industrial scale.
Used when you want to produce secondary metabolites.	Usually used when you want primary metabolites or the microorganisms themselves as the desired product.

Asepsis is Important when Culturing Microorganisms

1) **Asepsis** is the practice of **preventing contamination** of cultures by **unwanted microorganisms**.

2) It's important when culturing microorganisms because contamination can **affect** the **growth** of the microorganism that you're **interested in**.

3) Contaminated cultures in **laboratory experiments** give **inaccurate results**.

4) Contamination on an **industrial scale** can be **very costly** because **entire cultures** may have to be **thrown away**.

5) A number of **aseptic techniques** can be used when working with microorganisms:

- **Work surfaces** are **regularly disinfected** to minimise contamination.
- **Gloves should be worn** and **long hair** is **tied back** to prevent it from falling into anything.
- The **instruments** used to **transfer** cultures are **sterilised before** and **after** each use, e.g. **inoculation loops** (small wire loops) are **heated** using a **Bunsen burner** to **kill** any microorganisms on them.
- In laboratories, the **necks** of **culture containers** are **briefly flamed** before they're **opened** or **closed** — this causes **air** to **move out** of the container, **preventing** unwanted microorganisms from **falling in**.
- **Lids** are **held over** open containers after they're removed, instead of putting them on a work surface. This **prevents** unwanted microorganisms from **falling** onto the culture.

Practice Questions

Q1 Give one way that enzymes are immobilised.

Q2 Why is it important to maintain the pH level in a fermentation vessel?

Q3 Why is asepsis important when culturing microorganisms?

These questions cover pages 179-181.

Exam Question

Q1 Describe and explain the standard growth curve of microorganisms in a closed culture. [8 marks]

Calf stomachs, yeast and sterile conditions — biotechnology is sexy stuff...

Wow, biology and technology fused together — forget bionic arms, legs and eyes though, growing bacteria in a tank is where it's at. Just think of yourself like an immobilised enzyme in a column — the substrate going in is the information on these pages, then all the desired information will flow out of you (not as a liquid hopefully) onto the exam paper.

Common Techniques

This section is all about technologies used to investigate and fiddle about with genes.
So get your deerstalker hat on and your magnifying glass out...

Gene Technologies — Techniques Used to Study Genes

Gene technologies are basically all the **techniques** used to **study genes** and their **function**
— you need to learn some of these techniques for the exam. They include:

*   The **polymerase chain reaction** (**PCR**) (see below).

*   Cutting out DNA fragments using **restriction enzymes** (see next page).

*   **Gel electrophoresis** (see next page).

*   Finding specific sequences of DNA using **DNA probes** (see p. 189).

As well as helping us to study genes, these techniques have **other uses**,
such as in **genetic engineering** (see p. 184) and **gene therapy** (see p. 188).

*'I know all about jean
technology, baby...'*

Multiple Copies of a DNA Fragment can be Made Using PCR

The **polymerase chain reaction** (PCR) can be used to make **millions of copies** of a
fragment of DNA (containing the gene or bit of DNA you're interested in) in just a few
hours. PCR has **several stages** and is **repeated** over and over to make lots of copies:

1) A reaction mixture is set up that contains the **DNA
    sample, free nucleotides, primers** and **DNA polymerase**.
    *   **Primers** are short pieces of DNA that are **complementary**
        to the bases at the **start** of the fragment you want.
    *   **DNA polymerase** is an **enzyme** that creates new
        DNA strands.

2) The DNA mixture is **heated** to **95 °C** to break the
    hydrogen bonds between the two strands of DNA.

3) The mixture is then **cooled** to between **50** and **65 °C**
    so that the primers can **bind** (**anneal**) to the strands.

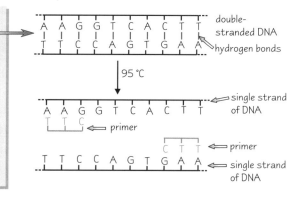

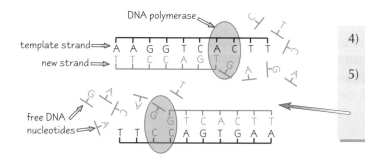

4) The reaction mixture is heated to **72 °C**,
    so **DNA polymerase** can **work**.

5) The DNA polymerase **lines up** free DNA
    nucleotides **alongside** each **template strand**.
    Complementary **base pairing** means **new
    complementary strands** are formed.

6) **Two new copies** of the fragment of DNA are formed and **one cycle** of PCR is **complete**.

7) The cycle starts again, with the mixture being heated to 95 °C and this time
    all four strands (two original and two new) are used as **templates**.

8) Each PCR cycle **doubles** the amount of DNA, e.g. **1st cycle = 2 × 2 = 4 DNA fragments**,
    2nd cycle = 4 × 2 = 8 DNA fragments, 3rd cycle = 8 × 2 = 16 DNA fragments, and so on.

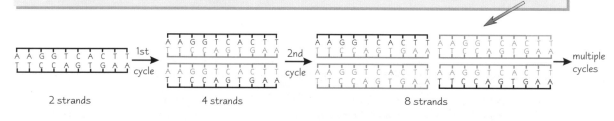

Common Techniques

Restriction Enzymes can be Used to Cut Out DNA Fragments

You can get a DNA fragment from an organism's DNA by using **restriction enzymes**:

1) Some sections of DNA have **palindromic** sequences of **nucleotides**. These sequences consist of **antiparallel base pairs** (base pairs that read the **same** in **opposite directions**).

2) **Restriction enzymes** are enzymes that **recognise specific** palindromic sequences (known as **recognition sequences**) and **cut** (**digest**) the DNA at these places.

3) Different restriction enzymes cut at **different specific** recognition sequences, because the **shape** of the recognition sequence is **complementary** to an enzyme's **active site**. E.g. the restriction enzyme *Eco*RI cuts at GAATTC, but *Hind*III cuts at AAGCTT.

4) If recognition sequences are present at **either side** of the DNA fragment you want, you can use restriction enzymes to **separate** it from the rest of the DNA.

5) The DNA sample is **incubated** with the specific restriction enzyme, which **cuts** the DNA fragment out via a **hydrolysis reaction**.

6) Sometimes the cut leaves **sticky ends** — **small tails** of **unpaired bases** at **each end** of the fragment. Sticky ends can be used to **bind** (**anneal**) the DNA fragment to another piece of DNA that has sticky ends with **complementary sequences**.

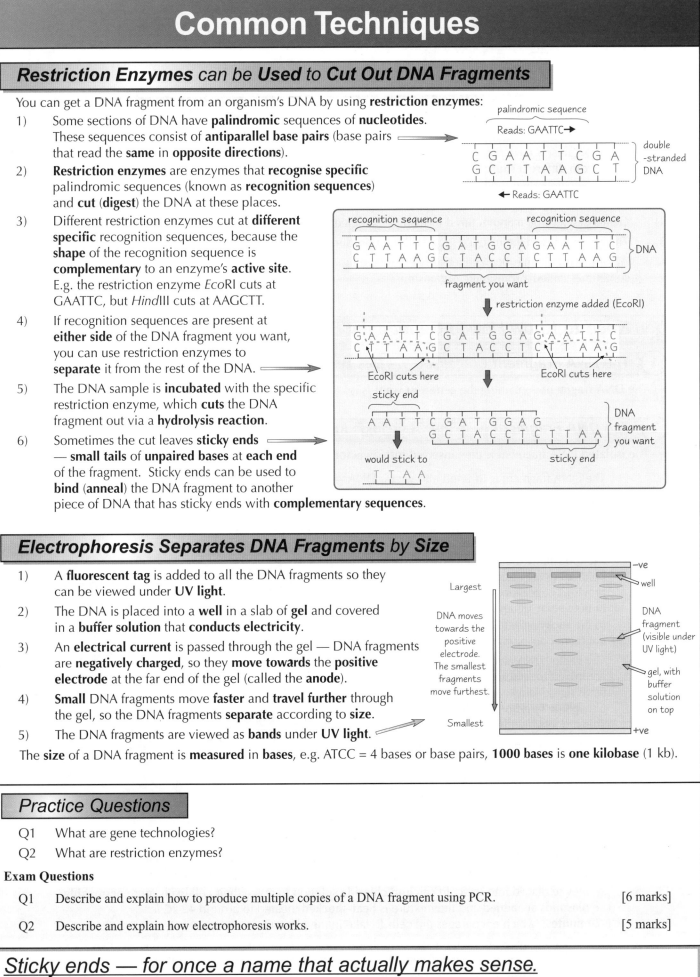

Electrophoresis Separates DNA Fragments by Size

1) A **fluorescent tag** is added to all the DNA fragments so they can be viewed under **UV light**.

2) The DNA is placed into a **well** in a slab of **gel** and covered in a **buffer solution** that **conducts electricity**.

3) An **electrical current** is passed through the gel — DNA fragments are **negatively charged**, so they **move towards** the **positive electrode** at the far end of the gel (called the **anode**).

4) **Small** DNA fragments move **faster** and **travel further** through the gel, so the DNA fragments **separate** according to **size**.

5) The DNA fragments are viewed as **bands** under **UV light**.

The **size** of a DNA fragment is **measured** in **bases**, e.g. ATCC = 4 bases or base pairs, **1000 bases** is **one kilobase** (1 kb).

Practice Questions

Q1   What are gene technologies?

Q2   What are restriction enzymes?

Exam Questions

Q1   Describe and explain how to produce multiple copies of a DNA fragment using PCR.   [6 marks]

Q2   Describe and explain how electrophoresis works.   [5 marks]

Sticky ends — for once a name that actually makes sense.

Gene technologies aren't the sort of technology you can buy in all good electrical stores, but they're still quite cool. Take PCR for example — you can throw in a DNA fragment and get out squillions of copies of it. Just like that. Amazing.

Genetic Engineering

Genetic engineering — you need to know what it is and how it's done... (unlucky)...

Genetic Engineering is the Manipulation of an Organism's DNA

1) Organisms that have had their **DNA altered** by genetic engineering are called **transformed organisms**.

2) These organisms have **recombinant DNA** — DNA formed by **joining together** DNA from **different sources**.

3) Genetic engineering usually involves **extracting** a **gene** from **one organism** and then **inserting** it **into another organism** (often one that's a **different species**).

4) Genes can also be **manufactured** instead of extracted from an organism.

5) The organism with the inserted gene will then **produce the protein** coded for by that gene.

6) An organism that has been genetically engineered to include a **gene** from a **different species** is sometimes called a **transgenic organism**.

Transformed organisms are also known as genetically engineered or genetically modified organisms.

You Need to Know How to Genetically Engineer a Microorganism

(1) The DNA Fragment Containing the Desired Gene is Obtained

The **DNA fragment** containing the **gene you want** is isolated using **restriction enzymes** (see previous page).

(2) The DNA Fragment (with the Gene in) is Inserted into a Vector

The **isolated** DNA fragment is then **inserted into** a **vector** using **restriction enzymes** and **ligase** (an enzyme):

1) The DNA fragment is inserted into vector DNA — a **vector** is something that's used to **transfer DNA** into a **cell**. They can be **plasmids** (**small**, **circular molecules** of DNA in **bacteria**) or **bacteriophages** (**viruses** that **infect** bacteria).

2) The vector DNA is **cut open** using the **same** restriction enzyme that was used to **isolate** the DNA fragment containing the desired gene (see previous page). So the **sticky ends** of the vector are **complementary** to the sticky ends of the DNA fragment containing the gene.

3) The vector DNA and DNA fragment are **mixed together** with DNA **ligase**. DNA ligase **joins up** the **sugar-phosphate backbones** of the two bits. This process is called **ligation**.

4) The new combination of bases in the DNA (vector DNA + DNA fragment) is called **recombinant DNA**.

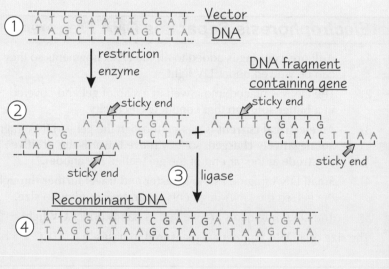

(3) The Vector Transfers the Gene into the Bacteria

1) The **vector** with the **recombinant DNA** is used to **transfer** the gene into the **bacterial cells**.

2) If a **plasmid vector** is used, the bacterial cells have to be **persuaded** to **take in** the plasmid vector and its DNA. E.g. they're placed into ice-cold **calcium chloride** solution to make their cell walls more **permeable**. The **plasmids** are **added** and the mixture is **heat-shocked** (heated to around **42 °C** for **1-2 minutes**), which encourages the cells to take in the plasmids.

3) With a **bacteriophage** vector, the bacteriophage will **infect** the bacterium by **injecting** its **DNA** into it. The phage DNA (with the desired gene in it) then **integrates** into the bacterial DNA.

4) **Cells** that **take up** the vectors containing the desired gene are genetically engineered, so are called **transformed**.

Genetic Engineering

(4) Identify the Transformed Bacteria

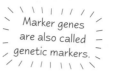

Marker genes are also called genetic markers.

Not all the bacteria will have **taken up** the vector.
Marker genes can be used to **identify** the ones that **have**:

1) **Marker genes** can be inserted into vectors at the **same time** as the desired gene.
This means any **transformed bacterial cells** will contain the desired gene **and** the marker gene.

2) The bacteria are **grown** on **agar plates** and each cell **divides** and **replicates** its DNA, creating a **colony of cells**.

3) Transformed cells will produce colonies where **all the cells** contain the desired gene and the marker gene.

4) The marker gene can code for **antibiotic resistance** — bacteria are grown on agar plates **containing** the **antibiotic**, so **only** cells that have the **marker gene** will **survive** and **grow**.

5) The marker gene can code for **fluorescence** — when the agar plate is placed under a **UV light** **only** transformed cells will **fluoresce**.

It's *Useful* for *Microorganisms* to be Able to *Take Up Plasmids*

Microorganisms can **take up plasmids** from their surroundings, which is **beneficial** because the plasmids often contain **useful genes**. This means the microorganisms gain **useful characteristics**, so they're more likely to have an **advantage** over other microorganisms, which **increases** their **chance** of **survival**. Plasmids may contain:

- Genes that code for **resistance** to **antibiotics**, e.g. genes for enzymes that **break down antibiotics**.

- Genes that help microorganisms **invade hosts**, e.g. genes for enzymes that **break down host tissues**.

- Genes that mean microorganisms can use **different nutrients**, e.g. genes for enzymes that break down **sugars** not normally used.

Practice Questions

Q1   What is the name for an organism that has had its DNA altered?

Q2   What is a vector?

Q3   Other than a plasmid, give an example of a vector.

Q4   Name the type of enzyme that can be used to cut DNA.

Q5   What is the name of the type of DNA formed from vector DNA and an inserted DNA fragment?

Q6   What is a marker gene?

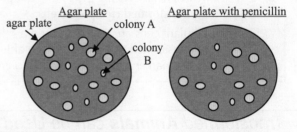

Exam Question

Q1   A scientist has genetically engineered some bacterial cells to contain a desired gene and a gene that gives resistance to penicillin. The cells were grown on an agar plate and then transferred to a plate containing penicillin. The two plates are shown above.
a) Explain why the scientist thinks colony A contains transformed bacterial cells, but colony B doesn't.   [2 marks]
b) Explain how the scientist might have inserted the desired gene into the plasmid.   [3 marks]
c) Explain why being able to take up plasmids is useful to bacteria.   [2 marks]

Examiners — genetically engineered to contain marker genes...

This stuff might seem tricky the first time you read it, but it's not too bad really — you get the gene you want and bung it in a vector, the vector gets the gene into the cell (it's kind of like a delivery boy), then all you have to do is figure out which cells have got the gene. Easy peasy. Unfortunately you need to know each stage in detail, so get learnin'.

Genetic Engineering

Genetic engineering can benefit humans in loads of different ways...

Transformed **Bacteria** can be used to **Produce Human Insulin**

See page 124 for more on Type 1 diabetes.

People with **Type 1 diabetes** need to **inject insulin** to **regulate** their **blood glucose concentration**. Insulin used to be obtained from the **pancreases** of dead animals, such as **pigs**. Nowadays we use **genetically engineered bacteria** to manufacture **human insulin**. Here's how the whole process works:

1) The **gene** for **human insulin** is **identified** and **isolated** using **restriction enzymes**.
2) A **plasmid** is **cut open** using the **same** restriction enzyme that was used to isolate the insulin gene.
3) The **insulin gene** is **inserted** into the **plasmid** (forming **recombinant DNA**).
4) The plasmid is **taken up** by bacteria and any **transformed** bacteria are **identified** using **marker genes**.
5) The bacteria are **grown** in a **fermenter** — human insulin is **produced** as the bacteria **grow** and **divide**.
6) The human insulin is **extracted** and **purified** so it can be **used in humans**.

These techniques are covered in more detail on page 184.

There are many **advantages** of using **genetically engineered human insulin** over **animal insulin**:

* It's **identical** to the insulin in our bodies, so it's **more effective** than animal insulin and there's **less risk** of an **allergic reaction**.

* It's **cheaper** and **faster** to produce than animal insulin, providing a **more reliable** and **larger supply** of insulin.

* Using genetically engineered insulin **overcomes** any **ethical** or **religious issues** arising from using animal insulin.

Transformed **Plants** can be Used to **Reduce Vitamin Deficiency**

Golden Rice is a type of **genetically engineered rice**. The rice is genetically engineered to contain a **gene** from a **maize plant** and a **gene** from a **soil bacterium**, which together enable the rice to produce **beta-carotene**. The beta-carotene is used by our bodies to produce **vitamin A**. *Golden Rice* is being developed to **reduce vitamin A deficiency** in areas where there's a **shortage** of **dietary vitamin A**, e.g. south Asia, parts of Africa. Here's how *Golden Rice* is produced:

1) The *psy* gene (from maize) and the *crtl* gene (from the soil bacterium) are **isolated** using **restriction enzymes**.
2) A **plasmid** is **removed** from the *Agrobacterium tumefaciens* **bacterium** and **cut open** with the **same** restriction enzymes.
3) The *psy* and *crtl* genes and a **marker gene** are **inserted** into the plasmid.
4) The **recombinant plasmid** is **put back into** the bacterium.
5) **Rice plant cells** are incubated with the **transformed** *A. tumefaciens* bacteria, which **infect** the rice plant cells.
6) *A. tumefaciens* **inserts** the **genes** into the **plant cells' DNA**, creating **transformed rice plant cells**.
7) The rice plant cells are then grown on a **selective medium** — only transformed rice plants will be able to **grow** because they contain the marker gene that's needed to grow on this medium.

Recombinant plasmid — marker gene — psy gene — ctrl gene

The plasmid is put back into A. tumefaciens.

A. tumefaciens infects rice plant cells.

Transgenic rice plant cells

Transformed **Animals** can be Used to **Produce Organs** for **Transplant**

1) **Organ failure** (e.g. kidney or liver failure) may be **treated** with an **organ transplant**.
2) However, there's a **shortage** of **donor organs** available for transplant in the UK, which means many people **die** whilst **waiting** for a suitable donor organ.
3) **Xenotransplantation** is the **transfer** of **cells**, **tissues** or **organs** from **one species** to **another**.
4) It's hoped that xenotransplantation can be used to provide **animal donor organs** for **humans**.
5) With any form of transplantation there's a chance of **rejection** — the **immune system** of the **recipient recognises proteins** on the **surface** of the transplanted cells as **foreign** and starts an **immune response** against them.
6) Rejection is an **even greater** problem with xenotransplantation because the **genetic differences** between organisms of **different species** are even **greater** than between organisms of the same species.

Genetic Engineering

7) Scientists are trying to **genetically engineer animals** so that their **organs aren't rejected** when transplanted into humans. Here's how:

> *Xenotransplantation hasn't been carried out in humans yet, but there's lots of research being done on it.*

1) Genes for HUMAN cell-surface proteins are INSERTED into the animal's DNA:

Human genes for **human cell-surface proteins** are **injected** into a **newly fertilised animal embryo**. The genes **integrate** into the **animal's DNA**. The animal then **produces human cell-surface proteins**, which reduces the risk of transplant rejection.

2) Genes for ANIMAL cell-surface proteins are 'KNOCKED OUT' — removed or inactivated:

- Animal genes involved in making cell-surface proteins are **removed** or **inactivated** in the **nucleus** of an **animal cell**. The nucleus is then **transferred** into an **unfertilised animal egg cell** (this is called **nuclear transfer**). The egg cell is then **stimulated** to **divide** into an embryo and the animal created **doesn't produce animal** cell-surface proteins, which reduces the risk of transplant rejection.

- For example, **pigs** have a sugar called **Gal-alpha(1,3)-Gal** attached to their cell-surface proteins, which humans don't. Scientists have developed a **knockout pig** that **doesn't produce** the **enzyme** needed to **make** this sugar.

There are Some **Ethical Issues** Surrounding **Genetic Engineering**

Genetic engineering can be used for **loads of things** other than producing insulin, reducing vitamin A deficiency and producing organs suitable for transplant from animals. For example it can be used to produce **pest-** or **herbicide-resistant crops** and **drugs** (and could even be used to genetically engineer **humans**). All these applications have ethical issues and concerns surrounding them:

1) Some people are worried that using **antibiotic-resistance** genes as **marker genes** may **increase** the number of **antibiotic-resistant**, **pathogenic** (disease-causing) **microorganisms** in our environment.

2) **Environmentalists** are worried that GM crops (like *Golden Rice*) may encourage **farmers** to carry out **monoculture** (where only one type of crop is planted). Monoculture **decreases biodiversity** and could leave the **whole crop vulnerable** to **disease**, because all the plants are **genetically identical**.

3) Some people are worried that genetically engineering **animals** for **xenotransplantation** may **cause them suffering**.

4) Some people are concerned about the possibility of '**superweeds**' — weeds that are **resistant** to **herbicides** because they've bred with **genetically engineered herbicide-resistant crops**.

5) Some people are concerned that large biotechnology companies may use GM crops to **exploit farmers** in **poor countries** — e.g. by selling them crops that they **can't** really **afford**.

6) Some people worry **humans** will be genetically engineered (e.g. to be more intelligent), creating a **genetic underclass**. This is currently **illegal** though.

Practice Questions

Q1 Give two advantages of using human insulin produced by genetic engineering compared to using animal insulin.

Q2 What is xenotransplantation?

Q3 How could xenotransplantation benefit humans?

Q4 Give two ethical issues surrounding genetic engineering.

Exam Questions

Q1 People with Type 1 diabetes need to inject insulin to regulate their blood glucose concentration. Describe how human insulin can be made using genetically engineered bacteria. [6 marks]

Q2 *Golden Rice* is a type of transformed rice. Outline the process used to create *Golden Rice*. [7 marks]

If only they could knockout the gene for smelly feet...

...or the gene for freckles... or spots... or a big nose... or chubby ankles... the list is endless. Not that I'm vain or anything. Anyway, make sure you know all the processes in detail — it's no good just knowing that Golden Rice is a genetically engineered crop, you need to know <u>how</u> it was genetically engineered too. So knuckle down and go over the page again...

Gene Therapy and DNA Probes

Now that you've seen how microorganisms, plants and animals can be genetically engineered it seems a shame to leave out humans and how gene therapy could be used to cure some disorders. Then you need to know all about DNA probes.

Gene Therapy Could be Used to Cure Genetic Disorders

Genetic disorders are **inherited disorders** caused by **abnormal genes** or **chromosomes**, e.g. cystic fibrosis. **Gene therapy** could be used to **cure** these disorders — it **isn't** being used yet but some treatments are undergoing **clinical trials**.

How it works:

1) Gene therapy involves **altering alleles** inside cells to cure **genetic disorders**.
2) How you do this depends on whether the genetic disorder is caused by a **dominant allele** or two **recessive alleles**:
   - If it's caused by two **recessive** alleles you can **add** a working **dominant allele** to make up for them.
   - If it's caused by a **dominant** allele you can 'silence' the **dominant allele** (e.g. by sticking a bit of DNA in the middle of the allele so it doesn't work any more).

See page 162 for more on dominant and recessive alleles.

A DNA-filled doughnut — surely the best way to deliver new alleles...

How you get the 'new' allele (DNA) inside the cell:

1) The allele is **inserted into cells** using **vectors**.
2) Different **vectors** can be used, e.g. altered **viruses**, **plasmids** or **liposomes** (spheres made of lipid).

There are two types of gene therapy:

1) **Somatic therapy** — this involves **altering** the **alleles** in **body cells**, particularly the cells that are **most affected** by the disorder. For example, **cystic fibrosis** (CF) is a genetic disorder that's very **damaging** to the **respiratory system**, so somatic therapy for CF **targets** the epithelial cells lining the lungs. Somatic therapy doesn't affect the individual's **sex cells** (sperm or eggs) though, so any **offspring** could still **inherit** the disease.
2) **Germ line therapy** — this involves **altering** the **alleles** in the **sex cells**. This means that **every cell** of **any offspring** produced from these cells will be **affected** by the gene therapy and they **won't suffer from the disease**. Germ line therapy in humans is currently **illegal** though.

There are Advantages and Disadvantages to Gene Therapy

ADVANTAGES	DISADVANTAGES
It could prolong the lives of people with genetic disorders.	The effects of the treatment may be short–lived (only in somatic therapy).
It could give people with genetic disorders a better quality of life.	The patient might have to undergo multiple treatments (only in somatic therapy).
Carriers of genetic disorders might be able to conceive a baby without that disorder or risk of cancer (only in germ line therapy).	It might be difficult to get the allele into specific body cells.
It could decrease the number of people that suffer from genetic disorders (only in germ line therapy).	The body could identify vectors as foreign bodies and start an immune response against them.
	An allele could be inserted into the wrong place in the DNA, possibly causing more problems, e.g. cancer.
	An inserted allele could get overexpressed, producing too much of the missing protein.
	Disorders caused by multiple genes (e.g. cancer) would be difficult to treat with this technique.

There are also many **ethical issues** associated with gene therapy. For example, some people are worried that the technology could be used in ways **other** than for **medical treatment**, such as for treating the **cosmetic effects** of **aging**. Other people worry that there's the potential to do **more harm** than good by using the technology (e.g. risk of overexpression of genes — see table). There's also the concern that gene therapy is **expensive** — some people believe that **health service resources** could be **better spent** on other treatments that have passed clinical trials.

Gene Therapy and DNA Probes

DNA Probes can be used to Identify Specific Base Sequences in DNA

1) **DNA probes** (also called **gene probes**) can be used to **identify DNA fragments** that contain **specific sequences** of bases, e.g. they can be used to **locate genes** on chromosomes or see if a person's DNA **contains** a **mutated gene** (e.g. a gene that causes a genetic disorder).

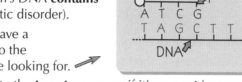
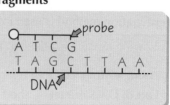

2) DNA probes are **short strands** of **DNA**. They have a **specific base sequence** that's **complementary** to the target sequence — the specific sequence you're looking for.

3) This means a DNA probe will **bind** (**hybridise**) to the **target sequence** if it's **present** in a **sample** of DNA.

4) A DNA probe also has a **label attached**, so that it can be **detected**. The two most common types of label are a **radioactive** label (detected using **X-ray film**) or a **fluorescent** label (detected using **UV light**).

5) For example, you can use a DNA probe to see if any members of a family have a **mutation** in a gene that causes a **genetic disorder**:

- A **sample** of **DNA** from each family member is **digested** into fragments using **restriction enzymes** (see page 183) and **separated** using **electrophoresis** (see page 183).

- The separated DNA fragments are then transferred to a **nylon membrane** and **incubated** with the **fluorescently labelled DNA probe**. The probe is **complementary** to the specific sequence of the mutated gene.

- If the specific sequence **is present** in one of the DNA fragments, the DNA probe will **hybridise** (**bind**) to it.

- The **membrane** is then **exposed** to **UV light** and if the specific sequence is present in one of the DNA fragments, then that band will **fluoresce** (**glow**).

- For example, **person three** has a **visible band**, so that family member has the specific sequence **in** one of their DNA fragments, which means they **have** the **mutated gene**.

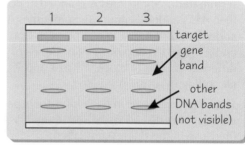

Practice Questions

Q1 How could gene therapy be used to supplement mutated recessive alleles?

Q2 How are supplementary alleles added to human DNA?

Q3 What does germ line gene therapy involve?

Q4 What is a DNA probe?

Q5 Name two types of label that can be attached to a DNA probe.

Exam Questions

Q1 A patient suffering from cystic fibrosis was offered gene therapy targeted at his lung epithelial cells to help treat the disease.

    a) What does gene therapy involve?   [1 mark]

    b) What type of gene therapy was the patient offered?   [1 mark]

Q2 Give three possible disadvantages of somatic gene therapy.   [3 marks]

Q3 Erin has a family history of breast cancer. She has agreed to be screened for the mutated BRCA1 gene, which can cause breast cancer. A sample of her DNA is digested and separated using gel electrophoresis. Describe how a DNA probe could be used to identify the mutated BRCA1 gene.   [4 marks]

DNA probes — don't worry, the DNA doesn't feel a thing...

You need to know exactly what gene therapy is and the differences between the two types ('somatic' means 'body', which should help you remember). How DNA probes work also needs to be etched in your memory — they can be used to tell if someone has a genetic disorder, but don't forget they can be used for other things too, like locating genes on chromosomes.

Sequencing Genes and Genomes

OK, these are the last two pages of the section, but sequencing is tricky business — so look sharp.

DNA can be Sequenced by the Chain-Termination Method

The **chain-termination method** is used to determine the **order** of **bases** in a section of **DNA** (gene):

1) The following mixture is added to **four separate** tubes:

   - A **single-stranded DNA template** — the DNA to sequence.
   - Lots of **DNA primer** — short pieces of DNA (see p. 182).
   - **DNA polymerase** — the enzyme that joins DNA nucleotides together.
   - **Free nucleotides** — lots of free A, T, C and G nucleotides.

   - **Fluorescently-labelled modified nucleotide** — like a normal nucleotide, but once it's added to a DNA strand, **no more** bases can be added after it. A **different** modified nucleotide is added to **each tube** (A*, T*, C*, G*).

2) The tubes undergo **PCR**, which produces many **strands of DNA**. The strands are **different lengths** because each one **terminates** at a **different point** depending on where the modified nucleotide was added.

3) For example, in tube A (with the **modified adenine** nucleotide A*) sometimes A* is **added** to the DNA at point 4 **instead** of A, **stopping** the **addition** of any more bases (the strand is **terminated**). Sometimes A is added at point 4, then **A*** is added at **point 5**. Sometimes A is added at **point 4**, A again at point 5, G at point 6 and **A*** is added at **point 7**. So strands of **three different lengths** (4 bases, 5 bases and 7 bases) all ending in **A*** are produced.

4) The DNA fragments in each tube are separated by **electrophoresis** and **visualised** under **UV light** (because of the **fluorescent label**).

5) The **complementary base sequence** can be **read** from the gel. The **smallest** nucleotide (e.g. one base) is at the **bottom** of the gel. Each band after this represents **one more base** added. So by reading the bands **from the bottom** of the gel **to the top**, you can build up the **DNA sequence** one base at a time.

Example — Tube A

A* added at point 4

A added, then A* added at point 5

2 As added, G added, then A* added at point 7

+ all other tubes (containing C*, G*, T*)

The complementary sequence is TTCAAGA, so the original sequence is AAGTTCT.

A Whole Genome can be Sequenced Using BACs

The **chain-termination method** can only be used for DNA fragments up to about **750 bp** long. So if you want to sequence the **entire genome** (all the DNA) of an organism, you need to chop it up into **smaller pieces** first. The smaller pieces are **sequenced** and then **put back in order** to give the sequence of the whole genome. Here's how it's done:

1) A genome is **cut** into **smaller fragments** (about 100 000 bp) using **restriction enzymes**.

2) The fragments are inserted into **bacterial artificial chromosomes (BACs)** — these are **man-made plasmids**. **Each** fragment in inserted into a **different BAC**.

3) The BACs are then **inserted** into **bacteria** — **each bacterium** contains a **BAC** with a **different DNA fragment**.

4) The bacteria **divide**, creating **colonies** of **cloned** (**identical**) cells that all contain a **specific DNA fragment**. Together the different colonies make a complete **genomic DNA library**.

5) **DNA** is **extracted** from **each colony** and **cut** up using restriction enzymes, producing **overlapping** pieces of DNA.

6) Each piece of DNA is **sequenced**, using the **chain-termination method**, and the pieces are **put back in order** to give the full sequence **from that BAC** (using **powerful computer systems**).

7) Finally the DNA fragments from **all the BACs** are **put back in order**, by computers, to **complete** the **entire genome**.

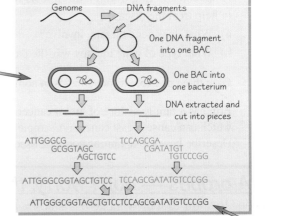

Sequencing Genes and Genomes

Sequenced Genomes can be Compared

Gene sequences and **whole genome** sequences can be compared **between** organisms of **different species** and between organisms of the **same species**. There are many reasons why we'd want to do this:

Look, when we stick our tongues out like this you can just TELL we're related, we don't need a genome comparison.

Comparing the genomes of DIFFERENT species can help us to:

1) Understand the **evolutionary relationships** between different species. **All** organisms **evolved** from **shared common ancestors** (relatives). **Closely related** species **evolved away** from each other more **recently** and so **share more DNA**. So DNA can tell us **how closely related** different species are. E.g. the genomes of **humans** and **chimpanzees** are about **94%** similar.

2) Understand the way in which **genes interact** during **development** and how they're **controlled**. For example, genome sequencing has shown that the **homeobox sequence** (see page 157) is the **same** in animals, plants and fungi. By studying how genes with the homeobox sequence work in the **Drosophila fruit fly** scientists can begin to piece together how they work in **humans** too.

3) Carry out **medical research**. **Human genes** that are associated with **disease**, like cancer or heart disease, can be found in the genomes of **other mammals**, such as mice and rats. This means mice or rats could be used as **animal models** for **research** into these diseases.

Comparing genomes of the SAME species can help us to:

1) Trace **early human migration**. For example, when different groups of early **humans separated** and **moved** to different parts of the world, their genomes **changed** in **slightly different ways**. By **comparing** the genomes of people from different parts of the world, it's possible to build up a picture of early human migration.

2) Study the **genetics** of **human diseases**. Some **gene mutations** have been **linked** to a **greater risk** of **disease** (e.g. mutations in the **BRCA1** gene are linked to **breast cancer**). Comparisons between the genomes of **sufferers** and **non-sufferers** can be used to **detect** particular **mutations** that could be responsible for the increased risk of disease.

3) Develop **medical treatments** for **particular genotypes**. The **same medicine** can be **more effective** in some patients than in others, which can be due to their **different genomes**. In the future, it may be possible to **sequence** a patient's genome so they can receive the **most effective medicine** for them.

Practice Questions

Q1 Give the name of a method used to sequence DNA.

Q2 What is a bacterial artificial chromosome?

Q3 Give two reasons why a scientist might want to compare the genomes of organisms from different species.

Q4 Give two reasons why a scientist might want to compare the genomes of organisms from the same species.

Exam Questions

Q1 To sequence a small DNA fragment, a single-stranded DNA template and DNA polymerase are needed.
   a) Name the other three reactants needed for a sequencing reaction.   [3 marks]
   b) Describe and explain the process of sequencing a small DNA fragment.   [6 marks]

Q2 The genomes of over 200 different species have been sequenced.
   Describe how a genome can be sequenced using BACs.   [8 marks]

Sequencing — so 80s...

Don't worry, the buzzing in your head is normal — it's due to information overload. So go get yourself a cuppa and a biccie and have a break. Then go over some of the difficult bits in this section again. Yes, I did say 'again'. But believe me, the more times you go over it the more things will click into place and you'll be even more prepared for the exam.

Ecosystems and the Nitrogen Cycle

All this ecology-type stuff is pretty wordy, so here are a nice few definitions to get you started.
This way, you'll know what I'm banging on about throughout the rest of the section, and that always helps I think.

You Need to **Learn Some Definitions** to get you **Started**

Ecosystem	—	**All** the **organisms** living in a **particular area** and all the **non-living** (abiotic) conditions, e.g. a freshwater ecosystem such as a lake. Ecosystems are **dynamic systems** — they're **changing** all the time.
Habitat	—	The **place** where an organism **lives**, e.g. a rocky shore or a field.
Population	—	**All** the organisms of **one species** in a **habitat**.
Abiotic factors	—	The **non-living** features of the ecosystem, e.g. **temperature** and **availability of water**.
Biotic factors	—	The **living** features of the ecosystem, e.g. the presence of **predators** or **food**.
Producer	—	An organism that **produces organic molecules** using sunlight energy, e.g. plants.
Consumer	—	An organism that **eats other organisms**, e.g. animals and birds.
Decomposer	—	An organism that **breaks down dead** or **undigested organic material**, e.g. bacteria and fungi.
Trophic level	—	A **stage** in a **food chain** occupied by a particular **group** of organisms, e.g. producers are the first trophic level in a food chain.

Being a member of the undead made it hard for Mumra to know whether he was a living or a non-living feature of the ecosystem.

Energy is **Transferred Through Ecosystems**

1) The **main route** by which energy **enters** an ecosystem is **photosynthesis** (e.g. by plants, see p. 134). (Some energy enters sea ecosystems when bacteria use chemicals from deep sea vents as an energy source.)

2) During photosynthesis plants **convert sunlight energy** into a form that can be **used** by other organisms — plants are called **producers** (see table above).

3) Energy is **transferred** through the **living organisms** of an ecosystem when organisms **eat** other organisms, e.g. producers are eaten by organisms called **primary consumers**. Primary consumers are then eaten by **secondary consumers** and secondary consumers are eaten by **tertiary consumers**.

4) **Food chains** and **food webs** show how energy is **transferred** through an ecosystem.

5) **Food chains** show **simple lines** of energy transfer.

6) **Food webs** show **lots** of **food chains** in an ecosystem and how they **overlap**.

7) Energy locked up in the things that **can't be eaten** (e.g. bones, faeces) gets recycled back into the ecosystem by **decomposers**.

Oak tree (producer) — Eaten by → Caterpillar (primary consumer) — Eaten by → Starling (secondary consumer) — Eaten by → Mr Cuddles (tertiary consumer)

Apple tree (producer) — Eaten by → Mouse (primary consumer) — Eaten by → Hawk (tertiary consumer)

Ecosystems and the Nitrogen Cycle

The Nitrogen Cycle shows how Nitrogen is Recycled in Ecosystems

Plants and animals **need** nitrogen to make **proteins** and **nucleic acids** (DNA and RNA). The atmosphere's made up of about 78% nitrogen, but plants and animals **can't use it** in that form — they need **bacteria** to **convert** it into **nitrogen compounds** first. The **nitrogen cycle** shows how nitrogen is **converted** into a useable form and then **passed** on between different **living** organisms and the **non-living** environment.

The nitrogen cycle includes **food chains** (nitrogen is passed on when organisms are eaten), and four different processes that involve bacteria — **nitrogen fixation**, **ammonification**, **nitrification** and **denitrification**:

1 **Nitrogen fixation**

- **Nitrogen fixation** is when nitrogen **gas** in the atmosphere is turned into **ammonia** by **bacteria** called *Rhizobium*. The ammonia can then be **used** by plants.

- *Rhizobium* are found inside **root nodules** (growths on the roots) of **leguminous** plants (e.g. peas, beans and clover).

- They form a **mutualistic** relationship with the plants — they provide the plant with **nitrogen compounds** and the plant provides them with **carbohydrates**.

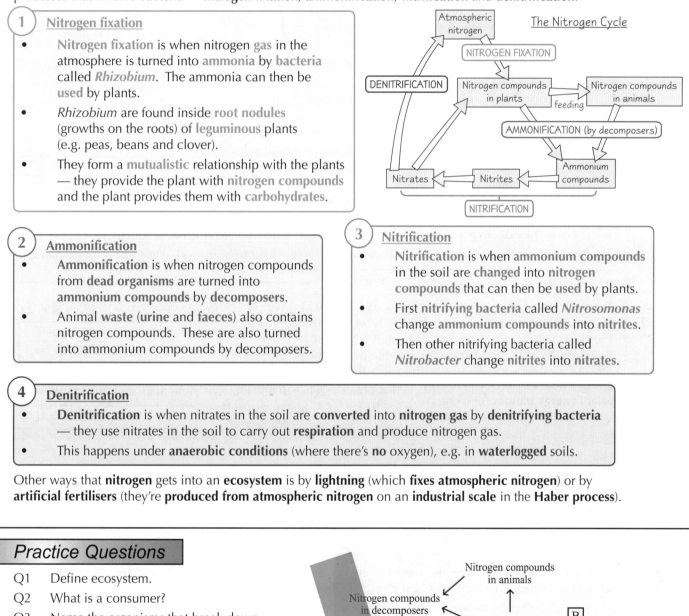

The Nitrogen Cycle

2 **Ammonification**

- **Ammonification** is when nitrogen compounds from **dead organisms** are turned into **ammonium compounds** by **decomposers**.

- Animal waste (**urine** and **faeces**) also contains nitrogen compounds. These are also turned into ammonium compounds by decomposers.

3 **Nitrification**

- **Nitrification** is when **ammonium compounds** in the soil are **changed** into **nitrogen compounds** that can then be **used** by plants.

- First **nitrifying bacteria** called *Nitrosomonas* change **ammonium compounds** into **nitrites**.

- Then other nitrifying bacteria called *Nitrobacter* change **nitrites** into **nitrates**.

4 **Denitrification**

- **Denitrification** is when nitrates in the soil are **converted** into **nitrogen gas** by **denitrifying bacteria** — they use nitrates in the soil to carry out **respiration** and produce nitrogen gas.

- This happens under **anaerobic conditions** (where there's **no** oxygen), e.g. in **waterlogged** soils.

Other ways that **nitrogen** gets into an **ecosystem** is by **lightning** (which **fixes atmospheric nitrogen**) or by **artificial fertilisers** (they're **produced from atmospheric nitrogen** on an **industrial scale** in the **Haber process**).

Practice Questions

Q1 Define ecosystem.
Q2 What is a consumer?
Q3 Name the organisms that break down dead organic material.
Q4 What is nitrification?

Exam Question

Q1 The diagram on the right shows the nitrogen cycle.
　　a) Name the processes labelled A and C in the diagram. [2 marks]
　　b) Name and describe process B in detail. [3 marks]

Nitrogen fixation — cheaper than a shoe fixation...

The nitrogen cycle's not as bad as it seems — divide up the four processes of nitrogen fixation, ammonification, nitrification and denitrification and learn them separately. Then before you know it, you'll have learnt the whole cycle. Easy peesy.

Energy Transfer Through an Ecosystem

Energy is lost along food chains (how careless, they should put it in a safe place if you ask me).

Not All Energy gets Transferred to the Next Trophic Level

1) **Not all** the energy (e.g. from sunlight or food) that's available to the organisms in a trophic level is **transferred** to the **next** trophic level — around **90%** of the **total available energy** is **lost** in various ways.

2) Some of the available energy (**60%**) is **never taken in** by the organisms in the first place. For example:
   - Plants **can't use** all the light energy that reaches their **leaves**, e.g. some is the **wrong wavelength**, some is **reflected**, and some **passes straight through** the leaves.
   - Some sunlight can't be used because it hits parts of the plant that **can't photosynthesise**, e.g. the bark of a tree.
   - Some **parts** of food, e.g. **roots** or **bones**, **aren't eaten** by organisms so the energy isn't taken in.
   - Some parts of food are **indigestible** so **pass through** organisms and come out as **waste**, e.g. **faeces**.

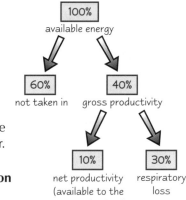

3) The rest of the available energy (**40%**) is **taken in** (absorbed) — this is called the **gross productivity**. But not all of this is available to the next trophic level either.
   - **30%** of the **total energy** available (75% of the gross productivity) is **lost to the environment** when organisms use energy produced from **respiration** for **movement** or body **heat**. This is called **respiratory loss**.
   - **10%** of the **total energy** available (25% of the gross productivity) becomes **biomass** (e.g. it's **stored** or used for **growth**) — this is called the **net productivity**.

4) **Net productivity** is the amount of energy that's **available** to the **next trophic level**. Here's how it's **calculated**:

> net productivity = gross productivity − respiratory loss
>
> **EXAMPLE:** The rabbits in an ecosystem receive **20 000 kJm⁻² yr⁻¹** of energy, but don't take in **12 000 kJm⁻² yr⁻¹** of it, so their gross productivity is **8000 kJm⁻² yr⁻¹** (20 000 − 12 000). They lose **6000 kJm⁻² yr⁻¹** using energy from **respiration**. You can use this to **calculate** the **net productivity** of the rabbits:
>
> net productivity = 8000 − 6000
> = 2000 kJm⁻² yr⁻¹

5) You might be asked to **calculate** how **efficient energy transfer** from one trophic level to another is: ➡ The rabbits receive **20 000 kJm⁻² yr⁻¹**, and their **net productivity** is **2000 kJm⁻² yr⁻¹**. So the **percentage efficiency** of energy transfer is: (2000 ÷ 20 000) × 100 = 10%

Energy Transfer Between Trophic Levels can be Measured

1) To **measure** the **energy transfer** between two trophic levels you need to **calculate** the **difference** between the amount of **energy** in each level (the net productivity of each level).

2) There are a couple of ways to **calculate** the **amount of energy** in a trophic level:

   1) You can **directly measure** the amount of **energy** (in **joules**) in the organisms by **burning** them in a **calorimeter**. The amount of **heat given off** tells you **how much** energy is in them.

   2) You can **indirectly measure** the amount of **energy** in the organisms by measuring their **dry mass** (their **biomass**). Biomass is created **using energy**, so it's an **indicator** of how much energy an organism **contains**.

3) First you calculate the amount of energy or biomass in a **sample** of the organisms, e.g. a 1 m² area of **wheat** or a single **mouse** that feeds on the wheat.

4) Then you **multiply** the results from the **sample** by the **size** of the **total population** (e.g. a 10 000 m² **field** of wheat or the **number** of mice in the population) to give the **total** amount of energy in the organisms at that **trophic level**.

5) The **difference** in **energy** between the trophic levels is the amount of energy **transferred**.

6) There are **problems** with this method though. For example, the consumers (mice) might have **taken in energy** from sources **other than** the producer measured (wheat). This means the difference between the two figures calculated **wouldn't** be an **accurate** estimate of the energy transferred between **only those two** organisms. For an **accurate estimate** you'd need to include **all** the individual organisms at each trophic level.

Energy Transfer Through an Ecosystem

Human Activities can Increase the Transfer of Energy Through an Ecosystem

Some **farming methods increase productivity** by **increasing** the **transfer** of **energy** through an **ecosystem**:

1) **Herbicides** kill **weeds** that **compete** with agricultural crops for **energy**. Reducing competition means crops receive **more energy**, so they grow **faster** and become **larger**, **increasing** productivity.

2) **Fungicides** kill **fungal infections** that **damage** agricultural crops. The crops **use more** energy for **growth** and **less** for fighting infection, so they grow **faster** and become **larger**, **increasing** productivity.

3) **Insecticides** kill **insect** pests that **eat** and **damage** crops. Killing insect pests means **less** biomass is **lost** from crops, so they grow to be **larger**, which means productivity is **greater**.

4) **Natural predators** introduced to the ecosystem **eat** the pest species, e.g. ladybirds eat greenfly. This means the crops lose **less energy** and **biomass**, **increasing** productivity.

5) **Fertilisers** are chemicals that provide crops with **minerals** needed **for growth**, e.g. **nitrates**. Crops **use up** minerals in the soil as they **grow**, so their growth is **limited** when there **aren't enough** minerals. Adding fertiliser **replaces** the lost minerals, so **more energy** from the ecosystem can be used to grow, **increasing** the **efficiency** of energy conversion.

6) Rearing livestock **intensively** involves **controlling** the **conditions** they live in, so **more** of their **energy** is used for **growth** and **less** is used for **other activities** — the **efficiency** of energy conversion is increased so **more biomass** is produced and productivity is **increased**. Here are a couple of **examples**:

> 1) Animals may be kept in **warm, indoor** pens where their **movement** is **restricted**. **Less energy** is **wasted** keeping **warm** and **moving around**.
>
> 2) Animals may be given **feed** that's **higher in energy** than their natural food. This **increases** the **energy input**, so **more energy** is available for **growth**.

The benefits are that **more food** can be produced in a **shorter** space of time, often at **lower cost**. However, enhancing productivity by intensive rearing raises **ethical issues**. For example, some people think the **conditions** intensively reared animals are kept in cause the animals **pain**, **distress** or restricts their **natural behaviour**, so it **shouldn't be done**.

Practice Questions

Q1 What is the equation for net productivity?

Q2 What do you need to calculate to find the energy transfer between two trophic levels?

Q3 Give one example of how farmers increase the productivity of crops.

Q4 Give one example of how farmers increase the productivity of animals.

Grass		Arctic hare		Arctic fox
13 883 kJm^{-2}yr^{-1}	→	2345 kJm^{-2}yr^{-1}	→	137 kJm^{-2}yr^{-1}

Exam Question

Q1 The diagram above shows the net productivity of different trophic levels in a food chain.

　　a) Explain why the net productivity of the Arctic hare is less than the net productivity of the grass. [4 marks]

　　b) Calculate the percentage efficiency of energy transfer from the Arctic hare to the Arctic fox. [2 marks]

I'm suffering from energy loss after those two pages...

Crikey, so farming's not just about getting up early to feed the chooks then — farmers are manipulating the transfer of energy to produce as much food as they can. And it's really important to remember that this transfer of energy isn't 100% efficient — most gets lost along the way so the next organisms don't get all the energy. Interesting, ve-ry interesting....

Succession

You've read that ecosystems are dynamic systems — they change over time. So now you need to know how they change.

Succession is the Process of Ecosystem Change

Succession is the process by which an **ecosystem changes** over **time**. The **biotic conditions** (e.g. **plant** and **animal communities**) change as the **abiotic conditions** change (e.g. **water** availability). There are **two** types of succession:

1) **Primary succession** — this happens on land that's been **newly formed** or **exposed**, e.g. where a **volcano** has erupted to form a **new rock surface**, or where **sea level** has **dropped** exposing a new area of land. There's **no soil** or **organic material** to start with, e.g. just bare rock.

2) **Secondary succession** — this happens on land that's been **cleared** of all the **plants**, but where the **soil remains**, e.g. after a **forest fire** or where a forest has been **cut down by humans**.

Succession Occurs in Stages called Seral Stages

1) **Primary succession** starts when species **colonise** a new land surface. **Seeds** and **spores** are blown in by the **wind** and begin to **grow**. The **first species** to colonise the area are called **pioneer species** — this is the **first seral stage**.

   - The **abiotic conditions** are hostile (**harsh**), e.g. there's no soil to **retain water**. Only pioneer species **grow** because they're **specialised** to cope with the harsh conditions, e.g. **marram grass** can grow on sand dunes near the sea because it has **deep roots** to get water and can **tolerate** the salty environment.

   - The pioneer species **change** the **abiotic conditions** — they **die** and **microorganisms decompose** the dead **organic material** (**humus**). This forms a **basic soil**.

   - This makes conditions **less hostile**, e.g. the basic soil helps to **retain water**, which means **new organisms** can move in and grow. These then die and are decomposed, adding **more** organic material, making the soil **deeper** and **richer in minerals**. This means **larger plants** like **shrubs** can start to grow in the deeper soil, which retains **even more** water. As **more plants** move in they create **more habitats**, so **more animals** move in.

2) **Secondary succession** happens in the **same way**, but because there's already a **soil layer** succession starts at a **later seral stage** — the pioneer species in secondary succession are **larger plants**, e.g. shrubs.

3) At each stage, **different** plants and animals that are **better adapted** for the improved conditions move in, **out-compete** the plants and animals that are already there, and become the **dominant species** in the ecosystem.

4) As succession goes on, the ecosystem becomes **more complex**. New species move in **alongside** existing species, which means the **species diversity** (the number of **different species** and the **abundance** of each species) **increases**.

5) The amount of **biomass** also **increases** because plants at later stages are **larger** and **more dense**, e.g. **woody trees**.

6) The **final seral stage** is called the **climax community** — the ecosystem is supporting the **largest** and **most complex** community of plants and animals it can. It **won't change** much more — it's in a **steady state**.

This example shows primary succession on bare rock, but succession also happens on sand dunes, salt marshes and even on lakes.

Example of primary succession — bare rock to woodland

1) **Pioneer species colonise** the rocks. E.g. **lichens** grow **on** and **break down** rocks, **releasing minerals**.

2) The lichens **die** and are **decomposed** helping to form a **thin soil**, which thickens as more **organic material** is formed. This means other species such as **mosses** can **grow**.

3) **Larger plants** that need **more water** can move in as the soil **deepens**, e.g. **grasses** and **small flowering plants**. The soil **continues to deepen** as the larger plants die and are decomposed.

4) **Shrubs, ferns** and **small trees** begin to grow, **out-competing** the grasses and smaller plants to become the **dominant** species. **Diversity increases**.

5) Finally, the soil is **deep** and **rich** enough in **nutrients** to support **large trees**. These become the dominant species, and the **climax community** is formed.

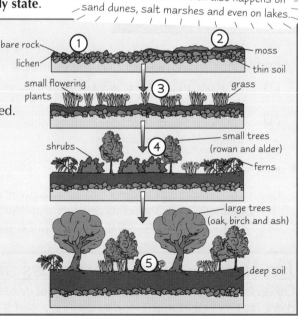

Succession

Different Ecosystems have Different Climax Communities

Which species make up the climax community depends on what the **climate's** like in an ecosystem. The climax community for a **particular** climate is called its **climatic climax**. For example:

> In a **temperate climate** there's **plenty** of **available water**, **mild temperatures** and not much **change** between the seasons. The climatic climax will contain **large trees** because they **can grow** in these conditions once **deep soils** have developed. In a **polar climate** there's **not much available water**, temperatures are **low** and there are **massive changes** between the seasons. Large trees **won't ever** be able to grow in these conditions, so the climatic climax contains only **herbs** or **shrubs**, but it's still the **climax community**.

Succession can be Prevented or Deflected

Human activities can **prevent succession**, stopping the normal climax community from **developing**. When succession is stopped **artificially** like this, the climax community is called a **plagioclimax**. **Deflected succession** is when succession is prevented by human activity, but the plagioclimax that develops is one that's **different** to any of the **natural seral stages** of the ecosystem — the path of succession has been **deflected** from its natural course. For example:

1) A **regularly mown** grassy field **won't develop** woody plants, even if the climate of the ecosystem could support them.

2) The **growing points** of the woody plants are **cut off** by the lawnmower, so larger plants **can't establish** themselves — only the grasses can **survive** being mowed, so the **climax community** is a **grassy field**.

3) A grassy field isn't a **natural seral stage** — there should also be things like small flowering plants, so succession has been **deflected**.

Man had been given a mighty weapon with which they would tame the forces of nature.

Grazing and burning have the same effect as mowing.

Practice Questions

Q1 What is the difference between primary and secondary succession?

Q2 What is the name given to species that are the first to colonise an area during succession?

Q3 What is meant by a climax community?

Exam Question

Q1 A farmer has a field where he plants crops every year. When the crops are fully grown he removes them all and then ploughs the field (churns up all the plants and soil so the field is left as bare soil). The farmer has decided not to plant crops or plough the field for several years.

a) Describe, in terms of succession, what will happen in the field over time. [6 marks]

b) Explain why succession doesn't usually take place in the farmer's field. [2 marks]

Revision succession — bare brain to a woodland of knowledge...

When answering questions on succession, examiners are pretty keen on you using the right terminology — that means saying "pioneer species" instead of "the first plants to grow there". If you can manage that, then you can manage succession.

Investigating Ecosystems

Examiners aren't happy unless you're freezing to death in the rain in a field somewhere in the middle of nowhere. Still, it's better than being stuck in the classroom being bored to death learning about fieldwork techniques...

You need to be able to **Investigate Populations** of **Organisms**

Investigating **populations** of organisms involves looking at the **abundance** and **distribution** of **species** in a particular **area**.

1) **Abundance** — the **number of individuals** of **one species** in a **particular area**.
The abundance of **mobile organisms** and **plants** can be estimated by simply counting the **number** of individuals in samples taken. **Percentage cover** can also be used to measure the abundance of plants — this is **how much** of the area you're investigating is **covered** by a species.

2) **Distribution** — this is **where** a particular species is within the **area you're investigating**.

You need to take a **Random Sample** from the **Area You're Investigating**

Most of the time it would be too **time-consuming** to measure the **number of individuals** and the **distribution** of every species in the **entire area** you're investigating, so instead you take **samples**:

1) **Choose an area** to **sample** — a **small** area **within** the area being investigated.

2) Samples should be **random** to **avoid bias**, e.g. if you were investigating a field you could pick random sample sites by dividing the field into a **grid** and using a **random number generator** to select **coordinates**.

3) Use an **appropriate technique** to take a sample of the population (see below and on the next page).

4) **Repeat** the process, taking as many samples as possible. This gives a more **reliable** estimate for the **whole area**.

5) The **number of individuals** for the **whole area** can then be **estimated** by taking an **average** of the data collected in each sample and **multiplying** it by the size of the whole area. The **percentage cover** for the whole area can be estimated by taking the average of all the samples.

Finally! 26 542 981 poppies. What do you mean I didn't need to count them all?

Frame Quadrats can be used to Investigate Plant Populations

1) A **frame quadrat** is a **square** frame divided into a **grid** of 100 **smaller squares** by strings attached across the frame.

2) They're **placed on the ground** at **random points** within the area you're investigating. This can be done by selecting **random coordinates** (see above).

3) The **number of individuals** of each species is recorded in **each quadrat**.

4) The **percentage cover** of a species can also be measured by counting how much of the quadrat is **covered** by the species — you count a square if it's **more than half-covered**. Percentage cover is a **quick** way to investigate populations and you **don't** have to **count** all the **individual** plants.

5) Frame quadrats are useful for **quickly** investigating areas with species that **fit** within a **small quadrat** — most frame quadrats are **1 m by 1 m**.

6) Areas with **larger plants** and **trees** need **very large** quadrats. Large quadrats **aren't** always in a frame — they can be marked out with a **tape measure**.

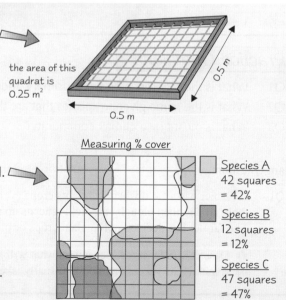

the area of this quadrat is 0.25 m²

0.5 m

0.5 m

Measuring % cover

Species A
42 squares
= 42%

Species B
12 squares
= 12%

Species C
47 squares
= 47%

Investigating Ecosystems

Point Quadrats can also be used to Investigate Plant Populations

1) A **point quadrat** is a **horizontal bar** on **two legs** with a series of holes at set intervals along its length.

2) Point quadrats are **placed on the ground** at **random points** within the area you're investigating.

3) **Pins** are dropped through the holes in the frame and **every plant** that each pin **touches** is **recorded**. If a pin touches several **overlapping** plants, **all** of them are recorded.

4) The **number of individuals** of each species is recorded in **each quadrat**.

5) The **percentage cover** of a species can also be measured by calculating the **number of times** a pin has touched a species as a **percentage** of the **total number** of pins dropped.

6) Point quadrats are especially useful in areas where there's lots of **dense vegetation** close to the ground.

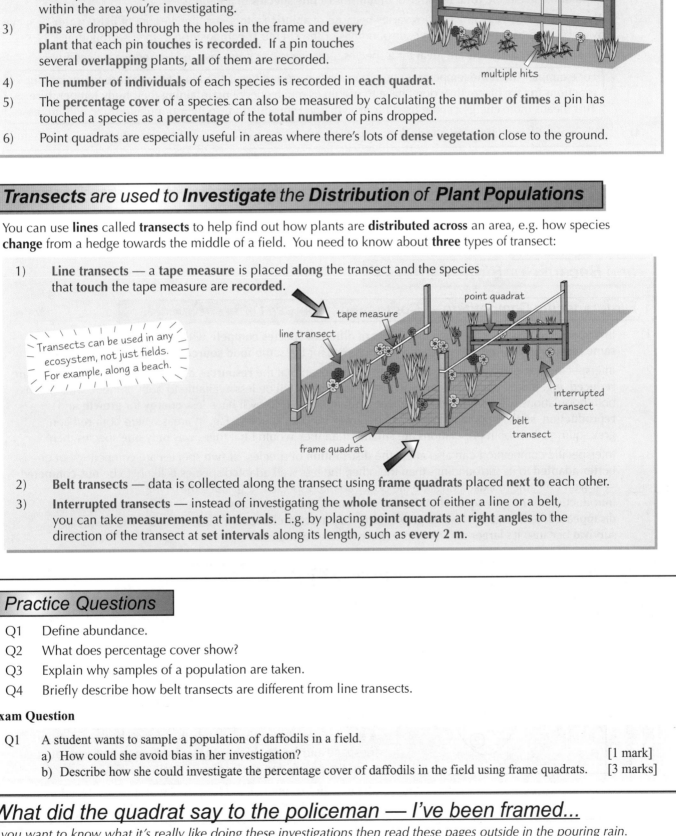

Transects are used to Investigate the Distribution of Plant Populations

You can use **lines** called **transects** to help find out how plants are **distributed across** an area, e.g. how species **change** from a hedge towards the middle of a field. You need to know about **three** types of transect:

1) **Line transects** — a **tape measure** is placed **along** the transect and the species that **touch** the tape measure are **recorded**.

> Transects can be used in any ecosystem, not just fields. For example, along a beach.

2) **Belt transects** — data is collected along the transect using **frame quadrats** placed **next to** each other.

3) **Interrupted transects** — instead of investigating the **whole transect** of either a line or a belt, you can take **measurements** at **intervals**. E.g. by placing **point quadrats** at **right angles** to the direction of the transect at **set intervals** along its length, such as **every 2 m**.

Practice Questions

Q1   Define abundance.

Q2   What does percentage cover show?

Q3   Explain why samples of a population are taken.

Q4   Briefly describe how belt transects are different from line transects.

Exam Question

Q1   A student wants to sample a population of daffodils in a field.
    a) How could she avoid bias in her investigation?   [1 mark]
    b) Describe how she could investigate the percentage cover of daffodils in the field using frame quadrats.   [3 marks]

What did the quadrat say to the policeman — I've been framed...

If you want to know what it's really like doing these investigations then read these pages outside in the pouring rain.
Doing it while you're tucked up in a nice warm, dry exam hall won't seem so bad after that, take my word for it.

Factors Affecting Population Size

Uh-oh, anyone who loves cute little bunny-wunnys look away now — these pages are about how the population sizes of organisms fluctuate and the reasons why. One of the reasons, I'm sad to say, is because the little rabbits get eaten.

Population Size Varies *Because of* Abiotic Factors...

Remember — abiotic factors are the non-living features of the ecosystem.

1) **Population size** is the **total number** of organisms of **one species** in a **habitat**.

2) The **population size** of any species **varies** because of **abiotic** factors, e.g. the amount of **light**, **water** or **space** available, the **temperature** of their surroundings or the **chemical composition** of their surroundings.

3) When abiotic conditions are **ideal** for a species, organisms can **grow fast** and **reproduce successfully**.

> For example, when the temperature of a mammal's surroundings is the ideal temperature for **metabolic reactions** to take place, they don't have to **use up** as much energy **maintaining** their **body temperature**. This means more energy can be used for **growth** and **reproduction**, so their population size will **increase**.

4) When abiotic conditions **aren't ideal** for a species, organisms **can't** grow as **fast** or reproduce as **successfully**.

> For example, when the temperature of a mammal's surroundings is significantly **lower** or **higher** than their **optimum** body temperature, they have to **use** a lot of **energy** to maintain the right **body temperature**. This means less energy will be available for **growth** and **reproduction**, so their population size will **decrease**.

...and *Because of* Biotic Factors

Biotic factors are the living features of the ecosystem.

1 Interspecific Competition — Competition *Between* Different Species

1) Interspecific competition is when organisms of **different species compete** with each other for the **same resources**, e.g. **red** and **grey** squirrels compete for the same **food sources** and **habitats** in the **UK**.

2) Interspecific competition between two species can mean that the **resources available** to **both** populations are **reduced**, e.g. if they share the **same** source of food, there will be **less** available to both of them. This means both populations will be **limited** by a lower amount of food. They'll have less **energy for growth** and **reproduction**, so the population sizes will be **lower** for both species. E.g. in areas where both **red** and **grey** squirrels live, both populations are **smaller** than they would be if there was **only one** species there.

3) Interspecific competition can also affect the **distribution** of species. If **two** species are competing but one is **better adapted** to its surroundings than the other, the less well adapted species is likely to be **out-competed** — it **won't** be able to **exist** alongside the better adapted species. E.g. since the introduction of the **grey squirrel** to the UK, the native **red squirrel** has **disappeared** from large areas. The grey squirrel has a better chance of **survival** because it's **larger** and can store **more fat** over winter.

Plants compete for things like minerals and light.

2 Intraspecific Competition — Competition *Within* a Species

Intraspecific competition is when organisms of the **same species compete** with each other for the **same resources**.

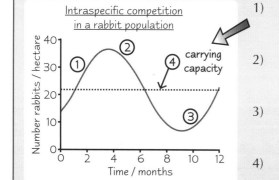

Intraspecific competition in a rabbit population

carrying capacity

1) The **population** of a species (e.g. rabbits) **increases** when resources are **plentiful**. As the population increases, there'll be **more** organisms competing for the **same amount** of space and food.

2) Eventually, resources such as food and space become **limiting** — there **isn't enough** for all the organisms. The population then begins to **decline**.

3) A **smaller** population then means that there's **less competition** for space and food, which is **better** for growth and reproduction — so the population starts to **grow** again.

4) The **maximum stable population size** of a species that an ecosystem can **support** is called the **carrying capacity**.

Factors Affecting Population Size

3) Predation — *Predator* and *Prey* Population Sizes are *Linked*

Predation is where an organism (the predator) kills and eats another organism (the prey), e.g. lions kill and eat (**predate** on) buffalo. The **population sizes** of predators and prey are **interlinked** — as the population of one **changes**, it **causes** the other population to **change**:

1) As the **prey** population **increases**, there's **more food** for predators, so the **predator** population **grows**. E.g. in the graph on the right the **lynx** population **grows** after the **snowshoe hare** population has **increased** because there's **more food** available.

2) As the **predator** population **increases**, **more prey** is **eaten** so the **prey** population then begins to **fall**. E.g. **greater numbers** of lynx eat lots of snowshoe hares, so their population **falls**.

3) This means there's **less food** for the **predators**, so their population **decreases**, and so on. E.g. **reduced** snowshoe hare numbers means there's **less food** for the lynx, so their population **falls**.

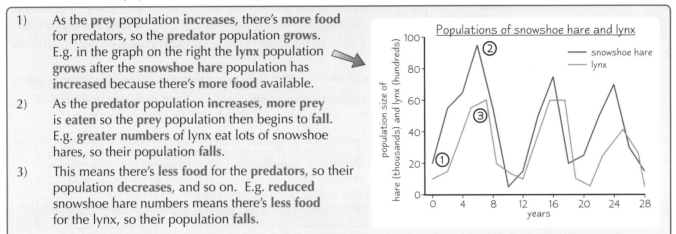

Predator-prey relationships are usually more **complicated** than this though because there are **other factors** involved, like availability of **food** for the **prey**. E.g. it's thought that the population of snowshoe hare initially begins to **decline** because there's **too many** of them for the amount of **food available**. This is then **accelerated** by **predation** from the lynx.

Limiting Factors *Stop* the *Population Size* of a *Species Increasing*

1) Limiting factors can be **abiotic**, e.g. the amount of **shelter** in an ecosystem **limits** the population size of a species because there's only enough shelter for a **certain number** of individuals.

2) Limiting factors can also be **biotic**, e.g. **interspecific competition limits** the population size of a species because the amount of **resources** available to a species is **reduced**.

Practice Questions

Q1 What is interspecific competition?
Q2 What will be the effect of interspecific competition on the population size of a species?
Q3 Define intraspecific competition.
Q4 What does 'carrying capacity' mean?
Q5 What is a limiting factor?

Exam Question

Q1 The graph on the right shows the population size of a predator species and a prey species over a period of 30 years.

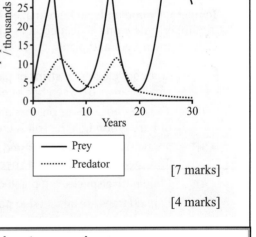

a) Using the graph, describe and explain how the population sizes of the predator and prey species vary over the first 20 years. [7 marks]

b) The numbers of species B declined after year 20 because of a disease. Describe and explain what happened to the population of species A. [4 marks]

Predator-prey relationships — they don't usually last very long...

You'd think they could have come up with names a little more different than inter- and intraspecific competition. I always remember it as int-er means diff-er-ent species. The factors that affect population size are divided up nicely for you here — abiotic factors, competition and predation — just like predators like to nicely divide up their prey into bitesize chunks.

Conservation of Ecosystems

It's important that ecosystems are conserved so the resources we use from them to make lots of nice things don't run out.

We Need to **Conserve Ecosystems**

1) **Conservation** is the **protection** and **management** of **ecosystems** so that the **natural resources** in them can be **used** without them **running out**. E.g. using rainforests for timber without any species becoming **extinct** and without any habitats being **destroyed**. This means the natural resources will still be available for **future generations**.

2) It's a **dynamic process** — conservation methods need to be **adapted** to the **constant changes** (caused **naturally** and by **humans**) that occur within ecosystems.

3) Conservation involves the **management** of ecosystems — controlling how **resources** are **used** and **replaced**.

4) Conservation can also involve **reclamation** — **restoring ecosystems** that have been **damaged** or **destroyed** so they can be **used again**, e.g. restoring **forests** that have been **cut down** so they can be used again.

5) Conservation is **important** for many reasons:

> **Economic** | **Ecosystems** provide **resources** for lots of things that **humans need**, e.g. **rainforests** contain species that provide things like **drugs, clothes** and **food**. These resources are **economically important** because they're **traded** on a **local** and **global** scale. If the ecosystems **aren't** conserved, the resources that we use now will be **lost**, so there will be **less trade** in the future.

> **Social** | Many ecosystems bring **joy** to lots of people because they're **attractive** to **look at** and people **use** them for **activities**, e.g. birdwatching and walking. The species and habitats in the ecosystems may be **lost** if they **aren't** conserved, so **future generations** won't be able to use and enjoy them.

> **Ethical** | 1) Some people think we should conserve ecosystems simply because it's the **right thing to do**, e.g. most people think organisms have a **right to exist**, so they shouldn't become extinct as a result of **human activity**.
> 2) Some people think we have a **moral responsibility** to conserve ecosystems for **future generations**, so they can enjoy and use them.

Cast your mind back to AS biology — the reasons for conservation are similar to the reasons for conserving biodiversity (see page 92).

6) **Preservation** is different from conservation — it's the **protection** of ecosystems so they're kept **exactly as they are**. Nothing is **removed** from a preserved ecosystem and they're only **used** for activities that **don't damage** them. For example, **Antarctica** is a preserved ecosystem because it's protected from **exploitation** by humans — it's only used for **limited tourism** and **scientific research**, not **mining** or other **industrial** activities.

Woodland Ecosystems can **Provide Resources** in a **Sustainable Way**

Ecosystems can be **managed** to provide resources in a way that's **sustainable** — this means enough resources are taken to meet the **needs** of people **today**, but without **reducing the ability** of people in the **future** to meet their own needs.

Temperate woodland can be managed in a **sustainable way** — for every tree that's **cut down** for timber, a **new one** is planted in its place. The woodland should never become **depleted**. Cutting down trees and planting new ones needs to be done **carefully** to be **successful**:

Temperate woodland is between the tropics and the polar circles.

1) Trees are cleared in **strips** or **patches** — woodland grows back **more quickly** in smaller areas between bits of **existing woodland** than it does in larger, **open areas**.

2) The cleared strips or patches aren't **too large** or **exposed** — lots of **soil erosion** can occur on large areas of **bare ground**. If the soil is eroded, newly planted trees **won't** be able to **grow**.

3) Timber is sometimes harvested by **coppicing** — **cutting** down trees in a way that lets them **grow back**. This means new trees don't need to be planted.

4) Only **native species** are planted — they grow most **successfully** because they're **adapted** to the climate.

5) Planted trees are attached to **posts** to provide **support**, and are grown in **plastic tubes** to stop them being **eaten** by grazing animals — this makes it **more likely** the trees will **survive** to become mature adults.

6) Trees **aren't** planted too **close together** — this means the trees aren't **competing** with each other for **space** or **resources**, so they're more likely to **survive**.

Conservation of Ecosystems

Human Activities Affect *Ecosystems* like the *Galapagos Islands*

Humans often need to **conserve** or **preserve** ecosystems because our **activities** have **badly affected** them, e.g. large areas of the **Amazon rainforest** have been **cleared** without being **replaced**, **destroying** the ecosystem.

Human activities have had a negative effect on the **Galapagos Islands**, a small group of islands in the **Pacific Ocean** about 1000 km off the coast of South America. Many species of animals and plants have evolved there that **can't** be found **anywhere else**, e.g. the **Galapagos giant tortoise** and the **Galapagos sea lion**. Here are some examples of how the **animal** and **plant populations** there have been affected by human activity:

1) Explorers and sailors that visited the Galapagos Islands in the 19th century directly affected the populations of some animals by eating them. For example, a type of giant tortoise found on Floreana Island was hunted to extinction for food.

2) Non-native animals introduced to the islands eat some native species. This has caused a decrease in the populations of native species. For example, non-native dogs, cats and black rats eat young giant tortoises and Galapagos land iguanas. Pigs also destroy the nests of the iguanas and eat their eggs. Goats have eaten much of the plant life on some of the islands.

3) Non-native plants have also been introduced to the islands. These compete with native plant species, causing a decrease in their populations. For example, quinine trees are taller than some native plants — they block out light to the native plants, which then struggle to survive.

4) Fishing has caused a decrease in the populations of some of the sea life around the Galapagos Islands. For example, the populations of sea cucumbers and hammerhead sharks have been reduced because of overfishing. Galapagos green turtle numbers have also been reduced by overfishing and they're also killed accidentally when they're caught in fishing nets. They're now an endangered species.

5) A recent increase in tourism (from 41 000 tourists in 1991 to around 160 000 in 2008) has led to an increase in development on the islands. For example, the airport on Baltra island has been redeveloped to receive more tourists. This causes damage to the ecosystems as more land is cleared and pollution is increased.

6) The population on the islands has also increased due to the increased opportunities from tourism. This could lead to further development and so more damage to the ecosystems.

Darwin (the sea lion) worried he was about to be affected by human activity.

Practice Questions

Q1 Why does conservation need to be dynamic?

Q2 What is meant by reclamation?

Q3 How is preservation different from conservation?

Q4 What does managing an ecosystem in a sustainable way mean?

Q5 Give one way that temperate woodlands are managed to make sure newly planted trees grow.

Exam Questions

Q1 Explain why conservation is important for economic, social and ethical reasons. [3 marks]

Q2 Explain how the following human activities have affected specific native animal or plant populations on the Galapagos Islands.

   a) Introduction of non-native animal species. [2 marks]

   b) Introduction of non-native plant species. [2 marks]

   c) Fishing. [2 marks]

If I can sustain this revision it'll be a miracle...

Never mind ecosystems, I'm more interested in preserving my sanity after all this hard work. I know it doesn't seem all that sciencey, but you can still study biology without a lab coat, some Petri dishes and a rack of test tubes. Sustainability's a funny one to get your head around, but luckily you just need to know about how it applies to temperate woodlands.

Plant Responses

You might not think that plants do much, but they respond to stimuli just like us. OK, not just like us (I can't picture a daisy boogying to cheesy music), but their responses are important all the same. So important there's four pages of em'...

Plants Need to Respond to Stimuli Too

1) Plants, like animals, **increase** their chances of **survival** by **responding** to changes in their **environment**, e.g:

> • They sense the direction of **light** and **grow** towards it to **maximise** light absorption for **photosynthesis**.
> • They can sense **gravity**, so their roots and shoots **grow** in the **right direction**.
> • **Climbing** plants have a sense of **touch**, so they can find things to climb and **reach** the **sunlight**.

2) Plants are more likely to survive if they **respond** to the presence of **predators** to **avoid being eaten**, e.g. some plants produce **toxic substances**:

> **White clover** is a plant that can produce substances that are **toxic** to **cattle**. Cattle start to **eat** lots of white clover when fields are **overgrazed** — the white clover **responds** by **producing toxins**, to **avoid** being **eaten**.

3) Plants are more likely to survive if they **respond** to **abiotic stress** — anything **harmful** that's **natural** but **non-living**, like a **drought**. E.g. some plants respond to **extreme cold** by **producing** their own form of **antifreeze**:

> **Carrots** produce **antifreeze proteins** at low temperatures — the proteins **bind** to **ice crystals** and **lower** the **temperature** that water **freezes** at, **stopping** more ice crystals from **growing**.

A Tropism is a Plant's Growth Response to an External Stimulus

1) A **tropism** is the **response** of a plant to a **directional stimulus** (a stimulus coming from a particular direction).
2) Plants respond to directional stimuli by **regulating** their **growth**.
3) A **p<u>o</u>sitive tropism** is growth **t<u>o</u>wards** the stimulus.
4) A **neg<u>a</u>tive tropism** is growth **<u>a</u>way** from the stimulus.
5) An example of a tropism is **phototropism** — the growth of a plant in response to **light**:

> • **Shoots** are positively phototropic and grow towards light.
> • **Roots** are negatively phototropic and grow away from light.

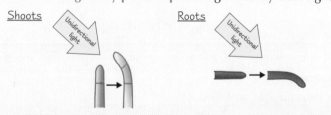

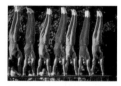

The men's gymnastics team were positively phototropic.

Responses are Brought About by Growth Hormones

> Growth hormones are also called growth substances.

1) Plants **respond** to stimuli using growth hormones — these are chemicals that speed up or slow down plant growth.
2) Growth hormones are produced in the growing regions of the plant (e.g. shoot tips, leaves) and they move to where they're needed in the other parts of the plant.
3) A growth hormone called gibberellin stimulates seed germination, stem elongation, side shoot formation and flowering.
4) Growth hormones called auxins stimulate the growth of shoots by cell elongation — this is where cell walls become loose and stretchy, so the cells get longer.
5) High concentrations of auxins inhibit growth in roots though.

Plant Responses

The *Uneven Distribution* of *Auxins* Causes *Uneven Growth*

1) **Auxins** are produced in the **tips** of **shoots** in flowering plants (called **apical buds**).

2) **Indoleacetic acid (IAA)** is an important **auxin** that's involved in **phototropism**.

3) Auxins (including IAA) are **moved** around the plant to **control tropisms** — they move by **diffusion** and **active transport** over short distances, and via the **phloem** over longer distances.

4) This results in **different parts** of the plants having **different amounts** of auxins. The **uneven distribution** of auxins means there's **uneven growth** of the plant, e.g:

> **Phototropism** — auxins move to the more **shaded** parts of the **shoots** and **roots**, so there's uneven growth.
>
> shoot — auxins move to this side — cells elongate and the shoot bends towards the light
>
> root — auxins move to this side — growth is inhibited so the root bends away from the light

Auxins are Involved in *Apical Dominance*

1) Auxins **stimulate** the **growth** of the **apical bud** and **inhibit** the **growth** of **side shoots**. This is called **apical dominance** — the apical bud is **dominant** over the side shoots.

> shoot tip grows but side shoots don't grow

2) Apical dominance prevents side shoots from growing — this **saves energy** and prevents side shoots from the same plant **competing** with the shoot tip for light.

3) Because energy **isn't** being used to grow side shoots, apical dominance allows a **plant** in an area where there are **loads of other plants** to **grow tall very fast**, past the smaller plants, to **reach** the **sunlight**.

4) If you **remove** the apical bud then the plant **won't produce auxins**, so the **side shoots** will **start growing** by **cell division** and **cell elongation**.

> tip removed
>
> side shoots no longer inhibited

5) Auxins become **less concentrated** as they **move away** from the apical bud to the rest of the plant. If a plant grows **very tall**, the bottom of the plant will have a **low auxin concentration** so side shoots will start to grow near the bottom.

The Role of *Auxins* in *Apical Dominance* Can be *Investigated Experimentally*

Here's an example of how you do it:

1) Plant **30 plants** (e.g. **pea plants**) that are a **similar age**, **height** and **weight** in pots.

2) **Count** and **record** the number of **side shoots** growing from the main stem of **each plant**.

3) For **10 plants**, **remove** the **tip** of the **shoot** and apply a **paste containing auxins** to the **top** of the **stem**.

4) For another 10 plants, remove the tip of the shoot and apply a **paste without auxins** to the top of the stem.

5) Leave the final 10 plants as they are — these are your untouched **controls**.

6) Remember, you **always** need to have controls (e.g. without the hormone, untouched) for **comparison** — so you know the **effect** you see is **likely** to be due to the **hormone** and **not any other factor**.

7) Let each group **grow** for about **six days**. You need to keep all the plants in the **same conditions** — the same **light intensity**, **water**, etc. This makes sure any **variables** that may affect your results are **controlled**, which makes your experiment **more reliable**.

8) After six days, **count** the number of **side shoots** growing from the main stem of **each** of your **plants**.

9) You might get **results** a bit like these:

10) The results in the **table** show that **removing** the **tips** of shoots caused **extra side shoots** to **grow**, but removing tips **and** applying **auxins** **reduced the number** of extra side shoots.

11) The results suggest auxins **inhibit** the **growth** of side shoots — suggesting that auxins are involved in **apical dominance**.

	plants left untreated (control group)	tips removed, paste with auxins applied	tips removed, paste without auxins applied
average no. of side shoots per plant at start of experiment	4	4	4
average no. of side shoots per plant at end of experiment	5	5	9

Plant Responses

Gibberellins and Auxins can Work Together

1) **Gibberellins** are produced in **young leaves** and in **seeds**.

2) They stimulate seed germination, stem elongation, side shoot formation and flowering.

3) Gibberellins **stimulate** the **stems** of plants to **grow** by **stem elongation** — this helps plants to grow **very tall**. If a **dwarf variety** of a plant is treated with gibberellin, it will grow to the **same height** as the **tall variety**.

4) Unlike auxins, gibberellins **don't inhibit** plant growth in any way.

5) **Auxins** and **gibberellins** sometimes **work together** to affect plant growth:

> Auxins and gibberellins are often synergistic — this means that they work together to have a really **big effect**. E.g. auxins and gibberellins work together to help plants grow **very tall**.

> Auxins and gibberellins are sometimes antagonistic — this means they **oppose** each other's actions. E.g. **gibberellins stimulate** the growth of **side shoots** but **auxins inhibit** the growth of side shoots.

The Role of Gibberellins in Stem Elongation Can be Investigated

Here's an example of how you do it:

1) Plant **40 plants** (e.g. **dwarf pea plants**) that are a **similar age**, **height** and **mass** in pots.

2) **Leave 20** plants as they are to grow, **watering** them **all** in the **same way** and keeping them **all** in the **same conditions** — these are your **controls**.

3) **Leave** the **other 20 plants** to grow in the **same conditions**, **except** water them with a **dilute solution** of gibberellin (e.g. **100 μg/ml** gibberellin).

4) Let the plants grow for about **28 days** and **measure** the **lengths** of all the **stems once each week**.

5) You might get **results** a bit like these:

6) The results in the **table** show that stems **grow more** when watered with a dilute solution of **gibberellin**.

7) The results suggest **gibberellin stimulates stem elongation**.

8) You might have to **calculate** the **rate of growth** of the plants in your exam, e.g:

	average stem length / cm	
time / days	plants watered normally	plants watered with gibberellin
0	14	14
7	15	17
14	18	27
21	19	38
28	23	46

- In **28 days** the plants **watered normally** grew an **average** of **9 cm** (23 cm − 14 cm), so they grew at an **average rate** of 9 ÷ 28 = **0.32 cm/day**.

- In **28 days** the plants **watered with gibberellin** grew an **average** of **32 cm** (46 cm − 14 cm), so they grew at an **average rate** of 32 ÷ 28 = **1.14 cm/day**.

Hormones are Involved in Leaf Loss in Deciduous Plants

1) **Deciduous plants** are plants that **lose** their **leaves** in **winter**.

2) Losing their leaves helps plants to **conserve water** (lost from leaves) during the cold part of the year, when it might be **difficult** to **absorb water** from the **soil** (the soil water may be **frozen**), and when there's **less light** for **photosynthesis**.

The technical term for leaf loss is abscission.

3) Leaf loss is **triggered** by the **shortening day length** in the autumn.

4) Leaf loss is **controlled** by hormones:

Auxins are antagonistic to ethene.

- **Auxins inhibit** leaf loss — auxins are produced by **young leaves**. As the leaf gets **older**, less auxin is produced, leading to **leaf loss**.

- **Ethene stimulates** leaf loss — ethene is produced by **ageing leaves**. As the leaves get **older**, **more ethene** is produced. A **layer of cells** (called the **abscission layer**) develops at the **bottom** of the **leaf stalk** (where the leaf joins the stem). The abscission layer **separates** the leaf from the rest of the plant. Ethene **stimulates** the cells in the abscission layer to **expand**, **breaking** the **cells walls** and causing the **leaf** to **fall off**.

Plant Responses

Plant Hormones have Many Commercial Uses

The **fruit industry** uses different **plant hormones** to **control** how different fruits develop, e.g:

Ethene stimulates the ripening of fruit

Ethene stimulates enzymes that **break down cell walls**, **break down chlorophyll** and convert **starch** into **sugars**. This makes the fruit **soft**, **ripe** and **ready to eat**.

E.g. **bananas** are harvested and transported **before** they're **ripe** because they're **less likely** to be **damaged** this way. They're then **exposed** to **ethene** on arrival so they **all ripen** at the **same time** on the **shelves** and in people's **homes**.

Auxins and gibberellins make fruit develop

Auxins and gibberellins are **sprayed** onto **unpollinated flowers**, which makes the **fruit develop without fertilisation**.

E.g. **seedless grapes** can be produced using **auxins** and **gibberellins**.

Auxins can prevent or trigger fruit drop

Applying a **low concentration** of auxins in the **early stages** of fruit production **prevents** the **fruit** from **dropping** off the plant. But applying a **high concentration** of auxins at a **later stage** of fruit production **triggers** the fruit to **drop**.

E.g. **apples** can be made to **drop off** the tree at **exactly** the **right time**.

Auxins are also used **commercially** by **farmers** and **gardeners**, for example:

Auxins are used in **selective weedkillers (herbicides)** — auxins make **weeds** produce **long stems** instead of lots of **leaves**. This makes the weeds **grow too fast**, so they **can't** get enough **water** or **nutrients**, so they **die**.

Auxins are used as **rooting hormones** — auxins make a **cutting** (part of the plant, e.g. a stem cutting) **grow roots**. The **cutting** can then be **planted** and **grown** into a new plant. **Many cuttings** can be taken from **just one original plant** and **treated** with **rooting hormones**, so **lots** of the same plant can be grown **quickly** and **cheaply** from just one plant.

Practice Questions

Q1   Give two reasons why plants need to respond to stimuli.
Q2   What is a tropism?
Q3   What is a plant growth hormone?
Q4   Give one function of gibberellins in a plant.
Q5   Which hormone inhibits leaf loss in deciduous plants?

These questions cover pages 204-207.

Exam Questions

Q1   Explain how the movement of auxins in a growing shoot enables the plant to grow towards the light.   [3 marks]

Q2   A gardener notices that one of the plants in his garden is showing apical dominance.
     a) Name the type of plant hormone that controls apical dominance.   [1 mark]
     b) Give two advantages of apical dominance.   [2 marks]

Q3   A tomato grower wants all her tomatoes to ripen at the same time, just before she sells them at a market.
     a) Name a plant hormone she could use to make the tomatoes ripen.   [1 mark]
     b) Explain how the plant hormone named in part a) makes tomatoes ripen.   [1 mark]
     c) Suggest a commercial advantage of being able to pick and transport tomatoes before they're ripe.   [1 mark]

The weeping willow — yep, that plant definitely has hormones...

See, told you plant responses were important — I didn't say exciting, I said important. Just wait till the next time you're in a supermarket — I bet you can't get round the whole shop without commenting on why the bananas are ripe...

Animal Responses

I'm afraid you're not seeing things — there's a little bit more about nervous and hormonal communication in this unit.

Responding to their Environment Helps Animals Survive

1) **Animals increase** their **chances** of **survival** by **responding** to **changes** in their **external environment**, e.g. by **avoiding harmful environments** such as places that are too hot or too cold.

2) They also **respond** to **changes** in their **internal environment** to make sure that the **conditions** are always **optimal** for their **metabolism** (all the chemical reactions that go on inside them).

3) Any **change** in the internal or external **environment** is called a **stimulus**.

You might remember a lot of this from Unit 4, but you have to know some of it for Unit 5 as well.

The Nervous and Hormonal Systems Coordinate Responses

1) **Receptors detect stimuli** and **effectors** bring about a **response** to a **stimulus**. Effectors include **muscle cells** and cells found in **glands**, e.g. the **pancreas**.

2) Receptors **communicate** with effectors via the **nervous system** or the **hormonal system**, or sometimes using **both**.

The Nervous System is Split into Two Main Systems

The **central nervous system (CNS)** — made up of the **brain** and the **spinal cord**.

The **peripheral nervous system** — made up of the neurones that connect the CNS to the **rest** of the **body**. It also has two different systems:

The **somatic nervous system** controls **conscious** activities, e.g. running and playing video games.

The **autonomic nervous system** controls **unconscious** activities, e.g. digestion. It's got two divisions that have **opposite effects** on the body:

The **sympathetic** nervous system gets the body **ready for action**. It's the '**fight or flight**' system. Sympathetic neurones release the neurotransmitter **noradrenaline**.

The **parasympathetic** nervous system **calms** the body down. It's the '**rest and digest**' system. Parasympathetic neurones release the neurotransmitter **acetylcholine**.

The Brain is Part of the Central Nervous System

You need to know the **location** and **function** of these **four brain structures**:

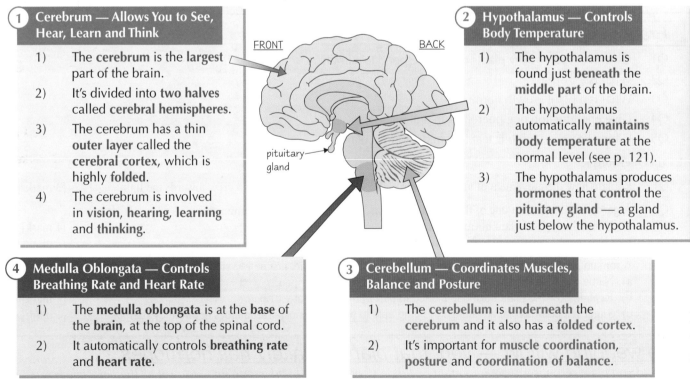

① Cerebrum — Allows You to See, Hear, Learn and Think

1) The **cerebrum** is the **largest** part of the brain.

2) It's divided into **two halves** called **cerebral hemispheres**.

3) The cerebrum has a thin **outer layer** called the **cerebral cortex**, which is highly **folded**.

4) The cerebrum is involved in **vision**, **hearing**, **learning** and **thinking**.

FRONT   BACK

pituitary gland

② Hypothalamus — Controls Body Temperature

1) The hypothalamus is found just **beneath** the **middle part** of the brain.

2) The hypothalamus automatically **maintains body temperature** at the normal level (see p. 121).

3) The hypothalamus produces **hormones** that **control** the **pituitary gland** — a gland just below the hypothalamus.

④ Medulla Oblongata — Controls Breathing Rate and Heart Rate

1) The **medulla oblongata** is at the **base** of the **brain**, at the top of the spinal cord.

2) It automatically controls **breathing rate** and **heart rate**.

③ Cerebellum — Coordinates Muscles, Balance and Posture

1) The **cerebellum** is **underneath** the **cerebrum** and it also has a **folded cortex**.

2) It's important for **muscle coordination**, **posture** and **coordination of balance**.

Animal Responses

The Nervous and Hormonal Systems Coordinate the 'Fight or Flight' Response

1) When an organism is **threatened** (e.g. by a predator) it responds by **preparing the body for action** (e.g. for fighting or running away). This **response** is called the **'fight or flight'** response.

2) The **nervous system** and **hormonal system coordinate** the fight or flight response.

Harold thought it was about time his sympathetic nervous system took over.

3) The **sympathetic** nervous system is **activated**, which also **triggers** the **release** of **adrenaline**. The sympathetic nervous system and adrenaline have the following effects:

> - **Heart rate** is **increased** — so blood is **pumped** around the body **faster**.
> - The **muscles** around the **bronchioles relax** — so **breathing is deeper**.
> - **Glycogen** is **converted** into **glucose** — so **more glucose** is **available** for **muscles** to **respire**.
> - Muscles in the **arterioles** supplying the **skin** and **gut constrict**, and muscles in the **arterioles** supplying the **heart, lungs** and **skeletal muscles dilate** — so **blood** is **diverted** from the skin and gut **to the heart, lungs** and **skeletal muscles**.

Practice Questions

Q1 Why do organisms respond to changes in their environment?

Q2 Which part of the nervous system controls unconscious activities?

Q3 What does the sympathetic nervous system do?

Q4 Which part of the brain is involved in learning?

Q5 Which part of the brain controls body temperature?

Exam Questions

Q1 The diagram on the right shows a cross-section of the brain from front to back.

a) Name structure A on the diagram of the brain. [1 mark]

b) Give two roles of structure B. [2 marks]

c) What effect might damage to structure C have on the body? [1 mark]

Q2 The nervous and hormonal systems coordinate the 'fight or flight' response.

a) What is the 'fight or flight' response? [1 mark]

b) Give an example of when it might occur. [1 mark]

c) Give one physiological effect of the response on the body. [1 mark]

The cere-mum part of the brain — coordinates dirty washing and clean clothes...

These pages aren't all bad — at least you've covered some of the information on them before, way back at the start of Unit 4. The difference here is that you need to know more about how the nervous system is organised, the structure of that big old squelchy mess in your skull, and the fight or flight response — so make sure you test yourself on these new bits.

Muscle Contraction

Muscles are effectors — they contract so you can respond to your environment. You need to know how they contract, but first you need to know a bit more about them and how they're involved in movement...

The **Central Nervous System** (CNS) **Coordinates Muscular Movement**

1) The **CNS** (**brain** and **spinal cord**) receives **sensory information** and **decides** what kind of **response** is needed.

2) If the response needed is **movement**, the CNS sends signals along **neurones** to tell **skeletal muscles** to **contract**.

3) Skeletal muscle (also called striated, striped or voluntary muscle) is the type of muscle you use to **move**, e.g. the biceps and triceps move the lower arm.

Movement Involves **Muscles**, **Tendons**, **Ligaments** and **Joints**

1) **Skeletal muscles** are attached to **bones** by **tendons**.

2) **Ligaments** attach **bones** to **other bones**, to hold them together.

3) The **structure** of the **joints** between your bones determines what **kind** of **movement** is possible:
   - **Ball and socket joints** (e.g. the **shoulder**) allow movement in **all directions**.
   - **Gliding joints** (e.g. the **wrist**) allow a **wide range** of movement because small bones slide over each other.
   - **Hinge joints** (e.g. the **elbow**) allow movement in **one plane only**, like up and down.

Here's how your **muscles** work to **bend** your **arm** at the **elbow**:

- The bones of your **lower arm** are attached to a **biceps** muscle and a **triceps** muscle by **tendons**.
- The biceps and triceps **work together** to move your arm — as one **contracts**, the other **relaxes**:

When your **biceps contracts** your **triceps relaxes**. This pulls the bone so your **arm bends** at the **elbow**.

biceps contracts

bending

triceps relaxes

When your **triceps contracts** your **biceps relaxes**. This pulls the bone so your **arm straightens** at the **elbow**.

biceps relaxes

straightening

triceps contracts

- Muscles that work together to move a bone are called **antagonistic pairs**.

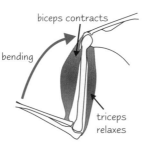
Muscles work in pairs because they can only pull (when they contract) — they can't push.

Skeletal Muscle is made up of **Long Muscle Fibres**

1) Skeletal muscle is made up of **large bundles** of **long cells**, called **muscle fibres**.

2) The cell membrane of muscle fibre cells is called the **sarcolemma**.

3) Bits of the sarcolemma **fold inwards** across the muscle fibre and stick into the **sarcoplasm** (a muscle cell's cytoplasm). These folds are called **transverse (T) tubules** and they help to **spread electrical impulses** throughout the sarcoplasm so they **reach** all parts of the **muscle fibre**.

4) A network of **internal membranes** called the **sarcoplasmic reticulum** runs through the sarcoplasm. The sarcoplasmic reticulum **stores** and **releases calcium ions** that are needed for muscle contraction (see p. 212).

5) Muscle fibres have lots of **mitochondria** to **provide** the **ATP** that's needed for **muscle contraction**.

6) They are **multinucleate** (contain many nuclei).

7) Muscle fibres have lots of **long, cylindrical organelles** called **myofibrils**. They're made up of proteins and are **highly specialised** for **contraction**.

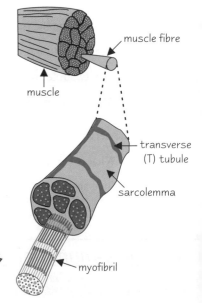

muscle fibre

muscle

transverse (T) tubule

sarcolemma

myofibril

Muscle Contraction

Myofibrils Contain Thick Myosin Filaments and Thin Actin Filaments

1) Myofibrils contain bundles of **thick** and **thin myofilaments** that **move past each other** to make muscles **contract**.

   • **Thick myofilaments** are made of the protein **myosin**.

   • Thin myofilaments are made of the protein actin.

2) If you look at a **myofibril** under an **electron microscope**, you'll see a pattern of alternating **dark** and **light bands**:

   • D<u>a</u>rk bands contain the **thick myosin filaments** and some overlapping thin actin filaments — these are called <u>A</u>-bands.

   • Light bands contain thin actin filaments only — these are called I-bands.

3) A myofibril is made up of many short units called **sarcomeres**.

4) The **ends** of each **sarcomere** are marked with a **Z-line**.

5) In the **middle** of each sarcomere is an **M-line**. The <u>M</u>-line is the **middle** of the **myosin** filaments.

6) **Around** the M-line is the **H-zone**. The H-zone **only** contains **myosin** filaments.

> There's more detail on actin and myosin on the next page.

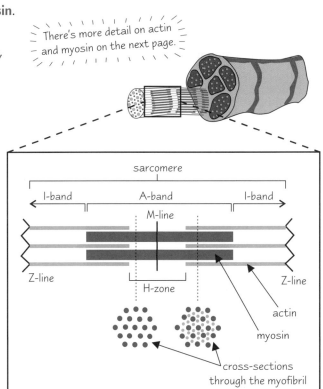

Derek was the proud winner of the biggest muscles AND the smallest pants.

Practice Questions

Q1 What is skeletal muscle?

Q2 When your biceps contracts, what happens to your triceps?

Q3 What are transverse (T) tubules?

Q4 Name the two proteins that make up myofibrils.

Q5 What are the light bands in a myofibril called?

Q6 Where is the M-line located in a sarcomere?

Exam Questions

Q1 Describe how myofilaments, muscle fibres, myofibrils and muscles are related to each other. [3 marks]

Q2 A muscle myofibril was examined under an electron microscope and a sketch was drawn (Figure 1).

   a) What are the correct names for labels A, B and C? [3 marks]

   b) The myofibril was then cut through the M-line (Figure 2). State which of the cross-section drawings you would expect to see and explain why. [3 marks]

Figure 1

Figure 2

Sarcomere — a French mother with a dry sense of humour...

Blimey, what a page. My head has A-bands, I-bands, what-bands and who-bands all swimming around in it. But I guess once you've learnt all these weird and wonderful names you'll never forget them — that's right, they'll take up vital brain space forever. But they'll also get you vital marks in your exam — providing you know what they all mean that is.

Muscle Contraction

Brace yourself — here comes the detail of muscle contraction...

Muscle Contraction is Explained by the Sliding Filament Theory

1) **Myosin** and **actin** filaments **slide** over one another to make the **sarcomeres contract** — the myofilaments themselves **don't** contract.

2) The **simultaneous contraction** of lots of **sarcomeres** means the **myofibrils** and **muscle fibres contract**.

3) Sarcomeres return to their **original length** as the muscle **relaxes**.

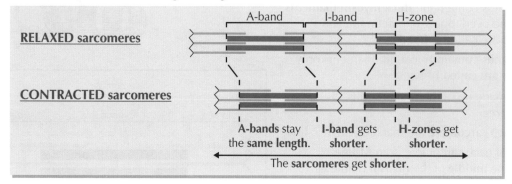

Myosin Filaments Have Globular Heads and Binding Sites

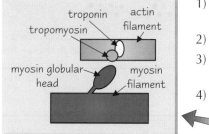

1) **Myosin filaments** have **globular heads** that are **hinged**, so they can move **back** and **forth**.

2) Each myosin head has a **binding site** for **actin** and a **binding site** for **ATP**.

3) **Actin filaments** have **binding sites** for **myosin heads**, called **actin-myosin** binding sites.

4) Two other **proteins** called **tropomyosin** and **troponin** are found between actin filaments. These proteins are **attached** to **each other** and they **help** myofilaments **move** past each other.

Binding Sites in Resting Muscles are Blocked by Tropomyosin

1) In a **resting** (unstimulated) muscle the **actin-myosin binding site** is **blocked** by **tropomyosin**, which is held in place by **troponin**.

2) So **myofilaments can't slide** past each other because the **myosin heads can't bind** to the actin-myosin binding site on the actin filaments.

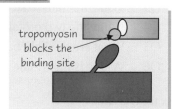

Muscle Contraction is Triggered by an Action Potential

① The Action Potential Triggers an Influx of Calcium Ions

1) When an action potential from a motor neurone **stimulates** a muscle cell, it **depolarises** the **sarcolemma**. Depolarisation **spreads** down the **T-tubules** to the **sarcoplasmic reticulum** (see p. 210).

2) This causes the **sarcoplasmic reticulum** to **release** stored **calcium ions** (Ca^{2+}) into the **sarcoplasm**.

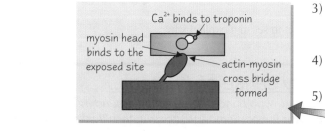

3) Calcium ions **bind** to **troponin**, causing it to **change shape**. This **pulls** the attached **tropomyosin out** of the **actin-myosin binding site** on the actin filament.

4) This **exposes** the **binding site**, which allows the **myosin head** to **bind**.

5) The bond formed when a **myosin head** binds to an **actin filament** is called an **actin-myosin cross bridge**.

Muscle Contraction

2) ATP Provides the Energy Needed to Move the Myosin Head...

1) **Calcium** ions also **activate** the enzyme **ATPase**, which **breaks down ATP** (into ADP + P$_i$) to **provide** the **energy** needed for muscle contraction.

2) The **energy** released from ATP **moves** the **myosin head**, which **pulls** the **actin filament** along in a kind of **rowing action**.

3) ...and to Break the Cross Bridge

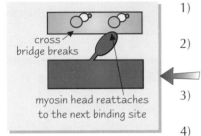
cross bridge breaks
myosin head reattaches to the next binding site

1) **ATP** also provides the **energy** to **break** the **actin-myosin cross bridge**, so the **myosin head detaches** from the actin filament **after** it's moved.

2) The **myosin head** then **reattaches** to a **different binding site** further along the actin filament. A **new actin-myosin cross bridge** is formed and the **cycle** is **repeated** (attach, move, detach, reattach to new binding site...).

3) **Many** cross bridges **form** and **break** very **rapidly**, pulling the actin filament along — which **shortens** the **sarcomere**, causing the **muscle** to **contract**.

4) The cycle will **continue** as long as **calcium ions** are **present** and **bound** to **troponin**.

When Excitation Stops, Calcium Ions Leave Troponin Molecules

1) When the muscle **stops** being **stimulated**, **calcium ions leave** their **binding sites** on the **troponin** molecules and are moved by **active transport** back into the **sarcoplasmic reticulum** (this needs **ATP** too).

2) The **troponin** molecules return to their **original shape**, pulling the attached **tropomyosin** molecules with them. This means the **tropomyosin** molecules **block** the actin-myosin **binding sites** again.

3) Muscles **aren't contracted** because **no myosin heads** are **attached** to **actin** filaments (so there are no actin-myosin cross bridges).

4) The **actin** filaments **slide back** to their **relaxed** position, which **lengthens** the **sarcomere**.

actin filaments slide back
tropomyosin blocks the binding sites again

Practice Questions

Q1 What happens to sarcomeres as a muscle relaxes?

Q2 Which molecule blocks the actin-myosin binding site in resting muscles?

Q3 What's the name of the bond that's formed when a myosin head binds to an actin filament?

Exam Questions

Q1 Describe how the lengths of the different bands in a myofibril change during muscle contraction. [2 marks]

Q2 Rigor mortis is the stiffening of muscles in the body after death. It happens when ATP reserves are exhausted. Explain why a lack of ATP leads to muscles being unable to relax. [3 marks]

Q3 Bepridil is a drug that blocks calcium ion channels. Describe and explain the effect this drug will have on muscle contraction. [3 marks]

What does muscle contraction cost? 80p...

Sorry, that's my favourite sciencey joke so I had to fit it in somewhere — a small distraction before you revisit this page. It's tough stuff but you know the best way to learn it. That's right, shut the book and scribble down what you can remember — if you can't remember much, read it again till you can (and if you can remember loads read it again anyway, just to be sure).

Muscle Contraction

Keep going, you've almost got muscles done and dusted — just a few more bits and pieces to learn about them.

ATP and PCr Provide the Energy for Muscle Contraction

So much **energy** is **needed** when muscles contract that **ATP** gets **used up very quickly**.
ATP has to be **continually generated** so exercise can continue — this happens in **three main ways**:

① Aerobic respiration

- **Most ATP** is generated via **oxidative phosphorylation** in the cell's **mitochondria**.
- **Aerobic** respiration only works when there's **oxygen** so it's good for **long periods** of **low-intensity exercise**, e.g. walking or jogging.

See pages 144-151 for more on aerobic and anaerobic respiration.

② Anaerobic respiration

- ATP is made **rapidly** by **glycolysis**.
- The **end product** of glycolysis is **pyruvate**, which is converted to **lactate** by **lactate fermentation**.
- Lactate can **quickly build up** in the muscles and cause **muscle fatigue**.
- Anaerobic respiration is good for **short periods** of **hard exercise**, e.g. a **400 m sprint**.

③ ATP-Phosphocreatine (PCr) System

- ATP is made by **phosphorylating ADP** — adding a phosphate group taken from **phosphocreatine (PCr)**.

$$\text{ADP} + \text{PCr} \rightarrow \text{ATP} + \text{Cr (creatine)}$$

Many activities use a combination of these systems.

- PCr is **stored** inside cells and the ATP-PCr system **generates ATP** very **quickly**.
- **PCr runs out** after a few seconds so it's used during **short bursts** of **vigorous exercise**, e.g. a **tennis serve**.
- The ATP-PCr system is **anaerobic** (it doesn't need oxygen) and it's **alactic** (it doesn't form any lactate).

There are Three Types of Muscle

❶ Voluntary muscle (skeletal muscle)

1) **Voluntary** muscle contraction is controlled **consciously** (you have to voluntarily decide to contract it).
2) It's made up of **many muscle fibres** that have **many nuclei**.
3) The muscle fibres can be **many centimetres long**.
4) You can see regular **cross-striations** (a striped pattern) under a **microscope**.
5) Some muscle fibres **contract very quickly** — they're used for **speed** and **strength** but **fatigue** (get tired) **quickly**.
6) Some muscle fibres **contract slowly** and **fatigue slowly** — they're used for **endurance** and **posture**.

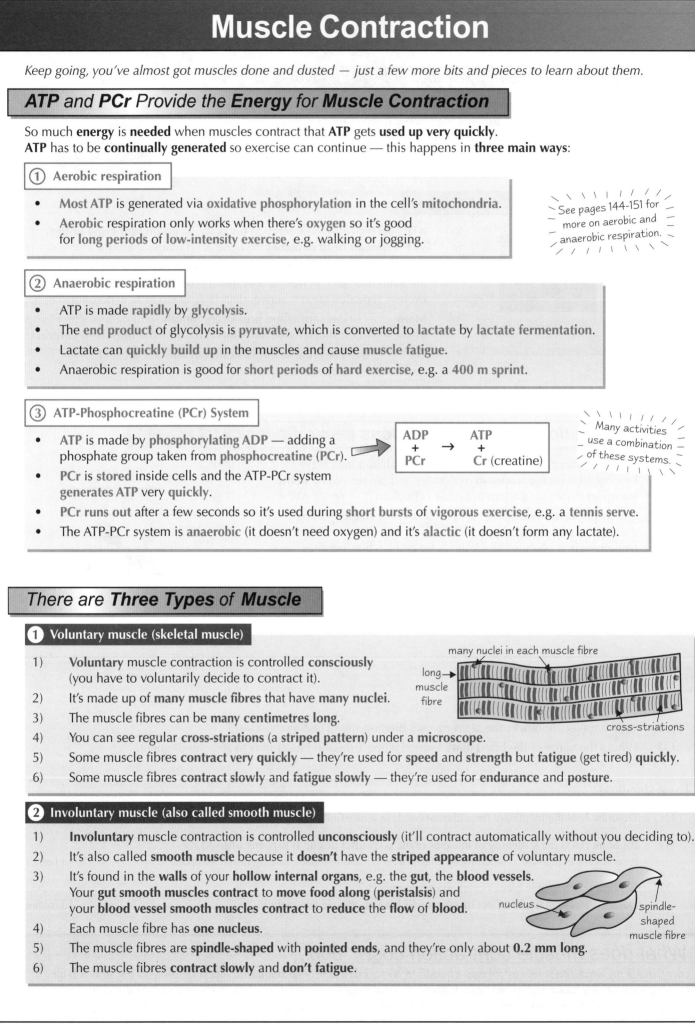

many nuclei in each muscle fibre

long muscle fibre

cross-striations

❷ Involuntary muscle (also called smooth muscle)

1) **Involuntary** muscle contraction is controlled **unconsciously** (it'll contract automatically without you deciding to).
2) It's also called **smooth muscle** because it **doesn't** have the **striped appearance** of voluntary muscle.
3) It's found in the **walls** of your **hollow internal organs**, e.g. the **gut**, the **blood vessels**. Your **gut smooth muscles contract** to **move food along** (peristalsis) and your **blood vessel smooth muscles contract** to **reduce** the **flow** of **blood**.
4) Each muscle fibre has **one nucleus**.
5) The muscle fibres are **spindle-shaped** with **pointed ends**, and they're only about **0.2 mm long**.
6) The muscle fibres **contract slowly** and **don't fatigue**.

nucleus

spindle-shaped muscle fibre

Muscle Contraction

3 Cardiac muscle (heart muscle)

1) **Cardiac** muscle **contracts** on its **own** — it's **myogenic** (but the **rate** of contraction is controlled involuntarily by the **autonomic nervous system**).

2) It's found in the **walls** of your **heart**.

3) It's made of muscle fibres **connected** by **intercalated discs**, which have **low electrical resistance** so nerve impulses pass **easily** between cells.

4) The muscle fibres are **branched** to allow **nerve impulses** to **spread quickly** through the whole muscle.

5) Each muscle fibre has **one nucleus**.

6) The muscle fibres are shaped like **cylinders** and they're about **0.2 mm long**.

7) You can see **some cross-striations** but the striped pattern **isn't** as **strong** as it is in voluntary muscle.

8) The muscle fibres **contract rhythmically** and **don't fatigue**.

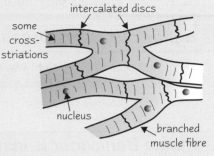

Neuromuscular Junctions are Synapses Between Neurones and Muscles

1) A **neuromuscular junction** is a **synapse** between a **motor neurone** and a **muscle cell**.

2) Neuromuscular junctions use the neurotransmitter **acetylcholine** (**ACh**), which binds to receptors called **nicotinic cholinergic receptors**.

3) Neuromuscular junctions **work** in the **same way** as **synapses between neurones** — they **release neurotransmitter**, which triggers **depolarisation** in the **postsynaptic cell** (see pages 116-117).

4) There are a few **differences** between neuromuscular junctions and synapses where two neurones meet:

	NEUROMUSCULAR JUNCTIONS	SYNAPSES (between neurones)
Neurotransmitter	Acetylcholine	Various
Postsynaptic receptors	Nicotinic cholinergic receptors	Various
Number of postsynaptic receptors	Lots	Fewer
Postsynaptic cell	Muscle cell	Neurone
Postsynaptic membrane	Has clefts containing AChE	Smooth
Effect of neurotransmitter binding to postsynaptic receptors	Muscle cell always contracts	Action potential may or may not fire in the next neurone
Removal of neurotransmitter	Broken down by AChE	Various ways (it depends on the neurotransmitter)

Practice Questions

Q1   What type of respiration provides energy for long periods of low-intensity exercise?

Q2   Which type of muscle has many nuclei in each muscle fibre?

Exam Questions

Q1   Compare the structure and function of involuntary muscle and cardiac muscle. [5 marks]

Q2   Describe three differences between neuromuscular junctions and synapses. [3 marks]

Smooth muscle — it has a way with the ladies...

There's a lot of information on these two pages (not unlike the past few) but you just have to sit down and learn it — there's no other way I'm afraid. But at least that's it for muscle contraction — now you just need to get through behaviour.

Behaviour

Behaviour is an organism's response to changes in its external environment. I thought there were only two types of behaviour — behaving and misbehaving. Turns out there are a few more...

Behaviour Helps Organisms to Survive and Reproduce

1) Responding in the **right way** to an environmental change helps organisms **survive** and **reproduce** (e.g. by finding food and a mate).

2) An organism's behaviour is influenced by both its **genes** and its **environment**.

Innate Behaviour is Instinctive and Inherited

1) **Innate** behaviour is **behaviour** that organisms do **instinctively**.

2) It's **genetically determined** — it's **inherited** from parents and it's **not** influenced by the **environment**.

3) It's also **stereotyped** — it's always carried out in the **same way** and by **all** the **individuals** in a species.

4) The **advantage** of innate behaviour is that organisms **respond** in the **right way** to the stimulus **straight away** because **no learning** is needed, e.g. newborn babies instinctively suckle from their mothers.

5) You need to know **three examples** of **innate behaviours**:

① **Escape reflexes** — the organisms **move away** from **potential danger**.

E.g. **cockroaches run away** when your foot's about to squash them.

Dave's escape reflex was about to kick in.

Taxes (**tactic** responses) and **kineses** (**kinetic** responses) allow simple organisms to move **away from unpleasant stimuli** and into **more favourable** environments:

② **Taxes** — the organisms move **towards** or **away from** a **directional stimulus**.

E.g. **woodlice** move **away from** a **light source**. This helps keep them **concealed** under stones where they're **safe** from predators, so it helps them **survive**.

③ **Kineses** — the organisms' **movement** response is affected by a **non-directional stimulus**, e.g. **intensity**.

E.g. **woodlice** show a **kinetic** response to **low humidity**. This helps them **move** from **drier air** to more **humid air**, and then **stay put**. This **reduces** their **water loss** so **improves** their **survival** chances.

Learned Behaviour is Behaviour that's Modified as a Result of Experience

Learned behaviour is **influenced** by the **environment**. It allows animals to **respond** to **changing conditions**, e.g. they **learn** to **avoid harmful food**. Here are some **examples** that you need to **learn**:

❶ Habituation

- **Habituation** is a **reduced response** to an **unimportant stimulus** after **repeated** exposure **over time**.

- An **unimportant stimulus** is a change that **isn't threatening or rewarding**. An animal quickly learns to **ignore** it so it **doesn't waste time** and **energy** responding to unimportant things, e.g. you **learn to sleep through traffic noise** at night.

- Animals **remain alert** to **unfamiliar stimuli** though, e.g. you instantly **wake up** if you hear an **unfamiliar noise**.

❷ Classical Conditioning

- **Classical conditioning** is **learning** to **respond naturally** to a **stimulus** that **doesn't normally** cause that response.

- A **natural stimulus** (called the **unconditioned** stimulus) can cause a **natural response** (called the unconditioned response). E.g. in dogs, **food** (an **unconditioned** stimulus) causes **salivation** (an unconditioned response).

- If another stimulus **coincides** with an **unconditioned** stimulus **enough times**, eventually this other stimulus will cause the **same response**. E.g. if a **bell** is rung **immediately before** dogs are given **food**, after a **time** the dogs will learn to **salivate** in **response** to the **bell only**.

The behaviour is automatic.

Behaviour

3 Operant Conditioning

- **Operant conditioning** is **learning** to **associate** a particular **response** with a **reward** or a **punishment**.
- When put in the **same situation lots of times**, an animal will work out **which response** gets a **reward** (e.g. pressing the right lever gets food) or a **punishment** (e.g. pressing the left lever gives a shock).
- The response must be **rewarded** (or punished) **straight away** — this **reinforces** the animal's behaviour so it's **more likely** to respond in the **same way** to get the **reward again** (or less likely to do it to be punished again).

  E.g. a **rat** was put in a cage with a **choice** of **levers**. Pressing one of the levers **rewarded** the rat with food **straight away**. The rat was **repeatedly** put in the **same cage**, so learned which **lever** to **press** to get the **reward**.

- Lots of mistakes are made at first, but animals **quickly learn** to make **fewer mistakes** by using **trial and error**.

4 Latent Learning

- **Latent** learning is **hidden** learning — an animal **doesn't immediately show** it's learned something.
- It involves **learning** through **repeatedly** doing the **same task**.
- The animal only **shows** it's learned something when it's given a **reward** or a **punishment**.

  E.g. **three groups** of **rats** were **repeatedly** put in the **same maze**:
  1) The first group of rats were **reinforced** with a **reward** each time they reached the **end** of the **maze** — they **quickly learned** their way around the maze.
  2) The second group of rats were **not reinforced** (they didn't receive a reward) — they continued to plod about the maze and **took ages** to reach the end.
  3) The third group of rats were **only rewarded** from the **11th time** they did the maze — after this they **very quickly reached the end**, with **hardly any errors**. The rats had been **learning** the maze all along **without reinforcement**, but they **didn't show** their learning **until** there **was a reward**.

5 Insight Learning

- **Insight** is learning to **solve** a **problem** by **working out** a **solution** using **previous experience**.
- Solving problems by **insight** is **quicker** than by trial and error because actions are **planned** and **worked out**.

  E.g. **chimpanzees** were put in a play area with **sticks**, **clubs** and **boxes**. Bunches of **bananas** were hung just **out of reach**. The chimps used their **previous experience** of playing with the objects to **work out** a **solution** — they **piled up** the boxes to reach the bananas, and used the sticks and clubs to **knock them down**.

Practice Questions

Q1 What is an escape reflex?

Q2 What's the difference between taxes and kineses?

Q3 What is habituation?

Exam Questions

Q1 When a postman puts a letter through Number 10, a dog barks loudly causing the postman's heart rate to increase. This happens for the next few days until the postman's heart rate increases as he approaches Number 10, even if the dog is not there. State what type of learning has occurred and give a reason for your answer. [2 marks]

Q2 Give an example of how operant conditioning could be used in dog training. [2 marks]

My hair's so shiny — it's classically conditioned...

Behaviour is a bit of a weird topic, really. It seems you can only find anything out by doing lots of strange experiments. Might be fun to work in this area of research though — it's certainly not your average day at the office. "How was your day, dear?" "Great thanks — the rats sped around the maze to get their chocolate." And who said science was boring...

Behaviour

All this studying of animal behaviour helps us to understand human behaviour. But animals are a bit different from us. Not many dogs study for exams, for a start. Mind you, they don't need A levels — they've already got a pe-degree...

Imprinting *is a Combination of* Innate *and* Learned *Behaviour*

1) **Imprinting** is a combination of a **learned** behaviour and an **innate** behaviour
   — e.g. an animal **learns to recognise its parents**, and **instinctively follows them**.

2) Imprinting occurs in several species, mainly **birds**, which are **able to move** very **soon** after they're **born**. A newly-born animal has an **innate instinct** to **follow** the **first moving object** it sees — usually this would be its **mother** or **father**, who would **provide warmth, shelter** and **food** (helping it to survive).

3) But the animal has **no innate instinct** of what its parents **look like** — they have to **learn** this.

4) Imprinting **only happens** during a certain period of time **soon after** the animal is **born**. This period of time is called the **critical period**.

> E.g. ducklings usually imprint on their parent ducks. But if ducklings are **reared from birth** (during the **critical period**) by a **human**, then the human is the **first moving object** the ducklings **see** — so the ducklings **imprint** on the human (they follow them).

"Who's your daddy..."

5) Once learned, imprinting is **fixed** and **irreversible**. Animals use imprinting later in life to **identify mates** from the **same species**.

The Dopamine Receptor D$_4$ *is* Linked *to* Human Behaviour

1) An animal's **behaviour** depends on the **structure** and **function** of its **brain** (e.g. neurotransmitters, synapses, receptors, etc.).

2) Even fairly **small differences** in the brain can produce **big differences** in **behaviour**.

3) Much of our **understanding** of **human behaviour** comes from **studying** people with **abnormal behaviour**, to see how their **brains** are **different** from the brains of people who behave 'normally'.

4) Any **differences** in the brain give scientists **clues** to understanding how normal behaviour is **controlled**. For example:

- The **D$_4$ receptor** is a receptor in the brain for a neurotransmitter called **dopamine**.

- Having **too many D$_4$ receptors** in the brain has been **linked** to **abnormal behaviour**, e.g. the abnormal behaviour seen in **schizophrenia** — a disorder that affects **thinking, perception, memory** and **emotions**.

> *See p. 116 if you can't remember about neurotransmitters and their receptors.*

- The **evidence** for this **link** includes:

  1. If **drugs** that **stimulate** dopamine receptors are given to **healthy people**, it **causes** the **abnormal behaviour** seen in **schizophrenia**.
  2. **Drugs** that **block** D$_4$ receptors **reduce symptoms** in people with schizophrenia.
  3. People with **schizophrenia** have a **higher density** of D$_4$ **receptors** in their brain.
  4. One of the drugs that's used to **treat** schizophrenia **binds** to D$_4$ receptors **better** than it binds to other dopamine receptors.

- The **link** between the **D$_4$ receptor** and **abnormal behaviour** helps us to understand the **role** that the D$_4$ receptor plays in **normal behaviour**, e.g. it's involved in **thinking, perception, memory** and **emotions**.

> *The D4 receptor protein is made by the DRD4 gene.*

Behaviour

Social Behaviour in Primates has Many Advantages

Many animals **live together** in large **groups**. Behaviour that involves members of the group **interacting** with each other is called **social behaviour**. The **primates** (e.g. baboons, apes, humans) have more developed **social behaviour** than other animals. Social behaviour has many **advantages**. Here are some **examples** of **social behaviour** in **baboons** and the **advantages** of the behaviours:

1) **Baboons** live in groups, with about 50 baboons in each group.

   A large group like this is **more efficient** at **hunting** for **food** — together the baboons can **search** a **large area** and **communicate** back to the group where there's a good source of **food**.

The kids knew they'd have to move up the hierarchy before they could enjoy their go on the slide.

2) Within each group there's a **clear-cut hierarchy** of **adult males**.

   This helps to **prevent fighting** (which **wastes energy**) because the males already **know** their **rank order** in the group.

3) As each group **moves through** its own **territory** hunting for food, baboons **cooperate** with each other — **infant baboons** stay with their **mother** in the **middle** of the group and the **adult males** stay on the **outside** of the group.

   Infants and the **females** are **protected** if they're on the **inside** of the group. The young baboons need to be kept **safe** and there needs to be **enough female baboons** for the males to **mate** with, to make sure that **reproduction** is **successful** and the group continues.

4) Members of the group **groom** each other (they **pick out small insects** and **dirt** from each other's **fur**).

   Grooming is **hygienic** and helps to **reinforce** the **social bonds** within the group.

Practice Questions

Q1 Give an example of a species that shows imprinting behaviour.
Q2 Can imprinting be reversed?
Q3 Name one behaviour that's linked to the D_4 receptor.
Q4 Give one example of social behaviour in primates.

Exam Questions

Q1 Goslings usually imprint on their parent geese. However, it's possible for a gosling to imprint on a human.

   a) Explain what is meant by imprinting. [1 mark]

   b) Explain how a gosling can imprint on a human. [2 marks]

Q2 Gorillas eat leaves, fruits and bark. They usually live in groups of 8-12 individuals. They exhibit many social behaviours that have many advantages.

   a) Describe what is meant by the term 'social behaviour'. [1 mark]

   b) Suggest a possible advantage to gorillas of:
   i)   working together to look for food. [1 mark]
   ii) grooming each other. [1 mark]

Dopamine — wasn't he one of the seven dwarfs...

More crazy behaviour stuff. Apparently, a duckling will imprint to almost anything that moves about and makes a noise — try it with a football next time you're near a pond. No, don't really. It'll only go and disturb every match you play. So forget the practical, concentrate on the theory — learn these pages and then you've finished the book. Give me a whoop whoop...

How to Interpret Experiment and Study Data

If you're thinking this looks slightly familiar, then you're right... you had to be able to interpret the results of an experiment or study (and spot a badly designed one) at AS Level. But those pesky examiners have gone and decided that you need to know it for your A2 Level exams as well. So here I am with some more lovely examples to stoke the fires of your memory.

Here Are Some **Things** You Might be **Asked** to do...

Here are three examples of the kind of data you could expect to get:

Study A

An agricultural scientist investigated the effect of three different pesticides on the number of pests in wheat fields. The number of pests was estimated in each of three fields, using ground traps, before and 1 month after application of one of the pesticides. The number of pests was also estimated in a control field where no pesticide had been applied. The table shows the results.

Pesticide	Number of pests	
	Before application	1 month after application
1	89	98
2	53	11
3	172	94
Control	70	77

Study B

Study B investigated the link between the number of bees in an area and the temperature of the area. The number of bees was estimated at ten 1-acre sites. The temperature was also recorded at each site. The results are shown in the scattergram below.

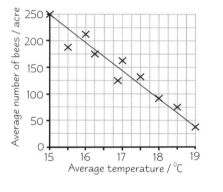

Experiment C

An experiment was conducted to investigate the effect of temperature on the rate of photosynthesis. The rate of photosynthesis in Canadian pondweed was measured at four different temperatures by measuring the volume of oxygen produced. All other variables were kept constant. The results are shown in the graph below.

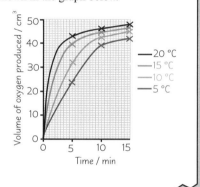

1) Describe and Manipulate the Data

You need to be able to **describe** any data you're given. The level of **detail** in your answer should be appropriate for the **number of marks** given. Loads of marks = more detail, few marks = less detail. You could also be asked to **manipulate** the data you're given (i.e. do some **calculations** on it). For the examples above:

Example — Study A

1) You could be asked to **calculate** the **percentage change** (**increase** or **decrease**) in the number of pests for each of the pesticides and the control. E.g. for pesticide 1: $(98 - 89) \div 89 = 0.10 = $ **10% increase**.

2) You can then use these values to **describe** what the **data** shows — the **percentage increase** in pests in the field treated with **pesticide 1 was the same as for the control** (10% increase) (1 mark). **Pesticide 3 reduced** pest numbers by **45%**, but **pesticide 2** reduced the pest numbers the **most** (79% decrease) (1 mark).

Example — Study B

The data shows a **negative correlation** between the average number of bees and the temperature (1 mark).

Correlation describes the **relationship** between two variables — e.g. the one that's been changed and the one that's been measured. Data can show **three** types of correlation:

1) **Positive** — as one variable **increases** the other **increases**.

2) **Negative** — as one variable **increases** the other **decreases**.

3) **None** — there is **no relationship** between the two variables.

To tell if some data in a table **is correlated** — draw a **scatter diagram** of one variable against the other and **draw a line of best fit**.

Example — Experiment C

You could be asked to calculate the initial rate of photosynthesis at each temperature: The **gradient = the rate of photosynthesis**:

$$\text{Gradient} = \frac{\text{Change in Y}}{\text{Change in X}}$$

How to Interpret Experiment and Study Data

2) Draw or Check a Conclusion

1) Ideally, only **two** quantities would ever change in any experiment or study — everything else would be **constant**.

2) If you can keep everything else constant and the results show a correlation then you **can** conclude that the change in one variable **does cause** the change in the other. ⟶

3) But usually all the variables **can't** be controlled, so other **factors** (that you **couldn't** keep constant) could be having an **effect**.

4) Because of this, scientists have to be very careful when **drawing conclusions**. Most results show a **link** (**correlation**) between the variables, but that **doesn't prove that a change in one causes the change in the other**. ⟶

Example — Experiment C

All other variables were **kept constant**. E.g. light intensity and CO_2 concentration **stayed the same** each time, so these **couldn't** have influenced the rate of reaction. So you **can say** that an increase in temperature up to 20 °C **causes** an increase in the rate of photosynthesis.

Example — Study B

There's a **negative correlation** between the average number of bees and temperature. But you **can't** conclude that the increase in temperature **causes** the decrease in bees. **Other factors** may have been involved, e.g. there may be **less food** in some areas, there may be **more bee predators** in some areas, or **something else** you hadn't thought of could have caused the pattern...

Example — Experiment C

A science magazine **concluded** from this data that the optimum temperature for photosynthesis is **20 °C**. The data **doesn't** support this. The rate **could** be greatest at 22 °C, or 18 °C, but you can't tell from the data because it doesn't go **higher** than 20 °C and **increases** of **5 °C** at a time were used. The rates of photosynthesis at in-between temperatures **weren't** measured.

5) The **data** should always **support** the conclusion. This may sound obvious but it's easy to **jump** to conclusions. Conclusions have to be **precise** — not make sweeping generalisations.

3) Explain the Evidence

You could also be asked to **explain** the **evidence** (the data and results) — basically use your **knowledge** of the subject to explain **why** those results were obtained. ⟶

Example — Experiment C

Temperature increases the rate of photosynthesis because it **increases** the **activity** of **enzymes** involved in photosynthesis, so reactions are catalysed more quickly.

4) Comment on the Reliability of the Results

Reliable means the results can be **consistently reproduced** when an experiment or study is repeated. And if the results are reproducible they're more likely to be **true**. If the data isn't reliable for whatever reason you **can't draw** a valid **conclusion**. Here are some of the things that affect the reliability of data:

1) **Size of the data set** — For experiments, the **more repeats** you do, the **more reliable** the data. If you get the **same result** twice, it could be the correct answer. But if you get the same result **20 times**, it's much more reliable. The general rule for **studies** is the larger the **sample size**, the more **reliable** the **data** is.

E.g. Study B is quite **small** — they only studied ten 1-acre sites. The **trend** shown by the data may not appear if you studied **50 or 100 sites**, or studied them for a longer period of time.

2) **The range of values in a data set** — The **closer** all the values are to the **mean**, the **more reliable** the data set.

E.g. Study A is **repeated three more times** for pesticides 2 and 3. The percentage decrease each time is: 79%, 85%, 98% and 65% for **pesticide 2** (**mean = 82%**) and 45%, 45%, 54% and 43% for **pesticide 3** (**mean = 47%**). The data values are **closer to the mean** for **pesticide 3** than pesticide 2, so that data set is **more reliable**. The **spread** of **values about the mean** can be shown by calculating the **standard deviation** (SD). ⟶

The **smaller the SD** the **closer** the values to the **mean** and the **more reliable the data**. SDs can be shown on a graph using **error bars**. The ends of the bars show one SD **above** and one SD **below** the **mean**.

2 has a larger error bar than 1 so the data is less reliable

How to Interpret Experiment and Study Data

3) <u>Variables</u> — The **more variables** you **control**, the **more reliable** your data is. In an experiment you would control all the variables. In a study you try to control **as many as possible**.

The hat, trousers, shirt and tie variables had been well controlled in this study.

E.g. ideally, all the sites in Study B would have a similar **type** of land, similar **weather**, have the same **plants** growing, etc. Then you could be more sure that the one factor being **investigated** (temperature) is having an **effect** on the thing being **measured** (number of bees).

4) <u>Data collection</u> — think about all the **problems** with the **method** and see if **bias** has slipped in.

E.g. in Study A, the traps were placed on the **ground**, so pests like moths or aphids weren't included. This could have affected the results.

5) <u>Controls</u> — without controls, it's very difficult to **draw valid conclusions**. **Negative controls** are used to make sure that nothing you're doing in the experiment has an effect, **other than** what you're testing.

E.g. in Experiment C, the **negative control** would be all the equipment set up as normal but **without** the pondweed. If **no oxygen** was produced at any temperature it would show that the variation in the volume of oxygen produced when there was pondweed was due to the **effect** of temperature on the pondweed, and **not** the effect of temperature on **anything else** in the experiment.

6) <u>Repetition by other scientists</u> — for theories to become accepted as 'fact' other scientists need to **repeat** the work (see page 1). If **multiple studies** or **experiments** come to the same conclusion, then that conclusion is **more reliable**.

E.g. if a second group of scientists repeated Study B and got the same results, the results would be **more reliable**.

There Are a Few Technical Terms You Need to Understand

I'm sure you probably know these all off by heart, but it's easy to get mixed up sometimes. So here's a quick recap of some words **commonly used** when assessing and analysing experiments and studies:

1) **Variable** — A variable is a **quantity** that has the **potential to change**, e.g. weight. There are two types of variable commonly referred to in experiments:

- **Independent variable** — the thing that's **changed** in an experiment.
- **Dependent variable** — the thing that you **measure** in an experiment.

When drawing graphs, the dependent variable should go on the **y-axis** (the vertical axis) and the independent on the **x-axis** (the horizontal axis).

2) **Accurate** — Accurate results are those that are **really close** to the **true** answer. The true answer is **without error**, so if you can reduce error as much as possible you'll get a more accurate result. The most **accurate** methods are those that produce as **error-free** results as possible.

3) **Precise results** — These are results taken using **sensitive instruments** that measure in **small increments**, e.g. pH measured with a meter (pH 7.692) will be **more precise** than pH measured with paper (pH 8).

It's possible for results to be precise **but not** accurate, e.g. a balance that weighs to 1/1000 th of a gram will give precise results, but if it's not **calibrated** properly the results won't be accurate.

4) **Qualitative** — A **qualitative** test tells you **what's** present, e.g. an acid or an alkali.

5) **Quantitative** — A **quantitative** test tells you **how much** is present, e.g. an acid that's pH 2.46.

There's enough evidence here to conclude that data interpretation is boring...

*These pages should give you a fair idea of how to interpret data. Just use your head and remember the four things you might be asked to do — **d**escribe the **d**ata, **c**heck the **c**onclusions, **e**xplain the **e**vidence and check the **r**esults are **r**eliable.*

AS-Level Answers

Unit 1: Section 1 — Cell Structure

Page 7 — Eukaryotic Cells and Organelles

1   Maximum of 4 marks available.
    cell wall *[1 mark]*, plasmodesmata *[1 mark]*, vacuole
    [1 mark], chloroplasts *[1 mark]*.

2 a) i) Maximum of 1 mark available.
       mitochondrion *[1 mark]*
    ii) Maximum of 1 mark available.
       Golgi apparatus *[1 mark]*
  b) Maximum of 2 marks available.
     Mitochondria are the site of aerobic respiration *[1 mark]*.
     The Golgi apparatus processes and packages new lipids and
     proteins / makes lysosomes *[1 mark]*.

Page 9 — Prokaryotic Cells

1 a) Maximum of 2 marks available
     Ribosomes *[1 mark]* because this is where protein
     synthesis occurs *[1 mark]*.
  b) Maximum of 3 mark available
     The rough endoplasmic reticulum *[1 mark]*, ribosomes
     [1 mark] and some vesicles *[1 mark]*.
  c) Maximum of 1 mark available
     Vesicles transport substances in and out of the cell and
     between organelles *[1 mark]*.

2   Maximum of 3 marks available, from any of the 4 points below.
    Supports the cell's organelles *[1 mark]*
    Strengthens the cell / maintains its shape *[1 mark]*
    Transports materials around the cell *[1 mark]*
    Enables cell movement *[1 mark]*

Page 11 — Studying Cells — Microscopes

1   Maximum of 2 marks available
    Magnification = length of image ÷ length of object
                 = 80 mm ÷ 0.5 mm *[1 mark]*
                 = × 160 *[1 mark]*
    Always remember to convert everything to the same units first —
    the insect is 0.5 mm long, so the length of the image needs to be
    changed from 8 cm to 80 mm.

2 a) Maximum of 3 marks available
     mitochondrion *[1 mark]* and nucleus *[1 mark]*
     The resolution of light microscopes is not good enough to show
     objects smaller than 0.2 µm *[1 mark]*.
  b) Maximum of 2 marks available
     All of the organelles in the table would be visible *[1 mark]*.
     SEMs can resolve objects down to about 5 nm (0.005 µm)
     [1 mark].

Unit 1: Section 2 — Cell Membranes

Page 13 — Cell Membranes — The Basics

1   Maximum of 2 marks available.
    The membrane is described as fluid because the phospholipids
    are constantly moving *[1 mark]*. It is described as a mosaic
    because the proteins are scattered throughout the membrane
    like tiles in a mosaic *[1 mark]*.

2   Maximum of 1 mark available.
    Cholesterol makes the membrane more rigid *[1 mark]*.

Page 15 — Cell Membranes — The Basics

1   Maximum of 3 marks available.
    Nicotine only binds to receptors with a complementary
    shape *[1 mark]*. Different cells have different membrane-bound
    receptors *[1 mark]*. Nicotine only affects nerve cells because
    they have the correct receptor for nicotine *[1 mark]*.

2 a) Maximum of 1 mark available.
     Tube 4 *[1 mark]*.
  b) Maximum of 4 marks available.
     There is a higher concentration of beetroot pigment in tube
     2 than in tube 1 *[1 mark]* because the membrane is more
     permeable at higher temperatures *[1 mark]*. The molecules
     in the membrane have more energy so can move more,
     increasing permeability *[1 mark]*. This caused more pigment to
     move out of the cells into the water than in tube 1 *[1 mark]*.
  c) Maximum of 4 marks available.
     There is a higher concentration of beetroot pigment in tube
     3 than in tube 2 *[1 mark]*. This is because the high temperature
     tube 3 was exposed to caused the membranes of the beetroot
     cells to break down *[1 mark]*, increasing their permeability
     [1 mark] and causing more pigment to move out of the cells
     into the water *[1 mark]*.
     For questions like this try to work out what the data in the table is
     telling you, using your own knowledge, before you attempt to answer
     the question. The table shows that the pieces of beetroot exposed
     to highest temperatures have released the most pigment. From your
     knowledge you know that very high temperatures damage cell
     membranes. If the cell membranes are damaged the cells become
     leaky, so they lose pigment.
  d) Maximum of 4 marks available
     The absorbance reading would have been high *[1 mark]*.
     At temperatures below 0 °C, channel proteins and carrier proteins
     denature *[1 mark]* and ice crystals form, which pierce the
     membrane *[1 mark]*. This makes the membrane highly
     permeable, so a lot of pigment would leak out into
     the solution *[1 mark]*.

Page 17 — Transport Across Cell Membranes

1 a) Maximum of 3 marks available.
     The water potential of the sucrose solution was higher than the
     water potential of the potato *[1 mark]*. Water moves by osmosis
     from a solution of higher water potential to a solution of lower
     water potential *[1 mark]*. So water moved into the potato,
     increasing its mass *[1 mark]*.
  b) Maximum of 1 mark available.
     The water potential of the potato and the water potential
     of the solution was the same *[1 mark]*.
  c) Maximum of 4 marks available.
     − 0.4 g *[1 mark]*. The potato has a higher water potential than
     the solution *[1 mark]* so net movement of water is out of the
     potato *[1 mark]*. The difference in water potential between the
     solution and the potato is the same as with the 1% solution,
     so the mass difference should be about the same *[1 mark]*.

Page 19 — Transport Across Cell Membranes

1   Maximum of 6 marks available.
    Facilitated diffusion involves channel proteins *[1 mark]*, which
    transport charged molecules across the membrane *[1 mark]*
    down their concentration gradient *[1 mark]*. It also involves
    carrier proteins *[1 mark]*, which transport large molecules across
    the membrane *[1 mark]* down their concentration gradient
    [1 mark].

AS-Level Answers

2   Maximum of 4 marks available.
    Endocytosis takes in substances from outside the cell *[1 mark]*
    via vesicles formed from the plasma membrane *[1 mark]*.
    Exocytosis secretes substances from the cell *[1 mark]* via vesicles
    made from the Golgi apparatus *[1 mark]*.
    Make sure you don't get these two processes mixed up
    — try to remember endo for 'in' and exo for 'out'.

Unit 1: Section 3 — Cell Division, Diversity and Organisation

Page 21 — Cell Division — Mitosis

1 a) Maximum of 6 marks available.
    A = Metaphase *[1 mark]*, because the chromosomes are lined
    up across the middle of the cell *[1 mark]*.
    B = Telophase *[1 mark]*, because there are now two nuclei and
    the cytoplasm is dividing to form two new cells *[1 mark]*.
    C = Anaphase *[1 mark]*, because the centromeres have divided
    and the chromatids are moving to opposite ends of the cell
    [1 mark].
    If you've learned the diagrams of what happens at each stage of
    mitosis, this should be a breeze. That's why it'd be a total disaster if
    you lost three marks for forgetting to give reasons for your answers.
    Always read the question properly and do exactly what it tells you
    to do.
  b) Maximum of 3 marks available:
    X = Nuclear envelope *[1 mark]*.
    Y = Cell membrane *[1 mark]*.
    Z = Centriole *[1 mark]*.

Page 23 — Cell Division and Reproduction

1 a) Maximum of 3 marks available.
    A bud has formed at the surface of the cell *[1 mark]*.
    The cell has undergone interphase *[1 mark]* and has
    started to divide by mitosis *[1 mark]*.
  b) Maximum of 2 marks available.
    The bud has separated off from the parent cell *[1 mark]*,
    producing a new, genetically identical yeast cell *[1 mark]*.

2   Maximum of 2 marks available.
    A pair of chromosomes, one from the mum and one from the
    dad *[1 mark]*, which have the same genes but could have
    different versions of those genes (alleles) *[1 mark]*.

Page 25 — Stem Cells and Differentiation

1   Maximum of 4 marks available.
    It has many chloroplasts *[1 mark]* to absorb light for
    photosynthesis *[1 mark]*. It has thin cell walls *[1 mark]*,
    so carbon dioxide can easily enter *[1 mark]*.

2   Maximum of 5 marks available.
    Stem cells divide to make new, specialised cells *[1 mark]*.
    In animals, adult stem cells are used to replace damaged
    cells *[1 mark]*, e.g. stem cells in the bone marrow differentiate/
    become specialised to make erythrocytes (red blood cells)/
    neutrophils (white blood cells) *[1 mark]*. In plants, stem cells
    are used to make new growing parts (roots and shoots) *[1 mark]*,
    e.g. stem cells in the cambium differentiate (become specialised)
    to make xylem/phloem *[1 mark]*.

Page 27 — Tissues, Organs and Systems

1   Maximum of 2 marks available.
    It's best described as an organ *[1 mark]* as it is made of
    many tissues working together to perform a particular function
    [1 mark].

2   Maximum of 3 marks available. 1 mark for naming an organ
    system. 1 mark for naming each organ contained in that system,
    up to a maximum of 2 marks.
    E.g. respiratory system — composed of the lungs, trachea, larynx,
    nose, mouth and diaphragm. / Circulatory system — composed
    of the heart, arteries, veins and capillaries.

Unit 1: Section 4 — Exchange Surfaces and Breathing

Page 29 — Gas Exchange

1   Maximum of 5 marks available.
    Humans are large multicellular organisms *[1 mark]*. There
    is a big distance between some cells and the environment
    [1 mark], so cells can't exchange substances directly quickly
    enough *[1 mark]*. Humans have a small surface area to volume
    ratio *[1 mark]*, which makes it impossible to exchange enough
    oxygen and carbon dioxide through their outer membranes to
    supply the body *[1 mark]*.

2   Maximum of 4 marks available.
    Oxygen diffuses out of the alveoli *[1 mark]* across the
    alveolar epithelium and the capillary endothelium *[1 mark]* and
    into the blood *[1 mark]*. Carbon dioxide diffuses from the blood
    into the alveoli *[1 mark]*.
    The mark for mentioning the alveolar epithelium and capillary
    endothelium would also be awarded if they were mentioned in
    reference to the diffusion of carbon dioxide.

Page 31 — The Gaseous Exchange System

1   Maximum of 5 marks available.
    Lungs contain many alveoli, giving a large surface area
    [1 mark]. Each alveolus has a good blood supply, maintaining
    a high concentration gradient *[1 mark]* by constantly removing
    oxygen and delivering carbon dioxide *[1 mark]*. The alveoli and
    capillary walls are each only one cell thick, so there is a short
    diffusion pathway *[1 mark]*. Concentration gradients are also
    maintained by breathing in and out, which refreshes the oxygen
    supply and removes carbon dioxide *[1 mark]*.

2   Maximum of 10 marks available.
    Goblet cells *[1 mark]* secrete mucus, which traps bacteria and
    dust so they don't reach the alveoli *[1 mark]*. Other cells have
    cilia *[1 mark]* which move the mucus towards the throat to be
    removed *[1 mark]*. Elastic fibres *[1 mark]* stretch when we
    breathe in, then recoil to help us breathe out *[1 mark]*. Smooth
    muscle tissue *[1 mark]* relaxes to make air passages wider and
    make breathing easier when exercising *[1 mark]*. Cartilage
    [1 mark] provides support and keeps the air passages open
    [1 mark].

Page 33 — Breathing

1   Maximum of 5 marks available.
    The intercostal muscles contract *[1 mark]*, making the ribs move
    up and out *[1 mark]*, and the diaphragm contracts/flattens
    [1 mark]. This increases the volume of the thorax *[1 mark]*, so
    the pressure inside decreases, drawing air into the lungs *[1 mark]*.

AS-Level Answers

Unit 1: Section 5 — Transport in Animals

Page 35 — The Circulatory System

1 Maximum of 1 mark available.
The blood flows through the body in vessels [1 mark].

2 Maximum of 2 marks available.
Insects have an open circulatory system [1 mark]. The blood is pumped into the body cavity where it circulates freely [1 mark].

3 a) It is a closed system [1 mark].
b) It is a single circulatory system, not a double one [1 mark].

Page 37 — The Heart

1 a) i) Maximum of 1 mark available.
D [1 mark]
The semi-lunar valve will only open if the pressure in the ventricle is higher than the pressure in the aorta (or pulmonary artery, if you're looking at the right side of the heart).
ii) Maximum of 1 mark available.
C [1 mark]
The atrioventricular valve will be forced closed when the pressure in the ventricle becomes higher than the pressure in the atrium.

b) Maximum of 2 marks available.
The graph should increase and decrease at the same times as the graph for the left side (because both ventricles contract together) [1 mark]. The pressure should be lower than for the left side of the heart at all times [1 mark].

E.g.

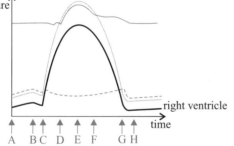

2 Maximum of 8 marks available.
When the heart muscles are relaxed, blood enters the atria from the veins [1 mark]. The semi-lunar valves prevent blood coming back into the ventricles from the arteries [1 mark]. Next, the atria contract [1 mark]. This pushes blood from the atria into the ventricles [1 mark] through the atrioventricular valves [1 mark]. Then the ventricles contract [1 mark]. This pushes blood out from the ventricles into the arteries [1 mark]. The atrioventricular valves shut to prevent blood going back into the atria [1 mark].

Page 39 — The Heart

1 a) Maximum of 1 mark available.
The sino-atrial node acts as a pacemaker/initiates heartbeats [1 mark].
b) Maximum of 1 mark available.
The Purkyne tissue conducts electrical impulses through the ventricle walls [1 mark].

2 Maximum of 2 marks available.
The ventricle is not contracting properly [1 mark]. This could be because of muscle damage / because the AVN is not conducting impulses to the ventricles properly [1 mark].

Page 41 — Blood Vessels

1 a) Maximum of 2 marks available.
Elastic tissue and a thick muscle layer allow the arteries to cope with the high pressure produced when the heart beats [1 mark]. The folded inner lining/endothelium allows arteries to expand to cope with high pressure [1 mark].
b) Maximum of 1 mark available.
Capillary walls are only one cell thick to increase diffusion [1 mark].
c) Maximum of 1 mark available.
Veins have valves to stop blood flowing backwards [1 mark].

2 Maximum of 4 marks available.
At the start of the capillary bed, the pressure in the capillaries is greater than the pressure in the tissue fluid outside the capillaries [1 mark]. This means fluid from the blood is forced out of the capillaries [1 mark]. Fluid loss causes the water potential of blood capillaries to become lower than that of tissue fluid [1 mark]. So fluid moves back into the capillaries at the vein end of the capillary bed by osmosis [1 mark].

Page 43 — Haemoglobin

1 Maximum of 3 marks available.
The fetus relies on oxygen from the mother's blood [1 mark]. By the time it reaches the fetus, the mother's blood is not fully oxygenated [1 mark]. Fetal haemoglobin must therefore have a higher affinity for oxygen than its mother's blood in order to take up enough oxygen [1 mark].

2 Maximum of 6 marks available.
Most of the CO_2 from respiring cells is converted to carbonic acid by the enzyme carbonic anhydrase [1 mark]. The carbonic acid splits up to form hydrogen ions and hydrogencarbonate ions [1 mark]. The hydrogencarbonate ions are transported in the blood plasma [1 mark]. Oxyhaemoglobin unloads some of its oxygen and binds to the hydrogen ions, forming haemoglobinic acid [1 mark]. At the lungs, the haemoglobin releases its hydrogen ions [1 mark], which recombine with the hydrogencarbonate ions to be breathed out as carbon dioxide [1 mark].

Unit 1: Section 6 — Transport in Plants

Page 45 — Xylem and Phloem

1 Maximum of 6 marks available.
The distribution can be explained in words or by diagrams — whichever you find easier. In either case, these are the key points: In the stem, the xylem and phloem are towards the outside, with the phloem outside the xylem [1 mark]. This provides a scaffold for the stem to reduce bending [1 mark]. In the root, the xylem and phloem are in the centre, with the phloem outside the xylem [1 mark]. This provides support for the root as it pushes through the soil [1 mark]. In the leaves, the veins run throughout the leaves, with the xylem above the phloem [1 mark]. This provides support for the thin leaves [1 mark].

2 Maximum of 8 marks available.
Xylem vessel cells have no end walls [1 mark], making an uninterrupted tube that allows water to pass through easily [1 mark]. The vessel cells are dead and contain no cytoplasm [1 mark], which allows water to pass through [1 mark]. Their walls are thickened with a woody substance called lignin [1 mark], which helps support the xylem vessels and stop them collapsing inwards [1 mark]. The vessel walls have small holes called pits where there's no lignin [1 mark]. This allows substances to pass in and out of the vessels [1 mark].

AS-Level Answers

Page 47 — Water Transport

1 Maximum of 4 marks available.
Loss of water from the leaves, due to transpiration, pulls more water into the leaves from the xylem *[1 mark]*. There are cohesive forces between water molecules *[1 mark]*. These cause water to be pulled up the xylem *[1 mark]*. Removing leaves means no transpiration occurs, so no water is pulled up the xylem *[1 mark]*.
It's pretty obvious (because there are 4 marks to get) that it's not enough just to say removing the leaves stops transpiration. You also need to explain why transpiration is so important in moving water through the xylem. It's always worth checking how many marks a question is worth — this gives you a clue about how much detail you need to include.

2 a) Maximum of 2 marks available.
In the symplast pathway, water moves through the cytoplasm *[1 mark]*. The cytoplasm of neighbouring cells is connected through plasmodesmata (small gaps in the cell walls) *[1 mark]*.
b) Maximum of 4 marks available.
In the apoplast pathway, water passes through the cell walls *[1 mark]*. The walls are very absorbent so water simply diffuses through them *[1 mark]*. In the endodermis layer of the root the Casparian strip inhibits the apoplast pathway *[1 mark]*. From here the water must take the symplast pathway *[1 mark]*.

Page 49 — Transpiration

1 Maximum of 8 marks available. 1 mark for each factor, and 1 mark for explaining each factor's effect.
Transpiration is increased when it's light *[1 mark]*, as the stomata open only when it's light *[1 mark]*. A high temperature increases transpiration *[1 mark]* because water evaporates from the cells inside the leaf faster/water diffuses out of the leaf faster *[1 mark]*. A low humidity level increases the rate of transpiration *[1 mark]* because it increases the water potential gradient between the leaf and the surrounding air *[1 mark]*. Transpiration is increased if it's windy *[1 mark]* because wind blows away water molecules from around the stomata, increasing the water potential gradient *[1 mark]*.

2 Maximum of 4 marks available.
'Hairs' on the epidermis *[1 mark]* trap moist air round the stomata, which reduces the water potential gradient and so reduces transpiration *[1 mark]*. Thick cuticle *[1 mark]* is waterproof so stops water evaporating *[1 mark]*.

Page 51 — Translocation

1 Maximum of 4 marks available.
Sugars are actively loaded into the sieve tubes at the source end *[1 mark]*. This lowers the water potential of the sieve tubes at the source end *[1 mark]*, which causes water to enter by osmosis *[1 mark]*. This causes a pressure increase inside the sieve tubes at the source end *[1 mark]*.
I think this is a pretty nasty question. If you got it all right first time you're probably a genius. If you didn't, you're probably not totally clear yet about the pressure idea. If there's a high concentration of sugar in a cell, this draws water in by osmosis, and so increases the pressure inside the cell.

Unit 2: Section 1 — Biological Molecules

Page 53 — Water

1 Maximum of 15 marks available.
Water molecules have two hydrogen atoms and one oxygen atom *[1 mark]*. The hydrogen and oxygen atoms are joined by shared electrons *[1 mark]*. Oxygen attracts the electrons more strongly than hydrogen *[1 mark]*. This makes water molecules polar *[1 mark]*. This polarity leads to the formation of hydrogen bonds between water molecules *[1 mark]*. The hydrogen bonds in water can absorb a lot of energy *[1 mark]*, giving water a high specific heat capacity *[1 mark]*. This allows living organisms to avoid rapid changes in temperature *[1 mark]*. It takes a lot of energy to break the hydrogen bonds in water *[1 mark]*, so water has a high latent heat of evaporation *[1 mark]*. This means water is good for cooling things *[1 mark]*. Water's polarity makes it very cohesive *[1 mark]*. This helps it to flow, allowing it to transport substances *[1 mark]*. Water's polarity allows it to dissolve other molecules *[1 mark]*. This allows water to act as a solvent so it can transport substances *[1 mark]*.

Page 55 — Proteins

1 Maximum of 9 marks available.
Proteins are made from amino acids *[1 mark]*. The amino acids are joined together in a long (polypeptide) chain *[1 mark]*. The sequence of amino acids is the protein's primary structure *[1 mark]*. The amino acid chain/polypeptide coils or folds in a certain way *[1 mark]*. The way it's coiled or folded is the protein's secondary structure *[1 mark]*. The coiled or folded chain is itself folded into a specific shape *[1 mark]*. This is the protein's tertiary structure *[1 mark]*. Different polypeptide chains can be joined together in the protein molecule *[1 mark]*. The way these chains are joined is the quaternary structure of the protein *[1 mark]*.

2 Maximum of 6 marks available, from any of the 7 points below.
Collagen is a fibrous protein *[1 mark]*.
For this mark, including the word 'fibrous' is essential.
It forms supportive tissues in the body, so it needs to be strong *[1 mark]*. Collagen is made of three polypeptide chains *[1 mark]*, tightly coiled to form a triple helix *[1 mark]*. The chains are interlinked by covalent bonds *[1 mark]*, which makes it strong *[1 mark]*. Minerals can bind to the triple helix, increasing its rigidity *[1 mark]*.

Page 57 — Carbohydrates

1 Maximum of 7 marks available.
Glycosidic bonds are formed when a hydrogen atom *[1 mark]* from one monosaccharide combines with a hydroxyl/OH group *[1 mark]* from another monosaccharide. This releases a molecule of water *[1 mark]*. Glycosidic bonds are broken by hydrolysis *[1 mark]*. A molecule of water reacts with the glycosidic bond to split the monosaccharide molecules apart *[1 mark]*. The last two marks are given for a diagram showing a reversible reaction with correct reactants (e.g. two glucose molecules) *[1 mark]* and correct products (e.g. water and maltose) *[1 mark]*.

Answers

2 Maximum of 12 marks available.
Starch is made of alpha-glucose molecules *[1 mark]* whereas cellulose is made of beta-glucose molecules *[1 mark]*. Cellulose is a single polysaccharide, whereas starch is made of two polysaccharides (amylose and amylopectin) *[1 mark]*. The amylose in starch is unbranched and coiled *[1 mark]* and the amylopectin is branched *[1 mark]*. In contrast, cellulose is straight and unbranched *[1 mark]* and the chains are linked together by hydrogen bonds to form strong fibres/microfibrils *[1 mark]*. Starch's structure makes it a good energy storage material in plants *[1 mark]*. The branches allow enzymes access to break the glycosidic bonds and release glucose quickly *[1 mark]*. It's insoluble, so it can be stored in cells without causing water to enter by osmosis, which would cause them to swell *[1 mark]*. Cellulose's structure makes it a good supporting structure in cell walls *[1 mark]*. The fibres provide strength *[1 mark]*.
The question asks you to compare and contrast, so you need to highlight how they differ from each other.

Page 59 — Lipids

1 a) Maximum of 2 marks available.
Hydrophilic — glycerol phosphate/phosphate group *[1 mark]*.
Hydrophobic — hydrocarbon tail/fatty acids *[1 mark]*.
  b) Maximum of 3 marks available.
They arrange themselves into a (phospholipid) bilayer/double layer *[1 mark]*, with fatty acid tails facing towards each other *[1 mark]*. This is because the fatty acid tails are hydrophobic (water-repelling), forcing them to face inwards, away from the water on either side of the membrane *[1 mark]*.

2 a) Maximum of 2 marks available.
The flattened shape allows them to fit in between the phospholipids, causing them to pack together more tightly *[1 mark]*, which makes the membrane less fluid and more rigid *[1 mark]*.
  b) Maximum of 2 marks available.
The hydrophobic tails force them to clump together in the cytoplasm as insoluble droplets *[1 mark]*. This means they can be stored in cells without affecting the cell's water potential *[1 mark]*.

Page 61 — Biochemical Tests for Molecules

1 a) Maximum of 1 mark available.
Solution C *[1 mark]*
Solution C has the lowest absorbance. It therefore has the least amount of Benedict's reagent <u>left</u> — so it had the most reducing sugar <u>before</u> the Benedict's test.
  b) Maximum of 1 mark available.
The colorimeter measures the amount of Benedict's reagent left after reacting with glucose. You therefore need to use an excessive amount of Benedict's reagent to make sure there's some left behind *[1 mark]*.
  c) Maximum of 2 marks available.
The amount of Benedict's reagent used in each test tube *[1 mark]*. The concentration of Benedict's reagent used *[1 mark]*. The length of time each solution is left for *[1 mark]*.

Unit 2: Section 2 — Nucleic Acids

Page 63 — DNA and RNA

1 Maximum of 1 mark available.

2 a) Maximum of 3 marks available, from any of the 4 points below.
DNA nucleotides consist of deoxyribose sugar *[1 mark]* joined to a phosphate group *[1 mark]* and a nitrogen-containing base *[1 mark]*. There are four possible bases in DNA — adenine (A), thymine (T), cytosine (C) or guanine (G) *[1 mark]*.

b) Maximum of 3 marks available.
RNA contains ribose sugar, not deoxyribose *[1 mark]*. RNA molecules are usually single stranded, not double stranded *[1 mark]*. The base uracil (U) is found in RNA instead of thymine (T) *[1 mark]*.

3 Maximum of 4 marks available, from any of the 6 points below.
Nucleotides are joined between the phosphate group of one nucleotide and the sugar of the next *[1 mark]*. The two polynucleotide strands join through hydrogen bonds *[1 mark]* between the base pairs *[1 mark]*. Complementary base pairing means adenine (A) always joins with thymine (T) and cytosine (C) always joins with guanine (G) *[1 mark]*. Three hydrogen bonds join C with G and two hydrogen bonds join A with T *[1 mark]*. One mark can be given for an accurate diagram showing at least one of the above points *[1 mark]*.
As the question asks for a diagram make sure you do at least one, e.g.:

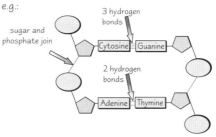

Page 65 — DNA Replication and Protein Synthesis

1 Maximum of 7 marks available.
The DNA helix unzips *[1 mark]*. Each strand acts as a template *[1 mark]*. Individual free DNA nucleotides join up along the template strand by complementary base pairing *[1 mark]*. DNA polymerase joins the individual nucleotides together *[1 mark]*. (Students often forget to mention this enzyme in their answers — make sure you don't forget.)
Hydrogen bonds then form between the bases on each strand *[1 mark]*. Two identical DNA molecules are produced *[1 mark]*. Each of the new molecules contains a single strand from the original DNA molecule and a single new strand *[1 mark]*.

2 Maximum of 2 marks available.
A gene is a sequence of DNA nucleotides *[1 mark]* that codes for a protein/polypeptide *[1 mark]*.

3 Maximum of 3 marks available.
DNA contains the instructions for making proteins *[1 mark]*. DNA is copied into RNA *[1 mark]*, which is used to make proteins *[1 mark]*.

Unit 2: Section 3 — Enzymes

Page 67 — Action of Enzymes

1 Maximum of 7 marks available.
In the 'lock and key' model the enzyme and the substrate have to fit together at the active site of the enzyme *[1 mark]*. This creates an enzyme-substrate complex *[1 mark]*. The active site then causes changes in the substrate *[1 mark]*. This mark could also be gained by explaining the change (e.g. bringing molecules closer together, or putting a strain on bonds).
The change results in the substrate being broken down/joined together *[1 mark]*. The 'induced fit' model has the same basic mechanism as the 'lock and key' model *[1 mark]*.
The difference is that the substrate is thought to cause a change in the enzyme's active site shape *[1 mark]*, which enables a better fit *[1 mark]*.

AS-Level Answers

Page 69 — Factors Affecting Enzyme Activity

1   Maximum of 8 marks available, from any of the 10 points below.
    If the solution is too cold, the enzyme will work very slowly
    [1 mark]. This is because, at low temperatures, the molecules
    have little kinetic energy, so move slowly, making collisions
    between enzyme and substrate molecules less likely **[1 mark]**.
    Also, fewer of the collisions will have enough energy to result
    in a reaction **[1 mark]**.
    The marks above could also be obtained by giving the reverse
    argument — a higher temperature is best to use because the
    molecules will move fast enough to give a reasonable chance of
    collisions and those collisions will have more energy, so more will
    result in a reaction.
    If the temperature gets too high, the reaction will stop **[1 mark]**.
    This is because the enzyme is denatured **[1 mark]** — the active
    site changes shape and will no longer fit the substrate **[1 mark]**.
    Denaturation is caused by increased vibration breaking bonds in
    the enzyme **[1 mark]**. Enzymes have an optimum pH **[1 mark]**.
    pH values too far from the optimum cause denaturation **[1 mark]**.
    Explanation of denaturation here will get a mark only if it hasn't been
    explained earlier.
    Denaturation by pH is caused by disruption of ionic and
    hydrogen bonds, which alters the enzyme's tertiary structure
    [1 mark].

Page 71 — Factors Affecting Enzyme Activity

1 a) Maximum of 2 marks available.
    Magnesium ions are a cofactor for hexokinase **[1 mark]**.
    They help the enzyme and substrate bind together **[1 mark]**.
  b) Maximum of 2 marks available.
    Aluminium ions are an enzyme inhibitor for hexokinase **[1 mark]**.
    They bind to the enzyme and prevent the enzyme-substrate
    complex from forming **[1 mark]**.
  c) Maximum of 1 mark available.
    Because they inhibit respiration, which is a metabolic reaction
    [1 mark].

2   Maximum of 5 marks available.
    Ritonavir will prevent the HIV virus from replicating **[1 mark]**,
    because the virus will not be able to break down the proteins
    needed to make new viruses **[1 mark]**. The Ritonavir molecules
    are a similar shape to the protease enzyme's substrate so it will
    act as a competitive inhibitor **[1 mark]**. It will bind to the active
    site of the enzyme **[1 mark]**, and block it so the substrate cannot
    fit in **[1 mark]**.

Unit 2: Section 4 — Diet and Food Production

Page 73 — Balanced Diet

1   Maximum of 4 marks available.
    Saturated fat increases blood cholesterol level **[1 mark]**,
    which increases the build up of fatty deposits in the arteries
    [1 mark]. This results in atherosclerosis/narrowing of the arteries
    [1 mark], which reduces blood flow to the heart **[1 mark]**.
2 a) Maximum of 2 marks available.
    The total blood cholesterol level would have decreased **[1 mark]**
    because there were more HDLs, which decrease blood
    cholesterol level by transporting cholesterol from the blood
    to the liver **[1 mark]**.
  b) Maximum of 1 mark available.
    The patient may have increased his polyunsaturated fat intake
    [1 mark].

Page 75 — Food Production

1 a) Maximum of 3 marks available.
    Plants with large grains were bred together **[1 mark]**. Then the
    offspring with the largest grains were bred together **[1 mark]**.
    This was repeated over generations **[1 mark]** to make the grains
    of modern wheat plants larger.
  b) Maximum of 3 marks available.
    Hessian fly infestation would reduce the crop yield by damaging
    the crops **[1 mark]**. A short-term solution would be to use a
    pesticide to kill the flies **[1 mark]**. A long-term solution would be
    to use selective breeding to create a wheat strain resistant to the
    fly **[1 mark]**.
    A lot of exam questions will be like this one — you have to use your
    knowledge and apply it to a real-life situation to show you've
    understood the principles. Make sure you refer to the situation the
    question has described.

Page 77 — Microorganisms and Food

1 a) Maximum of 2 marks available.
    It's heat-treated to kill any microorganisms **[1 mark]**,
    which extends its shelf life **[1 mark]**.
  b) Maximum of 3 marks available, from any of the 4 points below.
    The fungus can be grown faster than cows **[1 mark]**. The
    environment for growth of fungus can be more easily controlled,
    so they can potentially be grown anywhere **[1 mark]** and at any
    time of year **[1 mark]**. It's easier to create the right conditions for
    fungus to grow **[1 mark]**.

Unit 2: Section 5 — Health and Disease

Page 79 — Infectious Disease

1 a) Maximum of 4 marks available.
    It is caused by infection with Mycobacterium tuberculosis
    [1 mark]. It is transmitted by droplet infection **[1 mark]**. This is
    where an infected person coughs or sneezes and releases tiny
    droplets of saliva and mucus containing the bacteria from their
    mouth and nose **[1 mark]**. These droplets are then breathed in
    by other people **[1 mark]**.
  b) Maximum of 3 marks available, from any of the points below.
    Limited access to healthcare **[1 mark]**. Vaccinations or drugs not
    available **[1 mark]**. Less likely to be diagnosed **[1 mark]**.
    Overcrowding **[1 mark]**. Social disruption (which exacerbates
    other problems, such as access to healthcare) **[1 mark]**.
  c) Maximum of 2 marks available, from any of the points below.
    To find out where people are most at risk **[1 mark]**. To predict
    where epidemics are most likely to occur **[1 mark]**. To help
    research **[1 mark]**. To allow organisations to give aid where it is
    needed most **[1 mark]**.

2 a) Maximum of 1 mark available.
    HIV **[1 mark]**.
  b) Maximum of 4 marks available, from any of the points below.
    Educating people about safe sex practices **[1 mark]**. Making
    condoms available **[1 mark]**. Quick diagnosis, so that infected
    people won't pass it on unknowingly **[1 mark]**. Screening blood
    from donors **[1 mark]**. Sterilising needles and surgical equipment
    [1 mark]. Making alternatives to breast-feeding available for
    women with HIV **[1 mark]**. Providing needle exchanges **[1 mark]**.
    If you know how a disease is transmitted you should be able to figure
    out how to reduce its spread. Make sure you don't put down drug
    treatment for HIV, as this won't reduce the spread of the virus.

AS-Level Answers

Page 83 — The Immune System

1   Maximum of 6 marks available
    A phagocyte recognises the antigens on a pathogen *[1 mark]*.
    The phagocyte engulfs the pathogen *[1 mark]*. The pathogen is
    now contained in a phagocytic vacuole *[1 mark]*. A lysosome
    fuses with the phagocytic vacuole *[1 mark]* and digestive
    enzymes break down the pathogen *[1 mark]*. The phagocyte
    presents the antigens to T lymphocytes *[1 mark]*.

2   Maximum of 3 marks available.
    Antibodies agglutinate pathogens, so that phagocytes can get rid
    of a lot of the pathogens at once *[1 mark]*. Antibodies neutralise
    toxins produced by pathogens *[1 mark]*. Antibodies bind to
    pathogens to prevent them from binding to and infecting human
    cells *[1 mark]*.
    There are three marks available for this question so you need to think
    of three different functions.

3   Maximum of 10 marks available.
    When Emily caught chickenpox the first time *[1 mark]* her B and
    T lymphocytes produced memory cells *[1 mark]*, giving her
    immunological memory against the virus antigens *[1 mark]*.
    When exposed a second time *[1 mark]* the memory B
    lymphocytes divided into plasma cells *[1 mark]* to produce the
    right antibody to the virus *[1 mark]*. The memory T lymphocytes
    divided into the correct type of T lymphocyte *[1 mark]* to kill the
    virus *[1 mark]*. The secondary response was quicker and stronger
    [1 mark] and so got rid of the pathogen before she showed any
    symptoms *[1 mark]*.
    This question is asking about the secondary response and the
    immune system memory, so no detail is needed about how the
    primary response got rid of the infection.

Page 85 — Immunity and Vaccinations .

1 a) Maximum of 3 marks available.
    Different strains of the influenza virus are present in the
    population each year *[1 mark]*. Each different strain has different
    cell-surface antigens *[1 mark]*. So a new vaccine is made every
    year to protect against the most recently circulating strains of
    influenza *[1 mark]*.
  b) Maximum of 3 marks available.
    Samples of influenza viruses are collected by laboratories
    [1 mark]. The effectiveness of different vaccines is tested against
    these samples *[1 mark]* and the most effective vaccine is chosen
    [1 mark].

Page 87 — Smoking and Disease

1   Maximum of 12 marks available, 6 for each disease.
    Emphysema:
    Emphysema is caused by toxic particles from cigarette smoke
    becoming trapped in the alveoli of the lungs *[1 mark]*. This
    encourages phagocytes into the area *[1 mark]*, which release an
    enzyme that breaks down elastin in the walls of the alveoli
    [1 mark]. This reduces the surface area and elasticity of the
    alveoli, decreasing the rate of gas exchange *[1 mark]*. Sufferers
    have a shortness of breath because they can't breathe in enough
    oxygen *[1 mark]*. They may breathe faster than normal/
    hyperventilate to try to get enough oxygen into their body
    [1 mark]. People with emphysema may have an expanded lung
    as some air remains trapped in the alveoli *[1 mark]*.

Lung cancer:
    Lung cancer can be caused by the carcinogens present in
    cigarette smoke *[1 mark]*. These may cause mutations in the
    DNA of lung cells *[1 mark]*, which could lead to uncontrolled cell
    growth *[1 mark]*. This could cause malignant tumour growth
    [1 mark], which would block air flow to areas of the lungs,
    reducing gas exchange *[1 mark]*. Lung cancer leads to a
    shortness of breath as sufferers struggle to take in enough oxygen
    [1 mark]. It can also cause weight loss due to the tumour using
    up nutrients and energy *[1 mark]*.

Unit 2: Section 6 — Biodiversity
Page 89 — Studying Biodiversity

1 a) Maximum of 2 marks available.
    Species richness is the number of different species in an area
    [1 mark]. Species evenness is a measure of the relative
    abundance of each species in an area *[1 mark]*.
  b) Maximum of 4 marks available.
    They would take random samples from the area being studied
    [1 mark]. They would need to use an appropriate method to
    catch the millipedes, such as a pitfall trap *[1 mark]*. They would
    count the number of different species present *[1 mark]* and the
    number of individuals of each species in the sample *[1 mark]*.

Page 91 — Global Biodiversity

1 a) Maximum of 1 mark available, from any of the 3 points below.
    The total number of species on Earth is not known *[1 mark]*.
    Some species have not been discovered yet *[1 mark]*. It would
    be impossible *[1 mark]*.
  b) Maximum of 1 mark available.
    The Living Planet Index/biodiversity of Earth has decreased from
    1970 to 2000 *[1 mark]*.
  c) Maximum of 5 marks available.
    Climate change alters habitat conditions *[1 mark]*. Some species
    may be unable to survive in these conditions and become extinct,
    which decreases biodiversity *[1 mark]*. The ranges of some
    species that carry diseases may increase, which could cause
    population decline of other species, decreasing biodiversity
    [1 mark]. The ranges of some fungal diseases may increase,
    which could cause population decline of other species,
    decreasing biodiversity *[1 mark]*. Areas previously suitable for
    farming may become unsuitable, decreasing biodiversity
    [1 mark].
    The question asks about global biodiversity so you won't get marks
    for mentioning anything that affects local biodiversity but not overall
    biodiversity, e.g. migration.

Page 93 — Importance of Biodiversity

1   Maximum of 4 marks available.
    If one species is removed from a food chain it can affect all
    organisms further up the food chain *[1 mark]*. The loss of certain
    organisms (such as decomposers) can affect the nutrient cycle in
    the area, which will affect the growth of plants and reduce the
    amount of food available to animals *[1 mark]*. The loss of one
    habitat (such as a hedgerow) would affect other habitats as they
    may become isolated, so availability of food/nesting sites would
    be reduced *[1 mark]*. The destruction of species and habitats
    that store CO_2, like trees and peat bogs, contributes to climate
    change, which is reducing biodiversity *[1 mark]*.

A2-Level Answers

2   Maximum of 5 marks available.
Biodiversity provides a range of species that are used as food for people and livestock *[1 mark]*. Many crops are pollinated by a diverse range of insects *[1 mark]*, and other insects are used as natural predators of pest species *[1 mark]*. Cross-breeding with wild plants can create plants with new characteristics *[1 mark]*. A greater variety of crops grown means that food sources are less susceptible to disease or pests *[1 mark]*.

Page 95 — Conservation and Biodiversity

1 a) Maximum of 5 marks available.
In situ *methods could include protecting the turtles from hunters* *[1 mark]* and protecting their nesting sites *[1 mark]*. A national park/protected area could also be established to restrict human usage of the area *[1 mark]*. Ex situ *methods could include relocating the turtles or their eggs to a safer environment *[1 mark]* or to start a captive breeding programme *[1 mark]*.

  b) Maximum of 4 marks available.
It's only possible to conserve a limited number of individuals with ex situ *methods* *[1 mark]*. They can be very expensive *[1 mark]*. It may be difficult to sustain the environment for the turtle *[1 mark]*. They don't protect the habitat of the turtle *[1 mark]*.

  c) Maximum of 1 mark available.
International cooperation is important because it means that hunting endangered species is illegal in all countries — making hunting illegal in one country would have little use if it was legal in a neighbouring country *[1 mark]*.

Unit 2: Section 7 — Classification

Page 97 — Classification Basics

1 a) Maximum of 1 mark available.
The act of arranging organisms into groups based on their similarities and differences *[1 mark]*.

  b) Maximum of 1 mark available.
The study of classification *[1 mark]*.

  c) Maximum of 1 mark available.
The study of the evolutionary history/development of organisms *[1 mark]*.

2   Maximum of 3 marks available.
The binomial system gives all organisms an internationally accepted, two-word, scientific name in Latin *[1 mark]*. The first part is a genus name *[1 mark]*. The second part is the species name *[1 mark]*.

Page 99 — Dichotomous Keys

1 a) Maximum of 3 marks available.
A — Lyngbya *[1 mark]*.
B — Trichodesmium *[1 mark]*.
C — Anabaena *[1 mark]*.

  b) Maximum of 3 marks available, from any of the 4 points below.
RNA polymerase is different in the Archaea and Bacteria *[1 mark]*. Archaea, but not bacteria, have histones similar to Eukarya *[1 mark]*. The bonds of the lipids in the cell membranes of Archaea and Bacteria are different *[1 mark]*. The development and composition of flagellae are also different in the Archaea and Bacteria *[1 mark]*.

Unit 2: Section 8 — Evolution

Page 101 — Variation

1 a) Maximum of 3 marks available.
For species A, as the temperature increases the development time decreases *[1 mark]*. For species B the development time also decreases as the temperature increases *[1 mark]*.
The development time of species B is less affected by temperature than species A *[1 mark]*.

  b) Maximum of 4 marks available.
The variation between the species is mainly due to their different genes *[1 mark]*. Variation within a species is caused by both genetic and environmental factors *[1 mark]*. Individuals have different forms of the same genes (alleles), which causes genetic differences *[1 mark]*. Individuals may have the same genes, but environmental factors influence how some characteristics develop *[1 mark]*.

Page 102 — Adaptations

1   Maximum of 8 marks available.
Behavioural — It can roll into a ball when alarmed *[1 mark]*, which increases it chance of escaping attack *[1 mark]*. Physiological — It can hibernate over winter *[1 mark]*, which means it's more likely to survive the winter months when food is scarce *[1 mark]*.
For anatomical you can get any two from the list below, to a maximum of 4 marks — 1 mark for each adaptation and 1 mark for explaining why each adaptation increases survival.
Anatomical — Brown colour *[1 mark]*, camouflages it, so it's harder for predators to spot *[1 mark]*. Spiky fur *[1 mark]*, protects it from predators *[1 mark]*. Long fur *[1 mark]*, provides warmth *[1 mark]*. Small ears *[1 mark]*, help to reduce heat loss *[1 mark]*. Claws *[1 mark]*, are used to catch prey *[1 mark]*.

Page 105 — The Theory of Evolution

1   Maximum of 4 marks available.
Individuals within a population show variation *[1 mark]*. Predation, disease and competition create a struggle for survival *[1 mark]*. Individuals with better adaptations are more likely to survive, reproduce and pass on their advantageous adaptations to their offspring *[1 mark]*. Over time, the number of individuals with the advantageous adaptations increases and the adaptations become more common *[1 mark]*.

2 a) Maximum of 4 marks available.
Genetic mutations would have resulted in some moths being resistant to DDT *[1 mark]*. When the population was exposed to DDT, only those individuals who were resistant would survive to reproduce *[1 mark]*. The alleles which code for resistance would be passed on to the next generation *[1 mark]*. Over time, the number of individuals with DDT resistance would increase and it would become more common within the population *[1 mark]*.

  b) Maximum of 2 marks available, from any of the 3 points below.
Moth infestations would be harder to control *[1 mark]*. Broader pesticides might be used, which could kill beneficial insects *[1 mark]*. New pesticides might need to be developed if the moth develops resistance to all pesticides in use *[1 mark]*.

Unit 4: Section 1 — Communication and Homeostasis

Page 111 — Communication and Homeostasis Basics

1 a) Maximum of 1 mark available.
The maintenance of a constant internal environment *[1 mark]*.

  b) Maximum of 3 marks available.
Receptors detect when a level is too high or too low *[1 mark]*, and the information's communicated via the nervous system or the hormonal system to effectors *[1 mark]*. Effectors respond to counteract the change / to bring the level back to normal *[1 mark]*.

A2-Level Answers

Page 113 — The Nervous System and Neurones

1   Maximum of 5 marks available.
Receptors detect the stimulus [1 mark], e.g. light receptors/photoreceptors in the animal's eyes detect the bright light [1 mark]. The receptors send impulses along neurones via the CNS to the effectors [1 mark]. The effectors bring about a response [1 mark],
e.g. the circular iris muscles contract to constrict the pupils and protect the eyes [1 mark].

2   Maximum of 4 marks available.
A — receptor cell [1 mark]
B — dendrite [1 mark]
C — cell body [1 mark]
D — axon [1 mark]

Page 115 — Action Potentials

1 a) Maximum of 1 mark available.
Stimulus [1 mark].
  b) Maximum of 3 marks available.
A stimulus causes sodium ion channels in the neurone cell membrane to open [1 mark]. Sodium ions diffuse into the cell [1 mark], so the membrane becomes depolarised [1 mark].
  c) Maximum of 2 marks available.
The membrane was in the refractory period [1 mark], so the sodium ion channels were recovering and couldn't be opened [1 mark].

2   Maximum of 5 marks available.
Transmission of action potentials will be slower in neurones with damaged myelin sheaths [1 mark]. This is because myelin is an electrical insulator [1 mark], so increases the speed of action potential conduction [1 mark]. The action potentials 'jump' between the nodes of Ranvier/between the myelin sheaths [1 mark], where sodium ion channels are concentrated [1 mark].
Don't panic if a question mentions something you haven't learnt about. You might not know anything about multiple sclerosis but that's fine, because you're not supposed to. All you need to know to get full marks here is how myelination affects the speed of action potential conduction.

Page 117 — Synapses

1   Maximum of 5 marks available.
A — presynaptic membrane [1 mark]
B — vesicle/vesicle containing neurotransmitter [1 mark]
C — synaptic cleft [1 mark]
D — postsynaptic receptor [1 mark]
E — postsynaptic membrane [1 mark]

2   Maximum of 6 marks available, from any of the 10 points below.
The action potential arriving at the presynaptic membrane stimulates voltage-gated calcium ion channels to open [1 mark], so calcium ions diffuse into the neurone [1 mark]. This causes synaptic vesicles, containing neurotransmitter, to move to the presynaptic membrane [1 mark]. They then fuse with the presynaptic membrane [1 mark]. The vesicles release the neurotransmitter into the synaptic cleft [1 mark].
The neurotransmitter diffuses across the synaptic cleft [1 mark] and binds to specific receptors on the postsynaptic membrane [1 mark]. This causes sodium ion channels in the postsynaptic membrane to open [1 mark]. The influx of sodium ions causes depolarisation [1 mark]. This triggers a new action potential to be generated at the postsynaptic membrane [1 mark].

Page 119 — The Hormonal System and Glands

1   Maximum of 4 marks available.
The first messenger is a hormone [1 mark], which carries the message from an endocrine gland to the receptor on its target tissue [1 mark]. The second messenger is a signalling molecule [1 mark], which carries the message from the receptor to other parts of the cell and activates a cascade inside the cell [1 mark].

2   Maximum of 2 marks available.
Endocrine glands secrete chemicals directly into the blood, but exocrine glands secrete into ducts [1 mark].
Endocrine glands secrete hormones, but exocrine glands usually secrete enzymes [1 mark].

Page 121 — Homeostasis — Control of Body Temperature

1   Maximum of 4 marks available.
Snakes are ectotherms [1 mark]. They can't control their body temperature internally and depend on the temperature of their external environment [1 mark]. In cold climates, snakes will be less active [1 mark], which makes it harder to catch prey, avoid predators, find a mate, etc. [1 mark].
You need to use a bit of common sense to answer this question — you know that the activity level of an ectotherm depends on the temperature of the surroundings, so in a cold environment it won't be very active. And if it can't be very active it'll have trouble surviving.

2   Maximum of 4 marks available, from any of the 8 points below.
1 mark for each method, up to a maximum of 2 marks.
1 mark for each explanation, up to a maximum of 2 marks.
Vasoconstriction of blood vessels [1 mark] reduces heat loss because less blood flows through the capillaries in the surface layers of the dermis [1 mark]. Erector pili muscles contract to make hairs stand on end [1 mark], trapping an insulating layer of air to prevent heat loss [1 mark]. Muscles contract in spasms to make the body shiver [1 mark], so more heat is produced from increased respiration [1 mark]. Adrenaline and thyroxine are released [1 mark], which increase metabolism so more heat is produced [1 mark].

3   Maximum of 2 marks available.
Thermoreceptors/temperature receptors in the skin detect a higher external temperature than normal [1 mark].
The thermoreceptors/temperature receptors send impulses along sensory neurones to the hypothalamus [1 mark].

Page 123 — Homeostasis — Control of Blood Glucose

1   Maximum of 5 marks available, from any of the 7 points below.
High blood glucose concentration is detected by cells in the pancreas [1 mark]. Beta/b cells secrete insulin into the blood [1 mark], which binds to receptors on the cell membranes of liver and muscle cells [1 mark]. This increases the permeability of the cell membranes to glucose, so the cells take up more glucose [1 mark]. Insulin also activates glycogenesis [1 mark] and increases the rate that cells respire glucose [1 mark].
This lowers the concentration of glucose in the blood [1 mark].
You need to get the spelling of words like glycogenesis right in the exam or you'll miss out on marks.

2   Maximum of 2 marks available.
No insulin would be secreted [1 mark] because ATP wouldn't be produced, so the potassium ion channels in the b cell plasma membrane wouldn't close / the plasma membrane of b cell wouldn't be depolarised [1 mark].

A2-Level Answers

Page 125 — Diabetes and Control of Heart Rate

1   Maximum of 3 marks available.
    They have Type II diabetes *[1 mark]*. They produce insulin,
    but the insulin receptors on their cell membranes don't work
    properly, so the cells don't take up enough glucose *[1 mark]*.
    This means their blood glucose concentration remains higher
    than normal *[1 mark]*.

2   Maximum of 2 marks available, from any of the 4 points below.
    It's cheaper to produce insulin using GM bacteria than to extract
    it from animal pancreases *[1 mark]*. Large amounts of insulin can
    be made using GM bacteria, so there's enough insulin to treat
    everyone with Type I diabetes *[1 mark]*. GM bacteria make real
    human insulin, which is more effective and less likely to trigger an
    allergic response or be rejected by the immune system *[1 mark]*.
    Some people prefer insulin from GM bacteria for ethical or
    religious reasons *[1 mark]*.

3 a) Maximum of 5 marks available.
    High blood pressure is detected by pressure receptors in the
    aorta called baroreceptors *[1 mark]*. Impulses are sent along
    sensory neurones to the medulla *[1 mark]*. Impulses are then
    sent from the medulla to the SAN along the vagus nerve *[1 mark]*.
    The vagus nerve secretes acetylcholine, which binds to receptors
    on the sinoatrial node/SAN *[1 mark]*. This slows the heart rate
    (reducing blood pressure) *[1 mark]*.
  b) Maximum of 2 marks available.
    No impulses sent from the medulla would reach the SAN
    [1 mark], so the heart rate wouldn't increase or decrease/
    control of the heart rate would be lost *[1 mark]*.

Unit 4: Section 2 — Excretion

Page 127 — The Liver and Excretion

1   Maximum of 3 marks available.
    A — central vein *[1 mark]*, B — sinusoid *[1 mark]*,
    C — hepatocyte *[1 mark]*

2   Maximum of 6 marks available.
    The protein would be digested, producing amino acids *[1 mark]*.
    Amino acids contain nitrogen in their amino groups, but the body
    can't usually store nitrogenous substances, so if a lot of protein is
    eaten there could be an excess of amino acids that will need to
    be used or broken down and excreted *[1 mark]*. Excess amino
    acids are broken down in the liver into ammonia and organic
    acids in a process called deamination *[1 mark]*. Ammonia is
    then combined with CO_2 in the ornithine cycle to produce urea
    [1 mark]. Urea is then released into the blood and filtered out at
    the kidneys to produce urine *[1 mark]*. So if a large amount of
    protein is eaten, there may be excess amino acids that are broken
    down by the liver, producing a large amount of urea that's
    excreted in the urine *[1 mark]*.
    Don't forget to say that only excess amino acids are broken down.

Page 129 — The Kidneys and Excretion

1 a) Maximum of 4 marks available.
    A — nephron *[1 mark]*
    B — renal capsule / Bowman's capsule *[1 mark]*
    C — proximal convoluted tubule / PCT *[1 mark]*
    D — collecting duct *[1 mark]*
  b) Maximum of 1 mark available.
    B (renal capsule) *[1 mark]*

c) Maximum of 5 marks available.
    Ultrafiltration is when substances are filtered out of the blood
    and enter the tubules in the kidneys *[1 mark]*. Blood enters a
    glomerulus, a bundle of capillaries looped inside a hollow ball
    called a renal capsule/Bowman's capsule *[1 mark]*. The blood
    in the glomerulus is under high pressure because it enters
    through the afferent arteriole and leaves through the smaller
    efferent arteriole *[1 mark]*. The high pressure forces liquid and
    small molecules in the blood out of the capillary and into the
    renal capsule *[1 mark]*. The liquid and small molecules pass
    through the capillary wall, the basement membrane and slits in
    the epithelium of the renal capsule. But larger molecules like
    proteins and blood cells can't pass through and stay in the
    blood *[1 mark]*.

Page 131 — Controlling Water Content

1   Maximum of 6 marks available.
    Near the top of the ascending limb of the loop of Henle,
    sodium/Na^+ and chloride/Cl^- ions are actively pumped out into
    the medulla. This creates a low water potential in the medulla
    [1 mark]. There's now a lower water potential in the medulla
    than in the descending limb *[1 mark]*, so water moves out of
    the descending limb and into the medulla by osmosis *[1 mark]*.
    Near the bottom of the ascending limb sodium/Na^+ and chloride
    /Cl^- ions diffuse into the medulla, lowering the water potential
    of the medulla further *[1 mark]*. The low water potential in the
    medulla causes water to move out of the collecting duct by
    osmosis *[1 mark]*. The water in the medulla is then reabsorbed
    into the blood through the capillary network *[1 mark]*.

2   Maximum of 6 marks available.
    Strenuous exercise causes more sweating, so more water is lost
    [1 mark]. This decreases the water content of the blood,
    so its water potential drops *[1 mark]*. This is detected by
    osmoreceptors in the hypothalamus *[1 mark]*, which stimulates
    the posterior pituitary gland to release more ADH *[1 mark]*.
    The answer up to this point has explained the cause of the
    increase in ADH in the blood. After this, the answer explains the
    effect on the kidney.
    The ADH increases the permeability of the walls of the distal
    convoluted tubule and collecting duct *[1 mark]*. This means
    more water is reabsorbed into the medulla and into the blood
    by osmosis, so a small amount of concentrated urine is
    produced *[1 mark]*.

Page 133 — Kidney Failure and Detecting Hormones

1   Maximum of 5 marks available. For full marks answers must
    include at least 1 advantage and 1 disadvantage.
    Kidney transplants are cheaper in the long term than renal dialysis
    [1 mark]. Having a kidney transplant is more convenient for a
    person than regular dialysis sessions *[1 mark]*. A patient who
    has had a kidney transplant won't feel unwell between dialysis
    sessions *[1 mark]*. However, a transplant means the patient has
    to undergo a major operation, which is risky *[1 mark]*.
    The patient also has to take drugs to suppress the immune
    system, so it doesn't reject the transplant *[1 mark]*.

2   Maximum of 5 marks available.
    Steroids are removed from the blood in the urine, so urine can
    be tested to see if a person is using steroids *[1 mark]*. It's tested
    using a technique called gas chromatography, where the urine
    is vaporised and passed through a column containing a liquid
    [1 mark]. Different substances move through the column at
    different speeds *[1 mark]*. The time taken for substances in the
    sample to pass through the column is compared to the time taken
    for a steroid to pass through the column *[1 mark]*. If the time
    taken is the same then the sample contains the steroid *[1 mark]*.

A2-Level Answers

Unit 4: Section 3 — Photosynthesis and Respiration

Page 135 — Photosynthesis, Respiration and ATP

1 Maximum of 6 marks available, from any of the 8 points below.
In the cell, ATP is synthesised from ADP and inorganic phosphate/P_i *[1 mark]* using energy from an energy-releasing reaction, e.g. respiration *[1 mark]*. The energy is stored as chemical energy in the phosphate bond *[1 mark]*. ATP synthase catalyses this reaction *[1 mark]*. ATP then diffuses to the part of the cell that needs energy *[1 mark]*. Here, it's broken down back into ADP and inorganic phosphate/P_i *[1 mark]*, which is catalysed by ATPase *[1 mark]*. Chemical energy is released from the phosphate bond and used by the cell *[1 mark]*.
Make sure you don't get the two enzymes confused
— ATP **syn**thase **syn**thesises ATP, and ATPase breaks it down.

Page 139 — Photosynthesis

1 a) Maximum of 1 mark available.
The thylakoid membranes *[1 mark]*.
 b) Maximum of 1 mark available.
Photosystem II *[1 mark]*.
 c) Maximum of 4 marks available.
Light energy splits water *[1 mark]*.

H_2O *[1 mark]* $\rightarrow 2H^+ + \frac{1}{2} O_2$ *[1 mark]*.

The electrons from the water replace the electrons lost from chlorophyll *[1 mark]*.
The question asks you to explain the purpose of photolysis, so make sure you include why the water is split up — to replace the electrons lost from chlorophyll.
 d) Maximum of 1 mark available.
NADP *[1 mark]*.

2 a) Maximum of 6 marks available.
Ribulose bisphosphate/RuBP and carbon dioxide/CO_2 join together to form an unstable 6-carbon compound *[1 mark]*. This reaction is catalysed by the enzyme rubisco/ribulose bisphosphate carboxylase *[1 mark]*. The compound breaks down into two molecules of a 3-carbon compound called glycerate 3-phosphate/GP *[1 mark]*. Two molecules of glycerate 3-phosphate are then converted into two molecules of triose phosphate/TP *[1 mark]*. The energy for this reaction comes from ATP *[1 mark]* and the H^+ ions come from reduced NADP *[1 mark]*.
 b) Maximum of 2 marks available.
Ribulose bisphosphate is regenerated from triose phosphate/TP molecules *[1 mark]*. ATP provides the energy to do this *[1 mark]*.
This question is only worth two marks so only the main facts are needed, without the detail of the number of molecules.
 c) Maximum of 3 marks available.
No glycerate 3-phosphate/GP would be produced *[1 mark]*, so no triose phosphate/TP would be produced *[1 mark]*. This means there would be no glucose produced *[1 mark]*.

Page 141 — Limiting Factors in Photosynthesis

1 Maximum of 4 marks available.
25 °C *[1 mark]*. This is because photosynthesis involves enzymes *[1 mark]*, which become inactive at low temperatures/10 °C *[1 mark]* and denature at high temperatures/45 °C *[1 mark]*.

Page 143 — Limiting Factors in Photosynthesis

1 a) Maximum of 3 marks available.
The level of GP will rise and levels of TP and RuBP will fall *[1 mark]*. This is because there's less reduced NADP and ATP from the light-dependent reaction *[1 mark]*, so the conversion of GP to TP and RuBP is slow *[1 mark]*.

 b) Maximum of 3 marks available.
The levels of RuBP, GP and TP will fall *[1 mark]*. This is because the reactions in the Calvin cycle are slower *[1 mark]* due to all the enzymes working more slowly *[1 mark]*.

2 Maximum of 6 marks available, from any of the 8 points below.
A sample of pondweed would be placed in a test tube of water *[1 mark]*. The test tube would be placed in a beaker containing water at a known temperature *[1 mark]*. The test tube would be connected to a capillary tube of water *[1 mark]* and the capillary tube connected to a syringe *[1 mark]*. The pondweed would be allowed to photosynthesise for a set period of time *[1 mark]*. Afterwards, the syringe would be used to draw the bubble of oxygen produced up the capillary tube where its length would be measured using a ruler *[1 mark]*. The experiment is repeated and the mean length of gas bubble is calculated *[1 mark]*. Then the whole experiment is repeated at several different temperatures *[1 mark]*.

Page 145 — Aerobic Respiration

1 Maximum of 6 marks available, from any of the 8 points below.
First, the 6-carbon glucose molecule is phosphorylated *[1 mark]* by adding two phosphates from two molecules of ATP *[1 mark]*. This creates one molecule of 6-carbon hexose bisphosphate *[1 mark]* and two molecules of ADP *[1 mark]*. Then, the hexose bisphosphate is split up into two molecules of 3-carbon triose phosphate *[1 mark]*. Triose phosphate is oxidised (by removing hydrogen) to give two molecules of 3-carbon pyruvate *[1 mark]*. The hydrogen is accepted by two molecules of NAD, producing two molecules of reduced NAD *[1 mark]*. During oxidation four molecules of ATP are produced *[1 mark]*.
When describing glycolysis make sure you get the number of molecules correct — one glucose molecule produces one molecule of hexose bisphosphate, which produces two molecules of triose phosphate. You could draw a diagram in the exam to show the reactions.

2 a) Maximum of 3 marks available, from any of the 4 points below.
The 3-carbon pyruvate is decarboxylated *[1 mark]* and NAD is reduced to form acetate *[1 mark]*. Acetate combines with coenzyme A (CoA) to form acetyl coenzyme A (acetyl CoA) *[1 mark]*. No ATP is produced *[1 mark]*.
 b) Maximum of 2 marks available, from any of the 3 points below.
The inner membrane is folded into cristae, which increase the membrane's surface area and maximise respiration *[1 mark]*. There are lots of ATP synthase molecules on the inner membrane to produce lots of ATP in the final stage of respiration *[1 mark]*. The matrix contains all the reactants and enzymes needed for the Krebs cycle to take place *[1 mark]*.

Page 147 — Aerobic Respiration

1 a) Maximum of 2 mark available.
The transfer of electrons down the electron transport chain stops *[1 mark]*. So there's no energy released to phosphorylate ADP/produce ATP *[1 mark]*.
 b) Maximum of 2 marks available.
The Krebs cycle stops *[1 mark]* because there's no oxidised NAD/FAD coming from the electron transport chain *[1 mark]*.
Part b is a bit tricky — remember that when the electron transport chain is inhibited, the reactions that depend on the products of the chain are also affected.

Page 149 — Respiration Experiments

1 a) Maximum of 1 mark available.
Because there was no proton gradient *[1 mark]*.
 b) Maximum of 1 mark available.
3.7 *[1 mark]*

A2-Level Answers

c) *Maximum of 1 mark available.*
Yes, these results support the chemiosmotic theory because they show that a proton gradient can be used by mitochondria to synthesise ATP [1 mark].

2 a) *Maximum of 1 mark available.*
To make sure the results are only due to oxygen uptake by the woodlouse [1 mark].
b) *Maximum of 2 marks available.*
The oxygen taken up would be replaced by carbon dioxide given out / there would be no change in air volume in the test tube [1 mark]. This means there would be no movement of the liquid in the manometer [1 mark].
c) *Maximum of 1 mark available.*
Carbon dioxide/CO_2 [1 mark].

Page 151 — Aerobic and Anaerobic Respiration

1 *Maximum of 1 mark available.*
Because lactate fermentation doesn't involve electron carriers/ the electron transport chain/oxidative phosphorylation [1 mark].

2 *Maximum of 2 marks available.*
$RQ = CO_2 \div O_2$ [1 mark]
So the RQ of triolein = $57 \div 80 = 0.71$ [1 mark]
Award 2 marks for the correct answer of 0.71, without any working.

Unit 5: Section 1 — Protein Synthesis and Cellular Control

Page 153 — DNA, RNA and Protein Synthesis

1 *Maximum of 2 marks available.*
mRNA carries the genetic code from the DNA in the nucleus to the cytoplasm, where it's used to make a protein during translation [1 mark]. tRNA carries the amino acids that are used to make proteins to the ribosomes during translation [1 mark].

2 a) *Maximum of 1 mark available.*
5 amino acids [1 mark]
b) *Maximum of 2 marks available. Award 2 marks if all five amino acids are correct and in the correct order. Award 1 mark if four amino acids are correct and in the correct order.*
AGA = serine
ATA = tyrosine
CAC = valine
CGT = alanine
Correct sequence = serine, serine, tyrosine, valine, alanine.

Page 155 — Transcription and Translation

1 *Maximum of 2 marks available.*
The drug binds to DNA, preventing RNA polymerase from binding, so transcription can't take place and no mRNA can be made [1 mark]. This means there's no mRNA for translation and so protein synthesis is inhibited [1 mark].

2 a) *Maximum of 2 marks available.*
$10 \times 3 = 30$ nucleotides long [1 mark]. Each amino acid is coded for by three nucleotides (a codon), so the mRNA length in nucleotides is the number of amino acids multiplied by three [1 mark].

b) *Maximum of 6 marks available.*
The mRNA attaches itself to a ribosome and transfer RNA (tRNA) molecules carry amino acids to the ribosome [1 mark]. A tRNA molecule, with an anticodon that's complementary to the first codon on the mRNA (the start codon), attaches itself to the mRNA by complementary base pairing [1 mark]. A second tRNA molecule attaches itself to the next codon on the mRNA in the same way [1 mark]. The two amino acids attached to the tRNA molecules are joined by a peptide bond and the first tRNA molecule moves away, leaving its amino acid behind [1 mark]. A third tRNA molecule binds to the next codon on the mRNA and its amino acid binds to the first two and the second tRNA molecule moves away [1 mark]. This process continues, producing a chain of linked amino acids (a polypeptide chain), until there's a stop codon on the mRNA molecule [1 mark].

Page 157 — Control of Protein Synthesis and Body Plans

1 *Maximum of 4 marks available.*
When no lactose is present, the lac repressor binds to the operator site and blocks transcription [1 mark]. When lactose is present, it binds to the lac repressor [1 mark], changing its shape so that it can no longer bind to the operator site [1 mark]. RNA polymerase can now begin transcription of the structural genes, including the ones that code for β-galactosidase and lactose permease [1 mark].

Page 159 — Protein Activation and Gene Mutation

1 a) *Maximum of 1 mark available.*
Mutations are changes to the base sequence/nucleotide sequence of DNA [1 mark].
b) *Maximum of 2 marks available, from any of the 5 points below.*
Substitution — one base is swapped for another [1 mark].
Deletion — one base is removed [1 mark].
Insertion — one base is added [1 mark].
Duplication — one or more bases are repeated [1 mark].
Inversion — a sequence of bases is reversed [1 mark].

2 a) *Maximum of 1 mark available.*
ATGTATTCCGGCTGT [1 mark]
b) *Maximum of 3 marks available.*
The mutation changes a triplet in the gene from TCA to TCC [1 mark]. But the mutated triplet still codes for serine [1 mark], so the mutation would have a neutral effect on the protein that the gene codes for [1 mark].

Unit 5: Section 2 — Inheritance

Page 161 — Meiosis

1 a) *Maximum of 4 marks available.*
The chromosomes condense, getting shorter and fatter [1 mark]. Homologous chromosomes pair up [1 mark]. The centrioles start moving to opposite ends of the cell, forming a network of protein fibres across it called the spindle [1 mark]. The nuclear envelope breaks down [1 mark].
The question asks you to describe the nuclear envelope, chromosomes and centrioles, so make sure you include them all to get full marks.
b) *Maximum of 2 marks available.*
A — Telophase II [1 mark]
B — Anaphase II [1 mark]

A2-Level Answers

2 a) Maximum of 7 marks available.
Crossing-over of chromatids during prophase I causes genetic variation [1 mark]. The non-sister chromatids twist around each other and bits of the chromatids swap over [1 mark]. This means that each of the four daughter cells contain chromatids with different combinations of alleles [1 mark]. Independent assortment of chromosomes in metaphase I produces genetic variation [1 mark]. Different combinations of maternal and paternal chromosomes go into each daughter cell, so each cell ends up with a different combination of alleles [1 mark]. Independent assortment of chromatids in metaphase II also produces genetic variation [1 mark]. Different combinations of chromatids go into each daughter cell, so each cell ends up with a different combination of alleles [1 mark].

b) Maximum of 1 mark available.
Fertilisation increases genetic variation because any egg cell can fuse with any sperm cell [1 mark].

Page 163 — Inheritance

1 a) Maximum of 3 marks available.
Parents' genotypes identified as $X^H X^h$ and $X^h Y$ [1 mark].
Correct genetic diagram drawn with gametes' alleles identified as X^H, X^h and X^h, Y [1 mark] and gametes crossed to show $X^H X^h$, $X^H Y$, $X^h X^h$ and $X^h Y$ as the possible genotypes [1 mark].
The question specifically asks you to draw a genetic diagram, so make sure that you include one in your answer, e.g.

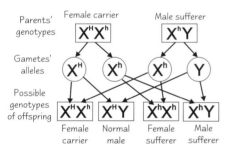

Parents' genotypes — Female carrier $X^H X^h$ — Male sufferer $X^h Y$
Gametes' alleles — X^H X^h X^h Y
Possible genotypes of offspring — $X^H X^h$ Female carrier — $X^H Y$ Normal male — $X^h X^h$ Female sufferer — $X^h Y$ Male sufferer

b) Maximum of 3 marks available.
Men only have one copy of the X chromosome (XY) but women have two (XX) [1 mark]. Haemophilia A is caused by a recessive allele so females would need two copies of the allele for them to have haemophilia A [1 mark]. As males only have one X chromosome they only need one recessive allele to have haemophilia A, which makes them more likely to have haemophilia A than females [1 mark].

Page 165 — Phenotypic Ratios and Epistasis

1 Maximum of 3 marks available.
Parents' genotypes identified as RRgg and rrGG [1 mark].
Correct genetic diagram drawn with gametes' alleles identified as Rg and rG [1 mark] and gametes crossed to show RrGg as the only possible genotype of the offspring [1 mark].
The question specifically asks you to draw a genetic diagram, so make sure that you include one in your answer, e.g.

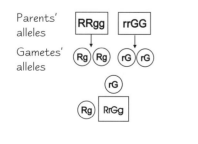

Parents' alleles — RRgg — rrGG
Gametes' alleles — Rg Rg — rG rG
— rG —
Rg — RrGg

2 Maximum of 4 marks available.
A cross between CCGG and ccgg will produce a 9 : 3 : 4 phenotypic ratio in the F_2 generation [1 mark] of coloured grey : coloured black : albino [1 mark]. This is because gene 1 has a recessive epistatic gene (c) [1 mark], and two copies of the recessive epistatic gene (cc) will mask the expression of the colour gene [1 mark].
You don't need to draw a genetic diagram to explain the phenotypic ratio that you'd expect from this cross. You can just state the ratio and explain it using your own knowledge.

3 Maximum of 3 marks available.
The table shows that a cross between hhss and HHSS produces a 36 : 9 : 3 or 12 : 3 : 1 phenotypic ratio in the F_2 generation of bald : straight hair : curly hair [1 mark]. This is because the hair gene has a dominant epistatic allele (H) [1 mark], which means having at least one copy of the dominant epistatic gene (Hh or HH) will result in a bald phenotype that masks the expression of the type of hair gene [1 mark].

Page 167 — The Chi-Squared Test

1 a) Maximum of 4 marks available.
(1 mark for each correct column and 1 mark for the answer).

Phenotype	Ratio	Expected Result (E)	Observed Result (O)	O – E	O – E²	$\frac{(O - E^2)}{E}$
Blue with white spots	9	135	131	−4	16	0.12
Purple with white spots	3	45	52	7	49	1.09
Blue with yellow spots	3	45	48	3	9	0.2
Purple with yellow spots	1	15	9	−6	36	2.4
						3.81

b) Maximum of 2 marks available.
The χ^2 value does support the null hypothesis [1 mark] because it's smaller than the critical value [1 mark].

Unit 5: Section 3 — Variation and Evolution

Page 169 — Variation

1 a) Maximum of 1 mark available.
Discontinuous variation [1 mark].

b) Maximum of 1 mark available.
18.99 − 9.25 = 9.74 kg [1 mark]

c) Maximum of 2 marks available.
Mass [1 mark] because it shows continuous variation [1 mark].

2 Maximum of 2 marks available.
E.g. body mass [1 mark] because large parents often have large children so it's affected by genotype, but body mass is also influenced by diet and exercise, which are environmental factors [1 mark].

Page 171 — Evolution by Natural Selection and Genetic Drift

1 Maximum of 5 marks available.
The dark moths were better camouflaged on the blackened trees than the pale moths [1 mark]. This means the dark moths were better adapted to avoid predation than the pale moths [1 mark]. Moths with the allele for a darker colour were more likely to survive, reproduce and pass on their alleles than pale moths [1 mark]. So a greater proportion of the next generation inherited the allele for a darker colour [1 mark]. The frequency of this allele then increased from generation to generation, causing an increase in the number of dark moths [1 mark].

A2-Level Answers

Page 173 — Hardy-Weinberg Principle and Artificial Selection

1   Maximum of 1 mark available.
     Frequency of the recessive allele (q) = 0.23, and p + q = 1
     So the frequency of the dominant allele (p)   = 1 − q
                                                   = 1 − 0.23
                                                   = 0.77 *[1 mark]*.

2   Maximum of 3 marks available.
     Farmers could have selected a male and female with a high meat yield and bred these two together *[1 mark]*. Then they could have selected the offspring with the highest meat yields and bred them together *[1 mark]*. This process could have been continued over several generations to produce cattle with a very high meat yield *[1 mark]*.

Page 175 — Speciation

1 a) Maximum of 1 mark available.
      The new species could not breed with each other *[1 mark]*.
  b) Maximum of 3 marks available.
      Different populations of flies were isolated and fed on different foods *[1 mark]*. This caused changes in allele frequencies between the populations *[1 mark]*, which made them reproductively isolated and eventually resulted in speciation *[1 mark]*.
  c) Maximum of 2 marks available, from any of the 3 points below.
      Seasonal changes (become sexually active at different times) *[1 mark]*. Mechanical changes (changes to genitalia) *[1 mark]*. Behavioural changes (changes in behaviour that prevent mating) *[1 mark]*.
  d) Maximum of 1 mark available, from any of the 5 points below or any other good point.
      E.g. geographical barrier *[1 mark]*, flood *[1 mark]*, volcanic eruption *[1 mark]*, earthquake *[1 mark]*, glacier *[1 mark]*.

Unit 5: Section 4 — Cloning and Biotechnology

Page 178 — Cloning

1 a) Maximum of 2 marks available.
      Reproductive cloning is used to make a complete organism that's genetically identical to another organism *[1 mark]*. Non-reproductive cloning is used to make embryonic stem cells that are genetically identical to another organism *[1 mark]*.
  b) Maximum of 6 marks available.
      The scientists could use nuclear transfer *[1 mark]*. They would take a body cell from an organism (organism A) and extract its nucleus *[1 mark]*. An egg cell would be taken from another organism (organism B) and its nucleus would be removed, forming an enucleated egg cell *[1 mark]*. The scientists would transfer the body cell nucleus into the enucleated egg cell *[1 mark]*. They would then stimulate the egg cell to divide *[1 mark]*. An embryo would form, which would be made up of stem cells that are genetically identical to the cells found in organism A *[1 mark]*.
      Don't forget — the technique of nuclear transfer is used in both reproductive and non-reproductive cloning.

Page 181 — Biotechnology

1   Maximum of 8 marks available.
     The first phase of the standard growth curve is the lag phase, when the microorganism population increases slowly *[1 mark]*. This is because the microorganisms need to make enzymes and other molecules before they can reproduce *[1 mark]*. The culture then enters the exponential phase, when the population size increases quickly *[1 mark]*. This is because there's lots of food and little competition *[1 mark]*. The next phase is the stationary phase, when the population size stays level *[1 mark]*. This is because the reproductive rate equals the death rate *[1 mark]*. The culture then enters the decline phase, when the population size begins to fall *[1 mark]*. This is because food is scarce and waste products are at toxic levels, causing microorganisms to die *[1 mark]*.

Unit 5: Section 5 — Gene Technologies

Page 183 — Common Techniques

1   Maximum of 6 marks available.
     The DNA sample is mixed with free nucleotides, primers and DNA polymerase *[1 mark]*. The mixture is heated to 95 °C to break the hydrogen bonds *[1 mark]*. The mixture is then cooled to between 50 – 65 °C to allow the primers to bind/anneal to the DNA *[1 mark]*. The primers bind/anneal to the DNA because they have a sequence that's complementary to the sequence at the start of the DNA fragment *[1 mark]*. The mixture is then heated to 72 °C and DNA polymerase lines up free nucleotides along each template strand, producing new strands of DNA *[1 mark]*. The cycle would be repeated over and over to produce lots of copies *[1 mark]*.
     This question asks you to describe and explain, so you need to give the reasons why each stage is done to gain full marks.

2   Maximum of 5 marks available.
     A fluorescent tag is added to all the DNA fragments in the mixture so they can be viewed under UV light *[1 mark]*. The DNA mixture is placed into a well in a slab of gel and covered in a buffer solution that conducts electricity *[1 mark]*. An electrical current is passed through the gel and the DNA fragments move towards the positive electrode because DNA fragments are negatively charged *[1 mark]*. The DNA fragments separate according to size because the small fragments move faster and travel further through the gel *[1 mark]*. The DNA fragments are viewed as bands under UV light *[1 mark]*.

Page 185 — Genetic Engineering

1 a) Maximum of 2 marks available.
      Colony A has grown on the agar plate containing penicillin *[1 mark]* so it contains the penicillin-resistance marker gene, which means it contains transformed cells *[1 mark]*.
  b) Maximum of 3 marks available.
      The plasmid vector DNA would have been cut open with the same restriction endonuclease that was used to isolate the DNA fragment containing the desired gene *[1 mark]*. The plasmid DNA and gene (DNA fragment) would have been mixed together with DNA ligase *[1 mark]*. DNA ligase joins the sugar-phosphate backbone of the two bits of DNA *[1 mark]*.
  c) Maximum of 2 marks available.
      It's useful for bacteria to take up plasmids because the plasmids may contain useful genes *[1 mark]* that increase their chance of survival *[1 mark]*.

A2-Level Answers

Page 187 — Genetic Engineering

1   Maximum of 6 marks available.
    The gene for human insulin is identified and isolated using restriction enzymes *[1 mark]*. A plasmid is cut open using the same restriction enzymes that were used to isolate the insulin gene *[1 mark]*. The insulin gene is inserted into the plasmid *[1 mark]*. The plasmid is taken up by bacteria and any transformed bacteria are identified using marker genes *[1 mark]*. The bacteria are grown in a fermenter and insulin is produced by the bacteria as they grow and divide *[1 mark]*. The insulin is extracted and purified so it can be used in humans *[1 mark]*.

2   Maximum of 7 marks available.
    The psy and crtl genes are isolated using restriction enzymes *[1 mark]*. A plasmid is removed from the Agrobacterium tumefaciens bacterium and cut open using the same restriction enzymes *[1 mark]*. The psy and crtl genes and a marker gene are inserted into the plasmid *[1 mark]*. The recombinant plasmid is put back into the A. tumefaciens bacterium *[1 mark]*. Rice plant cells are incubated with the transformed A. tumefaciens bacteria, which infect the rice plant cells *[1 mark]*. A. tumefaciens inserts the genes into the plant cells' DNA *[1 mark]*. The rice plant cells are then grown on a selective medium, so only the transformed rice plants will be able to grow *[1 mark]*.

Page 189 — Gene Therapy and DNA Probes

1 a) Maximum of 1 mark available.
    Gene therapy involves altering/supplementing defective genes (mutated alleles) inside cells to treat genetic disorders and cancer *[1 mark]*.
  b) Maximum of 1 mark available.
    Somatic gene therapy *[1 mark]*.

2   Maximum of 3 marks available, from any 6 of the points below.
    E.g. the effect of the treatment may be short-lived *[1 mark]*. The patient might have to undergo multiple treatments *[1 mark]*. It might be difficult to get the allele into specific body cells *[1 mark]*. The body may start an immune response against the vector *[1 mark]*. The allele may be inserted into the wrong place in the DNA, which could cause more problems *[1 mark]*. The allele may be overexpressed *[1 mark]*.

3   Maximum of 4 marks available.
    The separated DNA fragments are transferred to a nylon membrane and incubated with a fluorescently labelled DNA probe *[1 mark]*. The probe is complementary to the sequence of the mutated BRCA1 gene *[1 mark]*. If the sequence is present in one of the DNA fragments, the DNA probe will hybridise to it *[1 mark]*. The membrane is then exposed to UV light and if the sequence is present in one of the DNA fragments, then that band will fluoresce *[1 mark]*.

Page 191 — Sequencing Genes and Genomes

1 a) Maximum of 3 marks available.
    DNA primer *[1 mark]*, free nucleotides *[1 mark]* and fluorescently-labelled modified nucleotides *[1 mark]*.
  b) Maximum of 6 marks available.
    The reaction mixture is added to four tubes, with a different modified nucleotide in each tube *[1 mark]*. The tubes undergo PCR to produce lots of strands of DNA of different lengths *[1 mark]*. Each strand of DNA is a different length because each one terminates at a different point depending on where the modified nucleotide was added *[1 mark]*. The DNA fragments in each tube are separated by electrophoresis and visualised under UV light *[1 mark]*. The smallest nucleotide is at the bottom of the gel and each band after this represents one more base added *[1 mark]*. So the bands can be read from the bottom of the gel to the top, forming the base sequence of the DNA fragment *[1 mark]*.

2   Maximum of 8 marks available.
    The genome is cut up into smaller fragments using restriction enzymes *[1 mark]*. The individual fragments are inserted into bacterial artificial chromosomes/BACs, which are then inserted into bacteria *[1 mark]*. Each BAC contains a different DNA fragment, so each bacterium contains a BAC with a different DNA fragment *[1 mark]*. The bacteria divide, creating colonies of cloned cells that contain their specific DNA fragment *[1 mark]*. Together the different colonies make a complete genomic DNA library *[1 mark]*. DNA is extracted from each colony and cut up using restriction enzymes, producing overlapping pieces of DNA *[1 mark]*. Each piece of DNA is sequenced, using the chain-termination method, and the pieces are put back in order to give the full sequence from that BAC *[1 mark]*. Finally the DNA fragment from each different BAC is put back in order, using computers, to complete the entire genome *[1 mark]*.

Unit 5: Section 6 — Ecology

Page 193 — Ecosystems and the Nitrogen Cycle

1 a) Maximum of 2 marks available.
    A — ammonification *[1 mark]*, C — denitrification *[1 mark]*
  b) Maximum of 3 marks available.
    Process B is nitrogen fixation *[1 mark]*. Nitrogen fixation is where nitrogen gas in the atmosphere is turned into ammonia *[1 mark]* by bacteria *[1 mark]*.

Page 195 — Energy Transfer Through an Ecosystem

1 a) Maximum of 4 marks available.
    Because not all of the energy available from the grass is taken in by the Arctic hare *[1 mark]*. Some parts of the grass aren't eaten, so the energy isn't taken in *[1 mark]*, and some parts of the grass are indigestible, so they'll pass through the hares and come out as waste *[1 mark]*. Some energy is lost to the environment when the Arctic hare uses energy from respiration for things like movement or body heat *[1 mark]*.
  b) Maximum of 2 marks available.
    (137 ÷ 2345) × 100 = 5.8 *[1 mark]*
    Efficiency of energy transfer = 5.8% *[1 mark]*
    Award 2 marks for correct answer of 5.8% without any working.

Page 197 — Succession

1 a) Maximum of 6 marks available.
    This is an example of secondary succession, because there is already a soil layer present in the field *[1 mark]*. The first species to grow will be the pioneer species, which in this case will be larger plants *[1 mark]*. These will then be replaced with shrubs and smaller trees *[1 mark]*. At each stage, different plants and animals that are better adapted for the improved conditions will move in, out-compete the species already there, and become the dominant species *[1 mark]*. As succession goes on, the ecosystem becomes more complex, so species diversity (the number and abundance of different species) increases *[1 mark]*. Eventually large trees will grow, forming the climax community, which is the final seral stage *[1 mark]*.
  b) Maximum of 2 marks available.
    Ploughing destroys any plants that were growing *[1 mark]*, so larger plants may start to grow, but they won't have long enough to establish themselves before the field is ploughed again *[1 mark]*.

A2-Level Answers

Page 199 — Investigating Ecosystems

1 a) Maximum of 1 mark available.
By taking random samples of the population [1 mark].

b) Maximum of 3 marks available.
Several frame quadrats would be placed on the ground at random locations within the field [1 mark]. The percentage of each frame quadrat that's covered by daffodils would be recorded [1 mark]. The percentage cover for the whole field could then be estimated by averaging the data collected in all of the frame quadrats [1 mark].

Page 201 — Factors Affecting Population Size

1 a) Maximum of 7 marks available.
In the first three years, the population of prey increases from 5000 to 30 000. The population of predators increases slightly later (in the first five years), from 4000 to 11 000 [1 mark]. This is because there's more food available for the predators [1 mark]. The prey population then falls after year three to 3000 just before year 10 [1 mark], because lots are being eaten by the large population of predators [1 mark]. Shortly after the prey population falls, the predator population also falls (back to 4000 by just after year 10) [1 mark], because there's less food available [1 mark]. The same pattern is repeated in years 10-20 [1 mark].

b) Maximum of 4 marks available.
The population of prey increased to around 40 000 by year 26 [1 mark]. This is because there were fewer predators, so fewer prey were eaten [1 mark]. The population then decreased after year 26 to 25 000 by year 30 [1 mark]. This could be because of intraspecific competition [1 mark].

Page 203 — Conservation of Ecosystems

1 Maximum of 3 marks available, from any of the 4 points below.
For full marks, answers must contain at least one economic, one social and one ethical reason.
Conservation of ecosystems is important for economic reasons because ecosystems provide resources for things that are traded on a local and global scale, like clothes, drugs and food. If they're not conserved, the resources could be lost, causing large economic losses in the future [1 mark]. Many ecosystems bring joy to lots of people because they're attractive to look at and people use them for activities like birdwatching and walking. If they aren't conserved the ecosystems may be lost, so future generations won't be able to use and enjoy them [1 mark]. Some people think ecosystems should be conserved because it's the right thing to do. They think organisms have a right to exist, so they shouldn't become extinct because of human activity [1 mark]. Some people also think that humans have a moral responsibility to conserve ecosystems for future human generations, so they can enjoy and use them [1 mark].

2 a) Maximum of 2 marks available.
1 mark for an explanation and 1 mark for an example.
Non-native animal species eat some native species, causing a decrease in the populations of native species [1 mark]. For example, dogs, cats and black rats eat young giant tortoises and Galapagos land iguanas [1 mark] / pigs destroy the nests of Galapagos land iguanas and eat their eggs [1 mark] / goats have eaten a lot of the plant life on some of the islands [1 mark].

b) Maximum of 2 marks available.
Non-native plant species have decreased native plant populations because they compete with the native species [1 mark]. For example, quinine trees are taller than some native plants. They block out light to the native plants, which then struggle to survive [1 mark].

c) Maximum of 2 marks available.
1 mark for an explanation and 1 mark for an example.
Fishing has caused a decrease in the populations of some of the sea life around the Galapagos Islands [1 mark]. For example, sea cucumber and hammerhead shark populations have been reduced because of overfishing [1 mark] / Galapagos green turtle numbers have been reduced because of overfishing [1 mark] / Galapagos green turtle numbers have been reduced because they're killed accidentally when they're caught in fishing nets [1 mark].
You've been asked to explain how specific animals or plants have been affected, so you need to use named examples.

Unit 5: Section 7 — Responding to the Environment

Page 207 — Plant Responses

1 Maximum of 3 marks available.
Auxins are produced in the tip of shoots and they're moved around the plant, so different parts of the plant have different amounts of auxins [1 mark]. The uneven distribution of auxins means there's uneven growth of the plant [1 mark]. Auxins move to the more shaded parts of the shoots, making the cells there elongate, which makes the shoot bend towards the light [1 mark].

2 a) Maximum of 1 mark available.
Auxins [1 mark].

b) Maximum of 2 marks available.
Apical dominance saves energy as it stops side shoots growing. This allows a plant in an area where there are lots of other plants to grow tall very fast, past the smaller plants, to reach the sunlight [1 mark]. Apical dominance also prevents side shoots of the same plant from competing with the shoot tip for light [1 mark].

3 a) Maximum of 1 mark available.
Ethene [1 mark].

b) Maximum of 1 mark available.
Ethene stimulates enzymes that break down cell walls, break down chlorophyll and convert starch to sugars [1 mark].

c) Maximum of 1 mark available.
E.g. the tomatoes are less likely to be damaged in transport [1 mark].

Page 209 — Animal Responses

1 a) Maximum of 1 mark available.
Hypothalamus [1 mark].

b) Maximum of 2 marks available.
Control of breathing [1 mark]. Control of heart rate [1 mark].

c) Maximum of 1 mark available.
Lack of coordinated movement / balance / posture [1 mark].
You know that the cerebellum normally coordinates muscles, balance and posture, so damage to it is likely to cause a lack of coordinated movement, balance or posture.

2 a) Maximum of 1 mark available.
The 'fight or flight' response is when an organism prepares its body for action, e.g. to fight or run away [1 mark].

b) Maximum of 1 mark available.
E.g. when an organism is threatened by a predator [1 mark].

c) Maximum of 1 mark available, from any of the 5 points below.
E.g. heart rate increases [1 mark]. Muscles around the bronchioles relax [1 mark]. Glycogen is converted into glucose [1 mark]. Muscles in the arterioles supplying the skin and gut constrict [1 mark]. Muscles in the arterioles supplying the heart, lungs and skeletal muscles dilate [1 mark].

A2-Level Answers

Page 211 — Muscle Contraction

1   Maximum of 3 marks available.
     Muscles are made up of bundles of muscle fibres *[1 mark]*.
     Muscle fibres contain long organelles called myofibrils *[1 mark]*.
     Myofibrils contain bundles of myofilaments *[1 mark]*.

2 a) Maximum of 3 marks available.
     A = sarcomere *[1 mark]*, B = Z-line *[1 mark]*,
     C = H-zone *[1 mark]*.
  b) Maximum of 3 marks available.
     Drawing number 3 *[1 mark]* because the M-line connects
     the middle of the myosin filaments *[1 mark]*. The cross-section
     would only show myosin filaments, which are the thick
     filaments *[1 mark]*.
     The answer isn't drawing number 1 because all the dots in the cross-
     section are smaller, so the filaments shown are thin actin filaments
     — which aren't found at the M-line.

Page 213 — Muscle Contraction

1   Maximum of 2 marks available.
     The A-bands stay the same length during contraction *[1 mark]*.
     The I-bands get shorter *[1 mark]*.

2   Maximum of 3 marks available.
     Muscles need ATP to relax because ATP provides the energy
     to break the actin-myosin cross bridges *[1 mark]*. If the cross
     bridges can't be broken, the myosin heads will remain attached
     to the actin filaments *[1 mark]*, so the actin filaments can't slide
     back to their relaxed position *[1 mark]*.

3   Maximum of 3 marks available.
     The muscles won't contract *[1 mark]* because calcium ions won't
     be released into the sarcoplasm, so troponin won't be removed
     from its binding site *[1 mark]*. This means no actin-myosin cross
     bridges can be formed *[1 mark]*.

Page 215 — Muscle Contraction

1   Maximum of 5 marks available, from any of the 8 points below.
     Both types of muscle have one nucleus per muscle cell/fibre
     [1 mark]. Both types have cells/fibres that are small/about
     0.2 mm long *[1 mark]*. Neither type fatigues/gets tired quickly
     [1 mark]. Neither type is under conscious control *[1 mark]*.
     However, involuntary muscle is found in the walls of hollow
     internal organs like the gut, but cardiac muscle is found in the
     walls of the heart *[1 mark]*. Involuntary muscle fibres are
     spindle-shaped but cardiac muscle fibres are cylinder-shaped
     with intercalated discs *[1 mark]*. Cardiac muscle fibres are
     branched but involuntary muscles fibres aren't *[1 mark]*.
     Cardiac muscle fibres have some cross-striations but involuntary
     muscle fibres have a smooth appearance *[1 mark]*.

2   Maximum of 3 marks available, from any of the 6 points below.
     E.g. The neurotransmitter used at a neuromuscular junction
     is always acetylcholine, whereas various neurotransmitters can
     be used at a synapse *[1 mark]*. The postsynaptic receptors
     at a neuromuscular junction are always nicotinic cholinergic
     receptors, whereas they can be various receptors at a synapse
     depending on the type of neurotransmitter *[1 mark]*.
     Neuromuscular junctions have lots of postsynaptic receptors,
     whereas synapses have fewer *[1 mark]*. The postsynaptic cell
     at a neuromuscular junction is a muscle cell, whereas at a
     synapse it's a neurone *[1 mark]*. The postsynaptic membrane
     at a neuromuscular junction has clefts containing
     acetylcholinesterase/AChE, but the postsynaptic membrane
     at a synapse is smooth *[1 mark]*. At neuromuscular junctions
     acetylcholine is broken down by acetylcholinesterase/AChE,
     but at synapses the neurotransmitter is broken down in different
     ways depending on what it is *[1 mark]*.

Page 217 — Behaviour

1   Maximum of 2 marks available.
     Classical conditioning has occurred *[1 mark]*. The postman
     has learned to respond naturally to the stimulus of approaching
     Number 10, which wouldn't normally cause that response
     [1 mark].

2   Maximum of 2 marks available.
     A dog could be rewarded for good behaviour, e.g. it could be
     given a biscuit for sitting down when the trainer says, "Sit"
     [1 mark]. If the dog is repeatedly rewarded for sitting down
     then that behaviour will be reinforced, and the dog will learn
     to sit when told *[1 mark]*.
     You could answer this question by using an example of punishing
     a dog for bad behaviour instead.

Page 219 — Behaviour

1 a) Maximum of 1 mark available.
     Imprinting is where an animal learns to recognise its parents
     and instinctively follows them *[1 mark]*.
  b) Maximum of 2 marks available.
     A gosling can imprint on a human if the gosling is reared from
     birth/during the critical period by a human *[1 mark]*. The human
     will be the first moving object the gosling sees, so the gosling will
     imprint on the human/will follow the human *[1 mark]*.

2 a) Maximum of 1 mark available.
     Social behaviour is behaviour that involves members of a group
     interacting with each other *[1 mark]*.
  b) i) Maximum of 1 mark available.
        A large group is more efficient at finding food *[1 mark]*.
     ii) Maximum of 1 mark available, from any of the 2 points below.
        Grooming is hygienic *[1 mark]*. Grooming helps to reinforce
        the social bonds within the group *[1 mark]*.

Index

Index

Index

Index

Index